W9-DFN-706

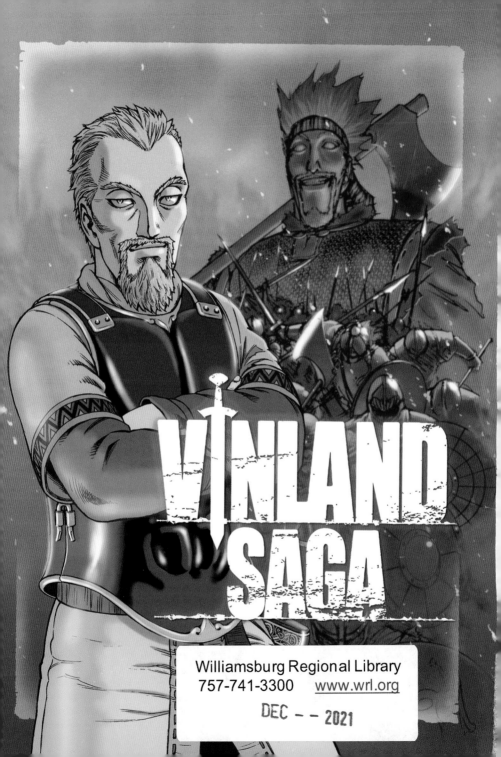

VINLAND
SAGA

TABLE OF CONTENTS

CHAPTER 17:   ENGLAND, 1008 A.D.   3

CHAPTER 18:   ENGLAND, 1013 A.D.   51

CHAPTER 19:   THE BATTLE OF
LONDON BRIDGE   91

CHAPTER 20:   RAGNAROK   131

CHAPTER 21:   VALHALLA   171

BONUS MATERIAL: YLVA AT WORK   205

CHAPTER 22:   THE TROLL'S SON   223

CHAPTER 23:   REINFORCEMENTS   259

CHAPTER 24:   THE LAND ON THE FAR BANK   285

CHAPTER 25:   BLUFF   317

CHAPTER 26:   ARTORIUS   339

CHAPTER 27:   THE WARRIORS AND THE MONK   371

CHAPTER 28:   NIGHT ATTACK   383

BONUS MATERIAL: VIKING GIRL YLVA,
HIDEO NISHIMOTO EDITION   422

TRANSLATION NOTES   424

BONUS STORY: FOR OUR FAREWELL IS
NEAR, PART 2   427

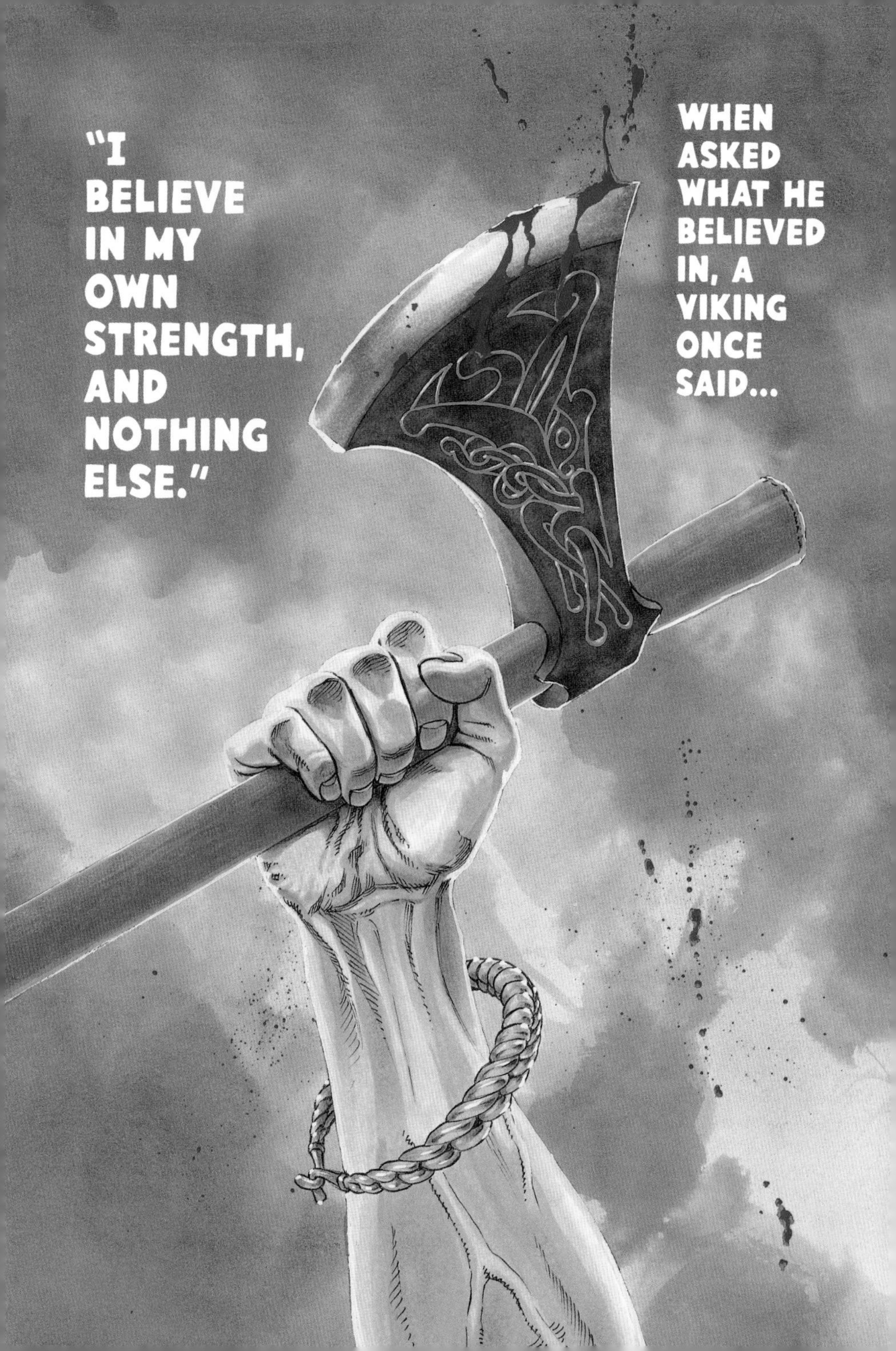
WHEN ASKED WHAT HE BELIEVED IN, A VIKING ONCE SAID...
"I BELIEVE IN MY OWN STRENGTH, AND NOTHING ELSE."

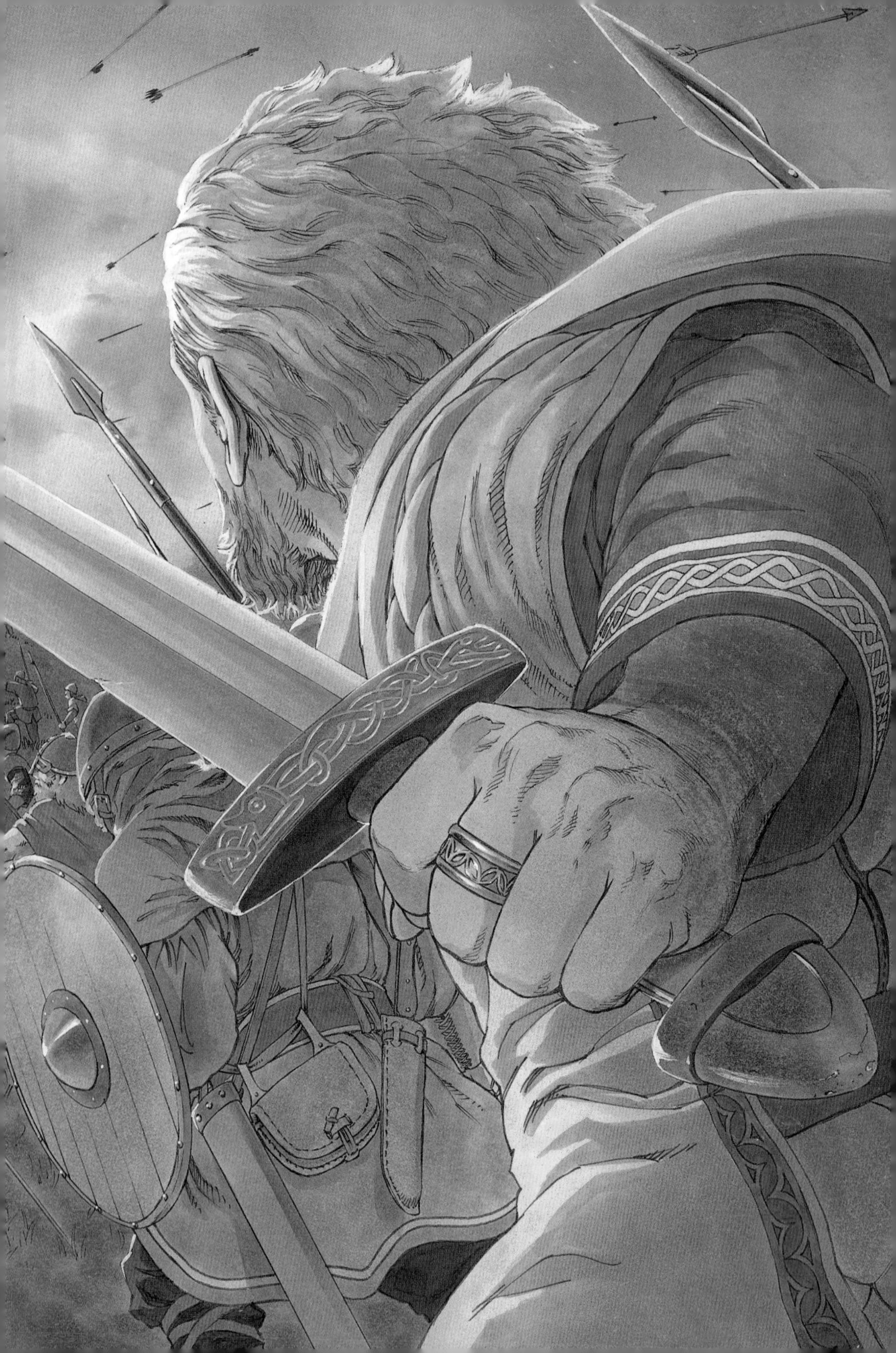

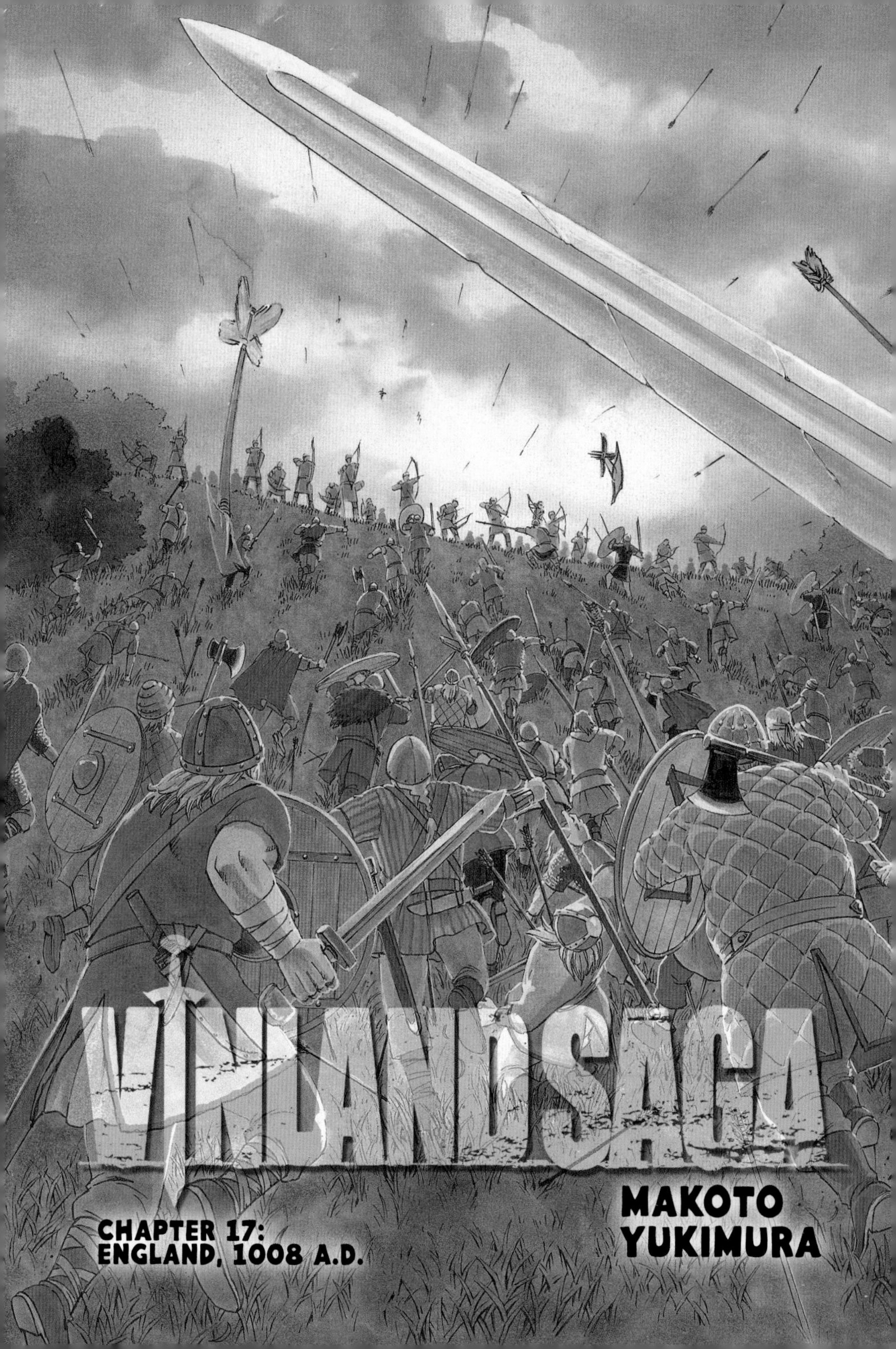
VINLAND SAGA
MAKOTO YUKIMURA
CHAPTER 17: ENGLAND, 1008 A.D.

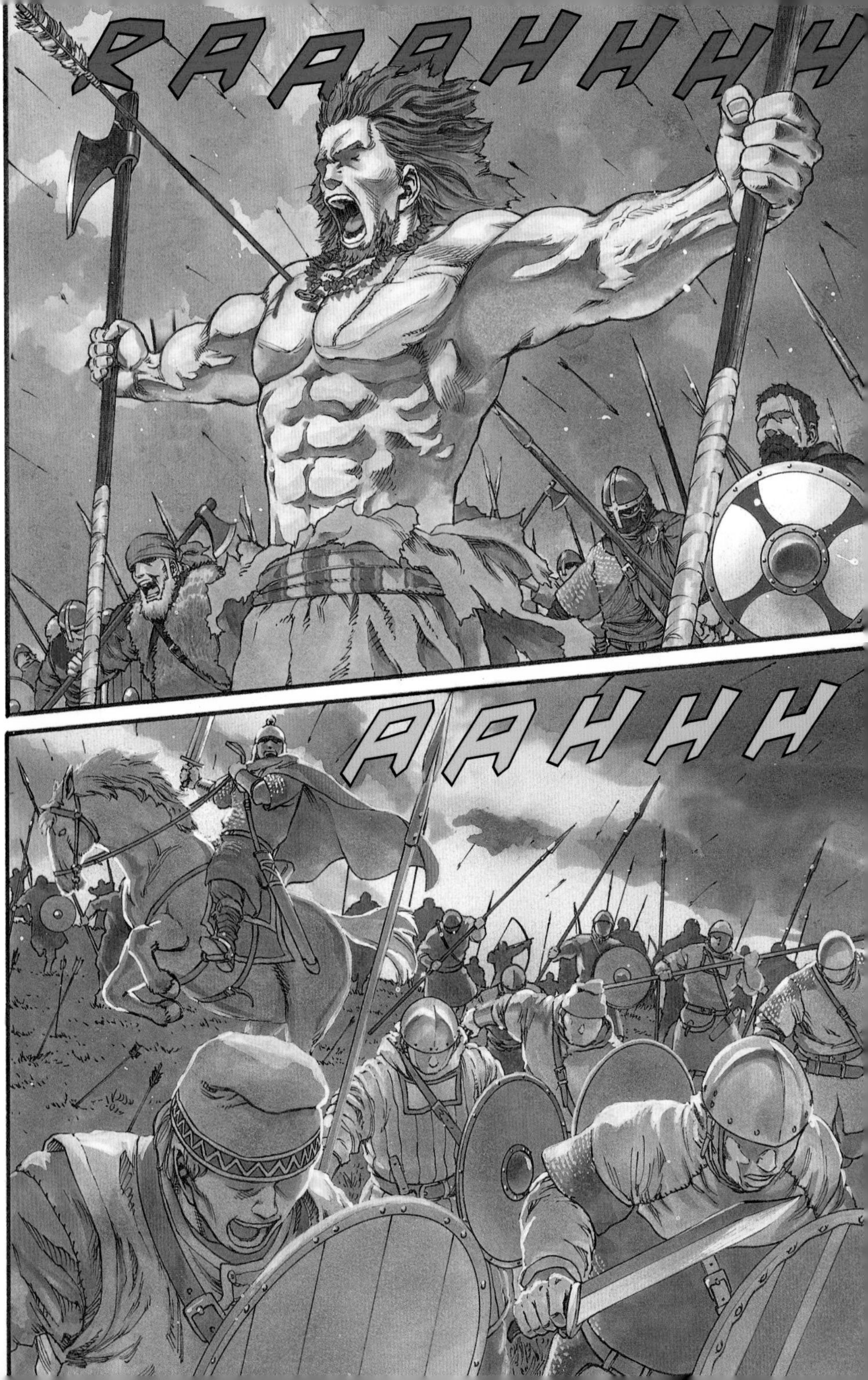
RAAAHHHH
AAHHH

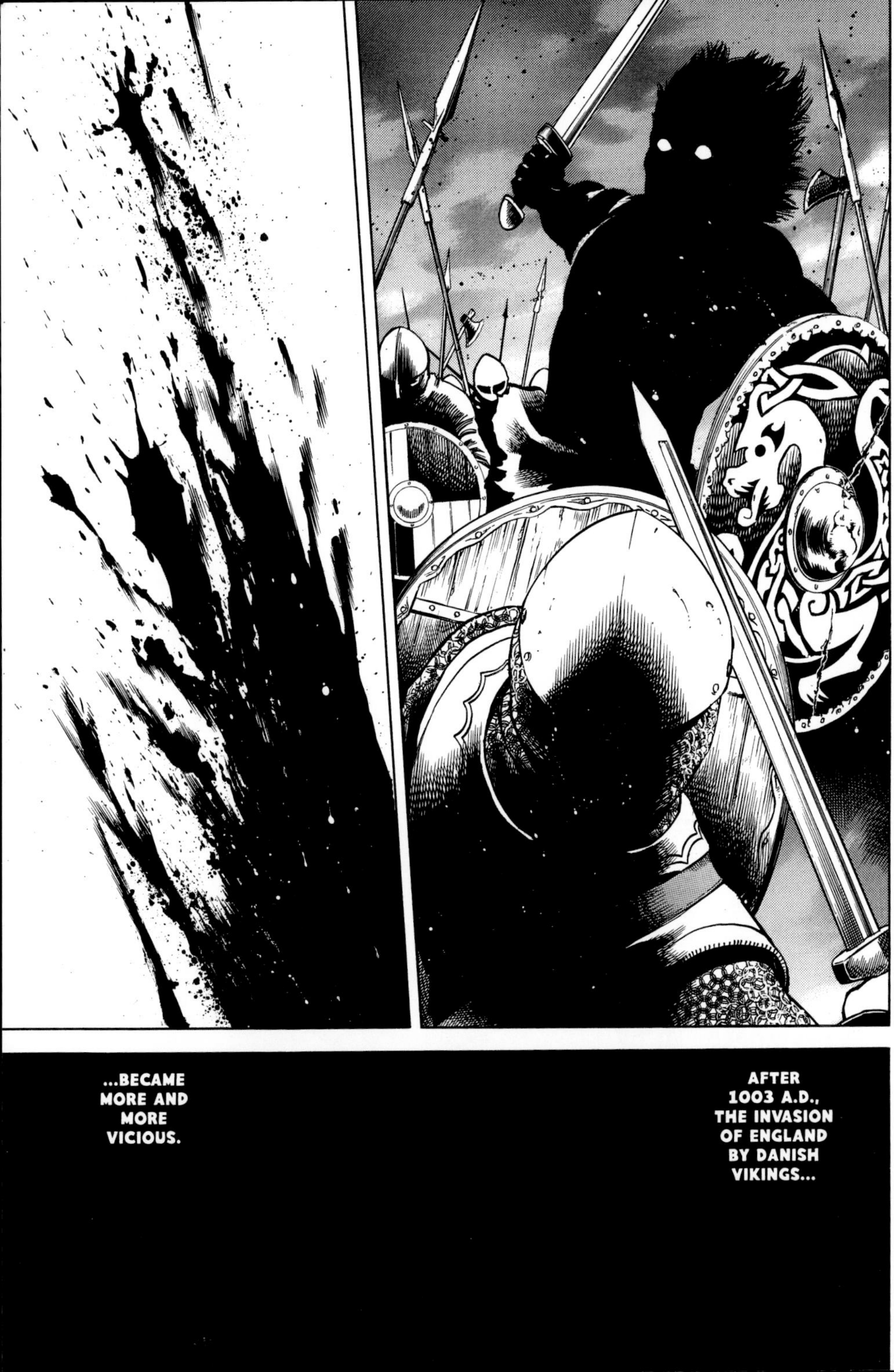
AFTER 1003 A.D., THE INVASION OF ENGLAND BY DANISH VIKINGS...
...BECAME MORE AND MORE VICIOUS.

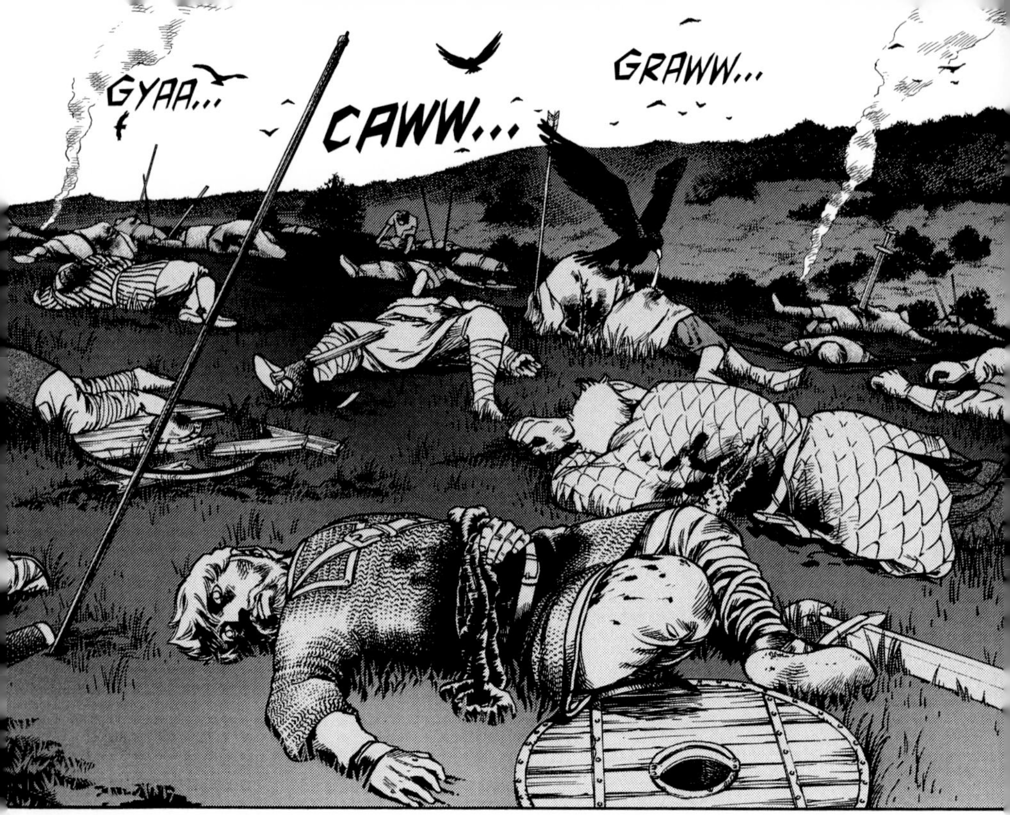
GRAWW...
CAWW...
GYAA...

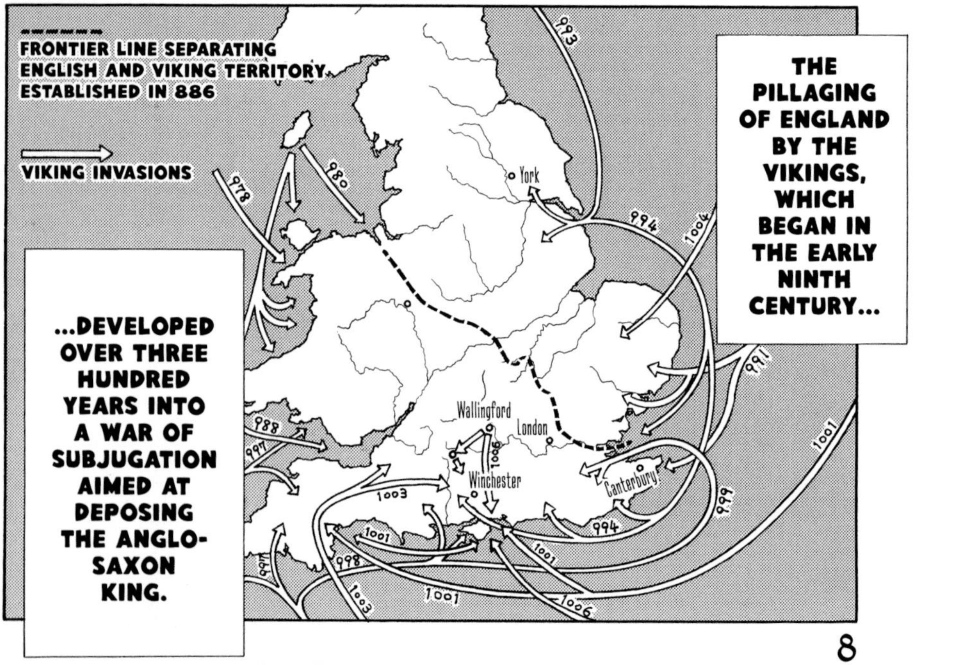
THE PILLAGING OF ENGLAND BY THE VIKINGS, WHICH BEGAN IN THE EARLY NINTH CENTURY...
...DEVELOPED OVER THREE HUNDRED YEARS INTO A WAR OF SUBJUGATION AIMED AT DEPOSING THE ANGLO-SAXON KING.
FRONTIER LINE SEPARATING ENGLISH AND VIKING TERRITORY ESTABLISHED IN 886
VIKING INVASIONS
York
Wallingford
London
Winchester
Canterbury
993
994
1006
991
1001
999
994
1001
1006
1001
1003
998
1001
1003
997
988
997
1006
978
980

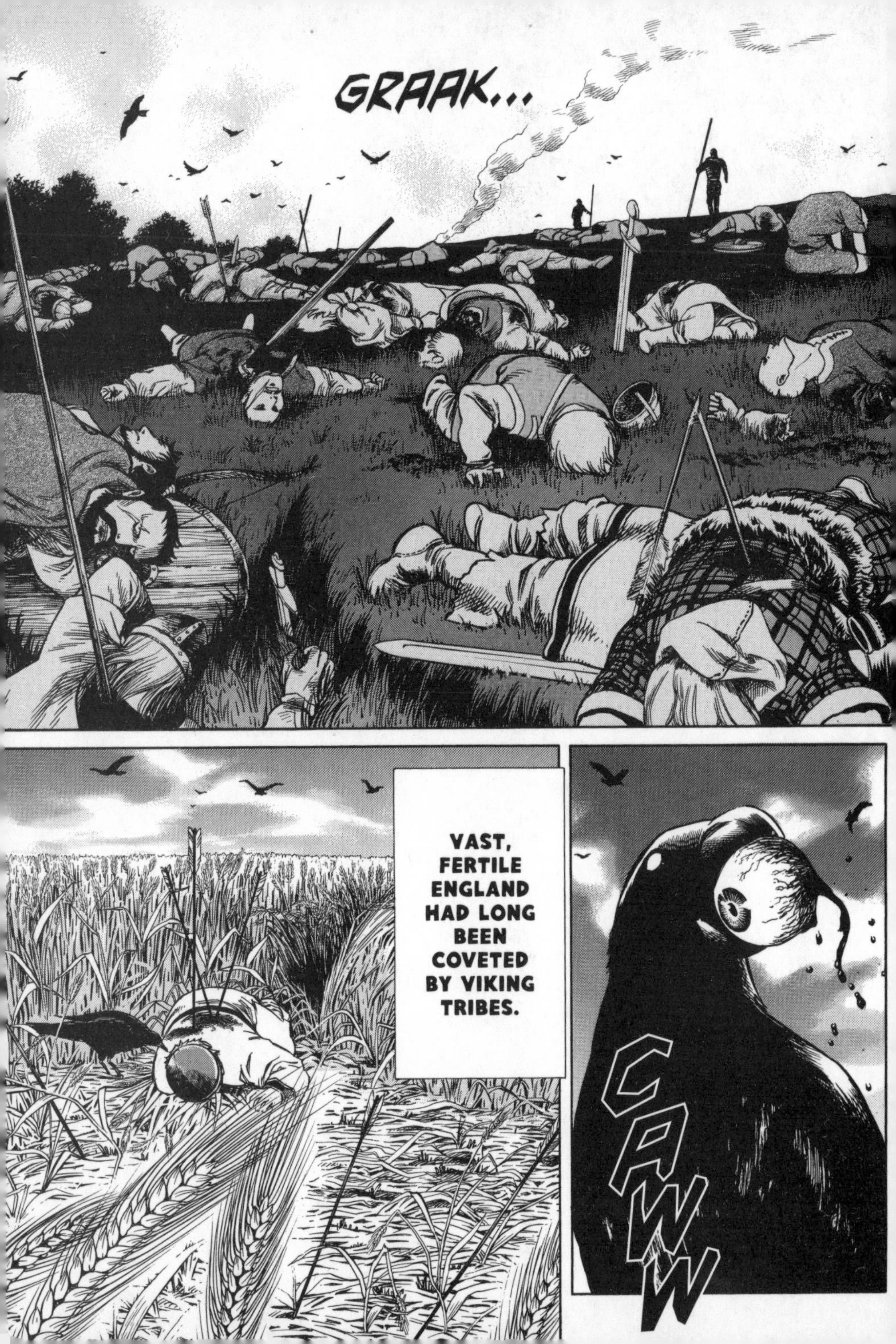
GRAAK...
CAWW
VAST, FERTILE ENGLAND HAD LONG BEEN COVETED BY VIKING TRIBES.

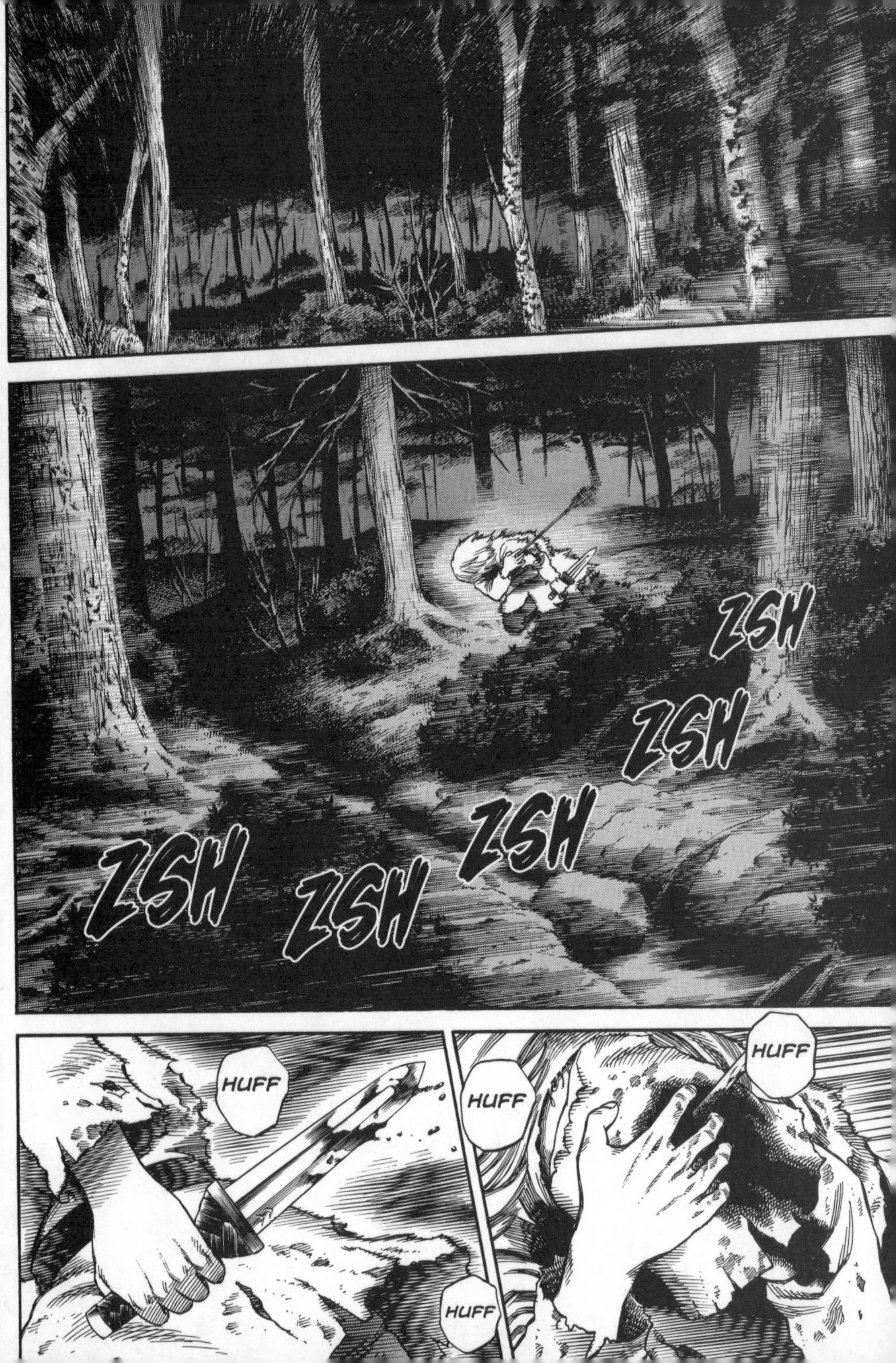
ZSH
ZSH
ZSH
ZSH
ZSH
HUFF
HUFF
HUFF
HUFF

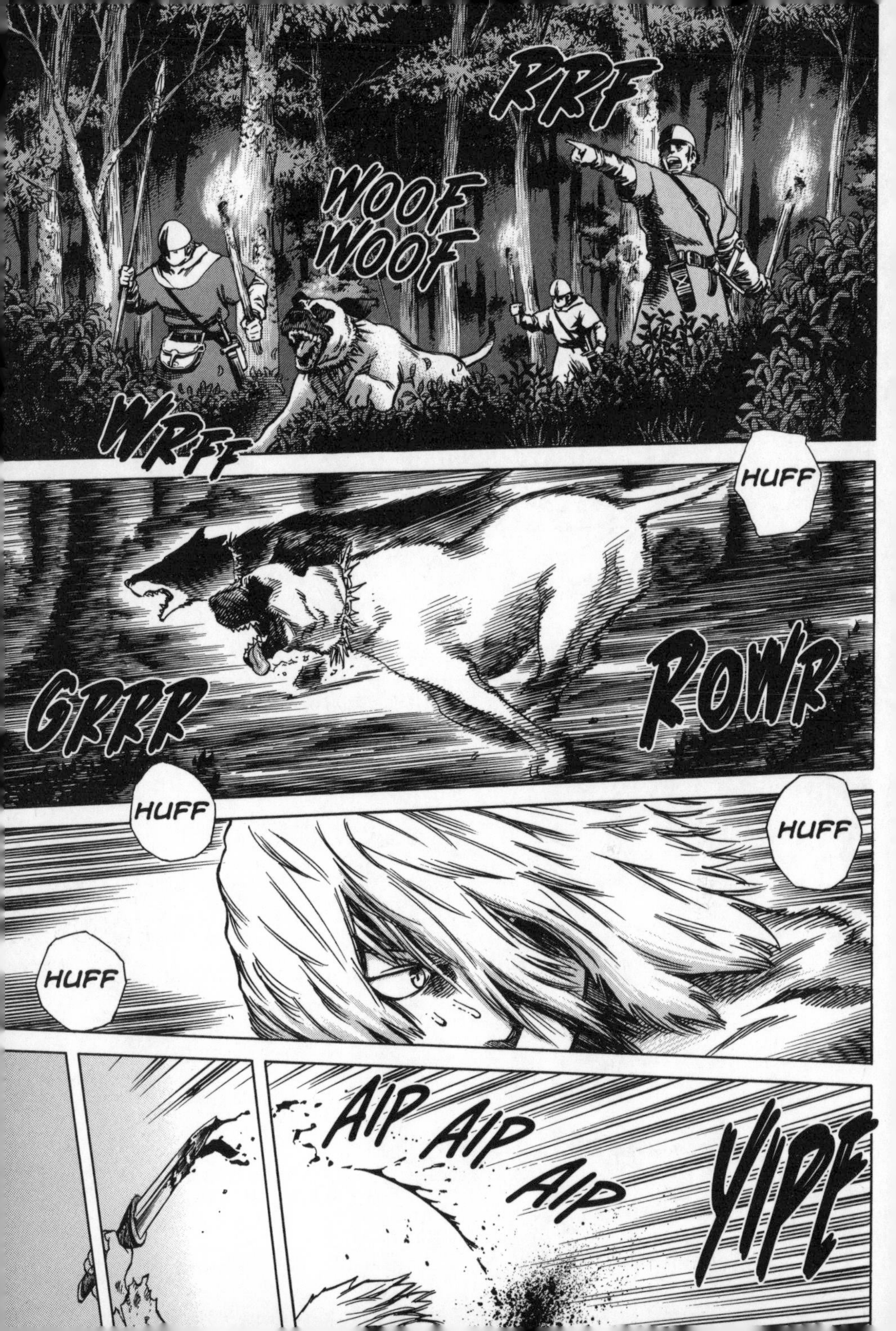
RRF
WOOF WOOF
WRFF
HUFF
ROWR
GRRR
HUFF
HUFF
HUFF
YIPE
AIP AIP AIP AIP

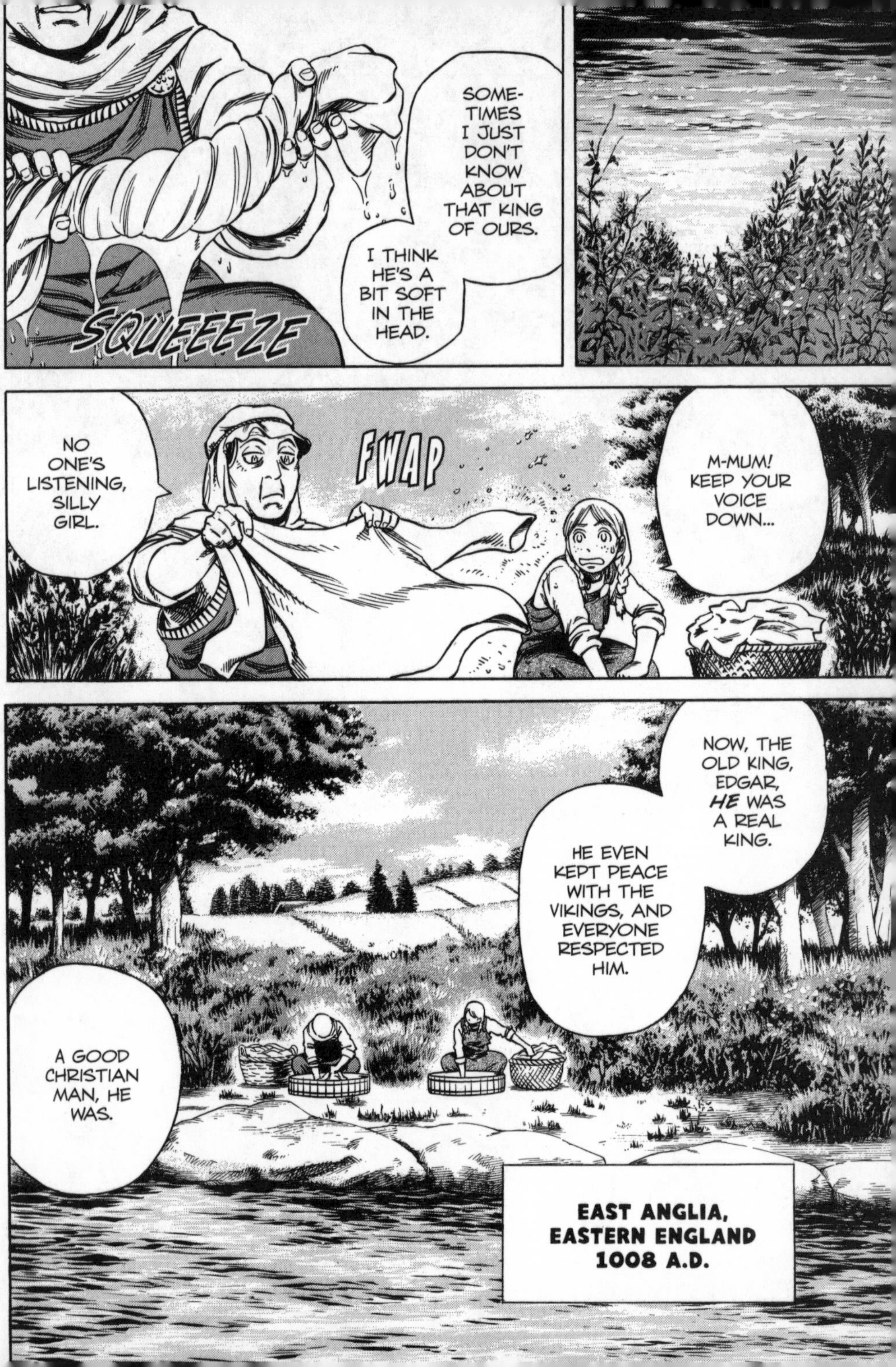
SOME-TIMES I JUST DON'T KNOW ABOUT THAT KING OF OURS.
I THINK HE'S A BIT SOFT IN THE HEAD.
SQUEEEEZE
M-MUM! KEEP YOUR VOICE DOWN...
FWAP
NO ONE'S LISTENING, SILLY GIRL.
NOW, THE OLD KING, EDGAR, *HE* WAS A REAL KING.
HE EVEN KEPT PEACE WITH THE VIKINGS, AND EVERYONE RESPECTED HIM.
A GOOD CHRISTIAN MAN, HE WAS.
EAST ANGLIA, EASTERN ENGLAND 1008 A.D.

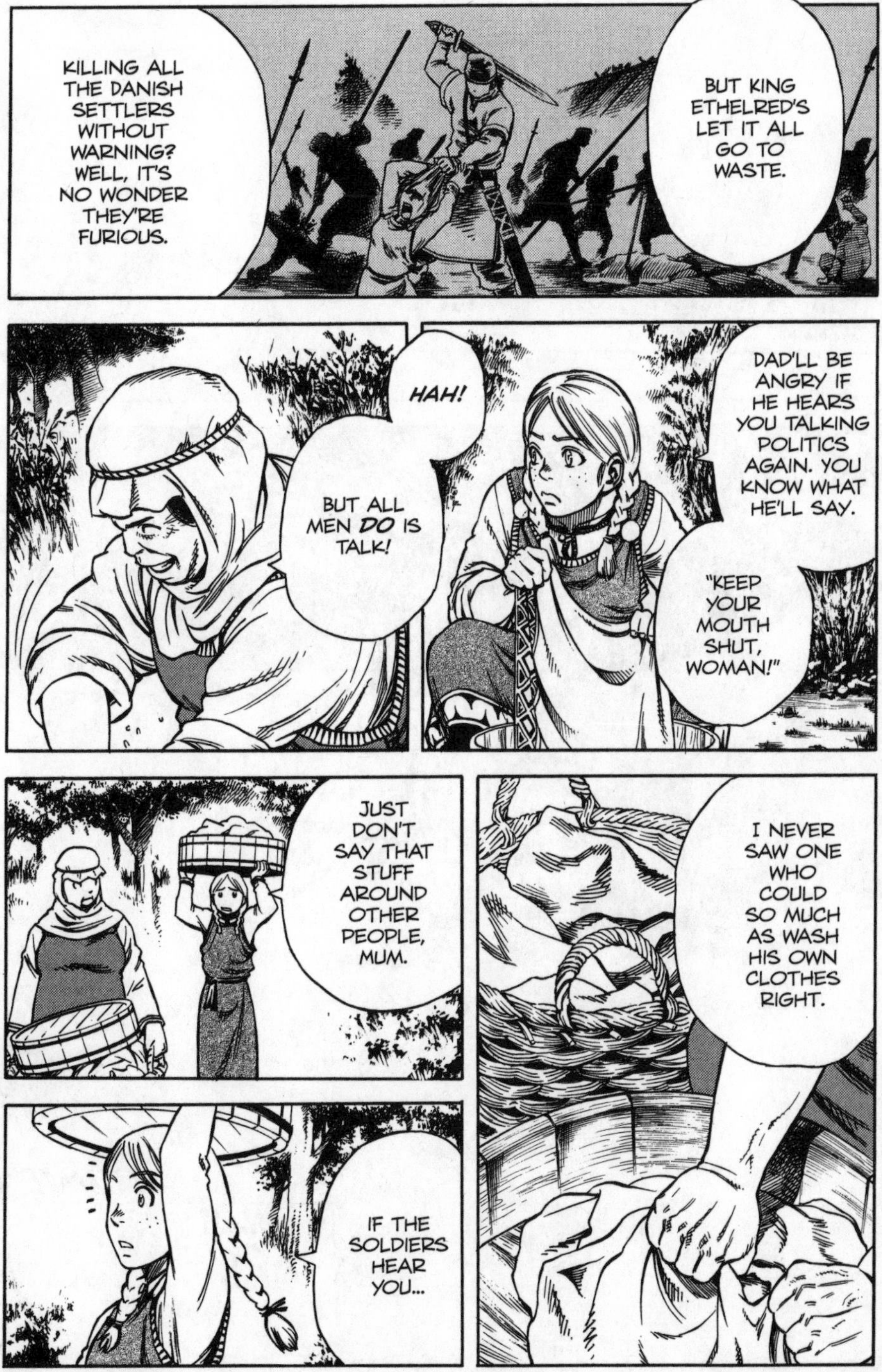
BUT KING ETHELRED'S LET IT ALL GO TO WASTE.
KILLING ALL THE DANISH SETTLERS WITHOUT WARNING? WELL, IT'S NO WONDER THEY'RE FURIOUS.
DAD'LL BE ANGRY IF HE HEARS YOU TALKING POLITICS AGAIN. YOU KNOW WHAT HE'LL SAY.
"KEEP YOUR MOUTH SHUT, WOMAN!"
HAH!
BUT ALL MEN *DO* IS TALK!
I NEVER SAW ONE WHO COULD SO MUCH AS WASH HIS OWN CLOTHES RIGHT.
JUST DON'T SAY THAT STUFF AROUND OTHER PEOPLE, MUM.
IF THE SOLDIERS HEAR YOU...

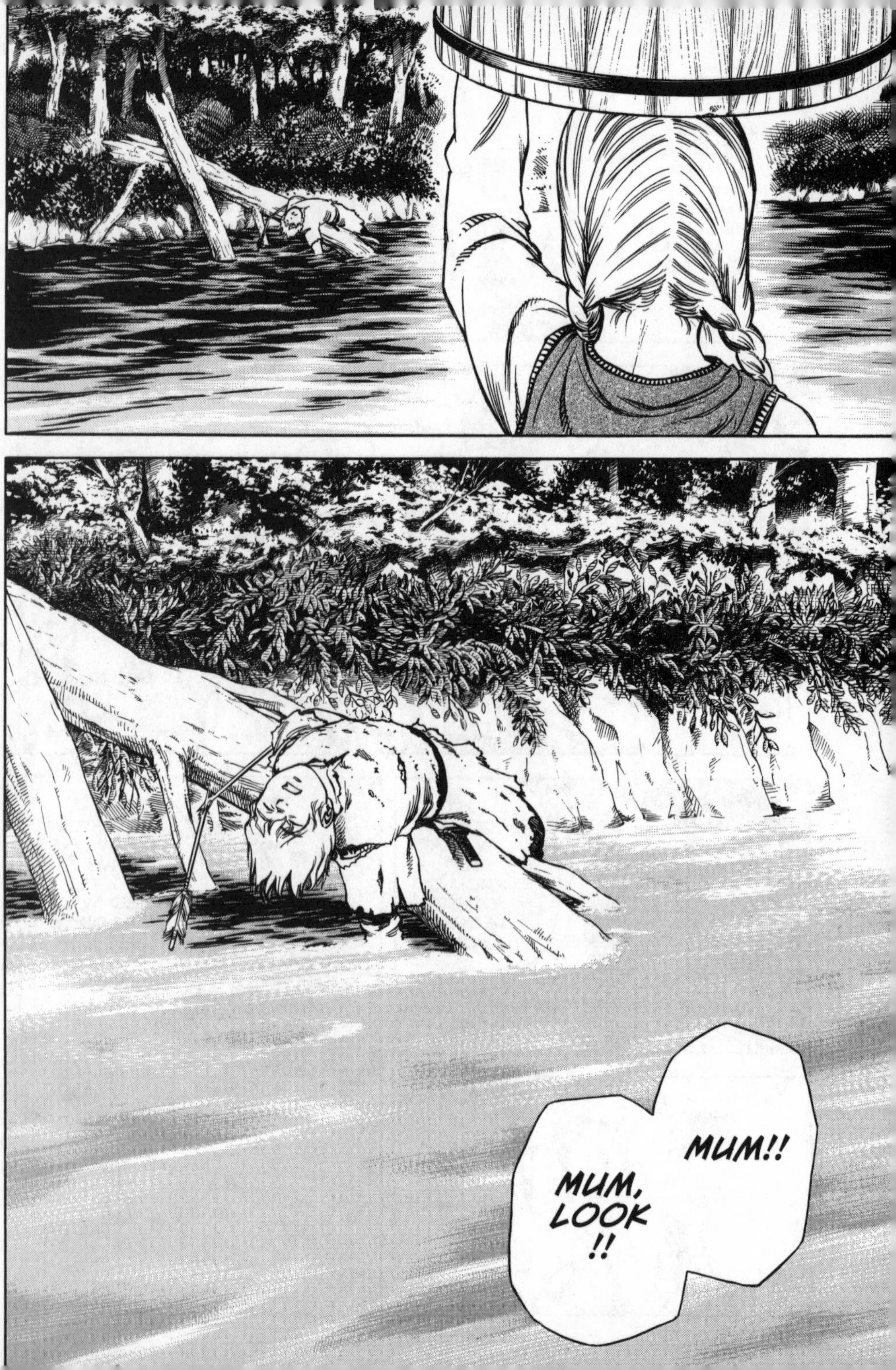
MUM!!
MUM, LOOK !!

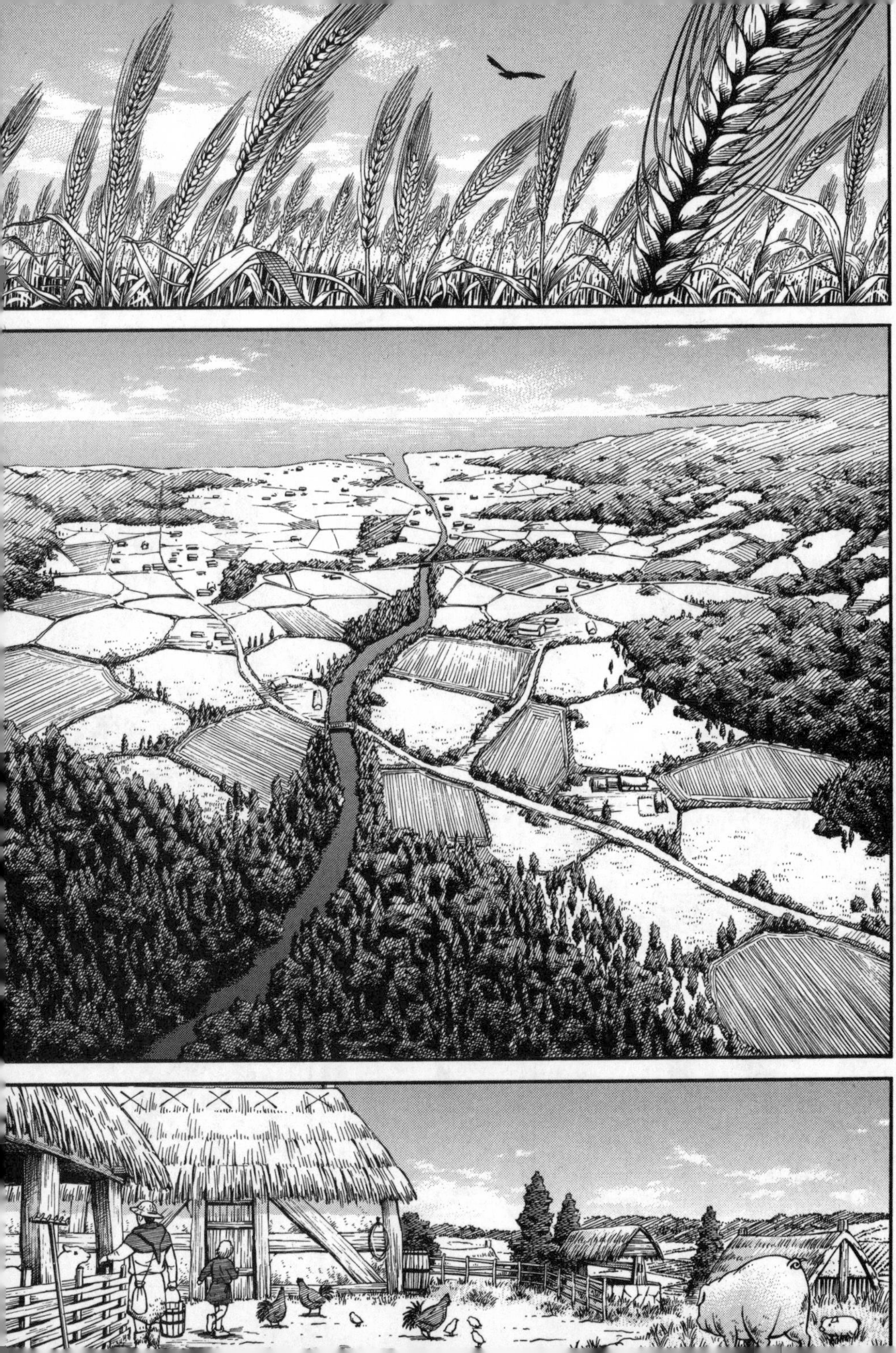

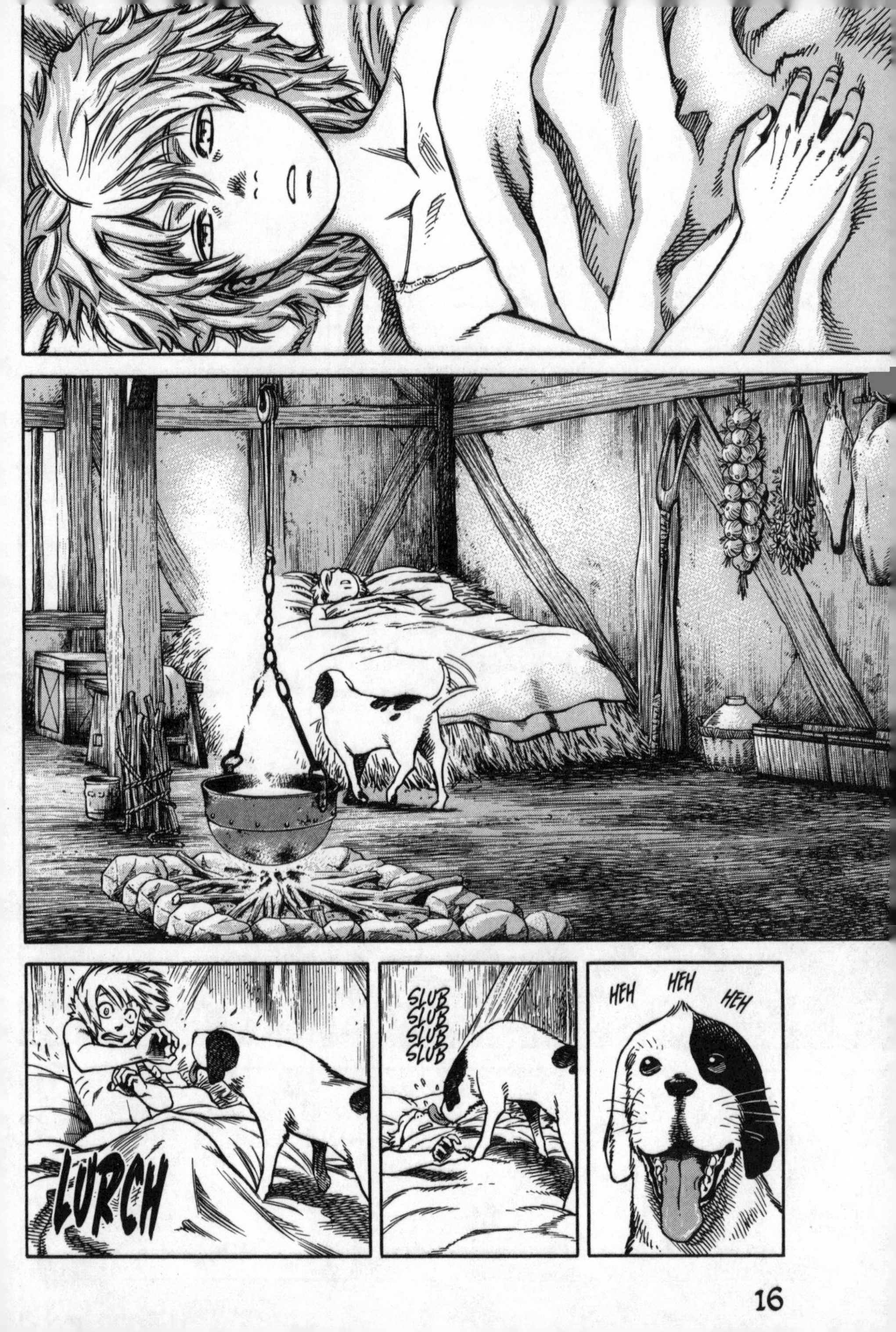
HEH
HEH
HEH
SLUB
SLUB
SLUB
SLUB
LURCH

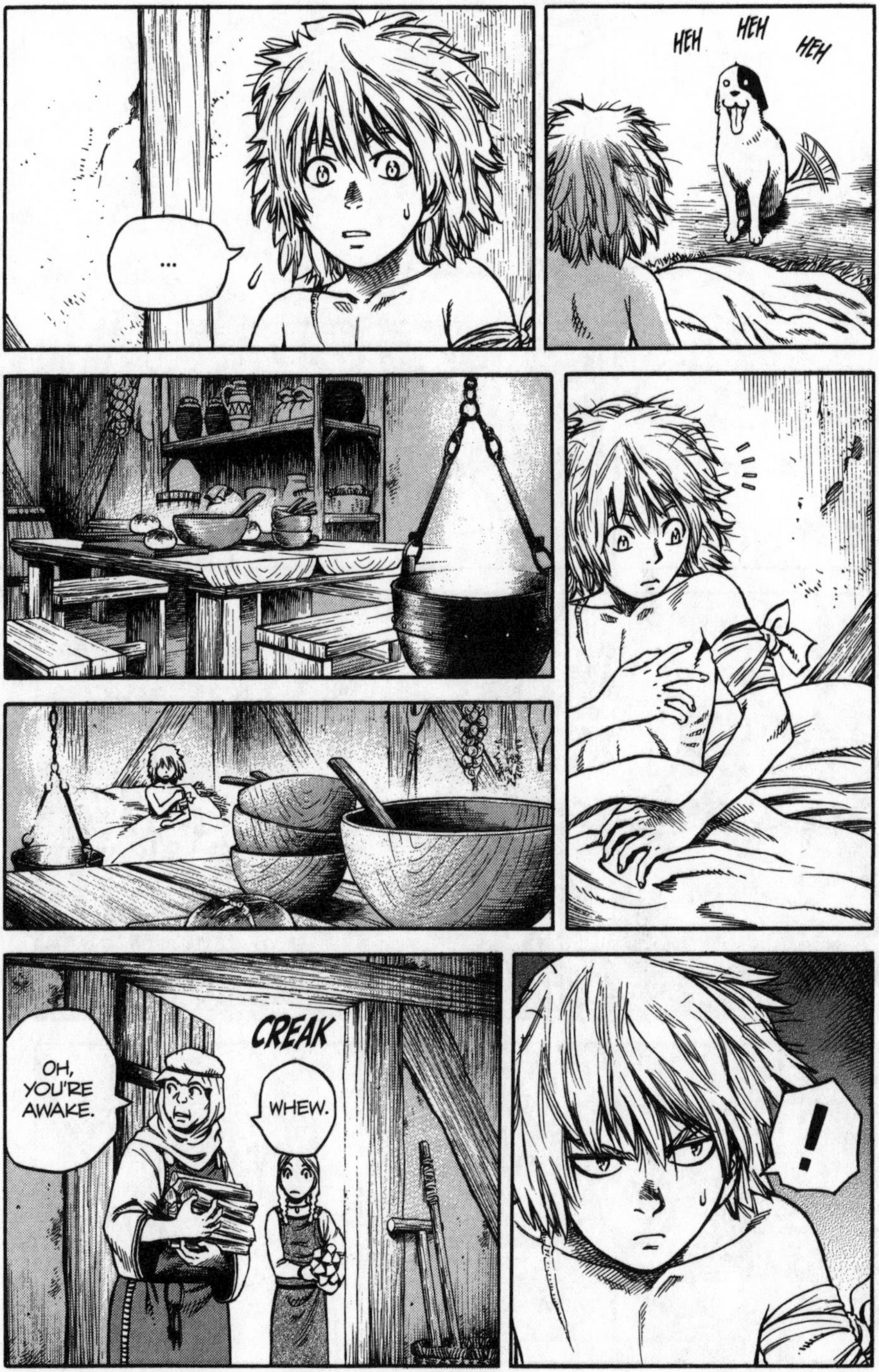
HEH HEH HEH
...
!
CREAK
OH, YOU'RE AWAKE.
WHEW.

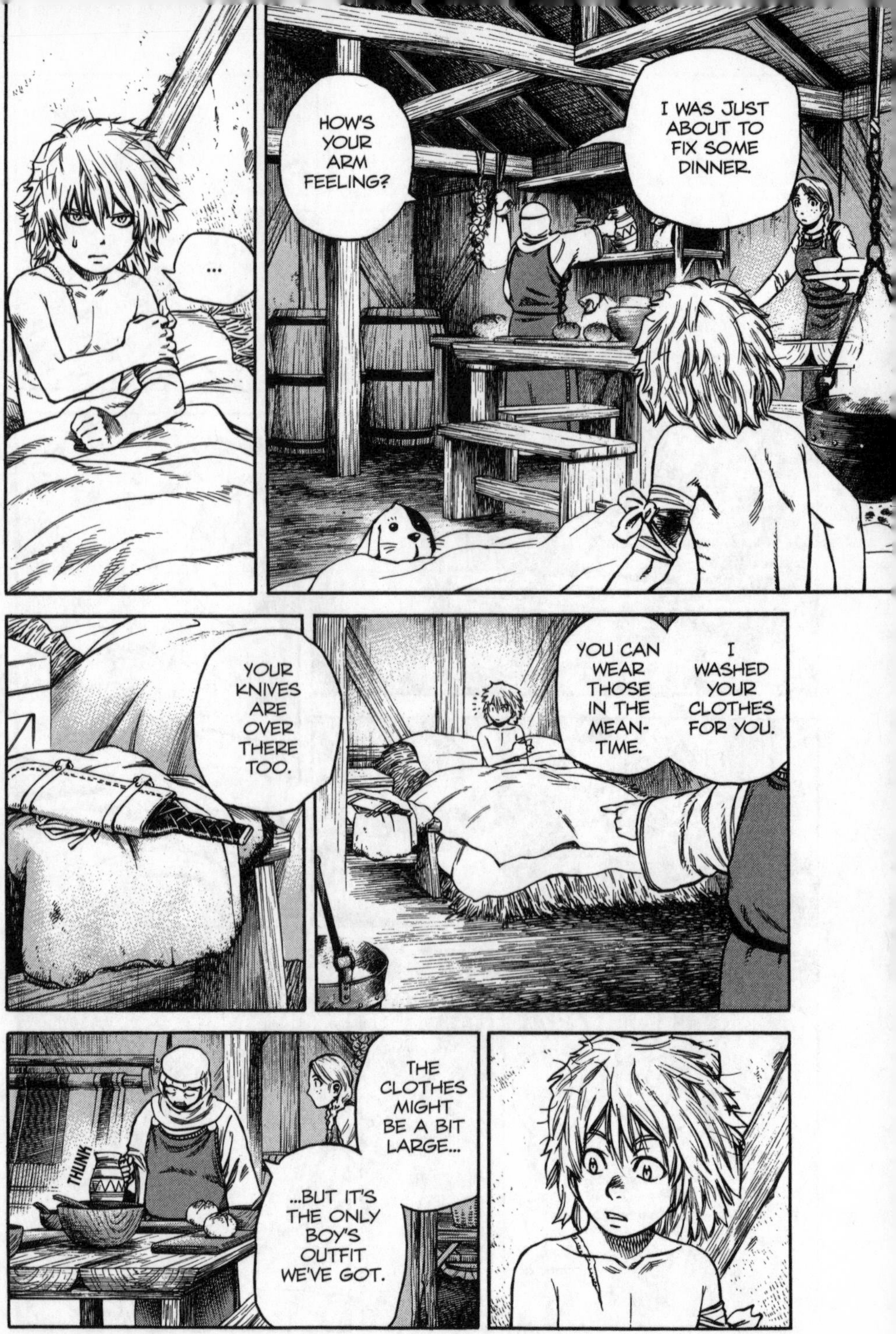
I WAS JUST ABOUT TO FIX SOME DINNER.
HOW'S YOUR ARM FEELING?
...
I WASHED YOUR CLOTHES FOR YOU.
YOU CAN WEAR THOSE IN THE MEAN-TIME.
YOUR KNIVES ARE OVER THERE TOO.
THE CLOTHES MIGHT BE A BIT LARGE...
...BUT IT'S THE ONLY BOY'S OUTFIT WE'VE GOT.
THUNK

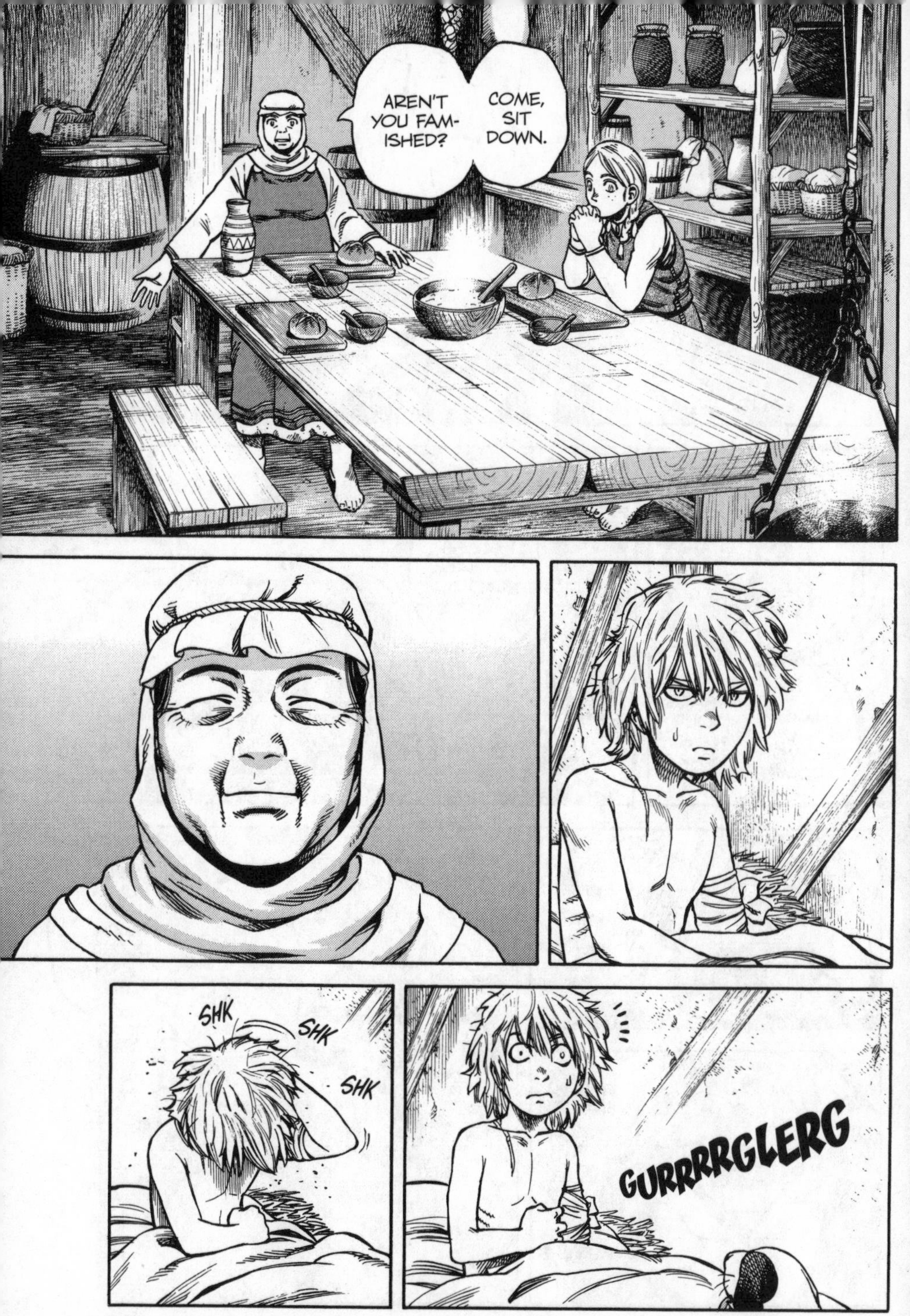
COME, SIT DOWN.
AREN'T YOU FAM-ISHED?
GURRRRGLERG
SHK
SHK
SHK

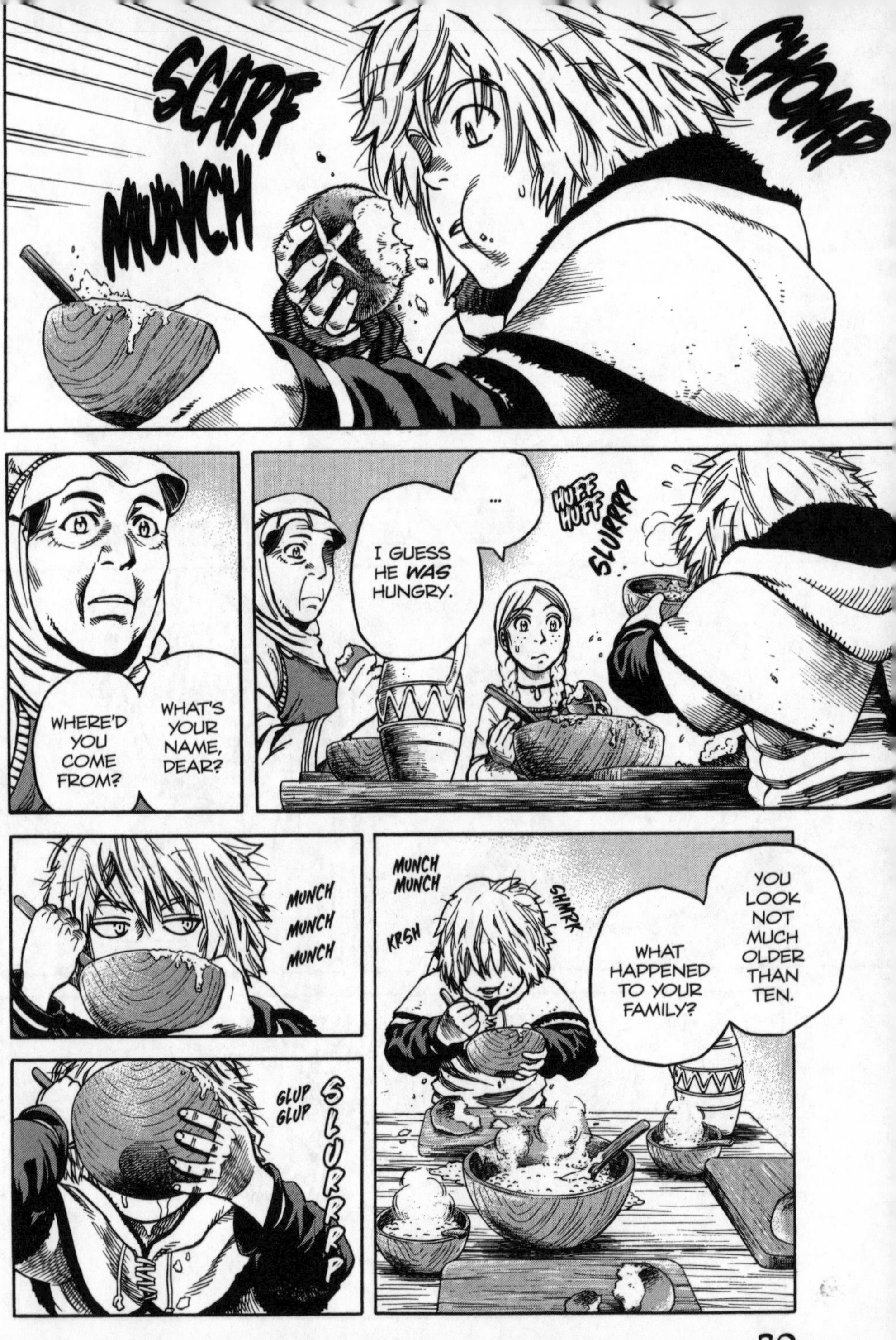
CHOMP
SCARF
MUNCH
HUFF HUFF
SLURRRP
...
I GUESS HE *WAS* HUNGRY.
WHAT'S YOUR NAME, DEAR?
WHERE'D YOU COME FROM?
YOU LOOK NOT MUCH OLDER THAN TEN.
WHAT HAPPENED TO YOUR FAMILY?
MUNCH MUNCH
SHMRK
KRSH
MUNCH MUNCH MUNCH
SLURRRP
GLUP GLUP

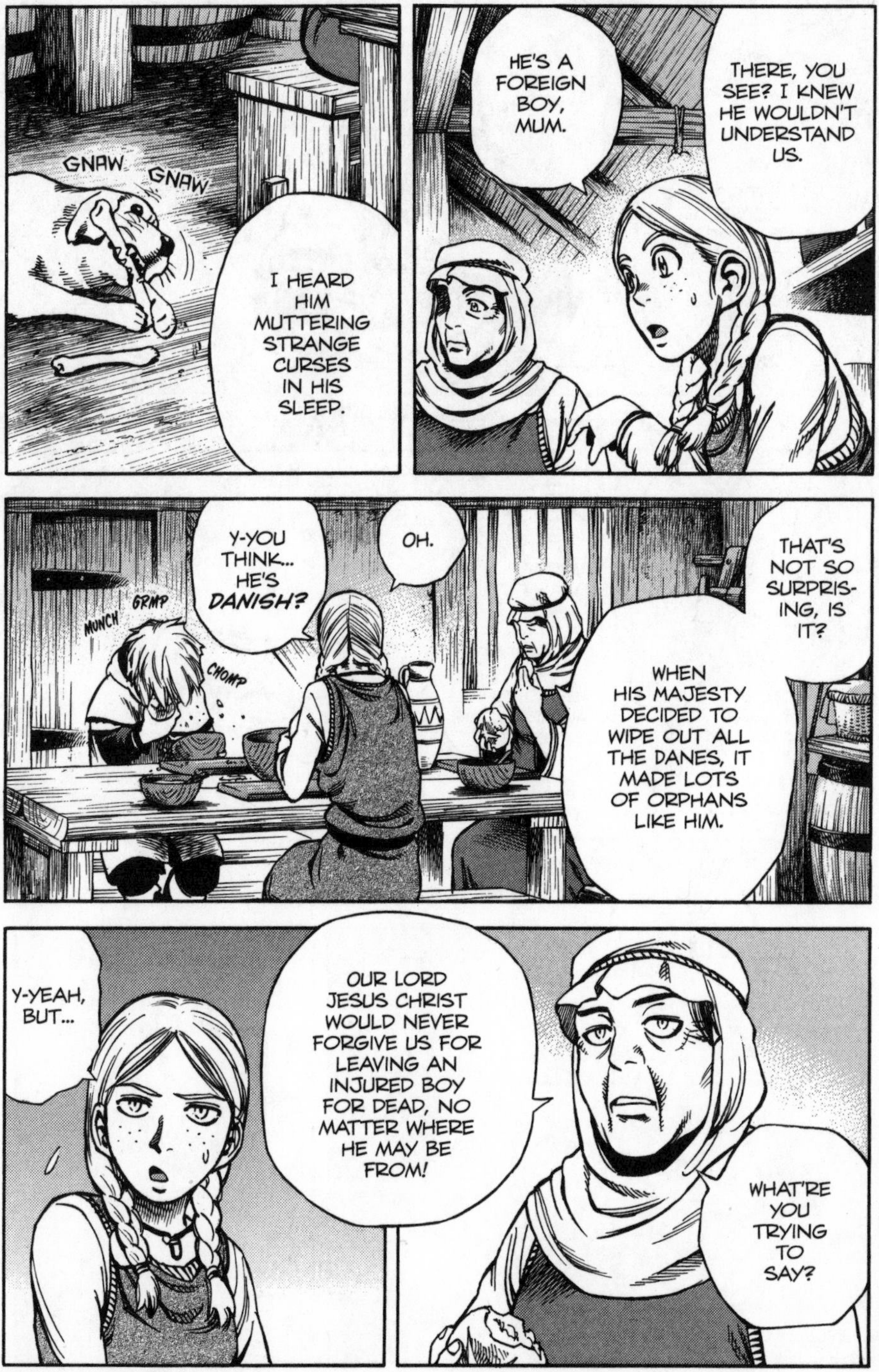
THERE, YOU SEE? I KNEW HE WOULDN'T UNDERSTAND US.
HE'S A FOREIGN BOY, MUM.
GNAW GNAW
I HEARD HIM MUTTERING STRANGE CURSES IN HIS SLEEP.
THAT'S NOT SO SURPRIS-ING, IS IT?
OH.
Y-YOU THINK... HE'S *DANISH?*
GRMP
MUNCH
CHOMP
WHEN HIS MAJESTY DECIDED TO WIPE OUT ALL THE DANES, IT MADE LOTS OF ORPHANS LIKE HIM.
WHAT'RE YOU TRYING TO SAY?
OUR LORD JESUS CHRIST WOULD NEVER FORGIVE US FOR LEAVING AN INJURED BOY FOR DEAD, NO MATTER WHERE HE MAY BE FROM!
Y-YEAH, BUT...

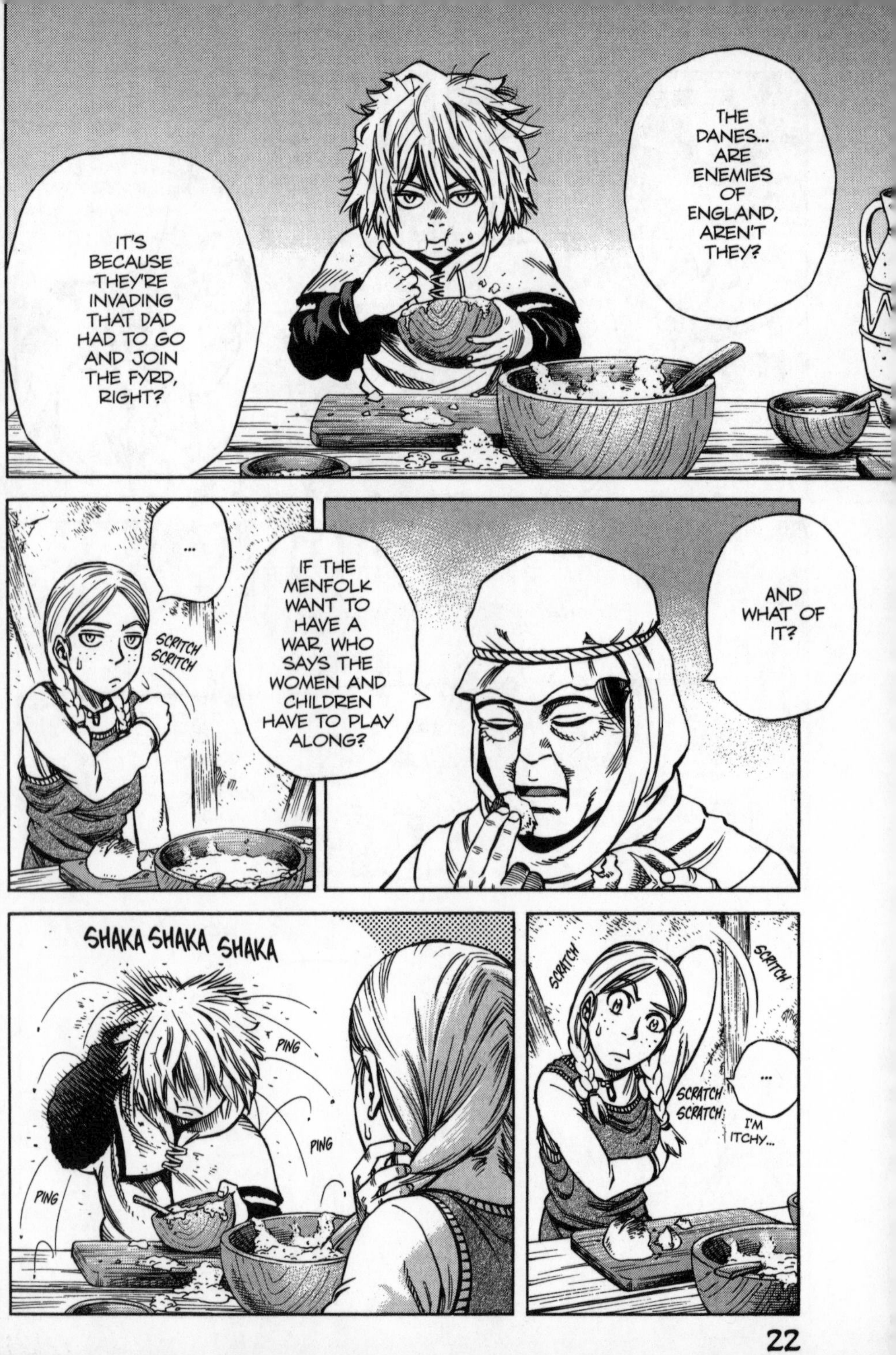
THE DANES... ARE ENEMIES OF ENGLAND, AREN'T THEY?
IT'S BECAUSE THEY'RE INVADING THAT DAD HAD TO GO AND JOIN THE FYRD, RIGHT?
AND WHAT OF IT?
IF THE MENFOLK WANT TO HAVE A WAR, WHO SAYS THE WOMEN AND CHILDREN HAVE TO PLAY ALONG?
...
SCRITCH SCRITCH
SCRATCH
SCRATCH
...
SCRATCH SCRATCH
I'M ITCHY...
SHAKA SHAKA SHAKA
PING
PING
PING

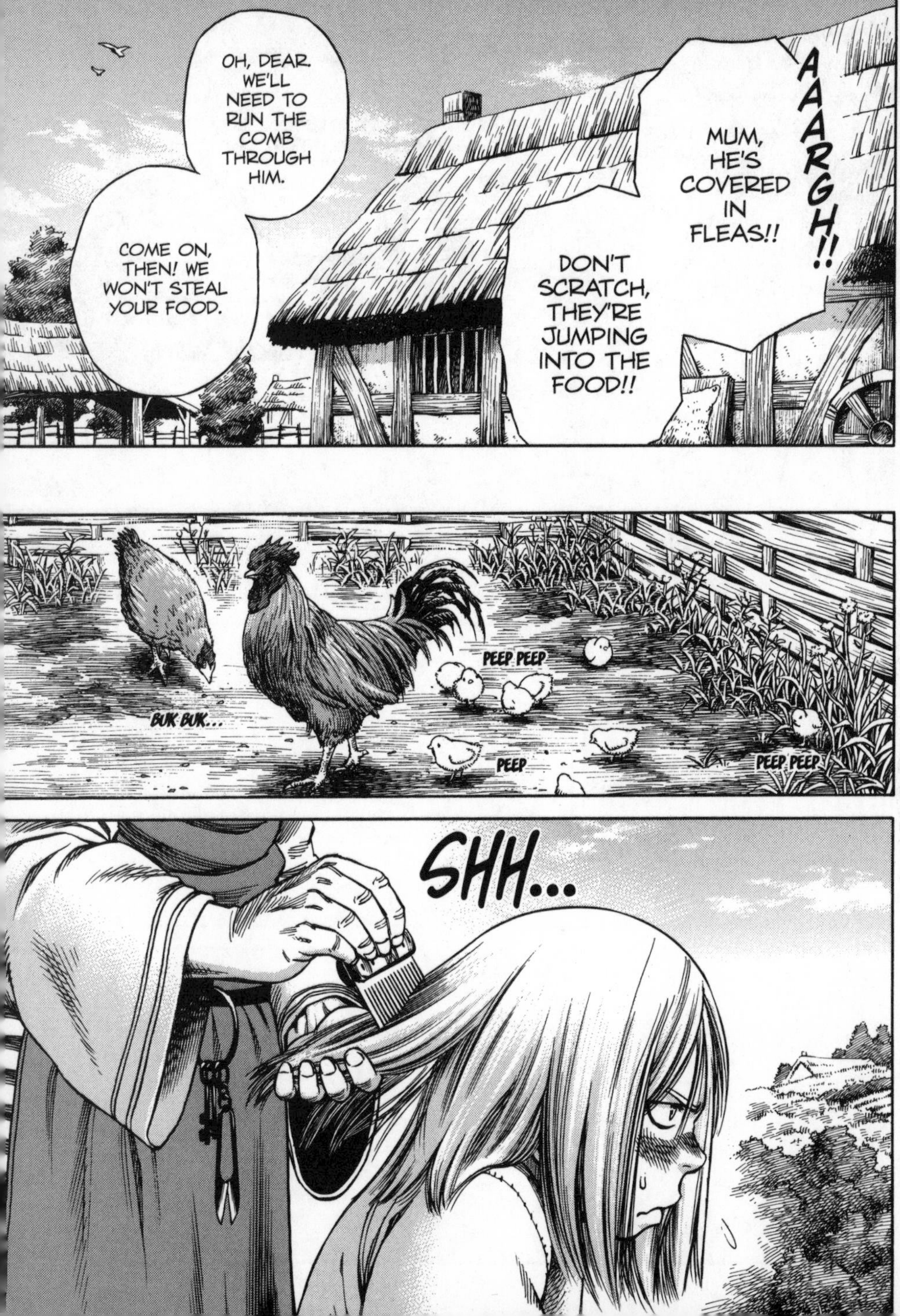
AAARGH!!
MUM, HE'S COVERED IN FLEAS!!
DON'T SCRATCH, THEY'RE JUMPING INTO THE FOOD!!
OH, DEAR. WE'LL NEED TO RUN THE COMB THROUGH HIM.
COME ON, THEN! WE WON'T STEAL YOUR FOOD.
PEEP PEEP
PEEP PEEP
PEEP
BUK BUK...
SHH...

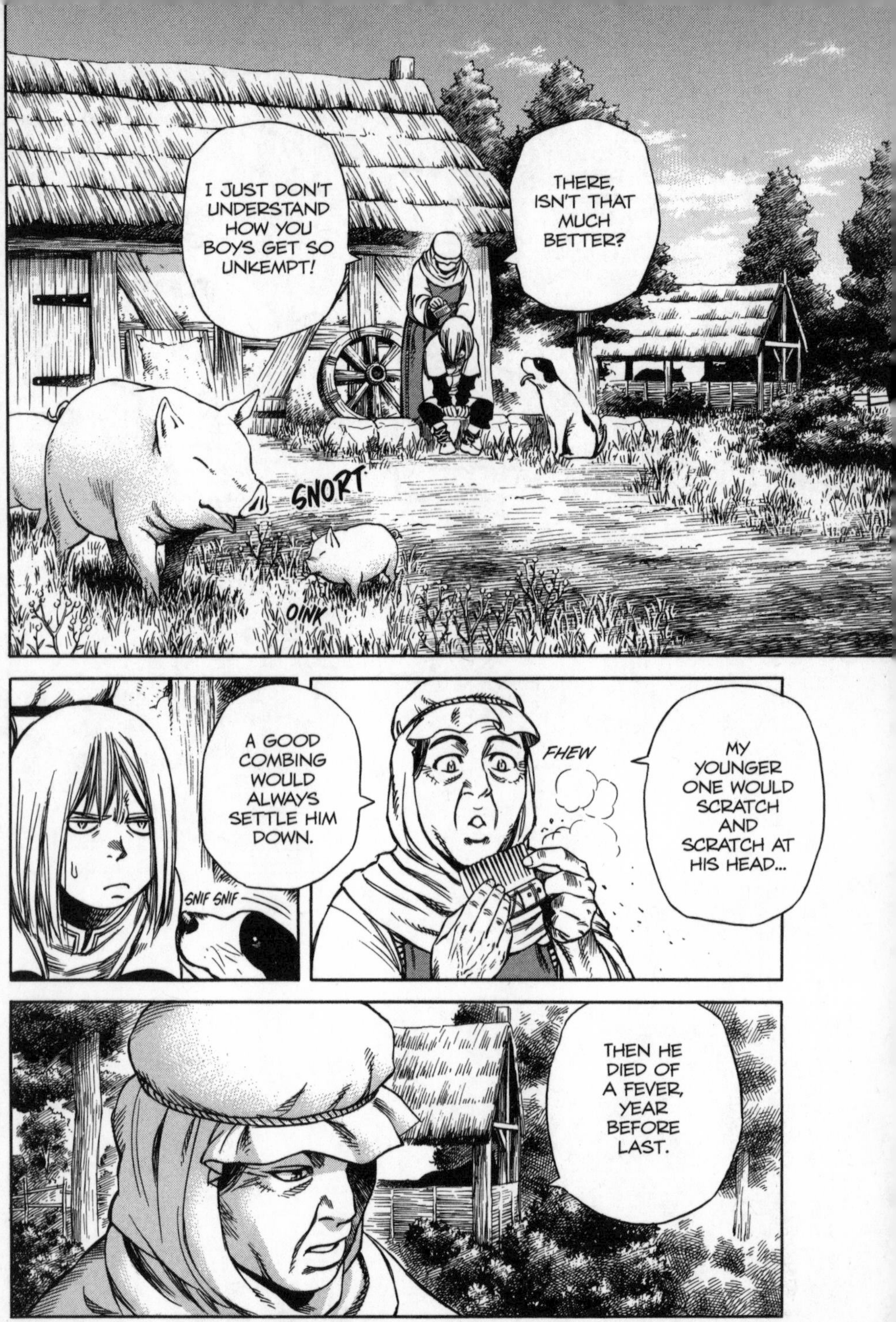
THERE, ISN'T THAT MUCH BETTER?
I JUST DON'T UNDERSTAND HOW YOU BOYS GET SO UNKEMPT!
SNORT
OINK
FHEW
MY YOUNGER ONE WOULD SCRATCH AND SCRATCH AT HIS HEAD...
A GOOD COMBING WOULD ALWAYS SETTLE HIM DOWN.
SNIF SNIF
THEN HE DIED OF A FEVER, YEAR BEFORE LAST.

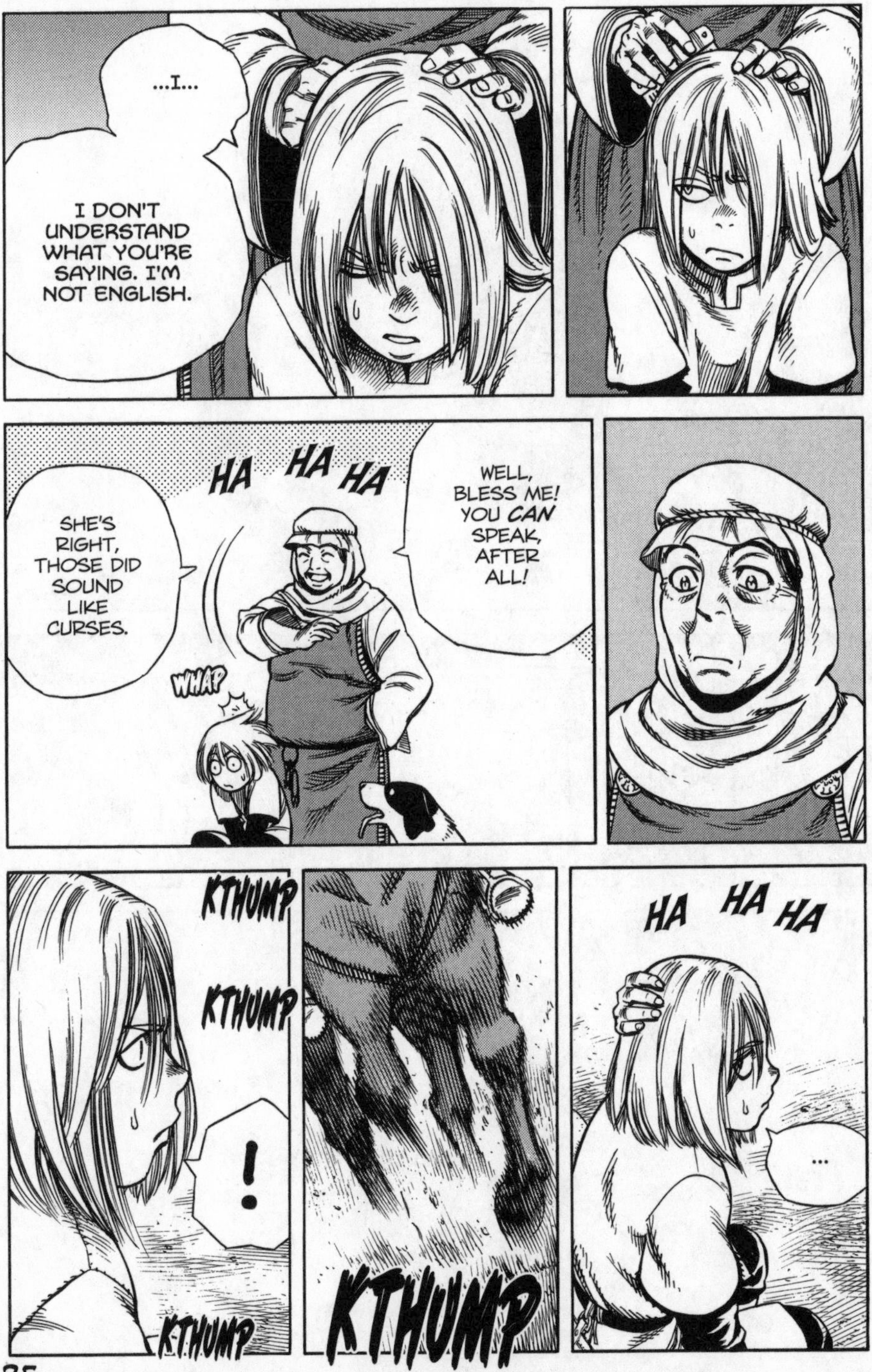
...I...
I DON'T UNDERSTAND WHAT YOU'RE SAYING. I'M NOT ENGLISH.
WELL, BLESS ME! YOU *CAN* SPEAK, AFTER ALL!
HA HA HA
SHE'S RIGHT, THOSE DID SOUND LIKE CURSES.
WHAP
HA HA HA
...
KTHUMP
KTHUMP
KTHUMP
!
KTHUMP

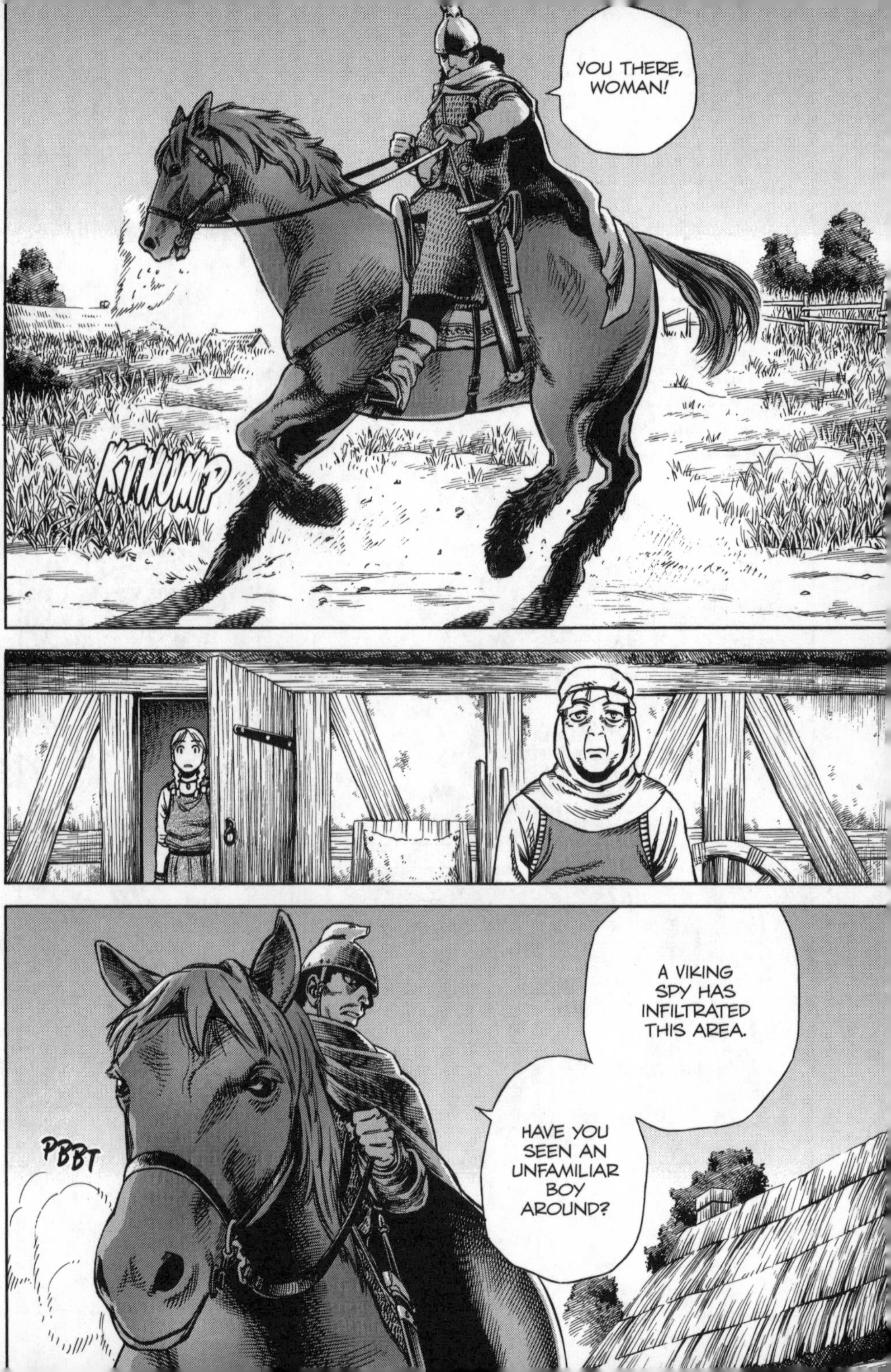
YOU THERE, WOMAN!
KTHUMP
A VIKING SPY HAS INFILTRATED THIS AREA.
HAVE YOU SEEN AN UNFAMILIAR BOY AROUND?
PBBT

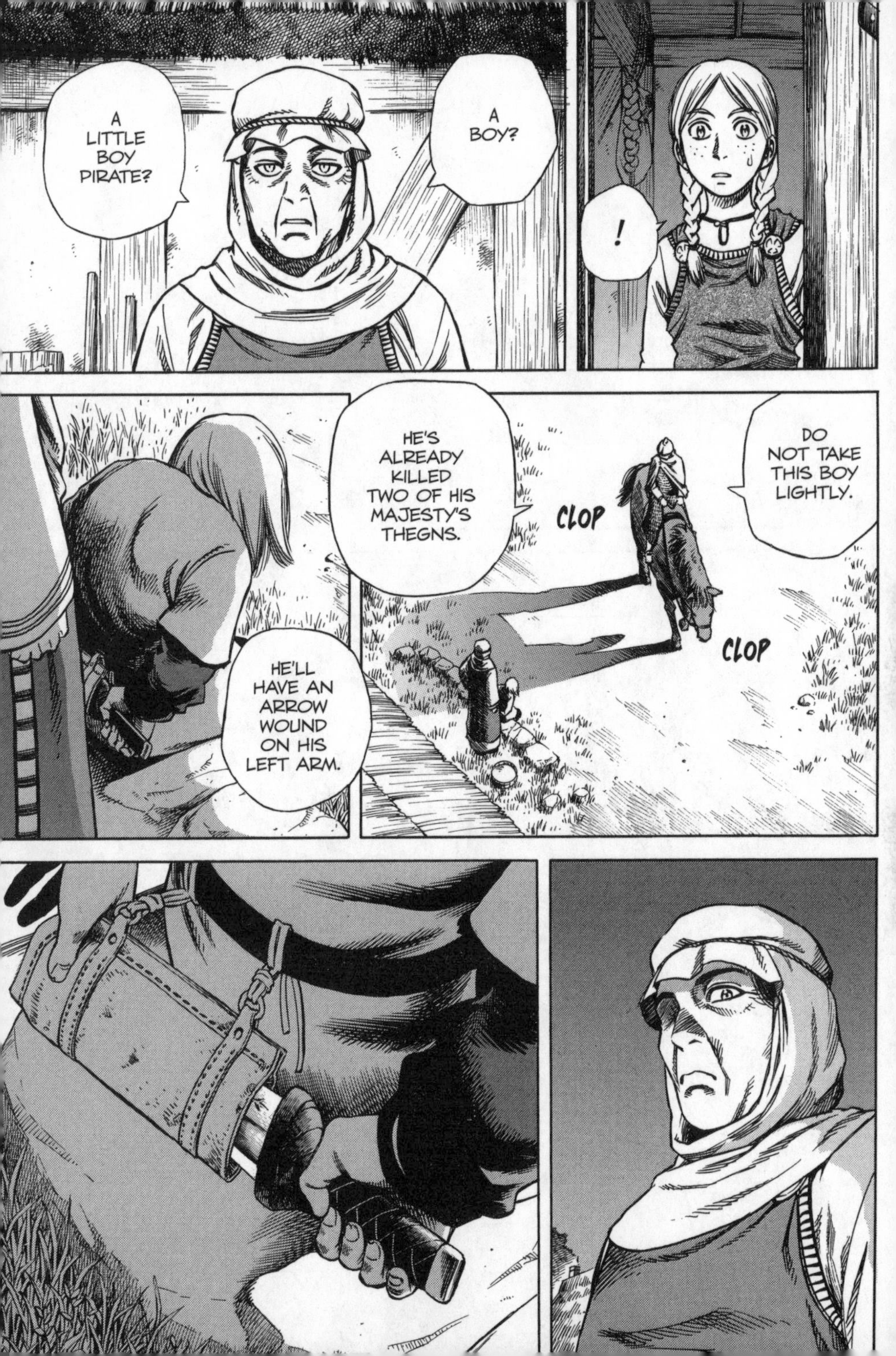
!
A BOY?
A LITTLE BOY PIRATE?
DO NOT TAKE THIS BOY LIGHTLY.
HE'S ALREADY KILLED TWO OF HIS MAJESTY'S THEGNS.
CLOP
CLOP
HE'LL HAVE AN ARROW WOUND ON HIS LEFT ARM.

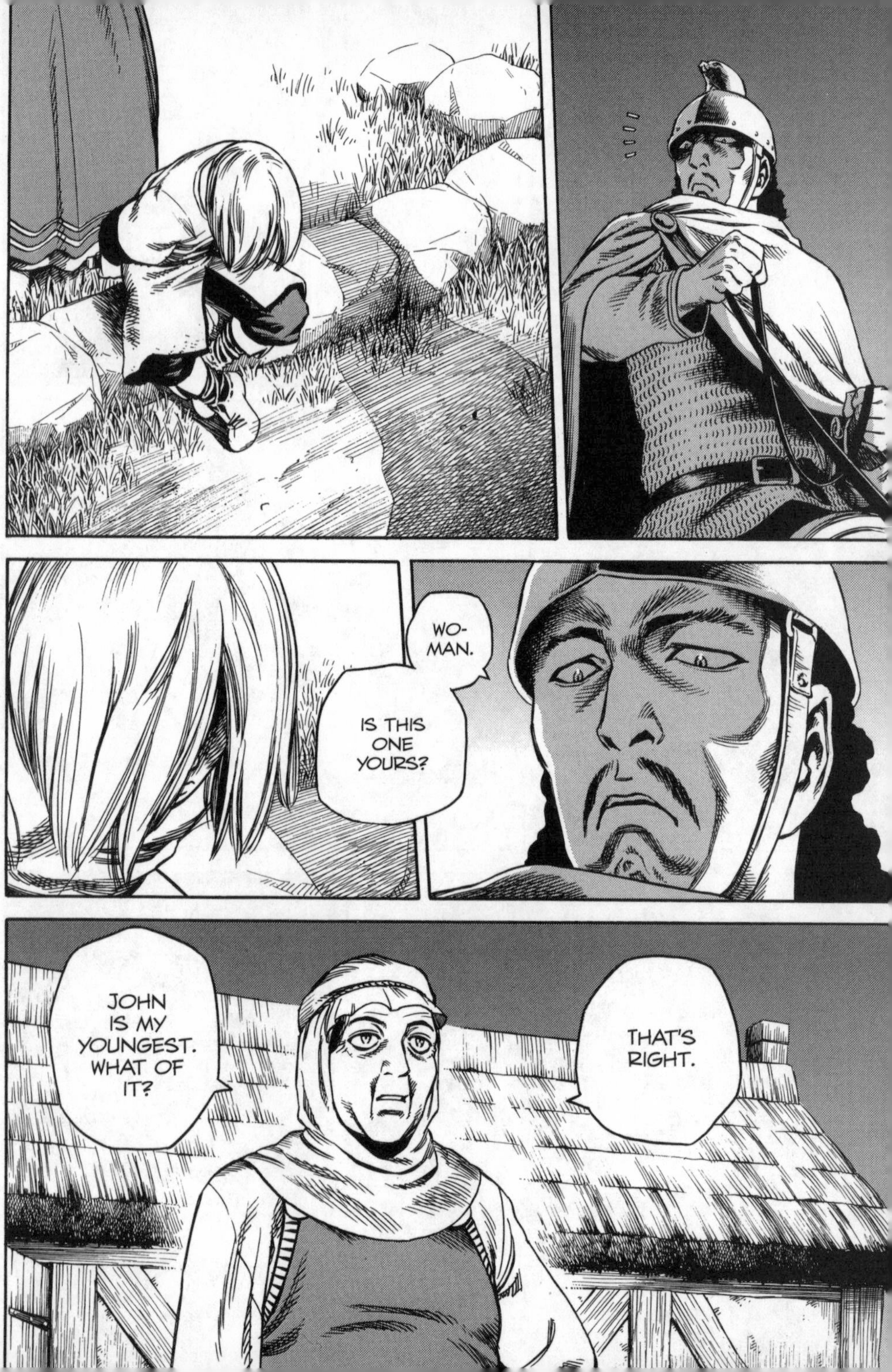
WO-MAN.
IS THIS ONE YOURS?
THAT'S RIGHT.
JOHN IS MY YOUNGEST. WHAT OF IT?

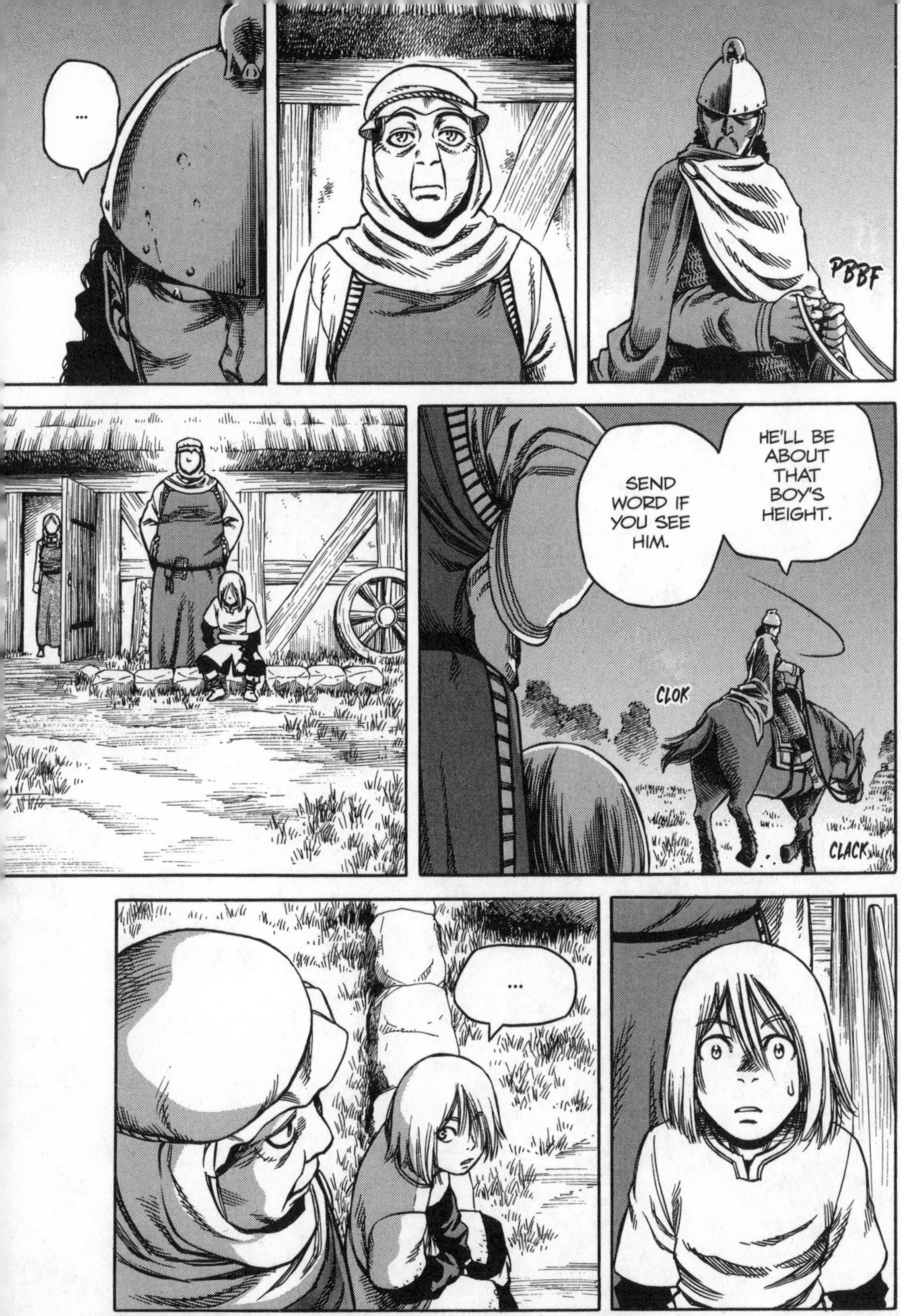
PBBF
...
HE'LL BE ABOUT THAT BOY'S HEIGHT.
SEND WORD IF YOU SEE HIM.
CLOK
CLACK
...

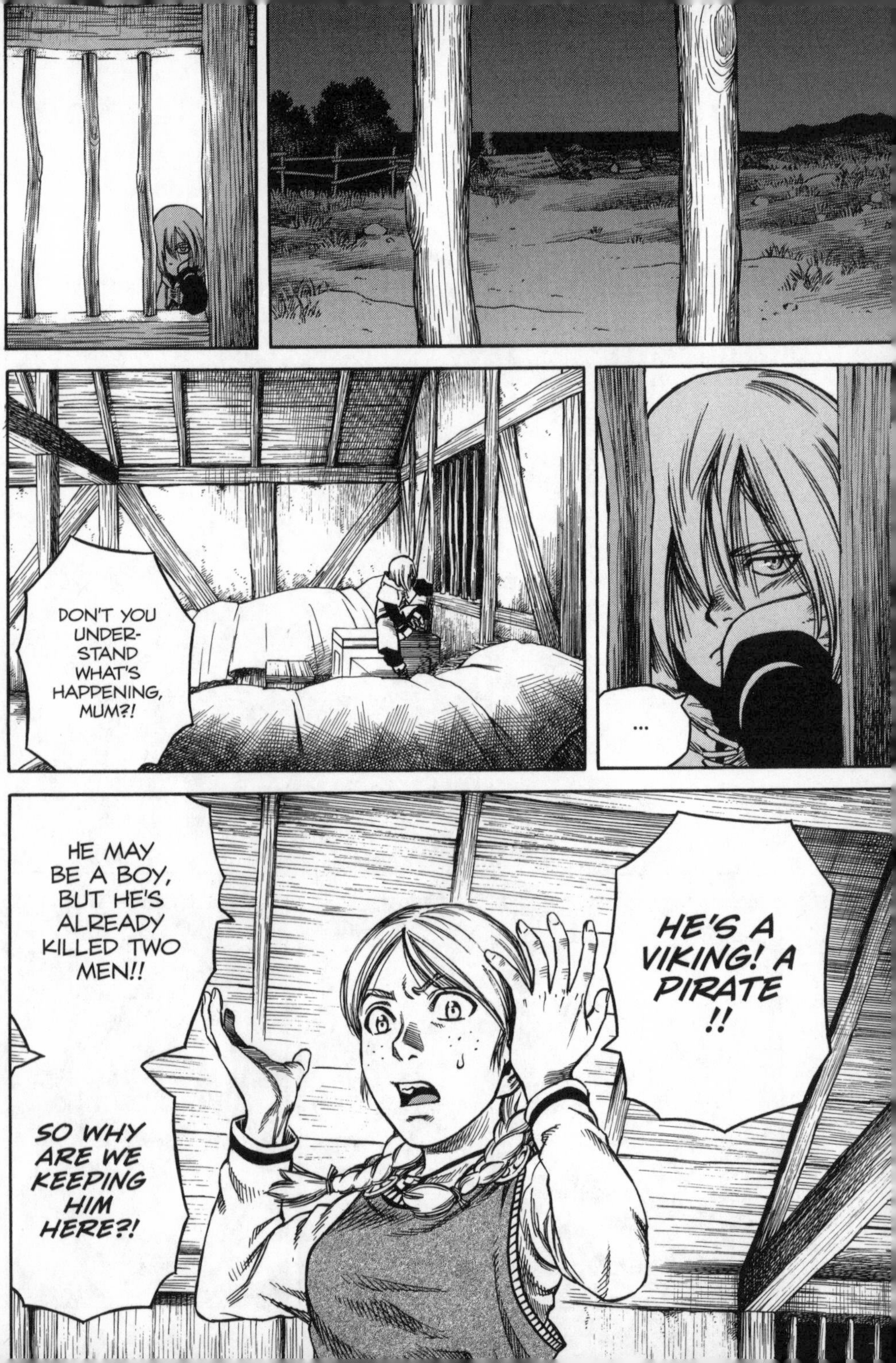
...
DON'T YOU UNDERSTAND WHAT'S HAPPENING, MUM?!
HE'S A VIKING! A PIRATE!!
HE MAY BE A BOY, BUT HE'S ALREADY KILLED TWO MEN!!
SO WHY ARE WE KEEPING HIM HERE?!

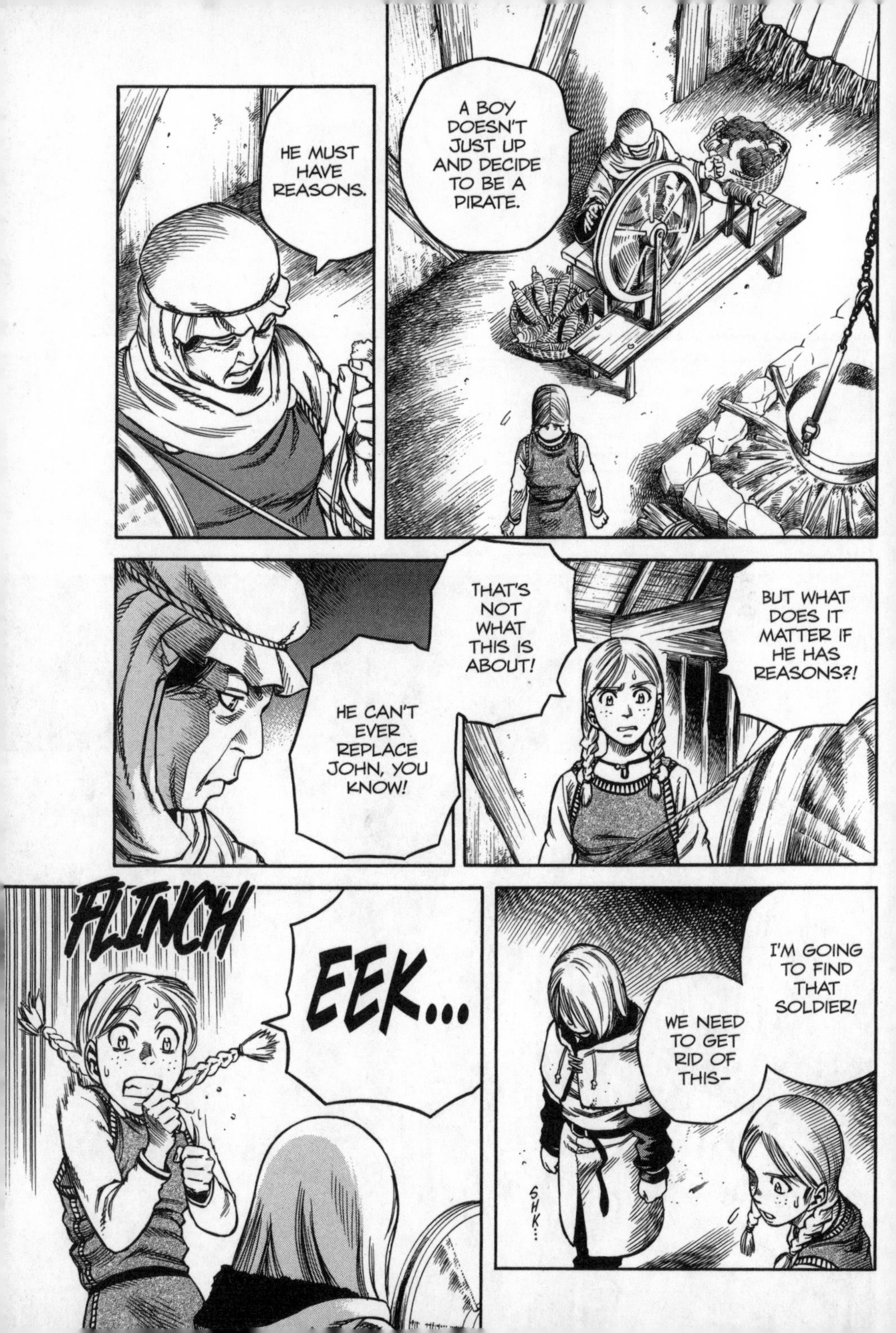
A BOY DOESN'T JUST UP AND DECIDE TO BE A PIRATE.
HE MUST HAVE REASONS.
BUT WHAT DOES IT MATTER IF HE HAS REASONS?!
THAT'S NOT WHAT THIS IS ABOUT!
HE CAN'T EVER REPLACE JOHN, YOU KNOW!
I'M GOING TO FIND THAT SOLDIER!
WE NEED TO GET RID OF THIS-
SHK...
FLINCH
EEK...

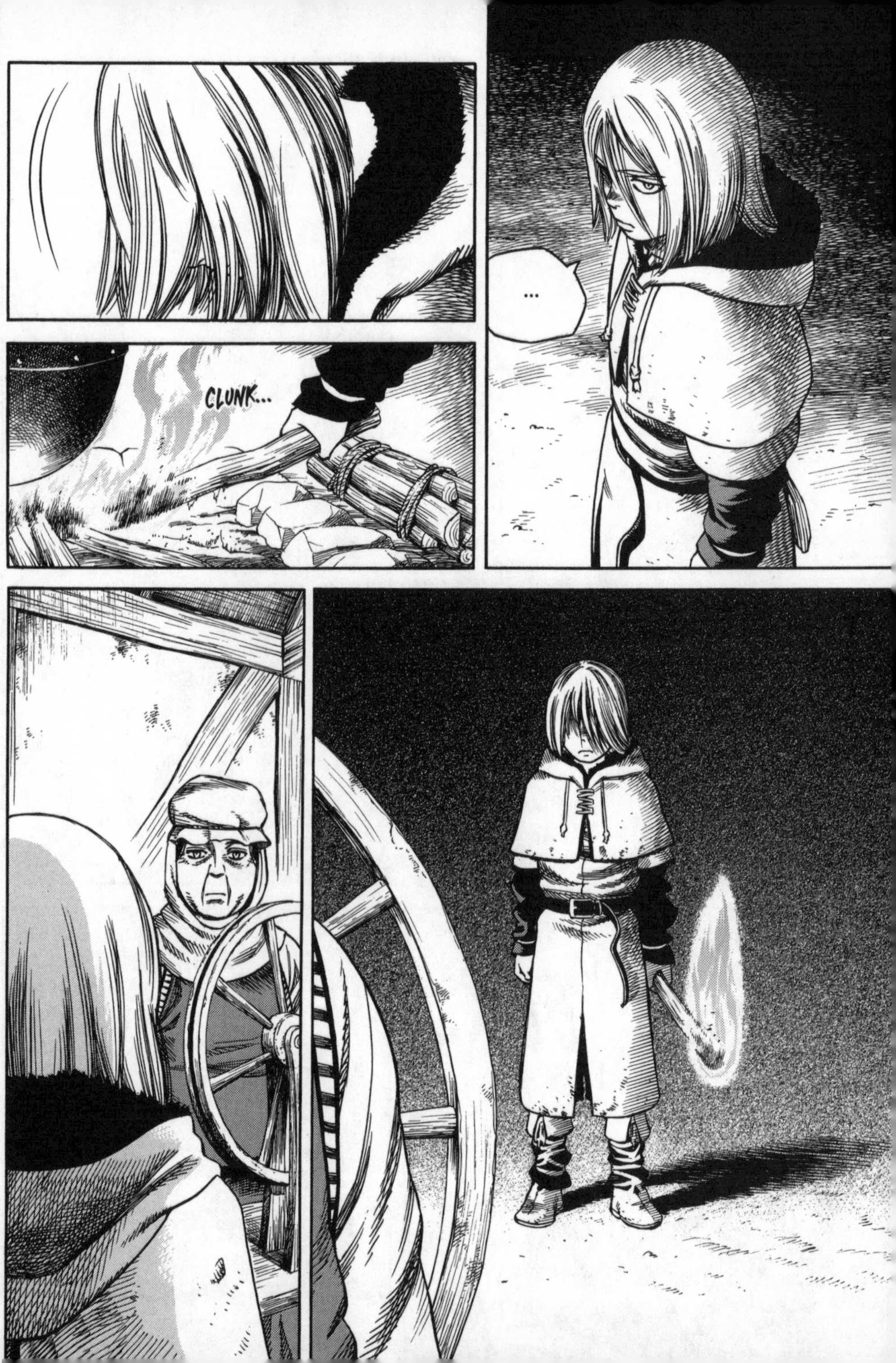
...
CLUNK...

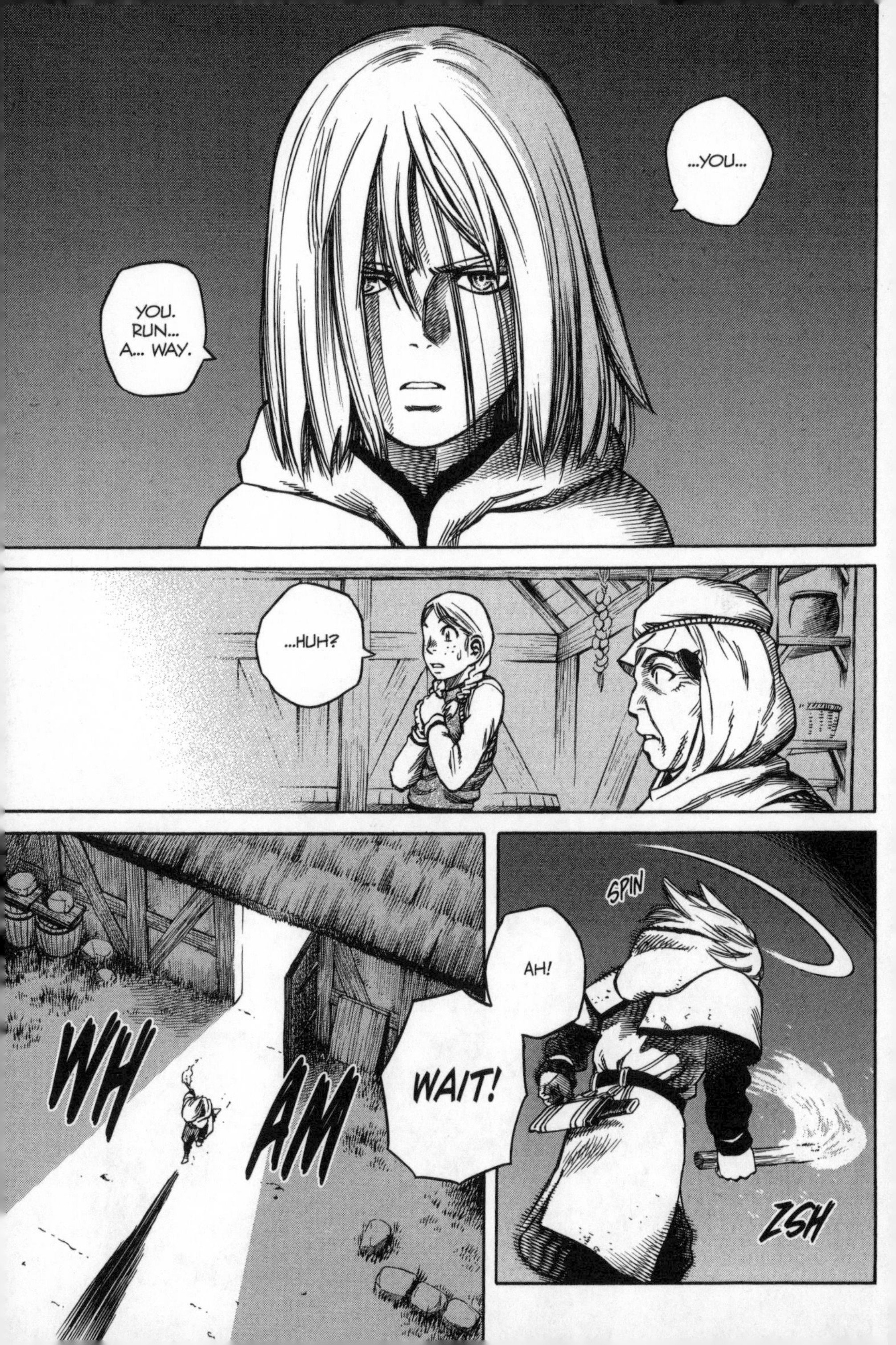
...YOU...
YOU. RUN... A... WAY.
...HUH?
SPIN
AH!
WAIT!
ZSH
WH AM

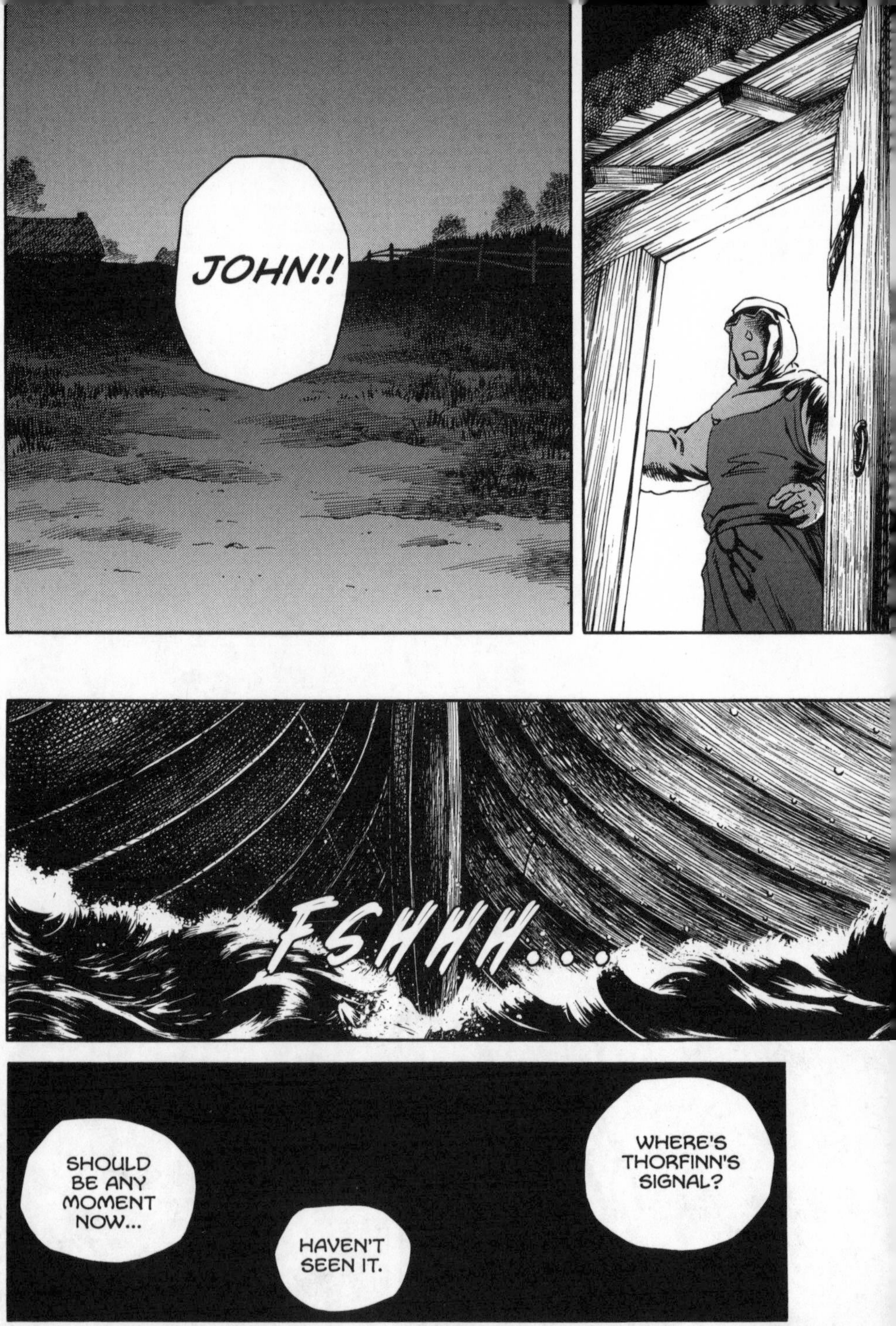
JOHN!!
FSHHH...
WHERE'S THORFINN'S SIGNAL?
HAVEN'T SEEN IT.
SHOULD BE ANY MOMENT NOW...

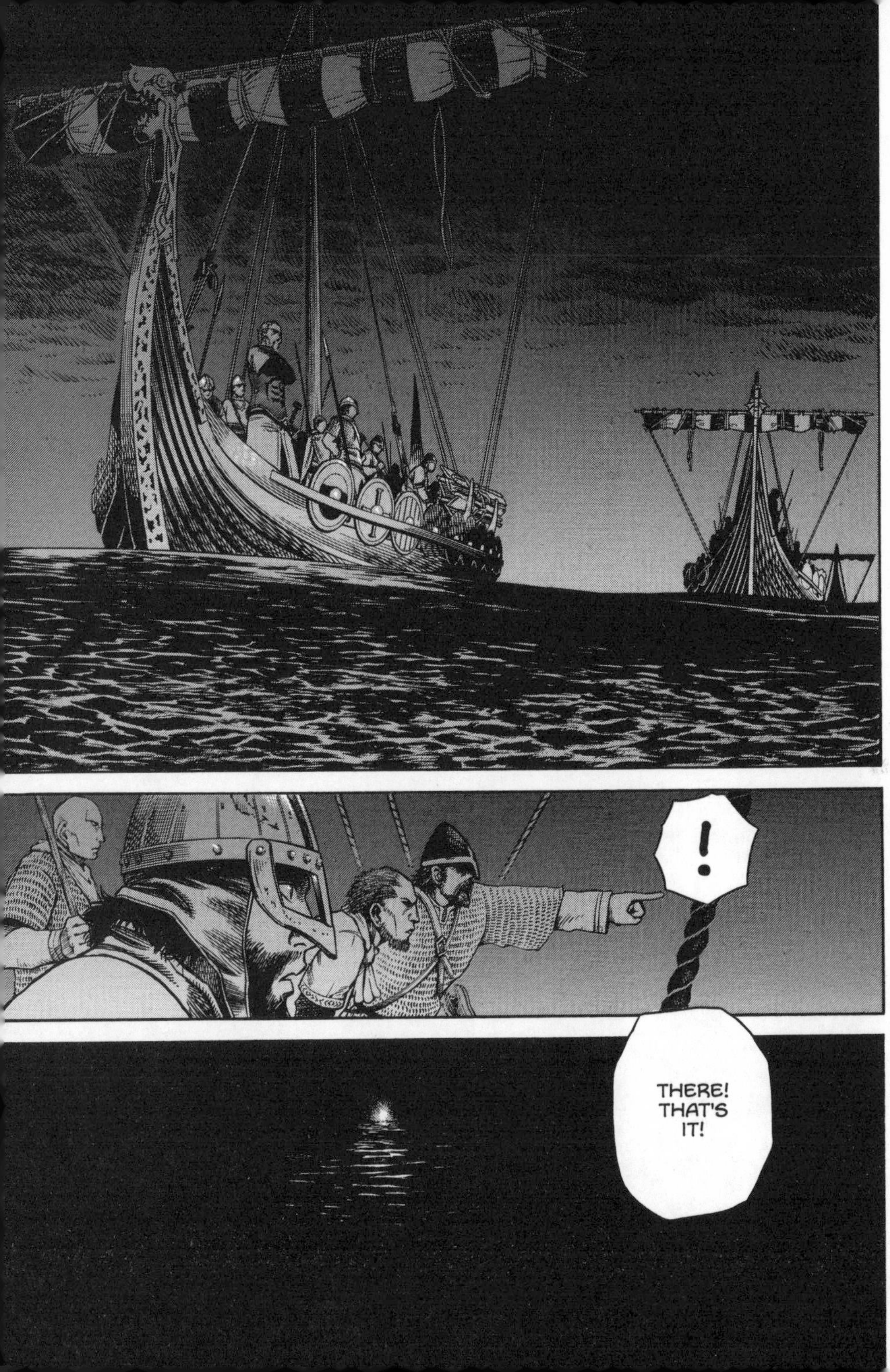
!
THERE! THAT'S IT!

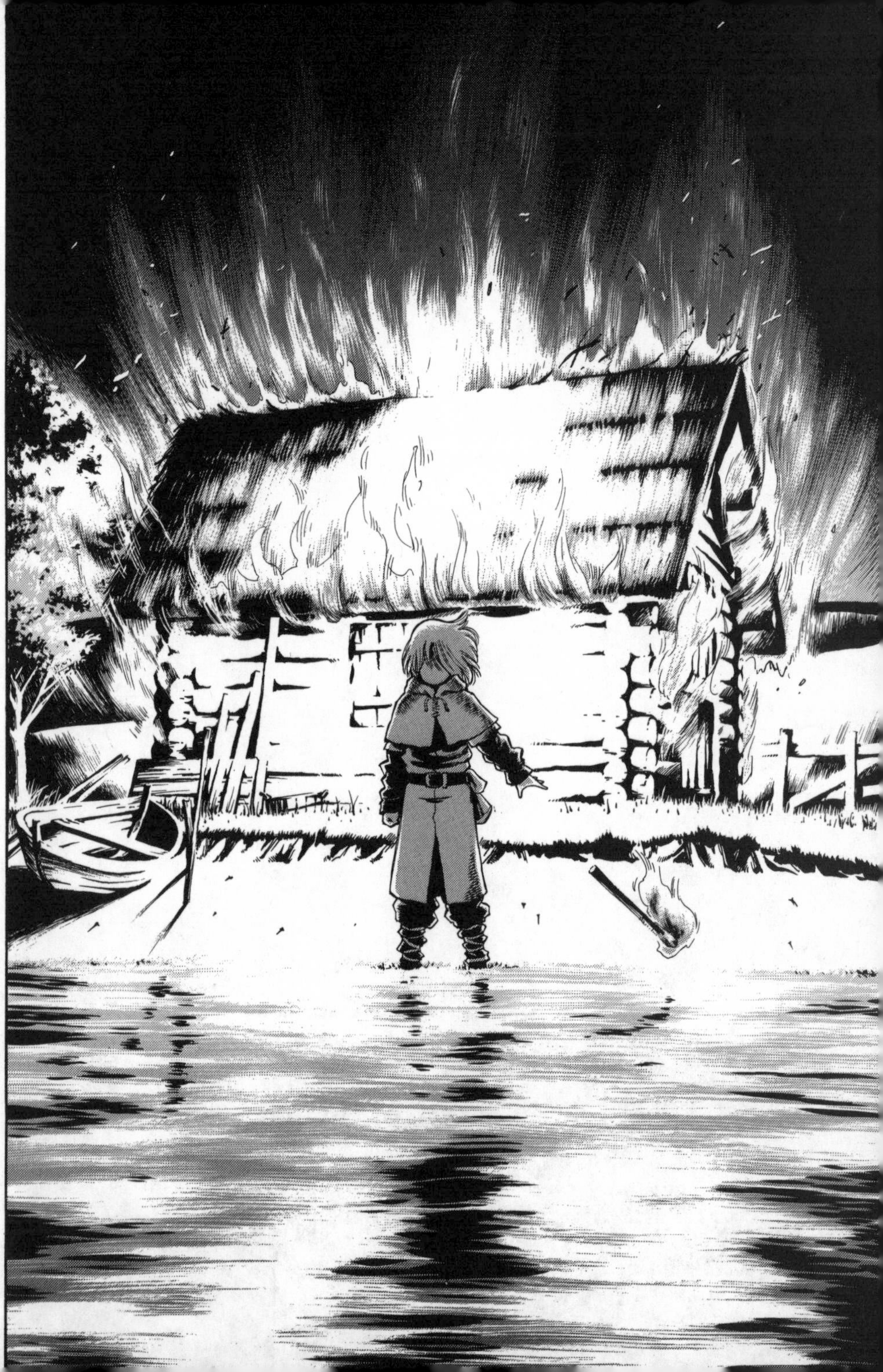

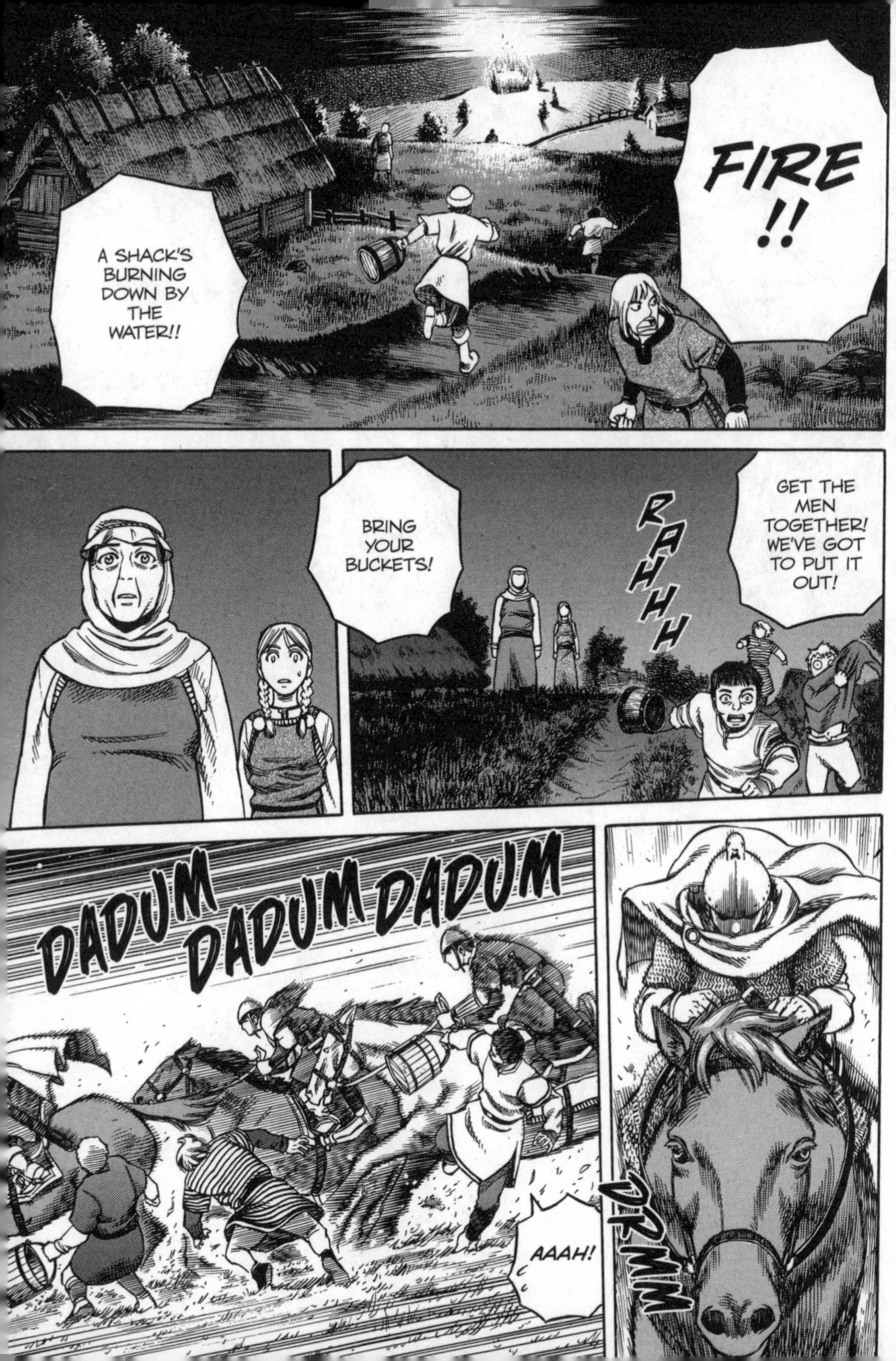
FIRE!!
A SHACK'S BURNING DOWN BY THE WATER!!
GET THE MEN TOGETHER! WE'VE GOT TO PUT IT OUT!
RAHHH
BRING YOUR BUCKETS!
DADUM DADUM DADUM
AAAH!

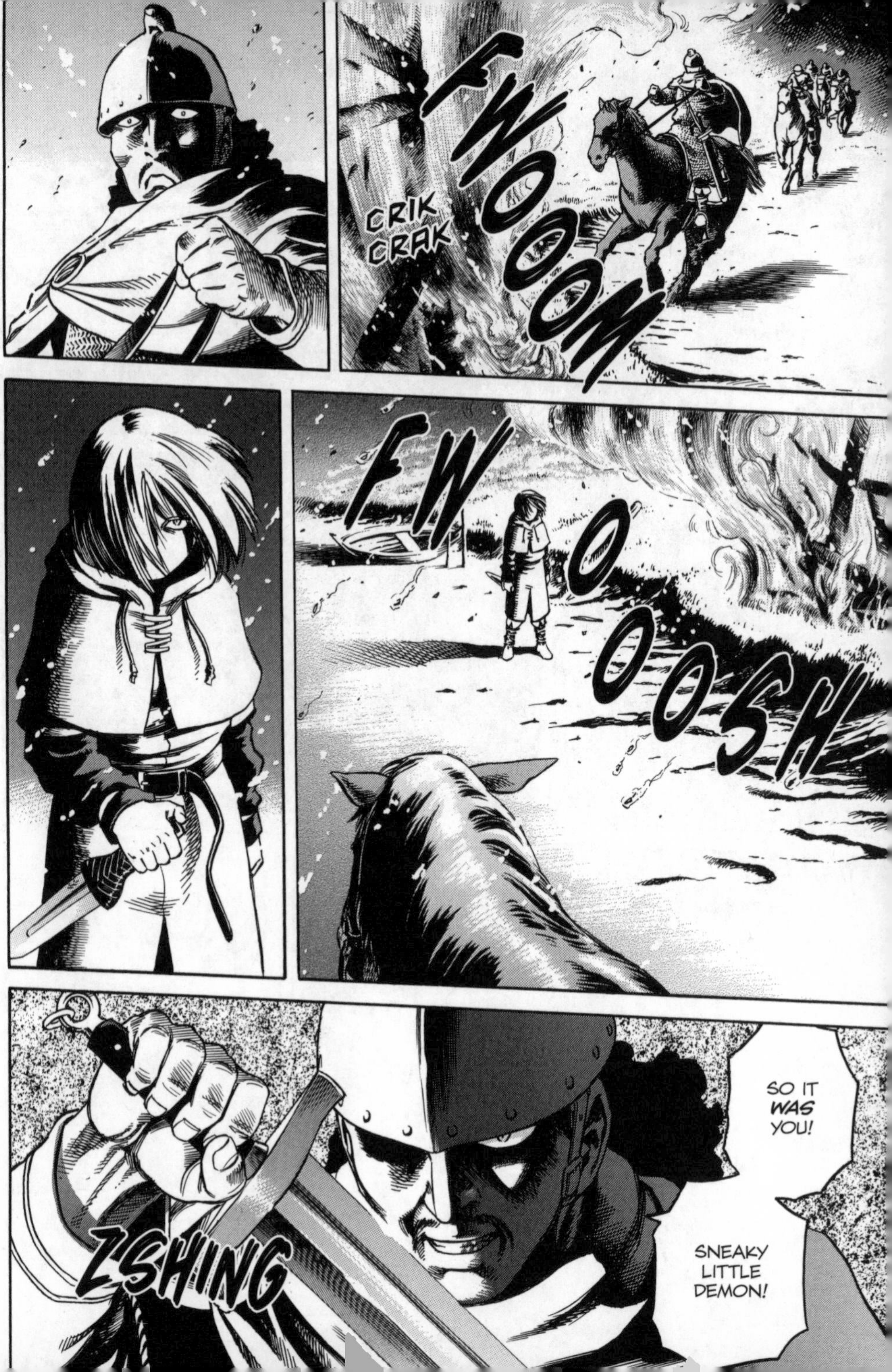
FWOOOM
CRIK CRAK
FWOOOOSH
SO IT WAS YOU!
SNEAKY LITTLE DEMON!
ZSHING

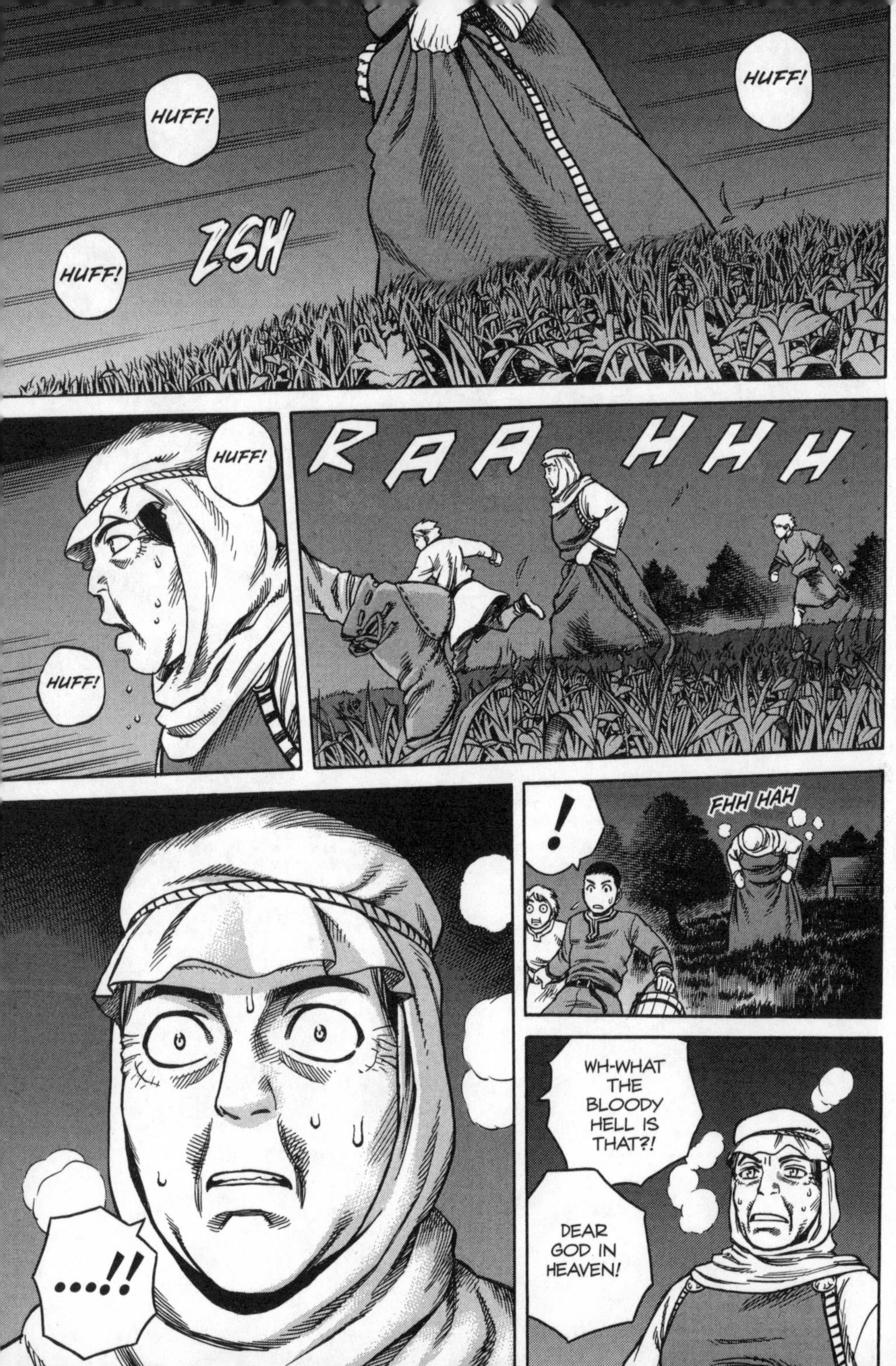
HUFF!
HUFF!
ZSH
HUFF!
RAAHHH
HUFF!
HUFF!
FHH HAH
!
WH-WHAT THE BLOODY HELL IS THAT?!
DEAR GOD IN HEAVEN!
...!!

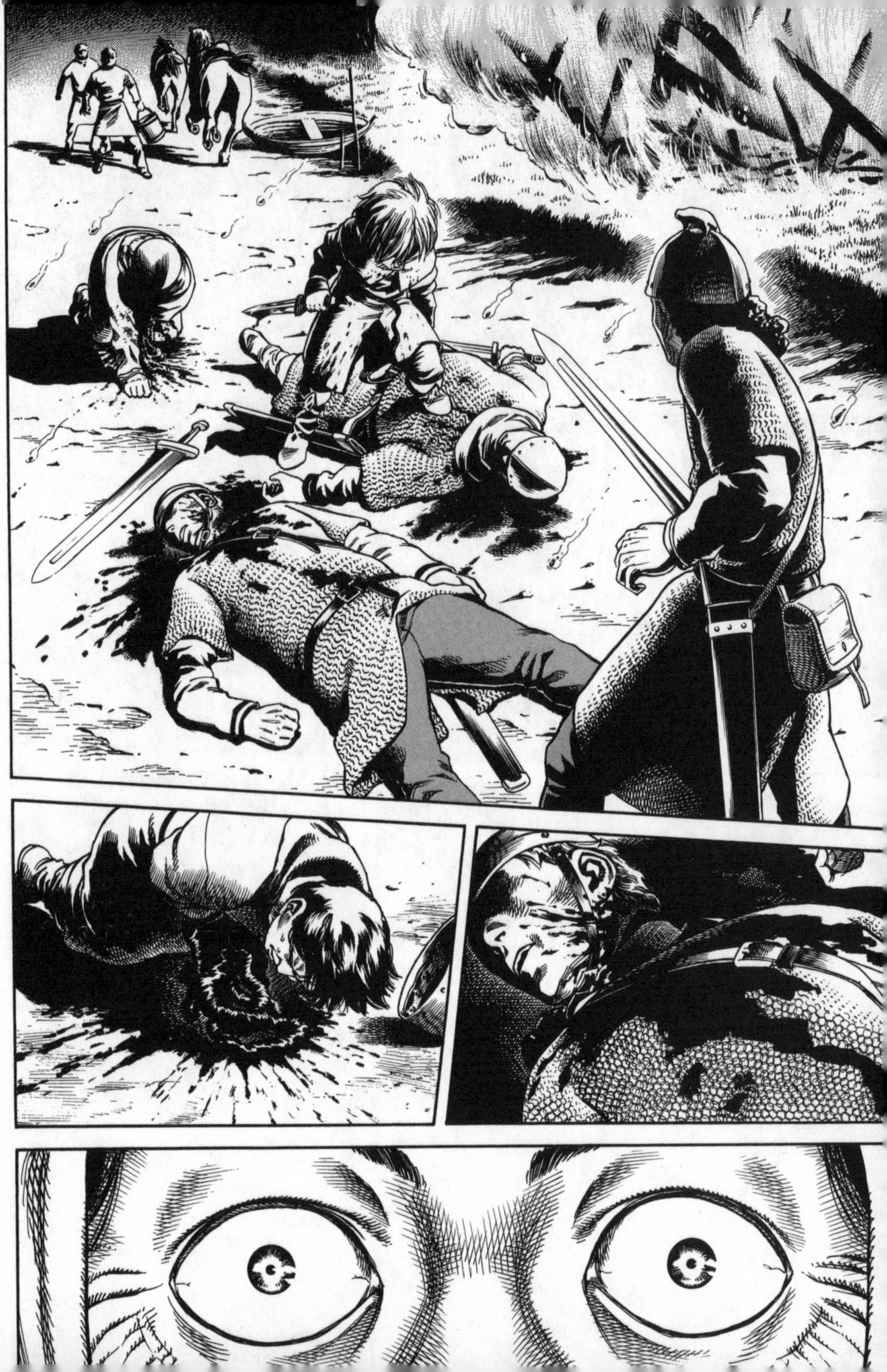

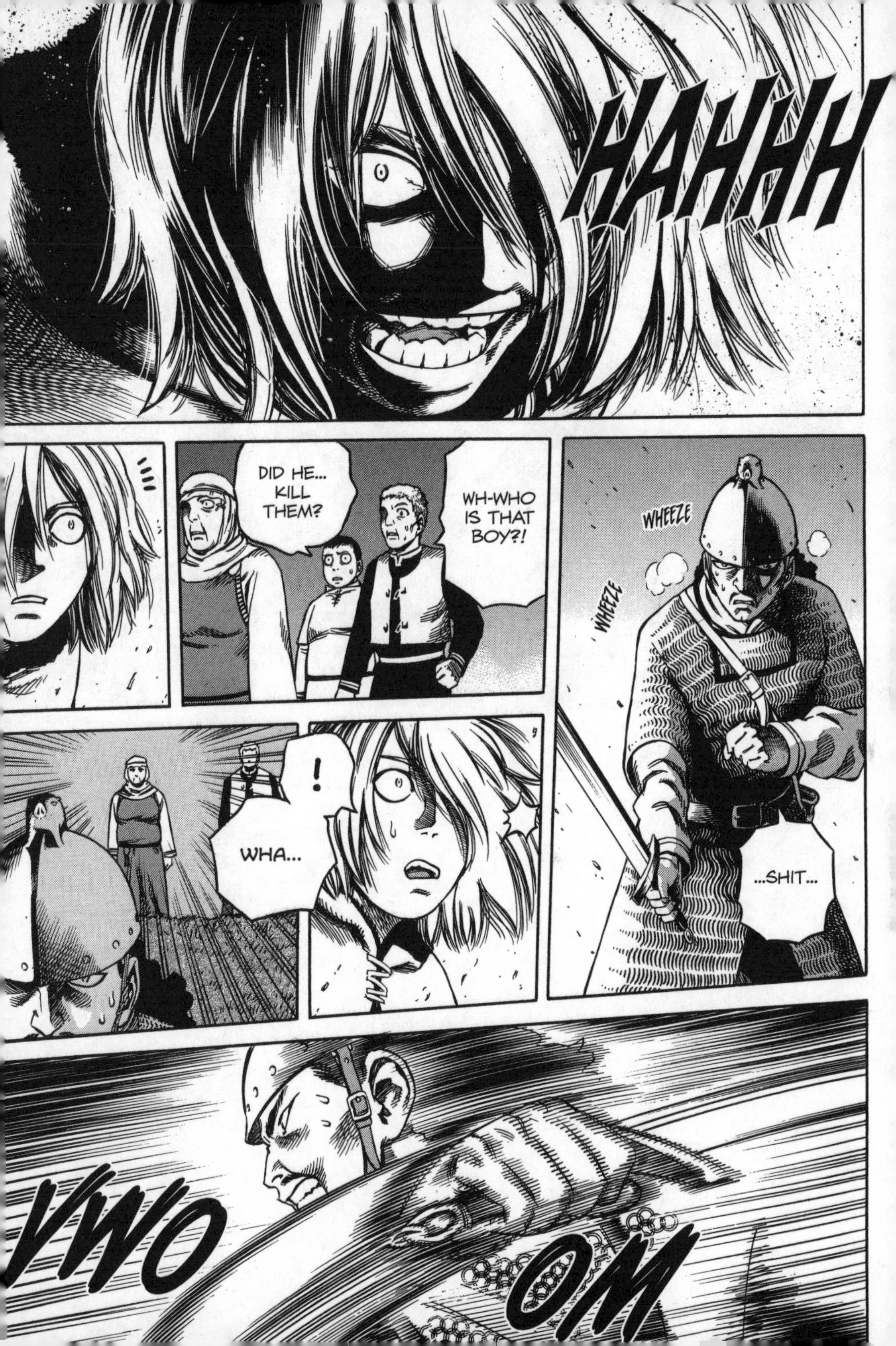

HAHHH
WHEEZE
WHEEZE
...SHIT...
WH-WHO IS THAT BOY?!
DID HE... KILL THEM?
!
WHA...
VWO
OM

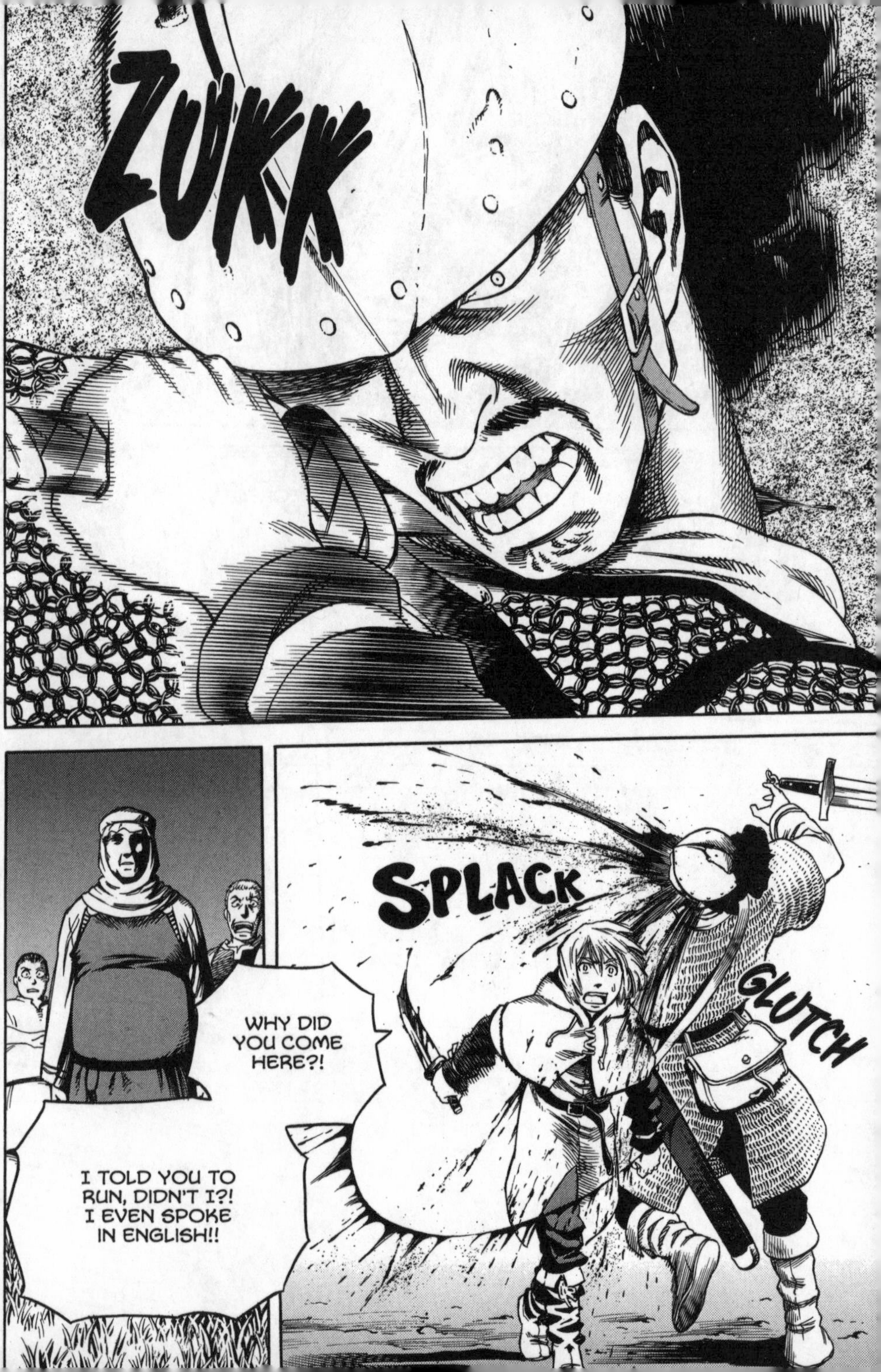
ZOKK
SPLACK
GLUTCH
WHY DID YOU COME HERE?!
I TOLD YOU TO RUN, DIDN'T I?! I EVEN SPOKE IN ENGLISH!!

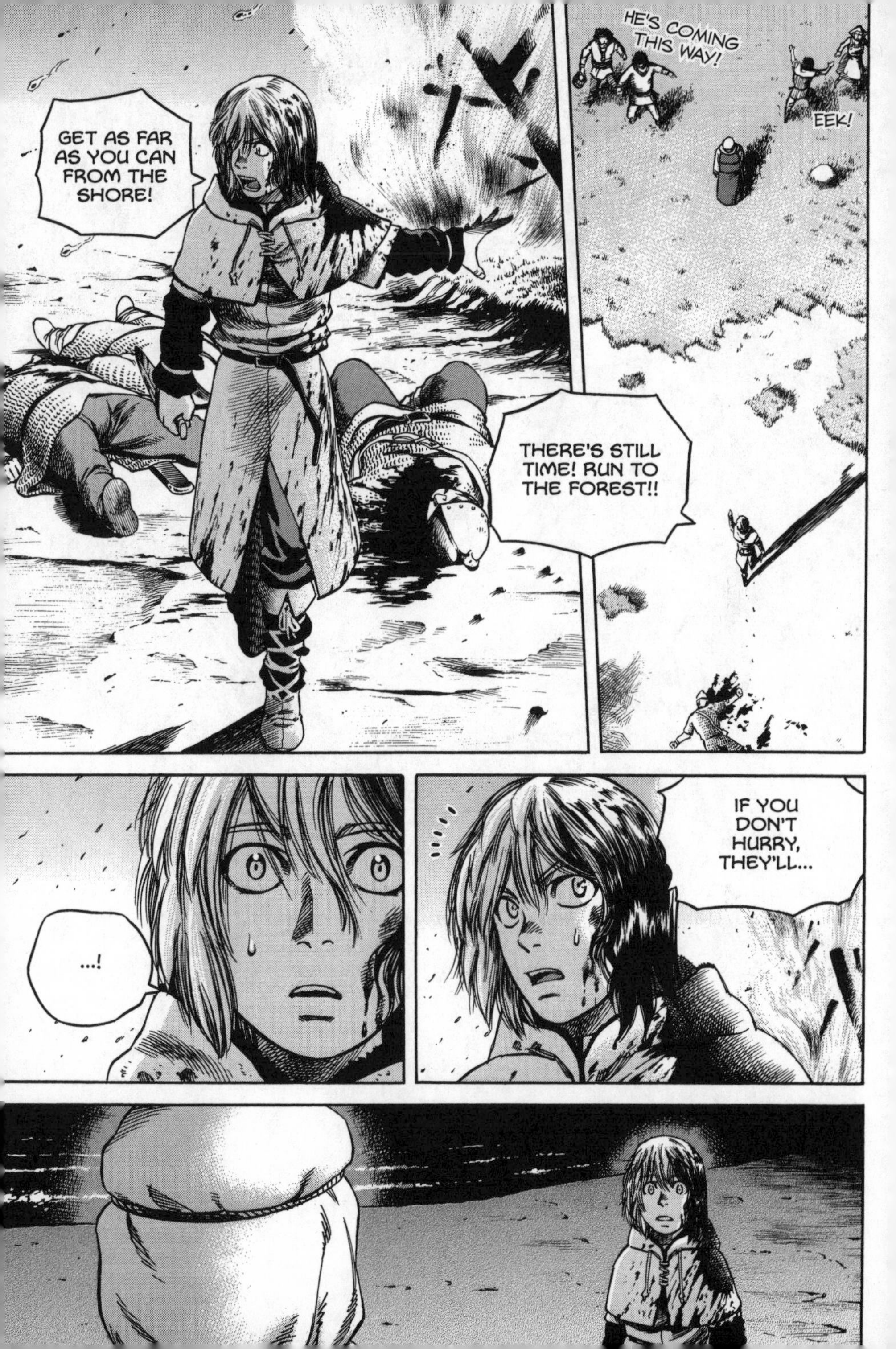
HE'S COMING THIS WAY!
EEK!
GET AS FAR AS YOU CAN FROM THE SHORE!
THERE'S STILL TIME! RUN TO THE FOREST!!
IF YOU DON'T HURRY, THEY'LL...
...!

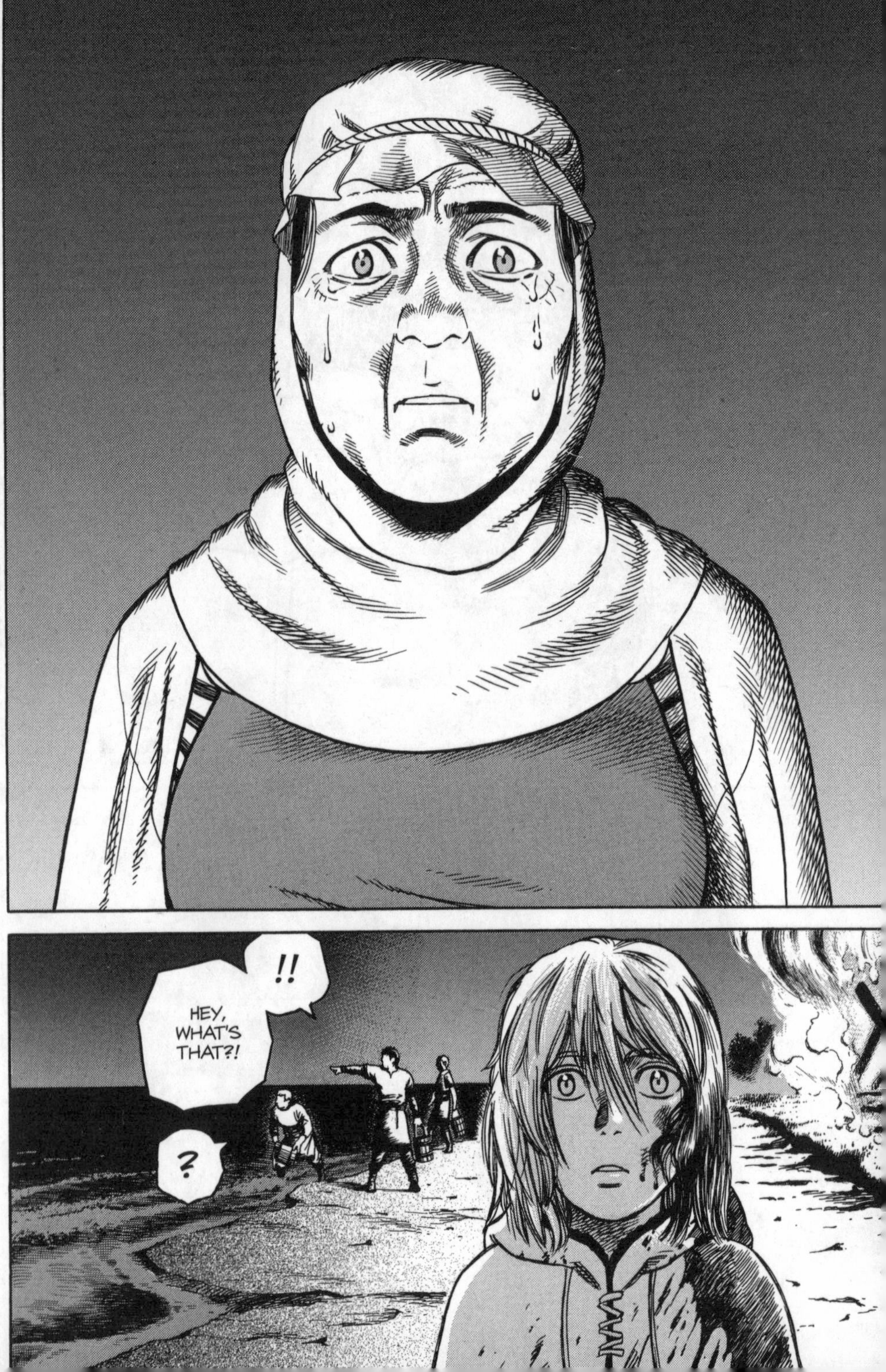
!!
HEY, WHAT'S THAT?!
?

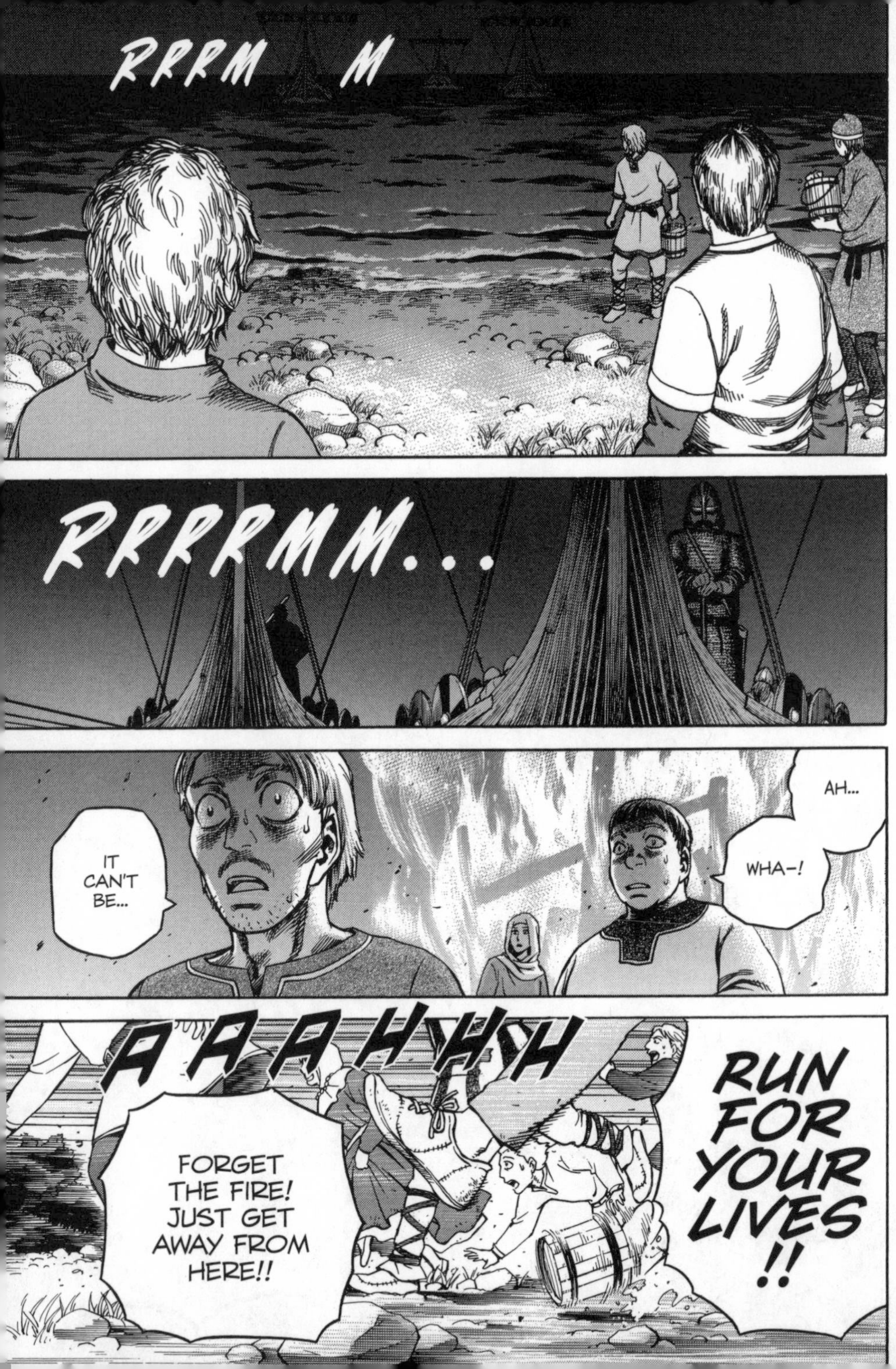
RRRM M
RRRRMM...
AH...
WHA-!
IT CAN'T BE...
RUN FOR YOUR LIVES!!
AAAHHHH
FORGET THE FIRE! JUST GET AWAY FROM HERE!!

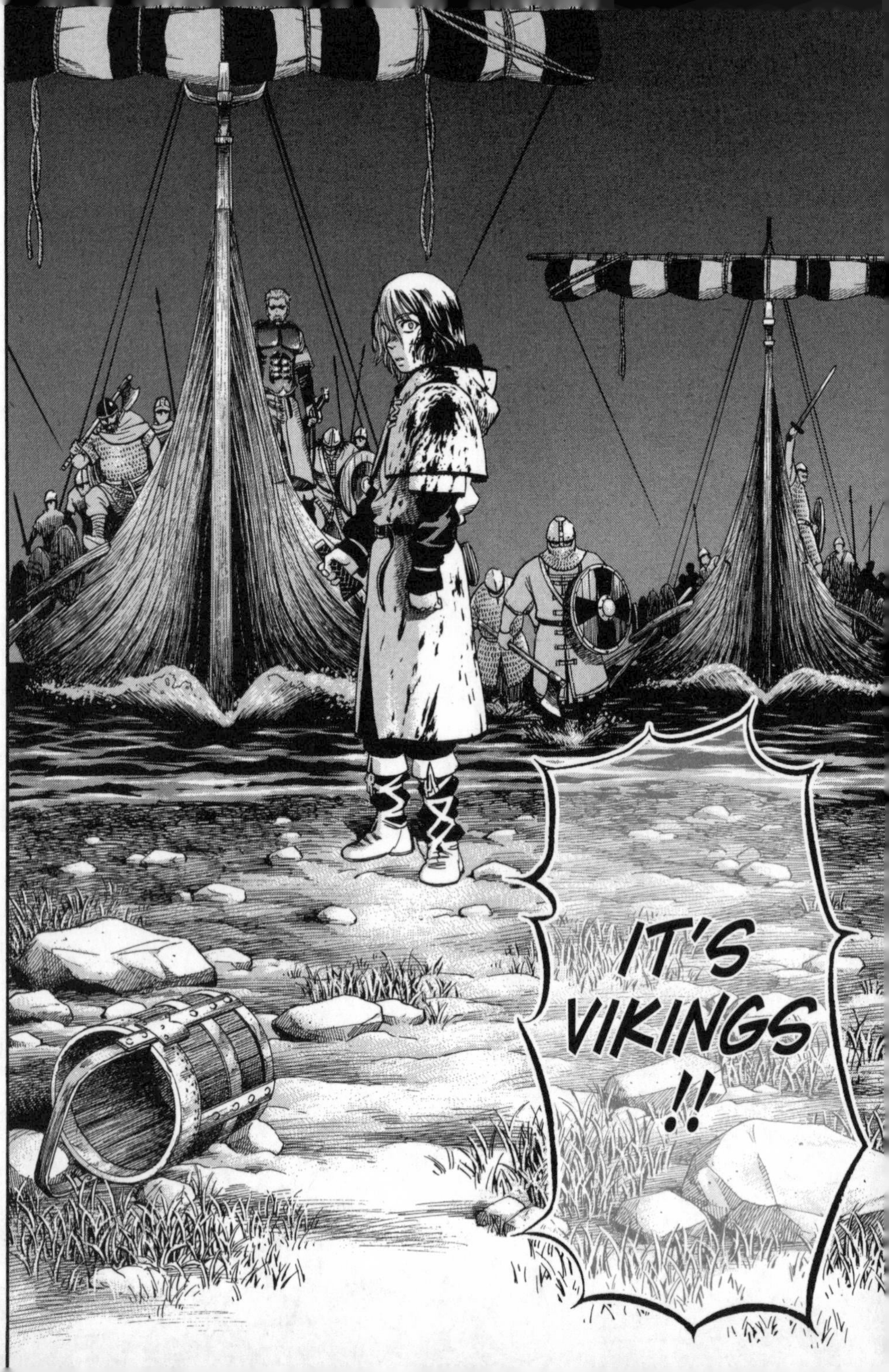
IT'S VIKINGS!!

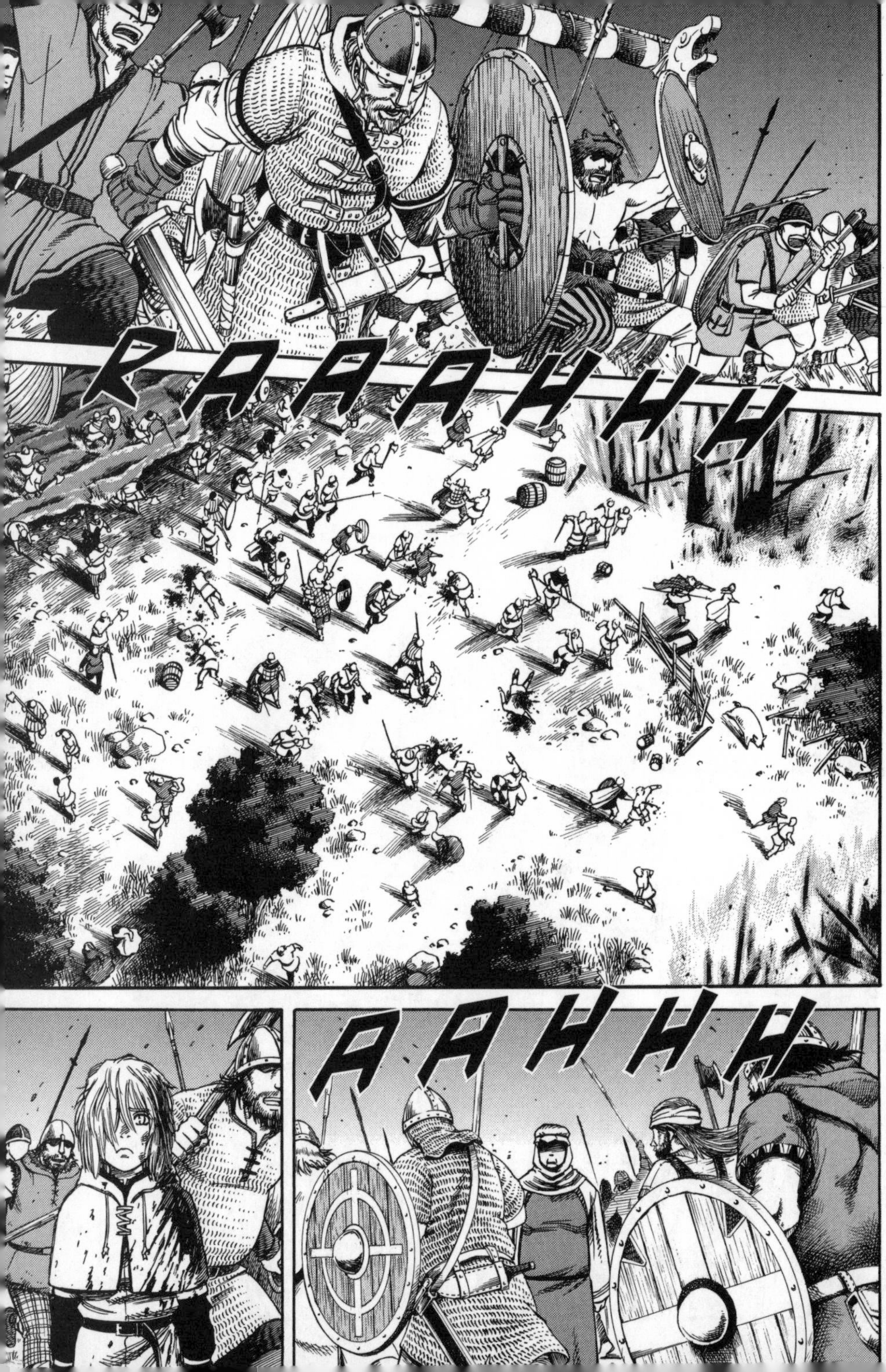
RAAAHHH
AAHHHH

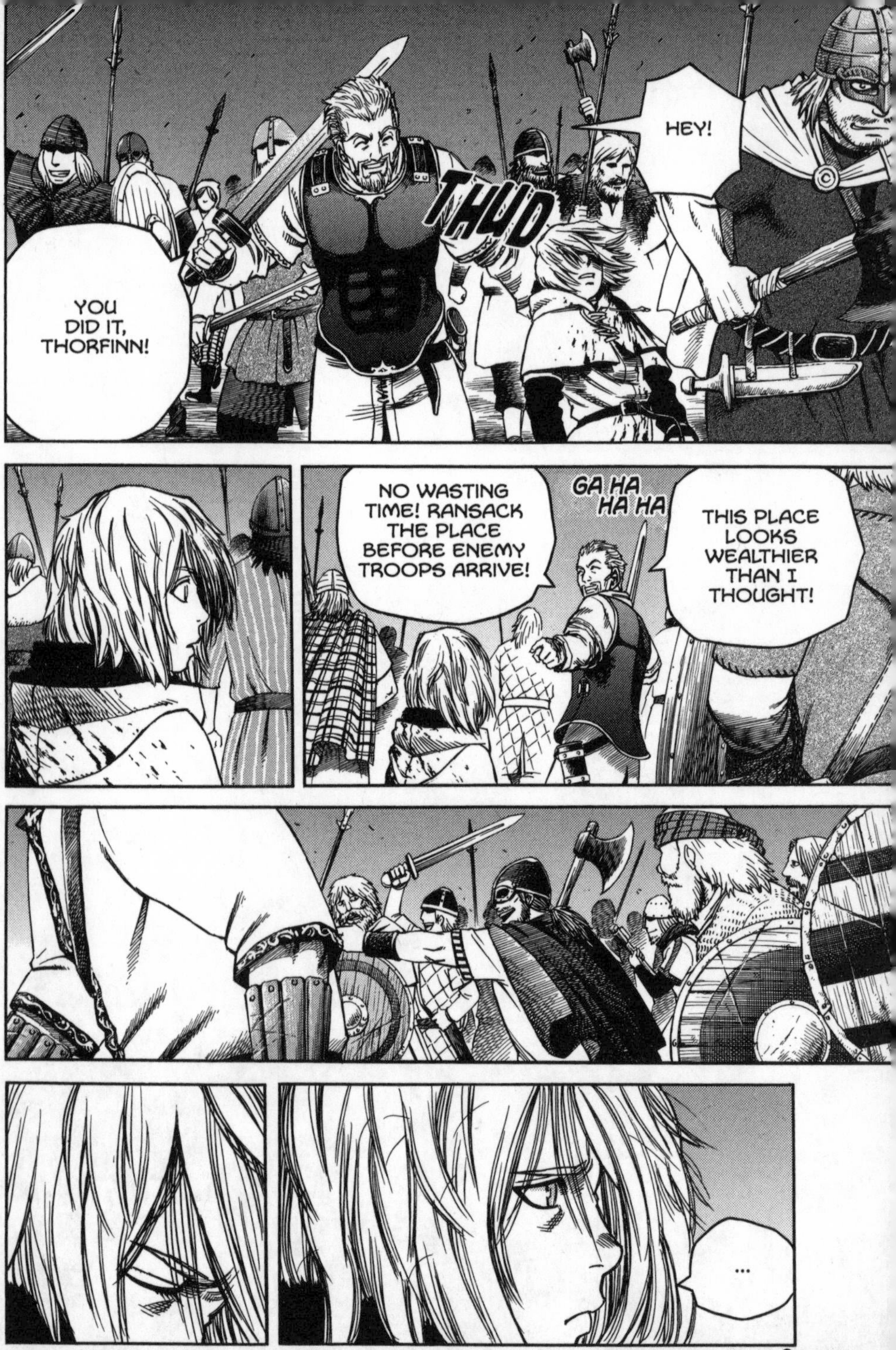
HEY!
THUD
YOU DID IT, THORFINN!
THIS PLACE LOOKS WEALTHIER THAN I THOUGHT!
GA HA HA HA
NO WASTING TIME! RANSACK THE PLACE BEFORE ENEMY TROOPS ARRIVE!
...

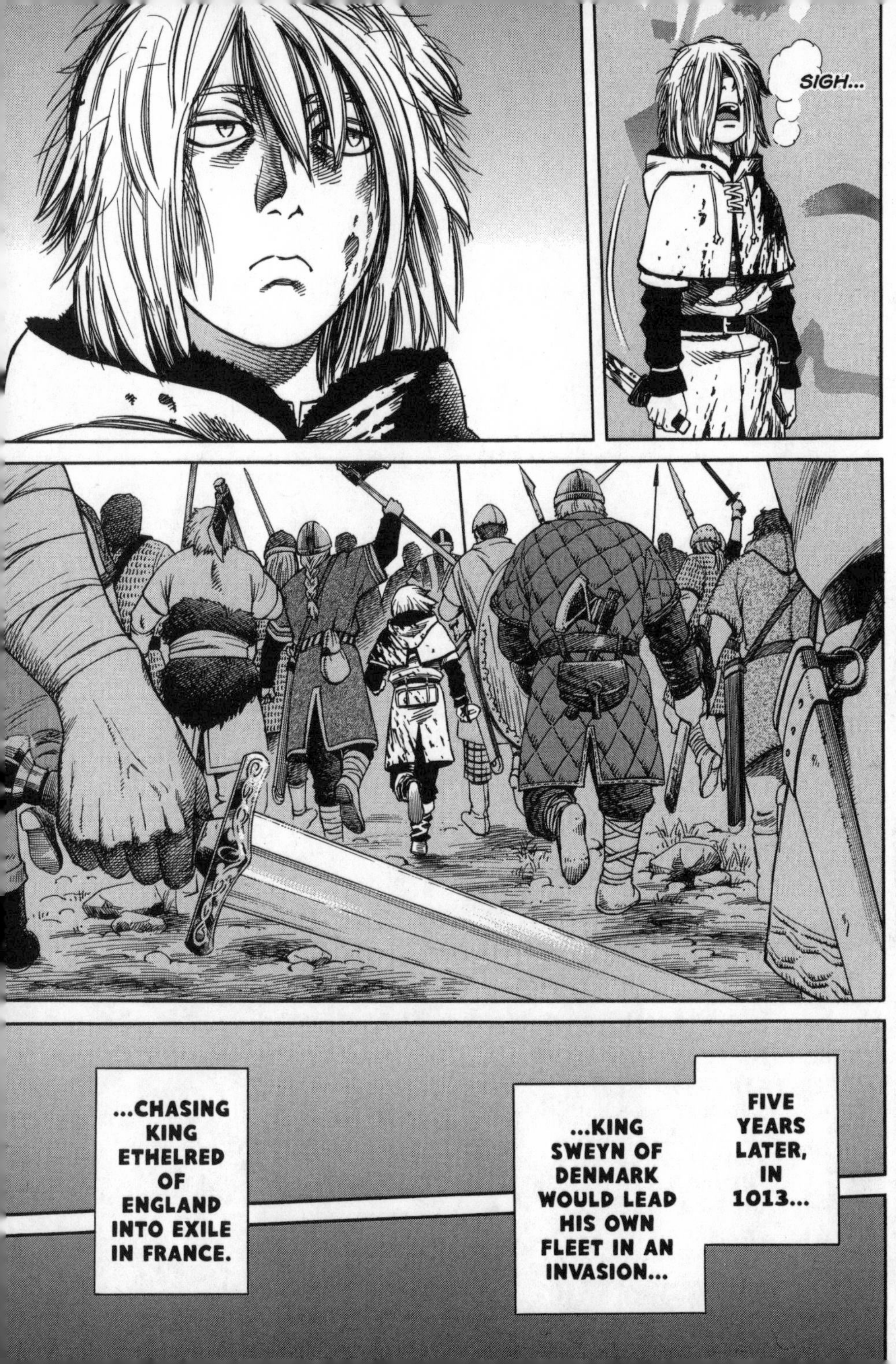
SIGH...
FIVE YEARS LATER, IN 1013...
...KING SWEYN OF DENMARK WOULD LEAD HIS OWN FLEET IN AN INVASION...
...CHASING KING ETHELRED OF ENGLAND INTO EXILE IN FRANCE.

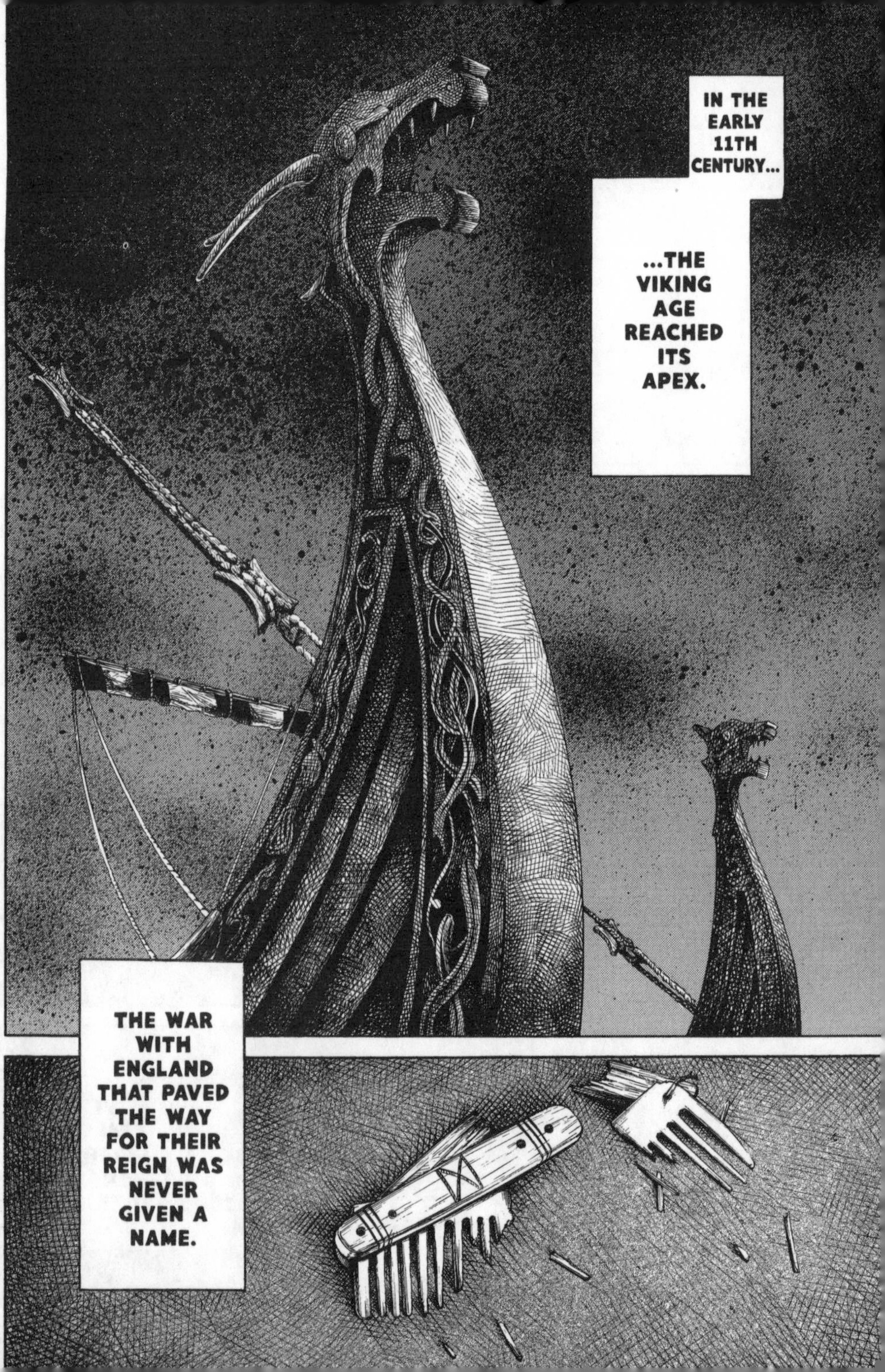
IN THE EARLY 11TH CENTURY...
...THE VIKING AGE REACHED ITS APEX.
THE WAR WITH ENGLAND THAT PAVED THE WAY FOR THEIR REIGN WAS NEVER GIVEN A NAME.

CHAPTER 17 • END

CHAPTER 18: ENGLAND, 1013 A.D.

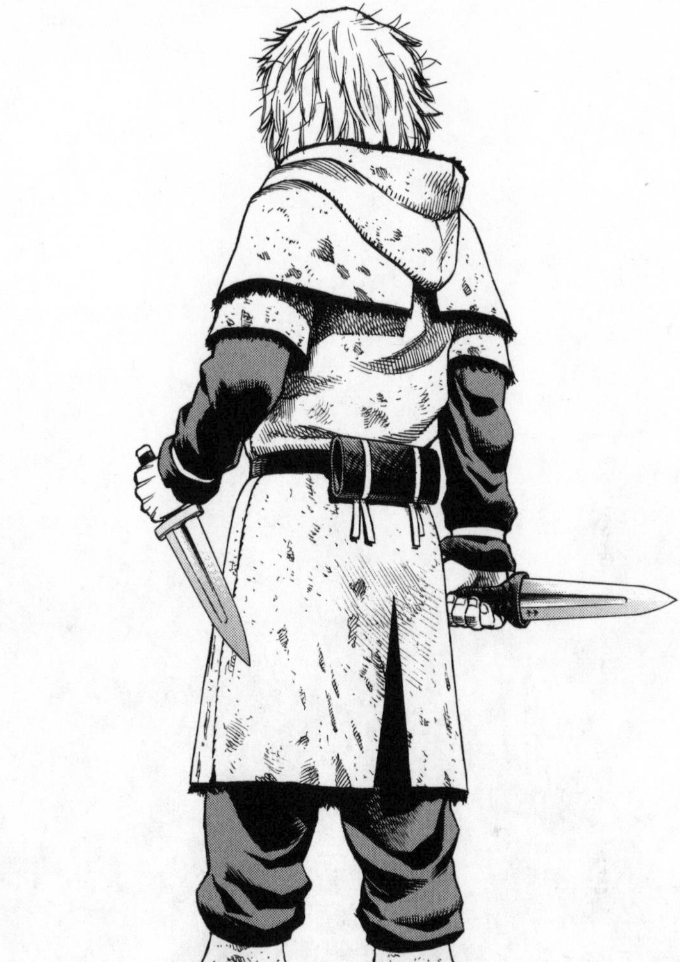

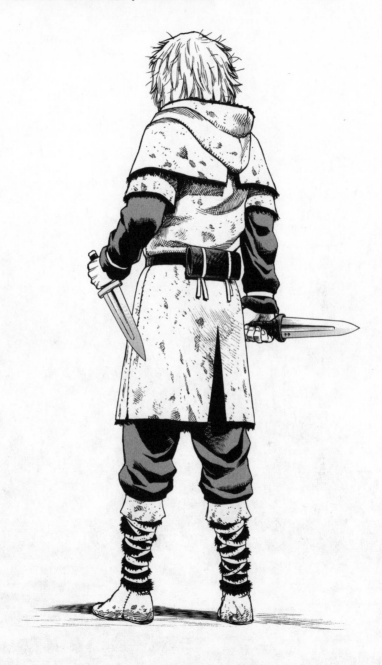

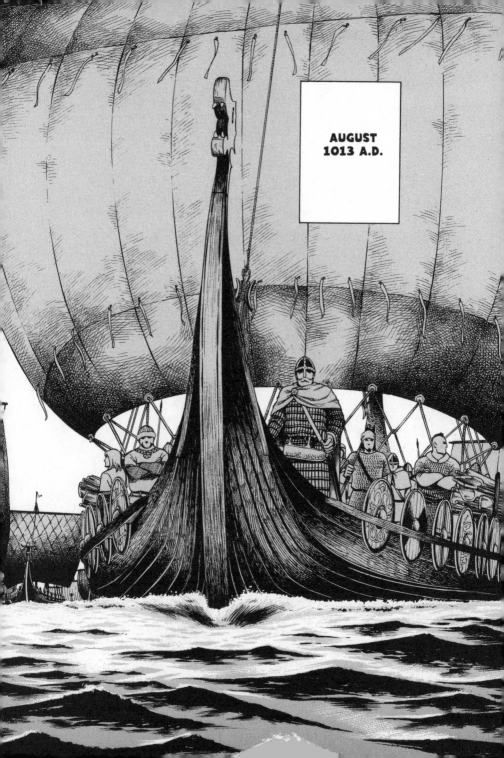

AUGUST
1013 A.D.

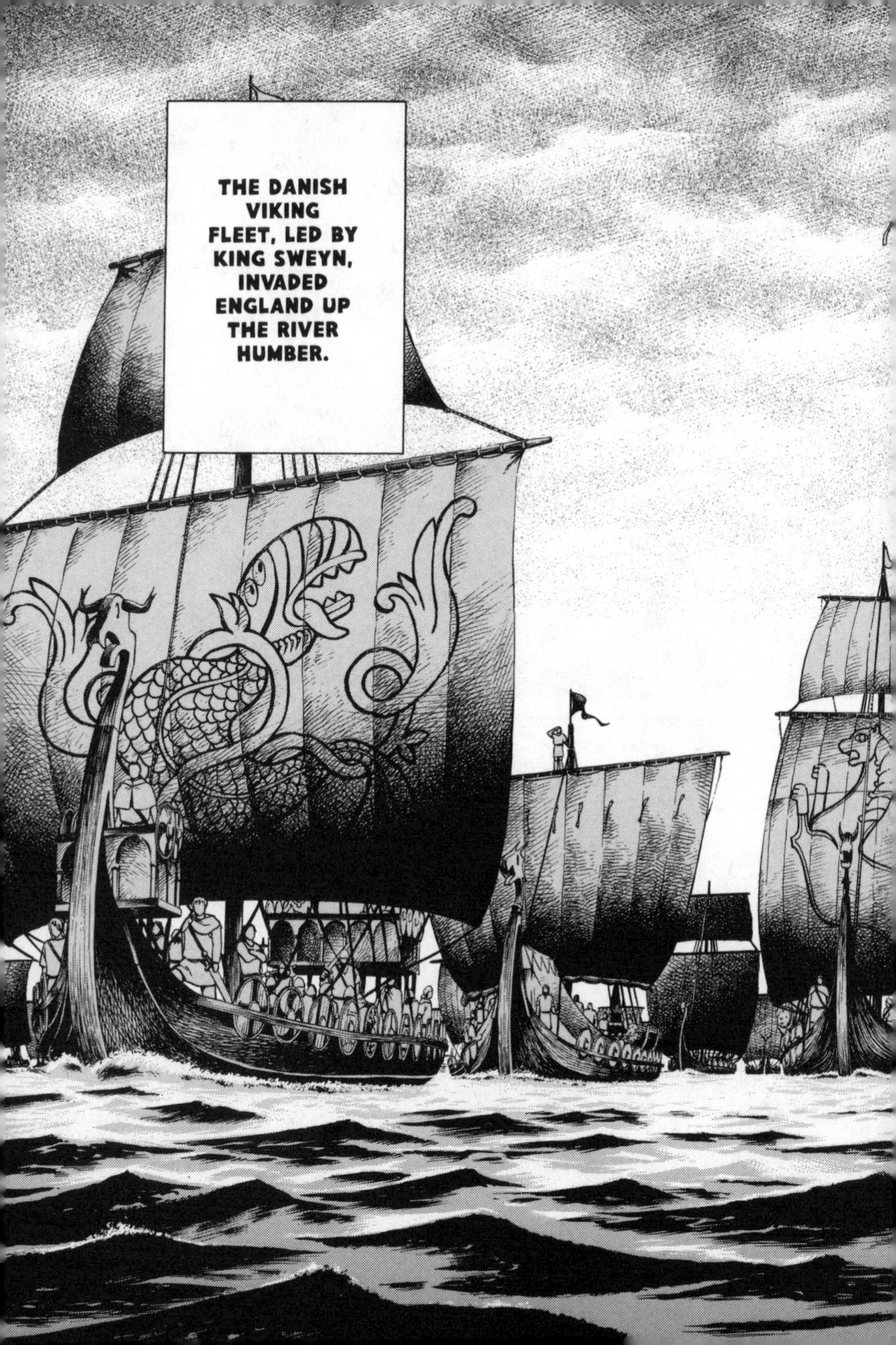
THE DANISH VIKING FLEET, LED BY KING SWEYN, INVADED ENGLAND UP THE RIVER HUMBER.

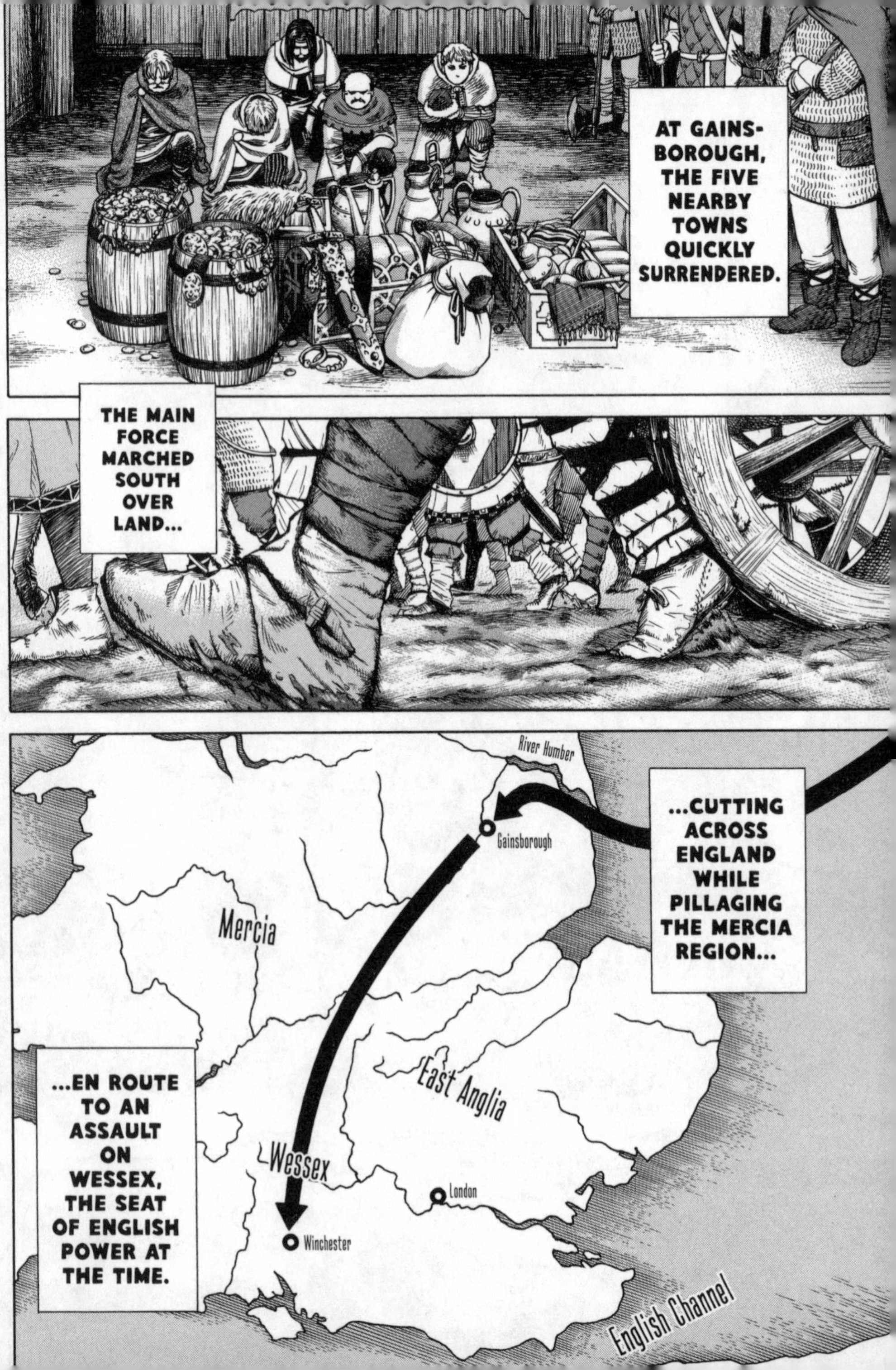
AT GAINSBOROUGH, THE FIVE NEARBY TOWNS QUICKLY SURRENDERED.
THE MAIN FORCE MARCHED SOUTH OVER LAND...
...CUTTING ACROSS ENGLAND WHILE PILLAGING THE MERCIA REGION...
River Humber
Gainsborough
Mercia
East Anglia
Wessex
London
Winchester
English Channel
...EN ROUTE TO AN ASSAULT ON WESSEX, THE SEAT OF ENGLISH POWER AT THE TIME.

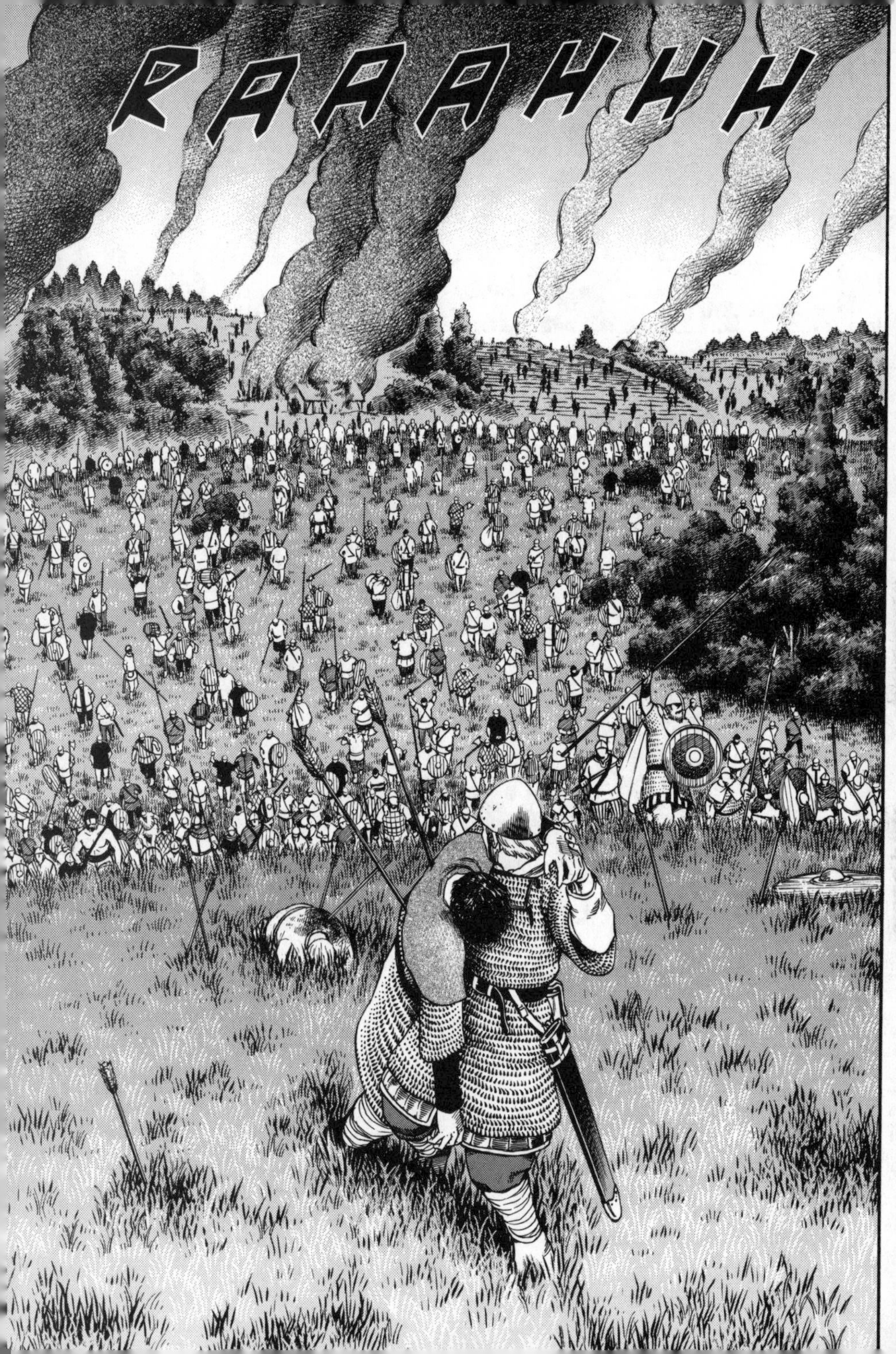
RAAAAHHH

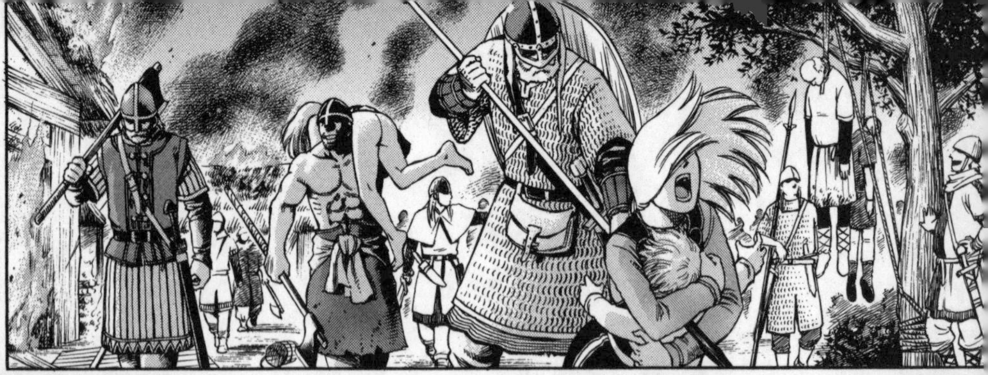

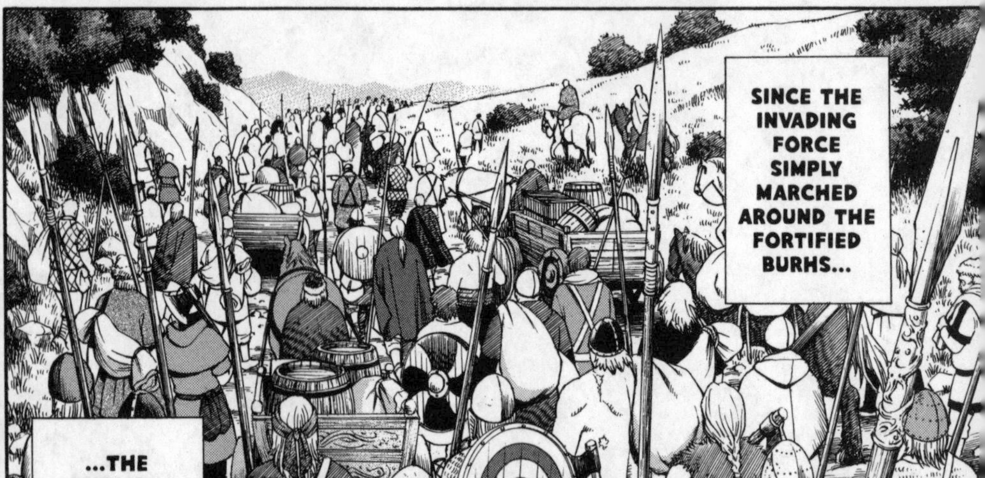
SINCE THE INVADING FORCE SIMPLY MARCHED AROUND THE FORTIFIED BURHS...
...THE ENGLISH SYSTEM OF FORTRESSES AND DEFENSES FAILED TO SERVE ITS PURPOSE.

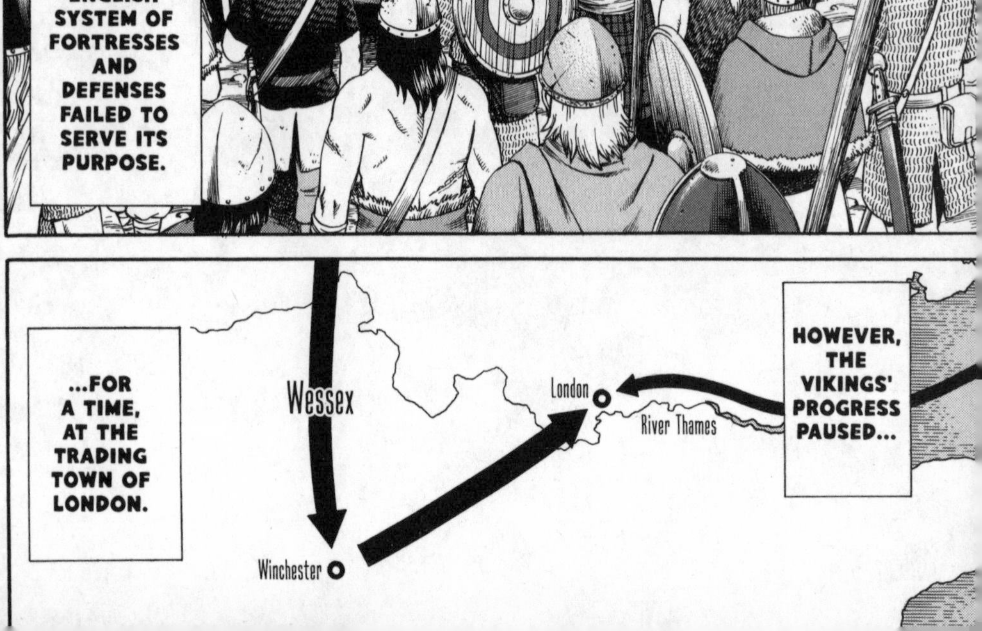
HOWEVER, THE VIKINGS' PROGRESS PAUSED...
London
River Thames
Wessex
Winchester
...FOR A TIME, AT THE TRADING TOWN OF LONDON.

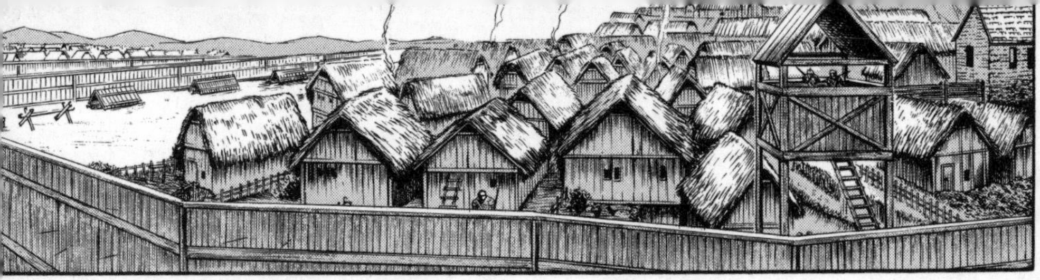
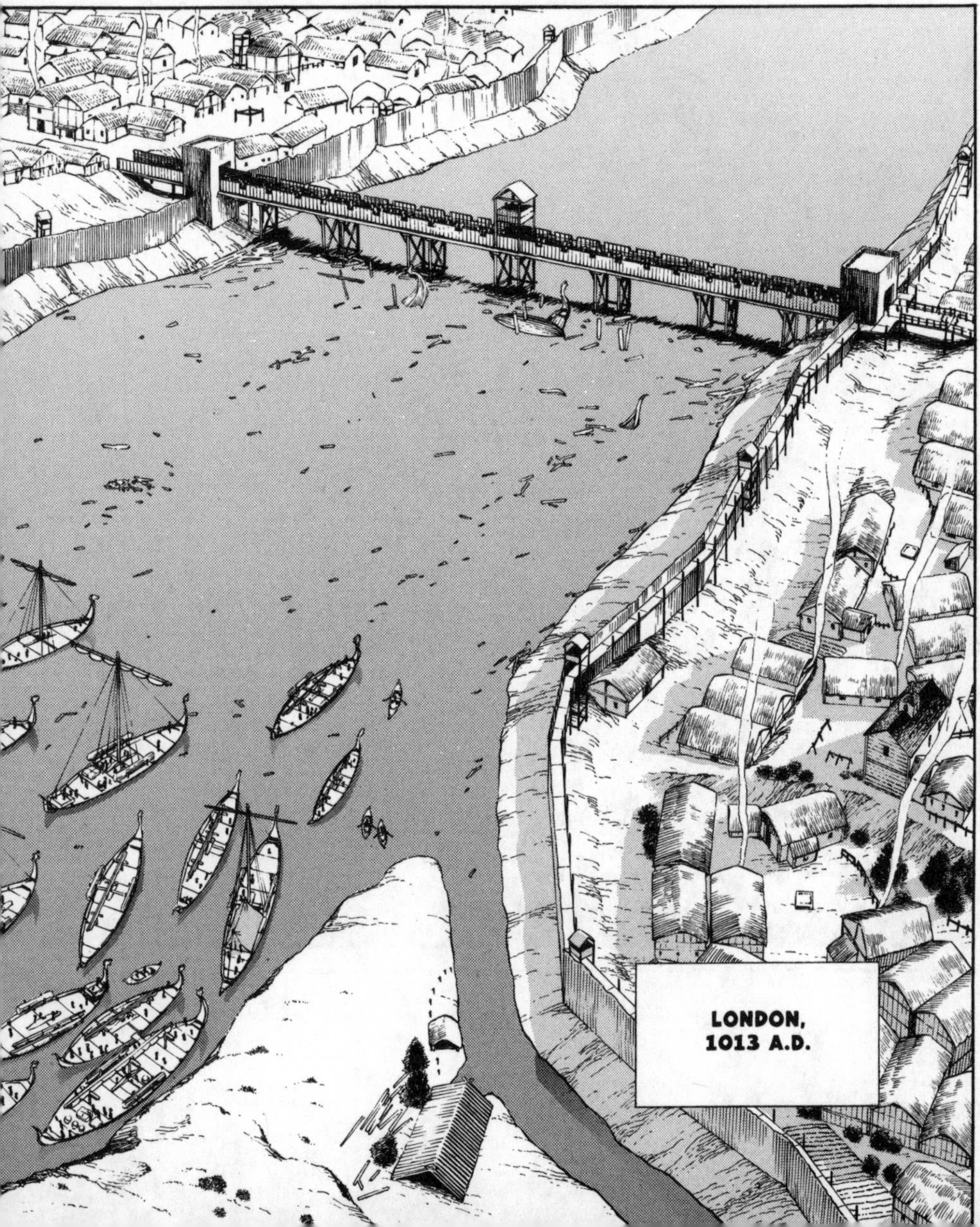
LONDON,
1013 A.D.

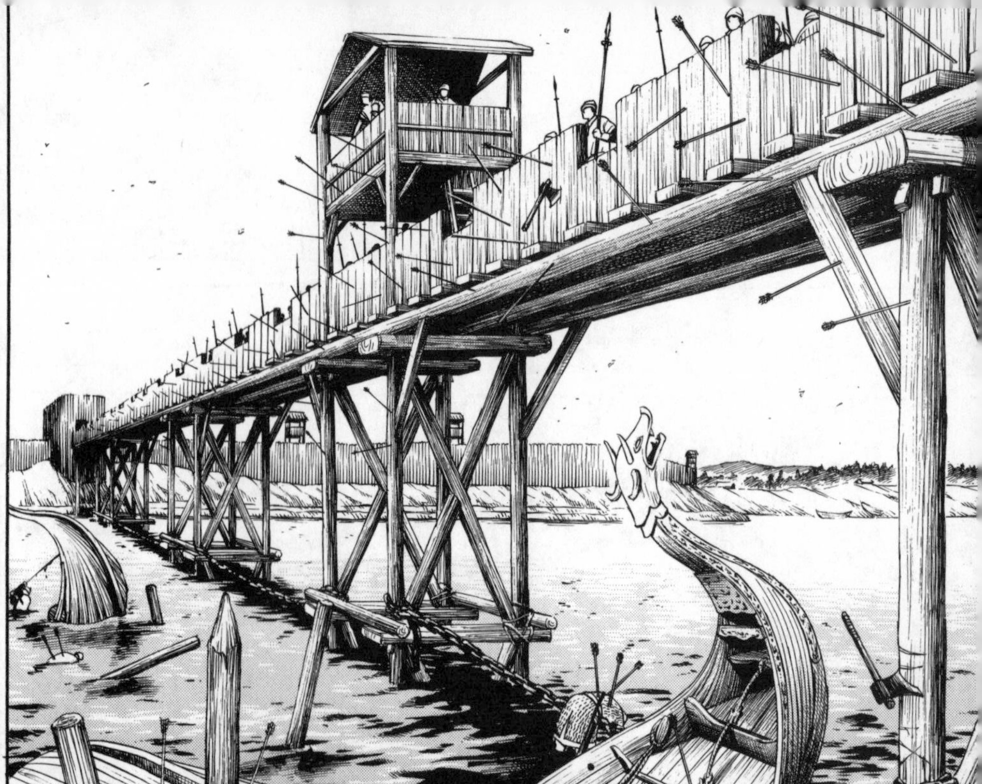
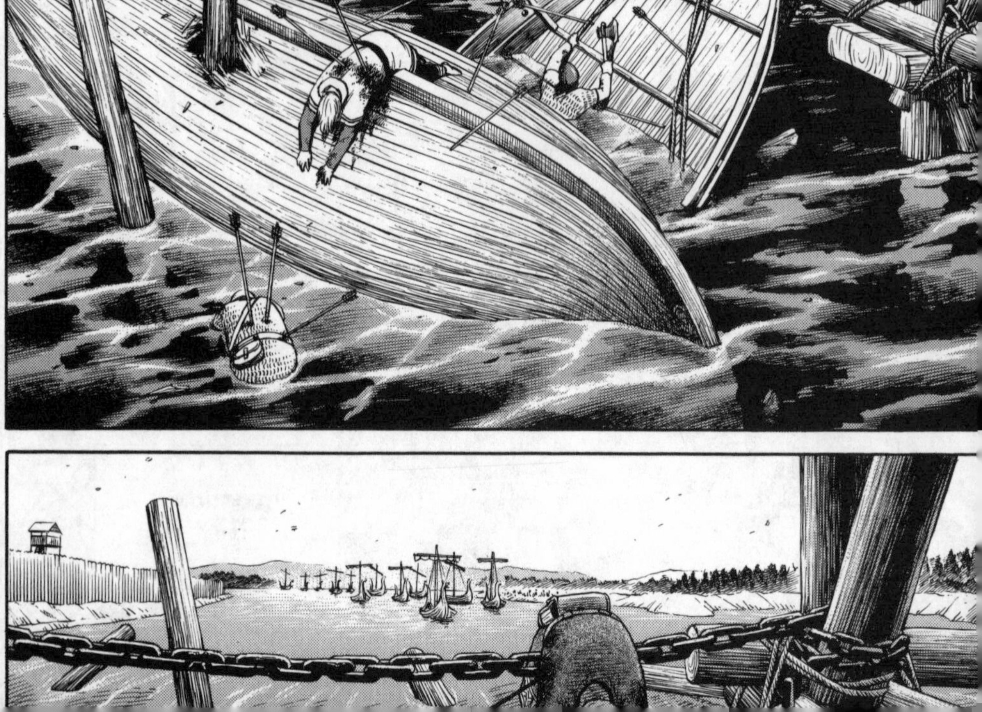

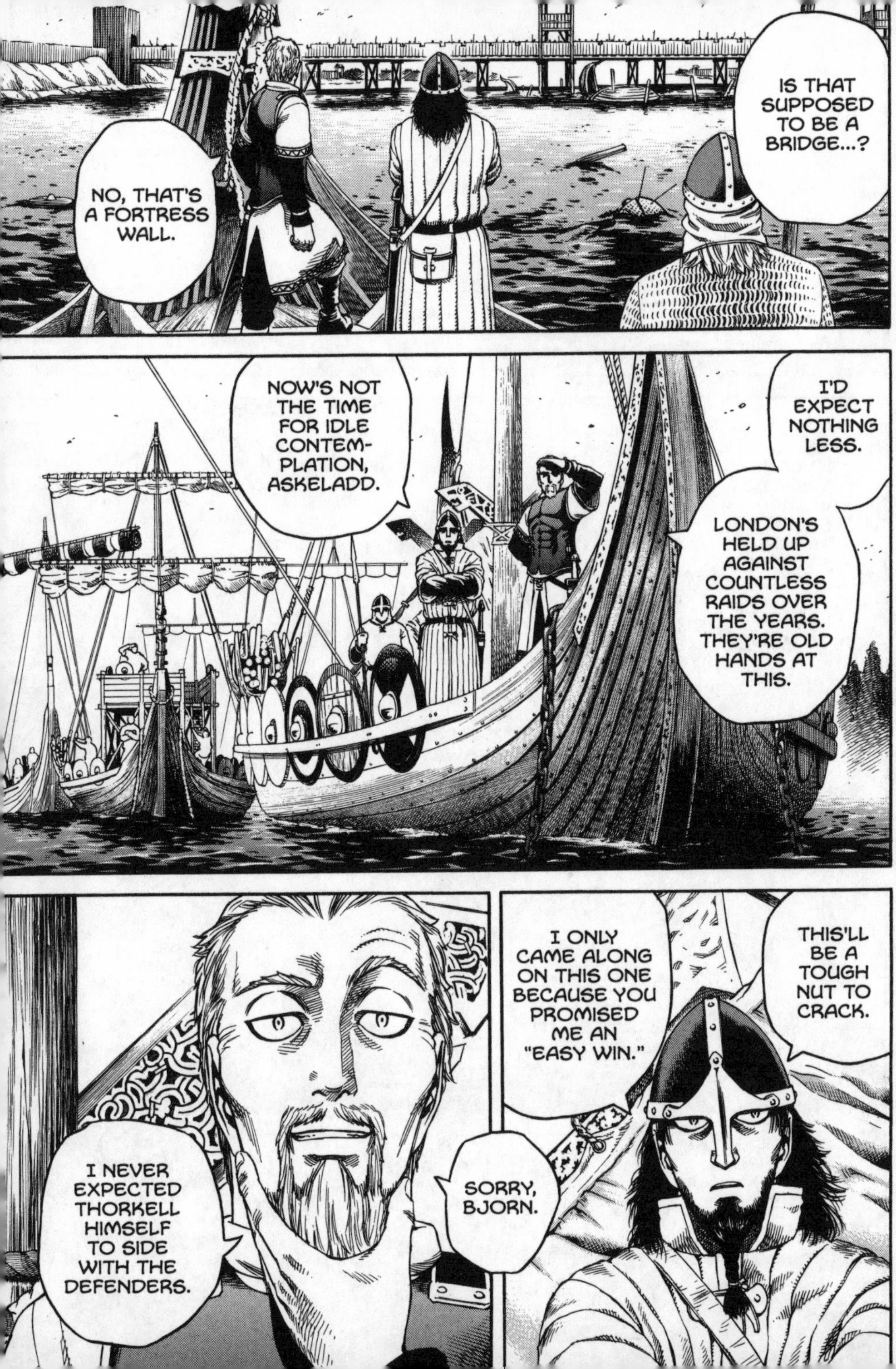

IS THAT SUPPOSED TO BE A BRIDGE...?
NO, THAT'S A FORTRESS WALL.
I'D EXPECT NOTHING LESS.
LONDON'S HELD UP AGAINST COUNTLESS RAIDS OVER THE YEARS. THEY'RE OLD HANDS AT THIS.
NOW'S NOT THE TIME FOR IDLE CONTEM-PLATION, ASKELADD.
THIS'LL BE A TOUGH NUT TO CRACK.
I ONLY CAME ALONG ON THIS ONE BECAUSE YOU PROMISED ME AN "EASY WIN."
SORRY, BJORN.
I NEVER EXPECTED THORKELL HIMSELF TO SIDE WITH THE DEFENDERS.

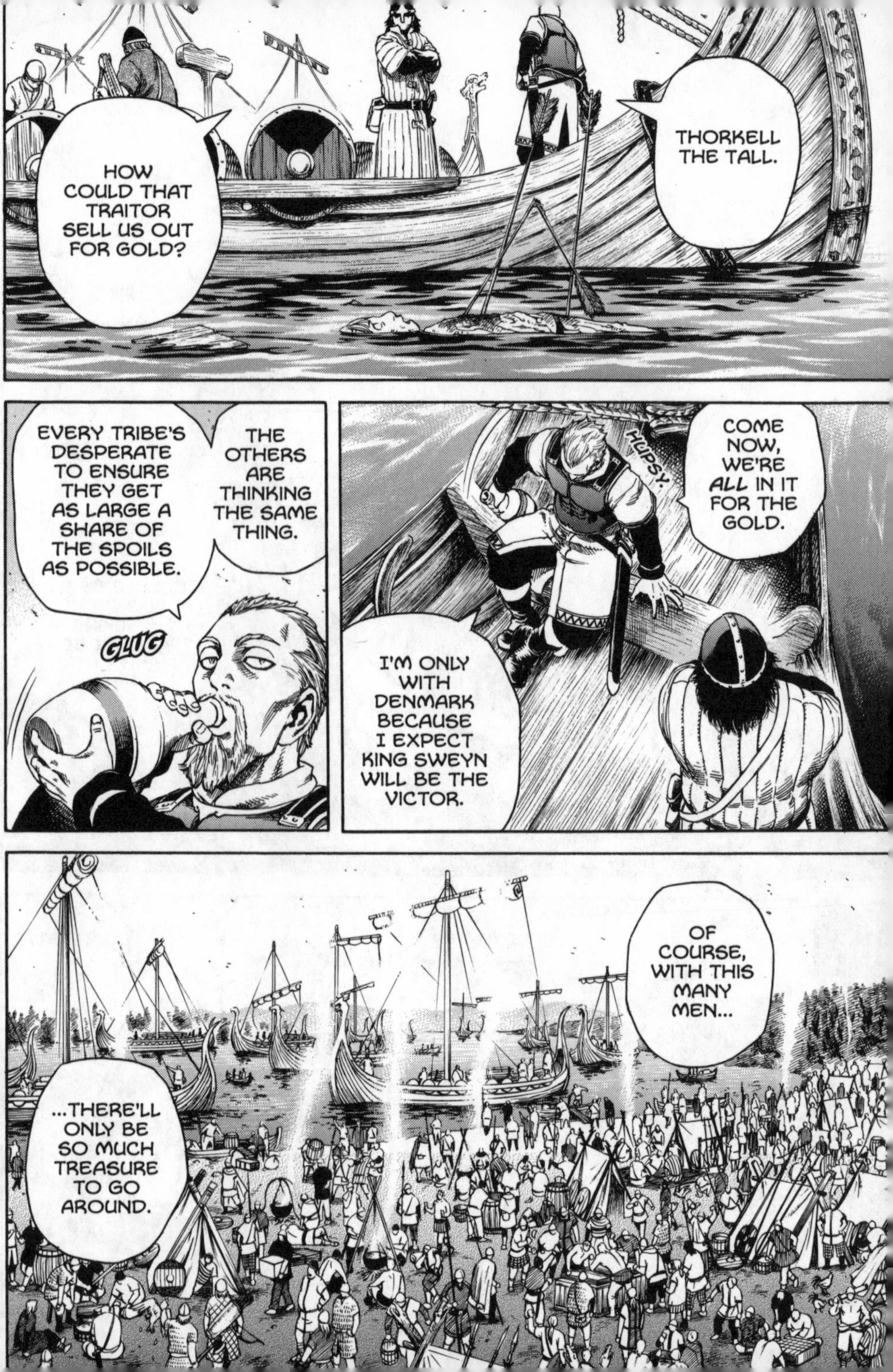
THORKELL THE TALL.
HOW COULD THAT TRAITOR SELL US OUT FOR GOLD?
COME NOW, WE'RE *ALL* IN IT FOR THE GOLD.
HUPSY.
I'M ONLY WITH DENMARK BECAUSE I EXPECT KING SWEYN WILL BE THE VICTOR.
THE OTHERS ARE THINKING THE SAME THING.
EVERY TRIBE'S DESPERATE TO ENSURE THEY GET AS LARGE A SHARE OF THE SPOILS AS POSSIBLE.
GLUG
OF COURSE, WITH THIS MANY MEN...
...THERE'LL ONLY BE SO MUCH TREASURE TO GO AROUND.

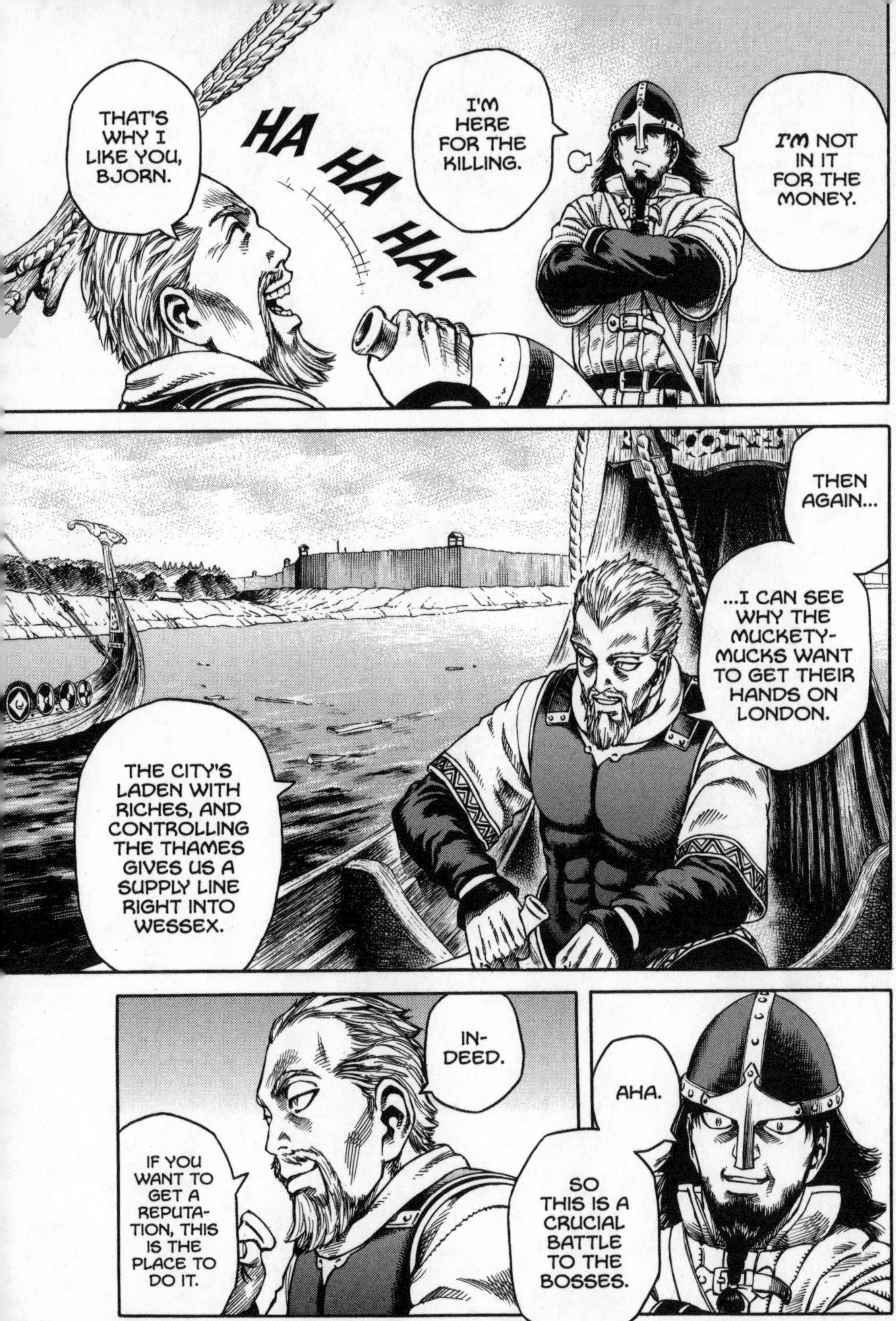
I'M NOT IN IT FOR THE MONEY.
I'M HERE FOR THE KILLING.
HA HA HA!
THAT'S WHY I LIKE YOU, BJORN.
THEN AGAIN...
...I CAN SEE WHY THE MUCKETY-MUCKS WANT TO GET THEIR HANDS ON LONDON.
THE CITY'S LADEN WITH RICHES, AND CONTROLLING THE THAMES GIVES US A SUPPLY LINE RIGHT INTO WESSEX.
AHA.
SO THIS IS A CRUCIAL BATTLE TO THE BOSSES.
IN-DEED.
IF YOU WANT TO GET A REPUTA-TION, THIS IS THE PLACE TO DO IT.

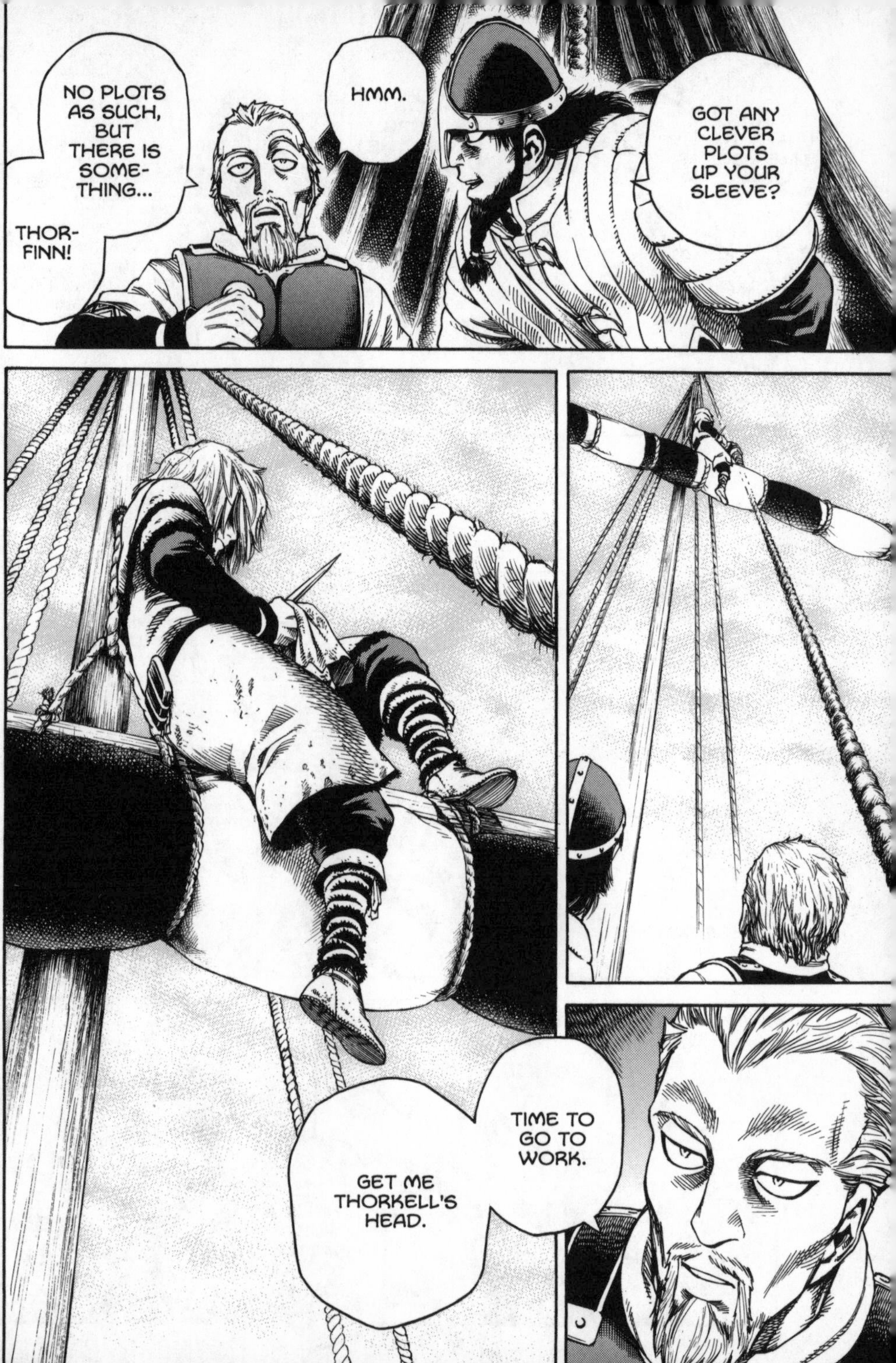
GOT ANY CLEVER PLOTS UP YOUR SLEEVE?
HMM.
NO PLOTS AS SUCH, BUT THERE IS SOME-THING...
THOR-FINN!
TIME TO GO TO WORK.
GET ME THORKELL'S HEAD.

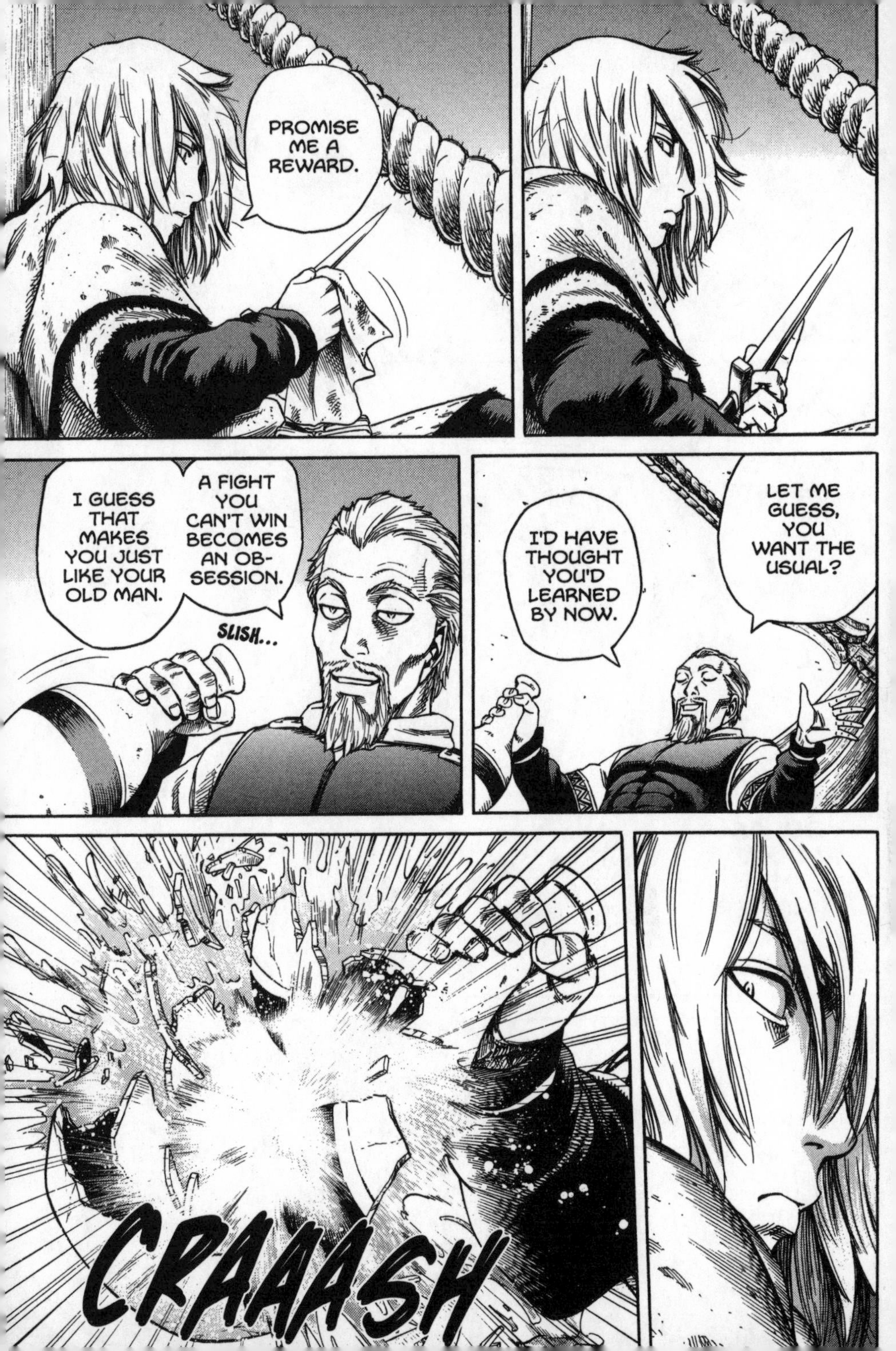
PROMISE ME A REWARD.
LET ME GUESS, YOU WANT THE USUAL?
I'D HAVE THOUGHT YOU'D LEARNED BY NOW.
A FIGHT YOU CAN'T WIN BECOMES AN OB-SESSION.
I GUESS THAT MAKES YOU JUST LIKE YOUR OLD MAN.
SLISH...
CRAAASH

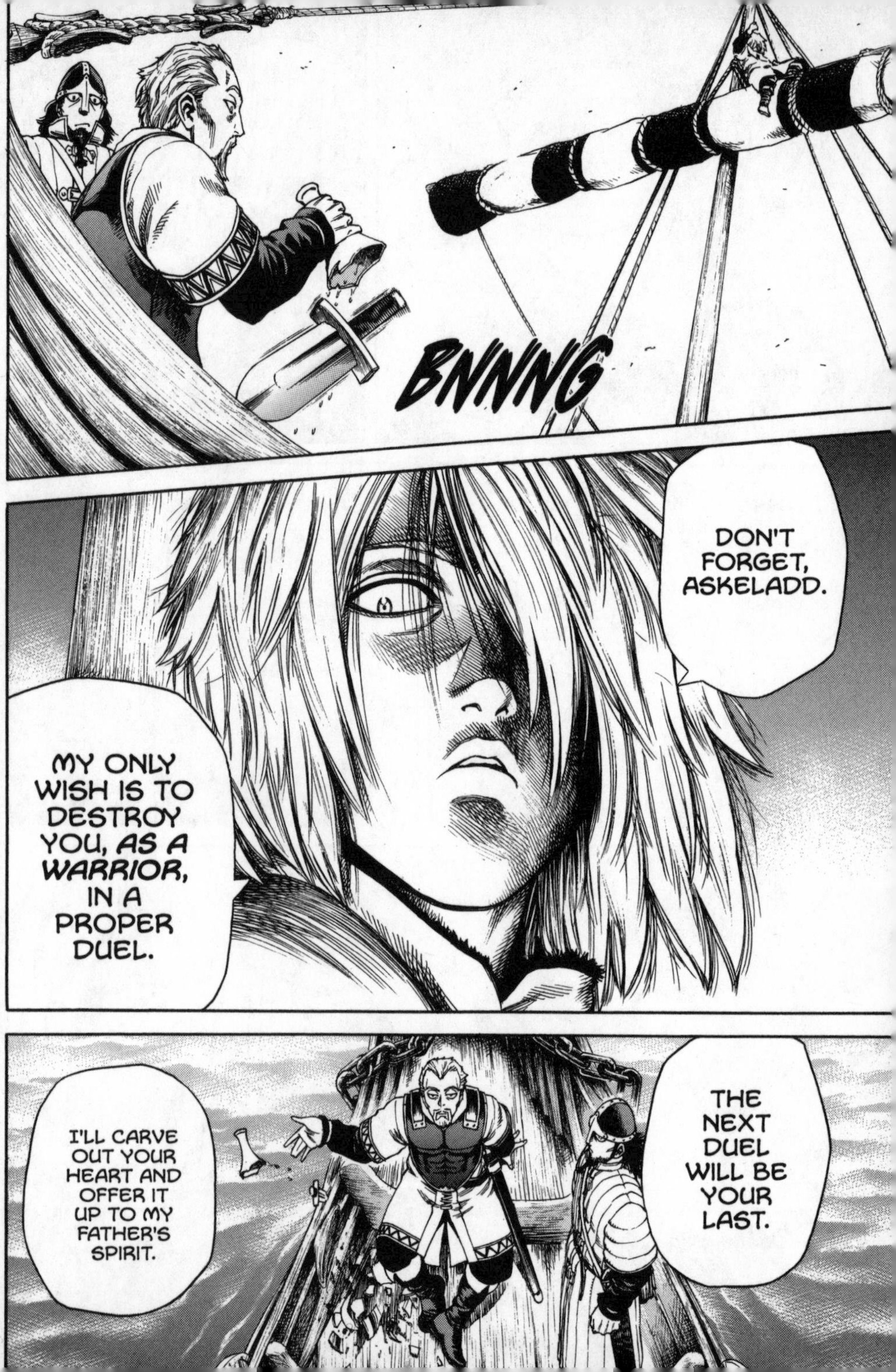
BNNNG
DON'T FORGET, ASKELADD.
MY ONLY WISH IS TO DESTROY YOU, *AS A WARRIOR*, IN A PROPER DUEL.
THE NEXT DUEL WILL BE YOUR LAST.
I'LL CARVE OUT YOUR HEART AND OFFER IT UP TO MY FATHER'S SPIRIT.

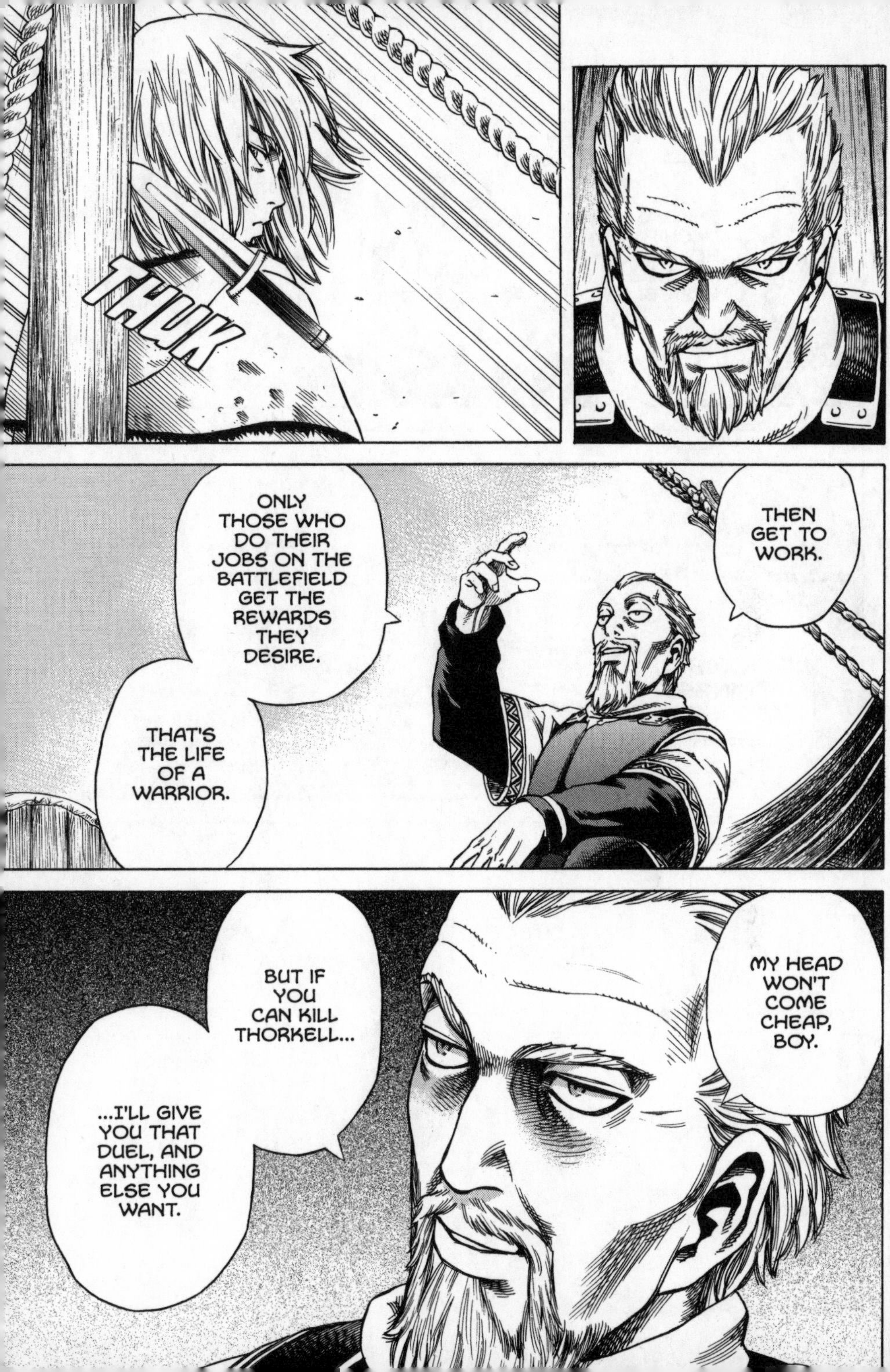
THUK
THEN GET TO WORK.
ONLY THOSE WHO DO THEIR JOBS ON THE BATTLEFIELD GET THE REWARDS THEY DESIRE.
THAT'S THE LIFE OF A WARRIOR.
MY HEAD WON'T COME CHEAP, BOY.
BUT IF YOU CAN KILL THORKELL...
...I'LL GIVE YOU THAT DUEL, AND ANYTHING ELSE YOU WANT.

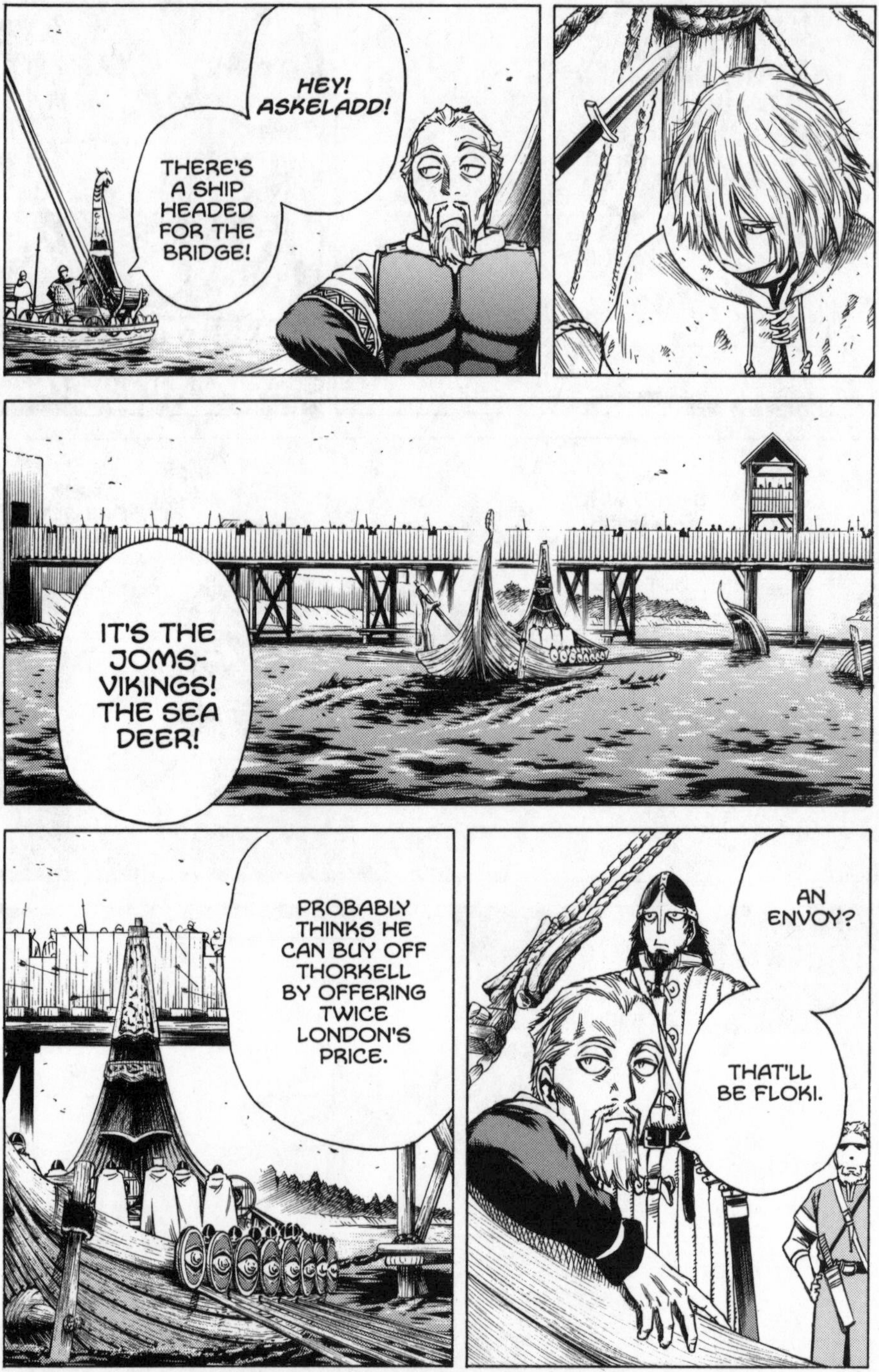
HEY! ASKELADD!
THERE'S A SHIP HEADED FOR THE BRIDGE!
IT'S THE JOMS-VIKINGS! THE SEA DEER!
AN ENVOY?
THAT'LL BE FLOKI.
PROBABLY THINKS HE CAN BUY OFF THORKELL BY OFFERING TWICE LONDON'S PRICE.

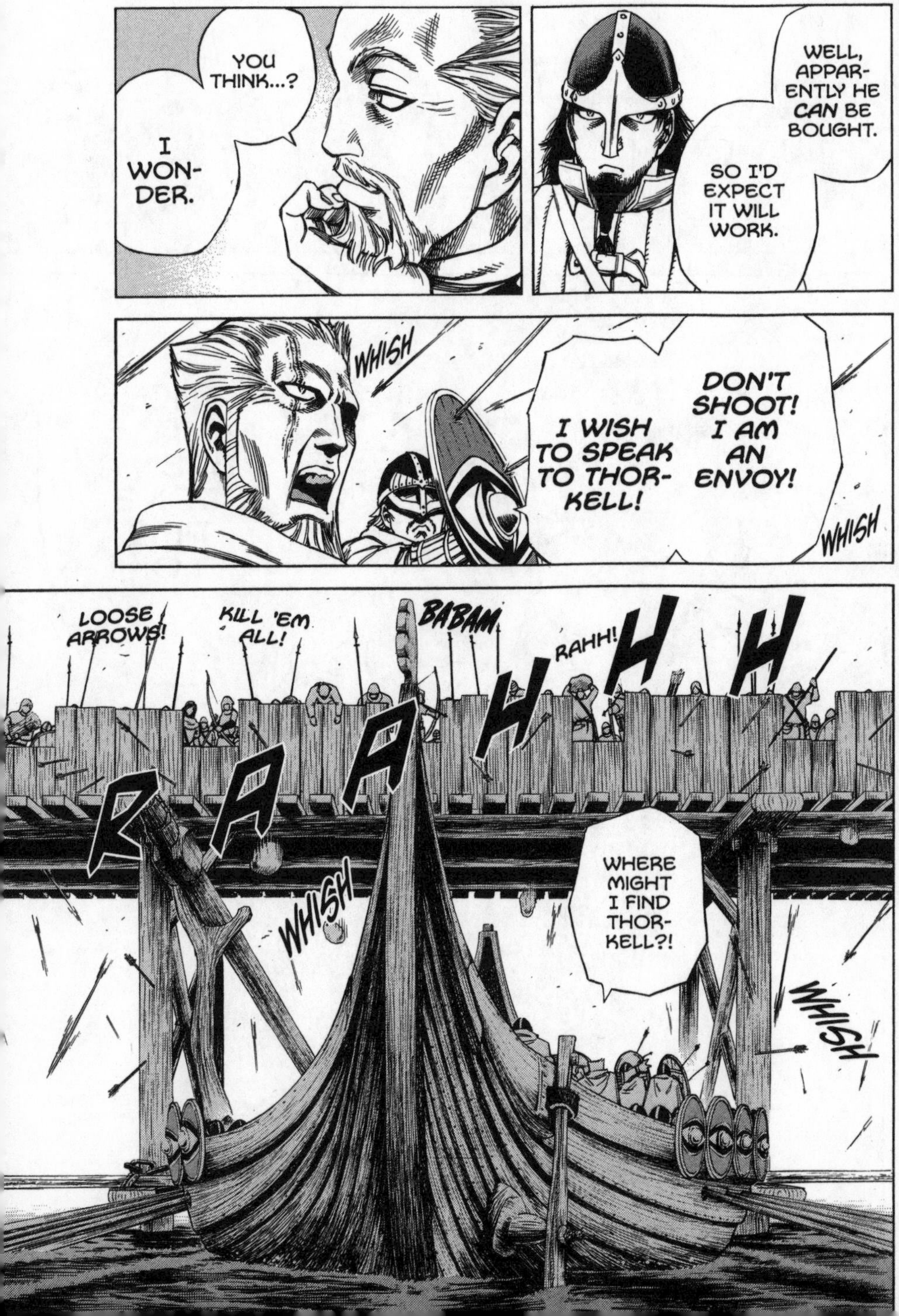
WELL, APPARENTLY HE CAN BE BOUGHT.
SO I'D EXPECT IT WILL WORK.
YOU THINK...?
I WONDER.
WHISH
DON'T SHOOT! I AM AN ENVOY!
I WISH TO SPEAK TO THORKELL!
WHISH
RAAAHHHH
RAHH!
BABAM
KILL 'EM ALL!
LOOSE ARROWS!
WHERE MIGHT I FIND THORKELL?!
WHISH
WHISH

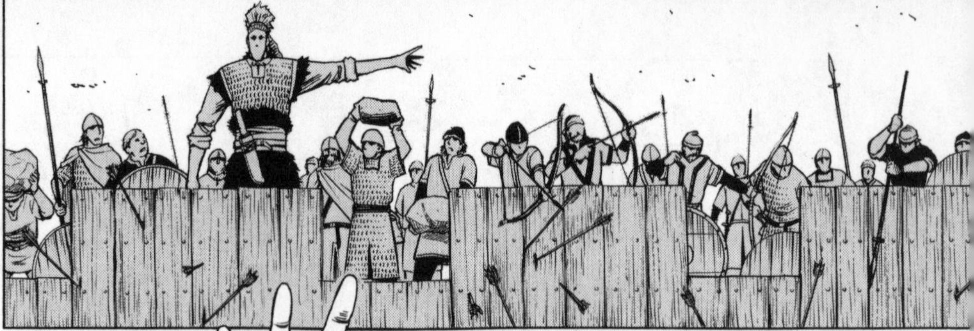

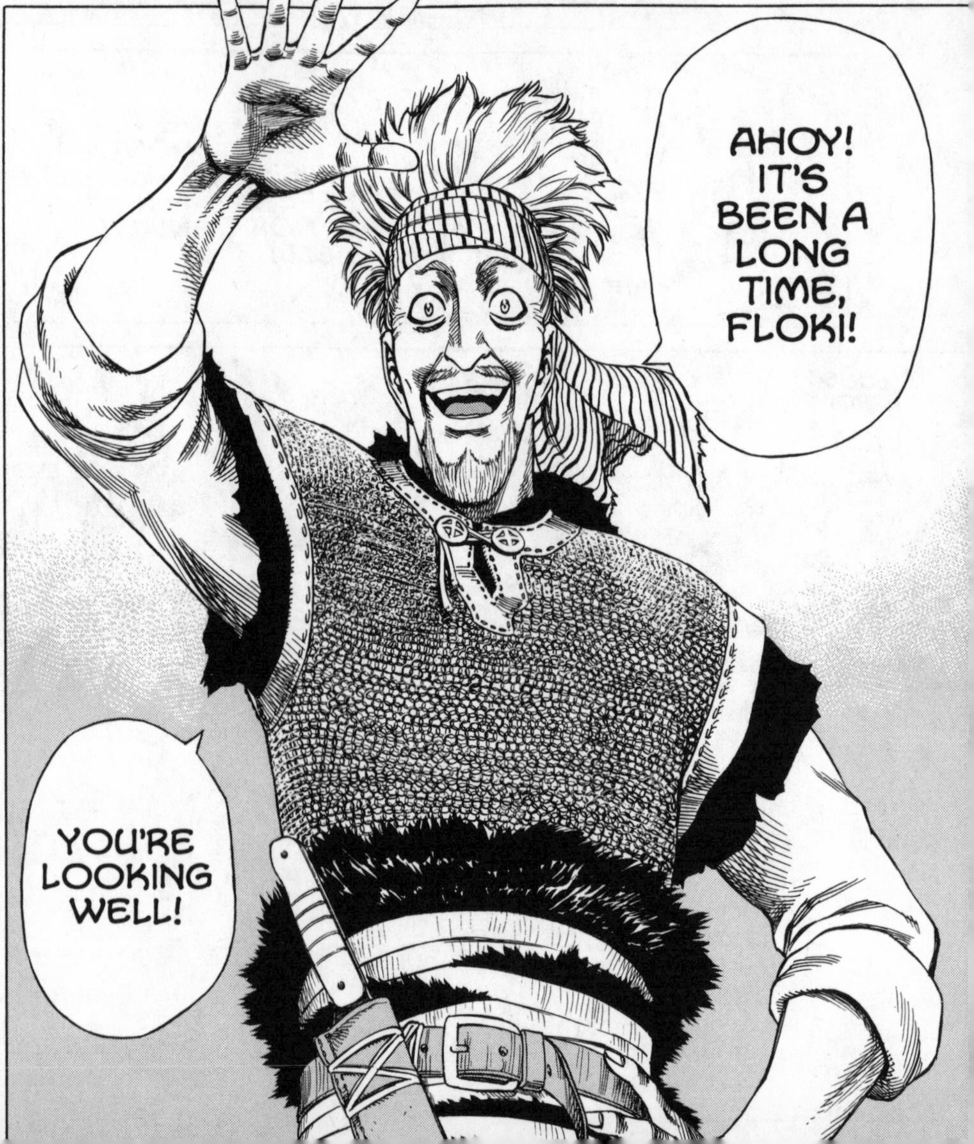
AHOY! IT'S BEEN A LONG TIME, FLOKI!
YOU'RE LOOKING WELL!

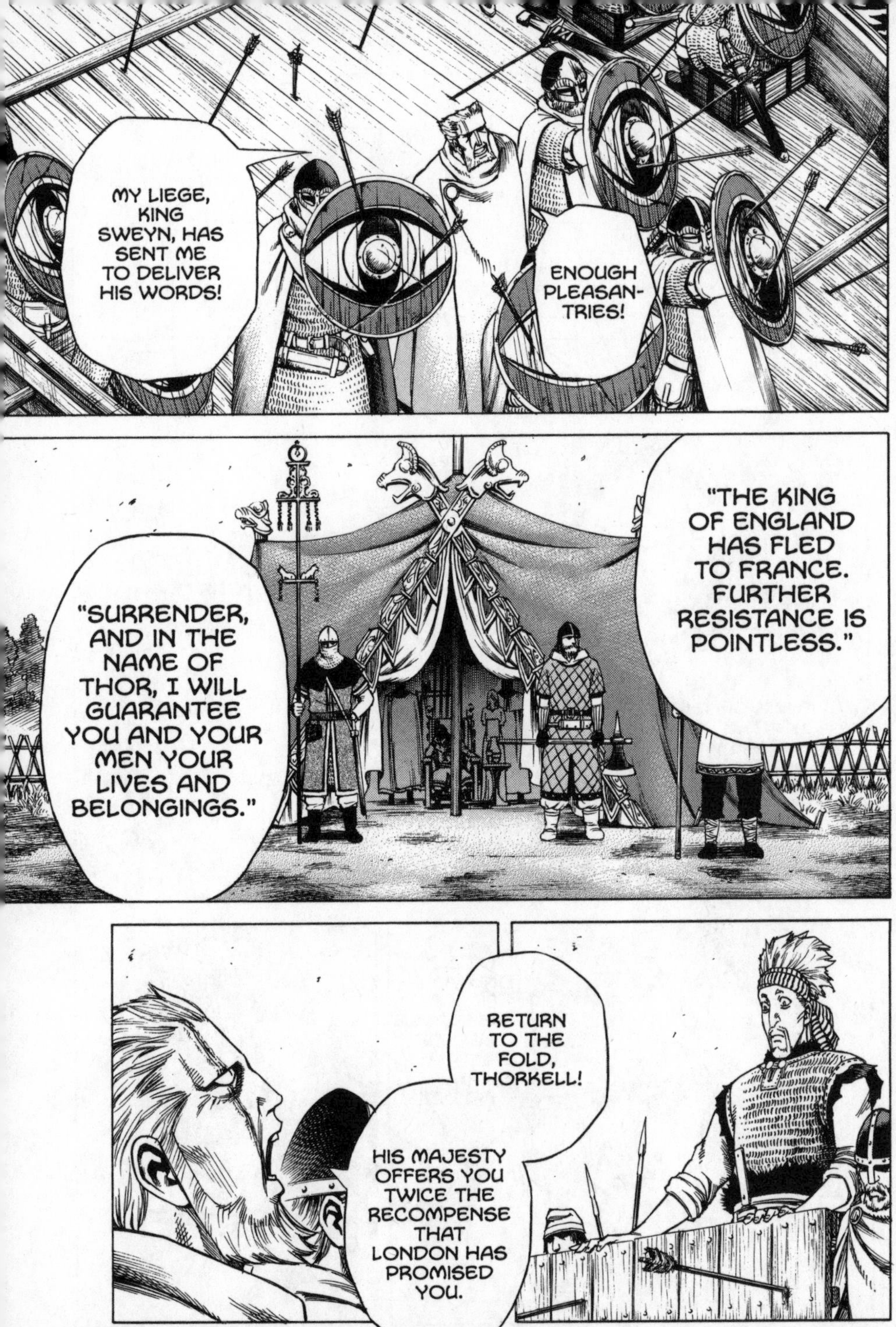
ENOUGH PLEASANTRIES!
MY LIEGE, KING SWEYN, HAS SENT ME TO DELIVER HIS WORDS!
"THE KING OF ENGLAND HAS FLED TO FRANCE. FURTHER RESISTANCE IS POINTLESS."
"SURRENDER, AND IN THE NAME OF THOR, I WILL GUARANTEE YOU AND YOUR MEN YOUR LIVES AND BELONGINGS."
RETURN TO THE FOLD, THORKELL!
HIS MAJESTY OFFERS YOU TWICE THE RECOMPENSE THAT LONDON HAS PROMISED YOU.

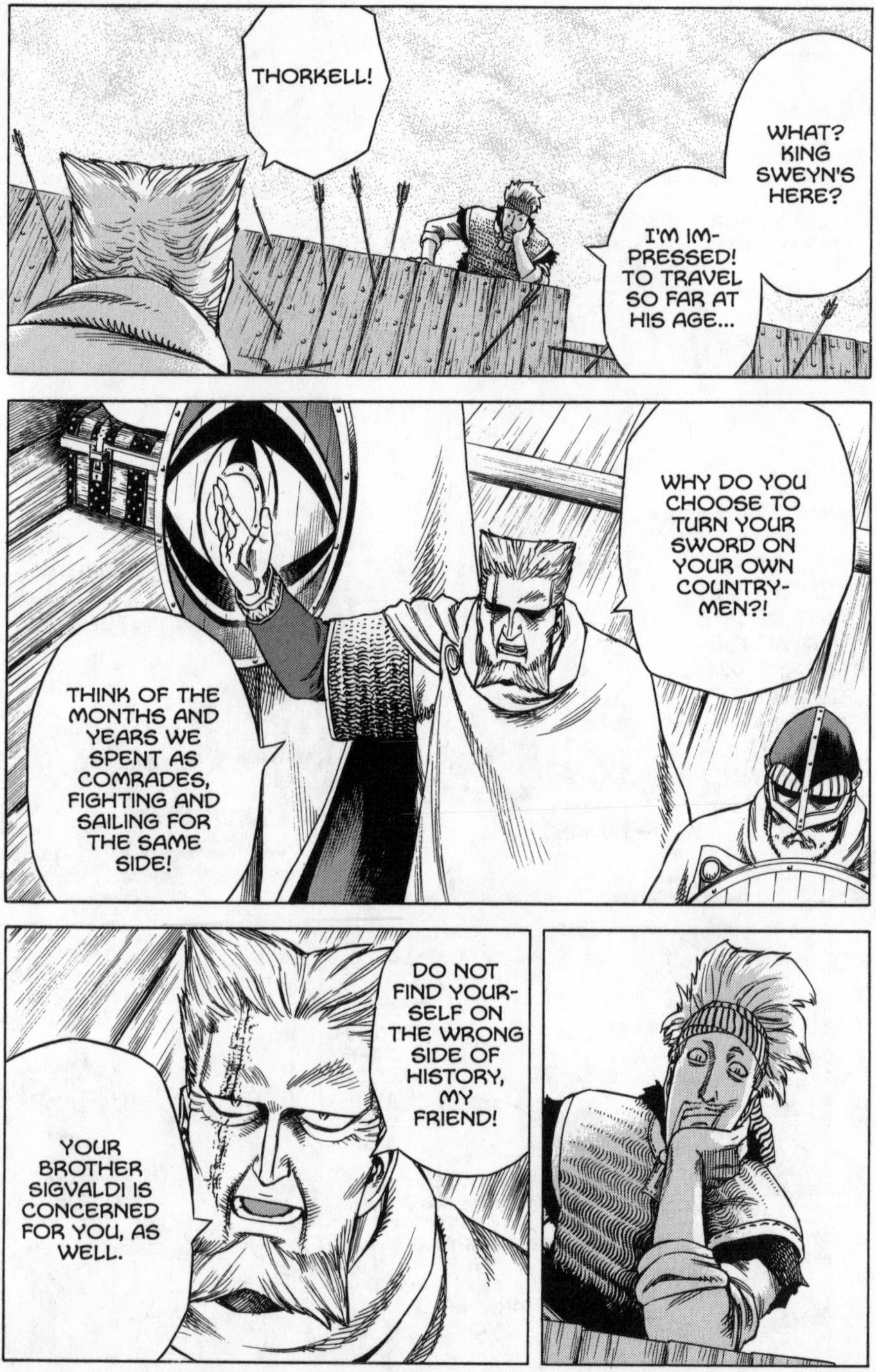
THORKELL!
WHAT? KING SWEYN'S HERE?
I'M IM-PRESSED! TO TRAVEL SO FAR AT HIS AGE...
WHY DO YOU CHOOSE TO TURN YOUR SWORD ON YOUR OWN COUNTRY-MEN?!
THINK OF THE MONTHS AND YEARS WE SPENT AS COMRADES, FIGHTING AND SAILING FOR THE SAME SIDE!
DO NOT FIND YOUR-SELF ON THE WRONG SIDE OF HISTORY, MY FRIEND!
YOUR BROTHER SIGVALDI IS CONCERNED FOR YOU, AS WELL.

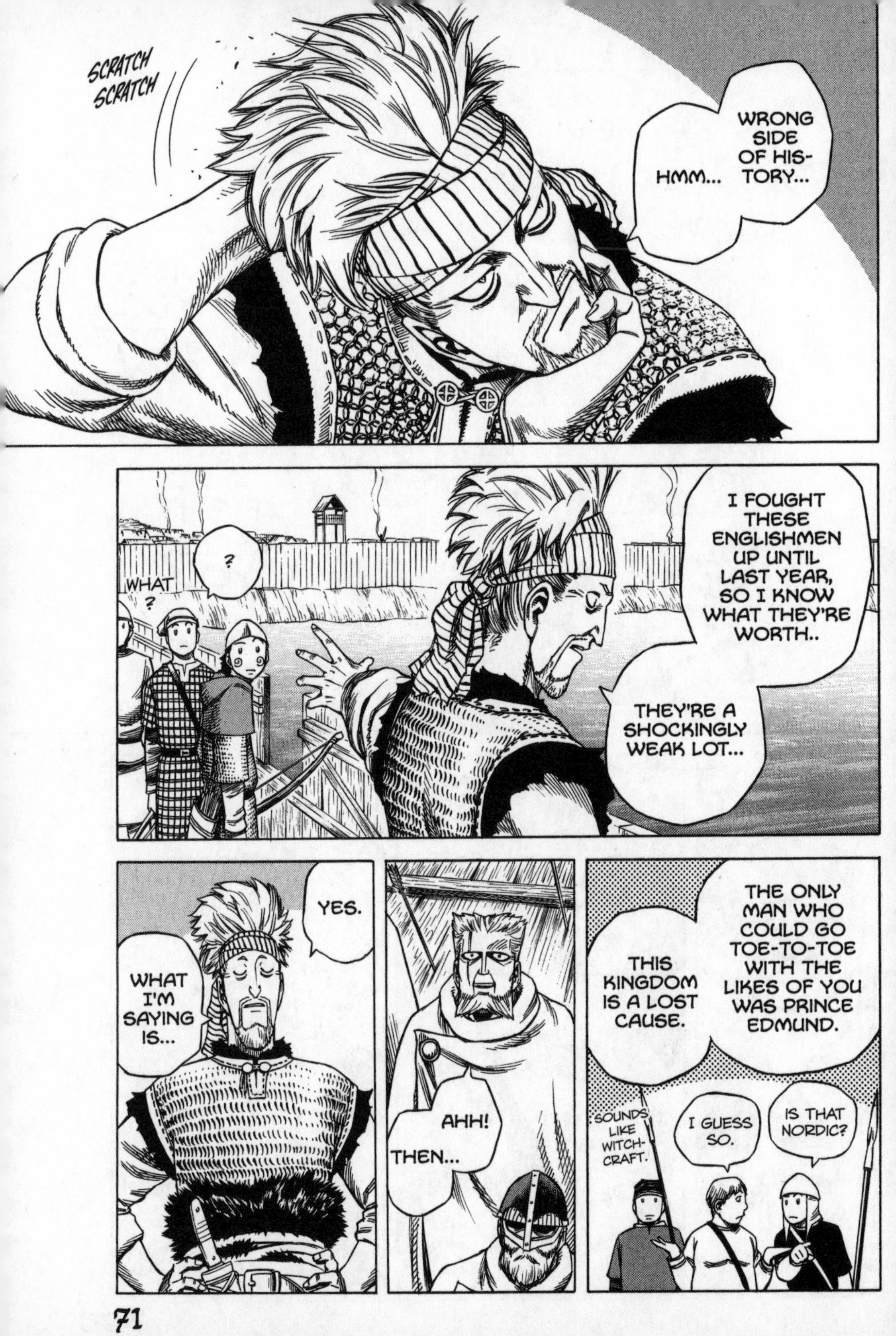
HMM... WRONG SIDE OF HISTORY...
SCRATCH SCRATCH
I FOUGHT THESE ENGLISHMEN UP UNTIL LAST YEAR, SO I KNOW WHAT THEY'RE WORTH..
THEY'RE A SHOCKINGLY WEAK LOT...
?
WHAT ?
THE ONLY MAN WHO COULD GO TOE-TO-TOE WITH THE LIKES OF YOU WAS PRINCE EDMUND.
THIS KINGDOM IS A LOST CAUSE.
IS THAT NORDIC?
I GUESS SO.
SOUNDS LIKE WITCH-CRAFT.
AHH!
THEN...
YES.
WHAT I'M SAYING IS...

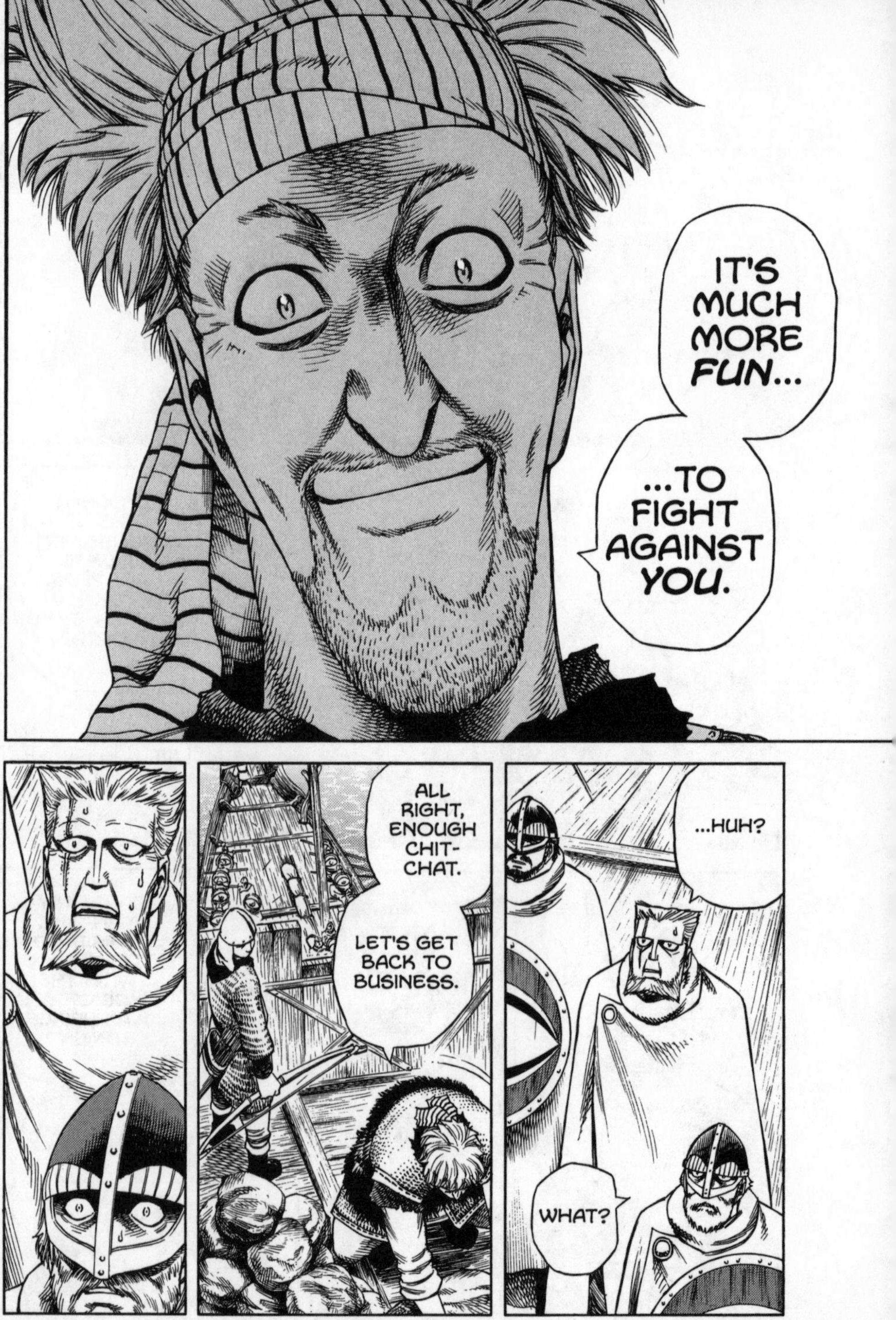
IT'S MUCH MORE FUN...
...TO FIGHT AGAINST YOU.
...HUH?
WHAT?
ALL RIGHT, ENOUGH CHIT-CHAT.
LET'S GET BACK TO BUSINESS.

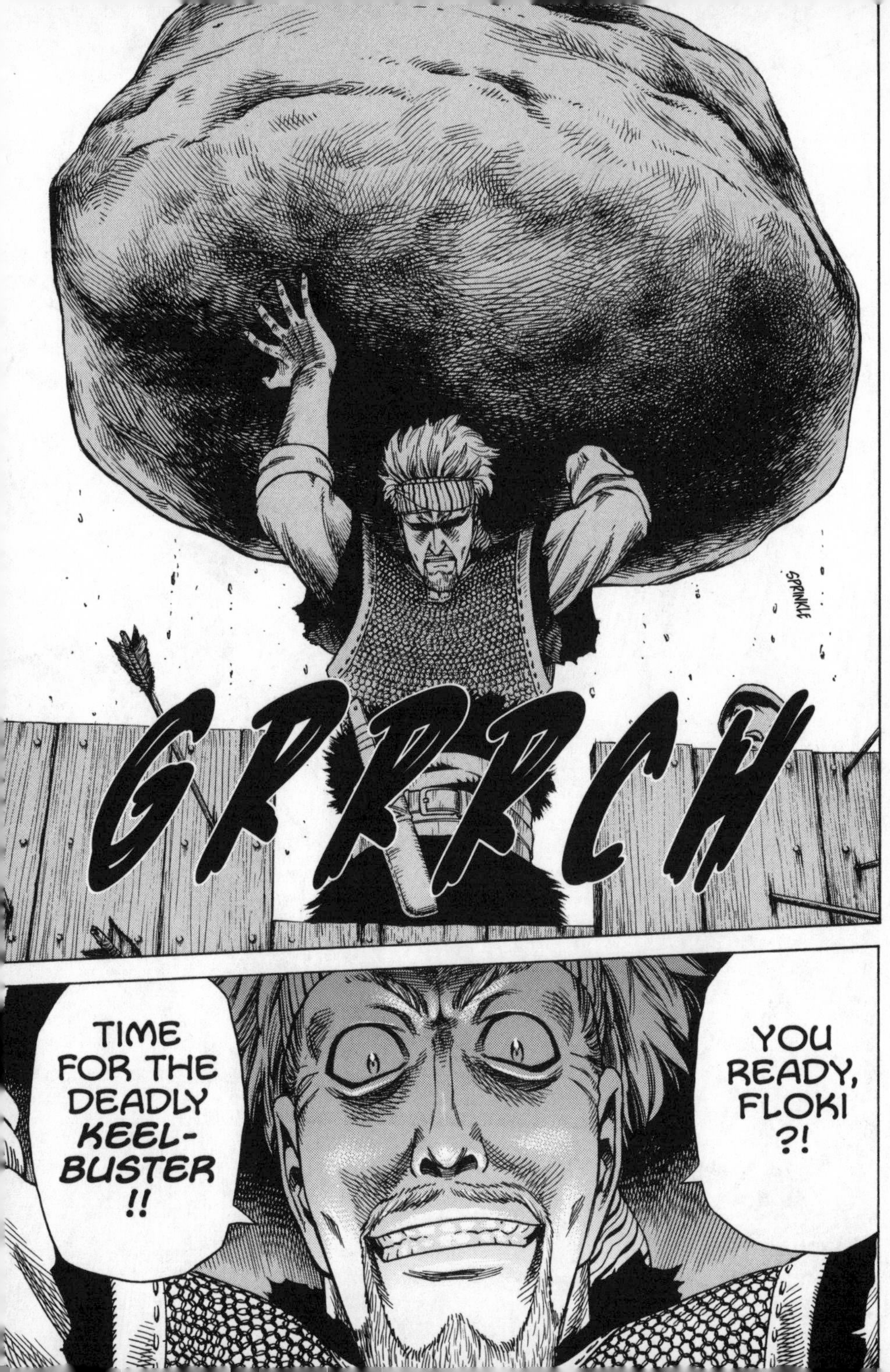
SPRINKLE
GRRRCH
YOU READY, FLOKI ?!
TIME FOR THE DEADLY KEEL-BUSTER !!

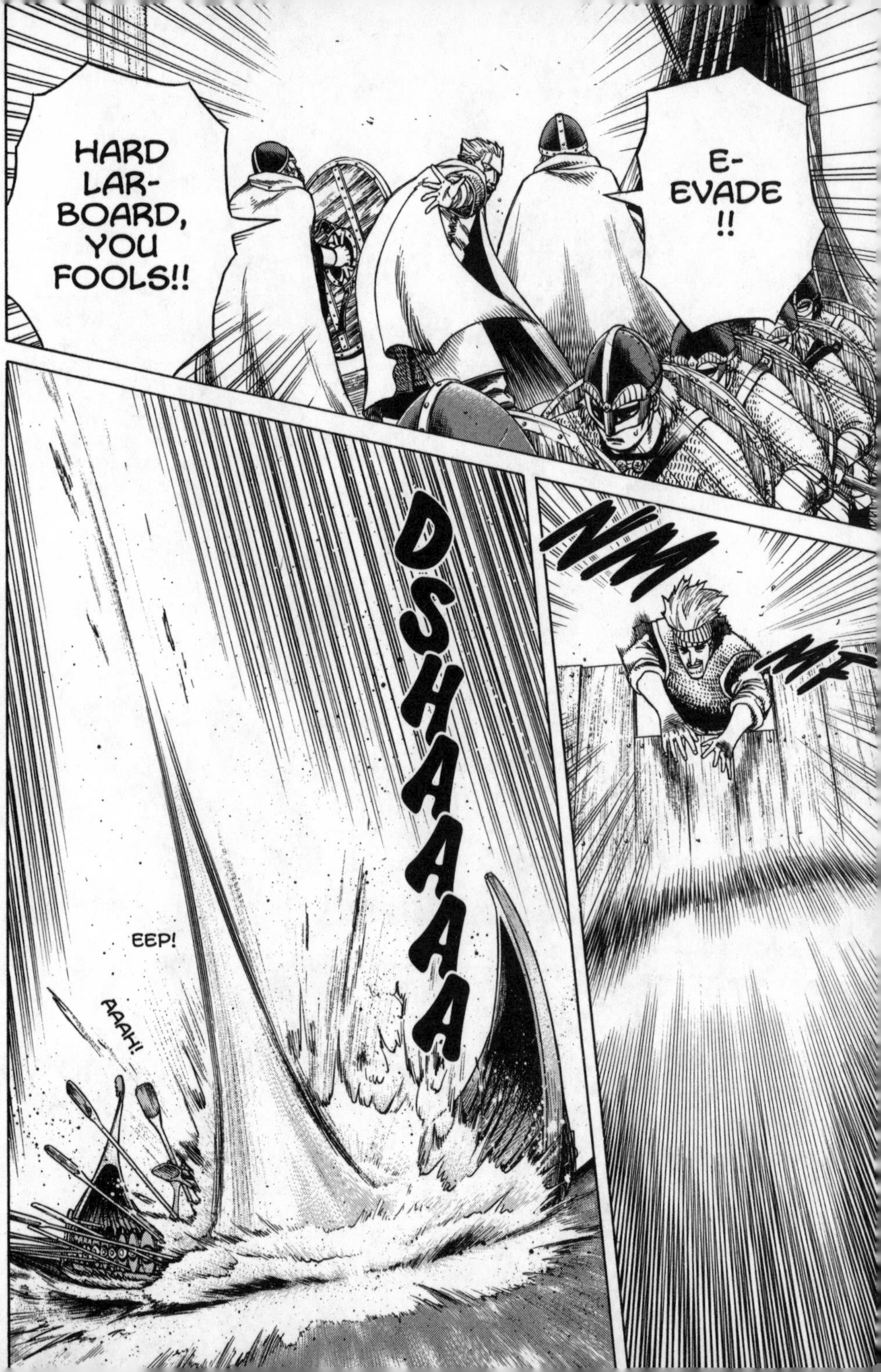
E- EVADE !!
HARD LAR- BOARD, YOU FOOLS!!
NNM
MF
DSHAAAA
EEP!
AAAH!

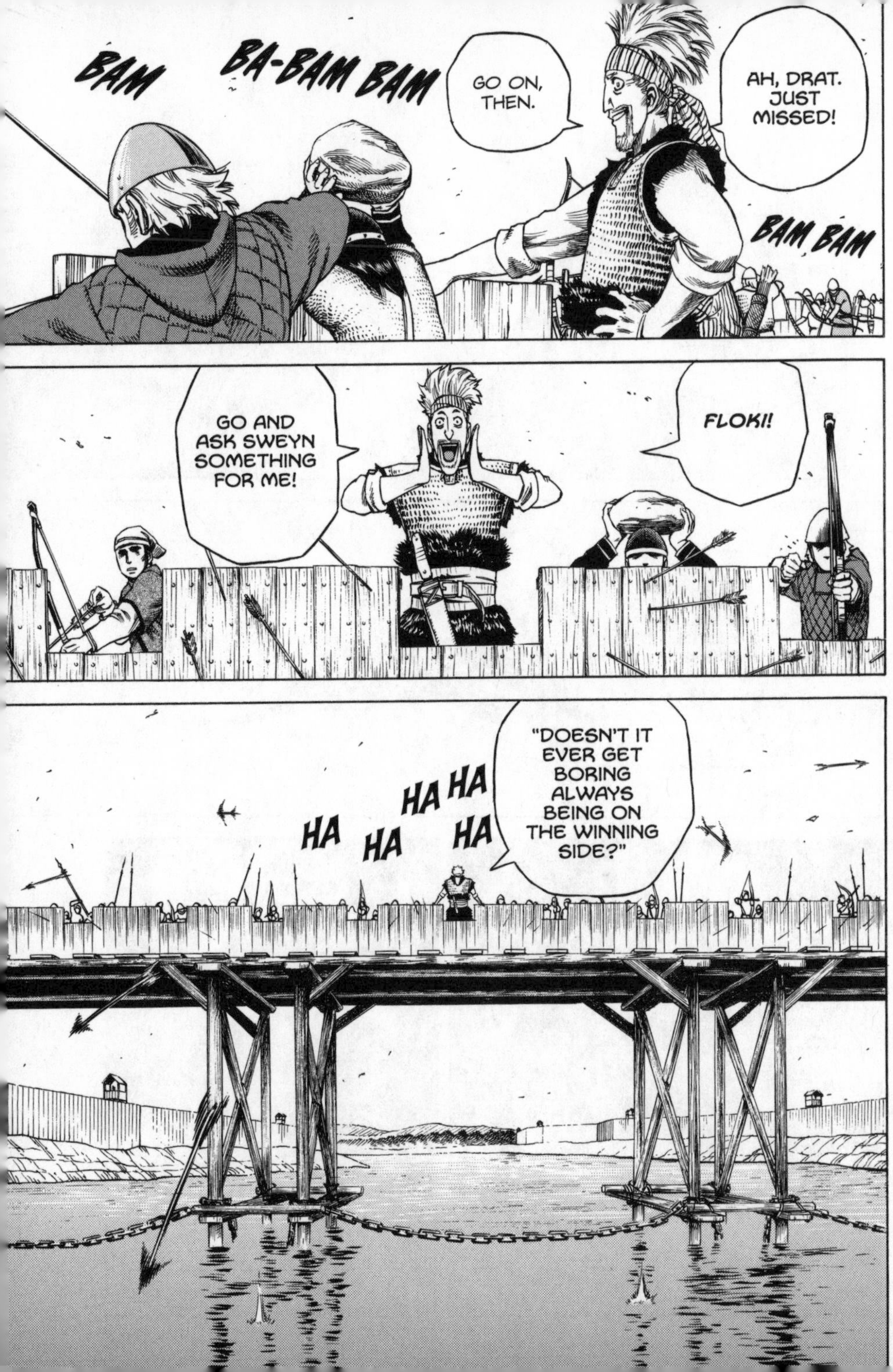
AH, DRAT. JUST MISSED!
GO ON, THEN.
BA-BAM BAM
BAM
BAM BAM
FLOKI!
GO AND ASK SWEYN SOMETHING FOR ME!
"DOESN'T IT EVER GET BORING ALWAYS BEING ON THE WINNING SIDE?"
HA HA
HA HA
HA

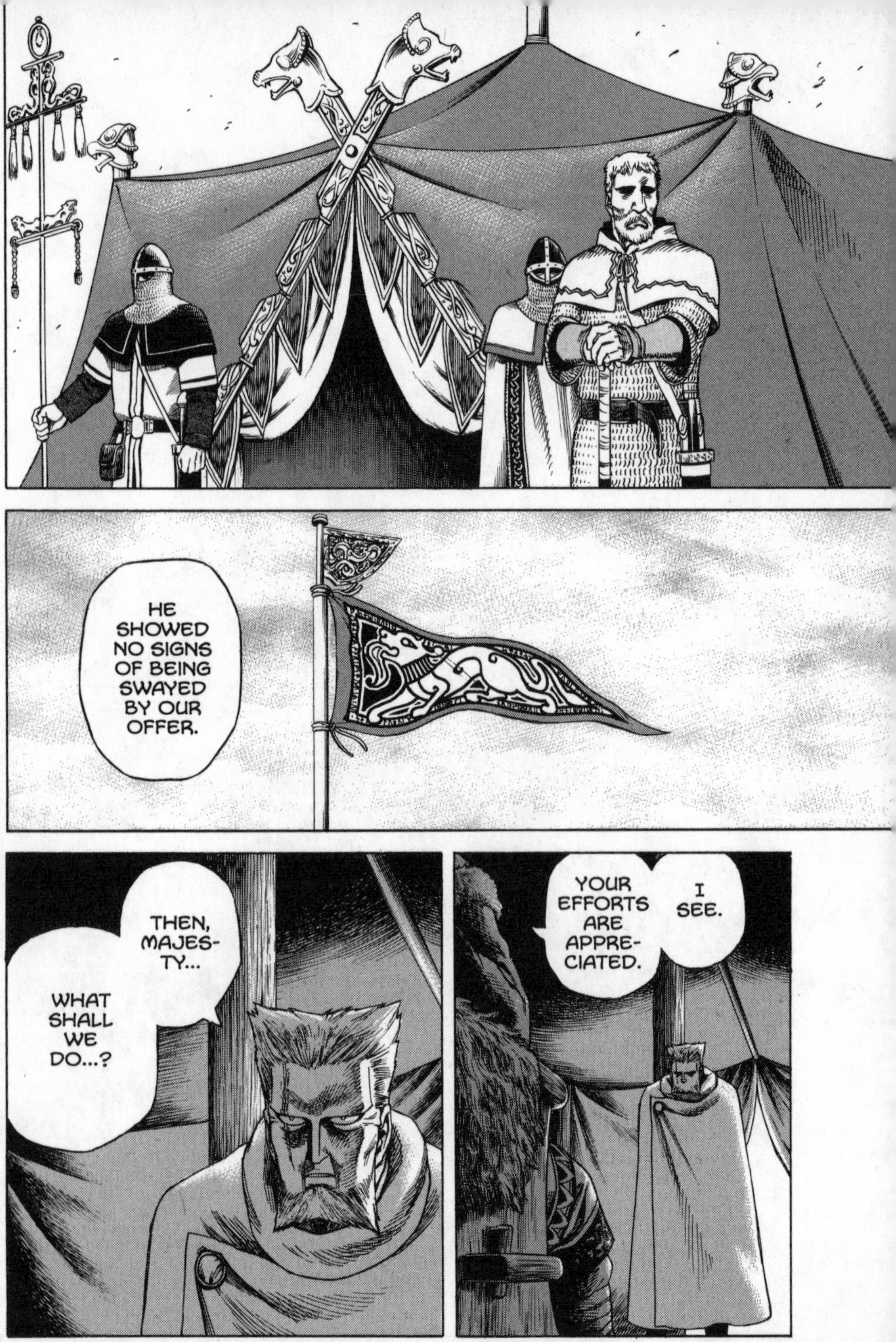
HE SHOWED NO SIGNS OF BEING SWAYED BY OUR OFFER.
I SEE.
YOUR EFFORTS ARE APPRE-CIATED.
THEN, MAJES-TY...
WHAT SHALL WE DO...?

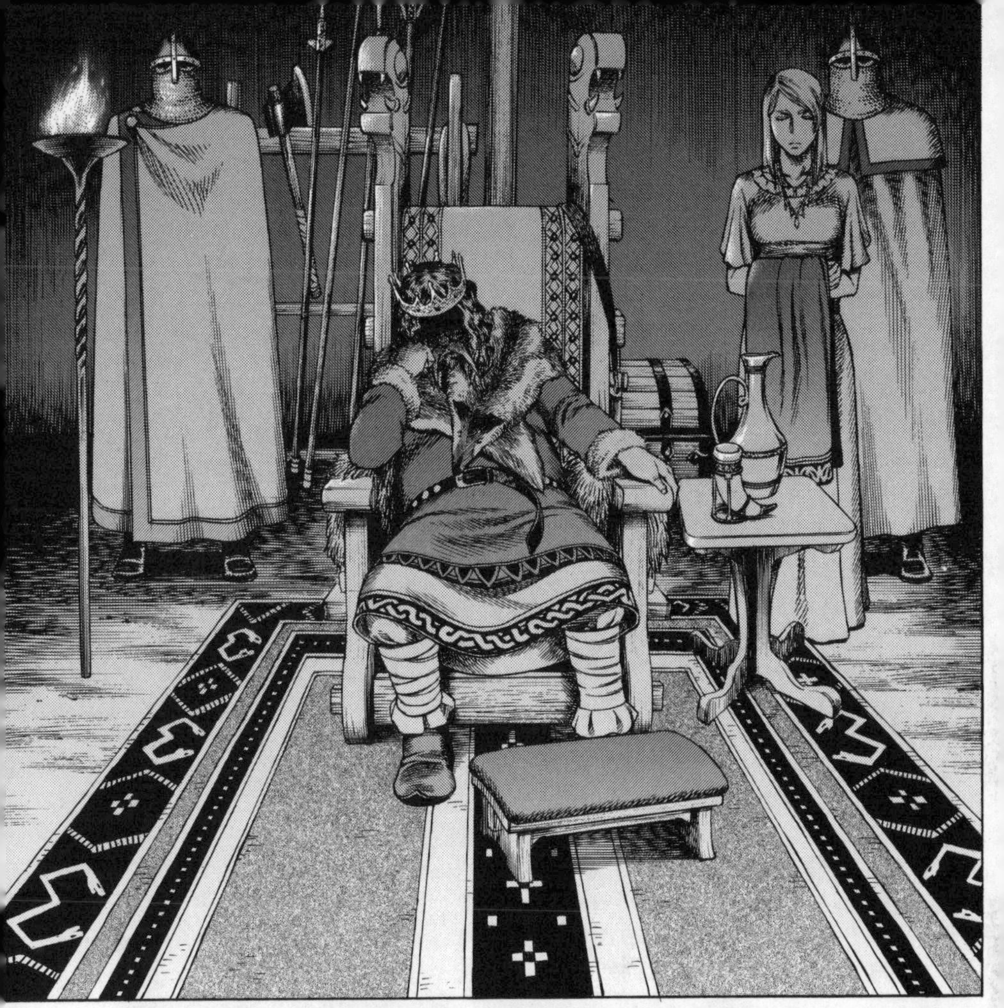

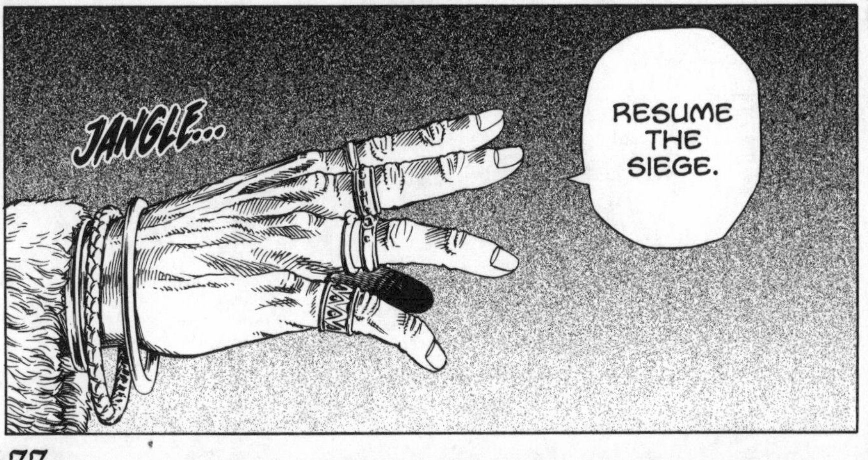
RESUME THE SIEGE.
JANGLE...

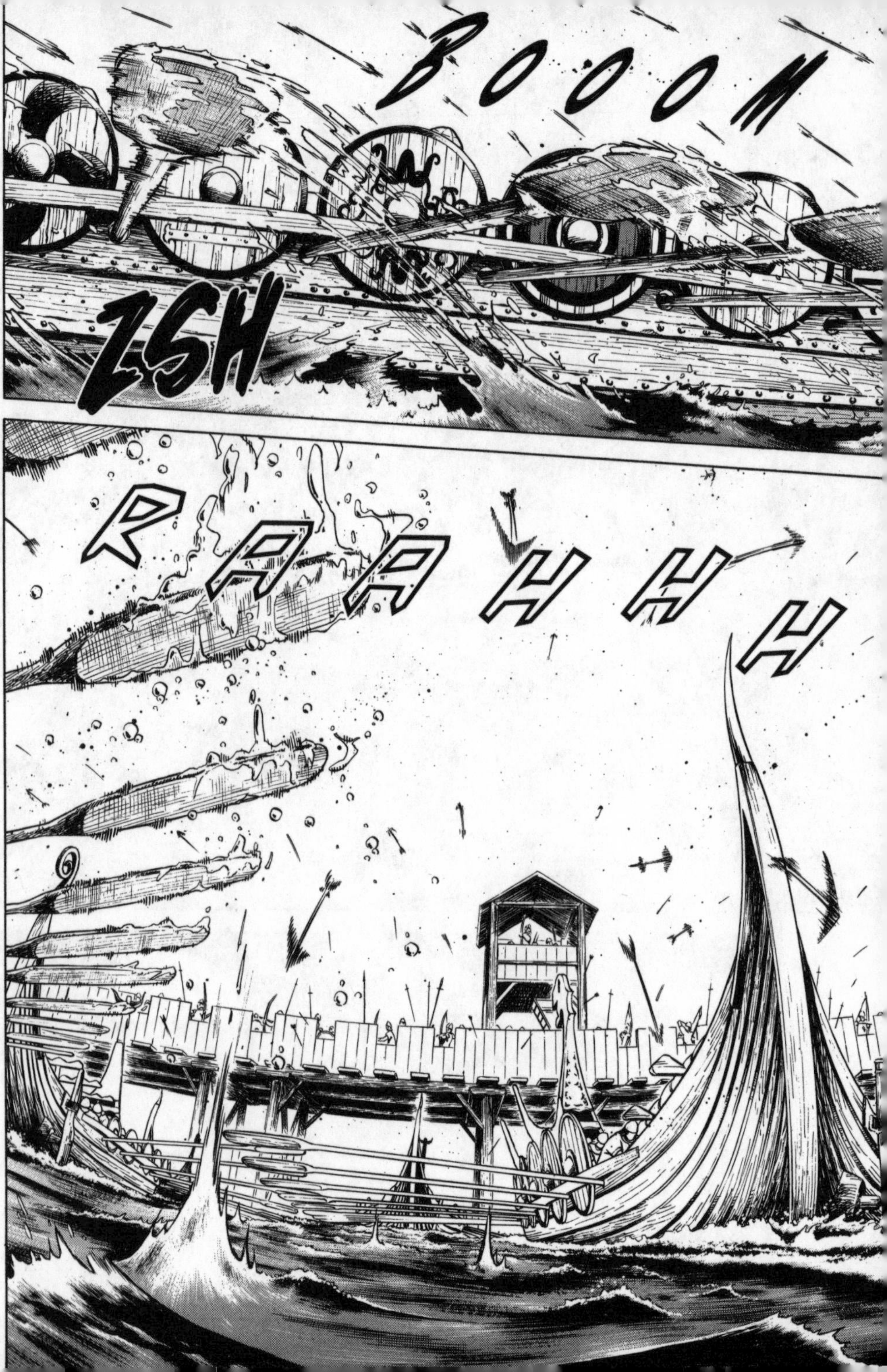
BOOOM
ZSH
RAAHHH

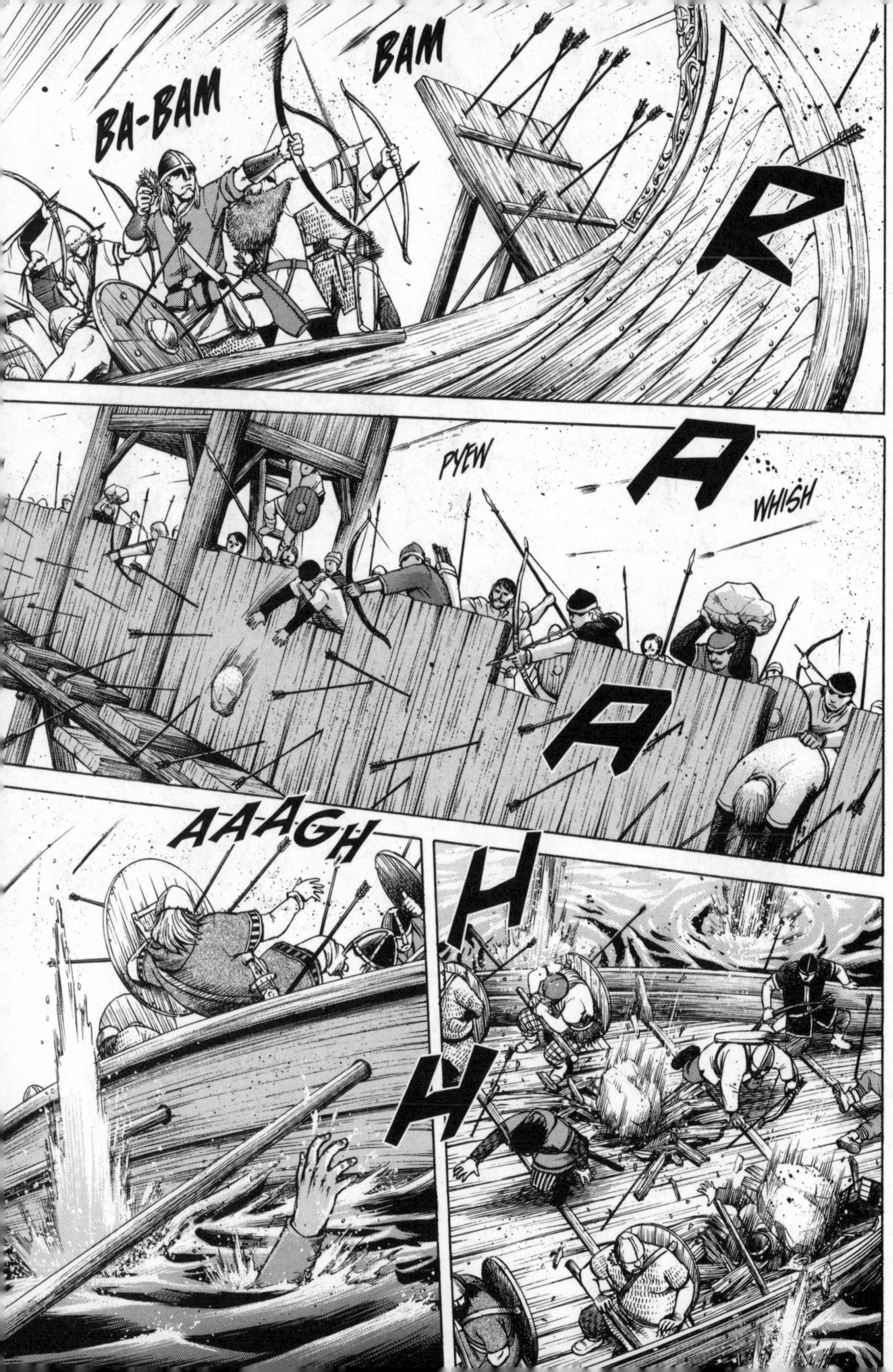
RAAHH
BAM
BA-BAM
WHISH
PYEW
AAAGH

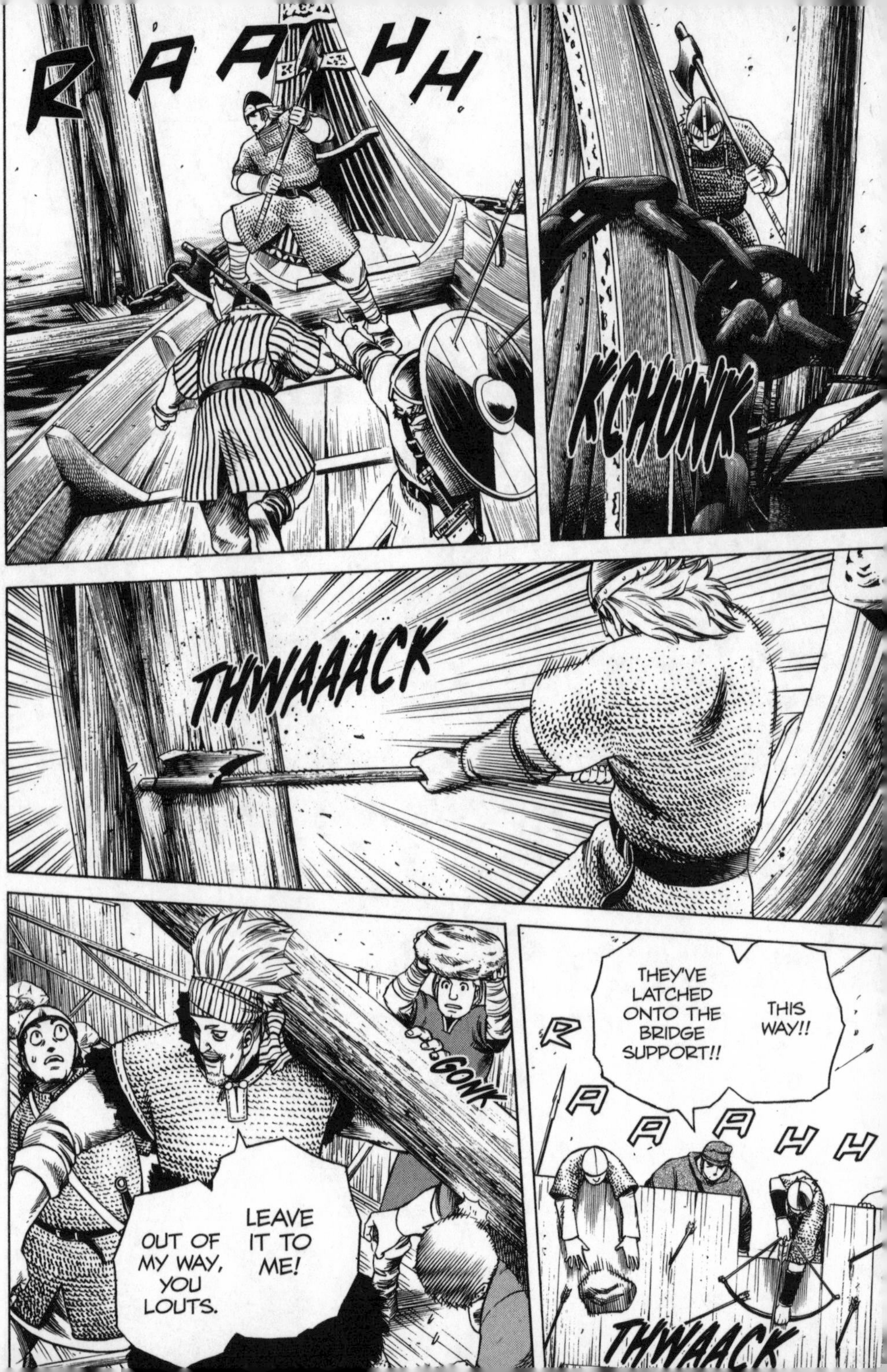
KCHUNK
RAAHH
THWAAACK
THEY'VE LATCHED ONTO THE BRIDGE SUPPORT!!
THIS WAY!!
RAAAHH
THWAACK
GONK
LEAVE IT TO ME!
OUT OF MY WAY, YOU LOUTS.

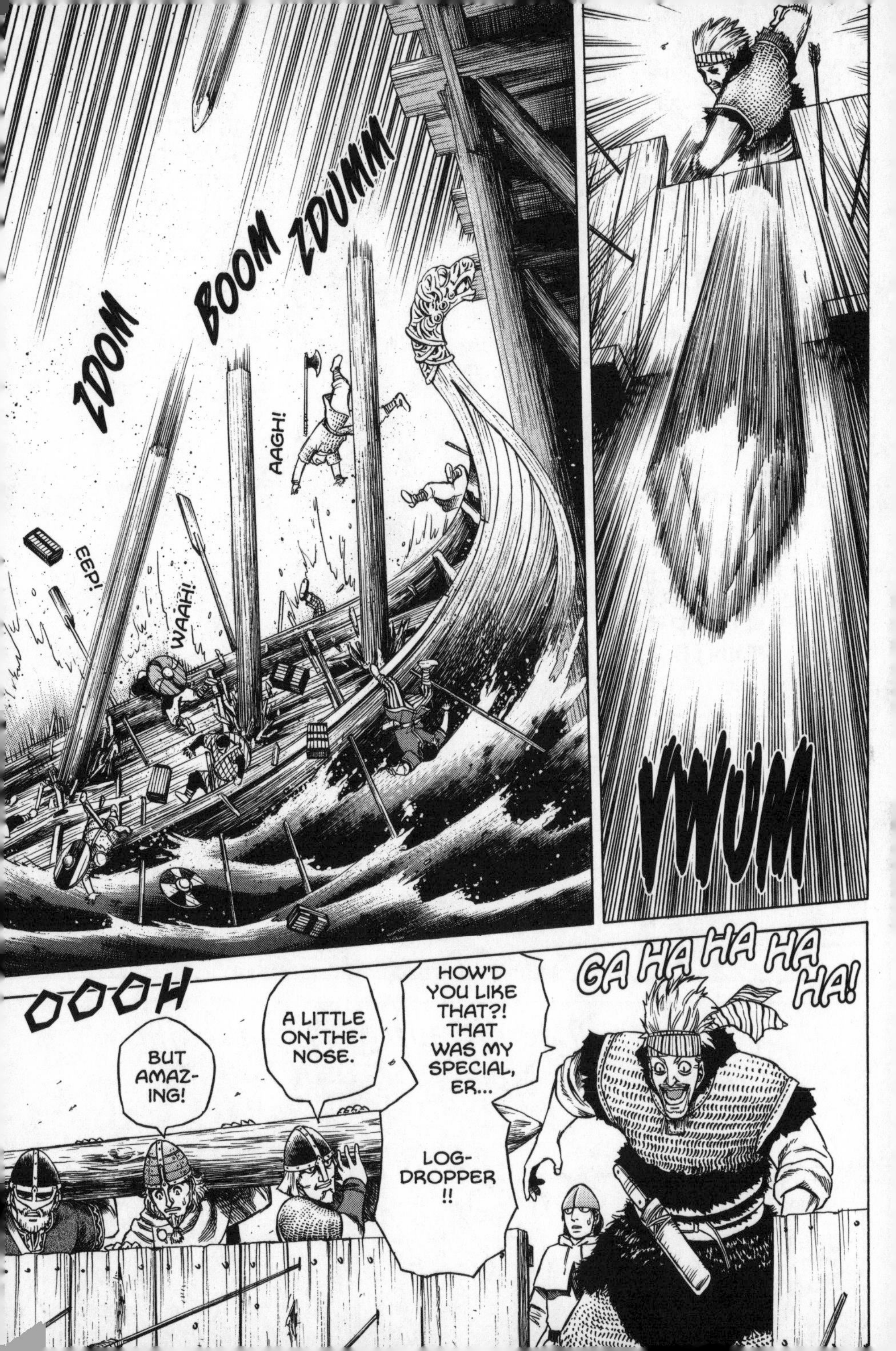
VWUM
ZDUMM
BOOM
ZDOM
AAGH!
EEP!
WAAAH!
GA HA HA HA HA HA!
HOW'D YOU LIKE THAT?! THAT WAS MY SPECIAL, ER...
LOG-DROPPER!!
A LITTLE ON-THE-NOSE.
BUT AMAZ-ING!
OOOH

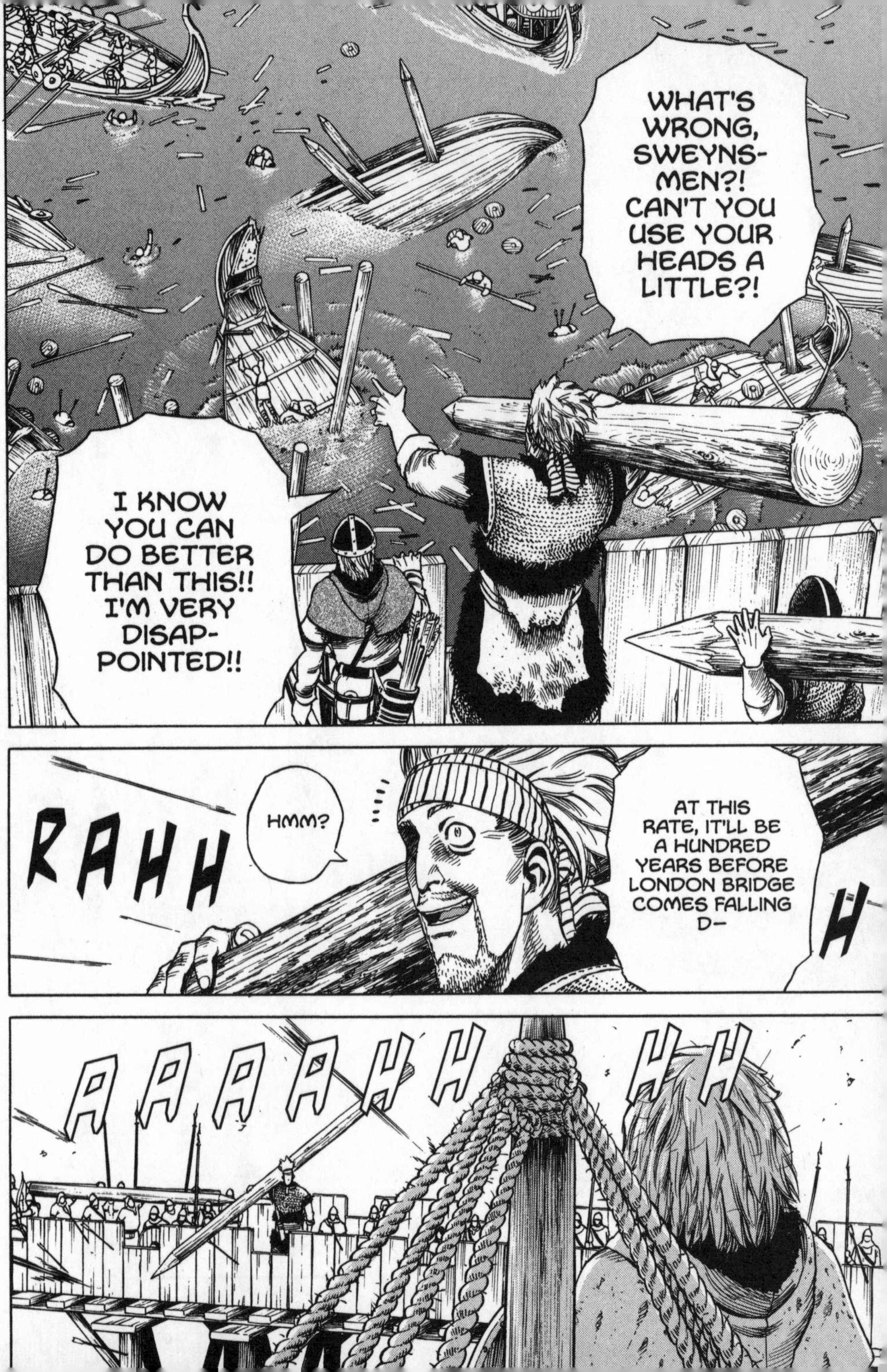
WHAT'S WRONG, SWEYNS-MEN?! CAN'T YOU USE YOUR HEADS A LITTLE?!
I KNOW YOU CAN DO BETTER THAN THIS!! I'M VERY DISAP-POINTED!!
AT THIS RATE, IT'LL BE A HUNDRED YEARS BEFORE LONDON BRIDGE COMES FALLING D—
H
HMM?
RAHH
AAAAHH HH

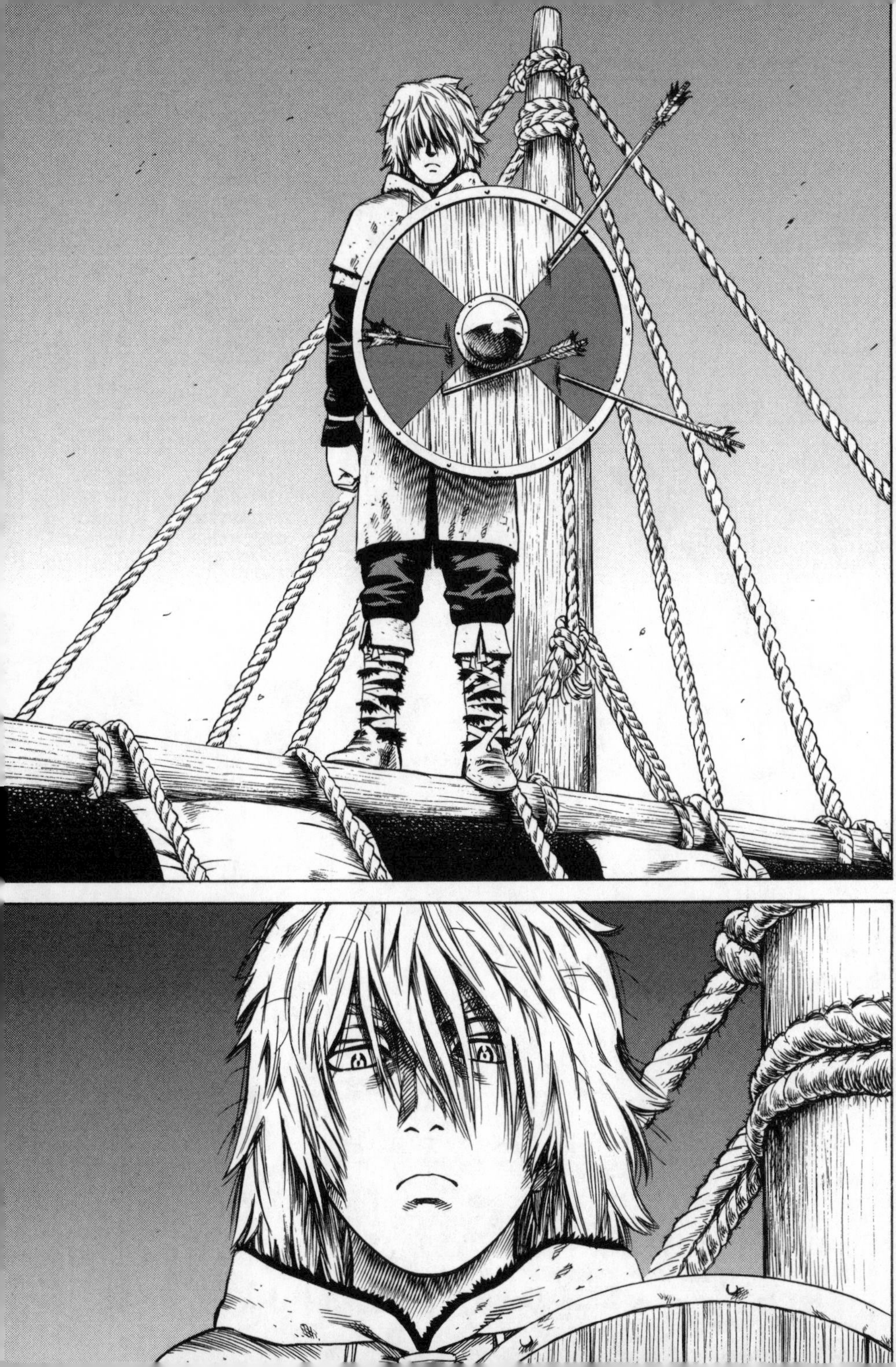

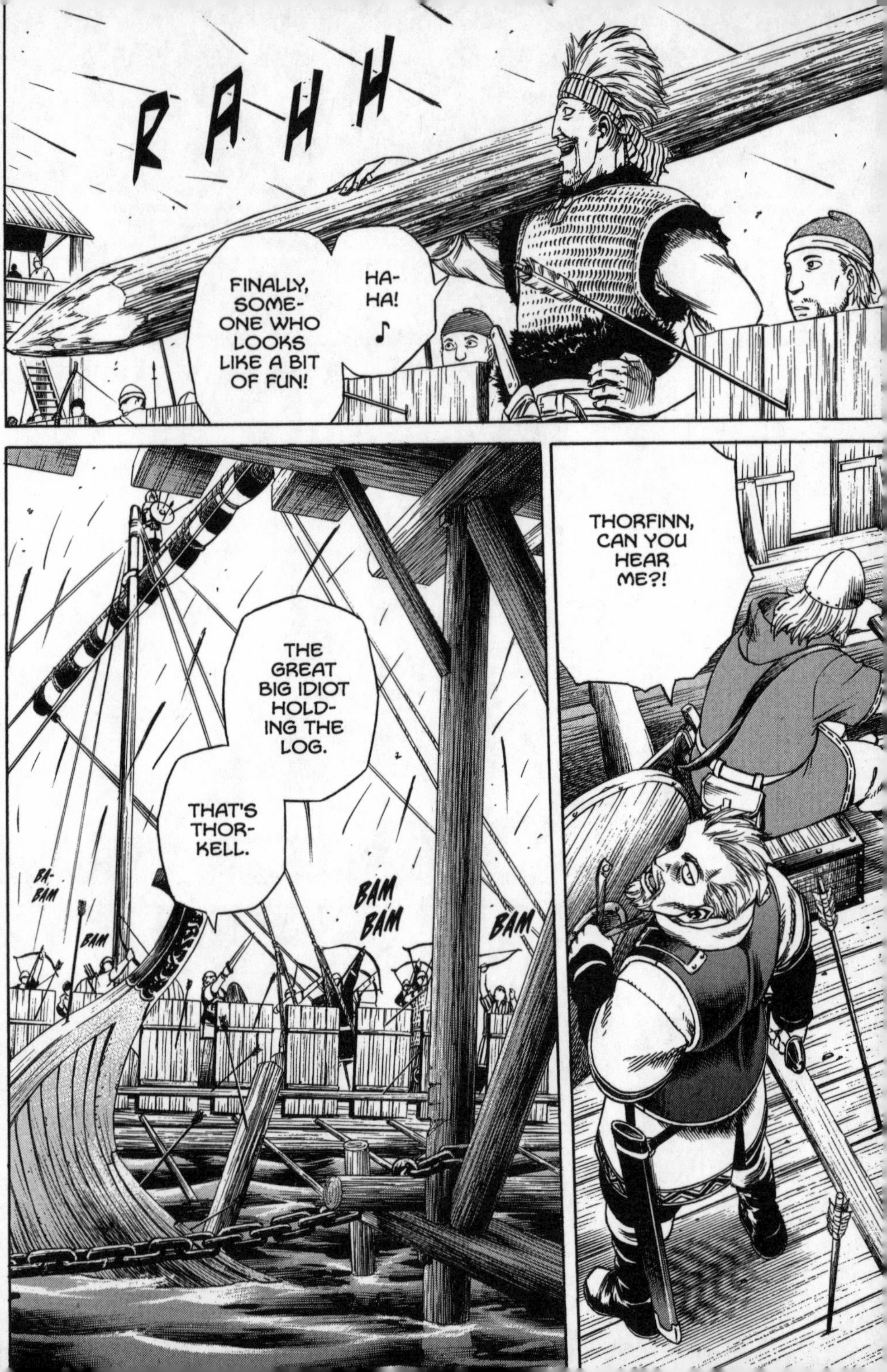
RAHH
HA-HA! ♪
FINALLY, SOME-ONE WHO LOOKS LIKE A BIT OF FUN!
THORFINN, CAN YOU HEAR ME?!
THE GREAT BIG IDIOT HOLD-ING THE LOG.
THAT'S THOR-KELL.
BAM
BAM BAM
BAM
BA-BAM

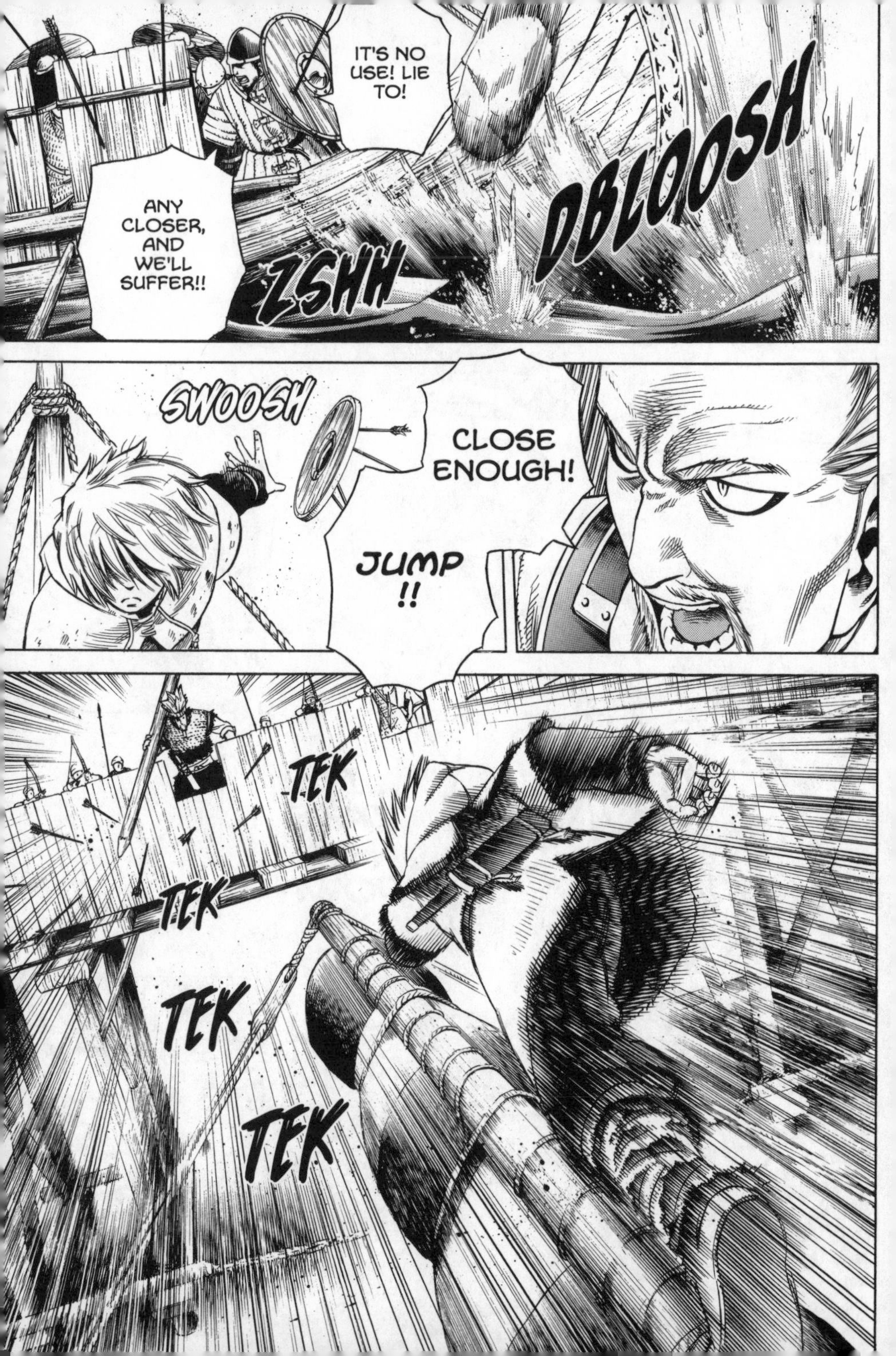
IT'S NO USE! LIE TO!
DBLOOSH
ANY CLOSER, AND WE'LL SUFFER!!
ZSHH
CLOSE ENOUGH!
JUMP !!
SWOOSH
TEK
TEK
TEK
TEK

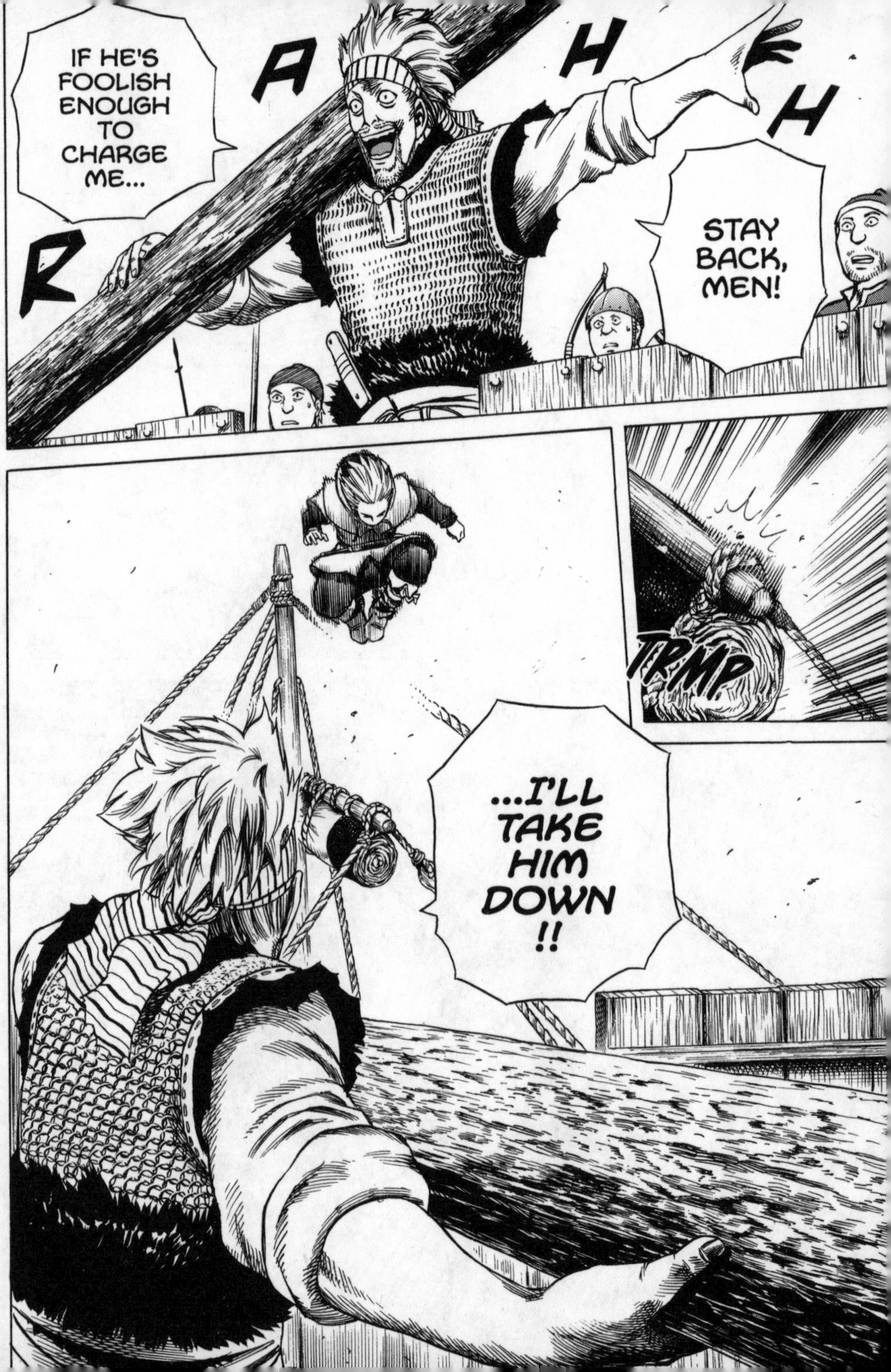
STAY BACK, MEN!
RAHH
IF HE'S FOOLISH ENOUGH TO CHARGE ME...
TRMP
...I'LL TAKE HIM DOWN!!

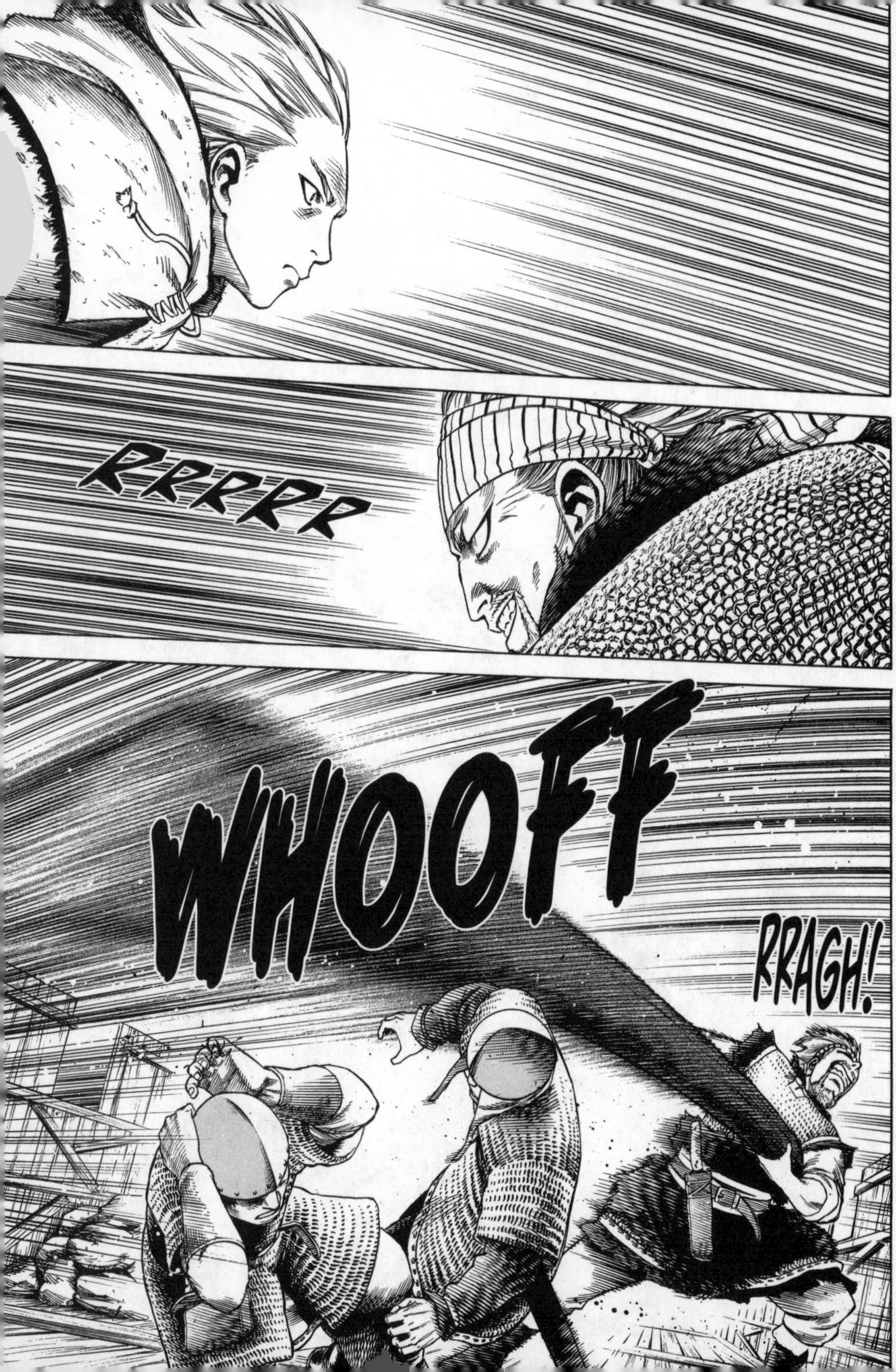
RRRRRR
WHOOFF
RRAGH!

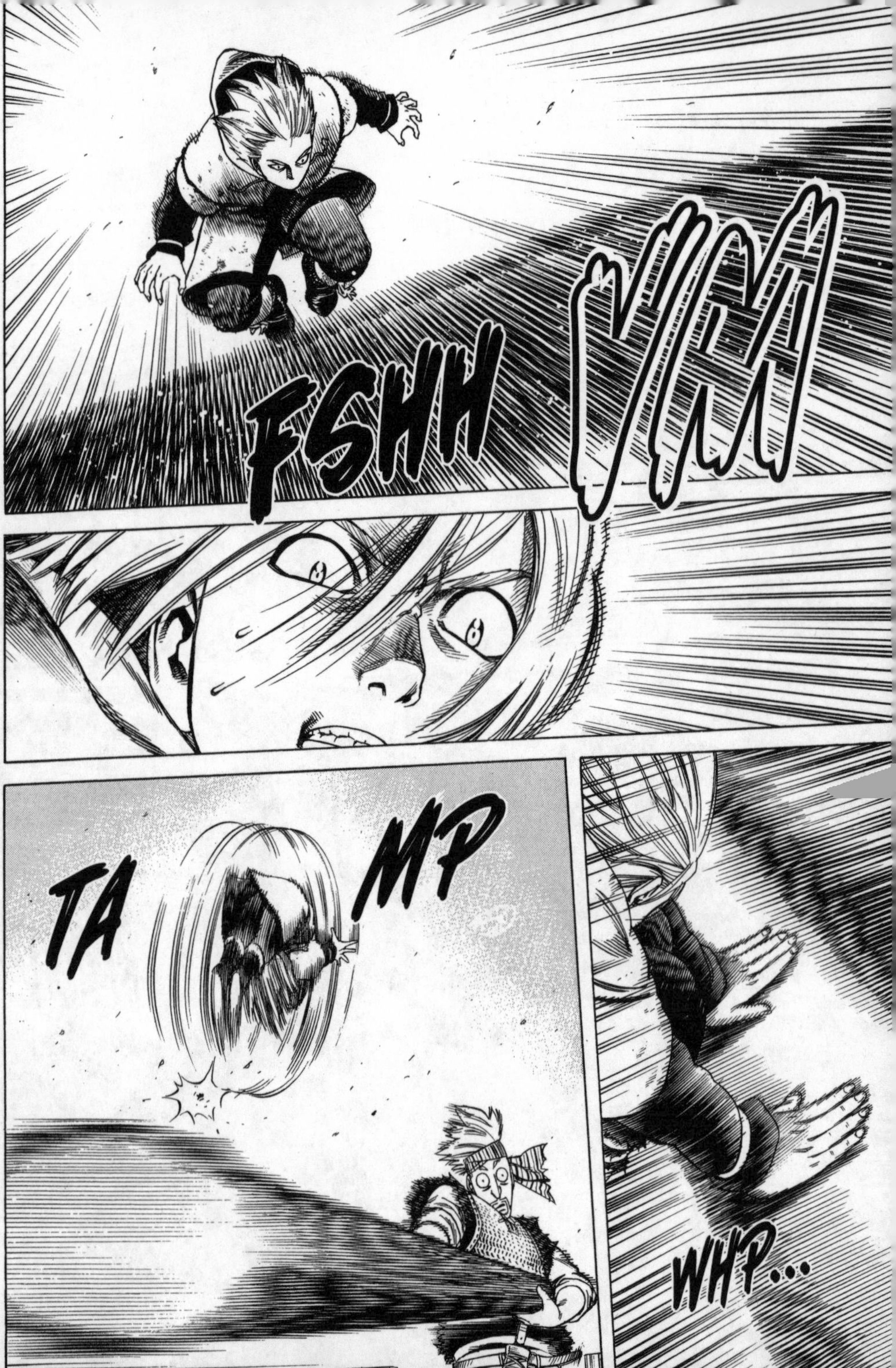
FSHH VMM
WHP...
TA MP

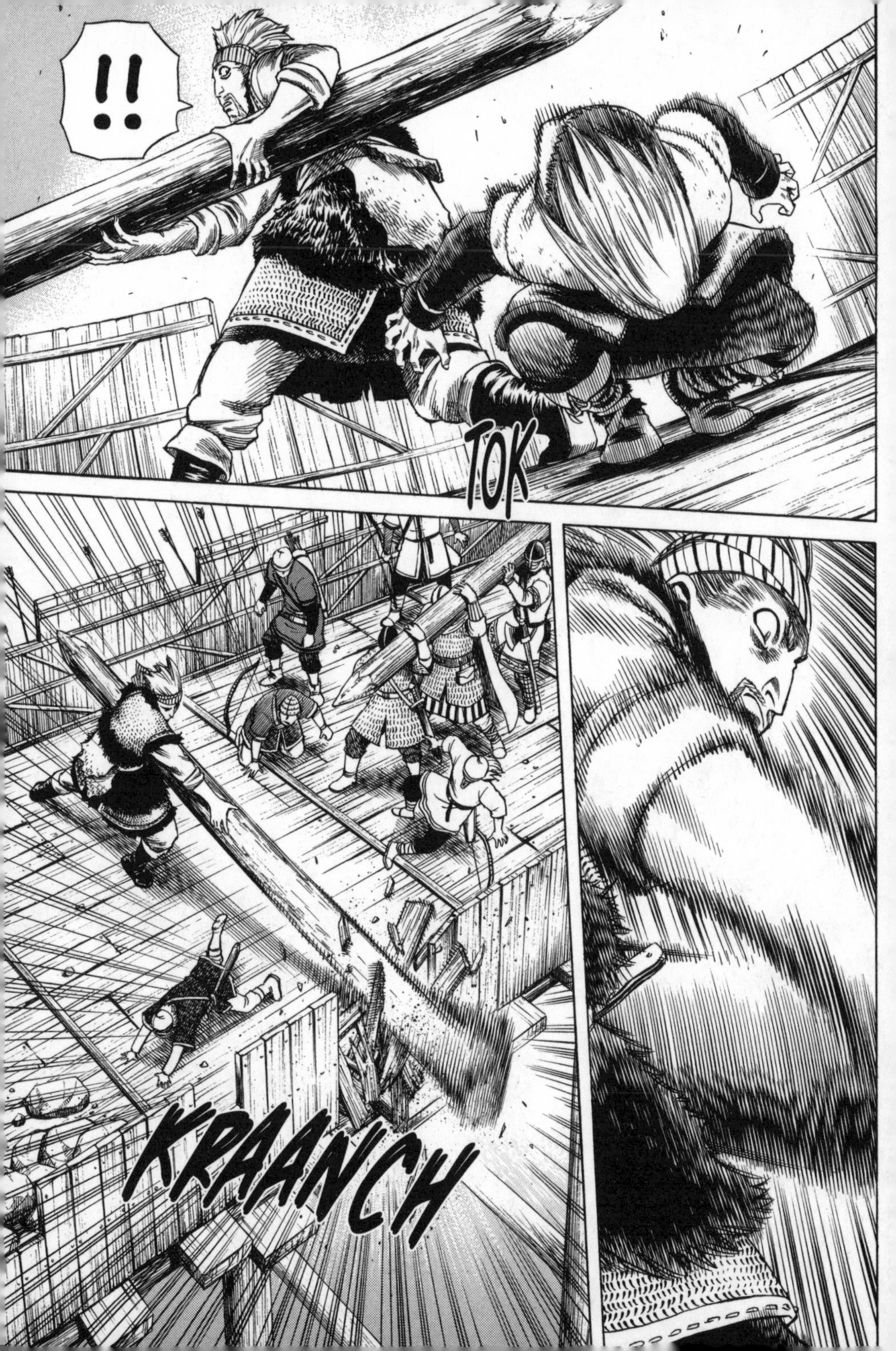
!!
TOK
KRAANCH

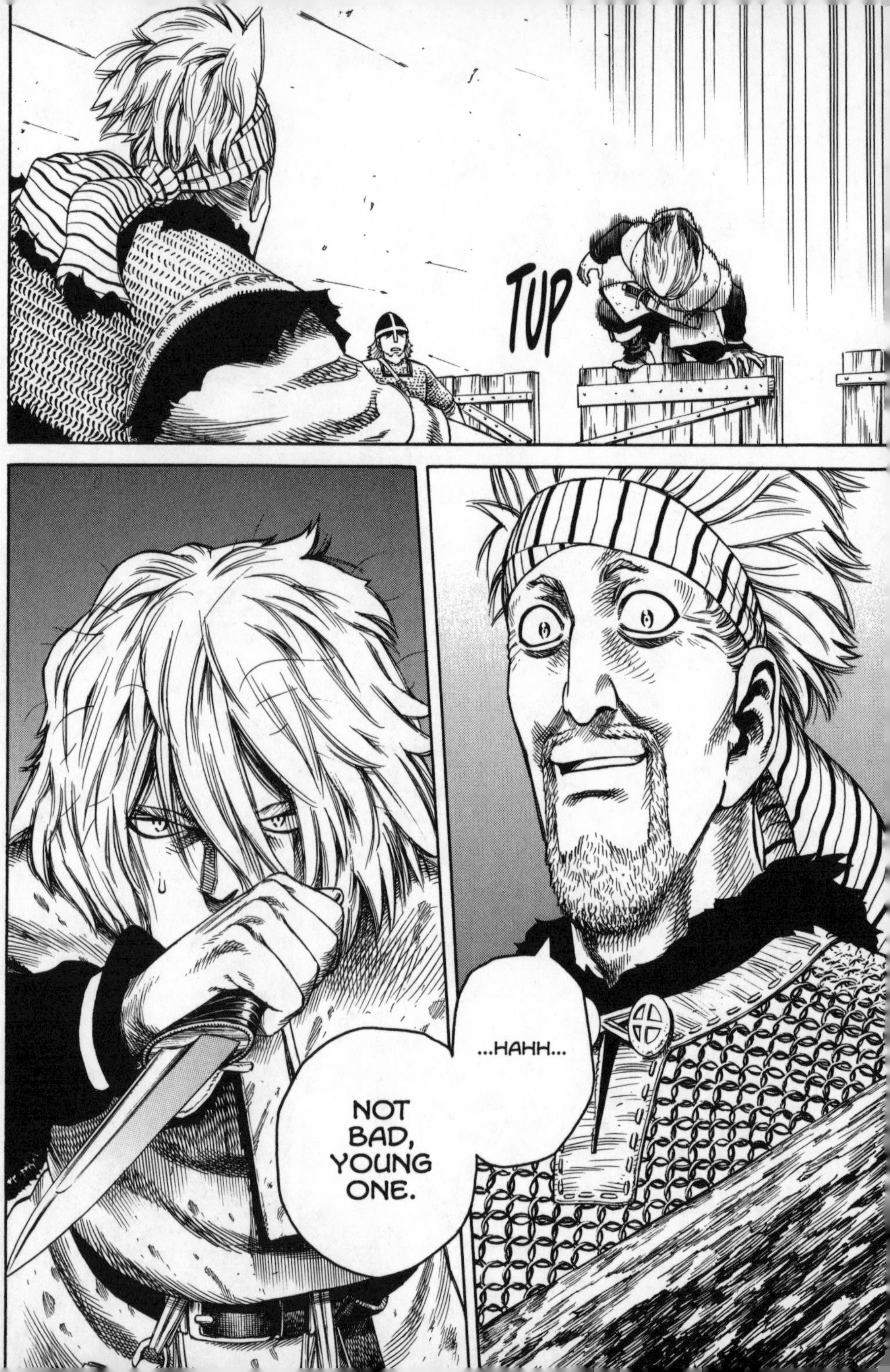
TUP
...HAHH...
NOT BAD, YOUNG ONE.

CHAPTER 19: THE BATTLE OF LONDON BRIDGE

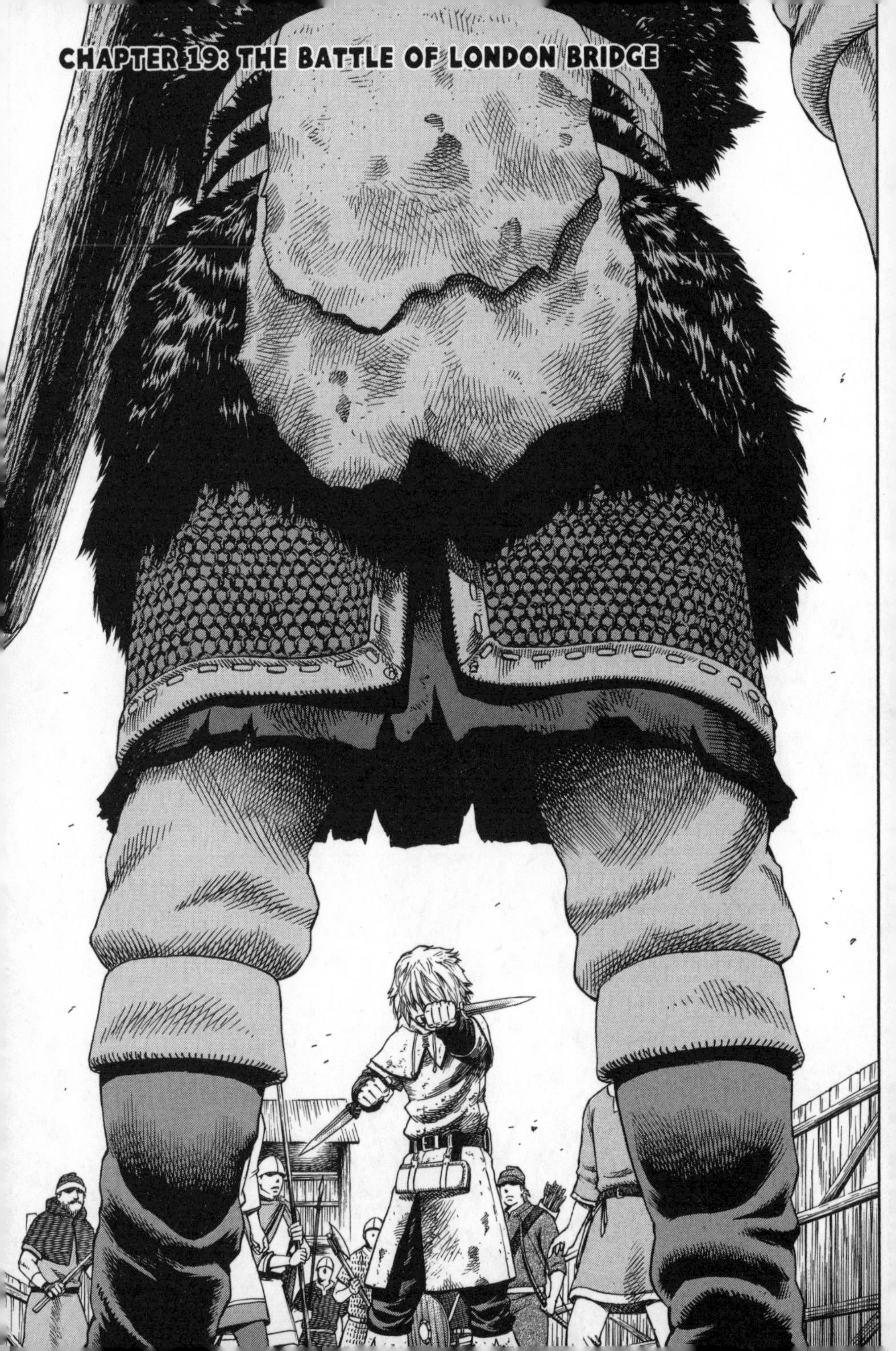

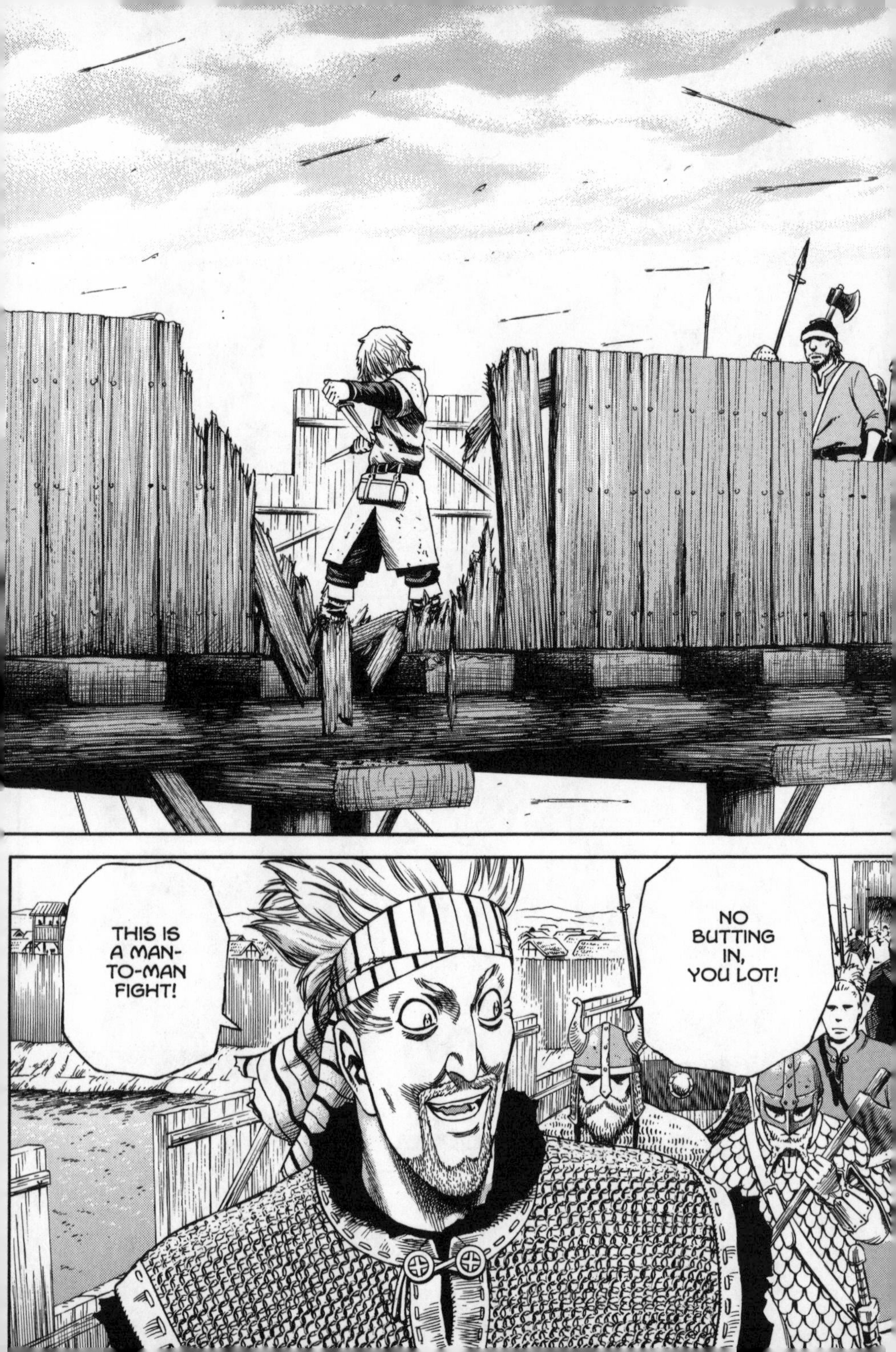
NO BUTTING IN, YOU LOT!
THIS IS A MAN-TO-MAN FIGHT!

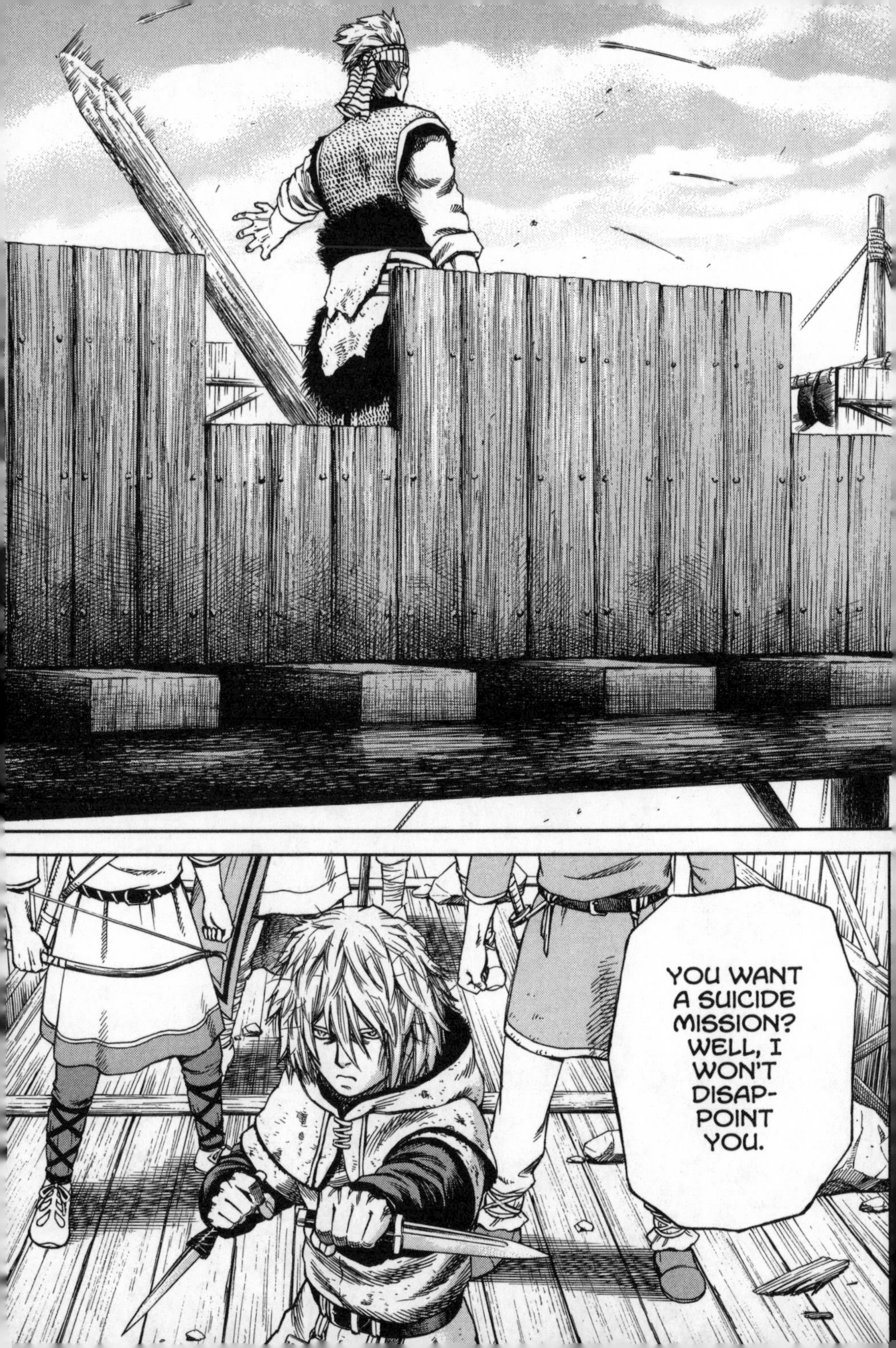
YOU WANT A SUICIDE MISSION? WELL, I WON'T DISAP-POINT YOU.

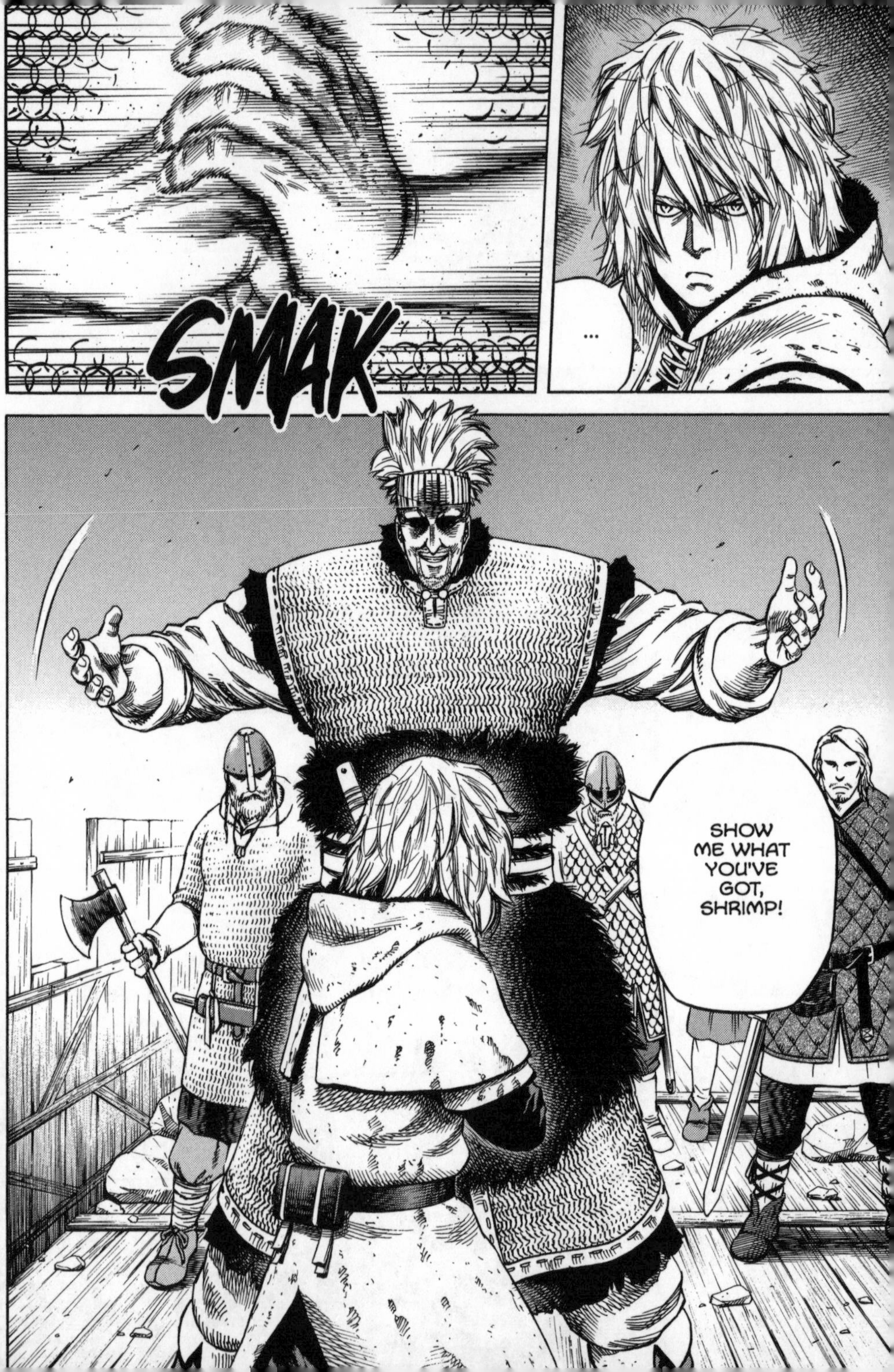
...
SMAK
SHOW ME WHAT YOU'VE GOT, SHRIMP!

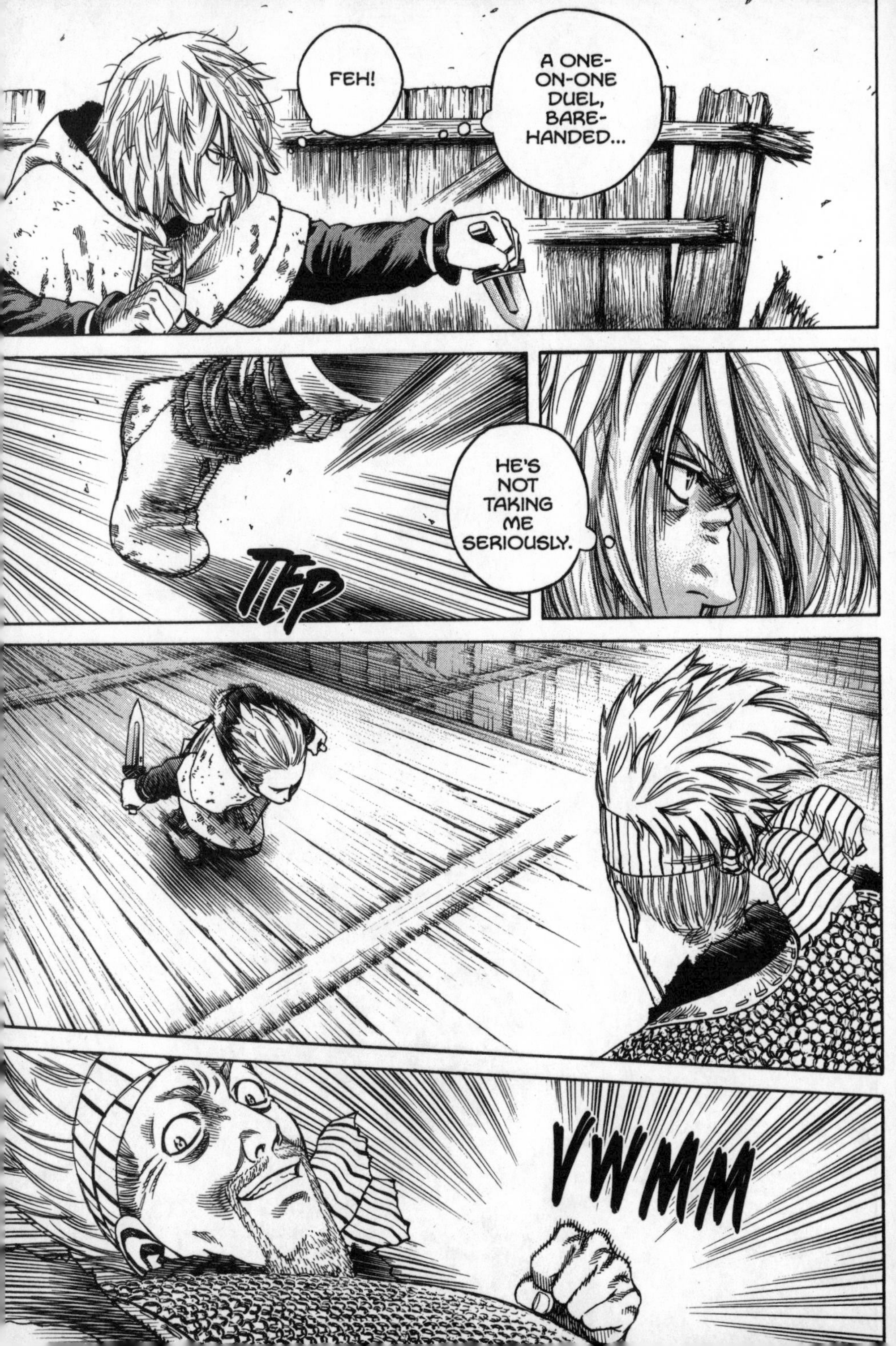
A ONE-ON-ONE DUEL, BARE-HANDED...
FEH!
HE'S NOT TAKING ME SERIOUSLY.
TEP
VWMM

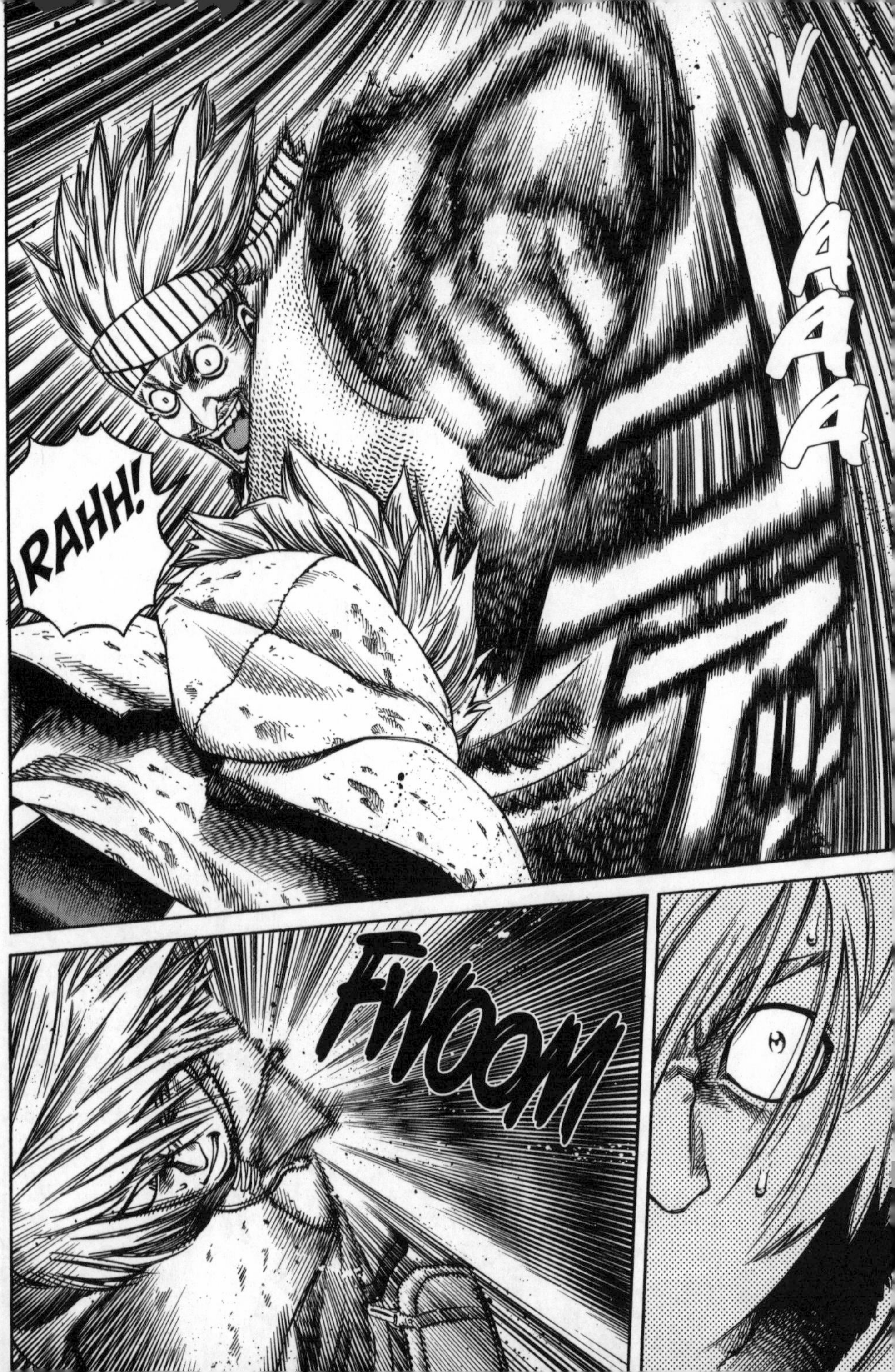
VWAAA
RAHH!
FWOOM

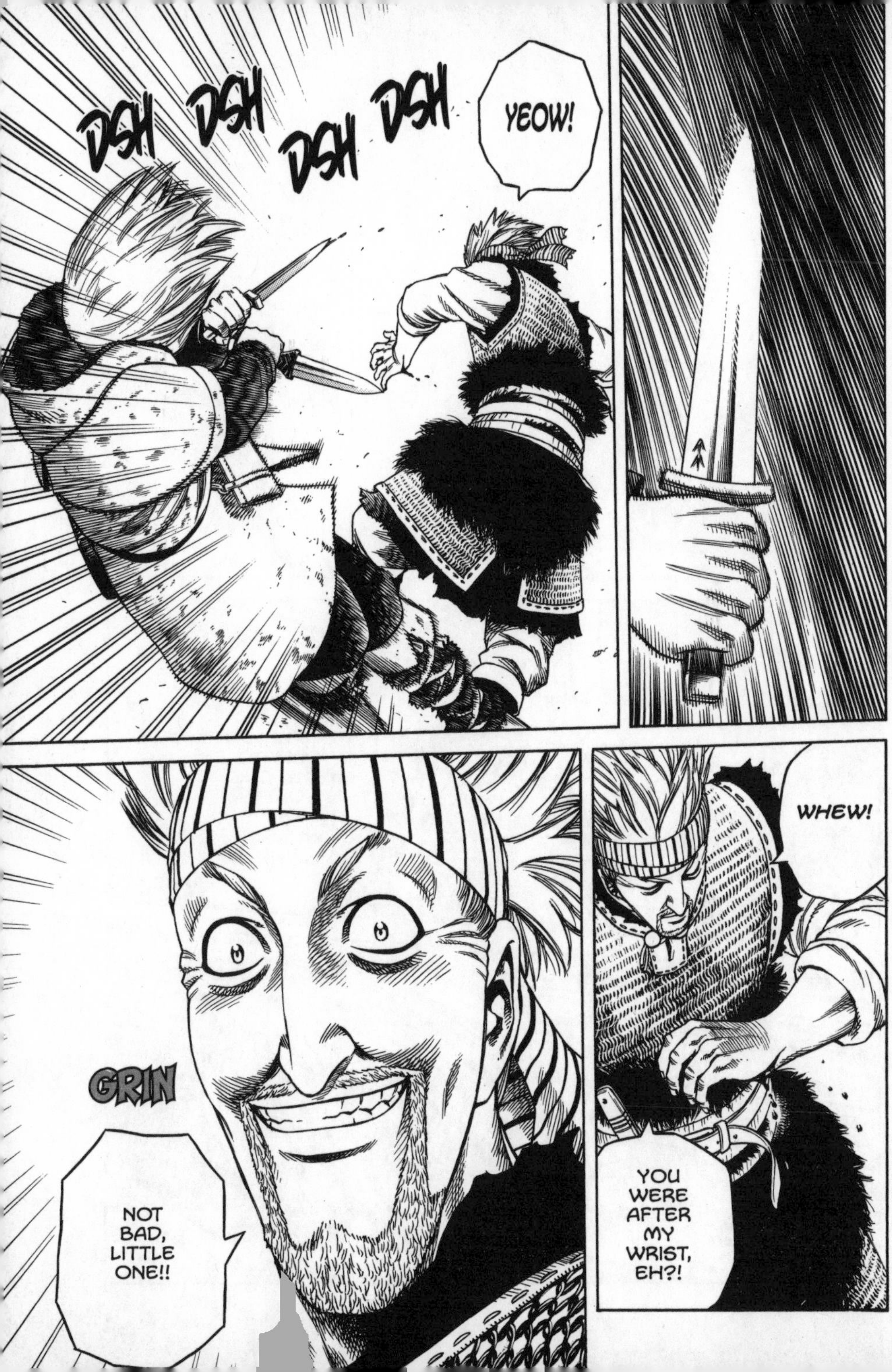
DSH DSH DSH DSH
YEOW!
WHEW!
YOU WERE AFTER MY WRIST, EH?!
GRIN
NOT BAD, LITTLE ONE!!

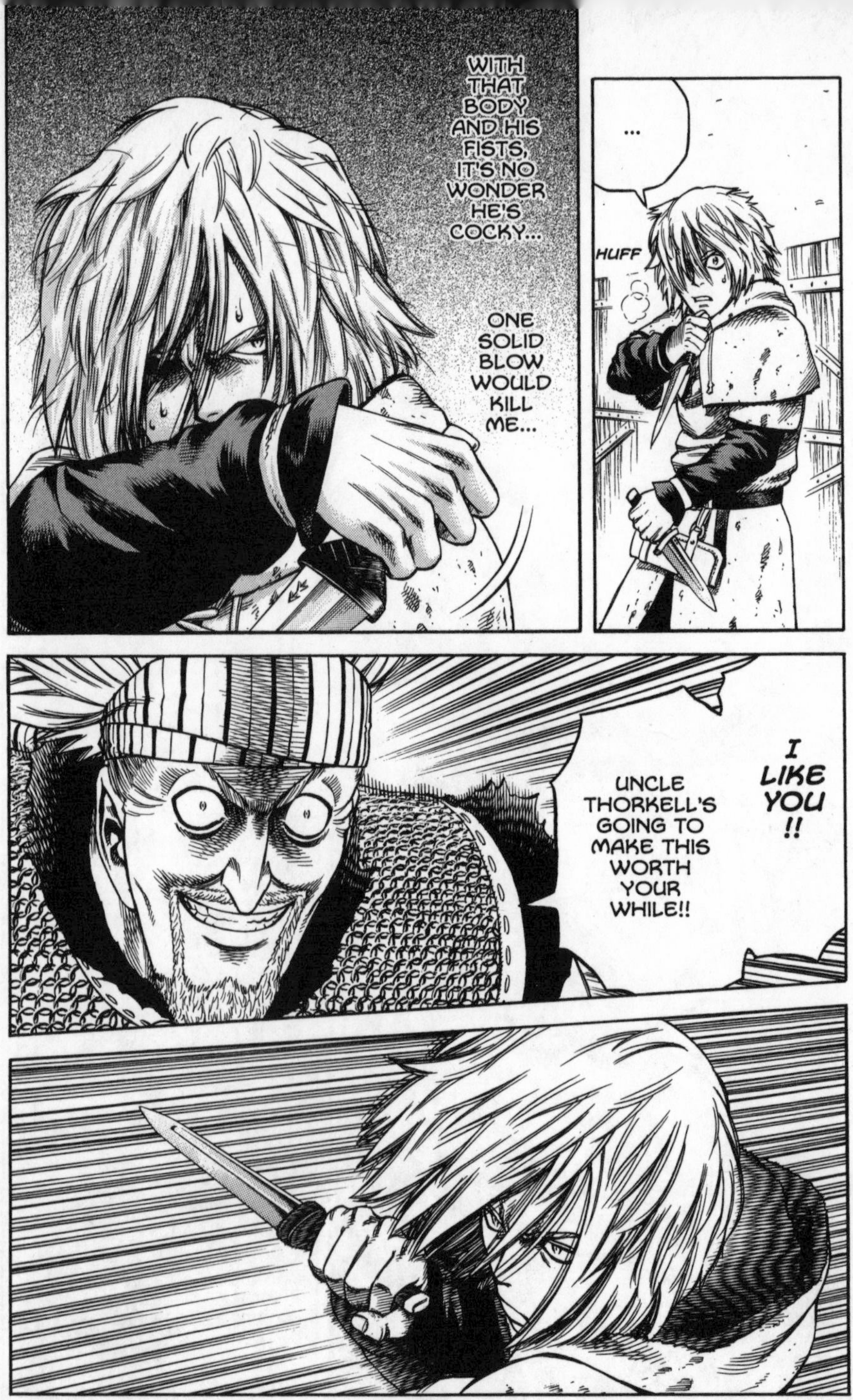
...
HUFF
WITH THAT BODY AND HIS FISTS, IT'S NO WONDER HE'S COCKY...
ONE SOLID BLOW WOULD KILL ME...
I LIKE YOU!!
UNCLE THORKELL'S GOING TO MAKE THIS WORTH YOUR WHILE!!

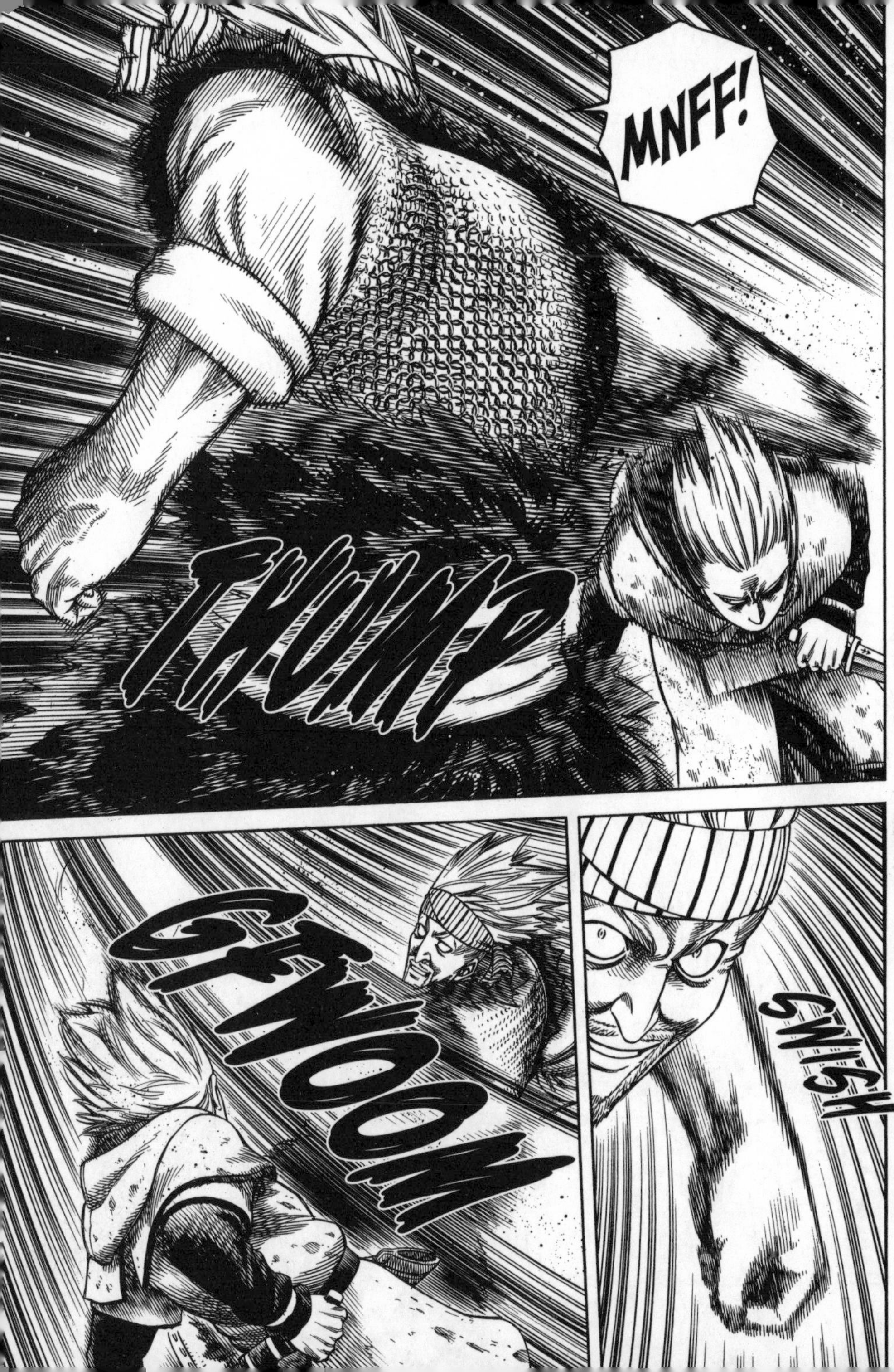
MNFF!
THUMP
SWISH
GFWOOM

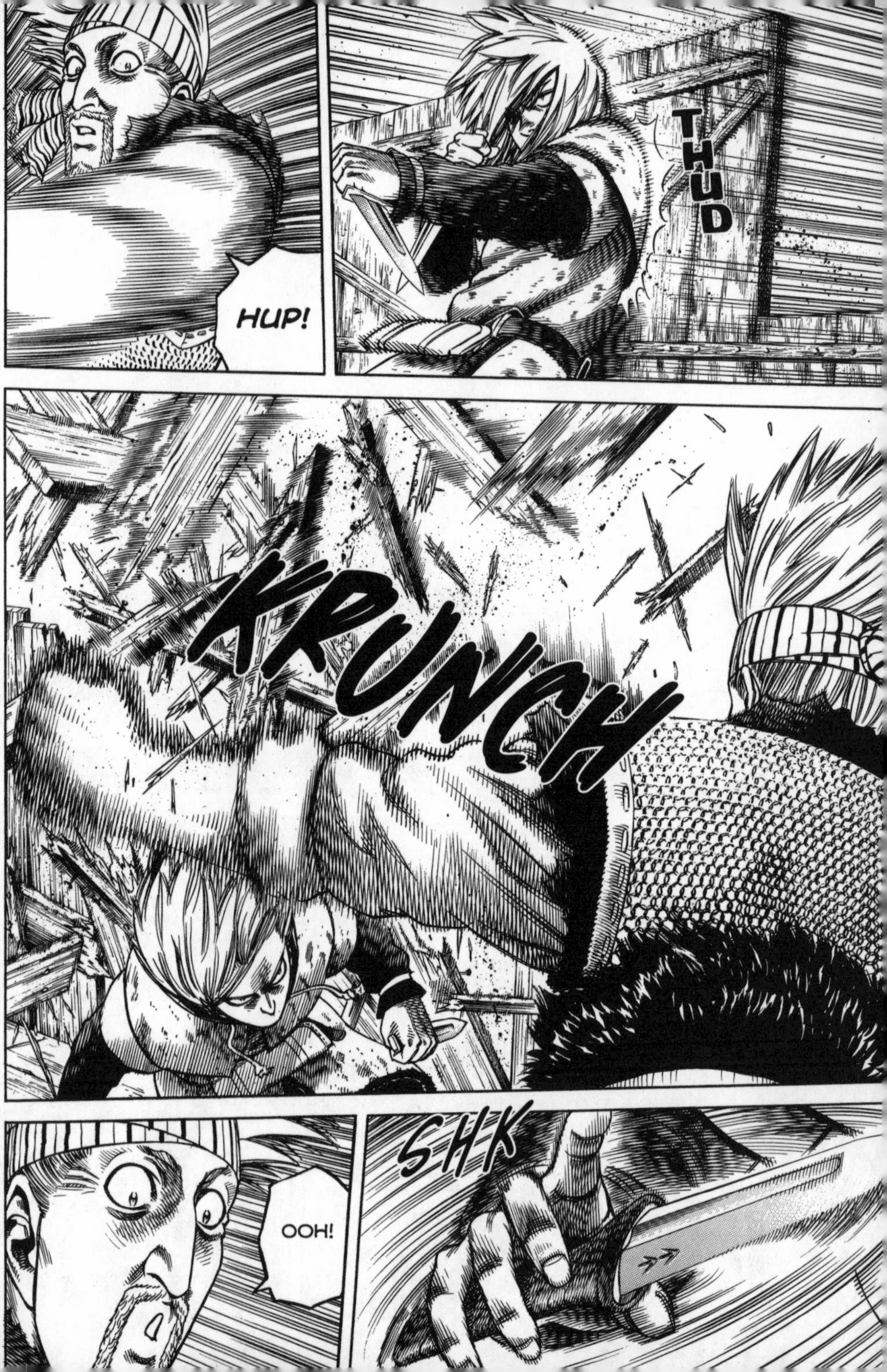
THUD
HUP!
KRUNCH
SHK
OOH!

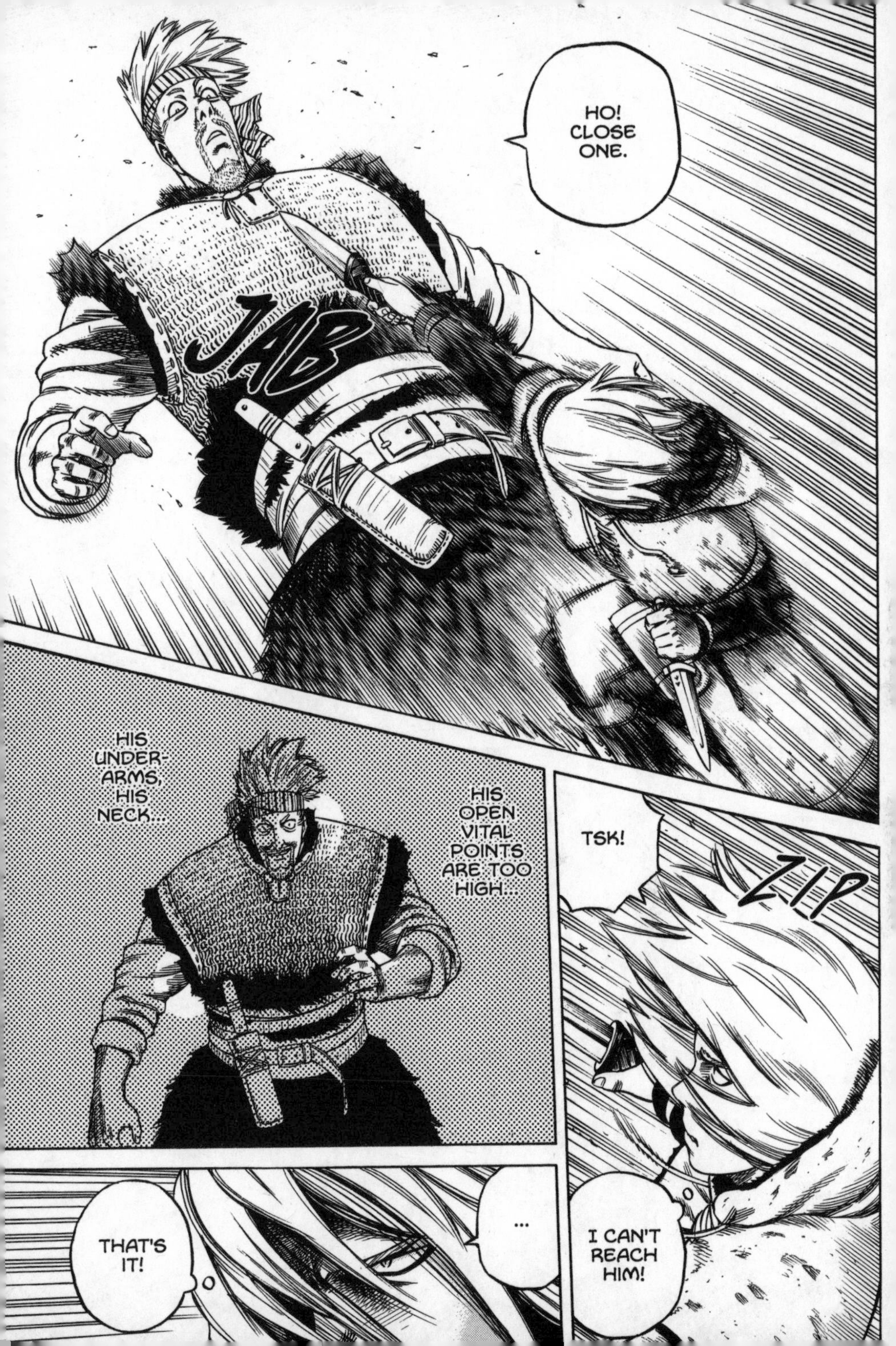
HO! CLOSE ONE.
JAB
TSK!
ZIP
I CAN'T REACH HIM!
HIS OPEN VITAL POINTS ARE TOO HIGH...
HIS UNDER-ARMS, HIS NECK...
...
THAT'S IT!

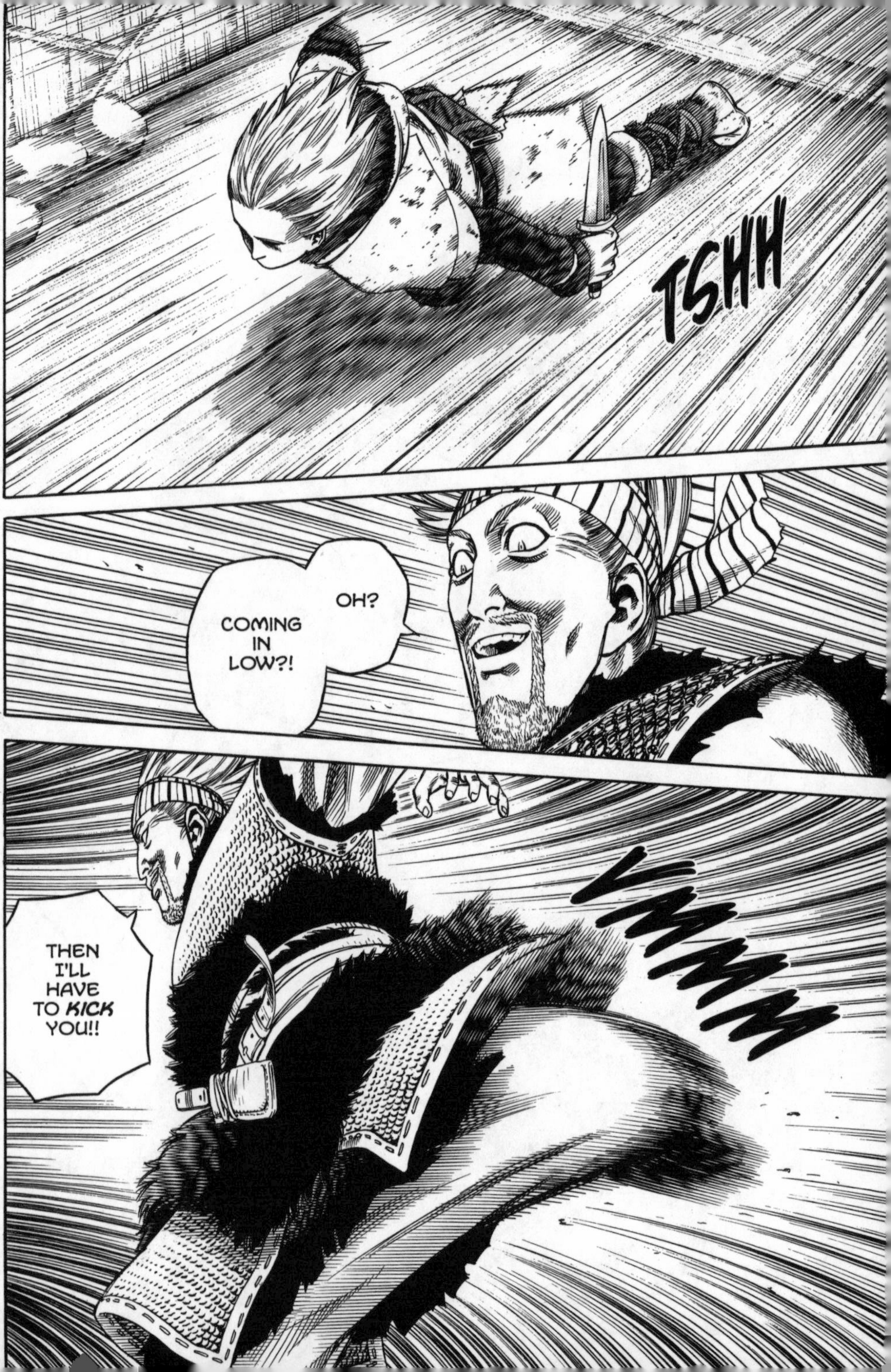
TSHH
OH? COMING IN LOW?!
VMMMM
THEN I'LL HAVE TO KICK YOU!!

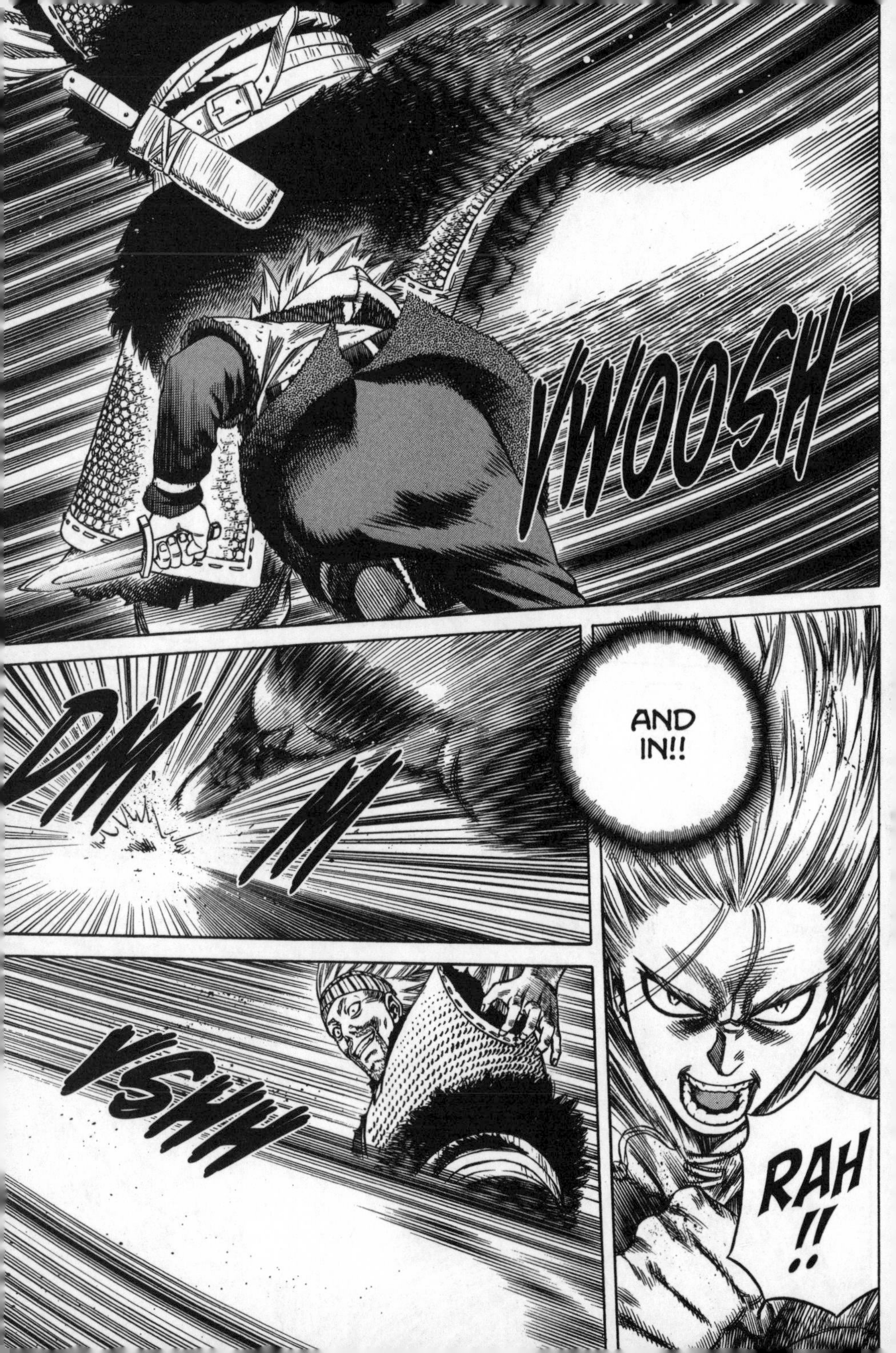
VWOOSH
AND IN!!
RAH!!
DMM
VSHH

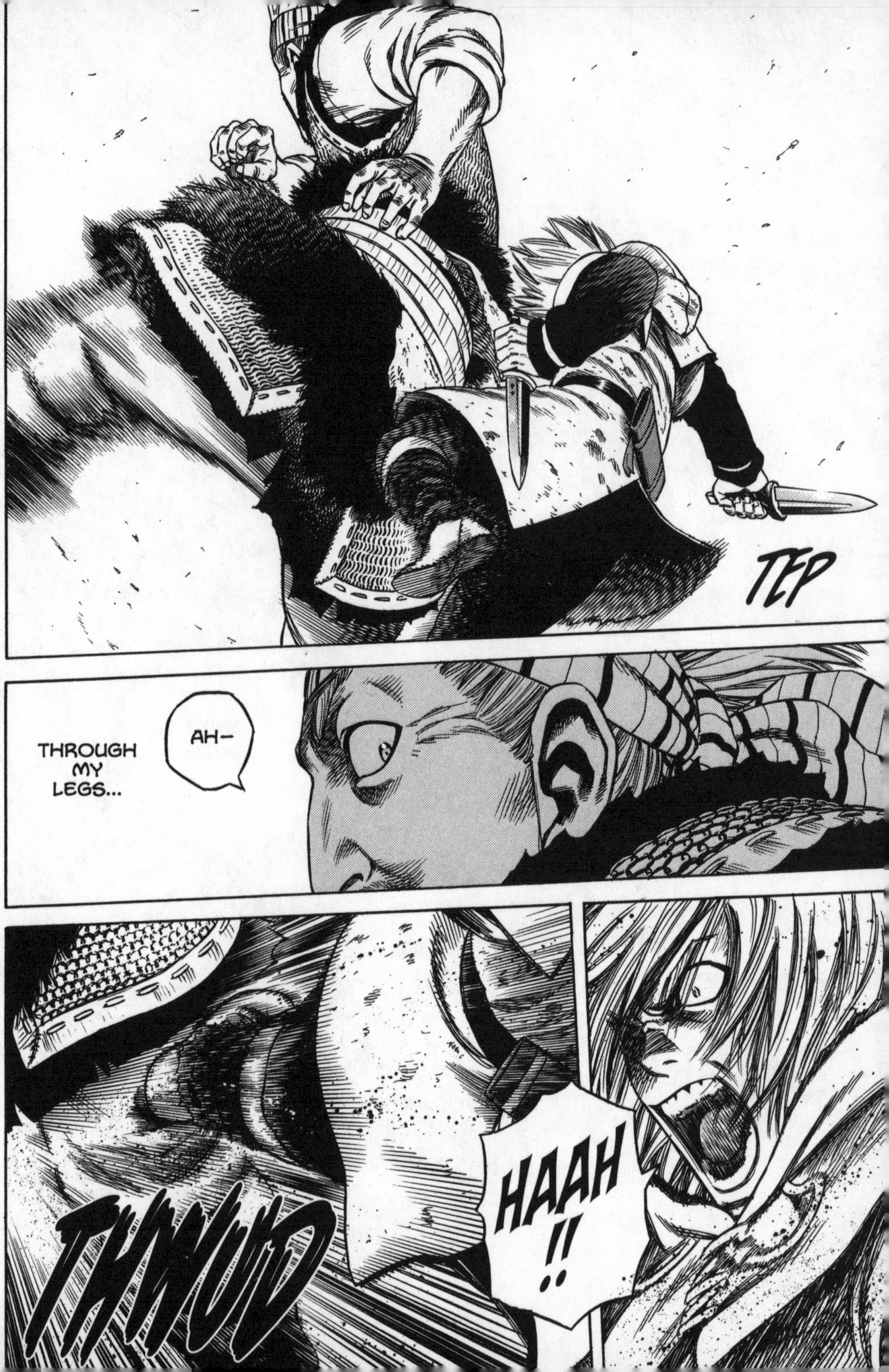
TEP
AH-
THROUGH MY LEGS...
HAAH !!
THWUD

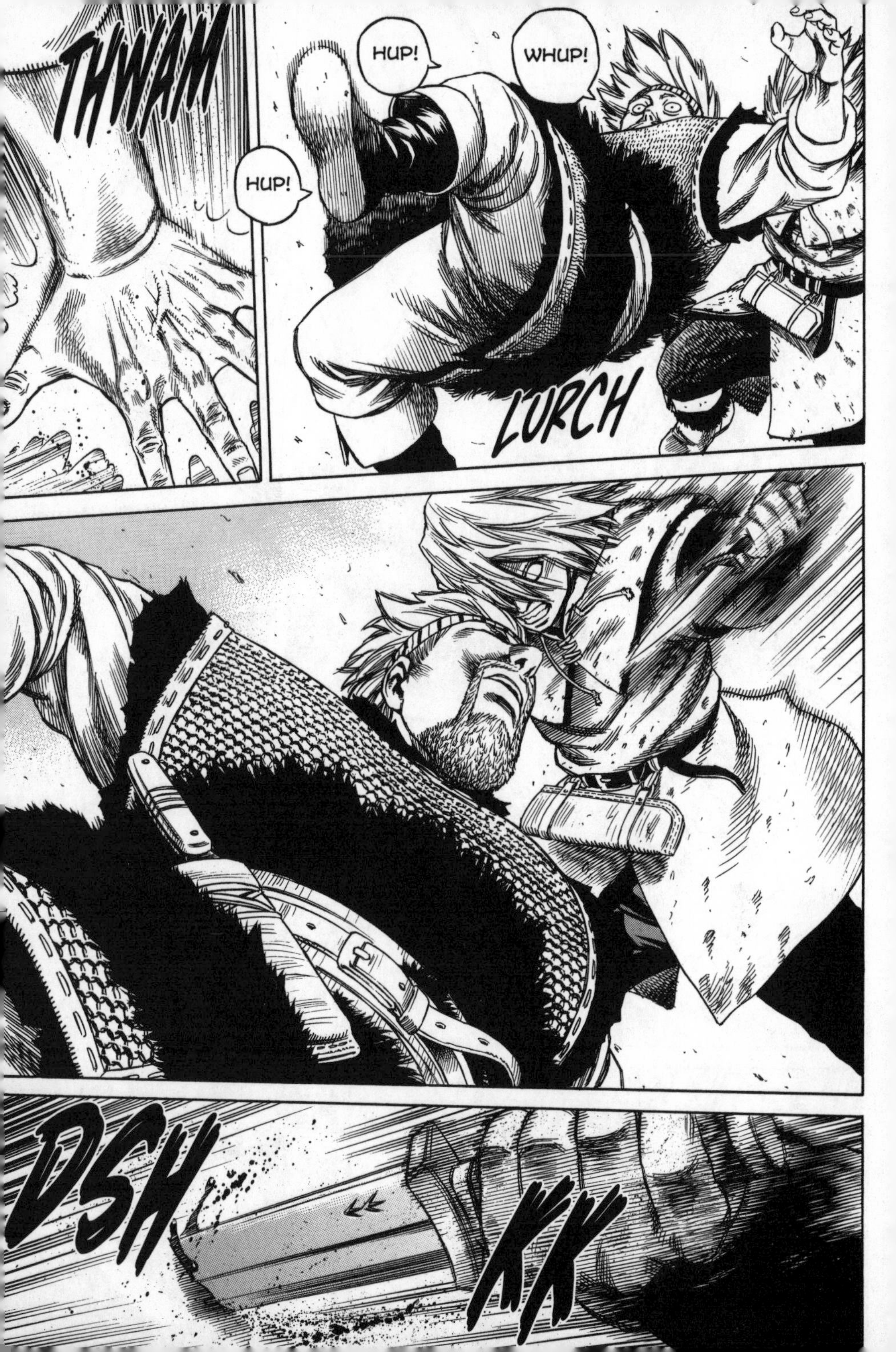
WHUP!
HUP!
HUP!
LURCH
THWAM
DSH
KK

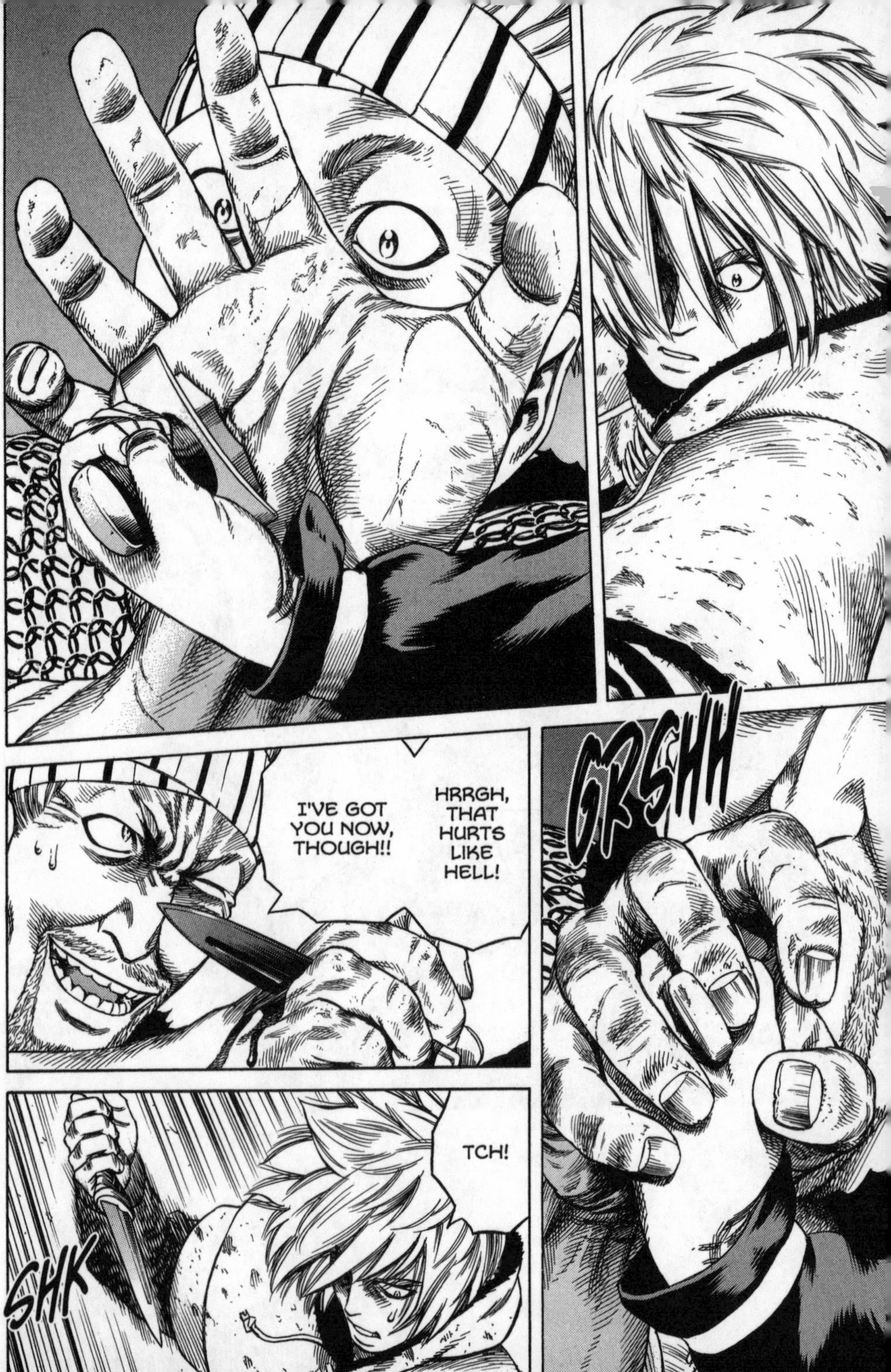
GRSHH
HRRGH, THAT HURTS LIKE HELL!
I'VE GOT YOU NOW, THOUGH!!
TCH!
SHK

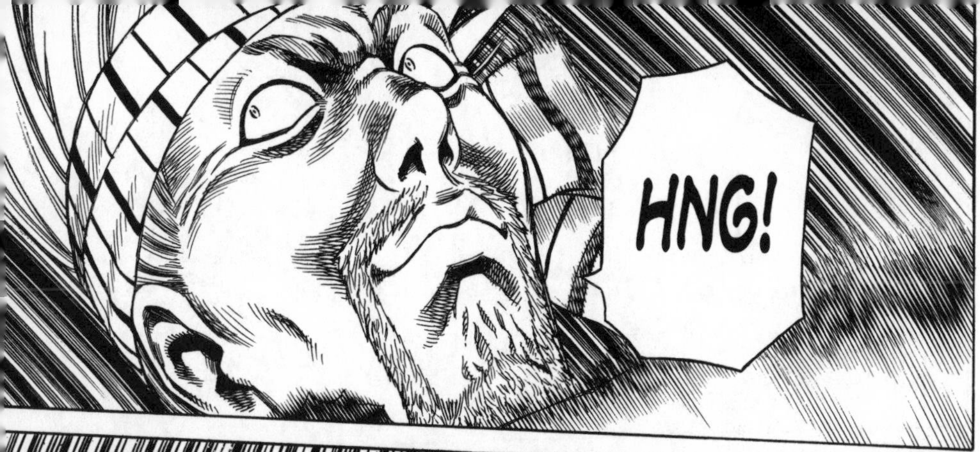
HNG!
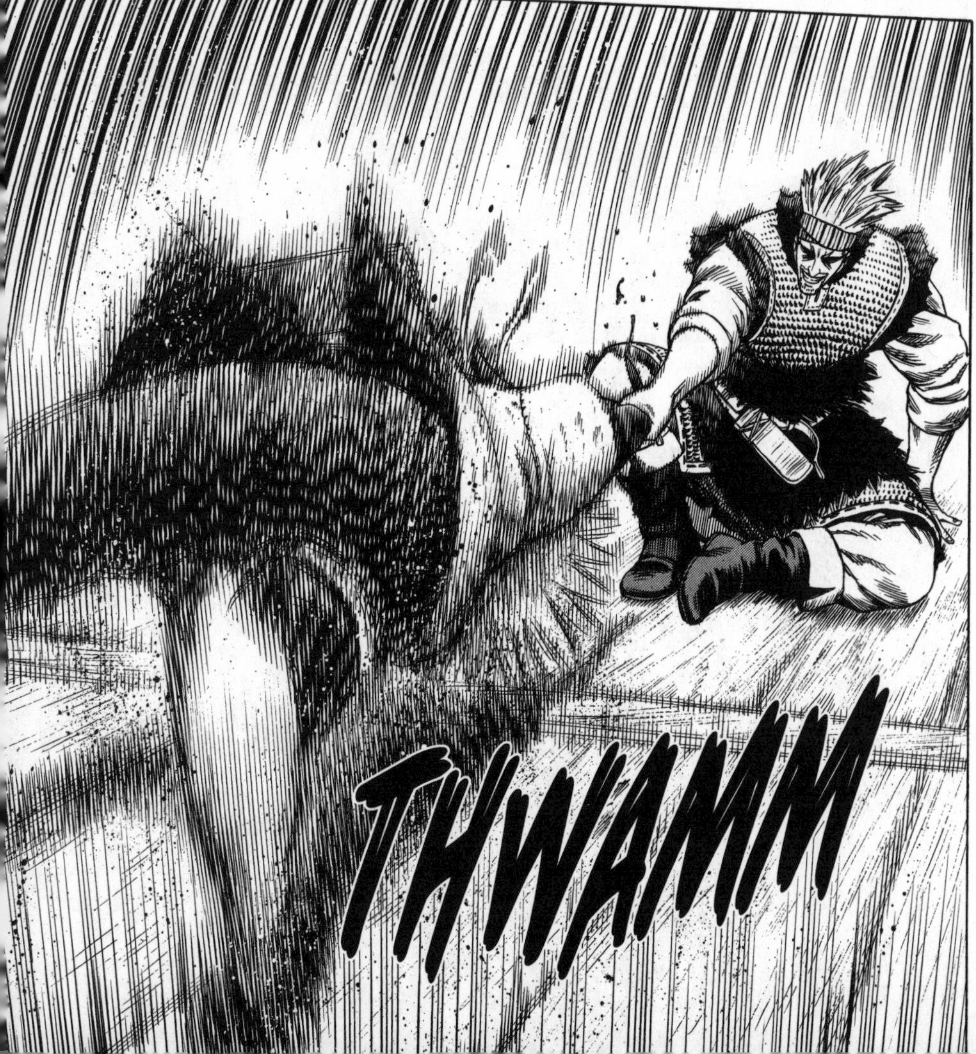
THWAMM

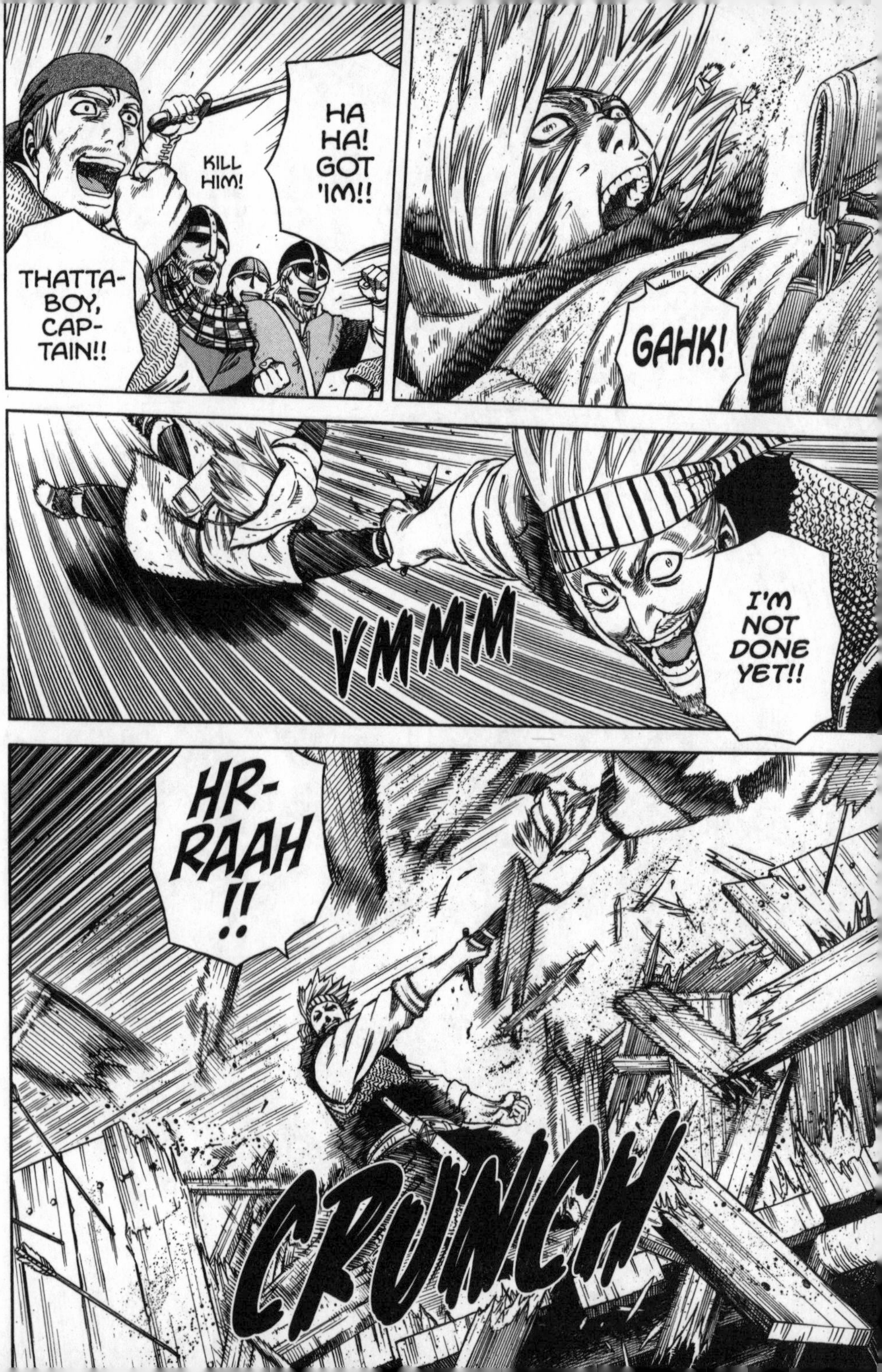
GAHK!
HA HA! GOT 'IM!!
KILL HIM!
THATTA-BOY, CAP-TAIN!!
I'M NOT DONE YET!!
VMMM
HR-RAAH!!
CRUNCH

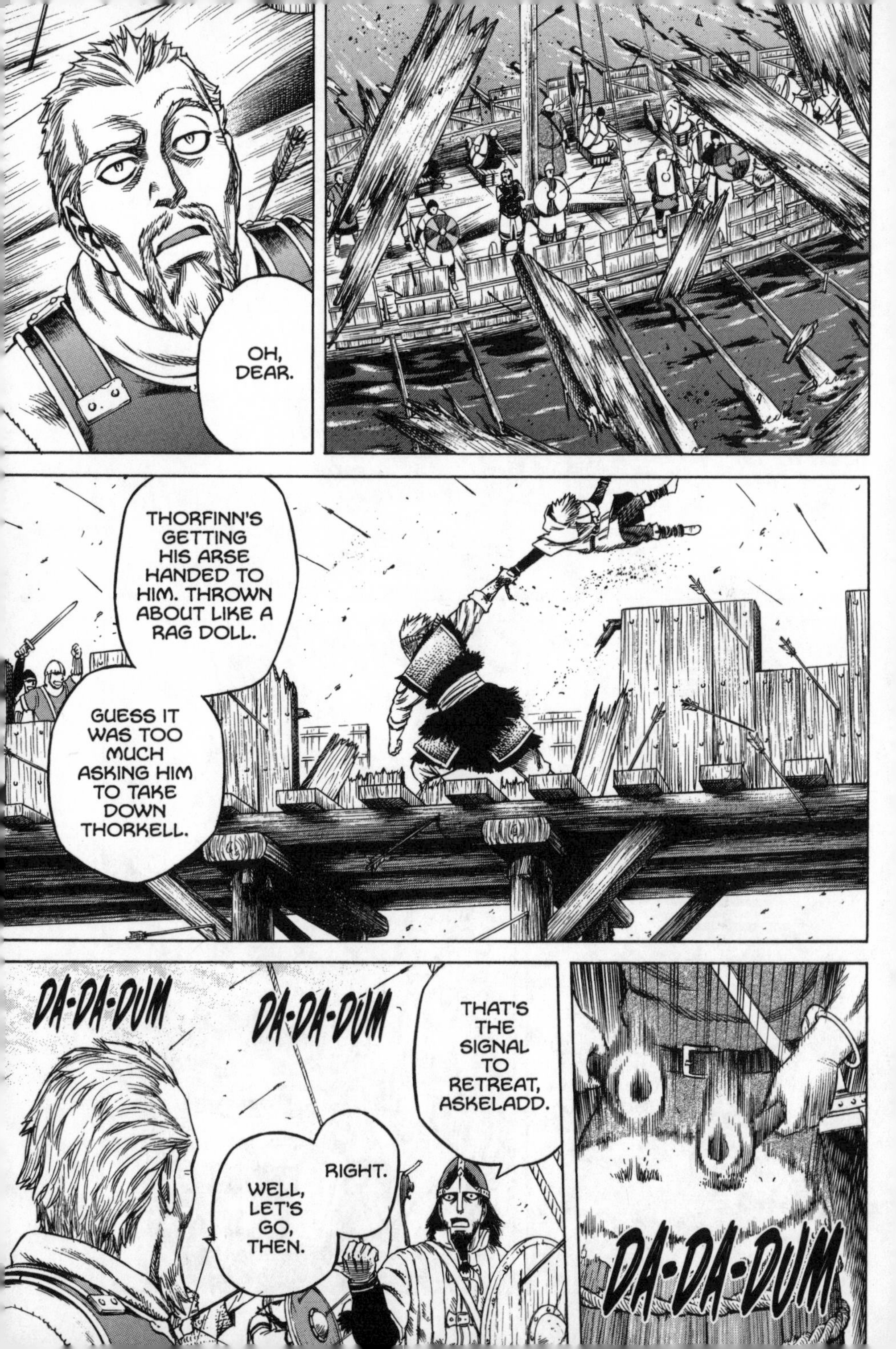
OH, DEAR.
THORFINN'S GETTING HIS ARSE HANDED TO HIM. THROWN ABOUT LIKE A RAG DOLL.
GUESS IT WAS TOO MUCH ASKING HIM TO TAKE DOWN THORKELL.
DA-DA-DUM
DA-DA-DUM
DA-DA-DUM
THAT'S THE SIGNAL TO RETREAT, ASKELADD.
RIGHT.
WELL, LET'S GO, THEN.

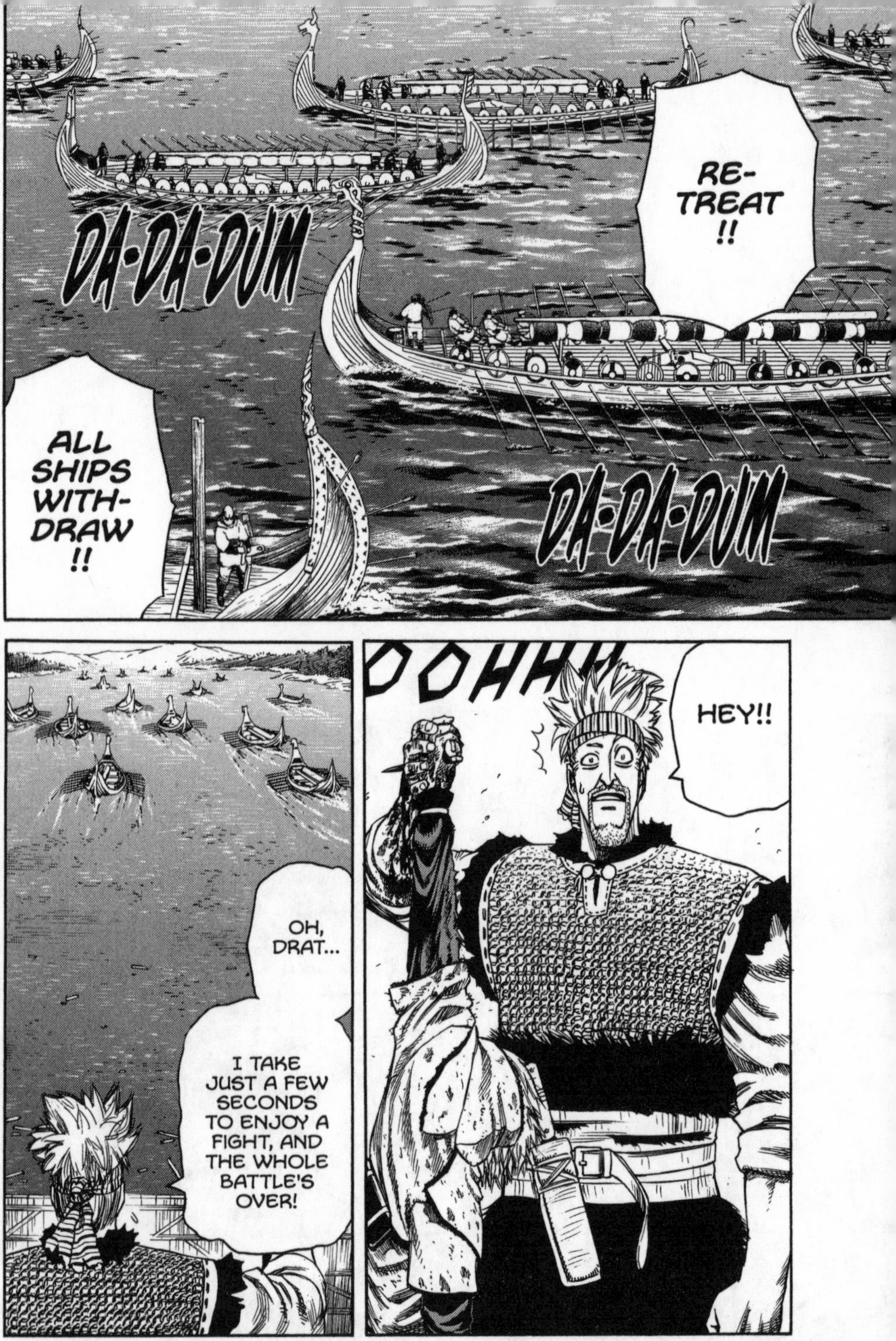
RE-TREAT!!
DA-DA-DUM
ALL SHIPS WITH-DRAW!!
DA-DA-DUM
DOHHH
HEY!!
OH, DRAT...
I TAKE JUST A FEW SECONDS TO ENJOY A FIGHT, AND THE WHOLE BATTLE'S OVER!

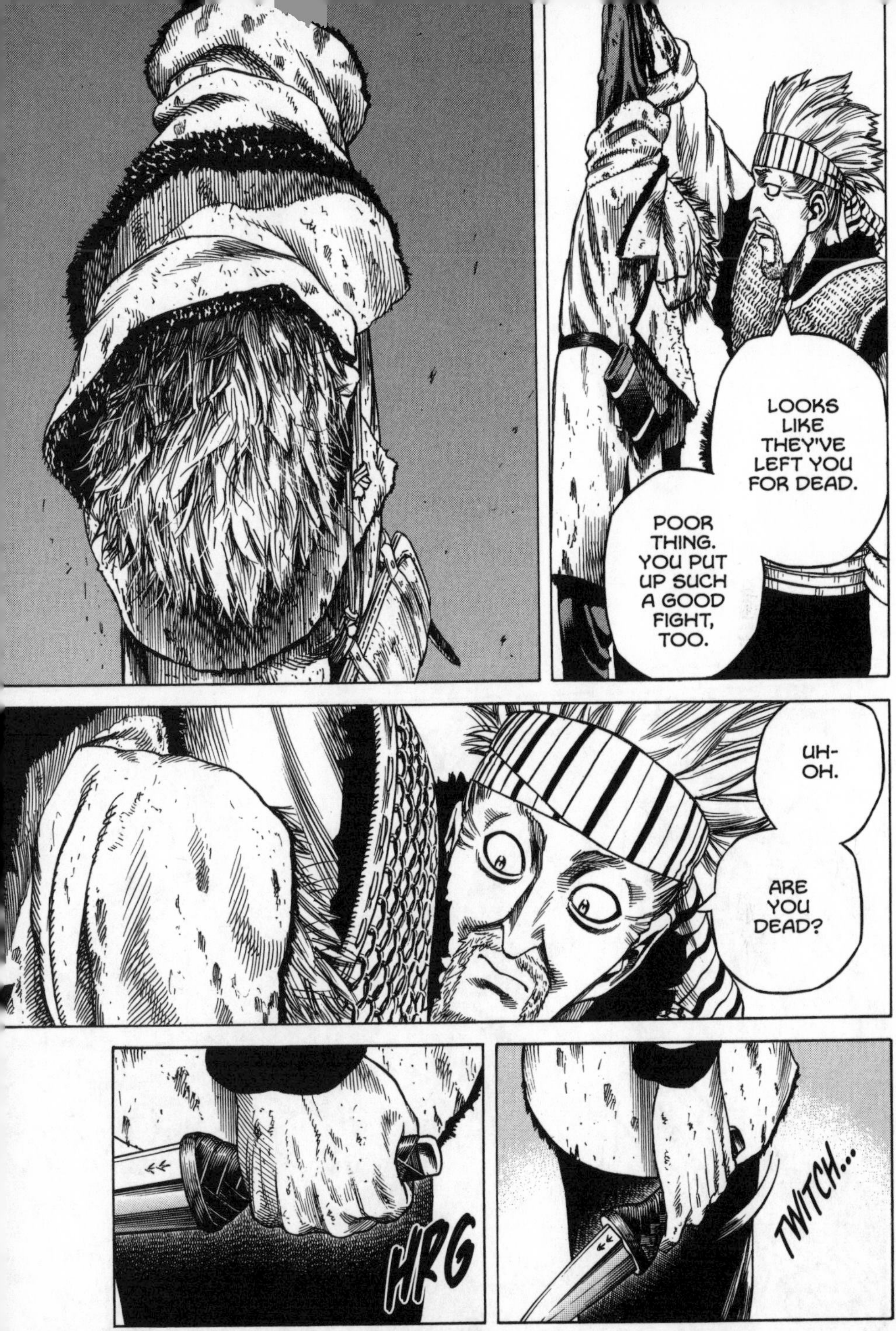
LOOKS LIKE THEY'VE LEFT YOU FOR DEAD.
POOR THING. YOU PUT UP SUCH A GOOD FIGHT, TOO.
UH-OH.
ARE YOU DEAD?
TWITCH...
HRG

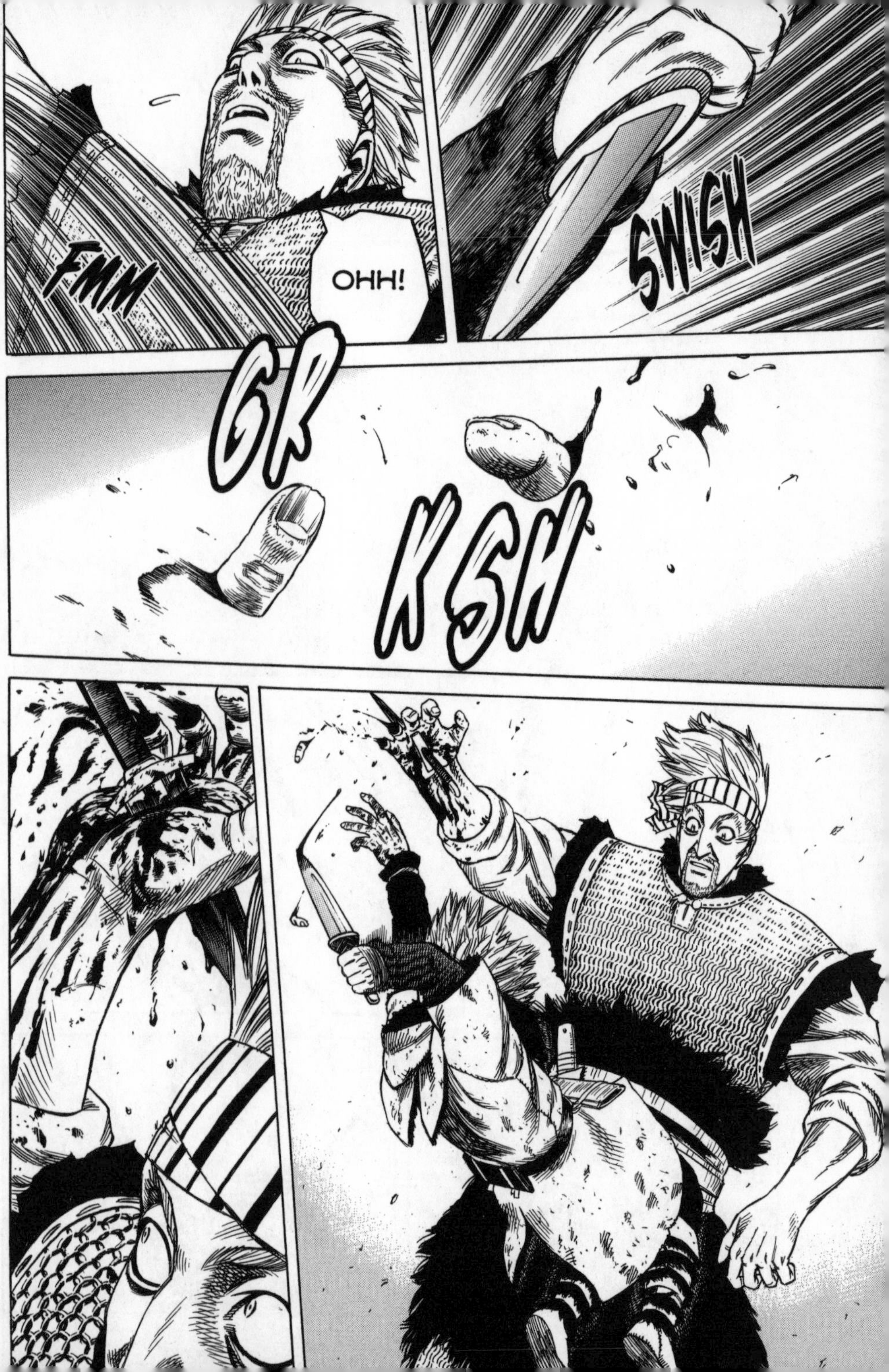
SWISH
OHH!
FMM
GR
KSH

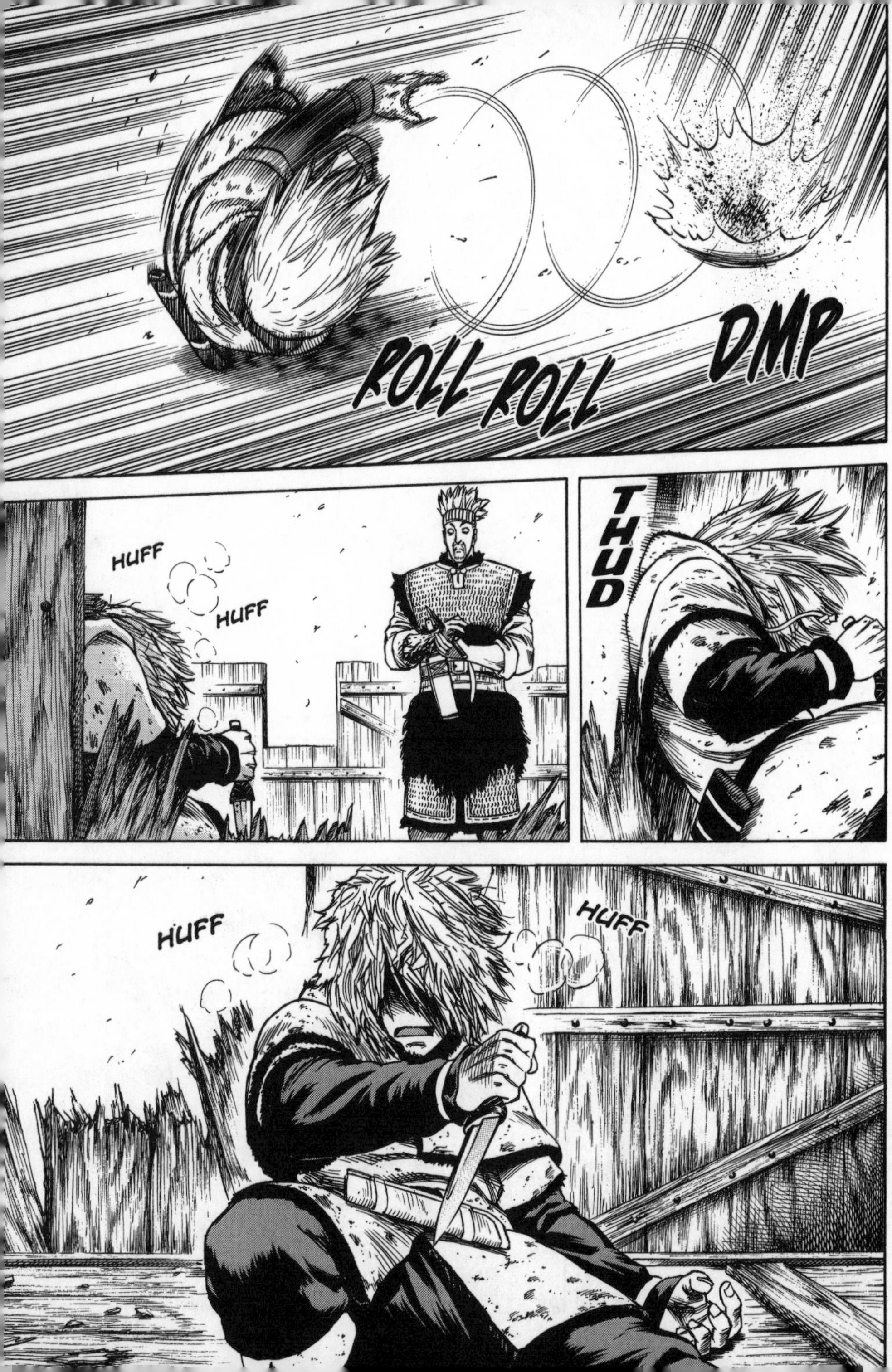
DMP
ROLL ROLL
THUD
HUFF
HUFF
HUFF
HUFF

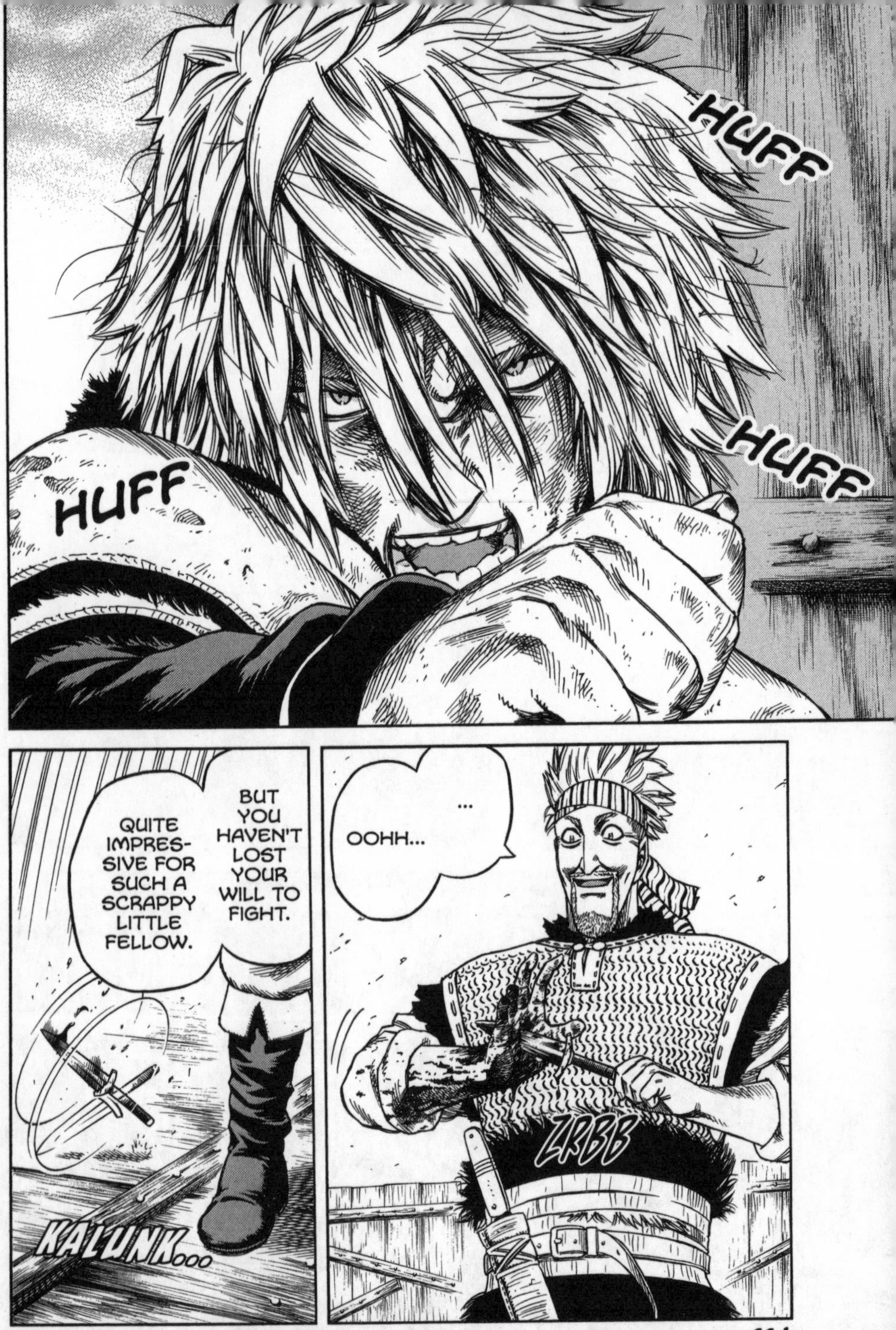

HUFF
HUFF
HUFF
...
OOHH...
ZRBB
QUITE IMPRESSIVE FOR SUCH A SCRAPPY LITTLE FELLOW.
BUT YOU HAVEN'T LOST YOUR WILL TO FIGHT.
KALUNK...

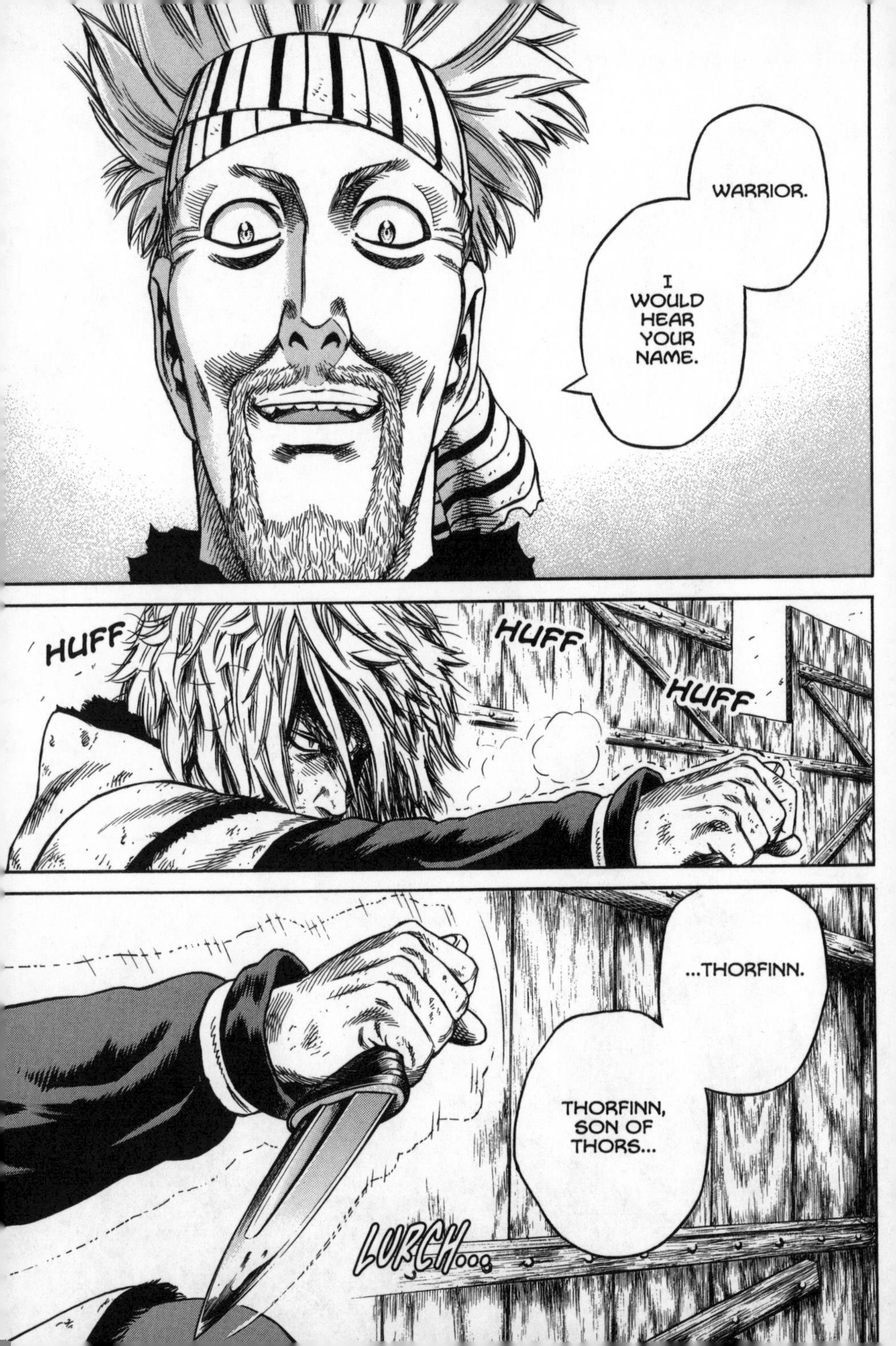
WARRIOR.
I WOULD HEAR YOUR NAME.
HUFF
HUFF
HUFF
...THORFINN.
THORFINN, SON OF THORS...
LURCH

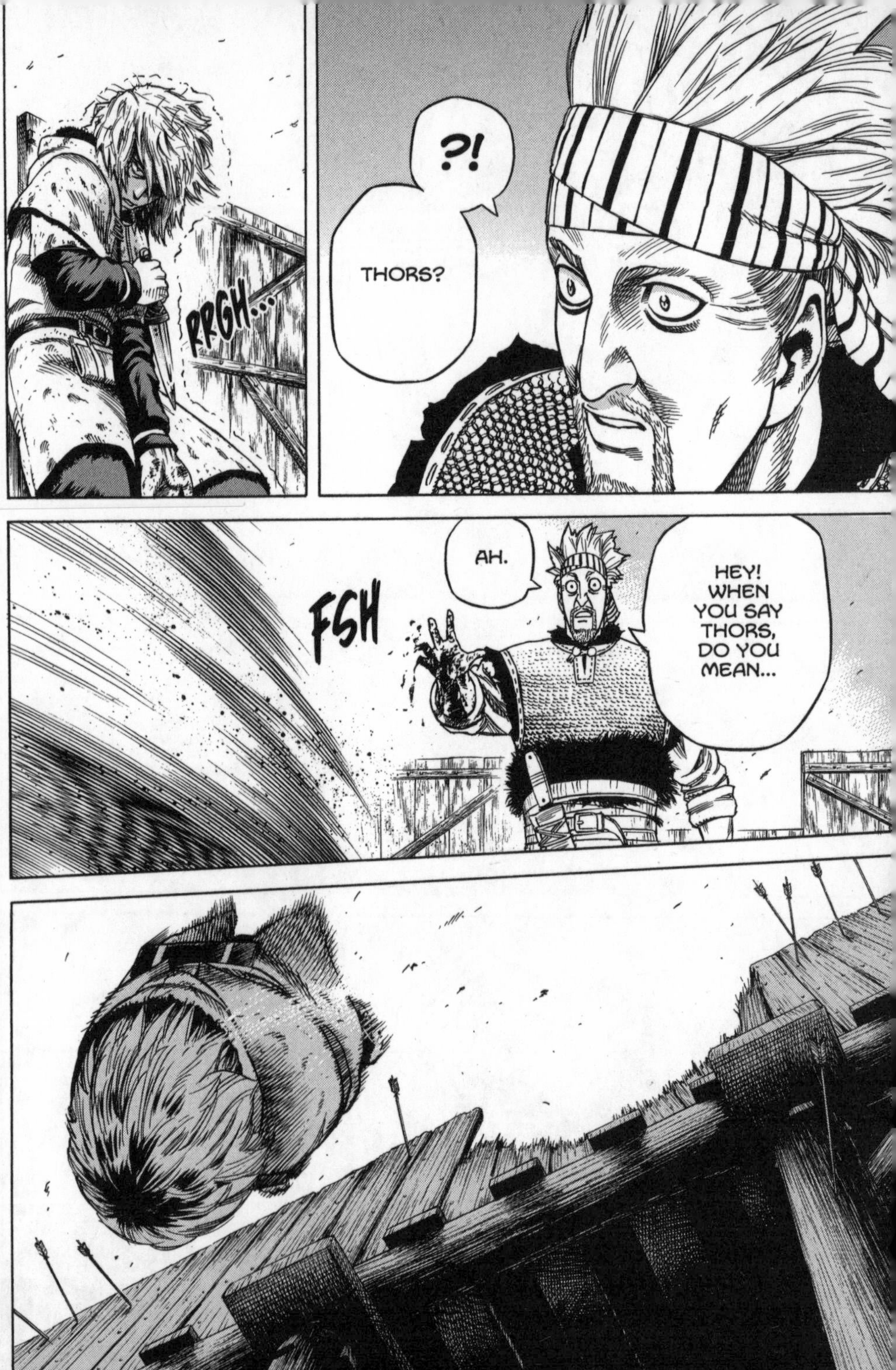
?!
THORS?
RRGH...
HEY! WHEN YOU SAY THORS, DO YOU MEAN...
AH.
FSH

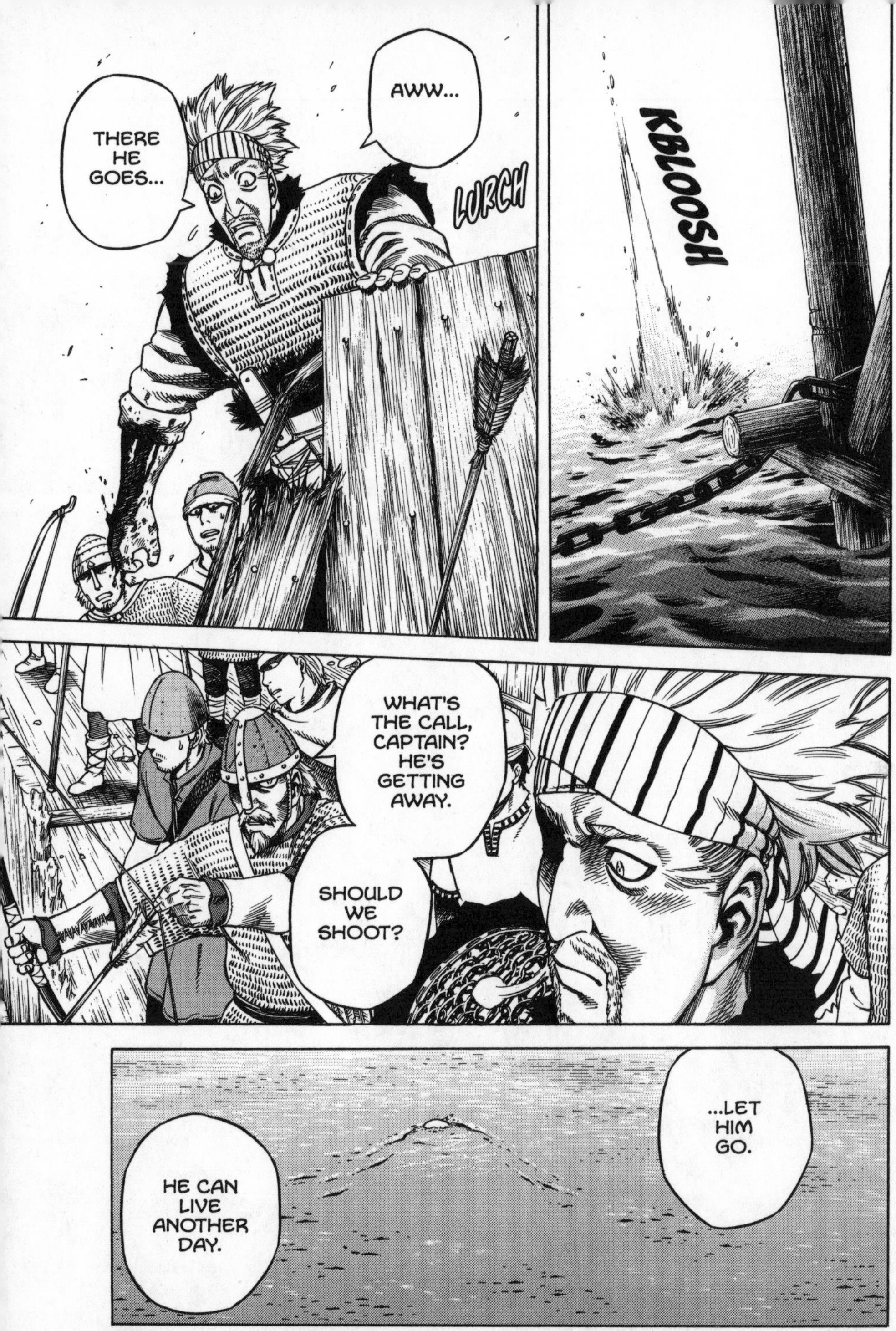
KBLOOSH
AWW...
LURCH
THERE HE GOES...
WHAT'S THE CALL, CAPTAIN? HE'S GETTING AWAY.
SHOULD WE SHOOT?
...LET HIM GO.
HE CAN LIVE ANOTHER DAY.

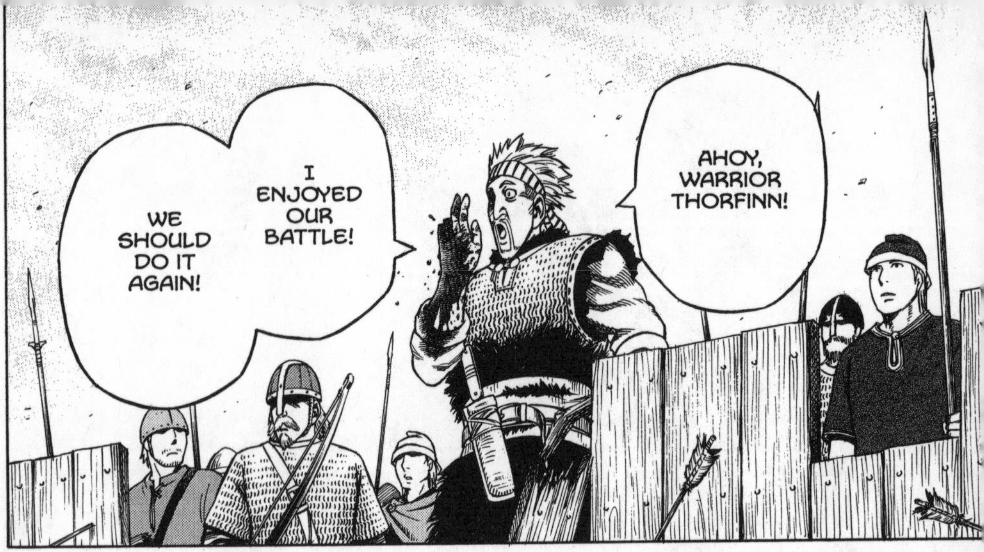
AHOY, WARRIOR THORFINN!
I ENJOYED OUR BATTLE!
WE SHOULD DO IT AGAIN!
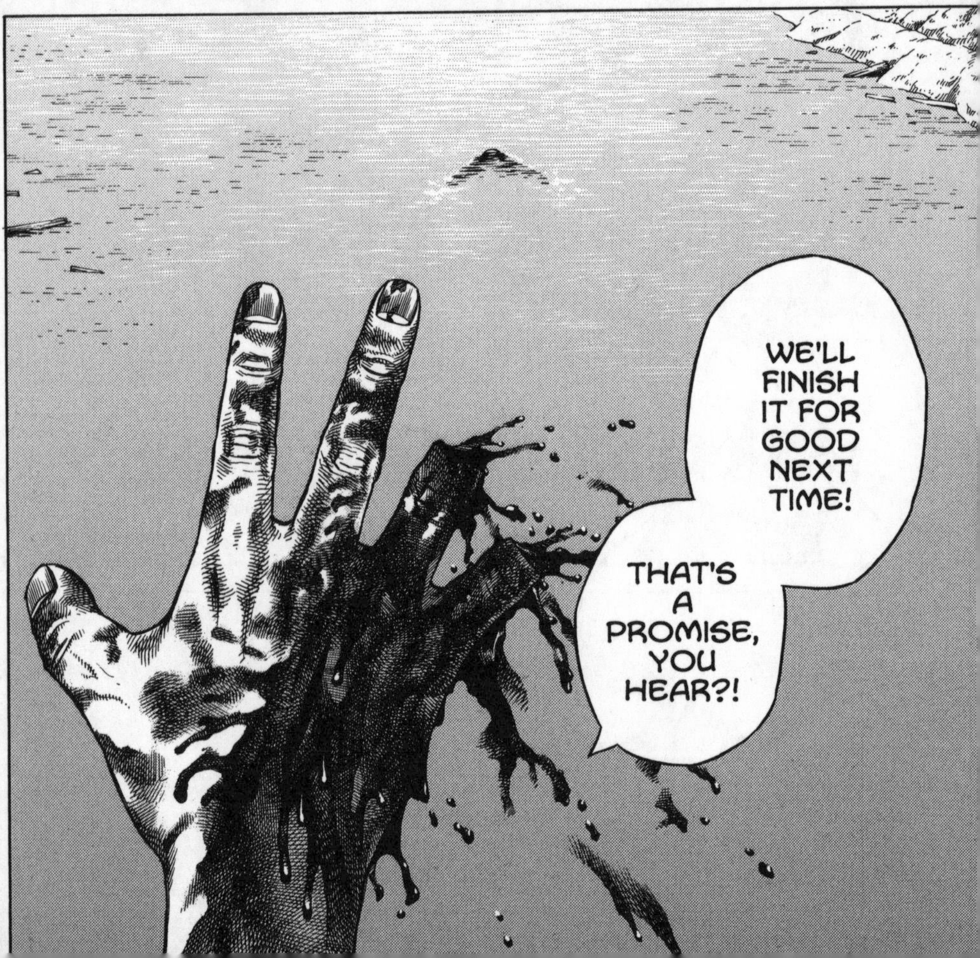
WE'LL FINISH IT FOR GOOD NEXT TIME!
THAT'S A PROMISE, YOU HEAR?!

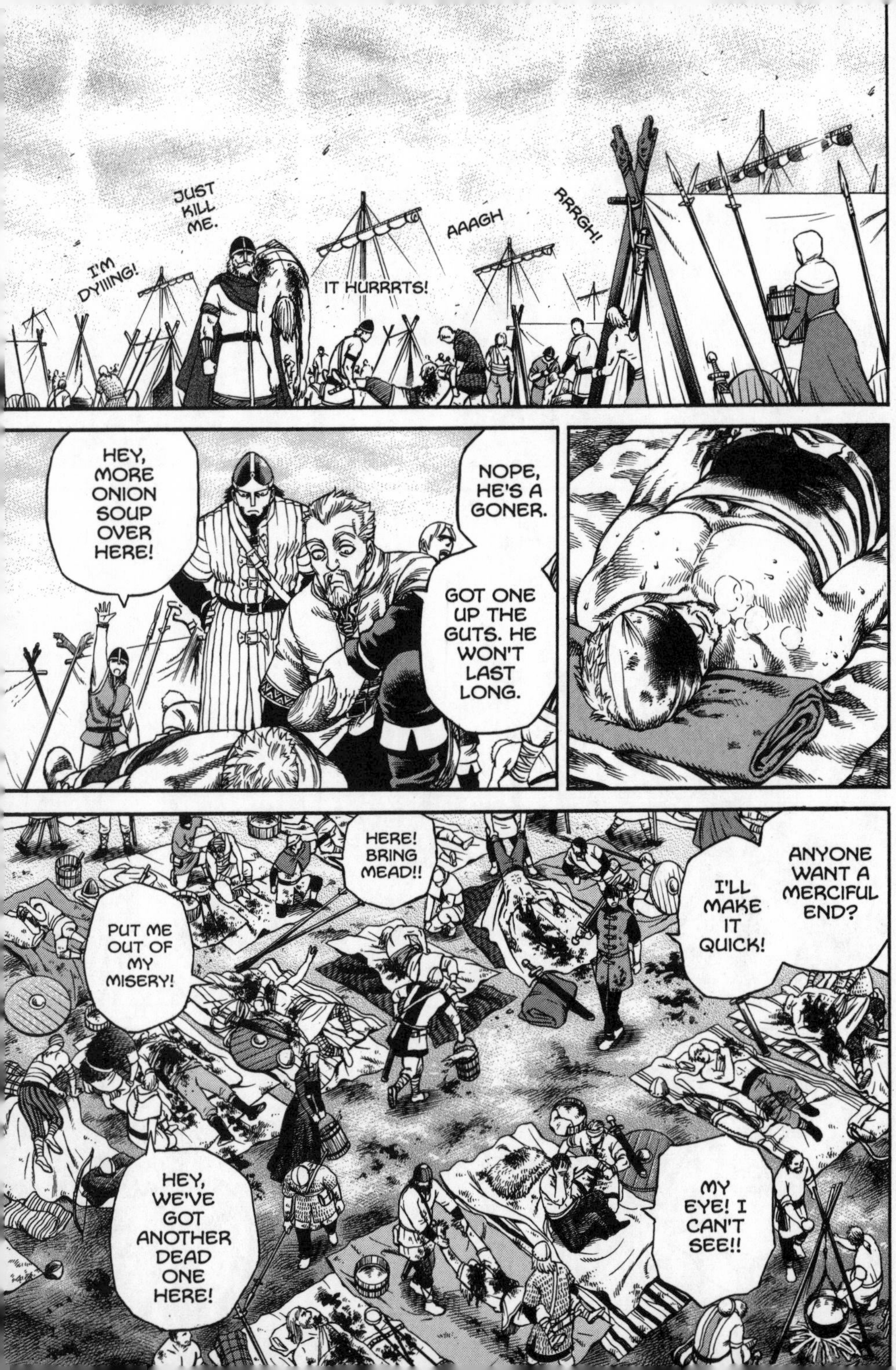
RRRGH!!
AAAGH
IT HURRRTS!
JUST KILL ME.
I'M DYIIING!
NOPE, HE'S A GONER.
GOT ONE UP THE GUTS. HE WON'T LAST LONG.
HEY, MORE ONION SOUP OVER HERE!
ANYONE WANT A MERCIFUL END?
I'LL MAKE IT QUICK!
HERE! BRING MEAD!!
PUT ME OUT OF MY MISERY!
MY EYE! I CAN'T SEE!!
HEY, WE'VE GOT ANOTHER DEAD ONE HERE!

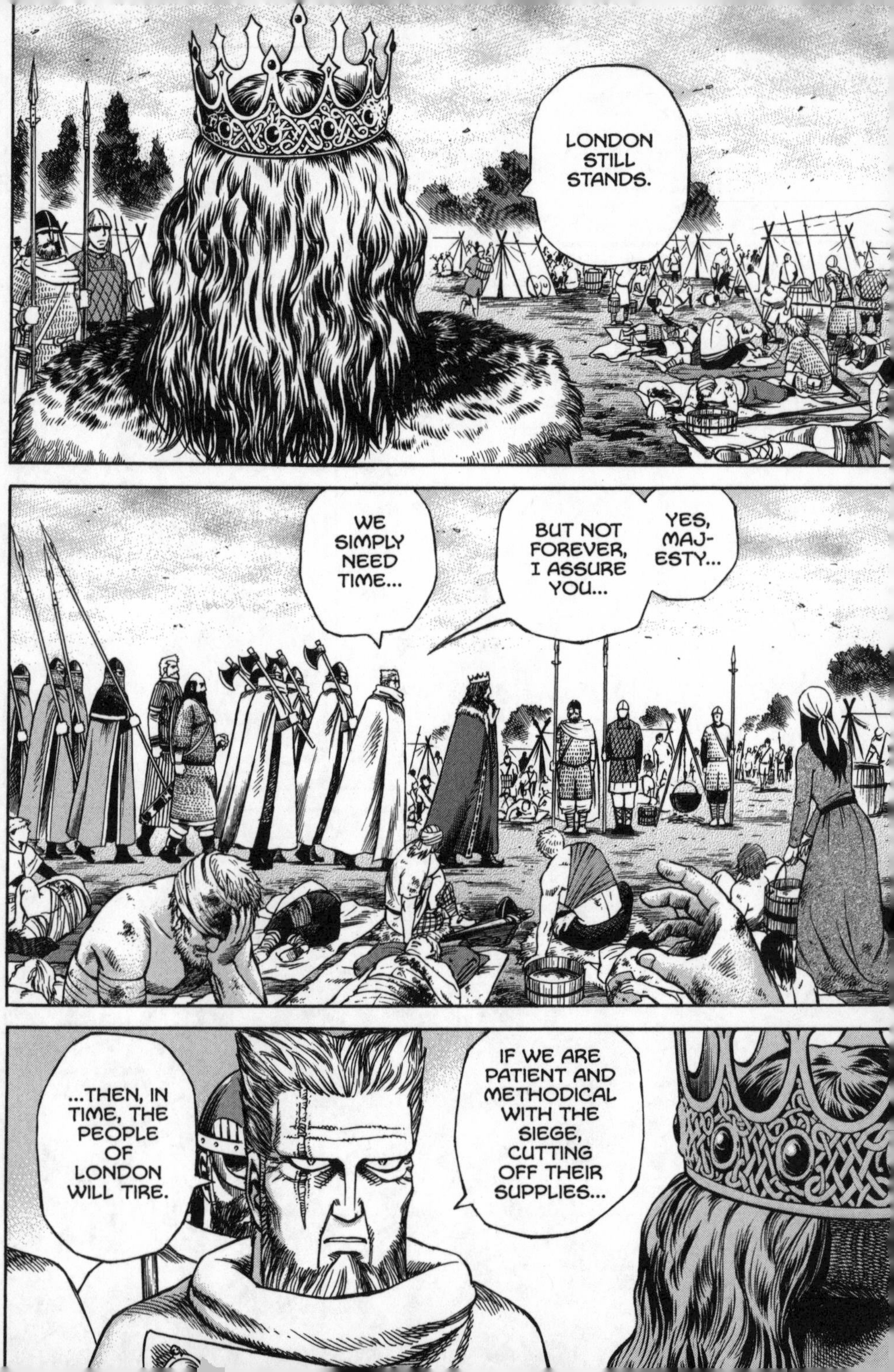
LONDON STILL STANDS.
YES, MAJ-ESTY...
BUT NOT FOREVER, I ASSURE YOU...
WE SIMPLY NEED TIME...
IF WE ARE PATIENT AND METHODICAL WITH THE SIEGE, CUTTING OFF THEIR SUPPLIES...
...THEN, IN TIME, THE PEOPLE OF LONDON WILL TIRE.

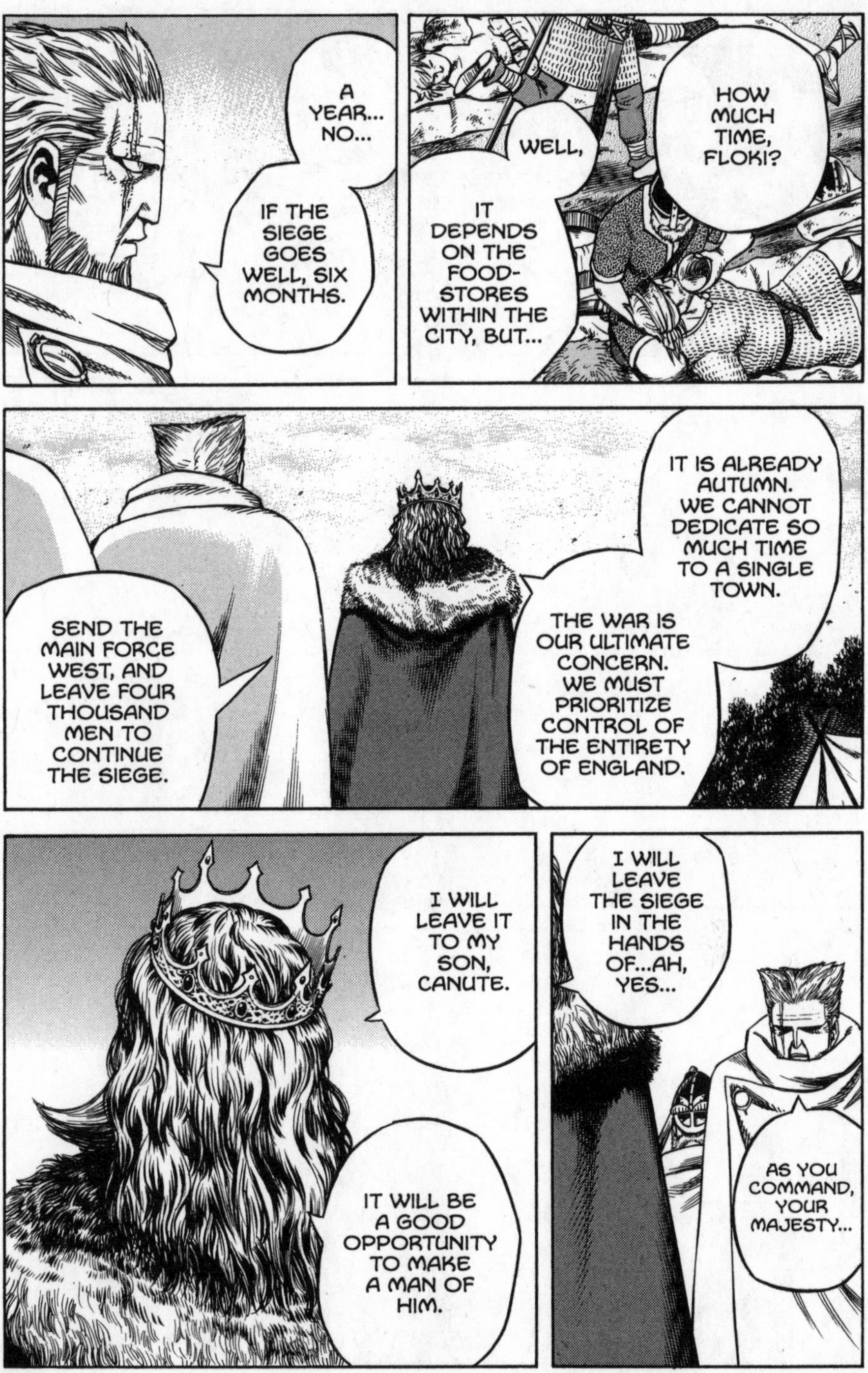
HOW MUCH TIME, FLOKI?
WELL,
IT DEPENDS ON THE FOOD-STORES WITHIN THE CITY, BUT...
A YEAR... NO...
IF THE SIEGE GOES WELL, SIX MONTHS.
IT IS ALREADY AUTUMN. WE CANNOT DEDICATE SO MUCH TIME TO A SINGLE TOWN.
THE WAR IS OUR ULTIMATE CONCERN. WE MUST PRIORITIZE CONTROL OF THE ENTIRETY OF ENGLAND.
SEND THE MAIN FORCE WEST, AND LEAVE FOUR THOUSAND MEN TO CONTINUE THE SIEGE.
I WILL LEAVE THE SIEGE IN THE HANDS OF...AH, YES...
AS YOU COMMAND, YOUR MAJESTY...
I WILL LEAVE IT TO MY SON, CANUTE.
IT WILL BE A GOOD OPPORTUNITY TO MAKE A MAN OF HIM.

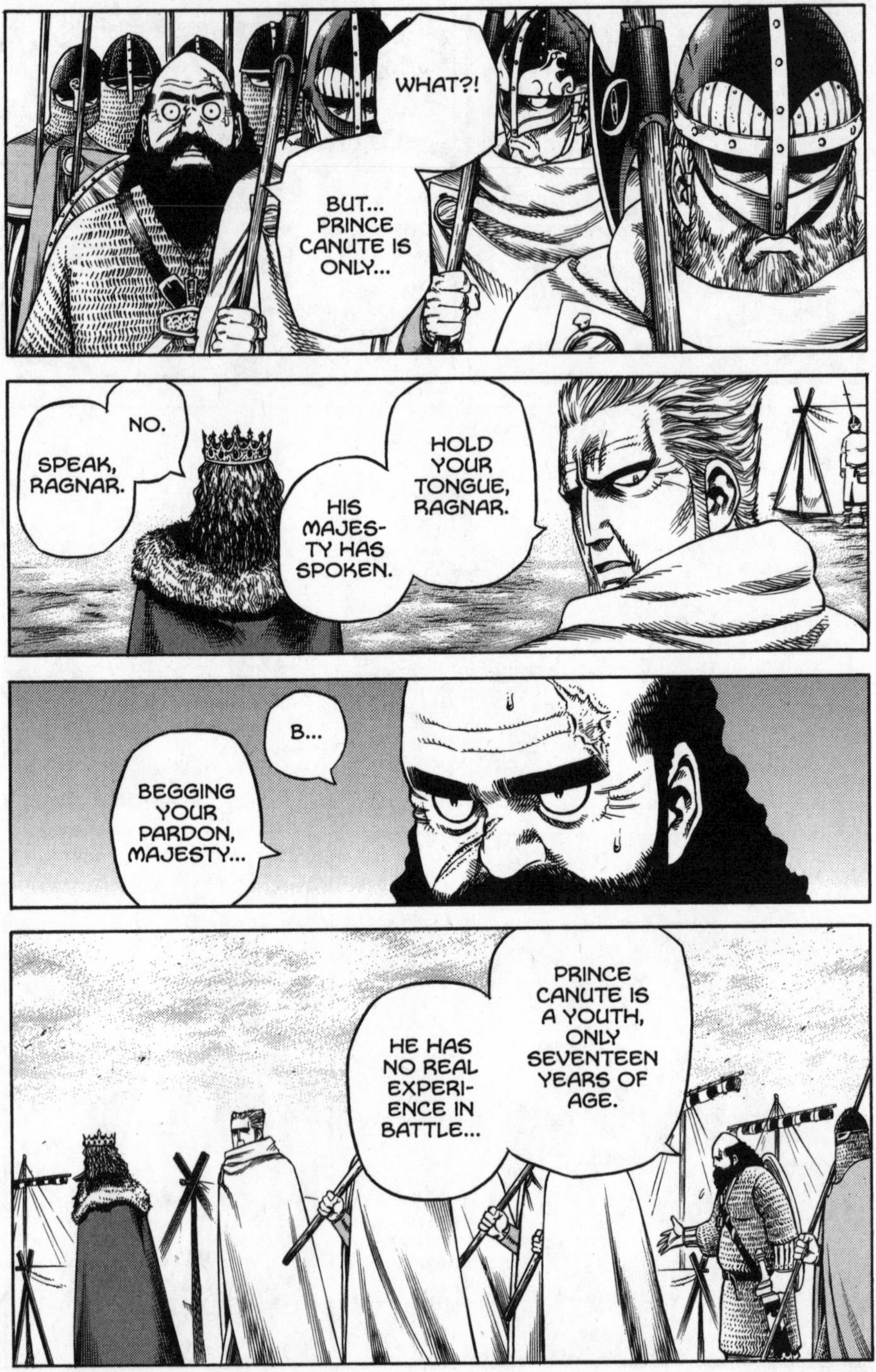
WHAT?!
BUT... PRINCE CANUTE IS ONLY...
HOLD YOUR TONGUE, RAGNAR.
HIS MAJES-TY HAS SPOKEN.
NO.
SPEAK, RAGNAR.
B...
BEGGING YOUR PARDON, MAJESTY...
PRINCE CANUTE IS A YOUTH, ONLY SEVENTEEN YEARS OF AGE.
HE HAS NO REAL EXPERI-ENCE IN BATTLE...

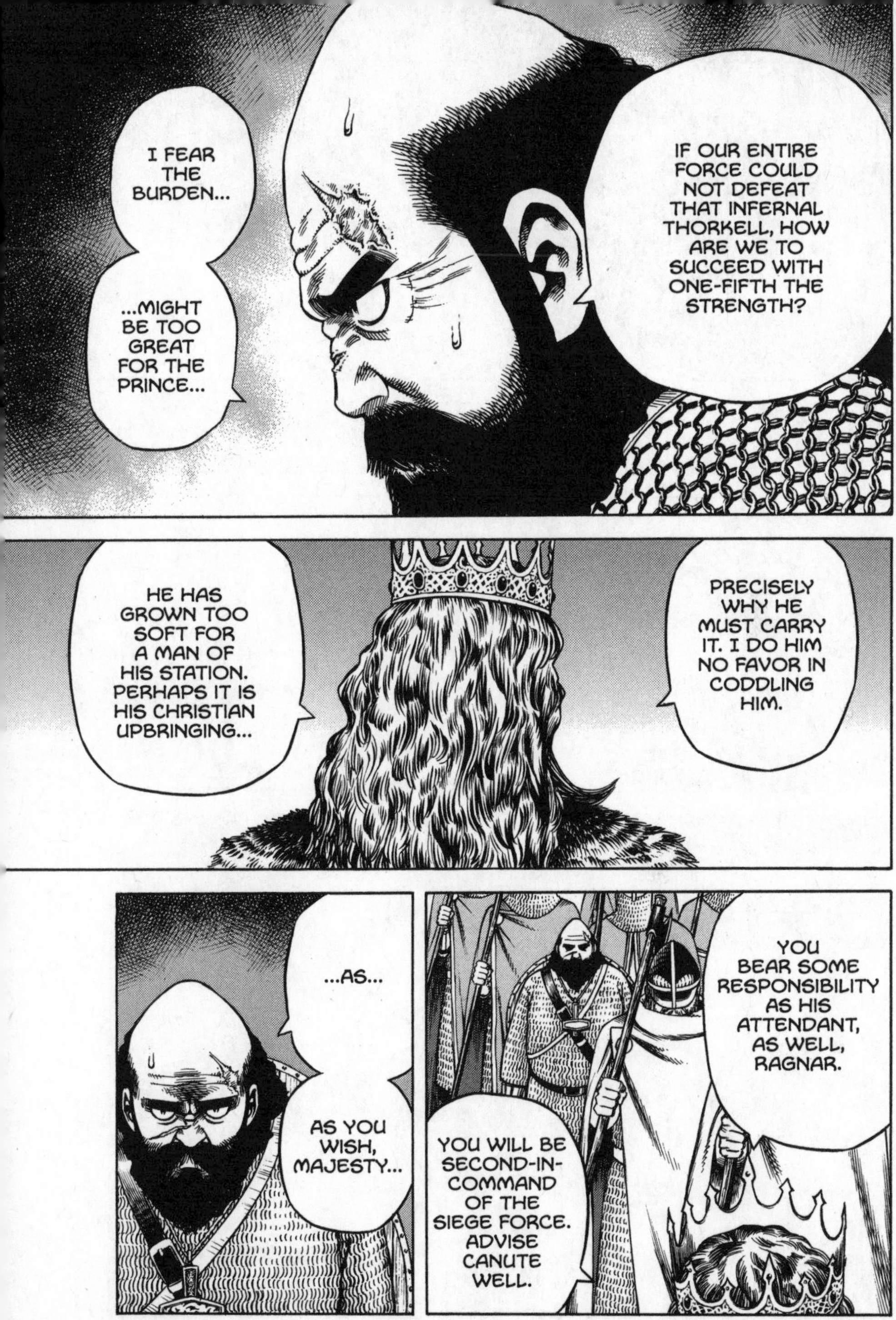
IF OUR ENTIRE FORCE COULD NOT DEFEAT THAT INFERNAL THORKELL, HOW ARE WE TO SUCCEED WITH ONE-FIFTH THE STRENGTH?
I FEAR THE BURDEN...
...MIGHT BE TOO GREAT FOR THE PRINCE...
PRECISELY WHY HE MUST CARRY IT. I DO HIM NO FAVOR IN CODDLING HIM.
HE HAS GROWN TOO SOFT FOR A MAN OF HIS STATION. PERHAPS IT IS HIS CHRISTIAN UPBRINGING...
YOU BEAR SOME RESPONSIBILITY AS HIS ATTENDANT, AS WELL, RAGNAR.
YOU WILL BE SECOND-IN-COMMAND OF THE SIEGE FORCE. ADVISE CANUTE WELL.
...AS...
AS YOU WISH, MAJESTY...

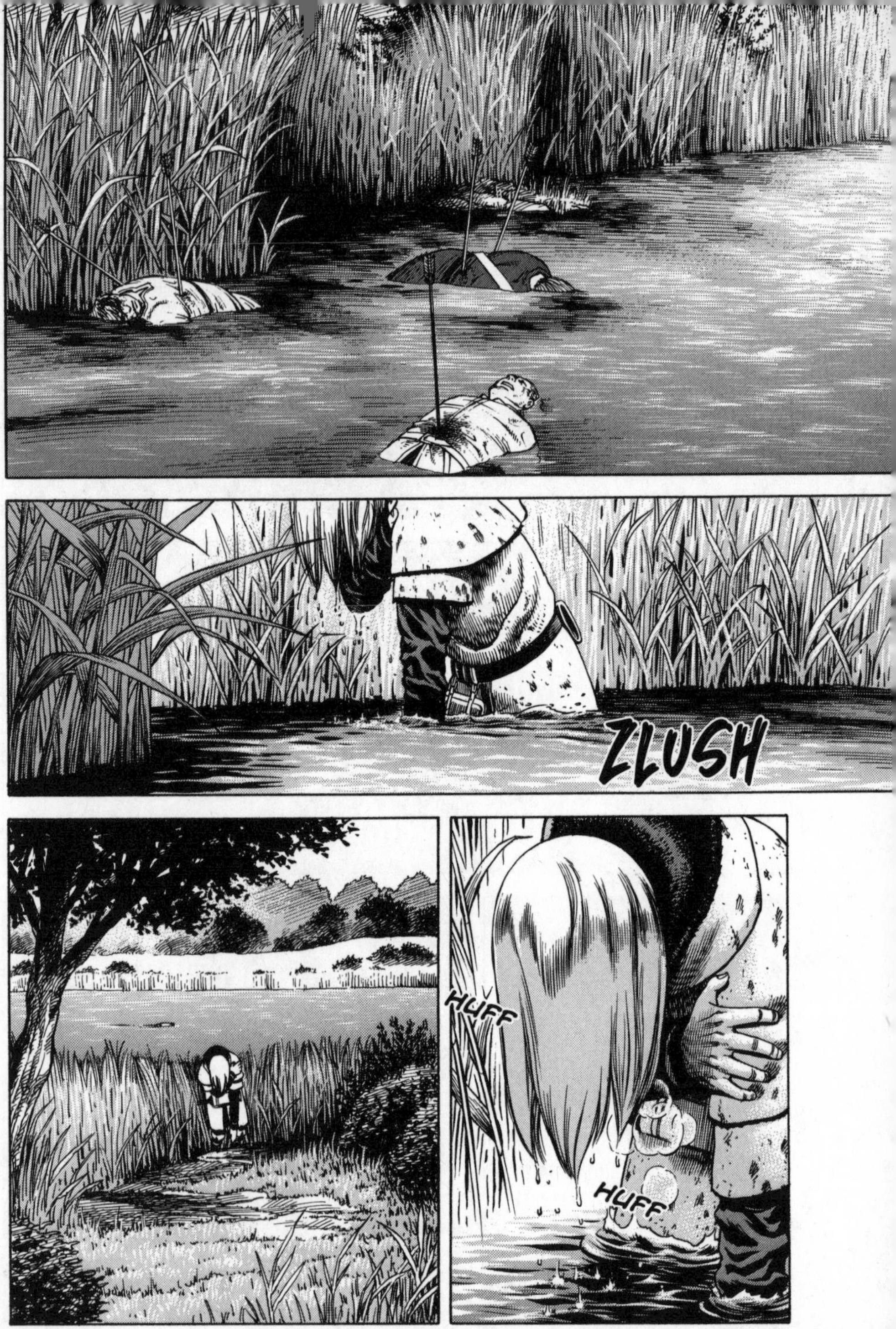
ZLUSH
HUFF
HUFF

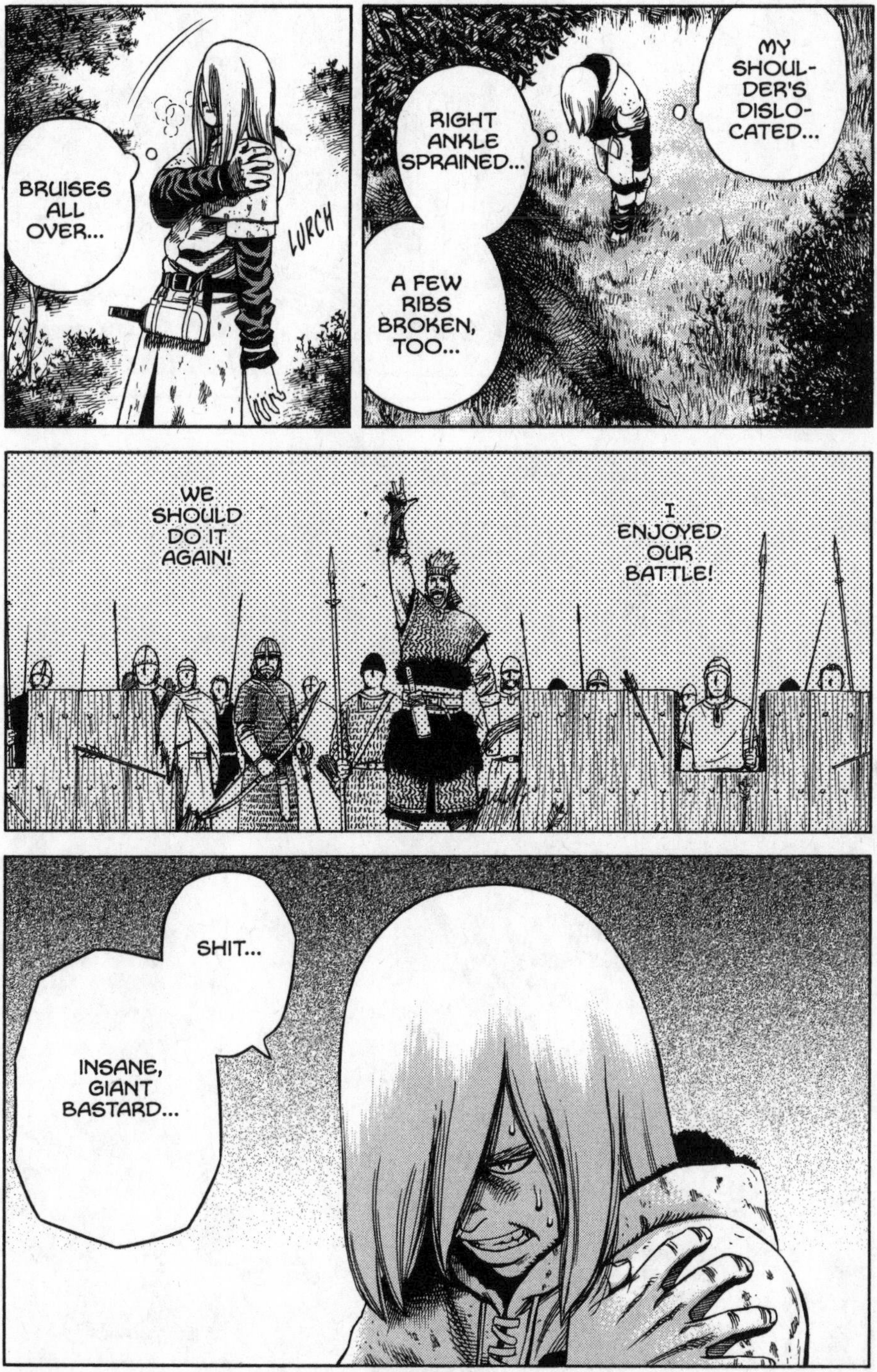
MY SHOULDER'S DISLOCATED...
RIGHT ANKLE SPRAINED...
A FEW RIBS BROKEN, TOO...
LURCH
BRUISES ALL OVER...
I ENJOYED OUR BATTLE!
WE SHOULD DO IT AGAIN!
SHIT...
INSANE, GIANT BASTARD...

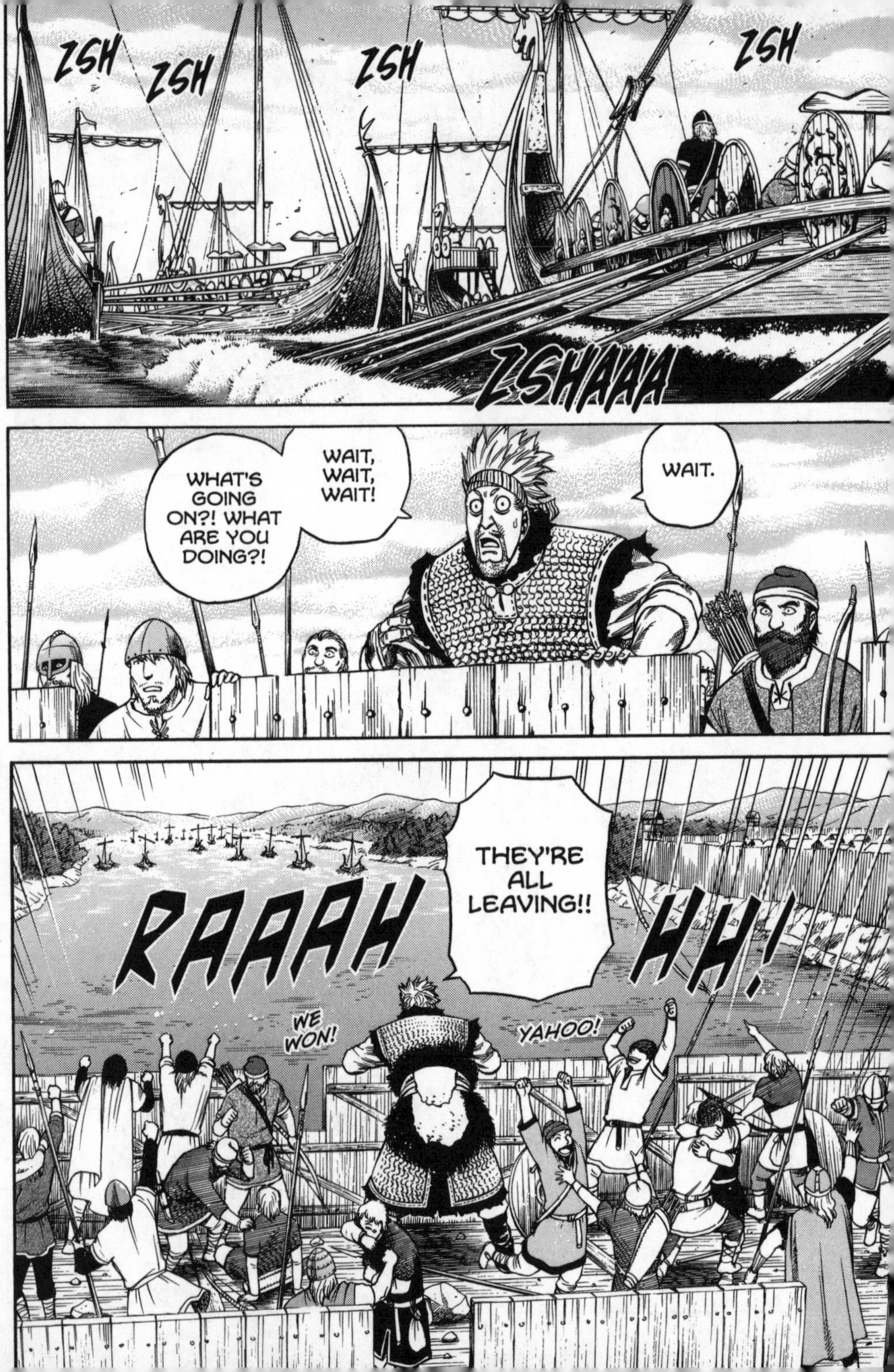
ZSH
ZSH
ZSH
ZSH
ZSHAAA
WAIT.
WAIT, WAIT, WAIT!
WHAT'S GOING ON?! WHAT ARE YOU DOING?!
THEY'RE ALL LEAVING!!
RAAAH HH!
YAHOO!
WE WON!

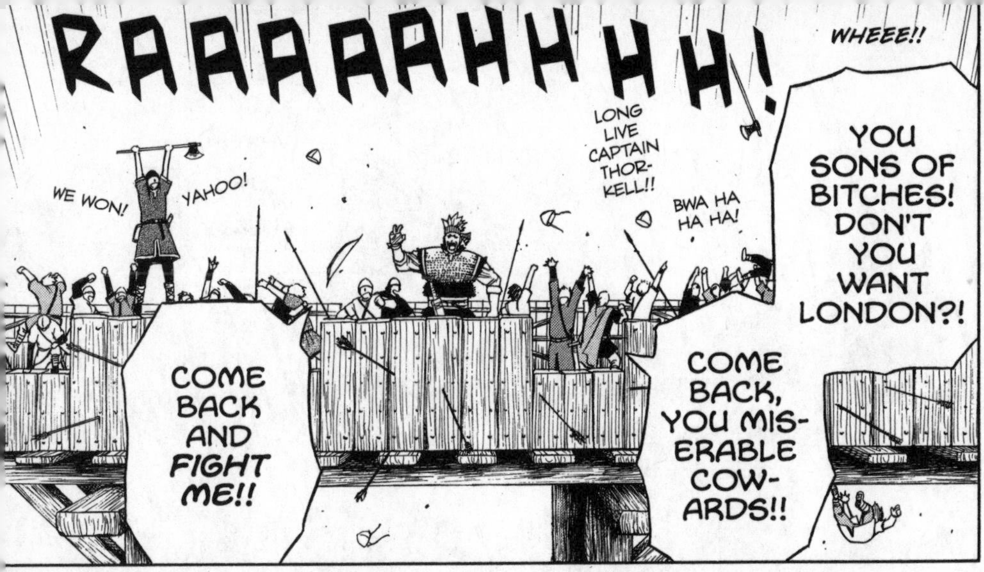
WHEEE!!
YOU SONS OF BITCHES! DON'T YOU WANT LONDON?!
RAAAAAHHHH!
LONG LIVE CAPTAIN THORKELL!!
BWA HA HA HA!
YAHOO!
WE WON!
COME BACK, YOU MISERABLE COWARDS!!
COME BACK AND FIGHT ME!!

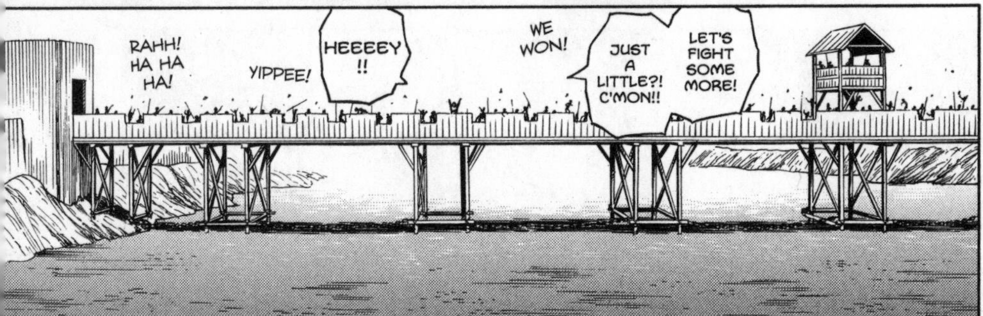
LET'S FIGHT SOME MORE!
JUST A LITTLE?! C'MON!!
WE WON!
HEEEEY!!
YIPPEE!
RAHH! HA HA HA!

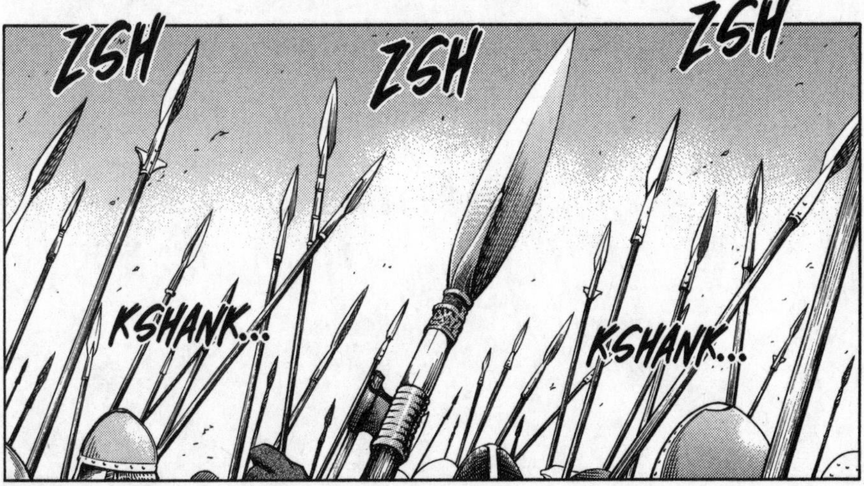
ZSH
ZSH
ZSH
KSHANK...
KSHANK...

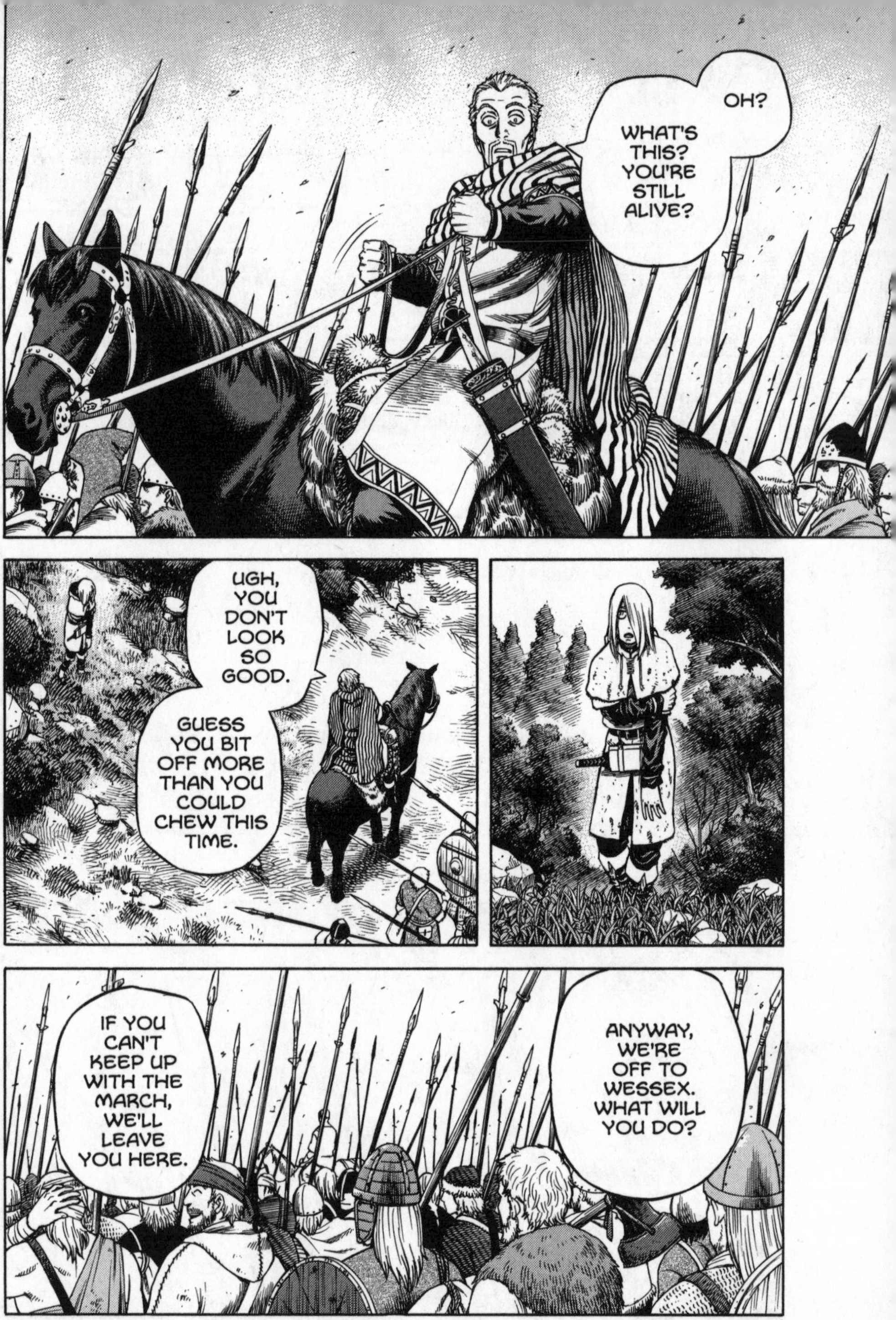
OH?
WHAT'S THIS? YOU'RE STILL ALIVE?
UGH, YOU DON'T LOOK SO GOOD.
GUESS YOU BIT OFF MORE THAN YOU COULD CHEW THIS TIME.
ANYWAY, WE'RE OFF TO WESSEX. WHAT WILL YOU DO?
IF YOU CAN'T KEEP UP WITH THE MARCH, WE'LL LEAVE YOU HERE.

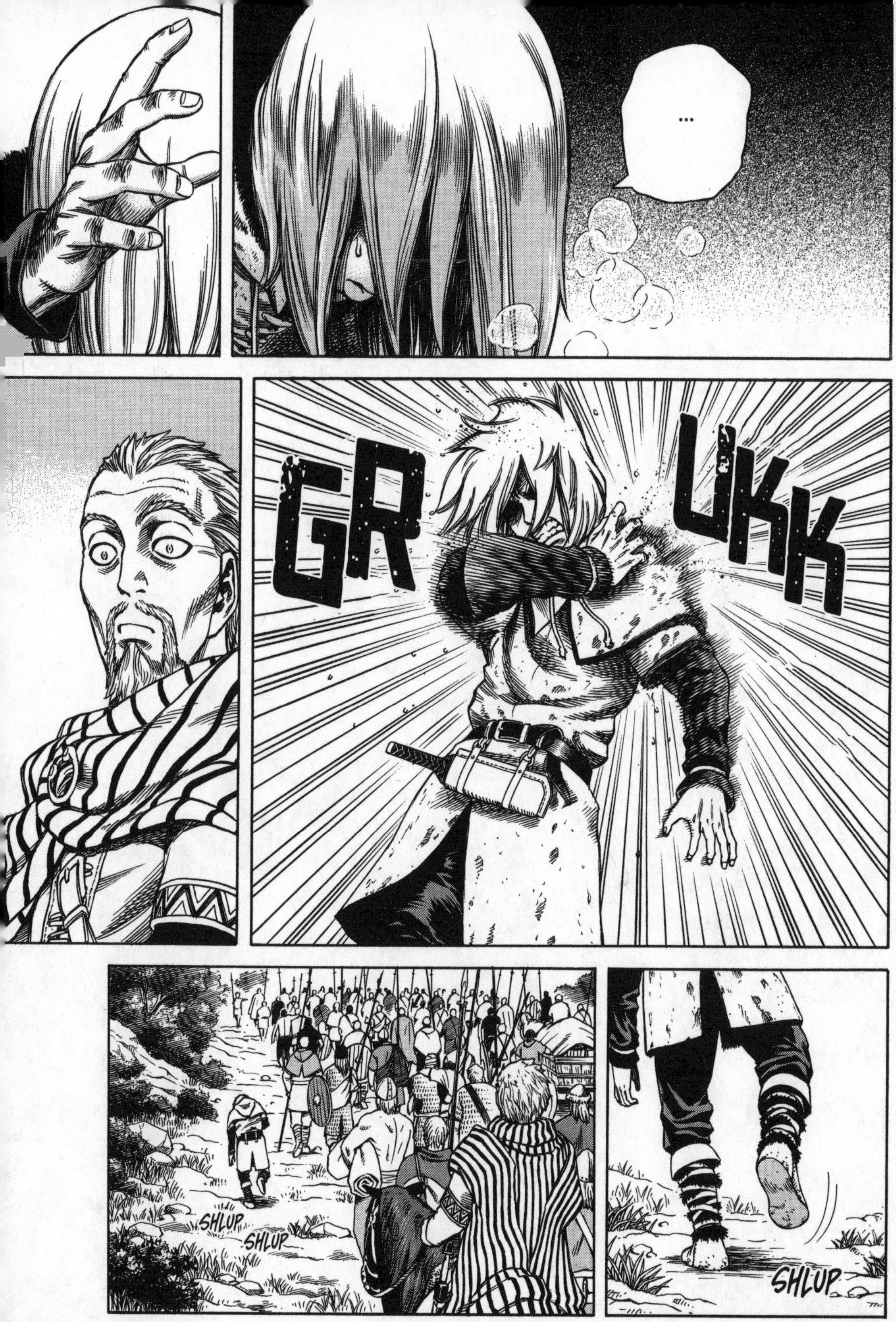
...
GRUKK
SHLUP
SHLUP
SHLUP

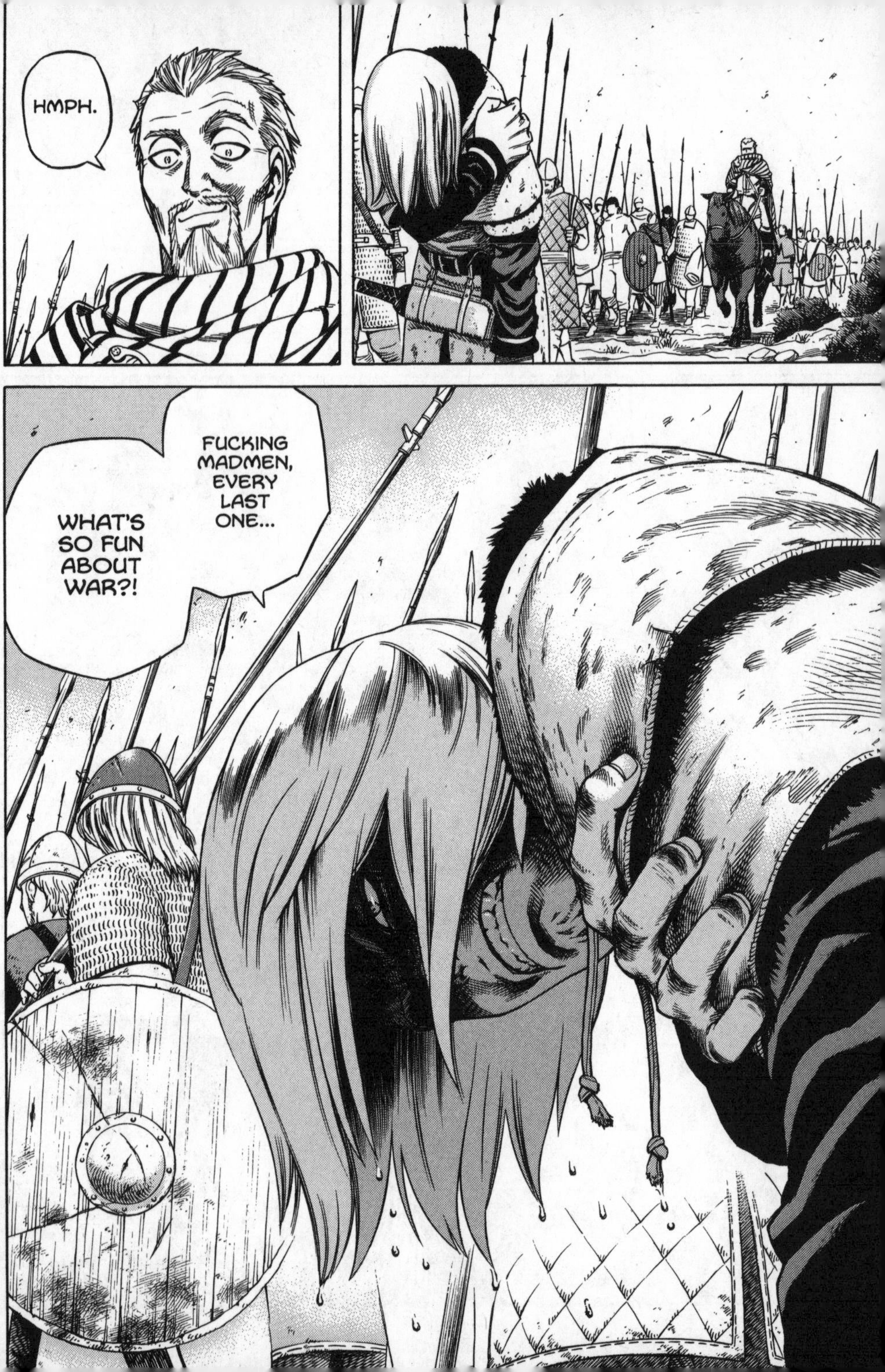
HMPH.
FUCKING MADMEN, EVERY LAST ONE...
WHAT'S SO FUN ABOUT WAR?!

CHAPTER 19 - END

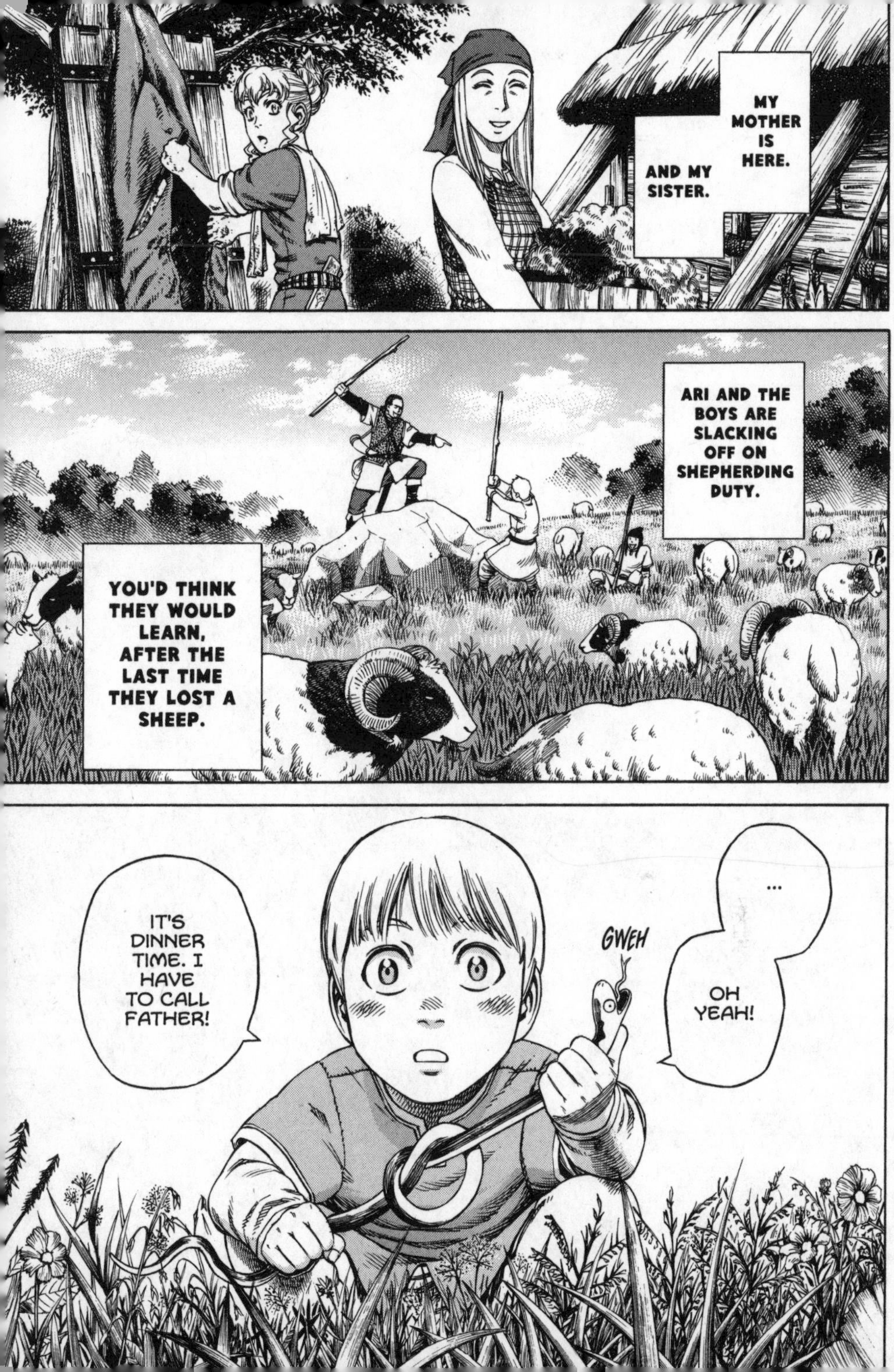
MY MOTHER IS HERE.
AND MY SISTER.
ARI AND THE BOYS ARE SLACKING OFF ON SHEPHERDING DUTY.
YOU'D THINK THEY WOULD LEARN, AFTER THE LAST TIME THEY LOST A SHEEP.
...
OH YEAH!
GWEH
IT'S DINNER TIME. I HAVE TO CALL FATHER!

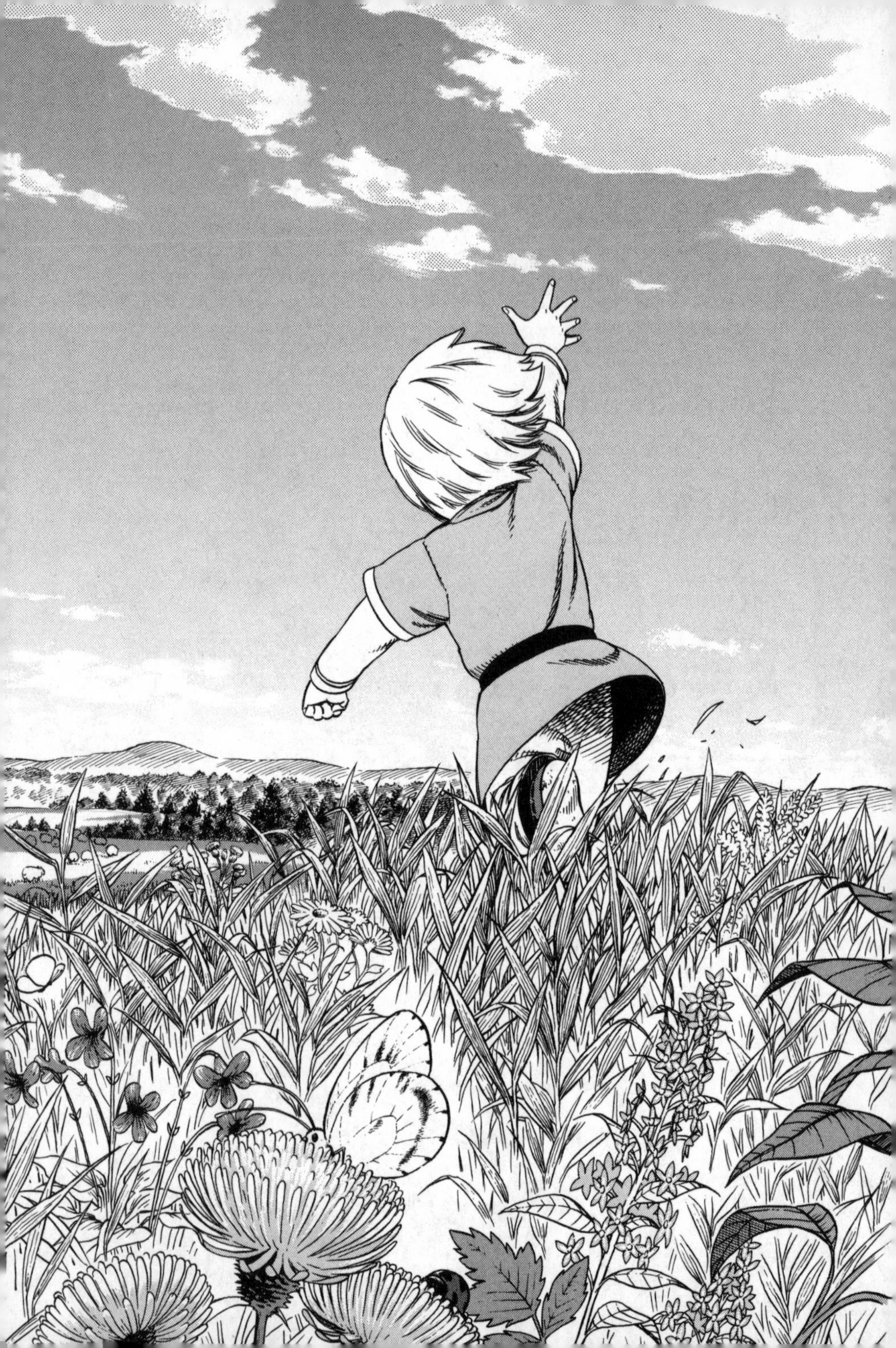

CHAPTER 20: RAGNAROK

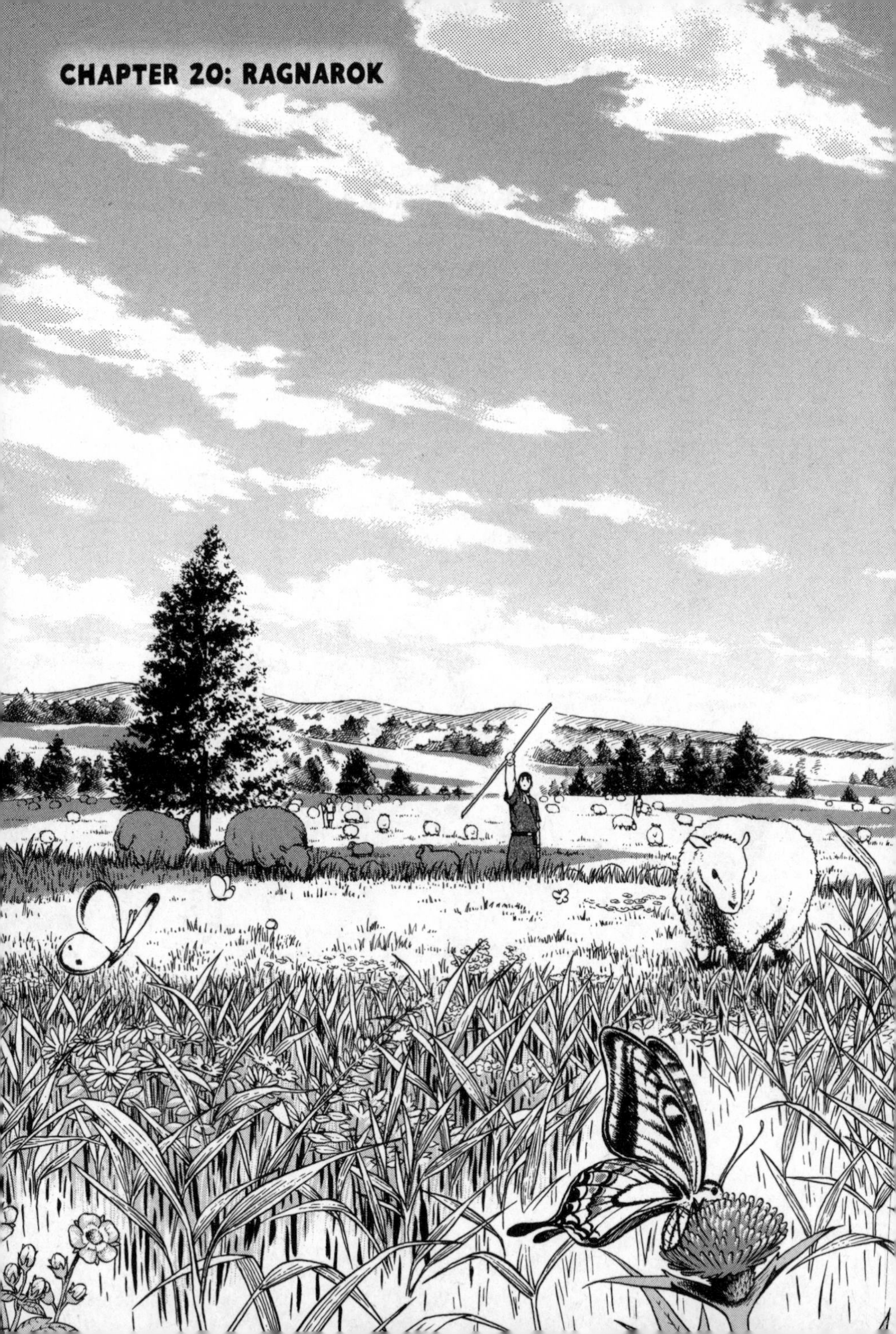

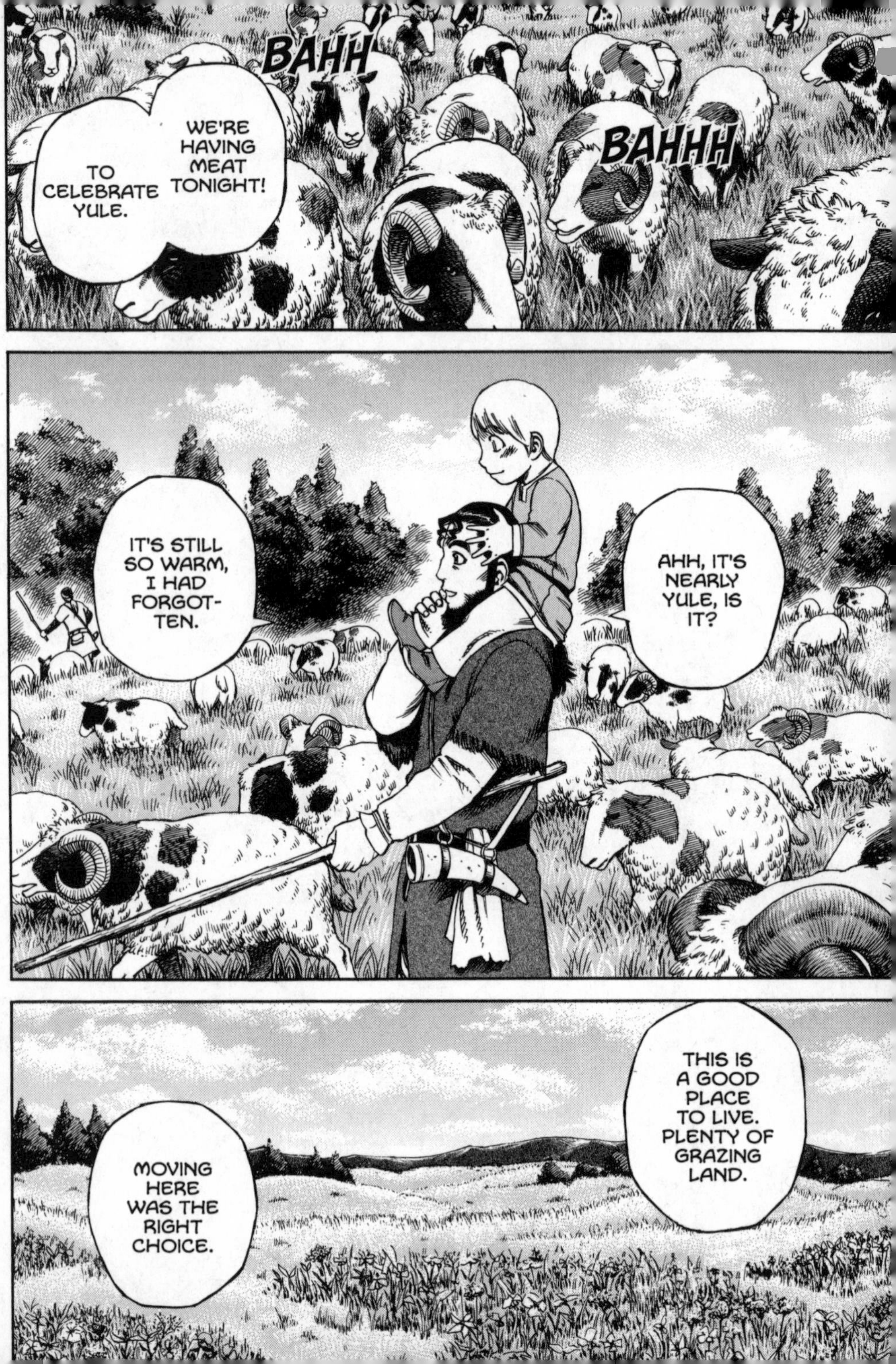
BAHH
BAHHH
WE'RE HAVING MEAT TONIGHT!
TO CELEBRATE YULE.
AHH, IT'S NEARLY YULE, IS IT?
IT'S STILL SO WARM, I HAD FORGOT-TEN.
THIS IS A GOOD PLACE TO LIVE. PLENTY OF GRAZING LAND.
MOVING HERE WAS THE RIGHT CHOICE.

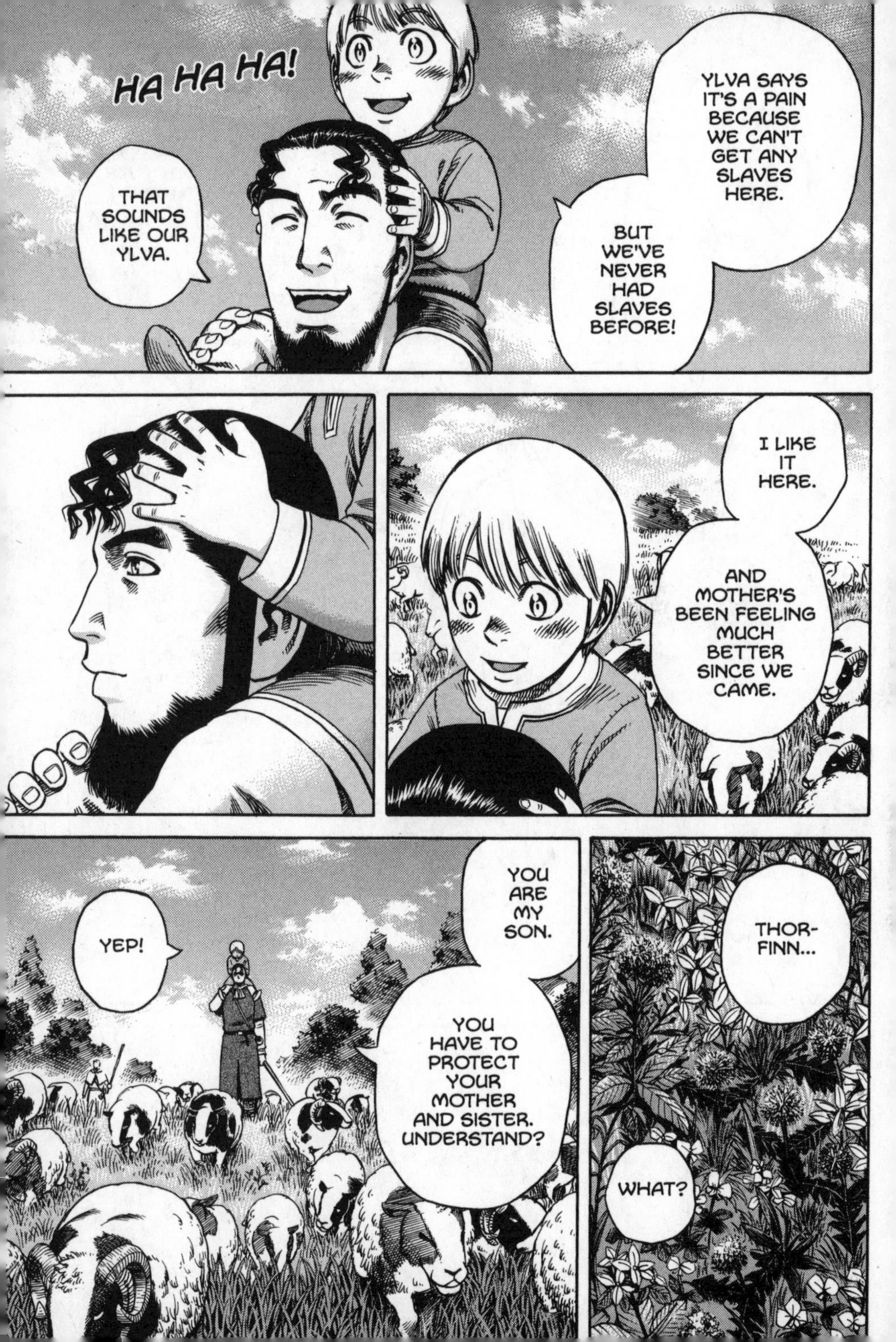
YLVA SAYS IT'S A PAIN BECAUSE WE CAN'T GET ANY SLAVES HERE.
BUT WE'VE NEVER HAD SLAVES BEFORE!
HA HA HA!
THAT SOUNDS LIKE OUR YLVA.
I LIKE IT HERE.
AND MOTHER'S BEEN FEELING MUCH BETTER SINCE WE CAME.
THOR-FINN...
WHAT?
YOU ARE MY SON.
YOU HAVE TO PROTECT YOUR MOTHER AND SISTER. UNDERSTAND?
YEP!

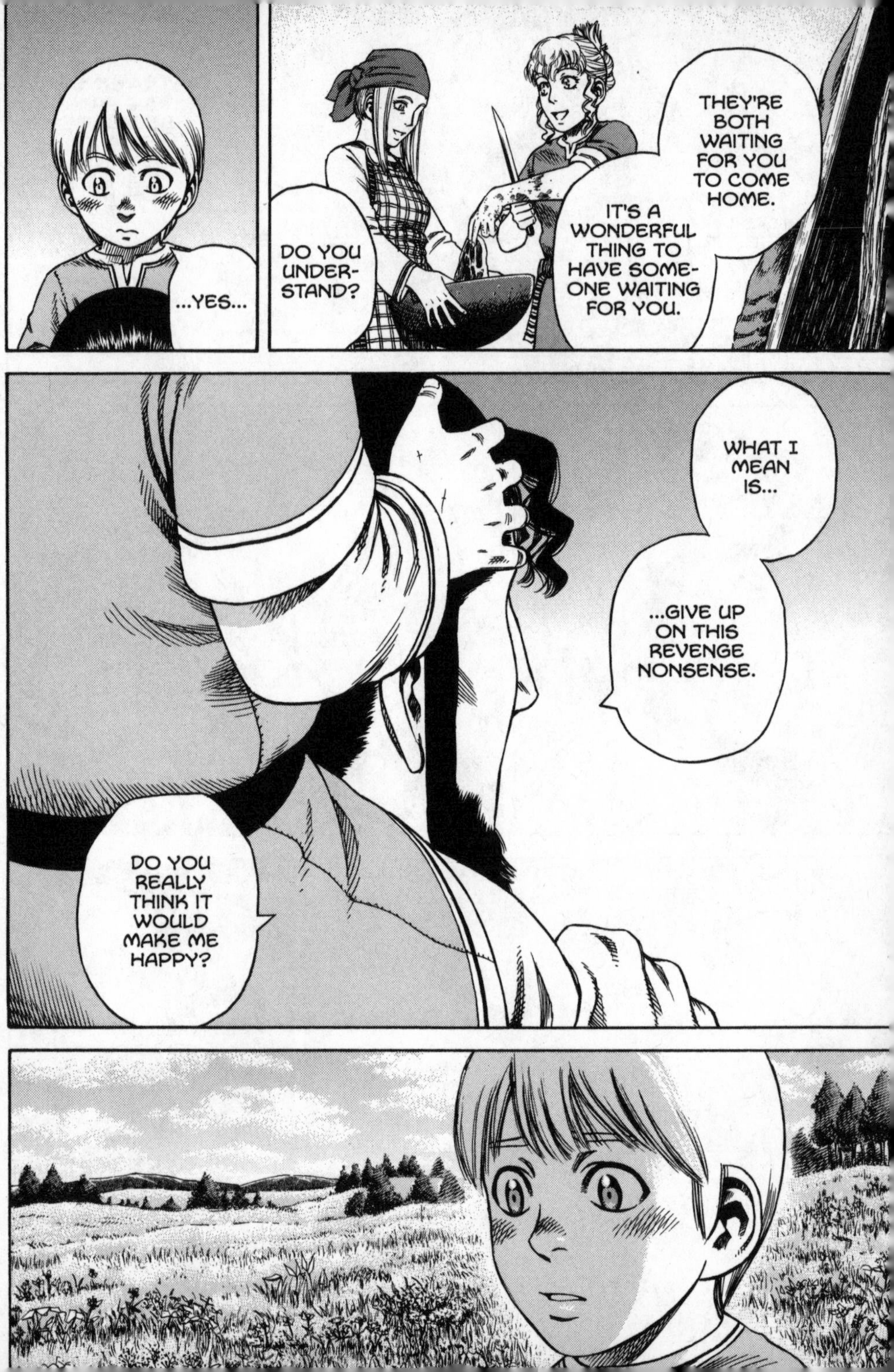
THEY'RE BOTH WAITING FOR YOU TO COME HOME.
IT'S A WONDERFUL THING TO HAVE SOME-ONE WAITING FOR YOU.
DO YOU UNDER-STAND?
...YES...
WHAT I MEAN IS...
...GIVE UP ON THIS REVENGE NONSENSE.
DO YOU REALLY THINK IT WOULD MAKE ME HAPPY?

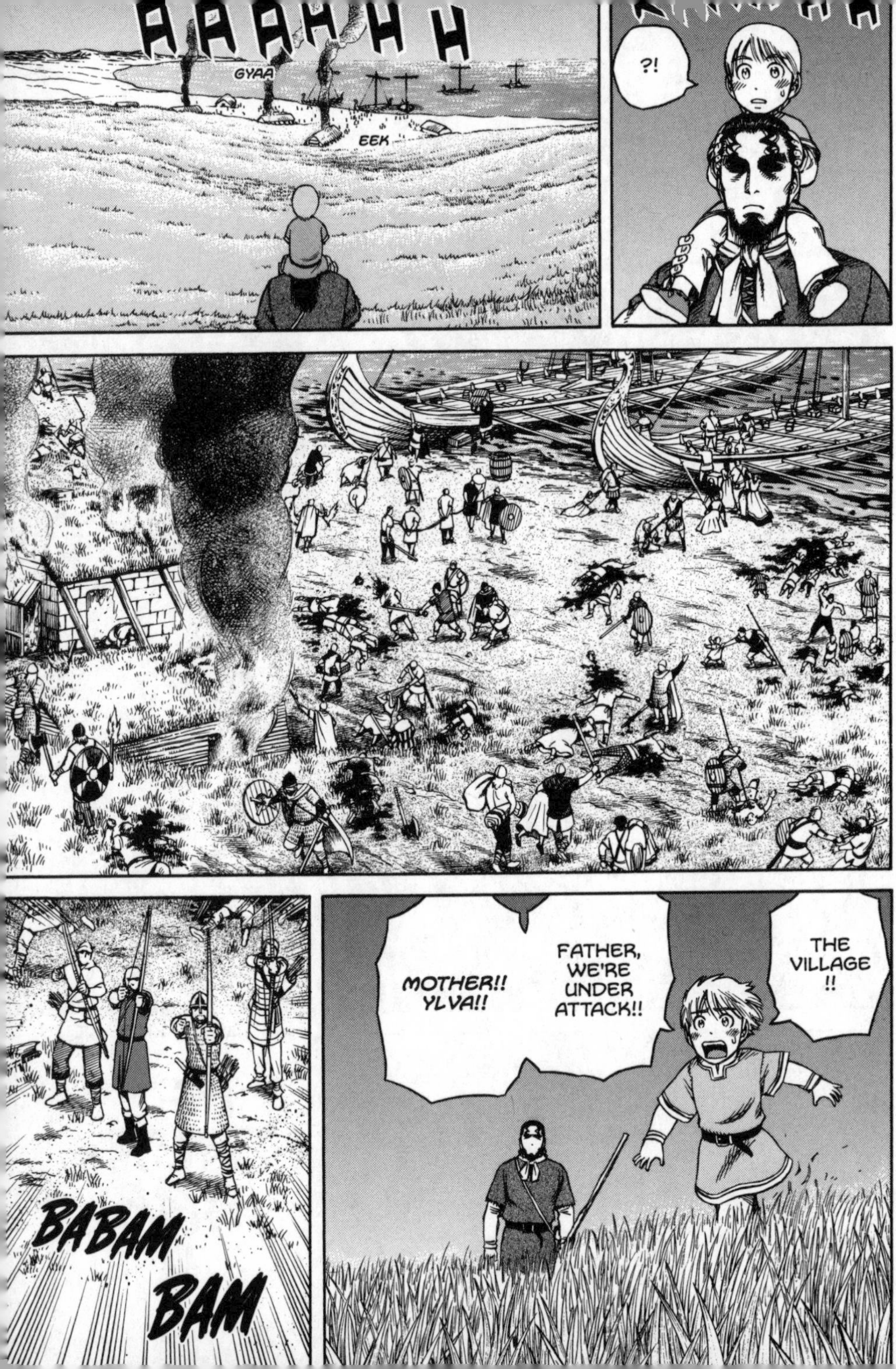
?!
AAAHHH
GYAA
EEK
THE VILLAGE !!
FATHER, WE'RE UNDER ATTACK!!
MOTHER!! YLVA!!
BABAM
BAM

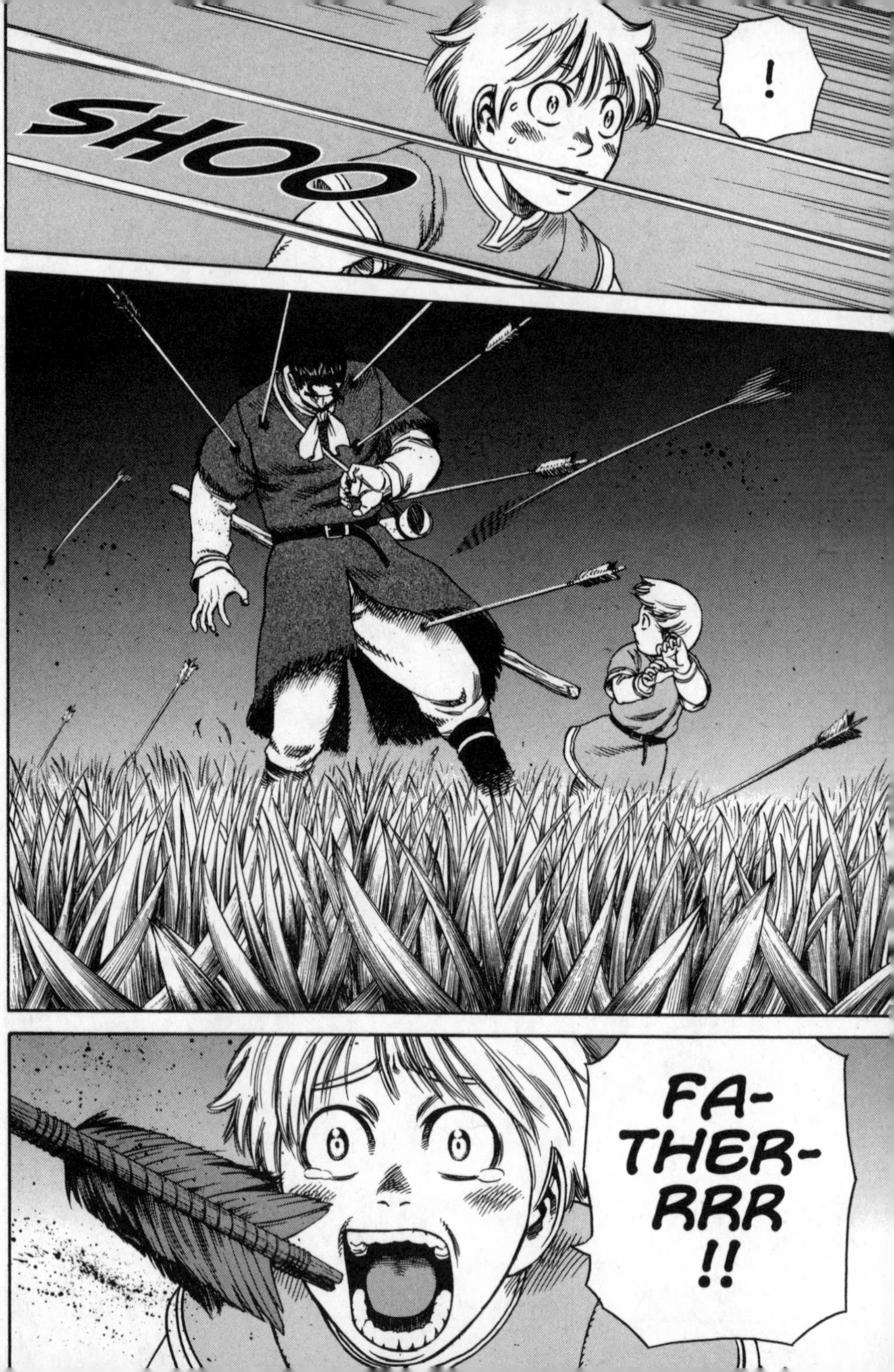
SHOO
!
FA-
THER-
RRR
!!

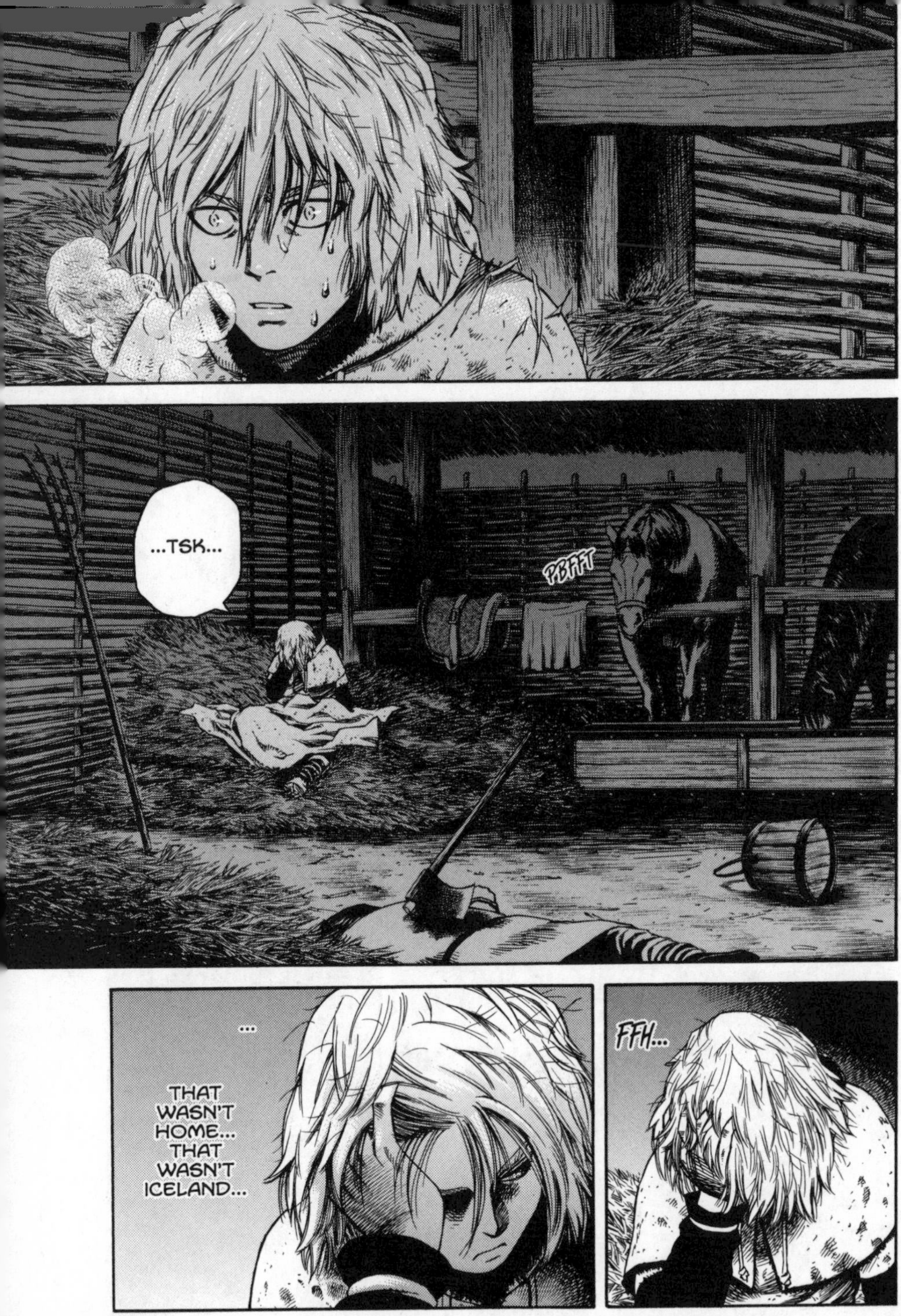
PBFFT
...TSK...
FFH...
...
THAT WASN'T HOME... THAT WASN'T ICELAND...

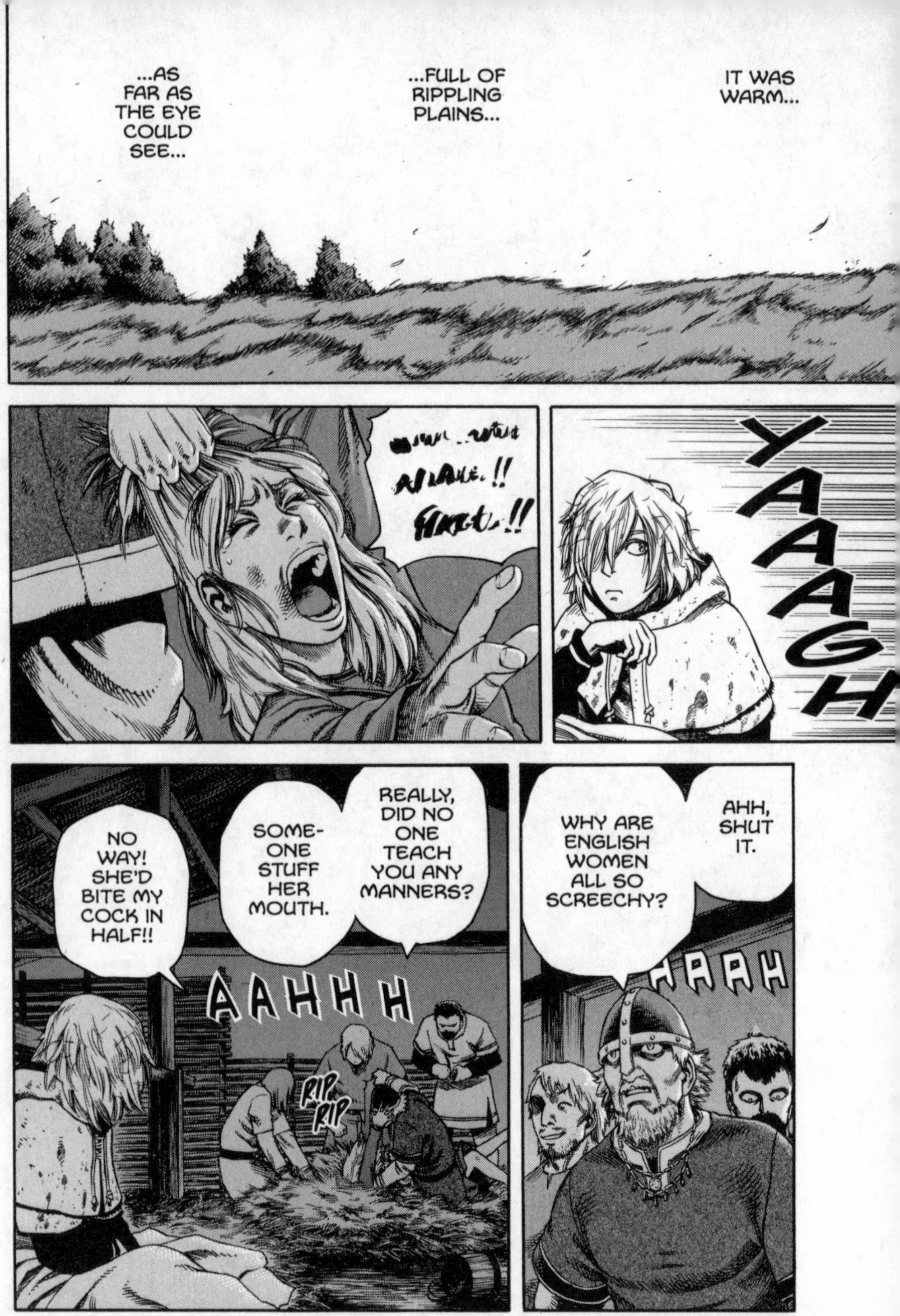
IT WAS WARM...
...FULL OF RIPPLING PLAINS...
...AS FAR AS THE EYE COULD SEE...
YAAAGH
AHH, SHUT IT.
WHY ARE ENGLISH WOMEN ALL SO SCREECHY?
REALLY, DID NO ONE TEACH YOU ANY MANNERS?
SOME-ONE STUFF HER MOUTH.
NO WAY! SHE'D BITE MY COCK IN HALF!!
AAHHH
RIP RIP

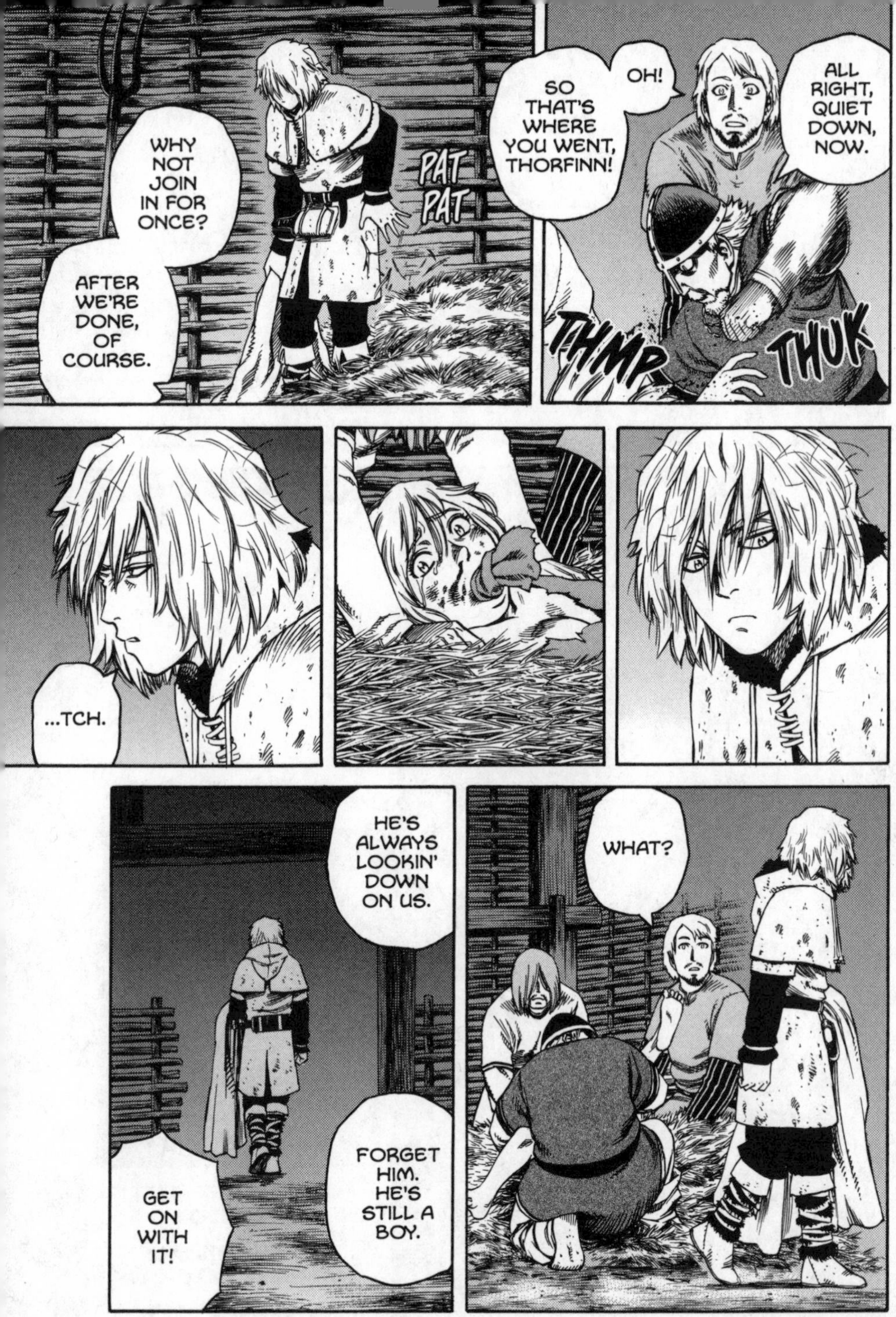
ALL RIGHT, QUIET DOWN, NOW.
OH!
SO THAT'S WHERE YOU WENT, THORFINN!
THUK
THMP
PAT PAT
WHY NOT JOIN IN FOR ONCE?
AFTER WE'RE DONE, OF COURSE.
...TCH.
WHAT?
HE'S ALWAYS LOOKIN' DOWN ON US.
FORGET HIM. HE'S STILL A BOY.
GET ON WITH IT!

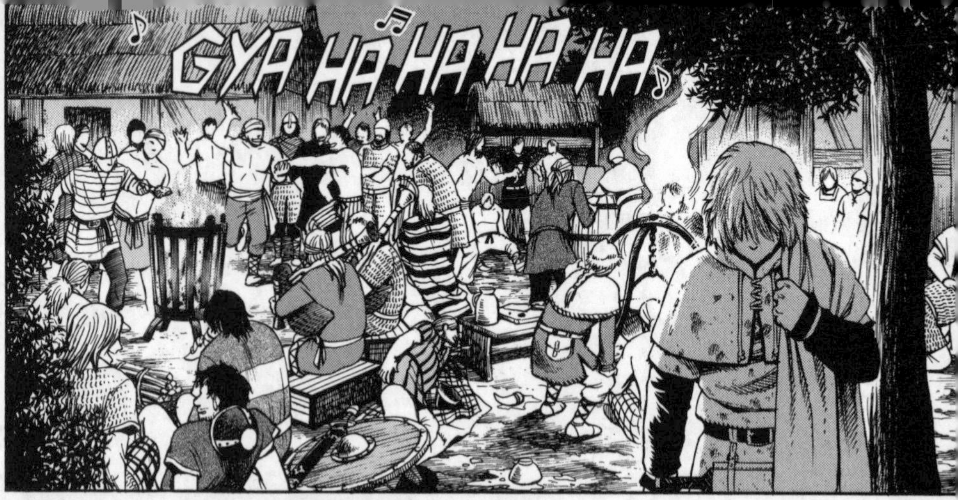
GYA HA HA HA HA

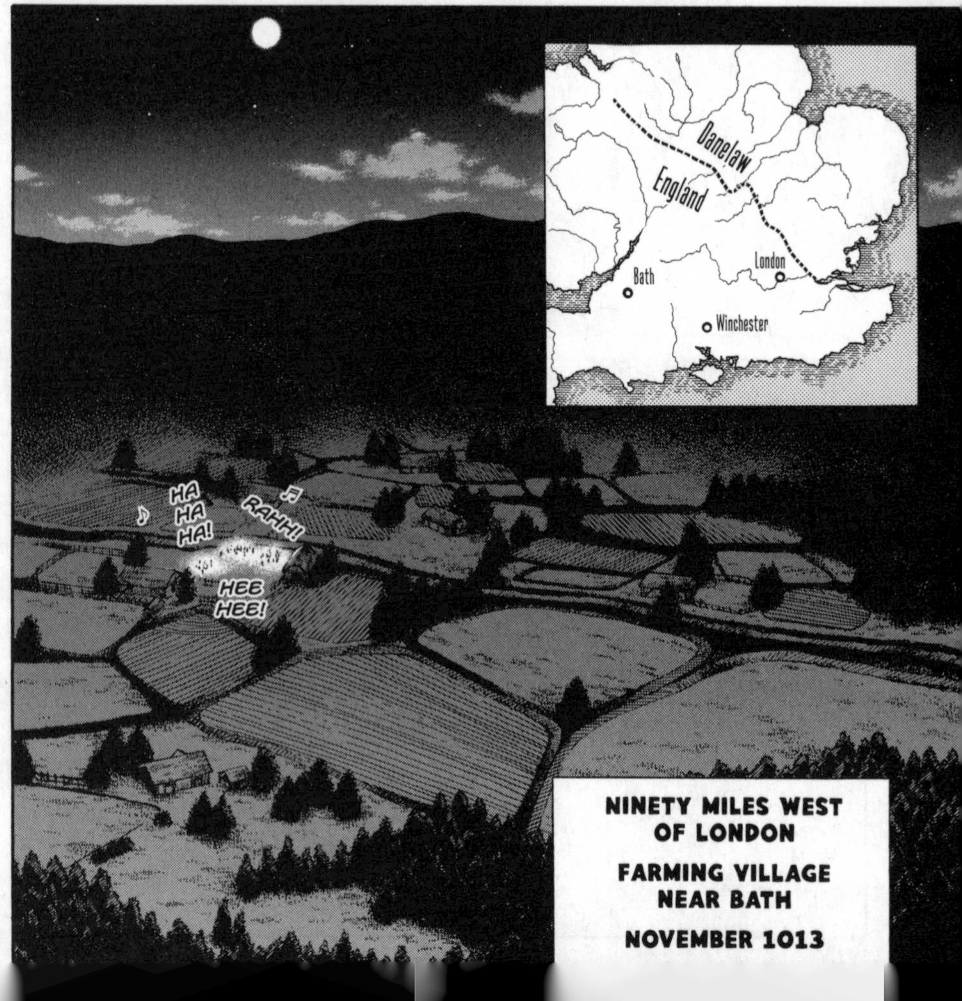
Danelaw
England
London
Bath
Winchester
HA HA HA!
RAHH!
HEE HEE!
NINETY MILES WEST OF LONDON
FARMING VILLAGE NEAR BATH
NOVEMBER 1013

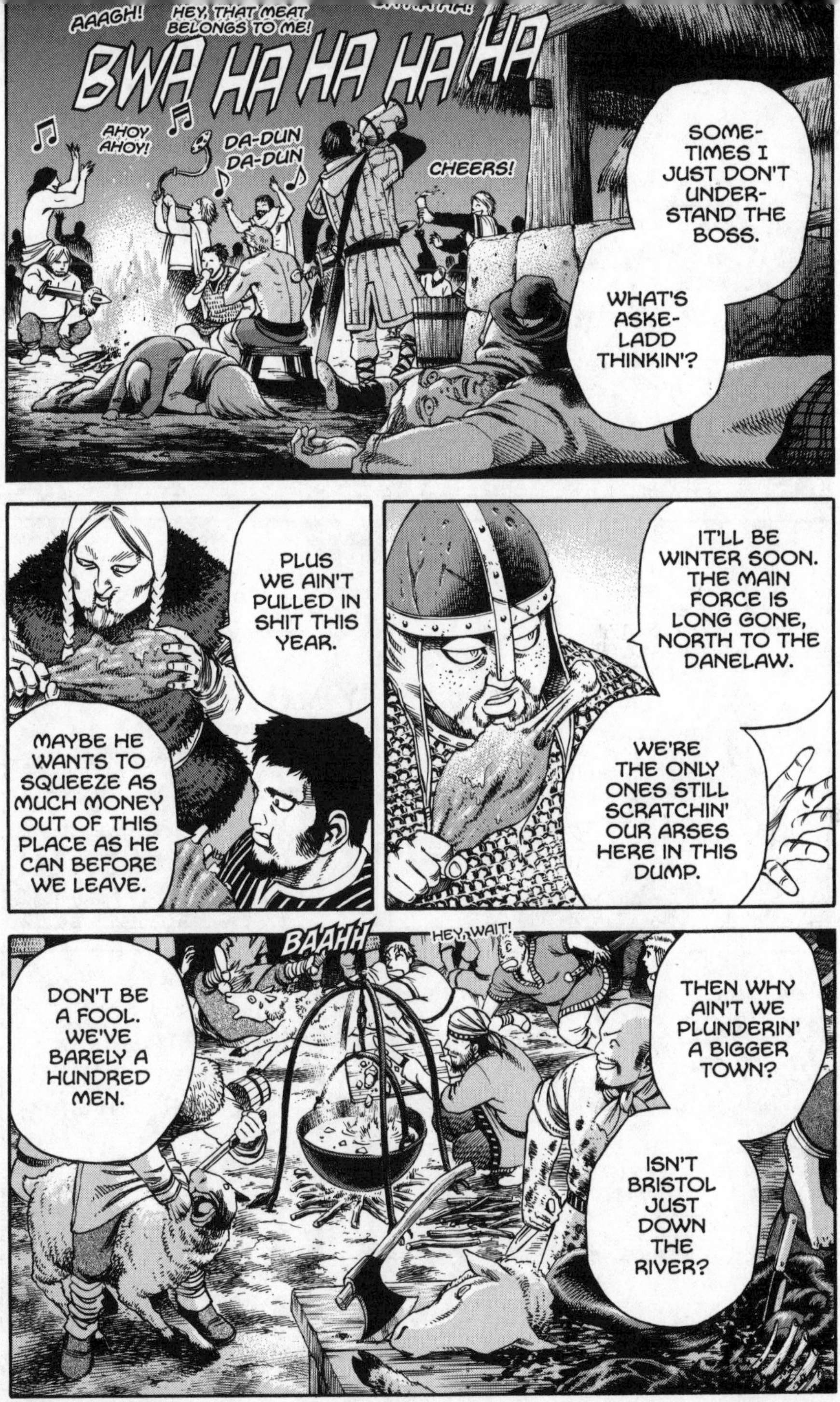
SOME-TIMES I JUST DON'T UNDER-STAND THE BOSS.
WHAT'S ASKE-LADD THINKIN'?
CHEERS!
HEY, THAT MEAT BELONGS TO ME!
BWA HA HA HA HA HA
DA-DUN DA-DUN
AHOY AHOY!
AAAGH!
IT'LL BE WINTER SOON. THE MAIN FORCE IS LONG GONE, NORTH TO THE DANELAW.
WE'RE THE ONLY ONES STILL SCRATCHIN' OUR ARSES HERE IN THIS DUMP.
PLUS WE AIN'T PULLED IN SHIT THIS YEAR.
MAYBE HE WANTS TO SQUEEZE AS MUCH MONEY OUT OF THIS PLACE AS HE CAN BEFORE WE LEAVE.
THEN WHY AIN'T WE PLUNDERIN' A BIGGER TOWN?
ISN'T BRISTOL JUST DOWN THE RIVER?
HEY, WAIT!
BAAHH
DON'T BE A FOOL. WE'VE BARELY A HUNDRED MEN.

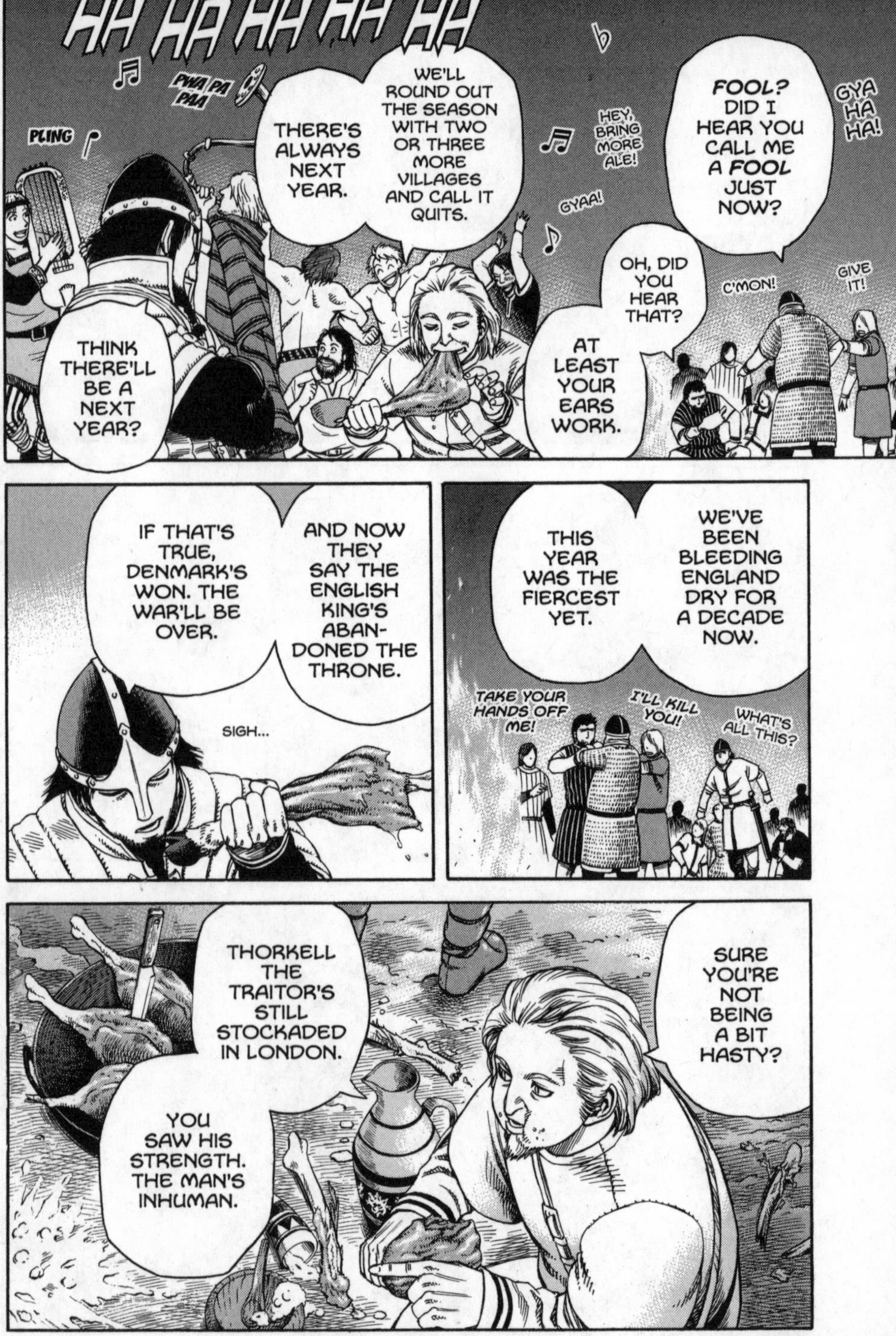
GYA HA HA!
FOOL? DID I HEAR YOU CALL ME A FOOL JUST NOW?
GIVE IT!
C'MON!
OH, DID YOU HEAR THAT?
AT LEAST YOUR EARS WORK.
HEY, BRING MORE ALE!
GYAA!
WE'LL ROUND OUT THE SEASON WITH TWO OR THREE MORE VILLAGES AND CALL IT QUITS.
THERE'S ALWAYS NEXT YEAR.
HA HA HA HA HA
PWA PA PAA
PLING
THINK THERE'LL BE A NEXT YEAR?
WE'VE BEEN BLEEDING ENGLAND DRY FOR A DECADE NOW.
THIS YEAR WAS THE FIERCEST YET.
WHAT'S ALL THIS?
I'LL KILL YOU!
TAKE YOUR HANDS OFF ME!
AND NOW THEY SAY THE ENGLISH KING'S ABAN-DONED THE THRONE.
IF THAT'S TRUE, DENMARK'S WON. THE WAR'LL BE OVER.
SIGH...
SURE YOU'RE NOT BEING A BIT HASTY?
THORKELL THE TRAITOR'S STILL STOCKADED IN LONDON.
YOU SAW HIS STRENGTH. THE MAN'S INHUMAN.

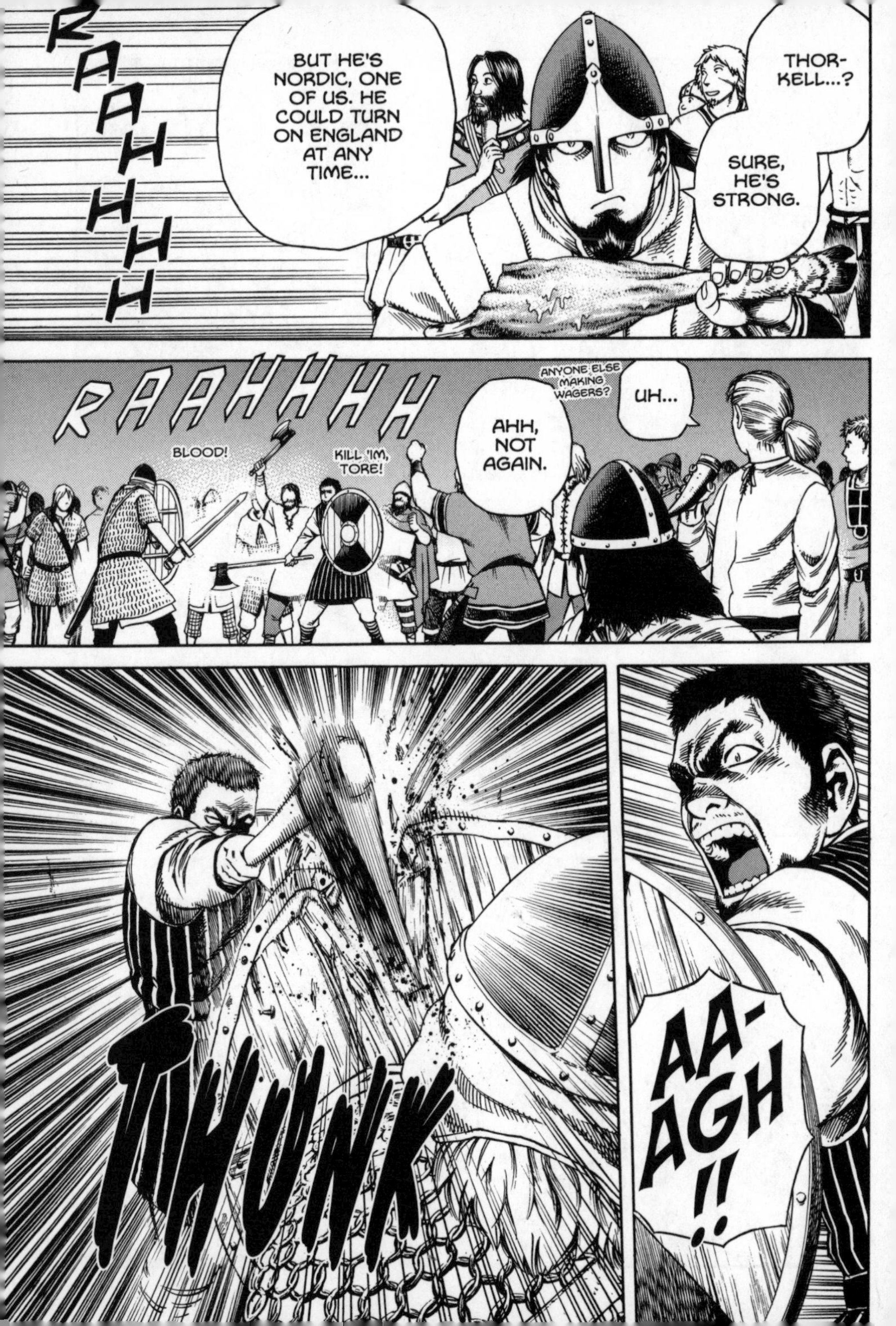
THOR-KELL...?
SURE, HE'S STRONG.
BUT HE'S NORDIC, ONE OF US. HE COULD TURN ON ENGLAND AT ANY TIME...
RAAHHHHH
UH...
ANYONE ELSE MAKING WAGERS?
AHH, NOT AGAIN.
KILL 'IM, TORE!
BLOOD!
RAAHHHHH
AA-AGH!!
THWUNK

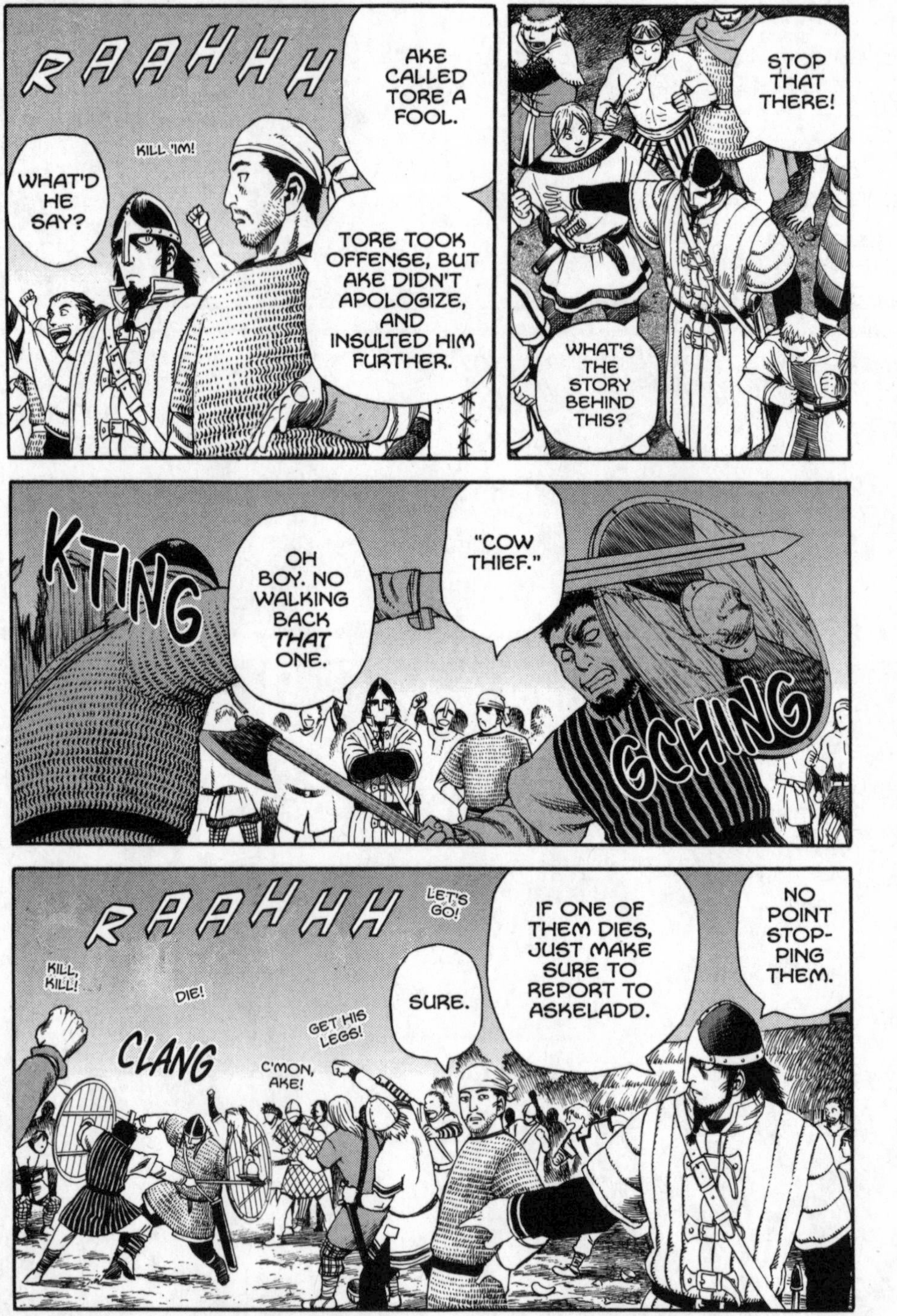
STOP THAT THERE!
WHAT'S THE STORY BEHIND THIS?
AKE CALLED TORE A FOOL.
TORE TOOK OFFENSE, BUT AKE DIDN'T APOLOGIZE, AND INSULTED HIM FURTHER.
RAAHHH
KILL 'IM!
WHAT'D HE SAY?
"COW THIEF."
OH BOY. NO WALKING BACK *THAT* ONE.
KTING
GCHING
NO POINT STOPPING THEM.
IF ONE OF THEM DIES, JUST MAKE SURE TO REPORT TO ASKELADD.
SURE.
LET'S GO!
RAAHHH
GET HIS LEGS!
C'MON, AKE!
DIE!
KILL, KILL!
CLANG

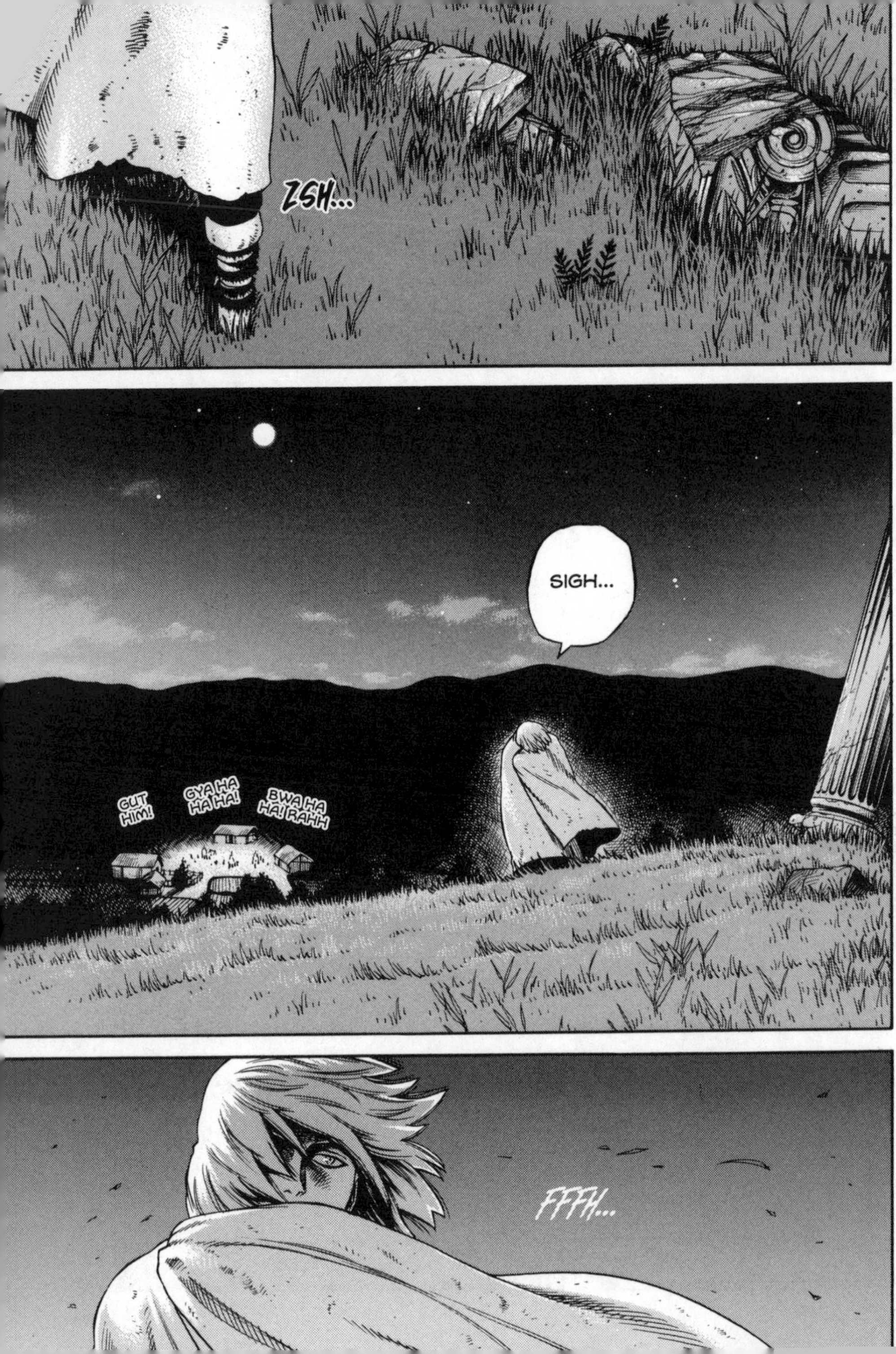
ZSH...
SIGH...
BWA HA HA! RAHH
GYA HA HA HA!
GUT HIM!
FFFH...

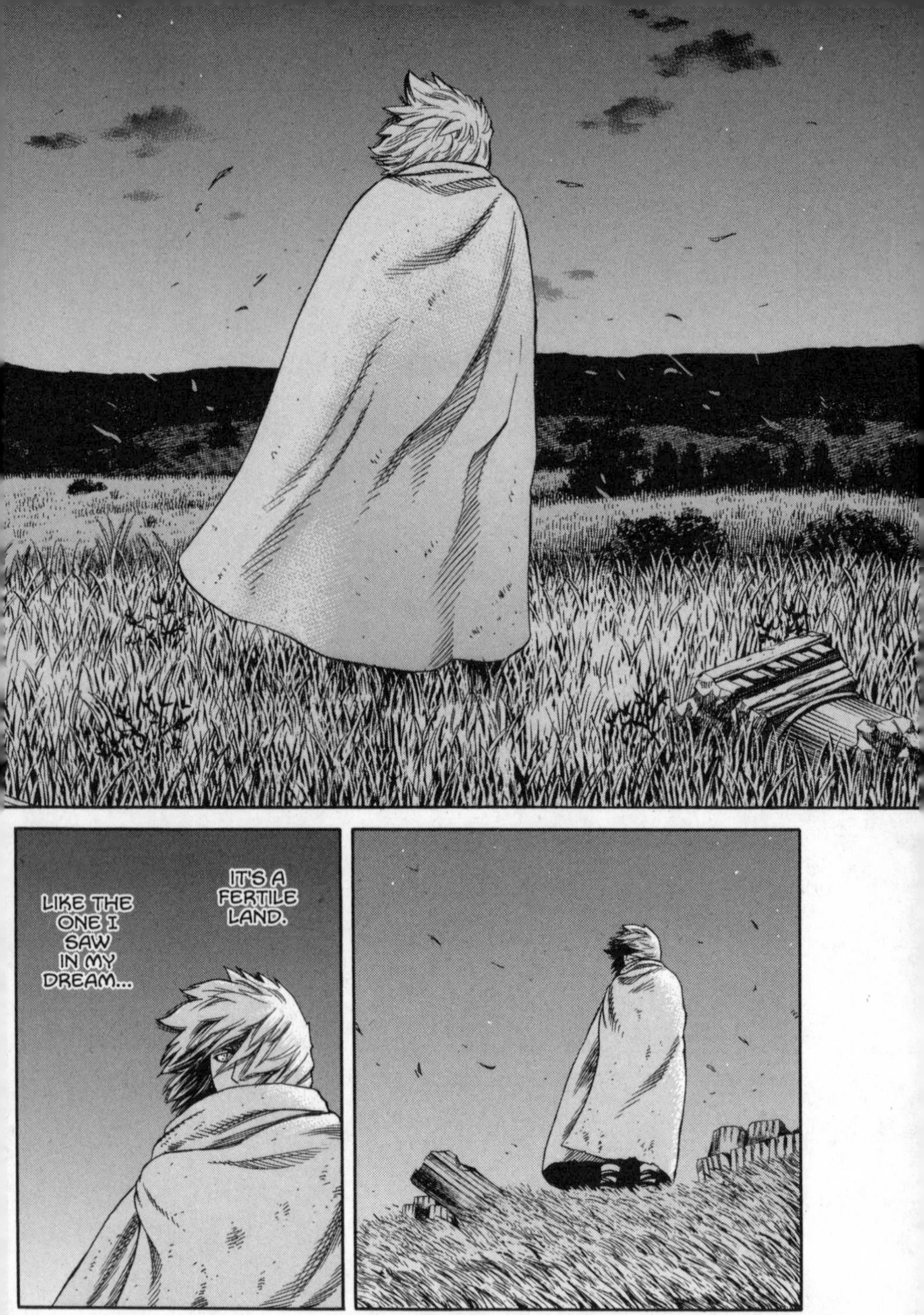
IT'S A FERTILE LAND.
LIKE THE ONE I SAW IN MY DREAM...

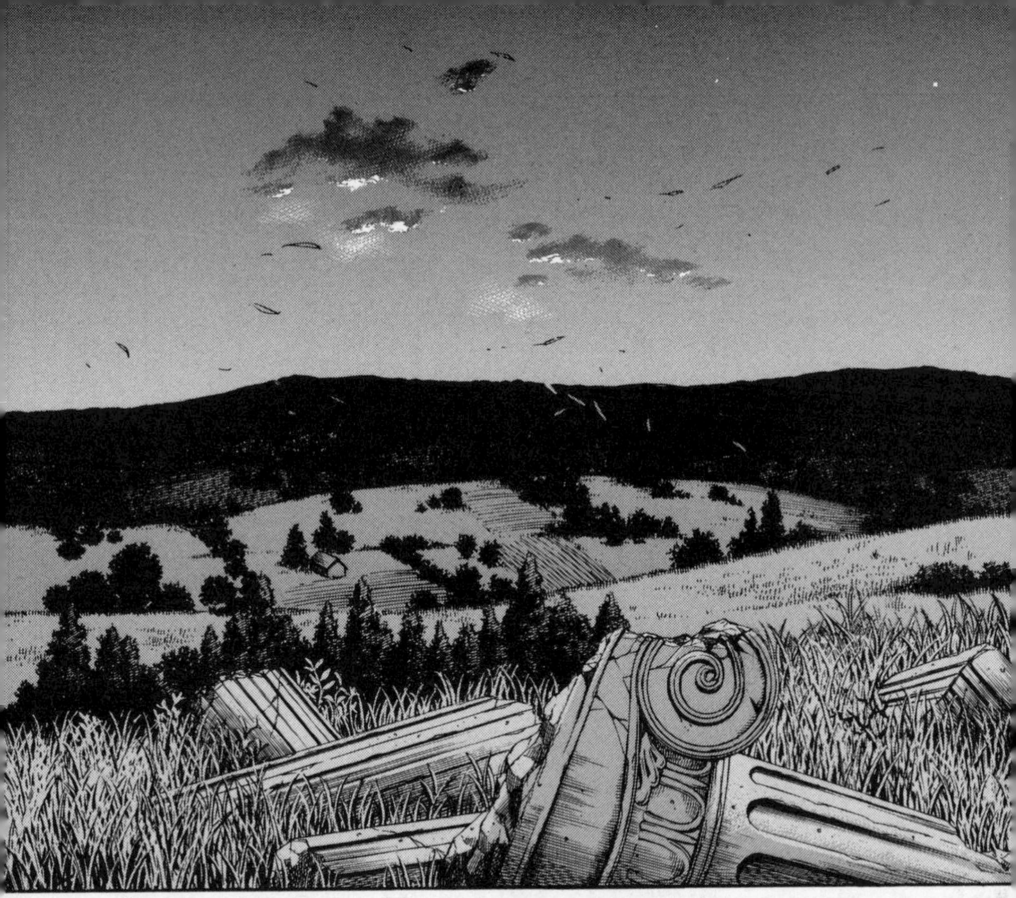

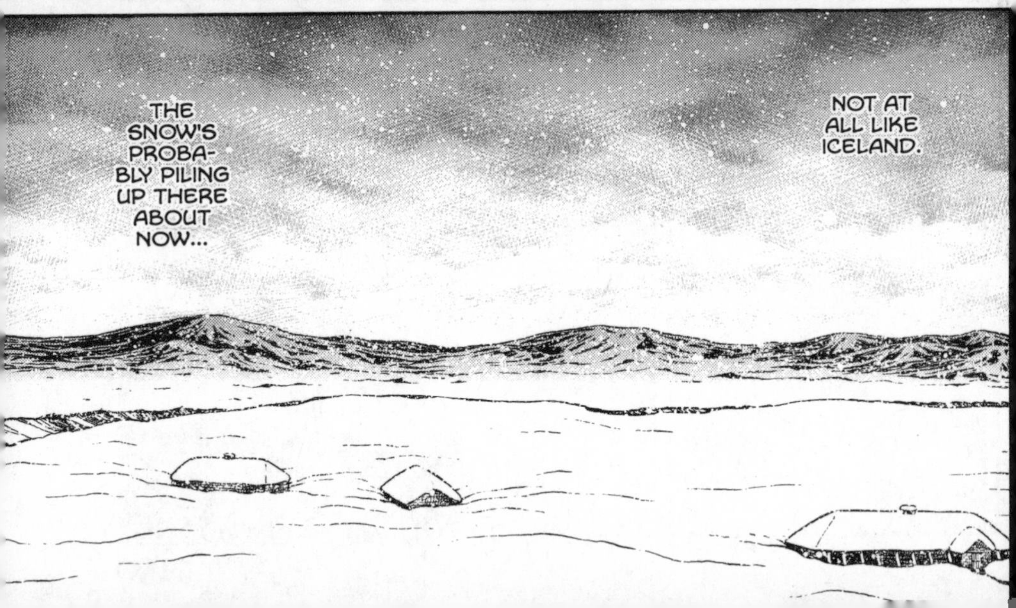
NOT AT ALL LIKE ICELAND.
THE SNOW'S PROBA-BLY PILING UP THERE ABOUT NOW...

TUG

YOU'RE UP EARLY, THOR-FINN.

NOT EVEN SUNRISE YET.

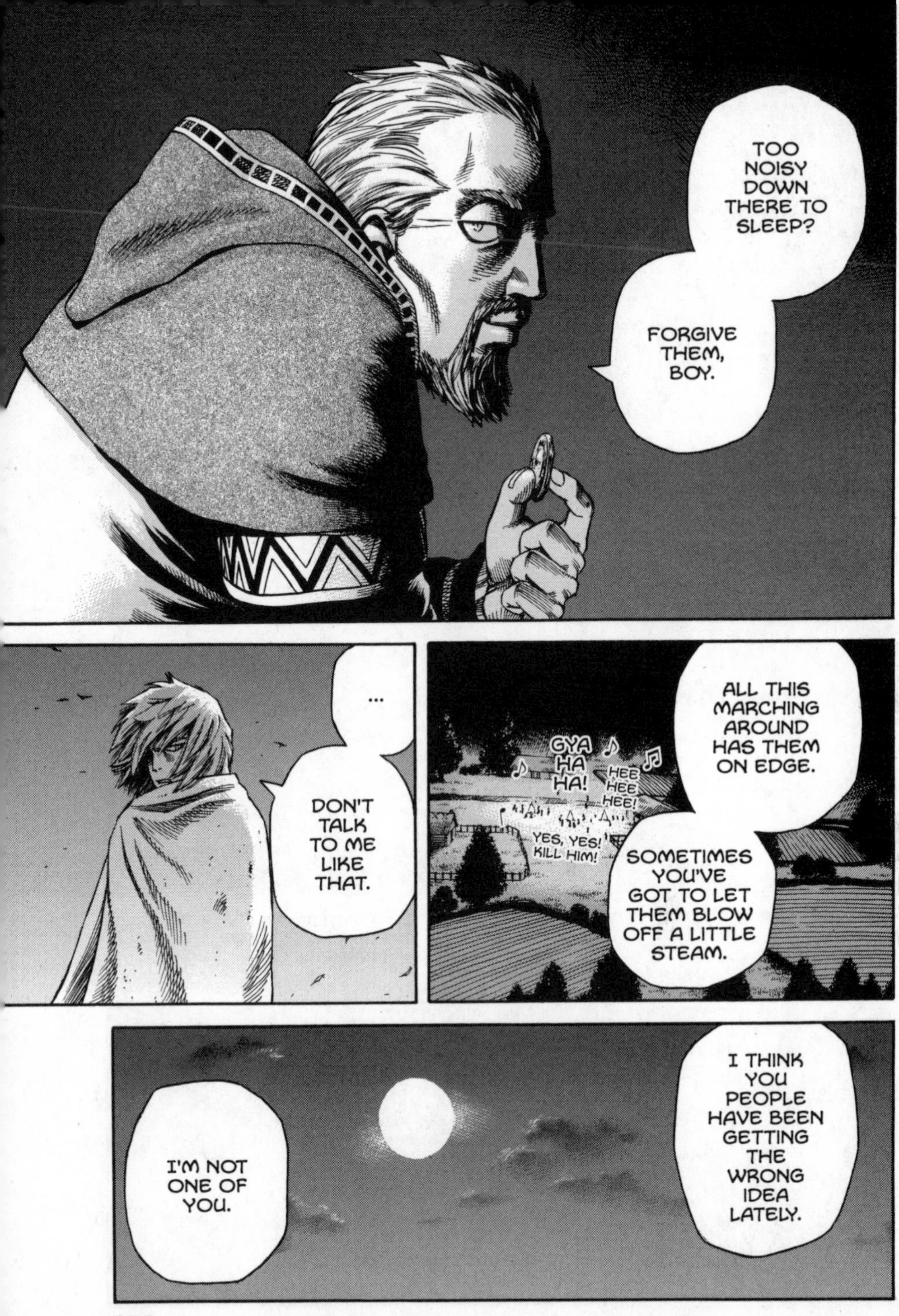
TOO NOISY DOWN THERE TO SLEEP?
FORGIVE THEM, BOY.
ALL THIS MARCHING AROUND HAS THEM ON EDGE.
HEE HEE HEE!
GYA HA HA!
YES, YES! KILL HIM!
SOMETIMES YOU'VE GOT TO LET THEM BLOW OFF A LITTLE STEAM.
...
DON'T TALK TO ME LIKE THAT.
I THINK YOU PEOPLE HAVE BEEN GETTING THE WRONG IDEA LATELY.
I'M NOT ONE OF YOU.

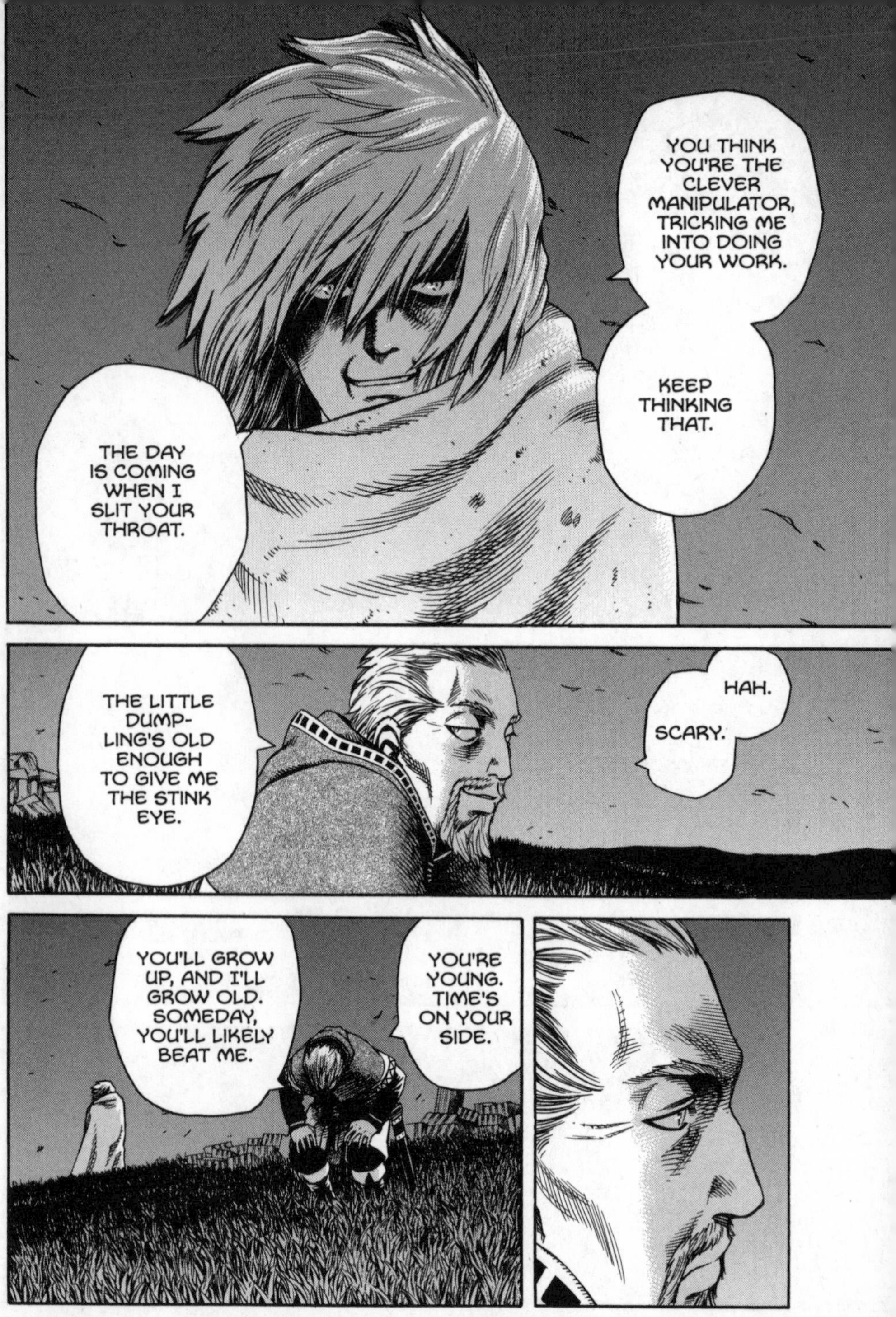
YOU THINK YOU'RE THE CLEVER MANIPULATOR, TRICKING ME INTO DOING YOUR WORK.
KEEP THINKING THAT.
THE DAY IS COMING WHEN I SLIT YOUR THROAT.
HAH.
SCARY.
THE LITTLE DUMP-LING'S OLD ENOUGH TO GIVE ME THE STINK EYE.
YOU'RE YOUNG. TIME'S ON YOUR SIDE.
YOU'LL GROW UP, AND I'LL GROW OLD. SOMEDAY, YOU'LL LIKELY BEAT ME.

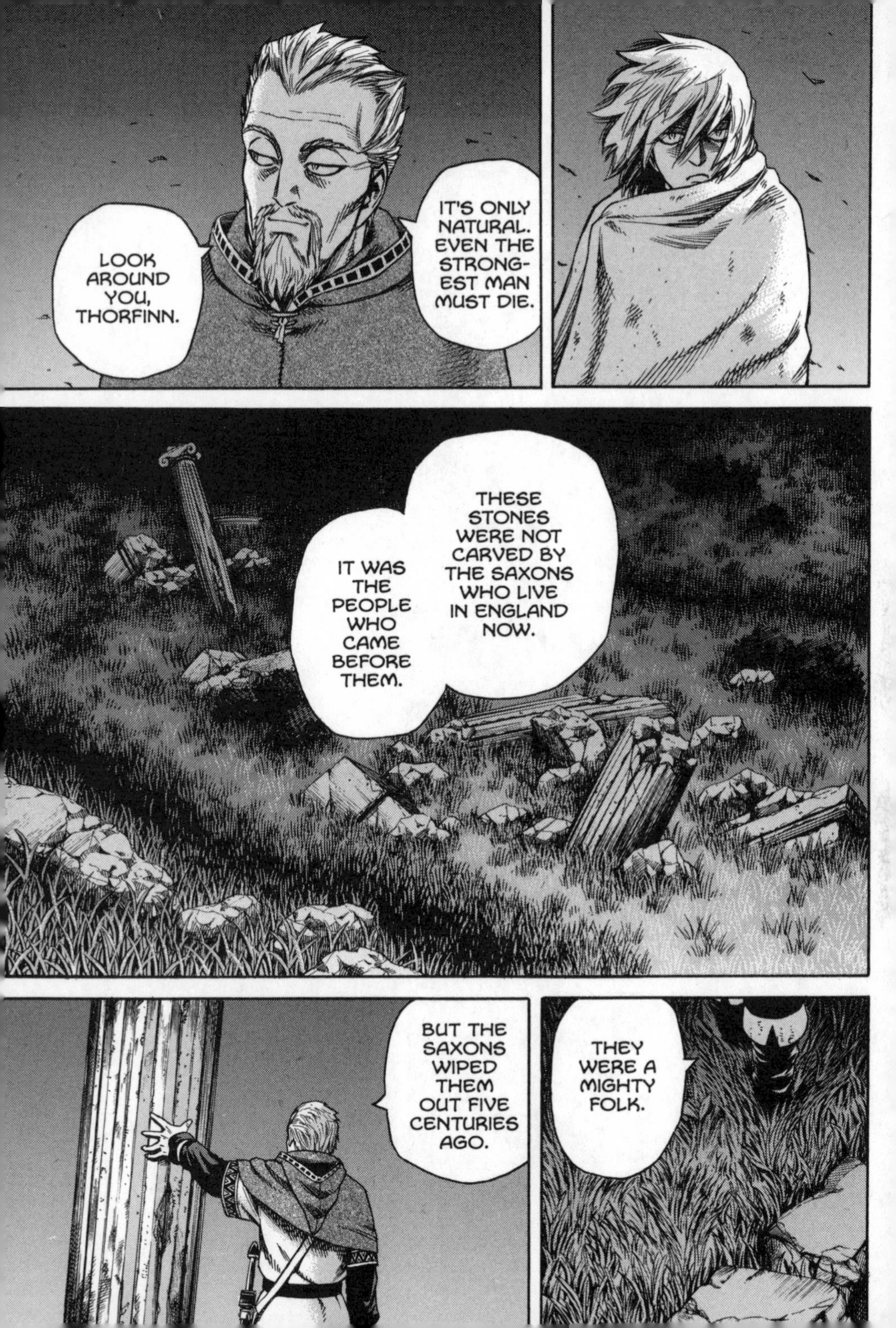
IT'S ONLY NATURAL. EVEN THE STRONGEST MAN MUST DIE.
LOOK AROUND YOU, THORFINN.
THESE STONES WERE NOT CARVED BY THE SAXONS WHO LIVE IN ENGLAND NOW.
IT WAS THE PEOPLE WHO CAME BEFORE THEM.
THEY WERE A MIGHTY FOLK.
BUT THE SAXONS WIPED THEM OUT FIVE CENTURIES AGO.

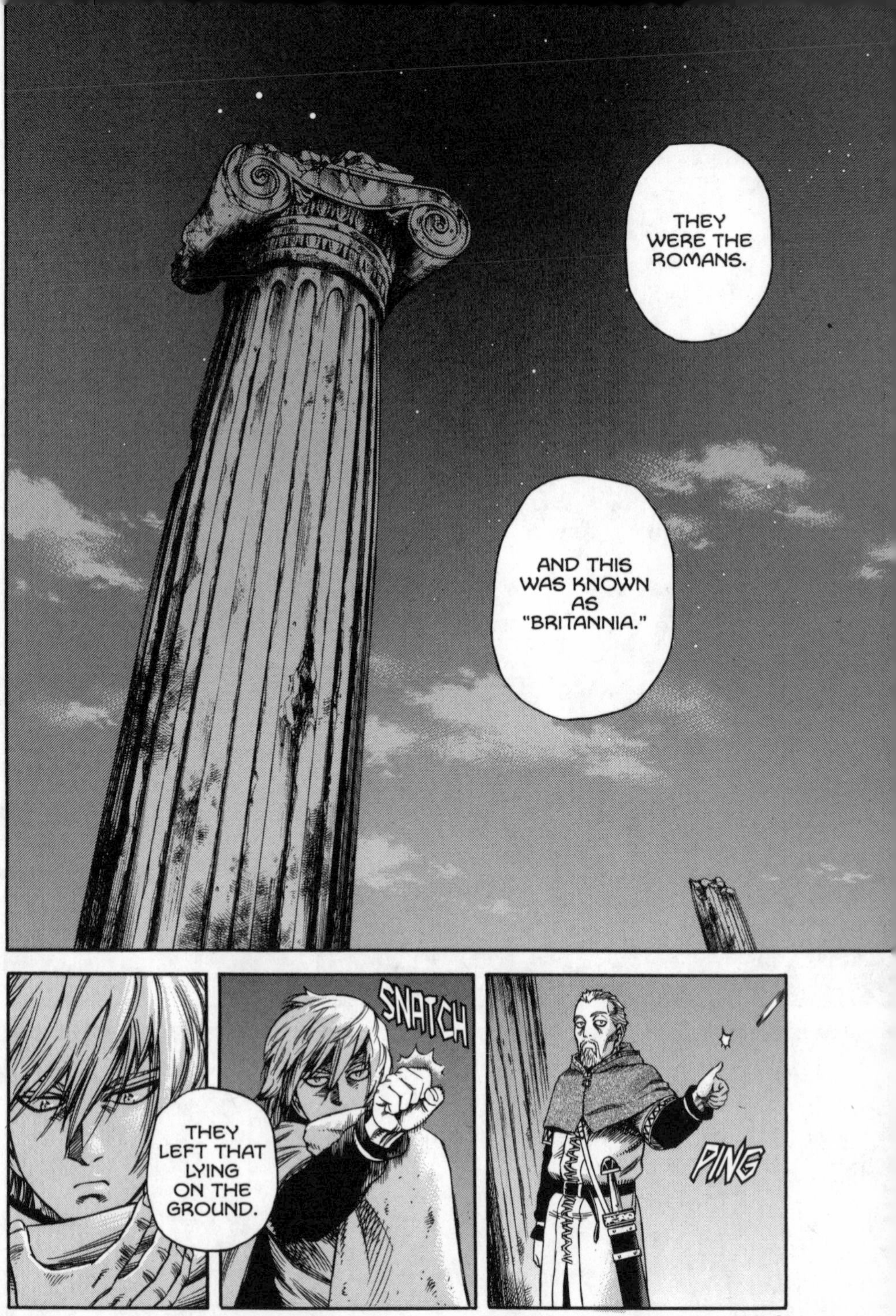
THEY WERE THE ROMANS.
AND THIS WAS KNOWN AS "BRITANNIA."
PING
SNATCH
THEY LEFT THAT LYING ON THE GROUND.

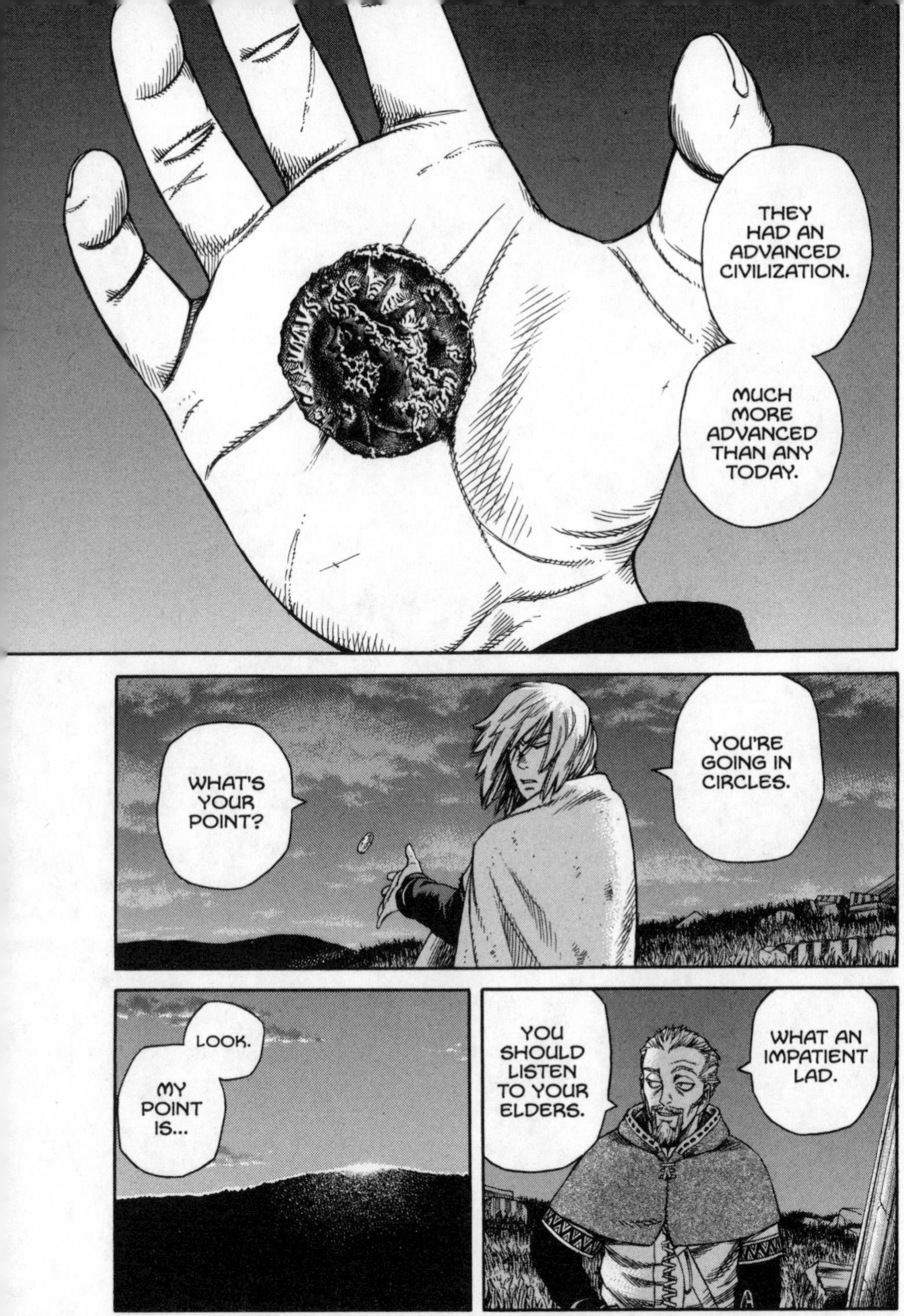
THEY HAD AN ADVANCED CIVILIZATION.
MUCH MORE ADVANCED THAN ANY TODAY.
YOU'RE GOING IN CIRCLES.
WHAT'S YOUR POINT?
WHAT AN IMPATIENT LAD.
YOU SHOULD LISTEN TO YOUR ELDERS.
LOOK.
MY POINT IS...

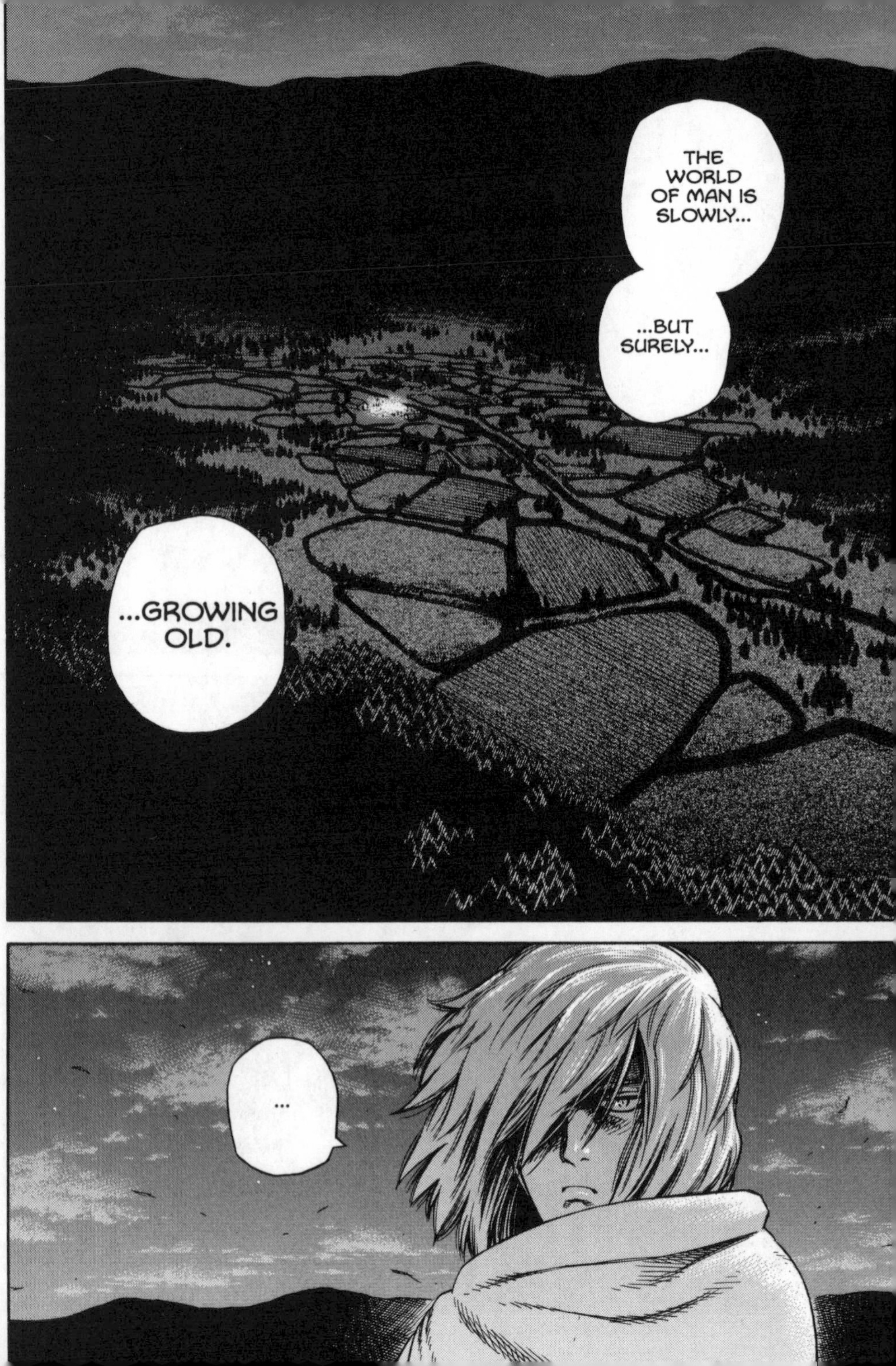
THE WORLD OF MAN IS SLOWLY...
...BUT SURELY...
...GROWING OLD.
...

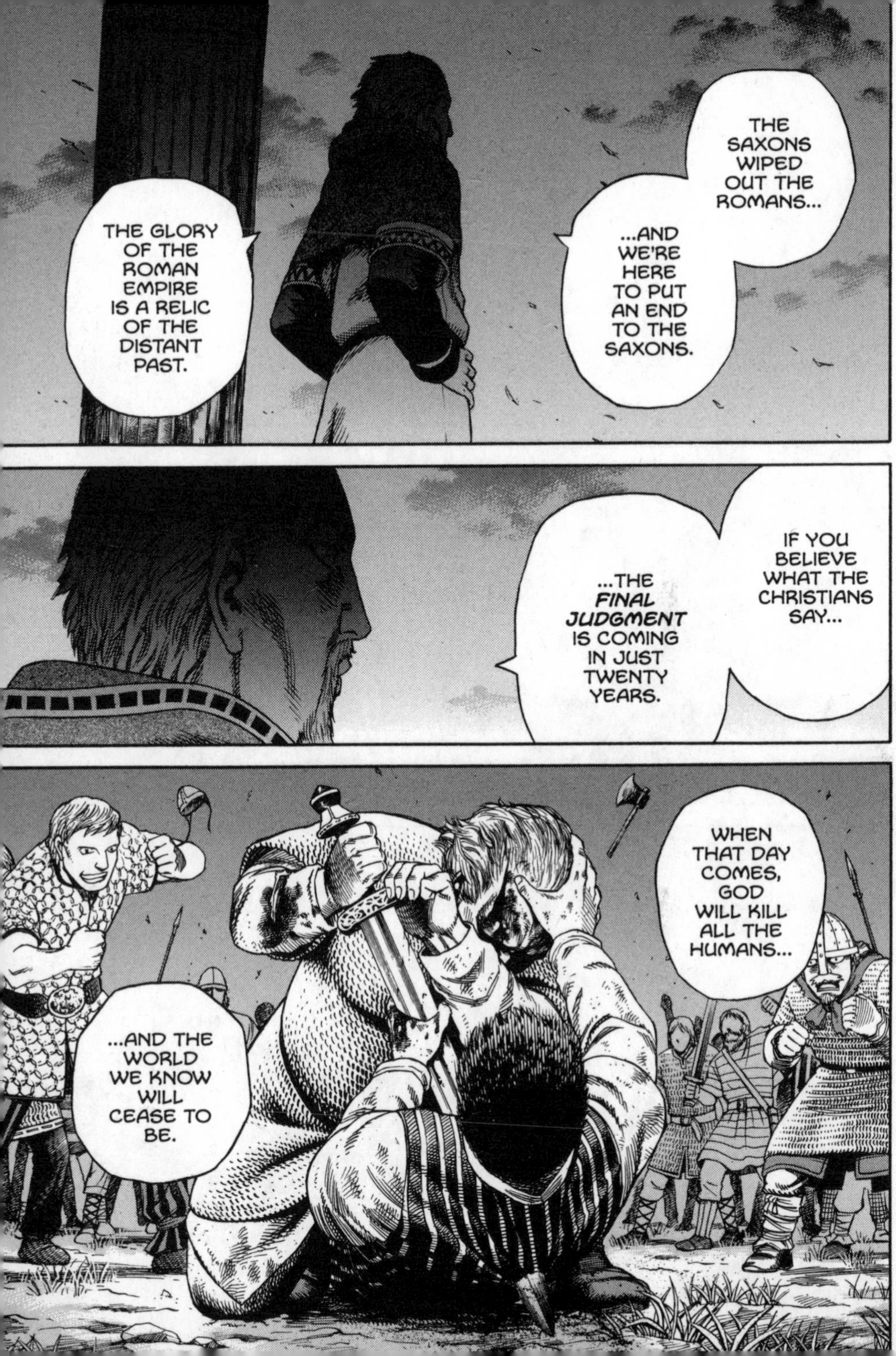
THE SAXONS WIPED OUT THE ROMANS...
...AND WE'RE HERE TO PUT AN END TO THE SAXONS.
THE GLORY OF THE ROMAN EMPIRE IS A RELIC OF THE DISTANT PAST.
IF YOU BELIEVE WHAT THE CHRISTIANS SAY...
...THE *FINAL JUDGMENT* IS COMING IN JUST TWENTY YEARS.
WHEN THAT DAY COMES, GOD WILL KILL ALL THE HUMANS...
...AND THE WORLD WE KNOW WILL CEASE TO BE.

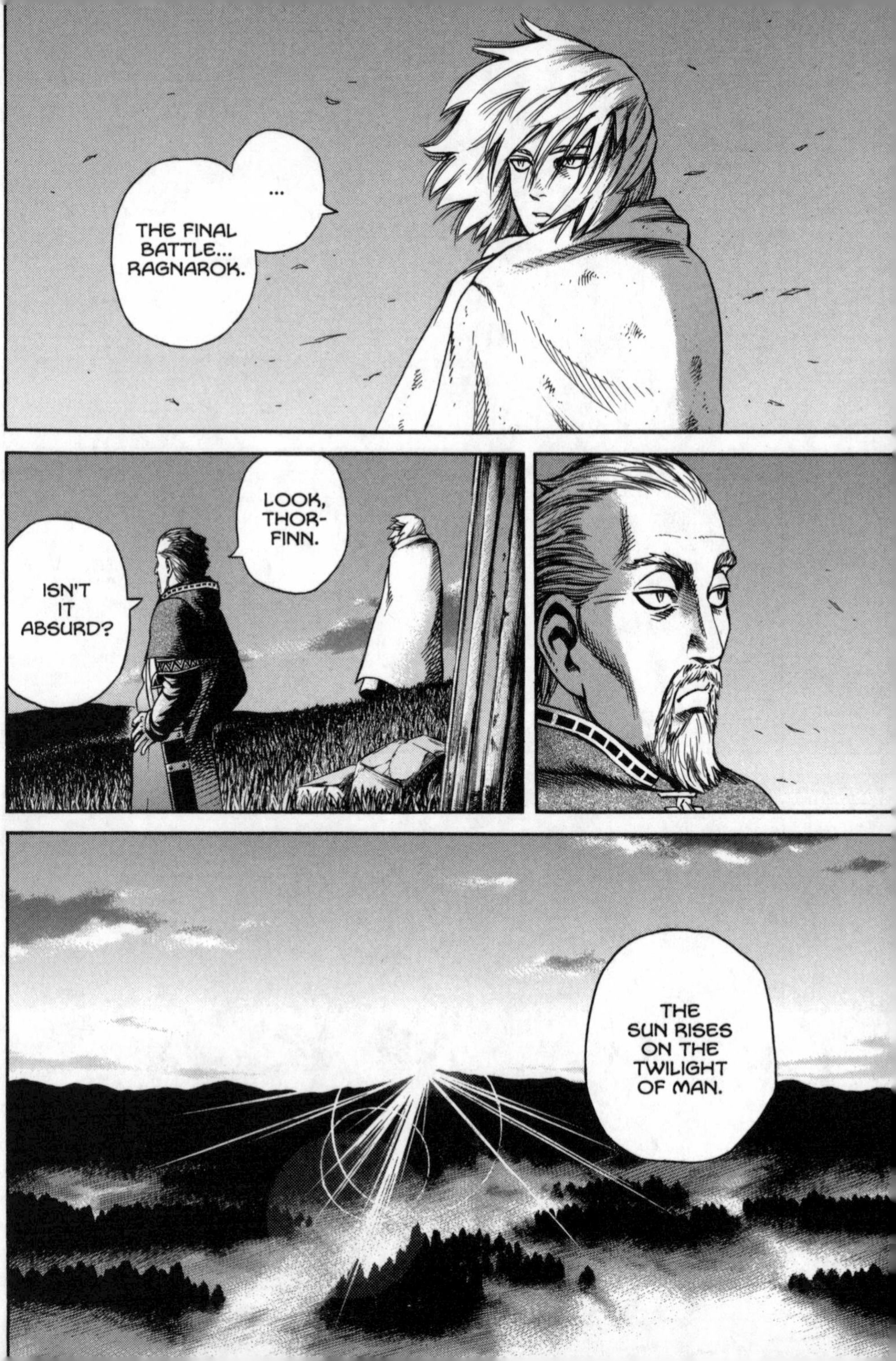
...
THE FINAL BATTLE... RAGNAROK.
LOOK, THORFINN.
ISN'T IT ABSURD?
THE SUN RISES ON THE TWILIGHT OF MAN.

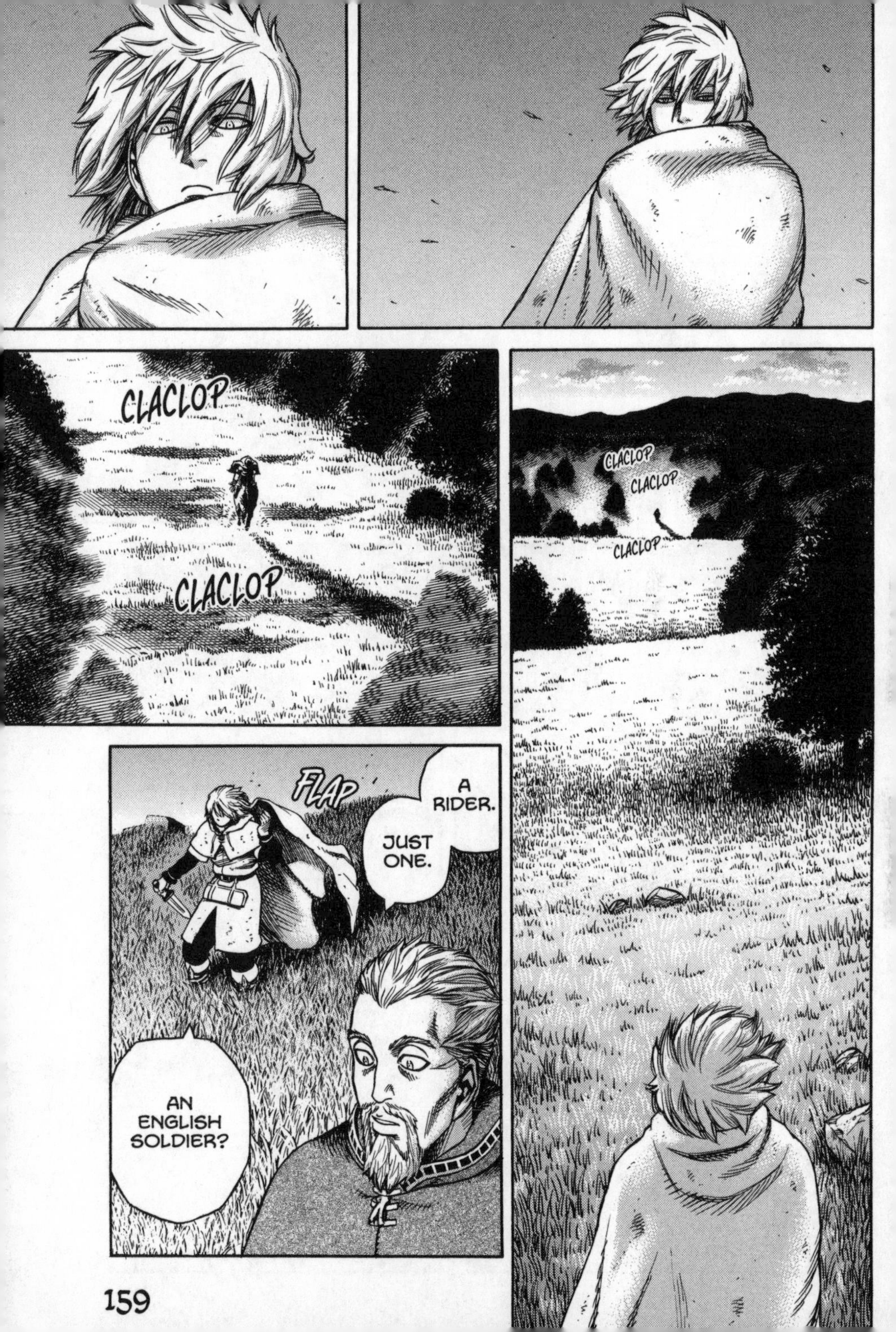
CLACLOP
CLACLOP
CLACLOP
CLACLOP
CLACLOP
FLAP
A RIDER.
JUST ONE.
AN ENGLISH SOLDIER?

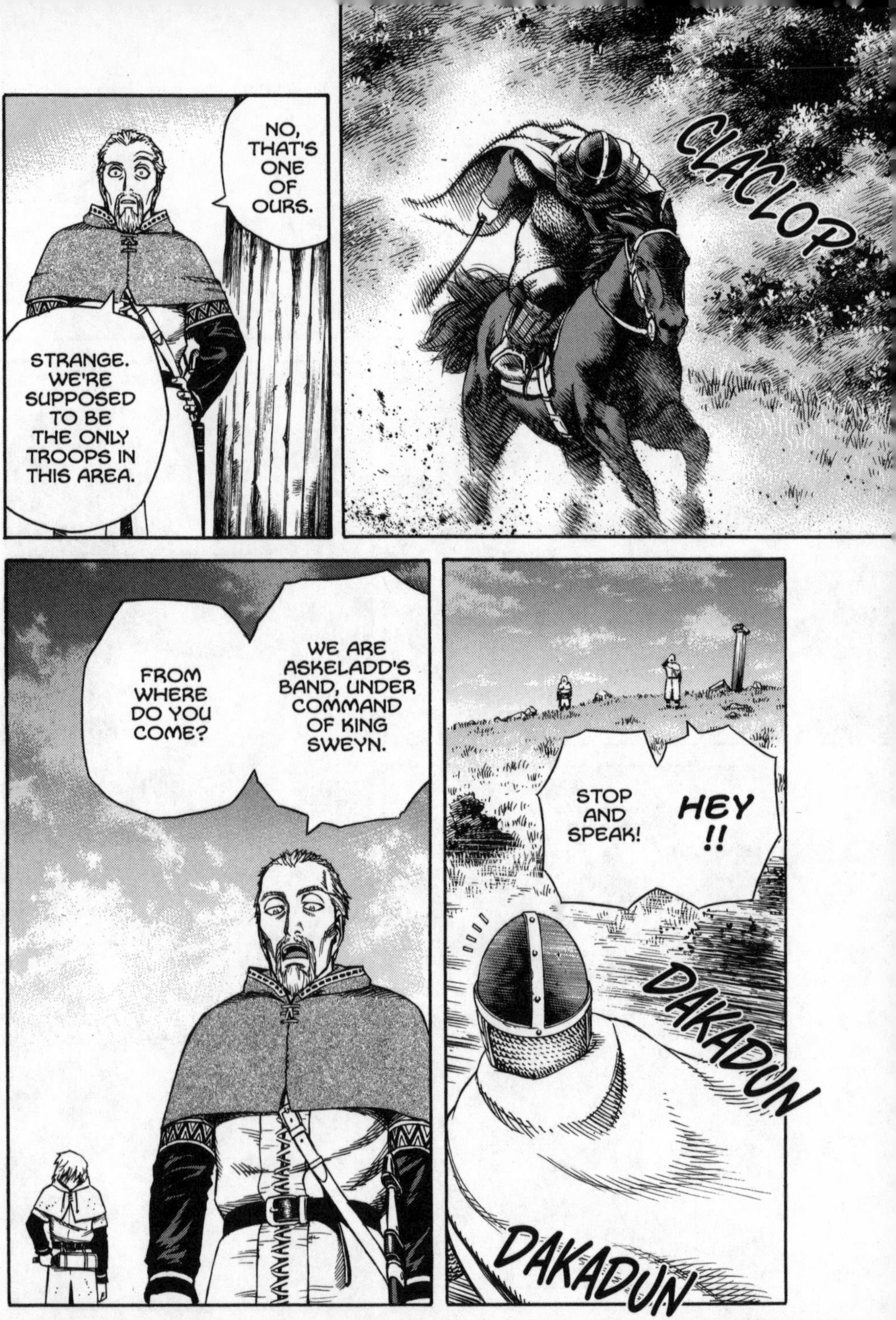
CLACLOP
NO, THAT'S ONE OF OURS.
STRANGE. WE'RE SUPPOSED TO BE THE ONLY TROOPS IN THIS AREA.
HEY!!
STOP AND SPEAK!
DAKADUN
DAKADUN
WE ARE ASKELADD'S BAND, UNDER COMMAND OF KING SWEYN.
FROM WHERE DO YOU COME?

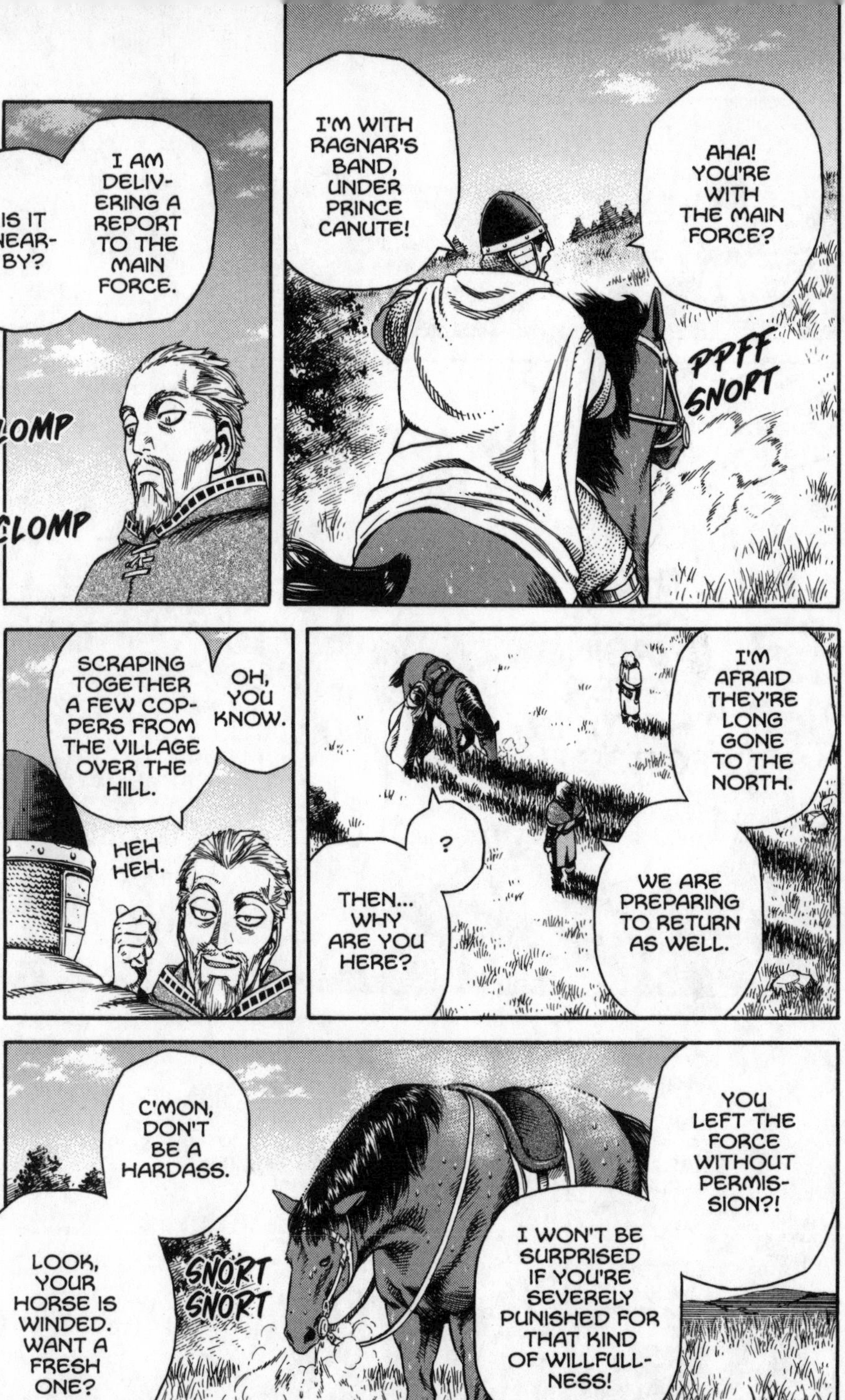
AHA! YOU'RE WITH THE MAIN FORCE?
I'M WITH RAGNAR'S BAND, UNDER PRINCE CANUTE!
PPFF SNORT
I AM DELIVERING A REPORT TO THE MAIN FORCE.
IS IT NEARBY?
CLOMP
CLOMP
I'M AFRAID THEY'RE LONG GONE TO THE NORTH.
WE ARE PREPARING TO RETURN AS WELL.
?
THEN... WHY ARE YOU HERE?
OH, YOU KNOW.
SCRAPING TOGETHER A FEW COPPERS FROM THE VILLAGE OVER THE HILL.
HEH HEH.
YOU LEFT THE FORCE WITHOUT PERMISSION?!
I WON'T BE SURPRISED IF YOU'RE SEVERELY PUNISHED FOR THAT KIND OF WILLFULLNESS!
SNORT SNORT
C'MON, DON'T BE A HARDASS.
LOOK, YOUR HORSE IS WINDED. WANT A FRESH ONE?

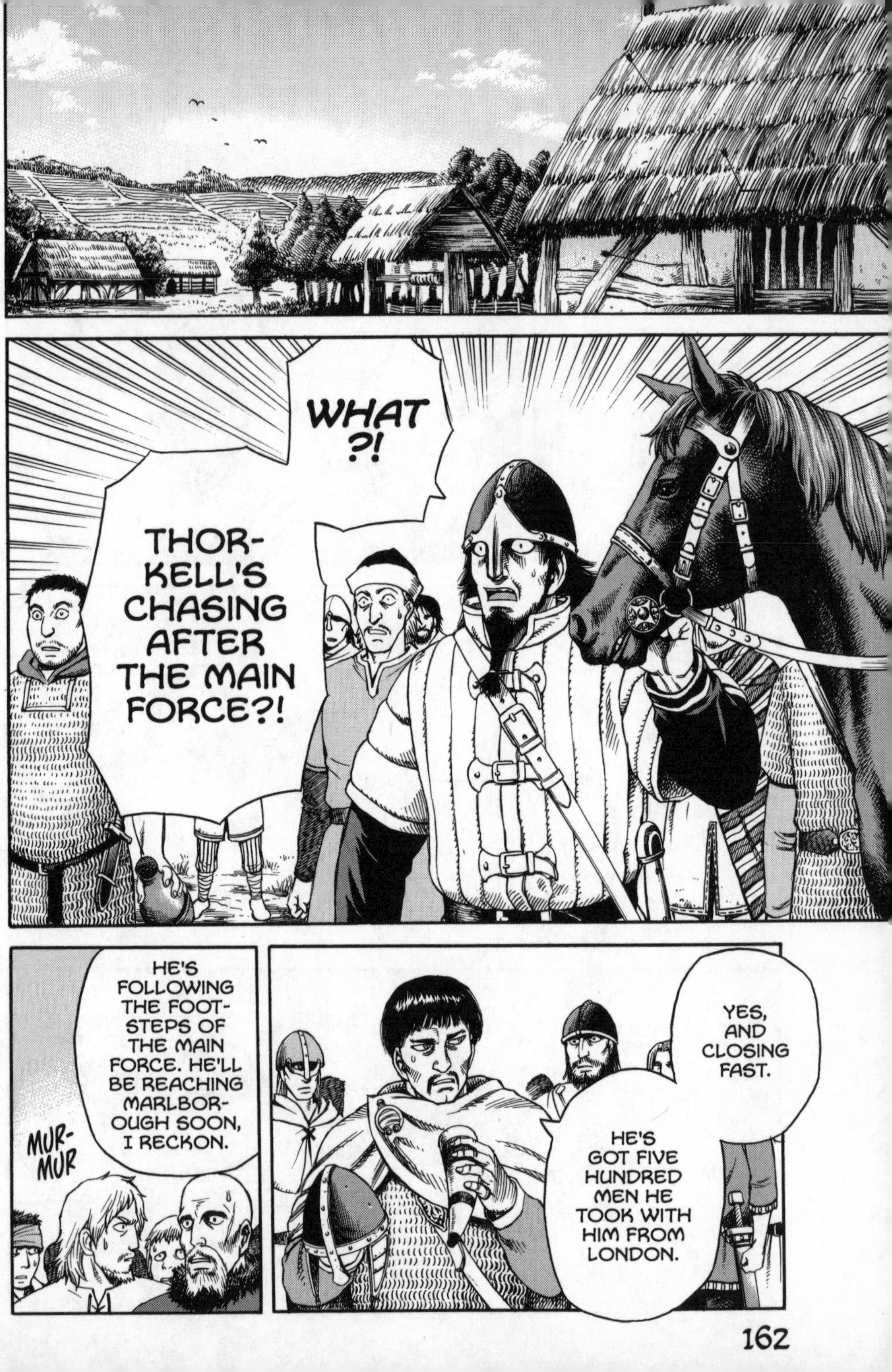
WHAT ?!
THOR-KELL'S CHASING AFTER THE MAIN FORCE?!
YES, AND CLOSING FAST.
HE'S GOT FIVE HUNDRED MEN HE TOOK WITH HIM FROM LONDON.
HE'S FOLLOWING THE FOOT-STEPS OF THE MAIN FORCE. HE'LL BE REACHING MARLBOR-OUGH SOON, I RECKON.
MUR-MUR

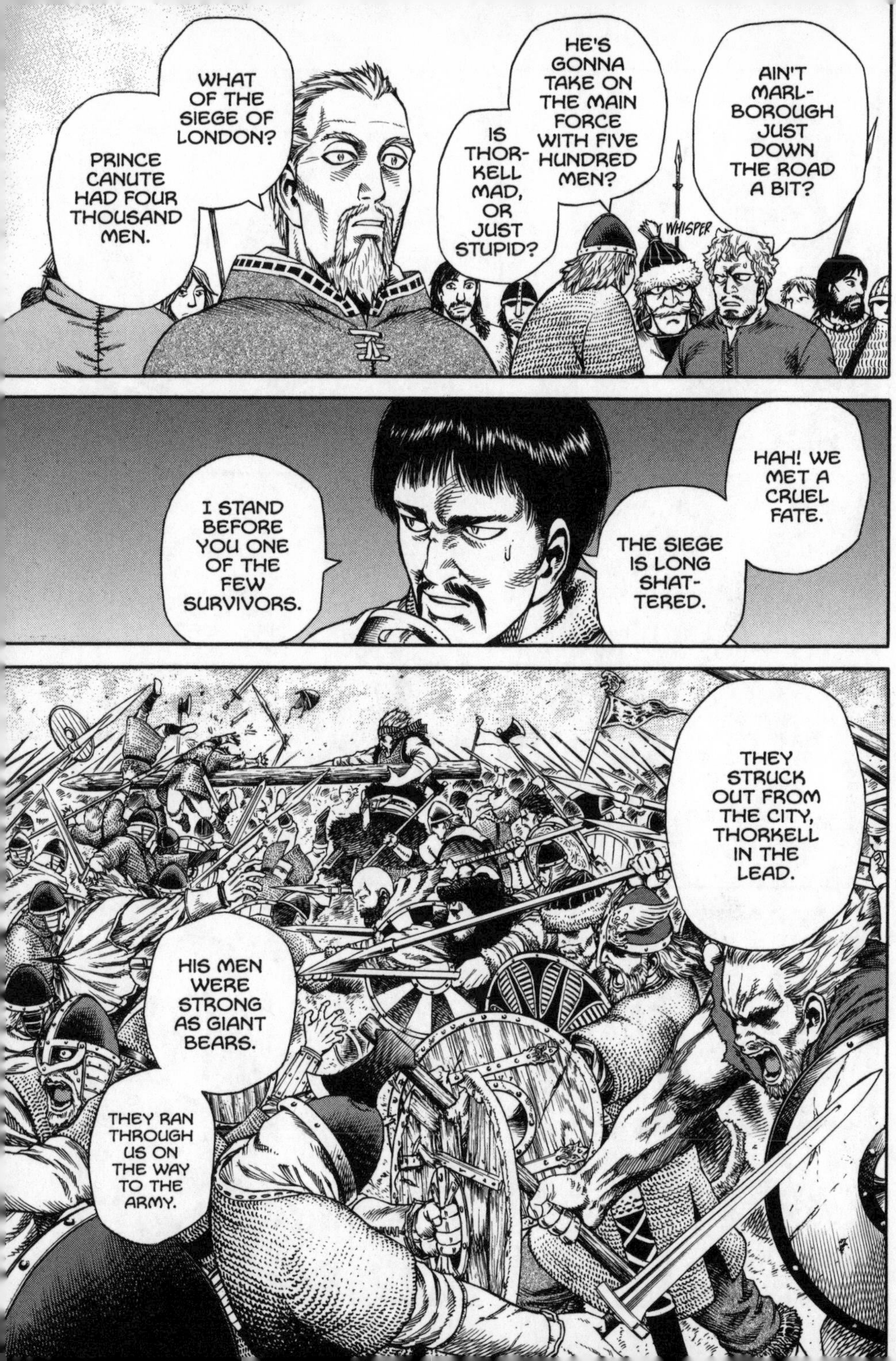
AIN'T MARL-BOROUGH JUST DOWN THE ROAD A BIT?
WHISPER
HE'S GONNA TAKE ON THE MAIN FORCE WITH FIVE HUNDRED MEN?
IS THOR-KELL MAD, OR JUST STUPID?
WHAT OF THE SIEGE OF LONDON?
PRINCE CANUTE HAD FOUR THOUSAND MEN.
HAH! WE MET A CRUEL FATE.
THE SIEGE IS LONG SHAT-TERED.
I STAND BEFORE YOU ONE OF THE FEW SURVIVORS.
THEY STRUCK OUT FROM THE CITY, THORKELL IN THE LEAD.
HIS MEN WERE STRONG AS GIANT BEARS.
THEY RAN THROUGH US ON THE WAY TO THE ARMY.

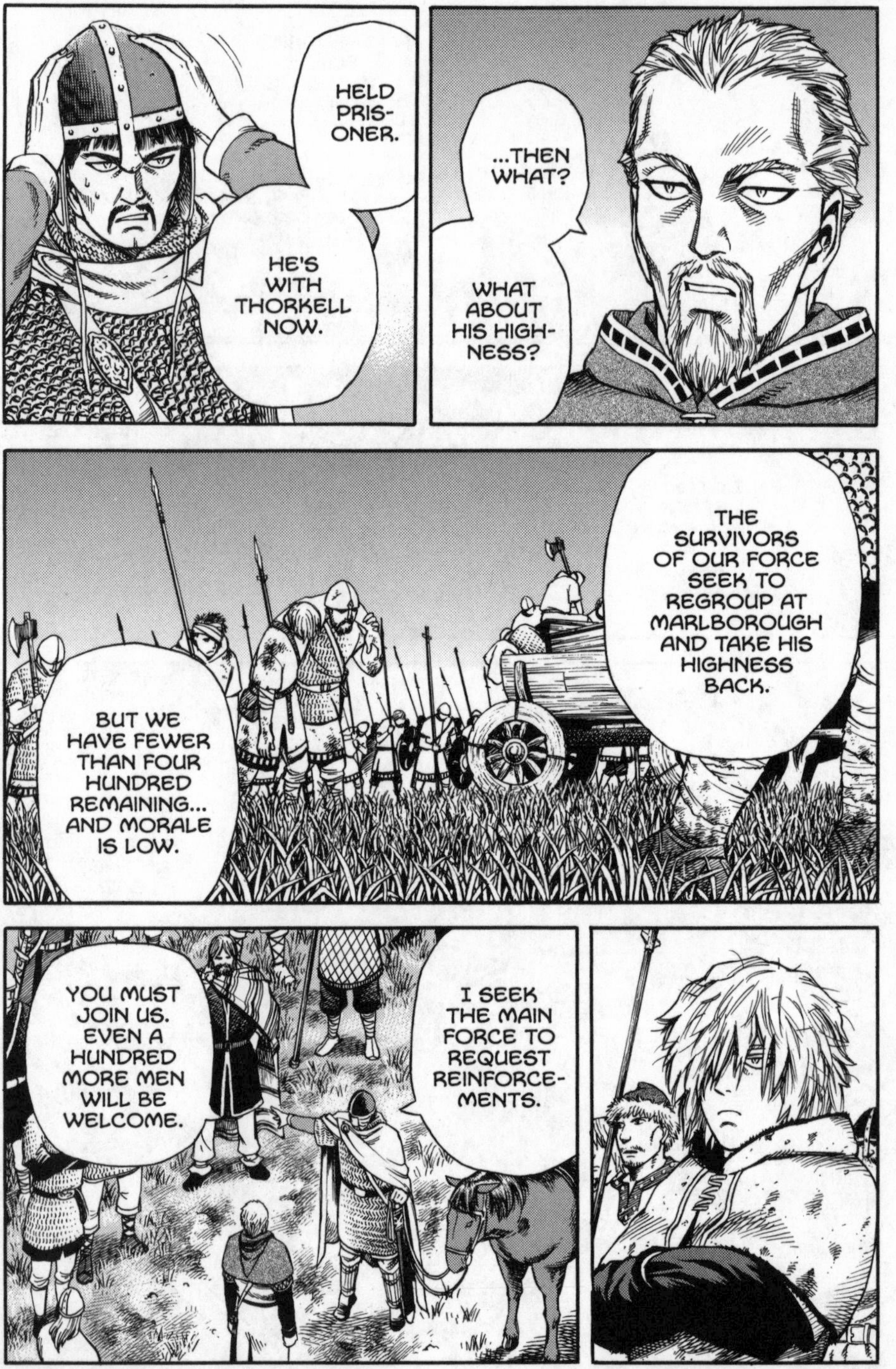
...THEN WHAT?
WHAT ABOUT HIS HIGH-NESS?
HELD PRIS-ONER.
HE'S WITH THORKELL NOW.
THE SURVIVORS OF OUR FORCE SEEK TO REGROUP AT MARLBOROUGH AND TAKE HIS HIGHNESS BACK.
BUT WE HAVE FEWER THAN FOUR HUNDRED REMAINING... AND MORALE IS LOW.
I SEEK THE MAIN FORCE TO REQUEST REINFORCE-MENTS.
YOU MUST JOIN US. EVEN A HUNDRED MORE MEN WILL BE WELCOME.

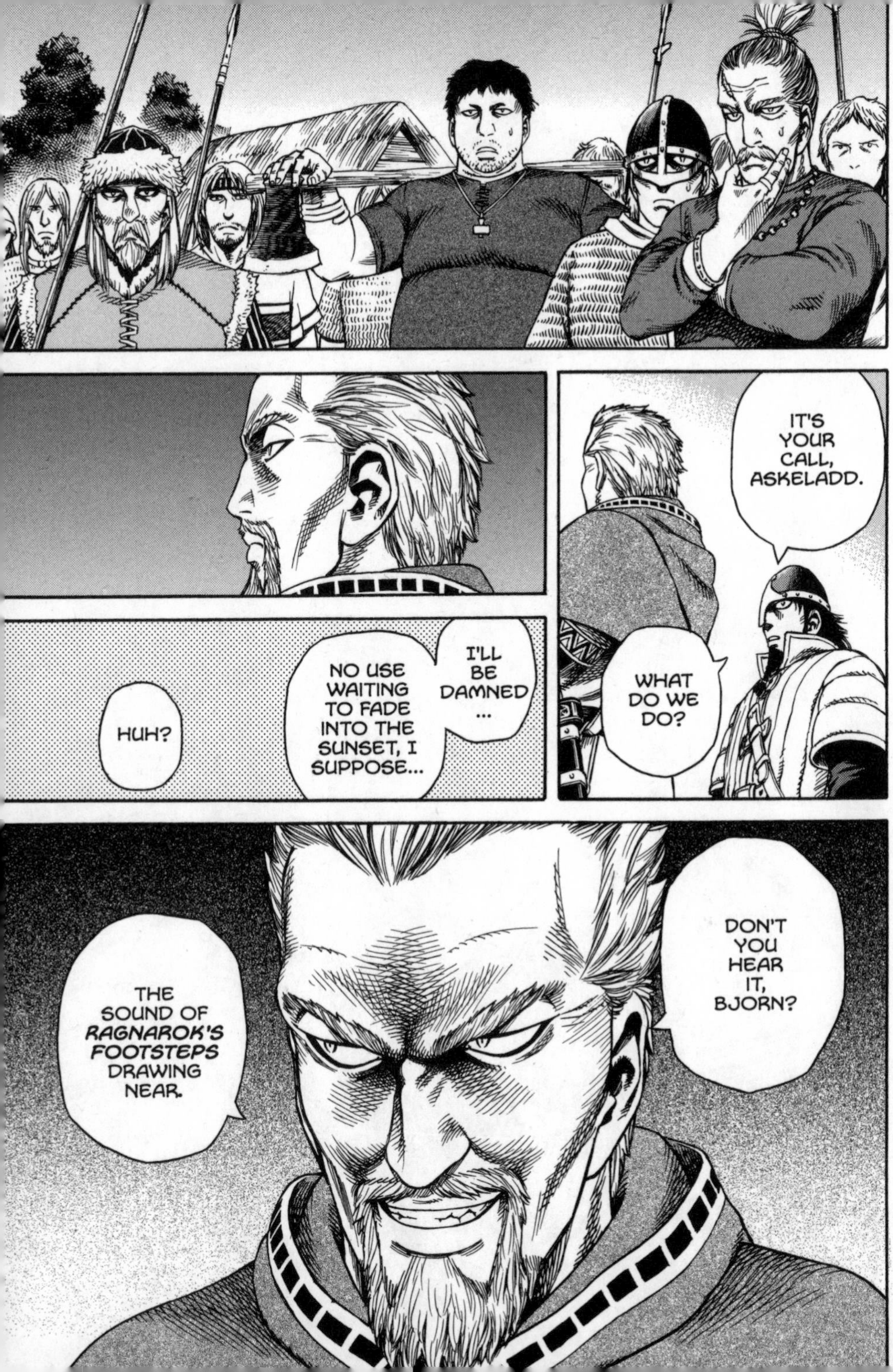
IT'S YOUR CALL, ASKELADD.
WHAT DO WE DO?
I'LL BE DAMNED...
NO USE WAITING TO FADE INTO THE SUNSET, I SUPPOSE...
HUH?
DON'T YOU HEAR IT, BJORN?
THE SOUND OF *RAGNAROK'S FOOTSTEPS* DRAWING NEAR.

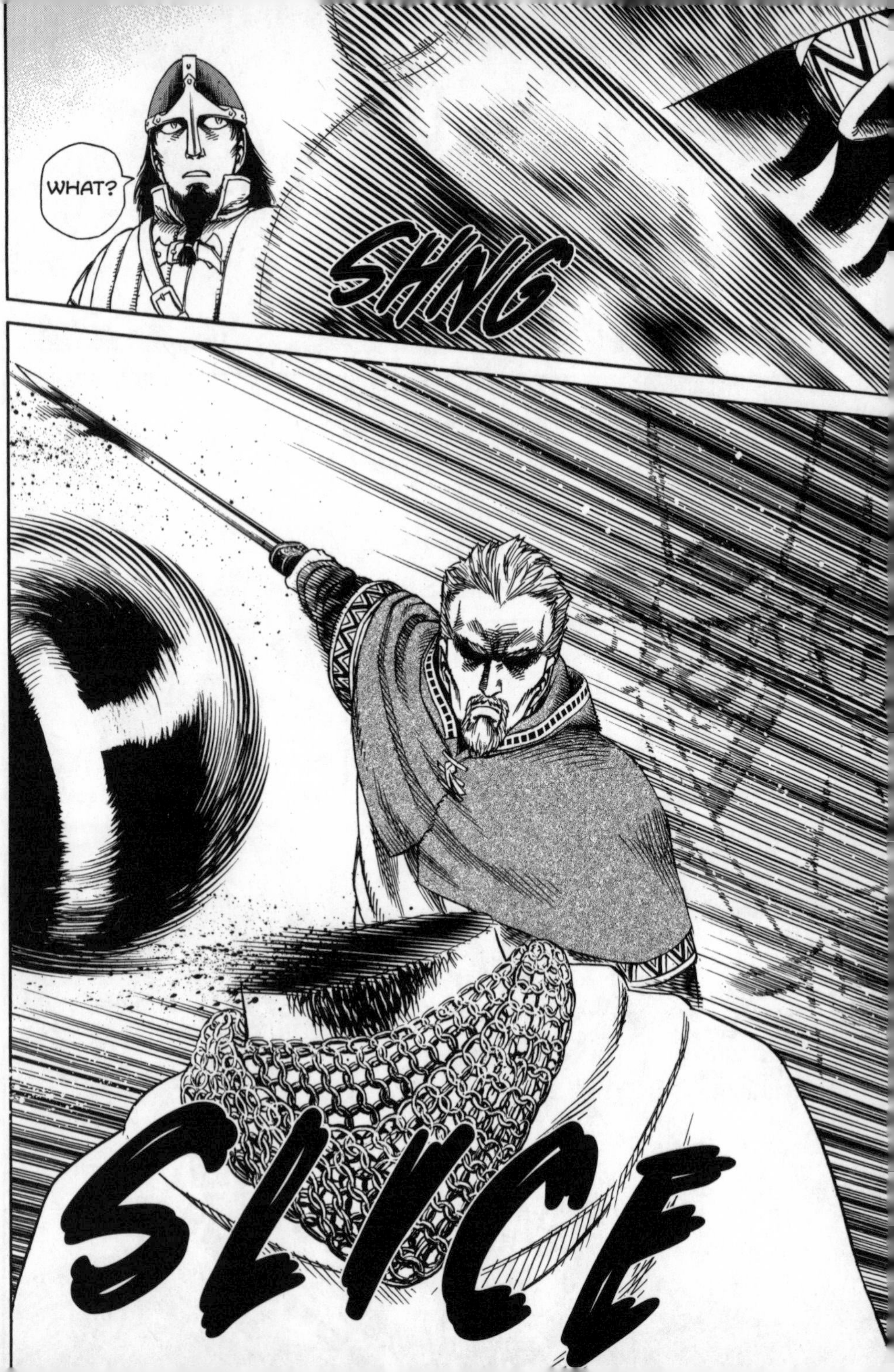
SHNG
WHAT?
SLICE

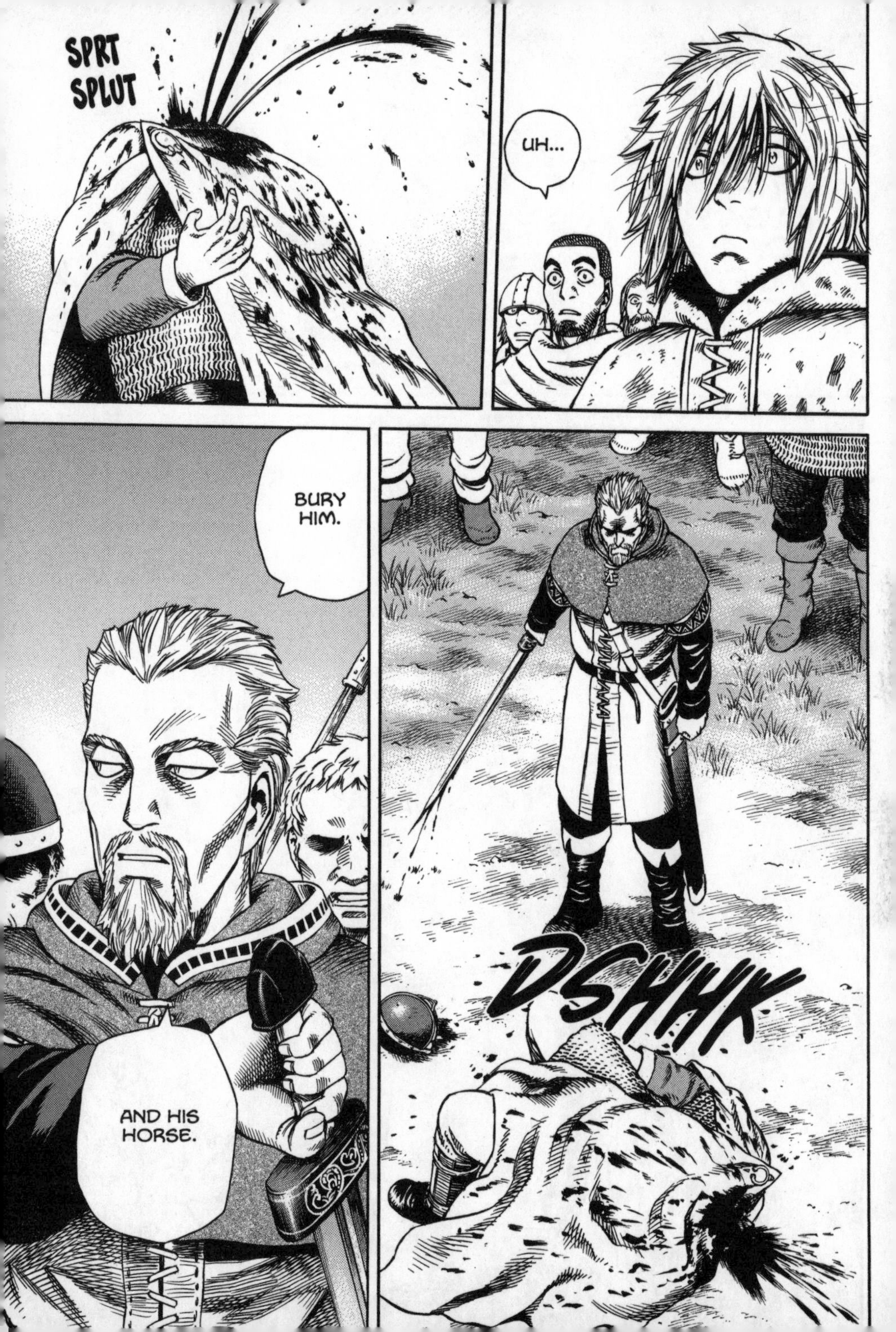
UH...
SPRT SPLUT
DSHHK
BURY HIM.
AND HIS HORSE.

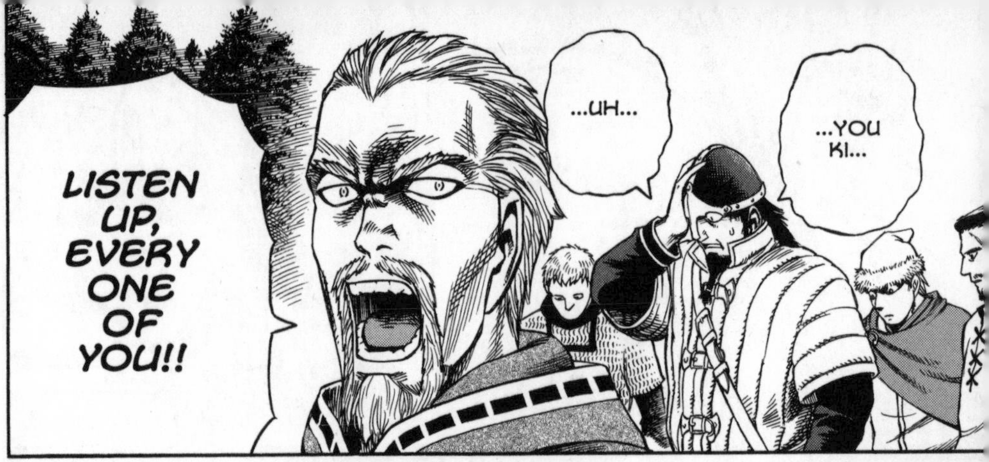
...YOU KI...
...UH...
LISTEN UP, EVERY ONE OF YOU!!

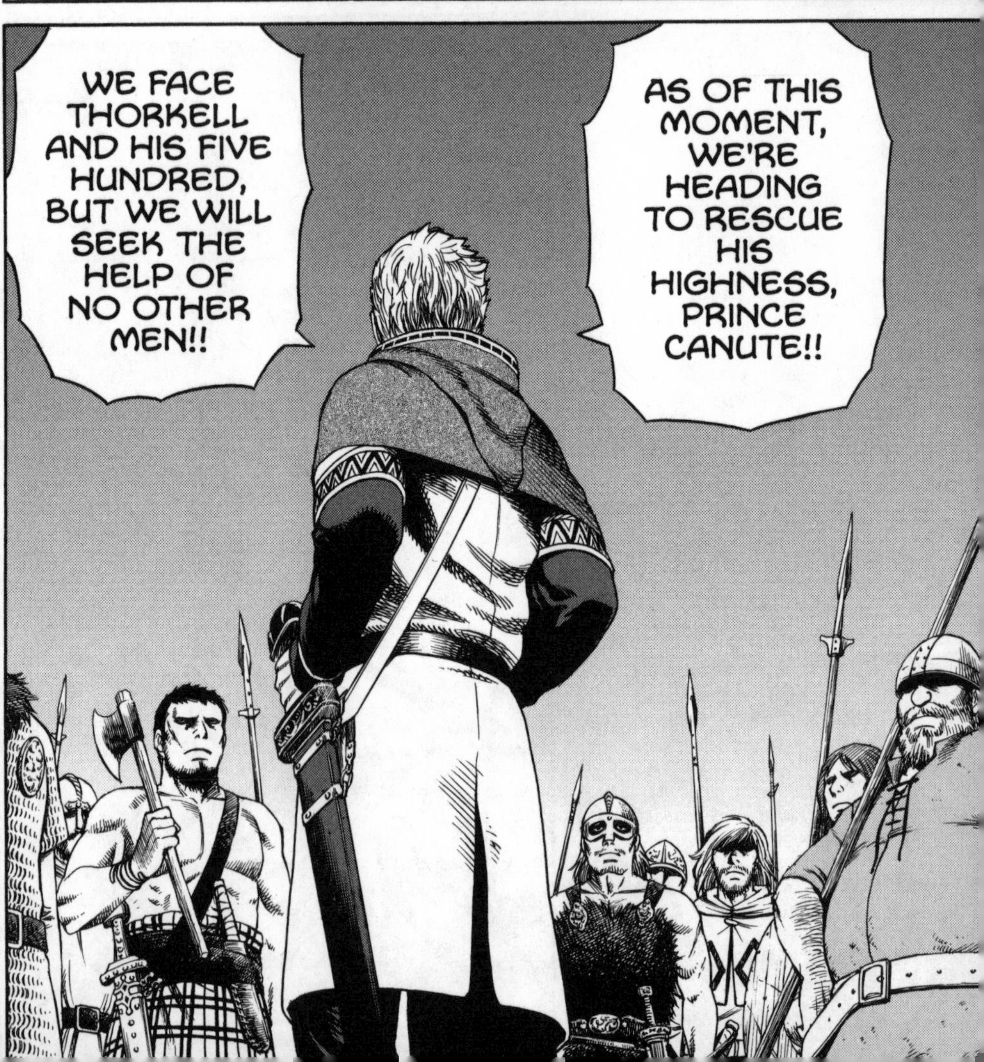
AS OF THIS MOMENT, WE'RE HEADING TO RESCUE HIS HIGHNESS, PRINCE CANUTE!!
WE FACE THORKELL AND HIS FIVE HUNDRED, BUT WE WILL SEEK THE HELP OF NO OTHER MEN!!

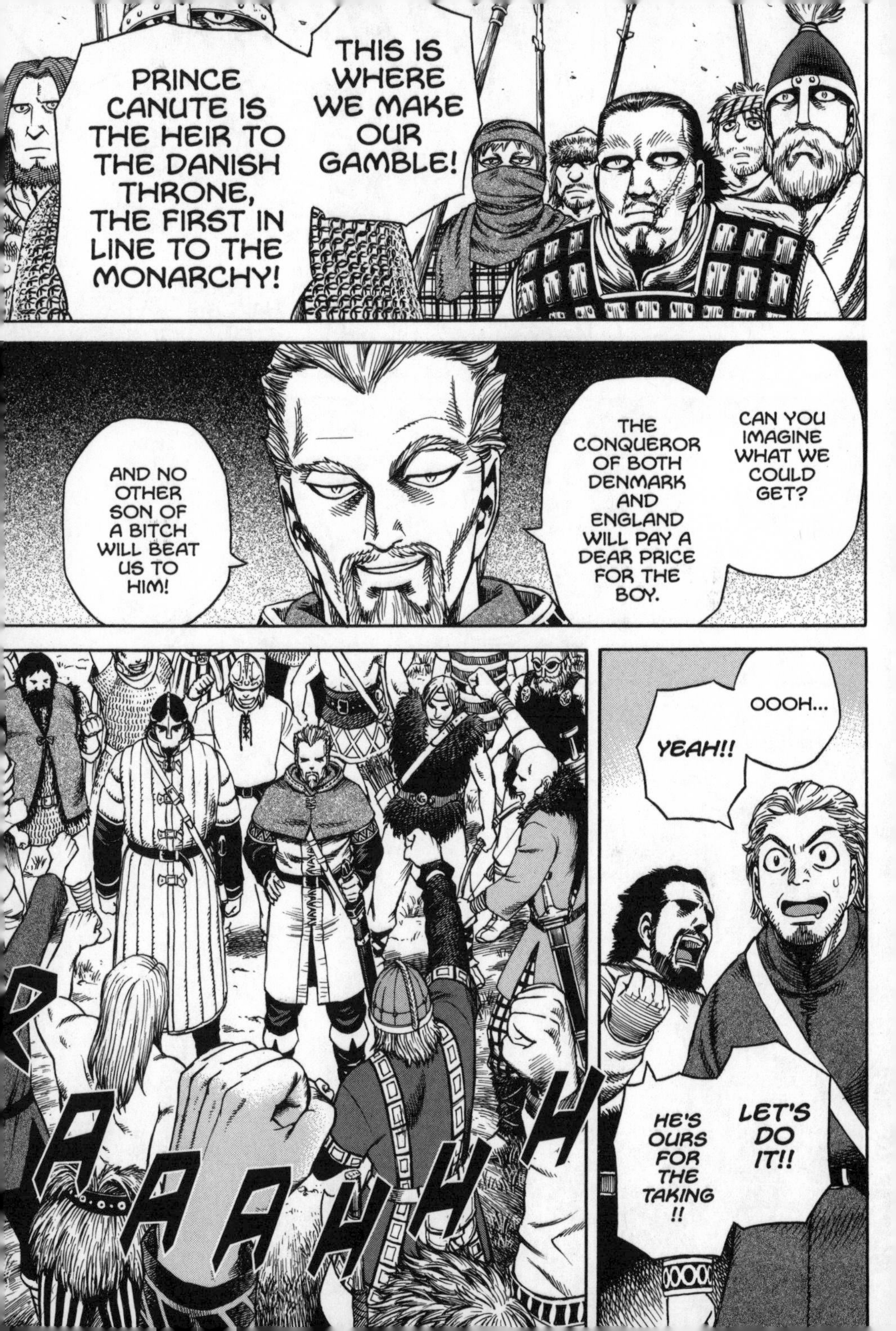
THIS IS WHERE WE MAKE OUR GAMBLE!
PRINCE CANUTE IS THE HEIR TO THE DANISH THRONE, THE FIRST IN LINE TO THE MONARCHY!
CAN YOU IMAGINE WHAT WE COULD GET?
THE CONQUEROR OF BOTH DENMARK AND ENGLAND WILL PAY A DEAR PRICE FOR THE BOY.
AND NO OTHER SON OF A BITCH WILL BEAT US TO HIM!
OOOH...
YEAH!!
LET'S DO IT!!
HE'S OURS FOR THE TAKING!!
AAAAHHHH

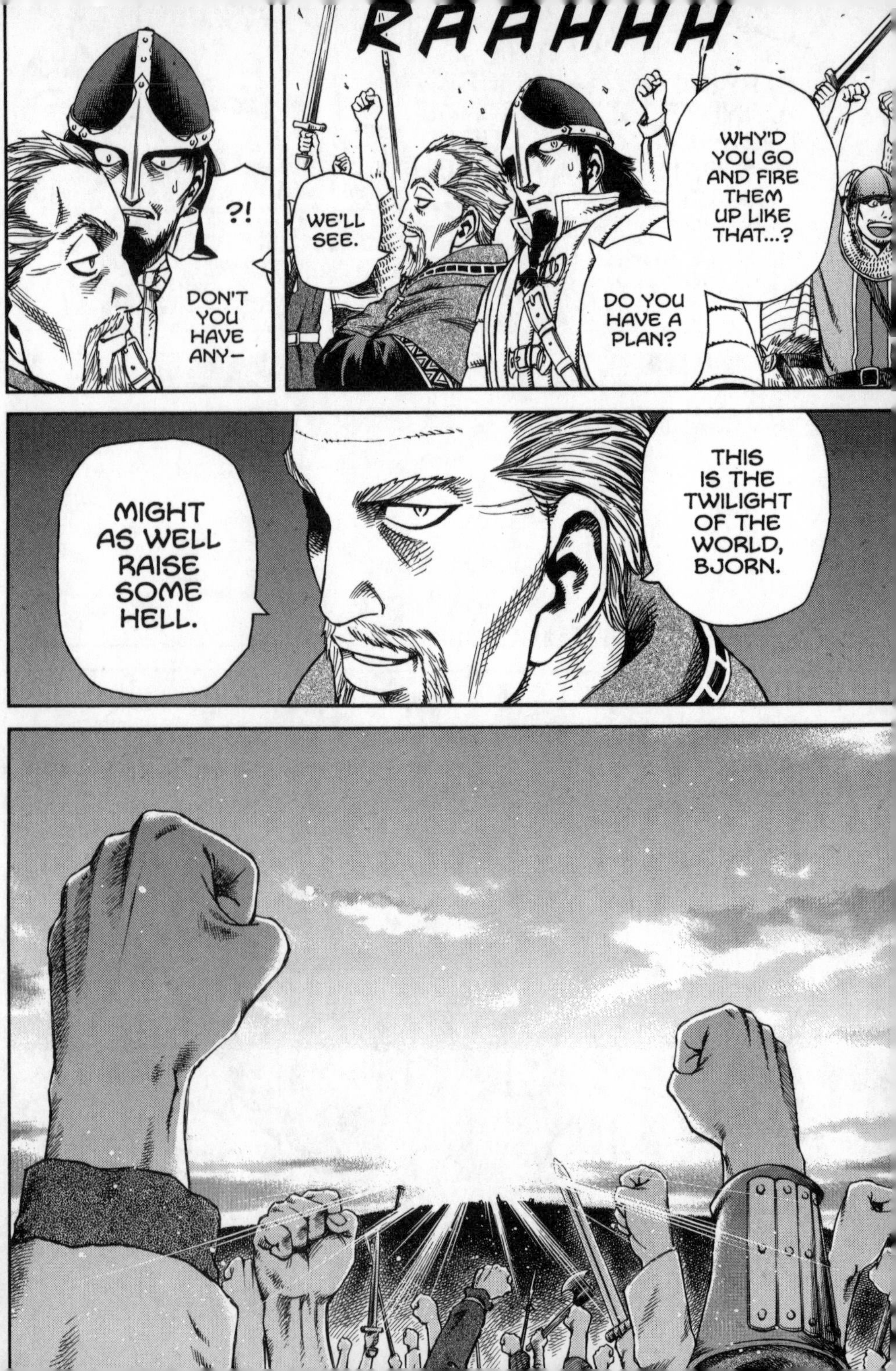
RAAHHH
WHY'D YOU GO AND FIRE THEM UP LIKE THAT...?
DO YOU HAVE A PLAN?
WE'LL SEE.
?!
DON'T YOU HAVE ANY–
THIS IS THE TWILIGHT OF THE WORLD, BJORN.
MIGHT AS WELL RAISE SOME HELL.

CHAPTER 20 - END

CHAPTER 21: VALHALLA

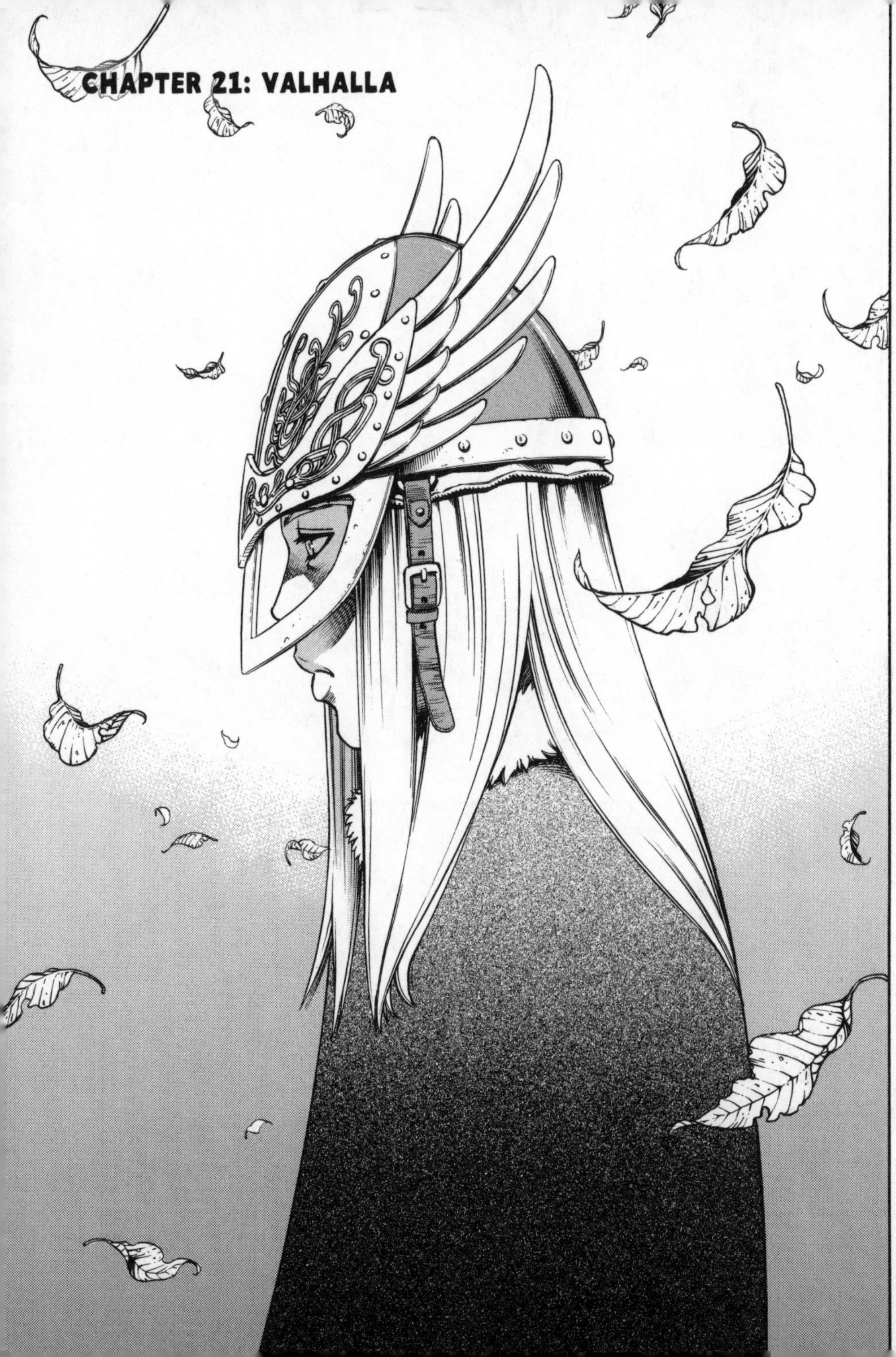

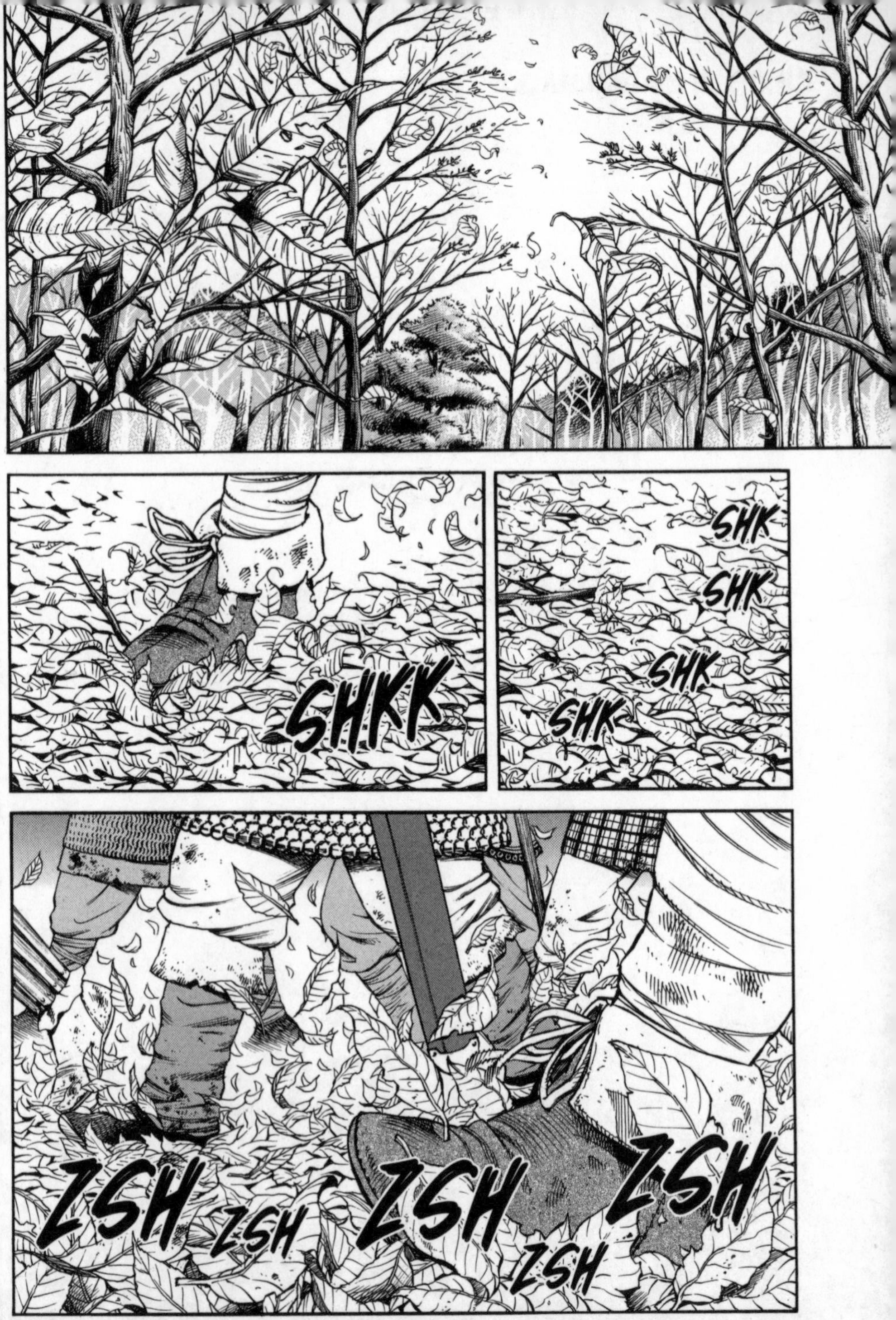
SHK
SHK
SHK
SHK
SHKK
ZSH
ZSH
ZSH
ZSH
ZSH

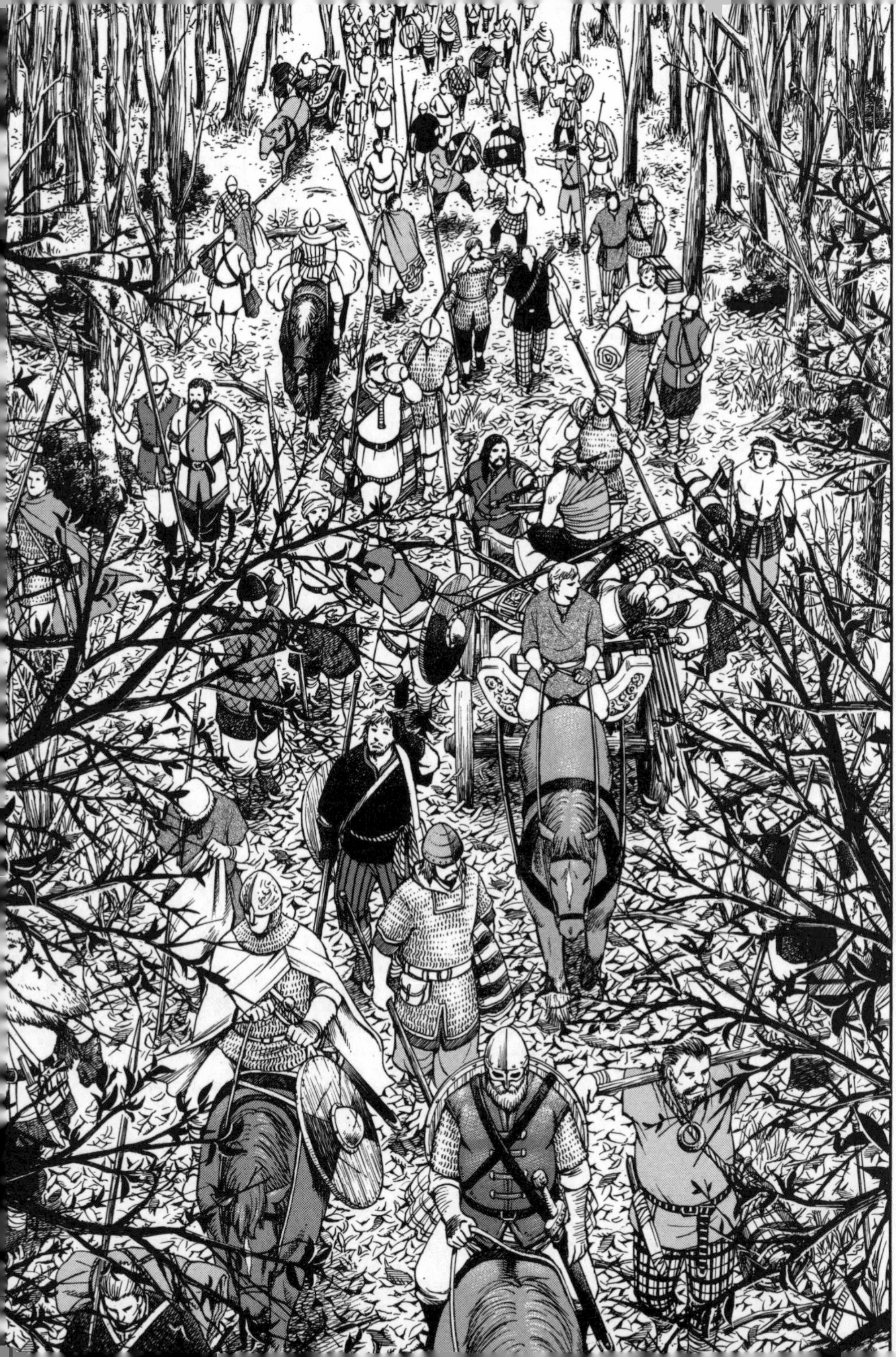

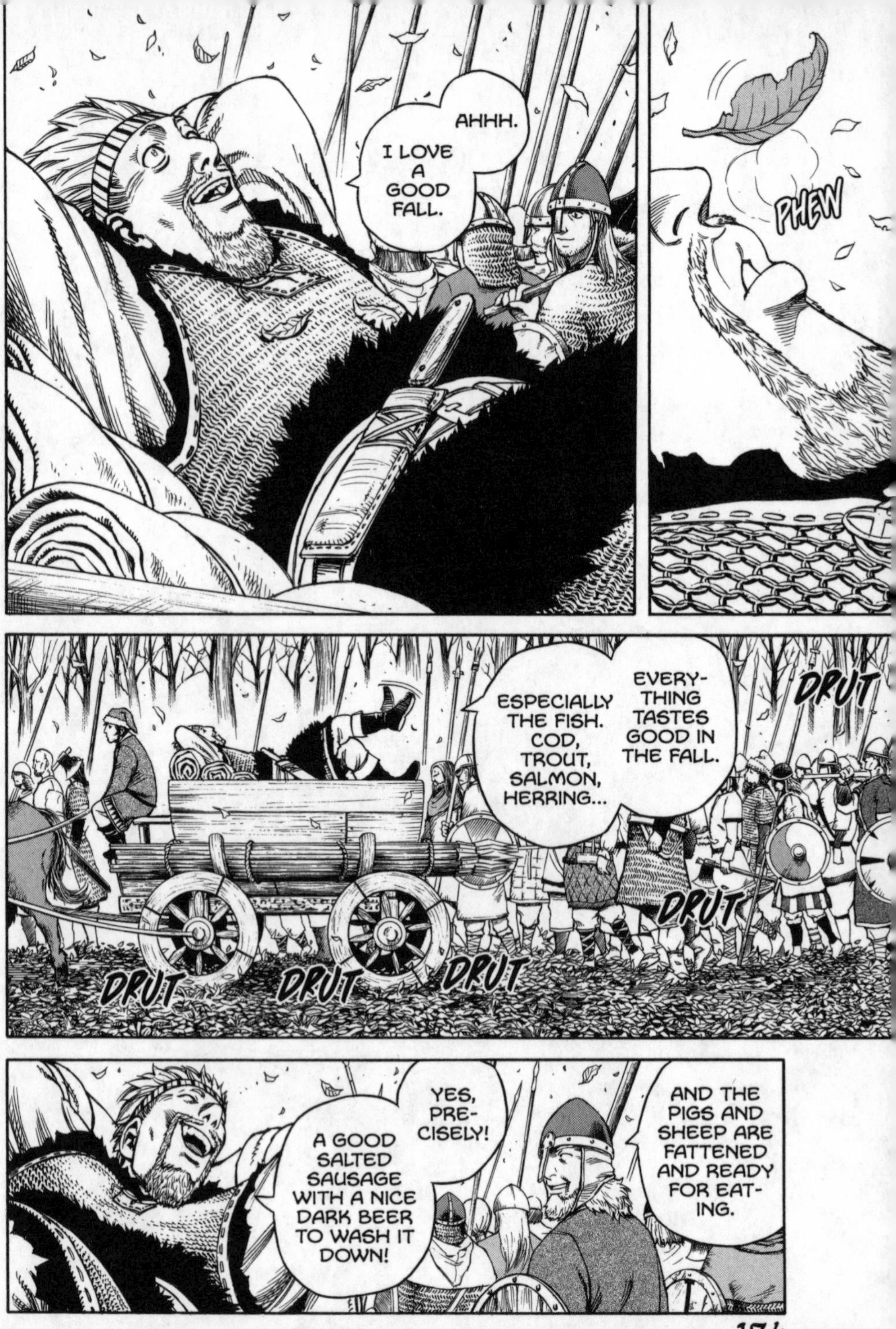
PHEW
AHHH.
I LOVE A GOOD FALL.
EVERY-THING TASTES GOOD IN THE FALL.
ESPECIALLY THE FISH. COD, TROUT, SALMON, HERRING...
DRUT
DRUT
DRUT
DRUT
DRUT
AND THE PIGS AND SHEEP ARE FATTENED AND READY FOR EAT-ING.
YES, PRE-CISELY!
A GOOD SALTED SAUSAGE WITH A NICE DARK BEER TO WASH IT DOWN!

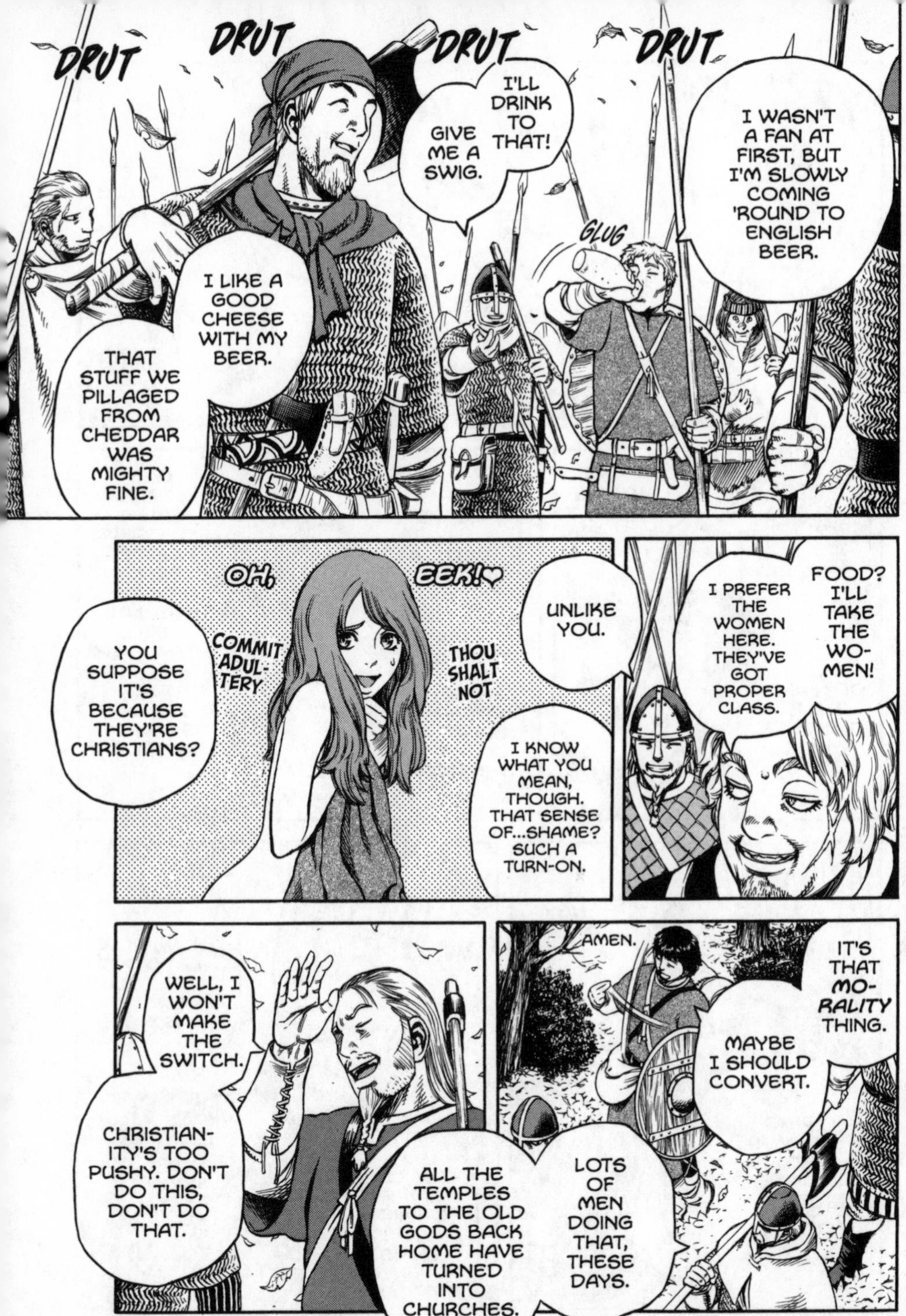
DRUT
DRUT
DRUT
DRUT
I WASN'T A FAN AT FIRST, BUT I'M SLOWLY COMING 'ROUND TO ENGLISH BEER.
I'LL DRINK TO THAT!
GIVE ME A SWIG.
GLUG
I LIKE A GOOD CHEESE WITH MY BEER.
THAT STUFF WE PILLAGED FROM CHEDDAR WAS MIGHTY FINE.
FOOD? I'LL TAKE THE WO-MEN!
I PREFER THE WOMEN HERE. THEY'VE GOT PROPER CLASS.
UNLIKE YOU.
I KNOW WHAT YOU MEAN, THOUGH. THAT SENSE OF...SHAME? SUCH A TURN-ON.
EEK!♡
THOU SHALT NOT
OH,
COMMIT ADUL-TERY
YOU SUPPOSE IT'S BECAUSE THEY'RE CHRISTIANS?
IT'S THAT MO-RALITY THING.
AMEN.
MAYBE I SHOULD CONVERT.
LOTS OF MEN DOING THAT, THESE DAYS.
ALL THE TEMPLES TO THE OLD GODS BACK HOME HAVE TURNED INTO CHURCHES.
WELL, I WON'T MAKE THE SWITCH.
CHRISTIAN-ITY'S TOO PUSHY. DON'T DO THIS, DON'T DO THAT.

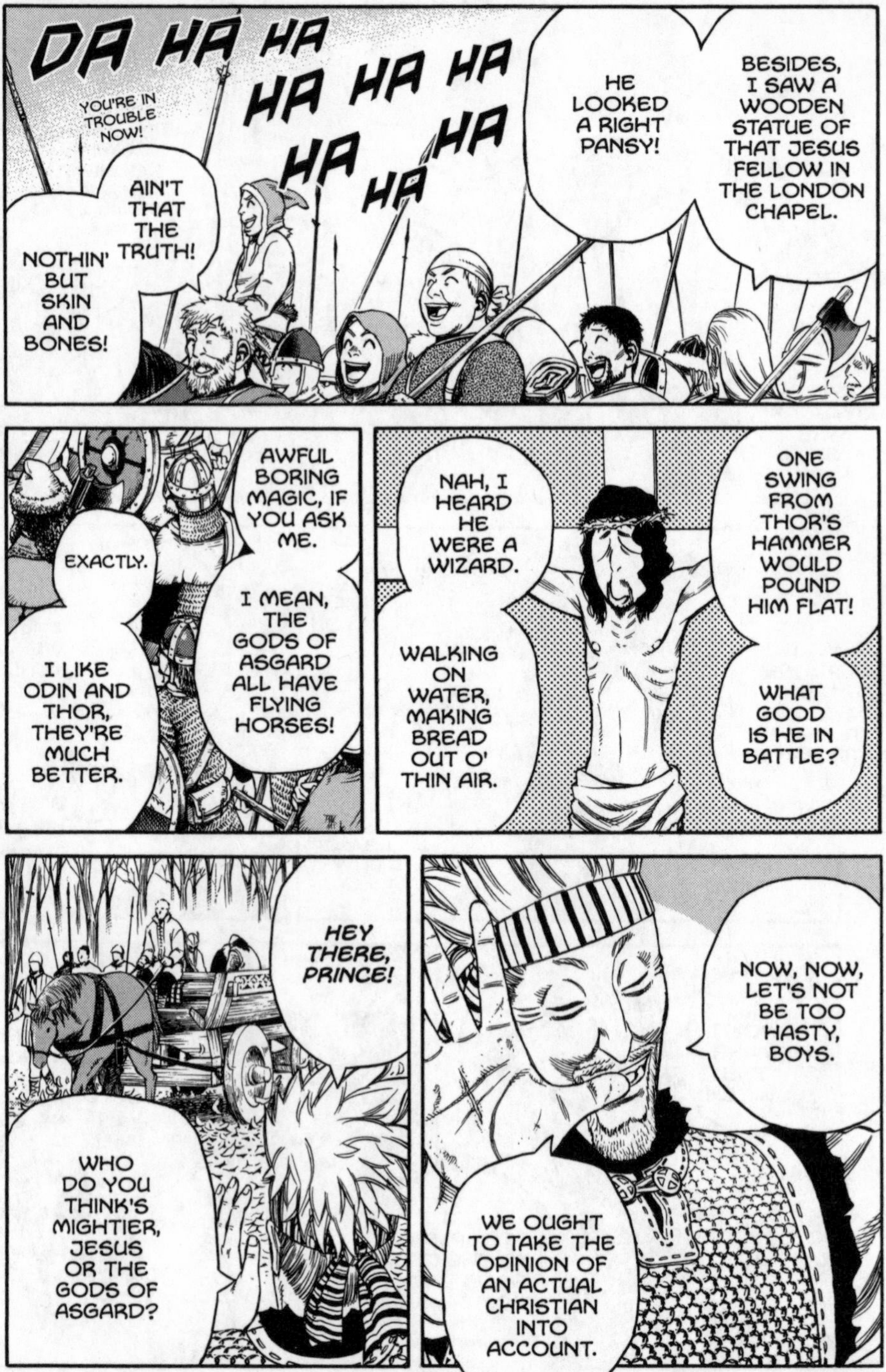
BESIDES, I SAW A WOODEN STATUE OF THAT JESUS FELLOW IN THE LONDON CHAPEL.
HE LOOKED A RIGHT PANSY!
DA HA HA HA HA HA HA HA HA HA
YOU'RE IN TROUBLE NOW!
AIN'T THAT THE TRUTH!
NOTHIN' BUT SKIN AND BONES!
ONE SWING FROM THOR'S HAMMER WOULD POUND HIM FLAT!
WHAT GOOD IS HE IN BATTLE?
NAH, I HEARD HE WERE A WIZARD.
WALKING ON WATER, MAKING BREAD OUT O' THIN AIR.
AWFUL BORING MAGIC, IF YOU ASK ME.
I MEAN, THE GODS OF ASGARD ALL HAVE FLYING HORSES!
EXACTLY.
I LIKE ODIN AND THOR, THEY'RE MUCH BETTER.
NOW, NOW, LET'S NOT BE TOO HASTY, BOYS.
WE OUGHT TO TAKE THE OPINION OF AN ACTUAL CHRISTIAN INTO ACCOUNT.
HEY THERE, PRINCE!
WHO DO YOU THINK'S MIGHTIER, JESUS OR THE GODS OF ASGARD?

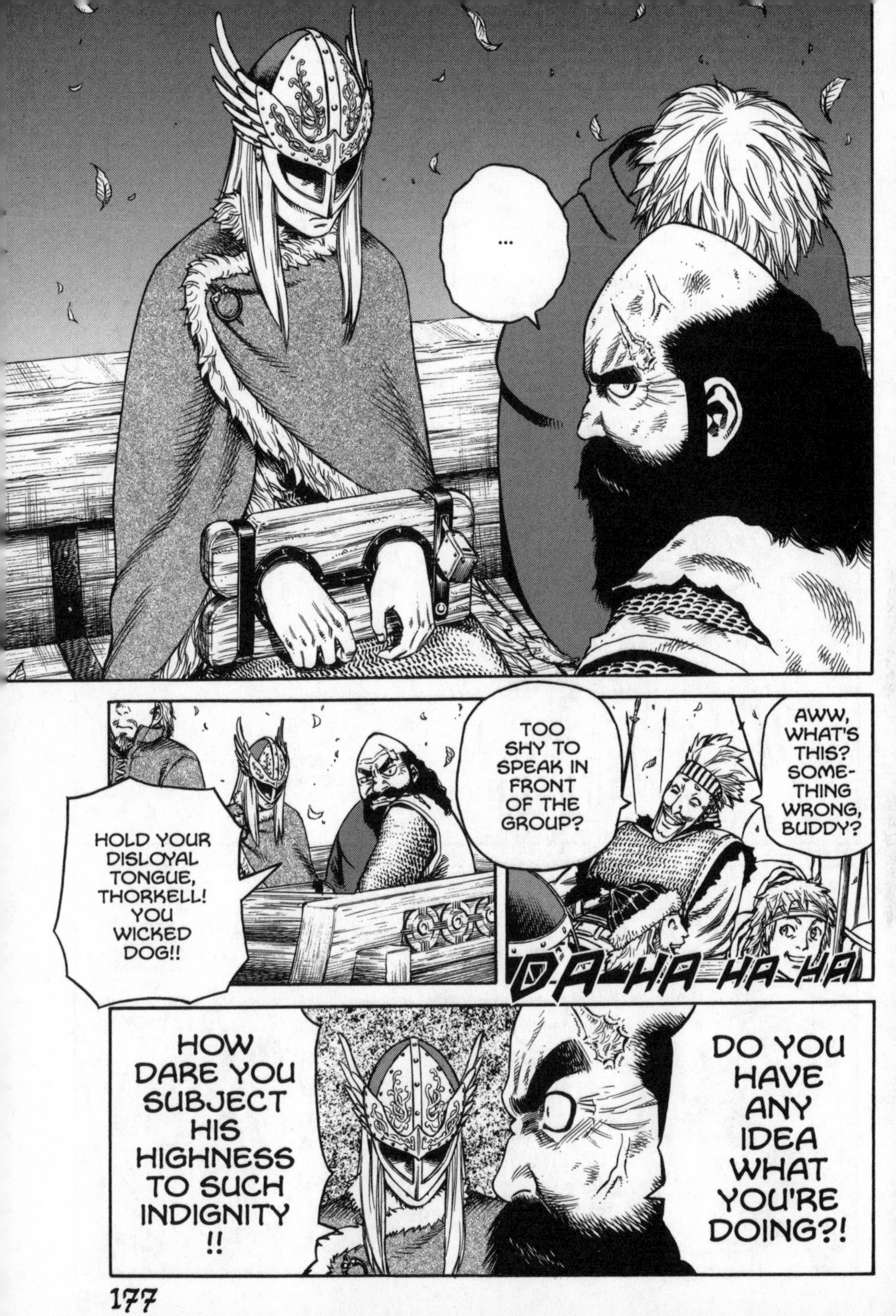
...
AWW, WHAT'S THIS? SOMETHING WRONG, BUDDY?
TOO SHY TO SPEAK IN FRONT OF THE GROUP?
DA-HA-HA-HA
HOLD YOUR DISLOYAL TONGUE, THORKELL! YOU WICKED DOG!!
DO YOU HAVE ANY IDEA WHAT YOU'RE DOING?!
HOW DARE YOU SUBJECT HIS HIGHNESS TO SUCH INDIGNITY !!

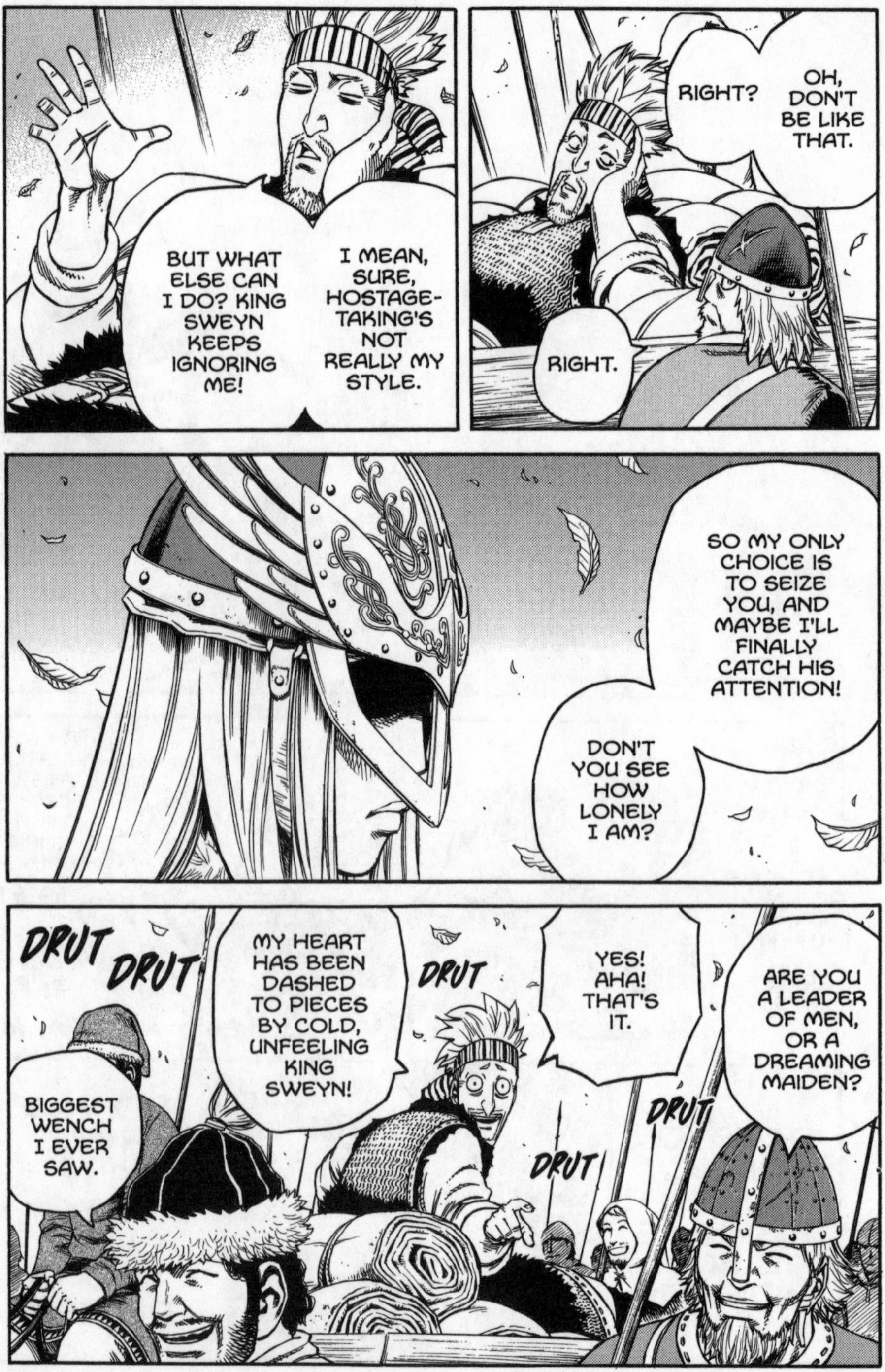
OH, DON'T BE LIKE THAT.
RIGHT?
RIGHT.
I MEAN, SURE, HOSTAGE-TAKING'S NOT REALLY MY STYLE.
BUT WHAT ELSE CAN I DO? KING SWEYN KEEPS IGNORING ME!
SO MY ONLY CHOICE IS TO SEIZE YOU, AND MAYBE I'LL FINALLY CATCH HIS ATTENTION!
DON'T YOU SEE HOW LONELY I AM?
ARE YOU A LEADER OF MEN, OR A DREAMING MAIDEN?
DRUT
DRUT
YES! AHA! THAT'S IT.
DRUT
MY HEART HAS BEEN DASHED TO PIECES BY COLD, UNFEELING KING SWEYN!
DRUT
DRUT
BIGGEST WENCH I EVER SAW.

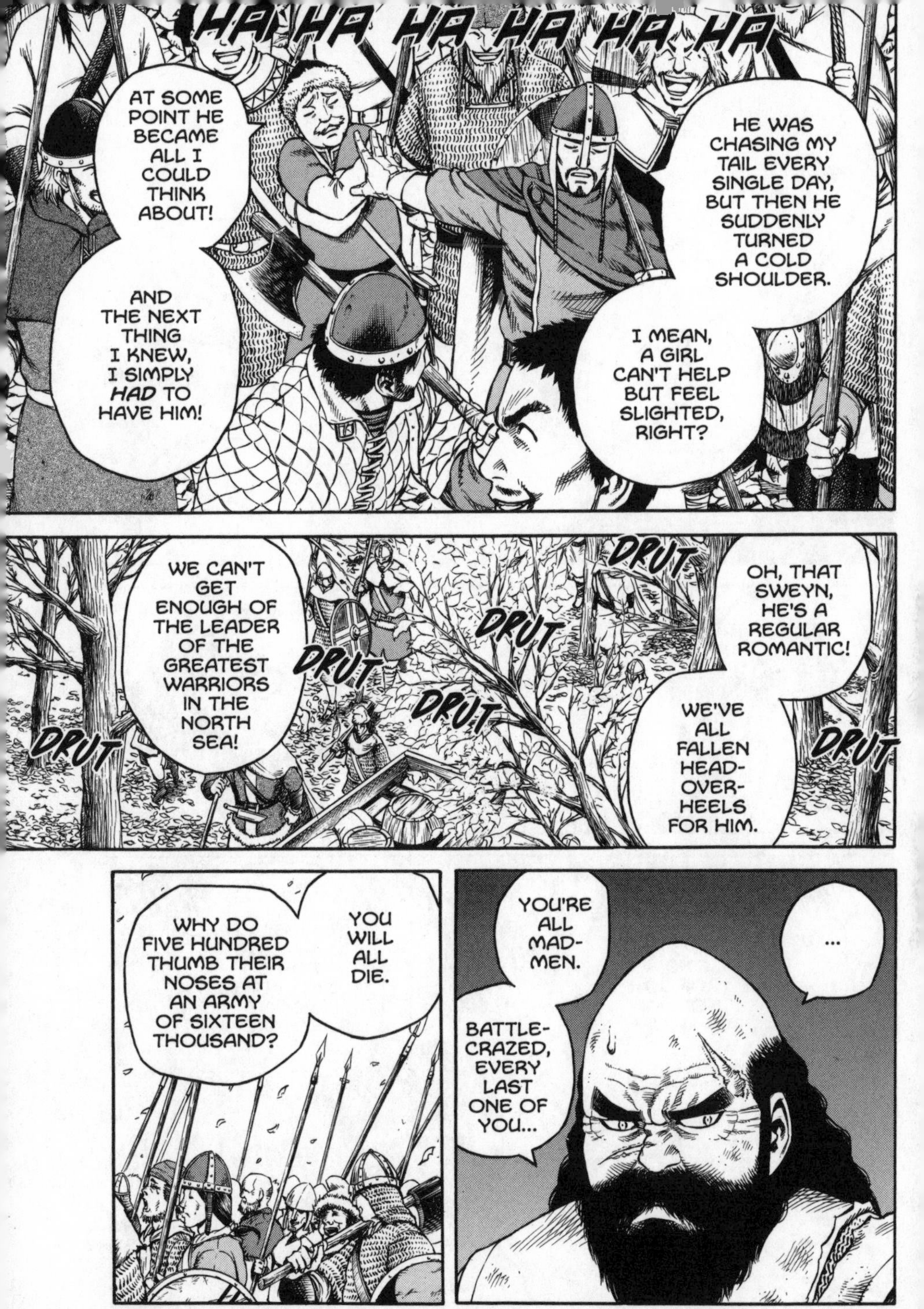
HA HA HA HA HA HA HA
HE WAS CHASING MY TAIL EVERY SINGLE DAY, BUT THEN HE SUDDENLY TURNED A COLD SHOULDER.
AT SOME POINT HE BECAME ALL I COULD THINK ABOUT!
I MEAN, A GIRL CAN'T HELP BUT FEEL SLIGHTED, RIGHT?
AND THE NEXT THING I KNEW, I SIMPLY *HAD* TO HAVE HIM!
DRUT
OH, THAT SWEYN, HE'S A REGULAR ROMANTIC!
WE'VE ALL FALLEN HEAD-OVER-HEELS FOR HIM.
DRUT
DRUT
DRUT
WE CAN'T GET ENOUGH OF THE LEADER OF THE GREATEST WARRIORS IN THE NORTH SEA!
DRUT
DRUT
...
YOU'RE ALL MAD-MEN.
BATTLE-CRAZED, EVERY LAST ONE OF YOU...
YOU WILL ALL DIE.
WHY DO FIVE HUNDRED THUMB THEIR NOSES AT AN ARMY OF SIXTEEN THOUSAND?

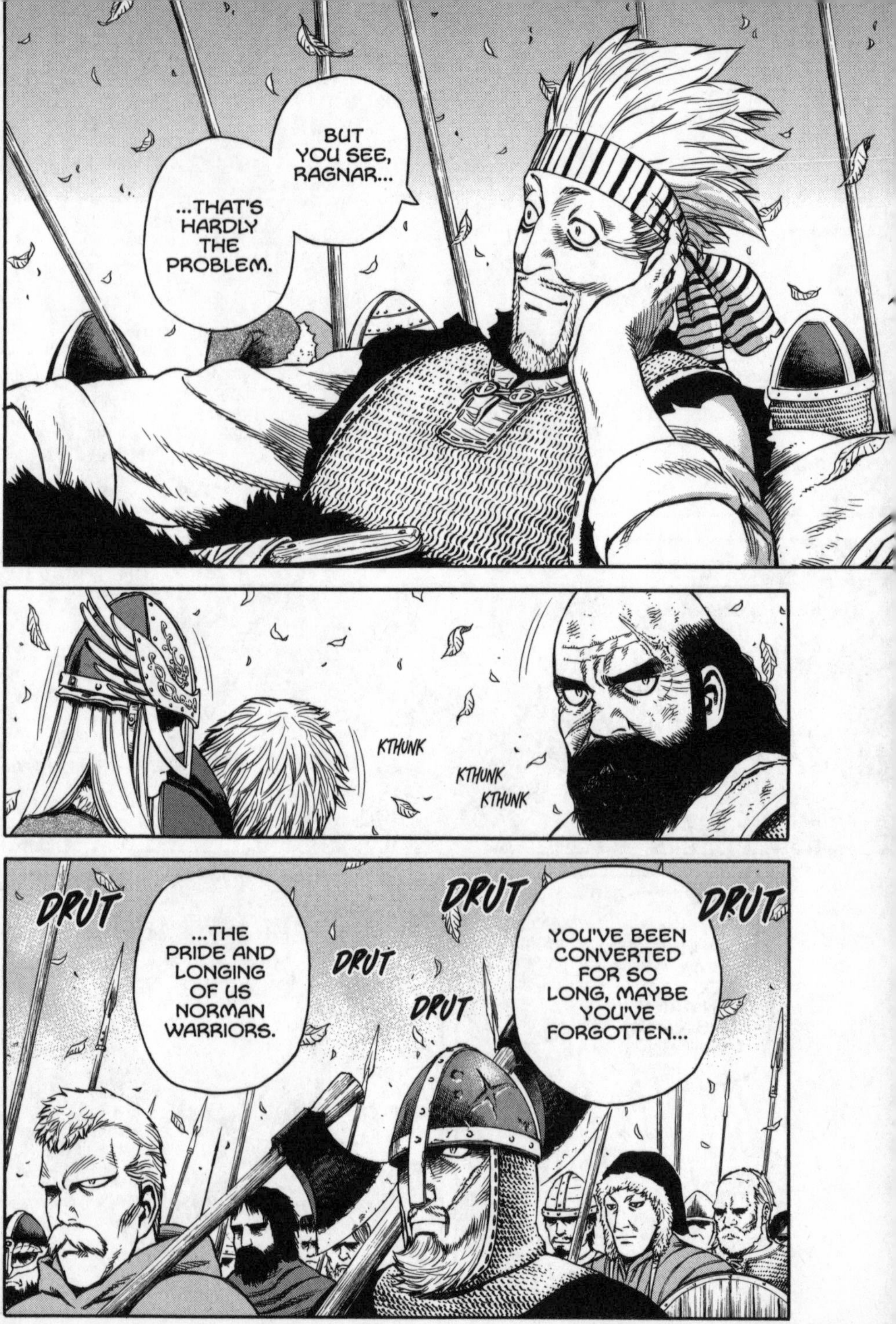
BUT YOU SEE, RAGNAR...
...THAT'S HARDLY THE PROBLEM.
KTHUNK
KTHUNK
KTHUNK
DRUT
DRUT
YOU'VE BEEN CONVERTED FOR SO LONG, MAYBE YOU'VE FORGOTTEN...
DRUT
DRUT
...THE PRIDE AND LONGING OF US NORMAN WARRIORS.
DRUT

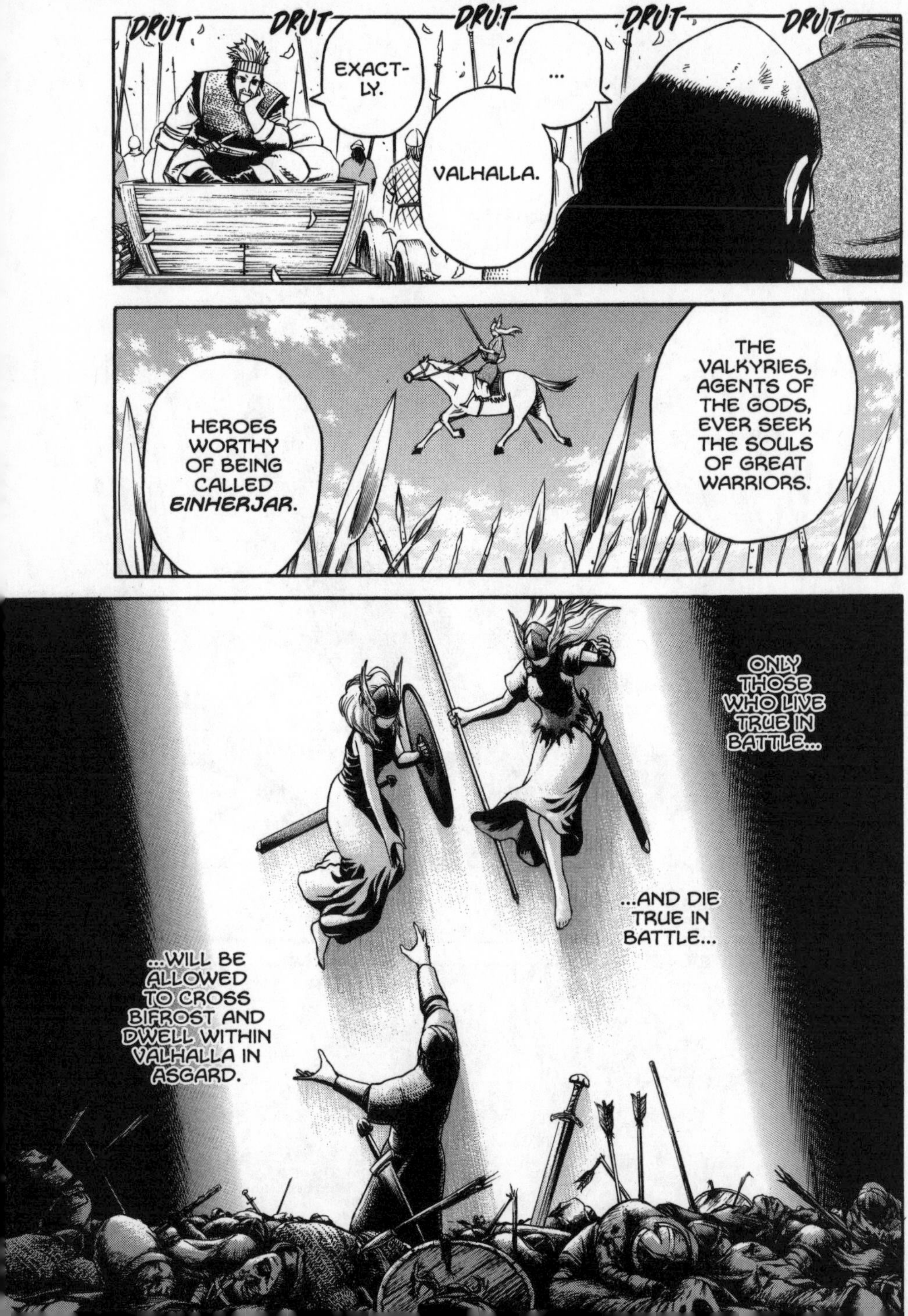
DRUT DRUT DRUT DRUT DRUT
...
VALHALLA.
EXACT-LY.
THE VALKYRIES, AGENTS OF THE GODS, EVER SEEK THE SOULS OF GREAT WARRIORS.
HEROES WORTHY OF BEING CALLED *EINHERJAR*.
ONLY THOSE WHO LIVE TRUE IN BATTLE...
...AND DIE TRUE IN BATTLE...
...WILL BE ALLOWED TO CROSS BIFROST AND DWELL WITHIN VALHALLA IN ASGARD.

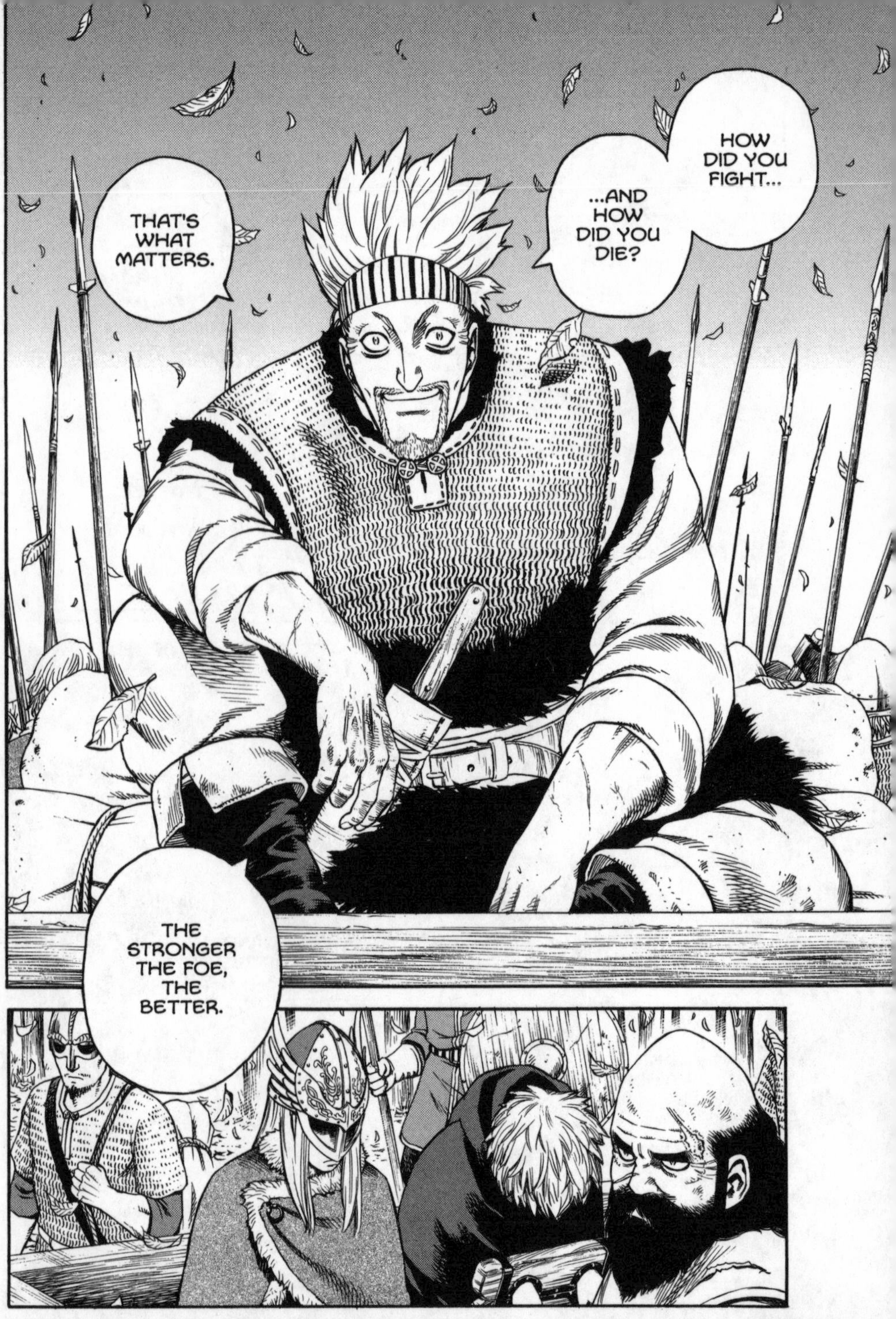
HOW DID YOU FIGHT...
...AND HOW DID YOU DIE?
THAT'S WHAT MATTERS.
THE STRONGER THE FOE, THE BETTER.

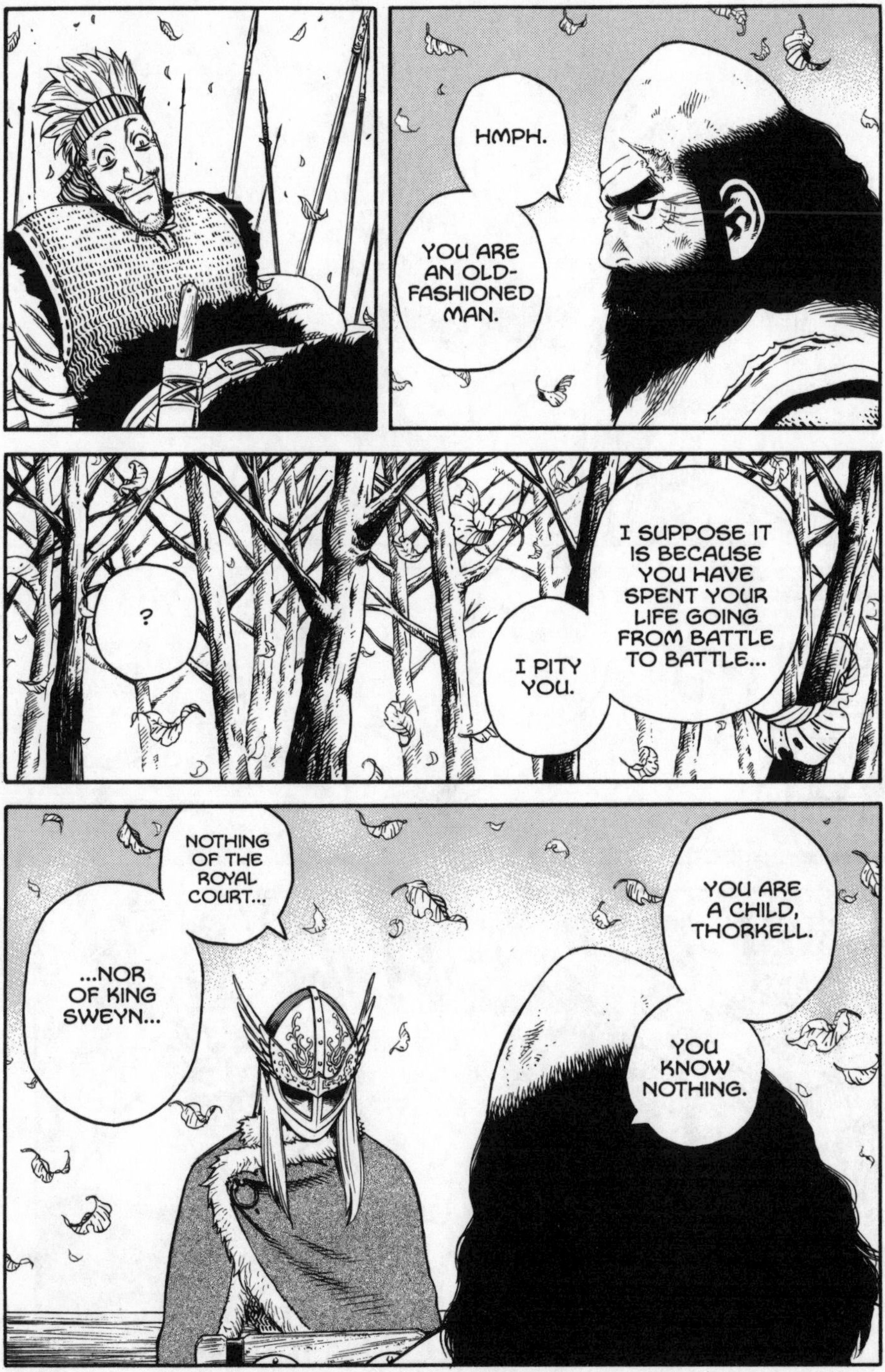
HMPH.
YOU ARE AN OLD-FASHIONED MAN.
I SUPPOSE IT IS BECAUSE YOU HAVE SPENT YOUR LIFE GOING FROM BATTLE TO BATTLE...
I PITY YOU.
?
YOU ARE A CHILD, THORKELL.
YOU KNOW NOTHING.
NOTHING OF THE ROYAL COURT...
...NOR OF KING SWEYN...

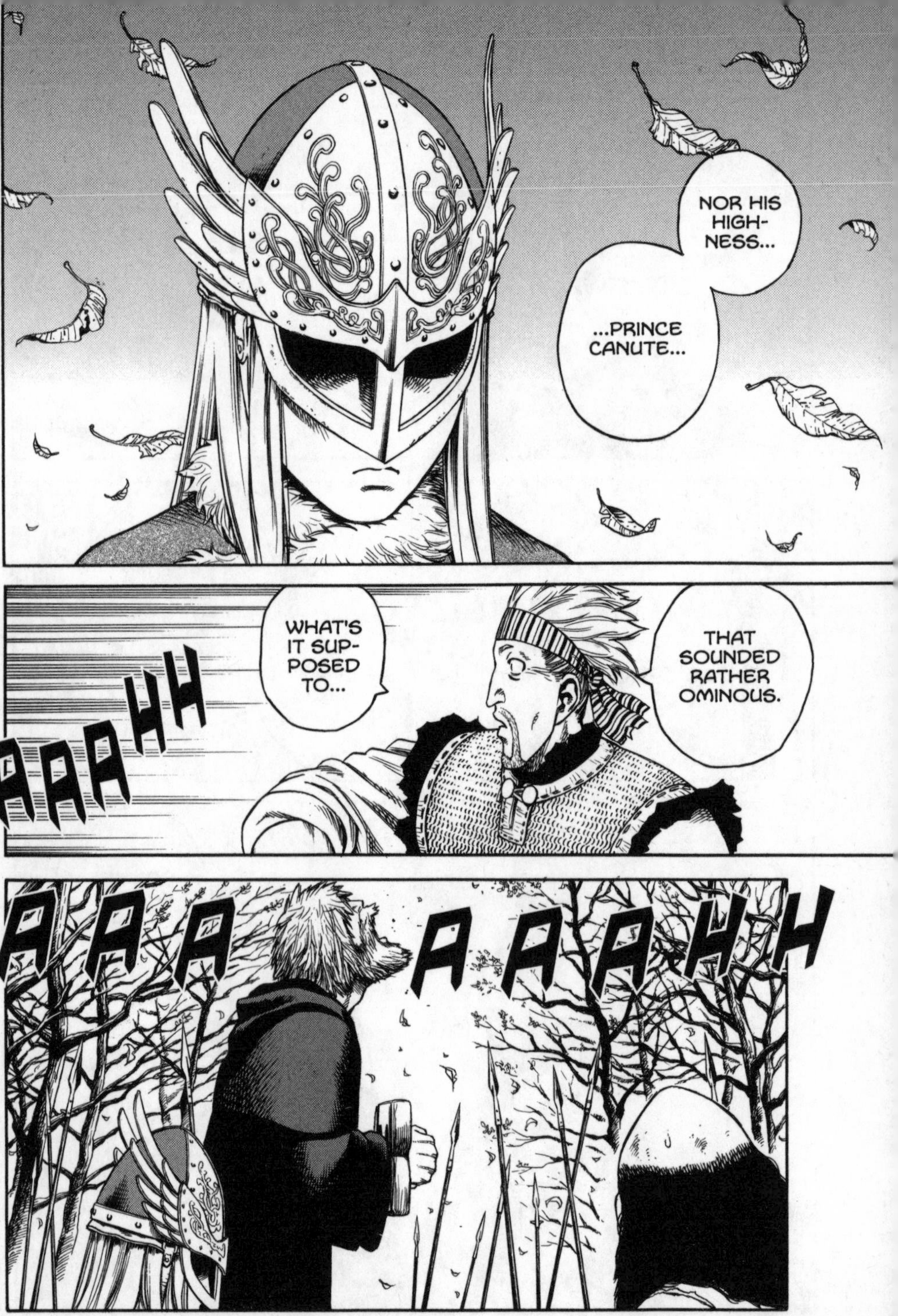
NOR HIS HIGH-NESS...
...PRINCE CANUTE...
THAT SOUNDED RATHER OMINOUS.
WHAT'S IT SUP-POSED TO...
AAAHH
AAA AAAAHH

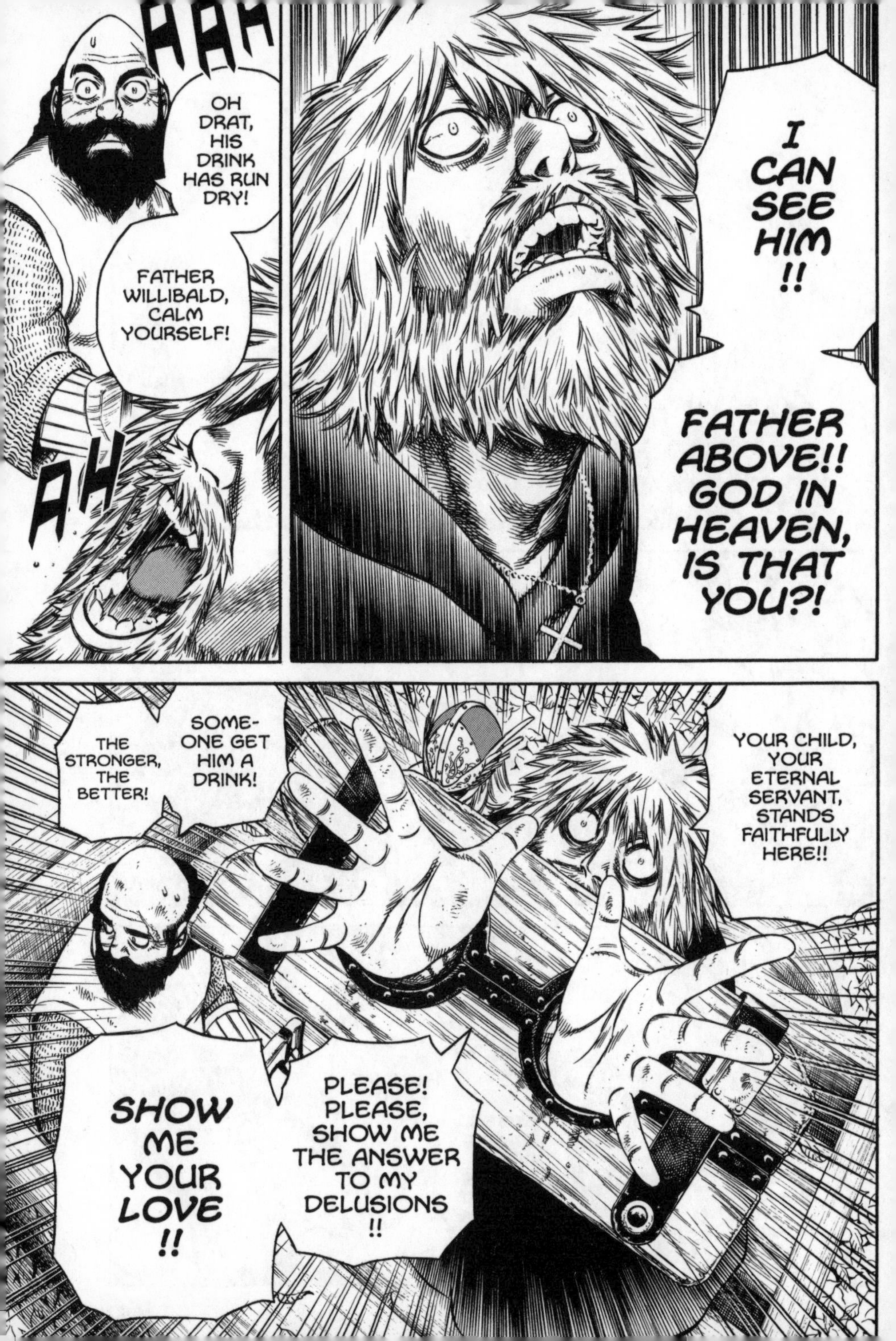
I CAN SEE HIM!!
FATHER ABOVE!! GOD IN HEAVEN, IS THAT YOU?!
AAA
OH DRAT, HIS DRINK HAS RUN DRY!
FATHER WILLIBALD, CALM YOURSELF!
AH
YOUR CHILD, YOUR ETERNAL SERVANT, STANDS FAITHFULLY HERE!!
SOME-ONE GET HIM A DRINK!
THE STRONGER, THE BETTER!
PLEASE! PLEASE, SHOW ME THE ANSWER TO MY DELUSIONS!!
SHOW ME YOUR LOVE!!

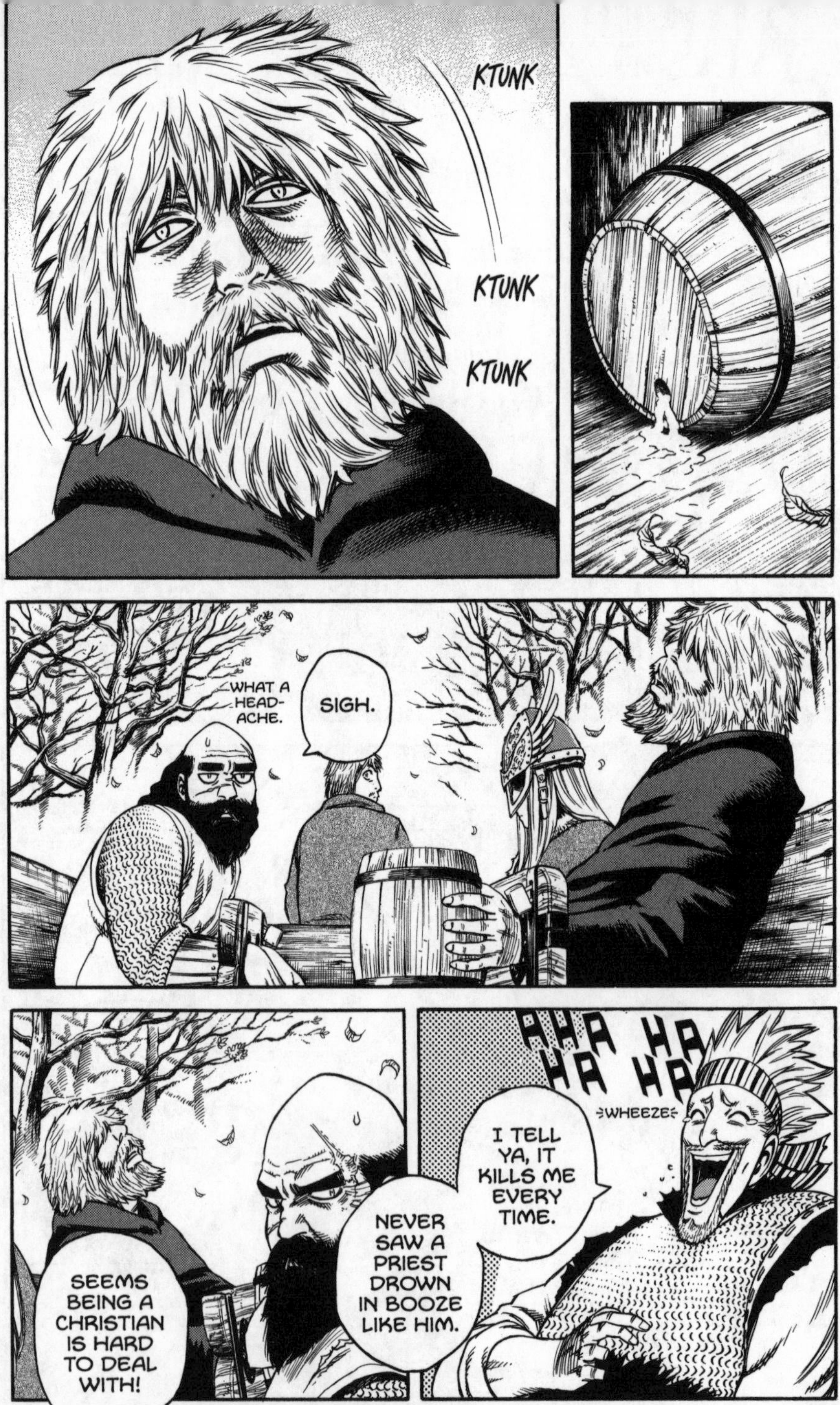
KTUNK
KTUNK
KTUNK
SIGH.
WHAT A HEAD-ACHE.
HA HA HA HA HA HA
WHEEZE
I TELL YA, IT KILLS ME EVERY TIME.
NEVER SAW A PRIEST DROWN IN BOOZE LIKE HIM.
SEEMS BEING A CHRISTIAN IS HARD TO DEAL WITH!

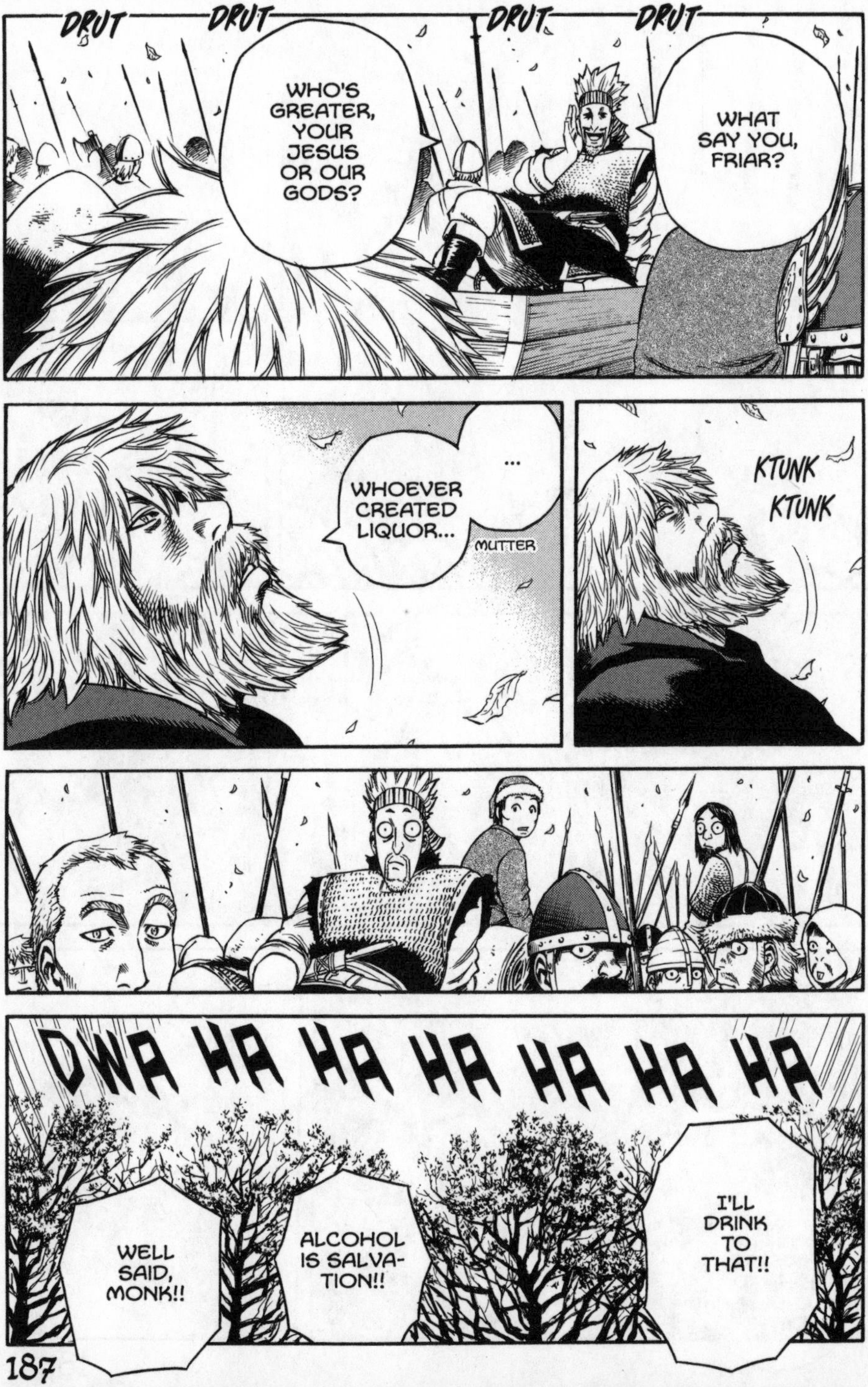
DRUT DRUT DRUT DRUT
WHAT SAY YOU, FRIAR?
WHO'S GREATER, YOUR JESUS OR OUR GODS?
KTUNK KTUNK
...
WHOEVER CREATED LIQUOR...
MUTTER
DWA HA HA HA HA HA HA
I'LL DRINK TO THAT!!
ALCOHOL IS SALVATION!!
WELL SAID, MONK!!

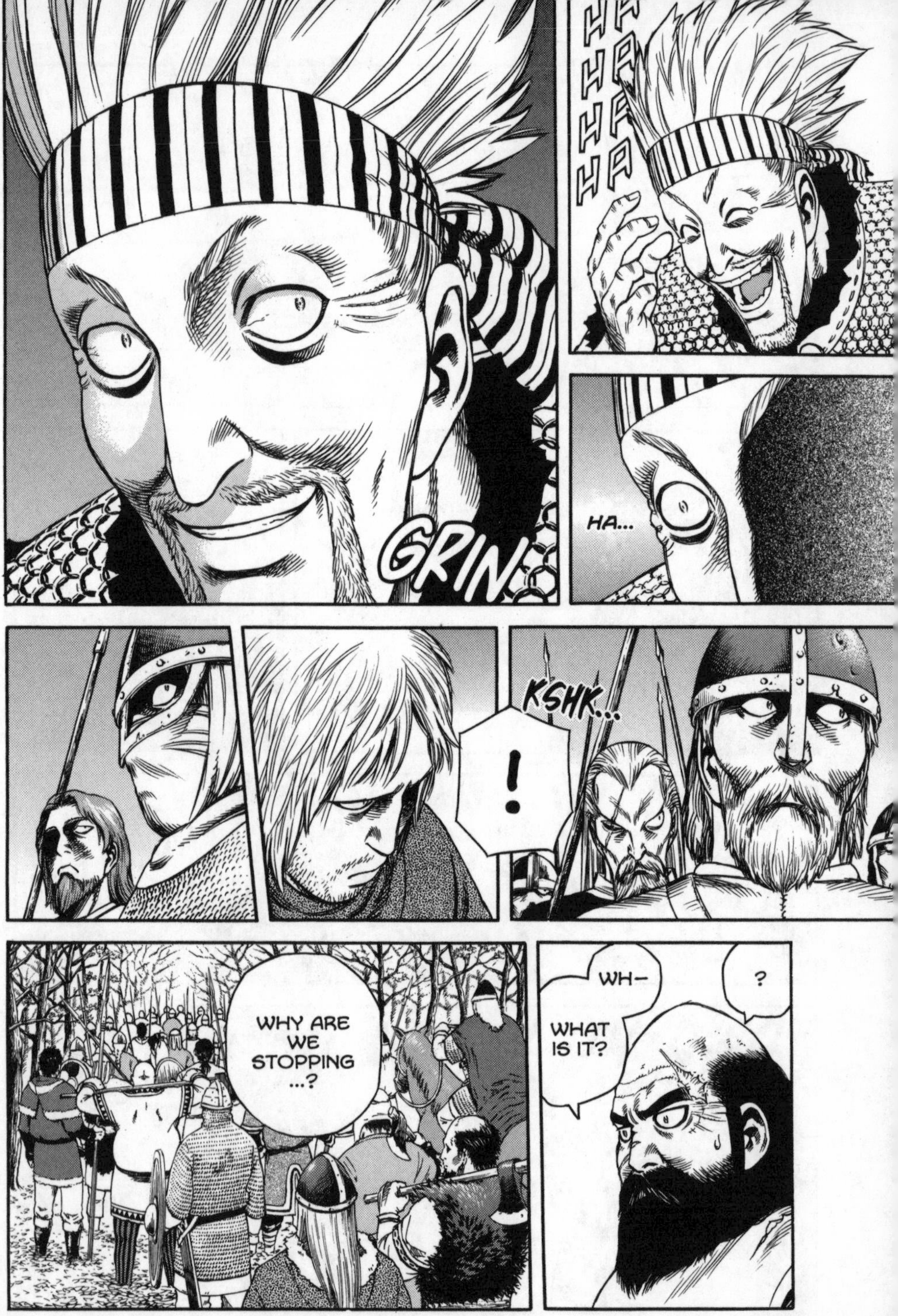
HA HA HA HA HA
HA...
GRIN
KSHK...
!
?
WH—
WHAT IS IT?
WHY ARE WE STOPPING ...?

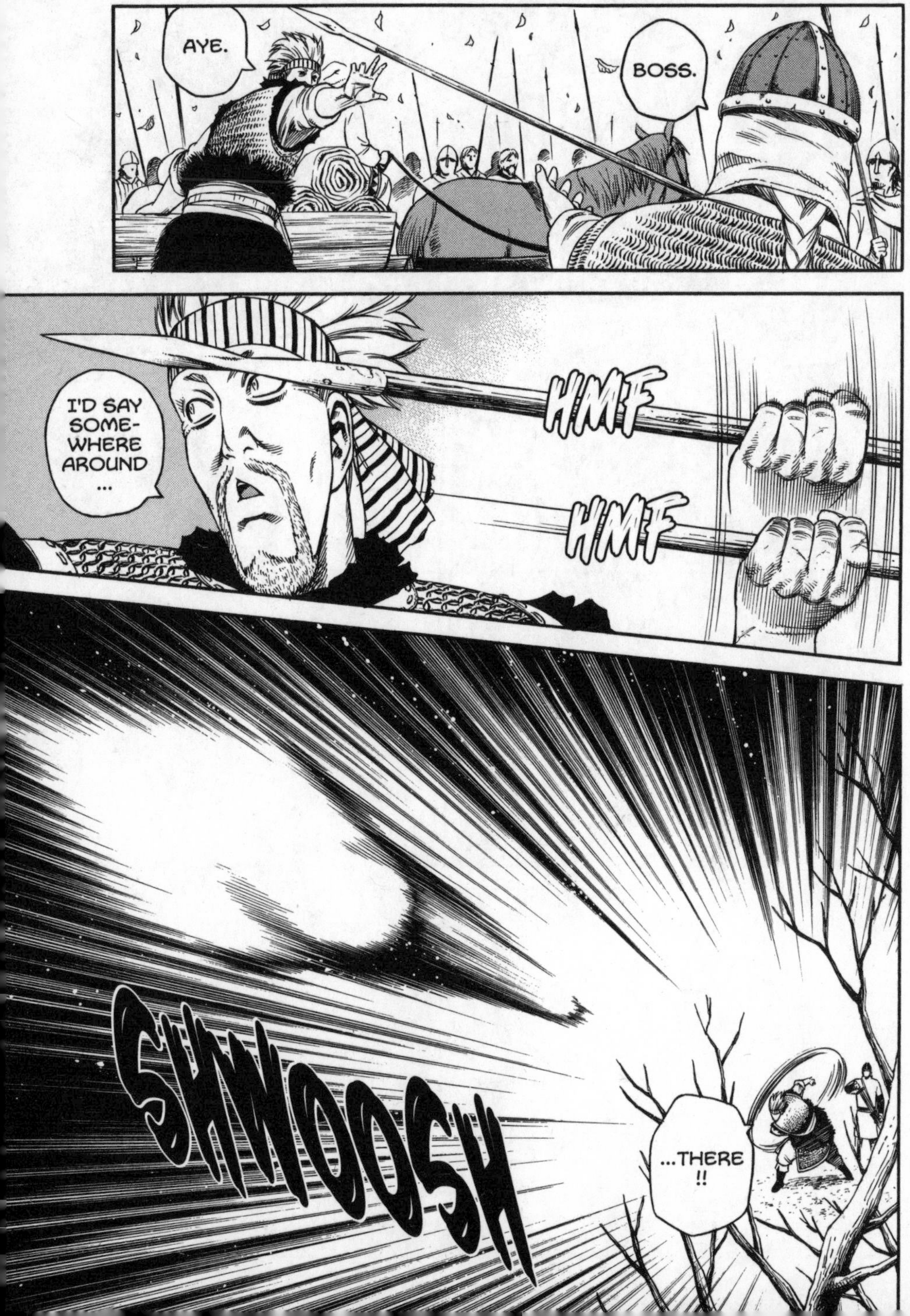
BOSS.
AYE.
I'D SAY SOME-WHERE AROUND ...
HMF
HMF
...THERE !!
SHWOOSH

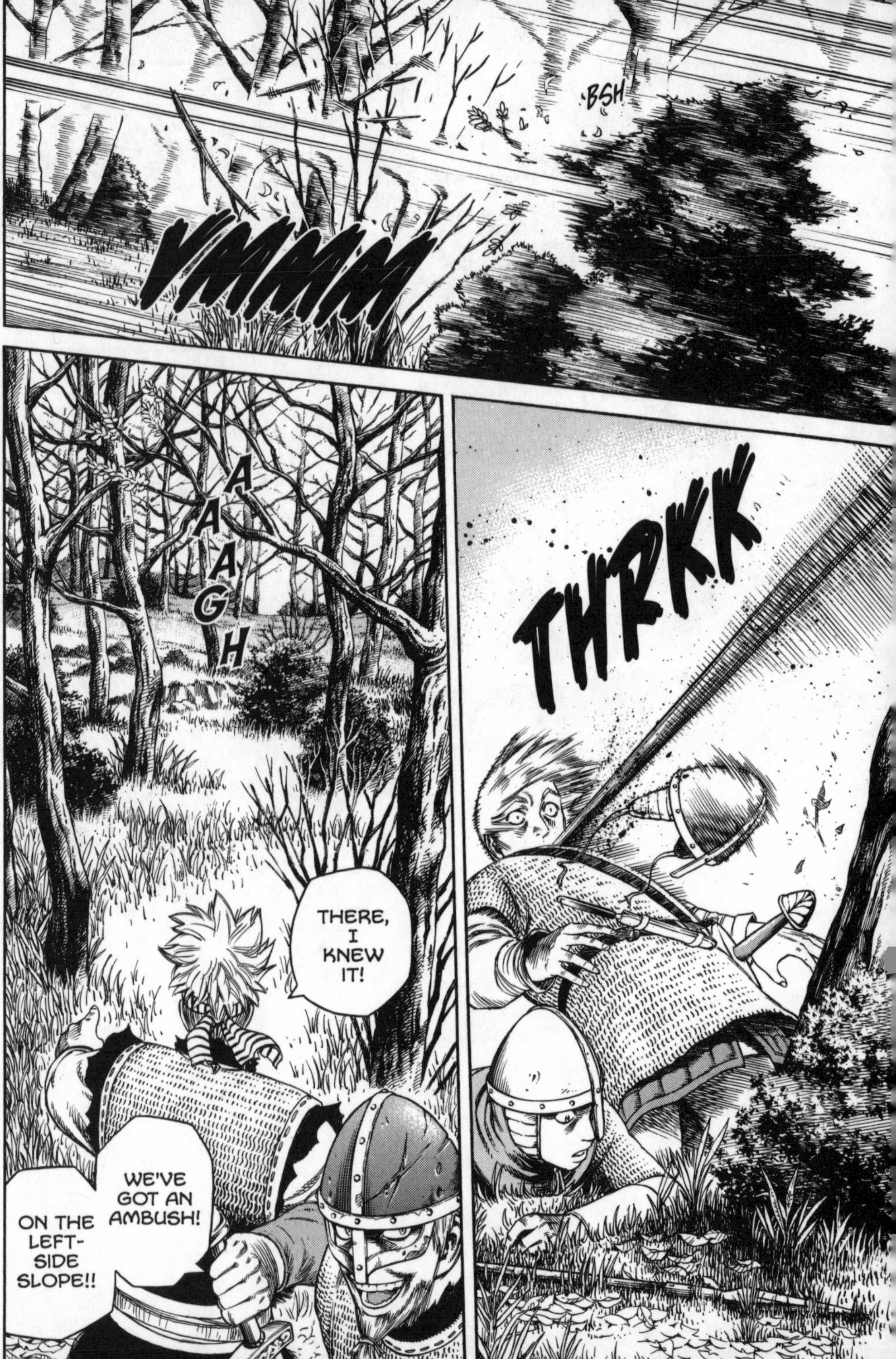
BSH
VMMMM
THRKK
AAAAGH
THERE, I KNEW IT!
WE'VE GOT AN AMBUSH!
ON THE LEFT-SIDE SLOPE!!

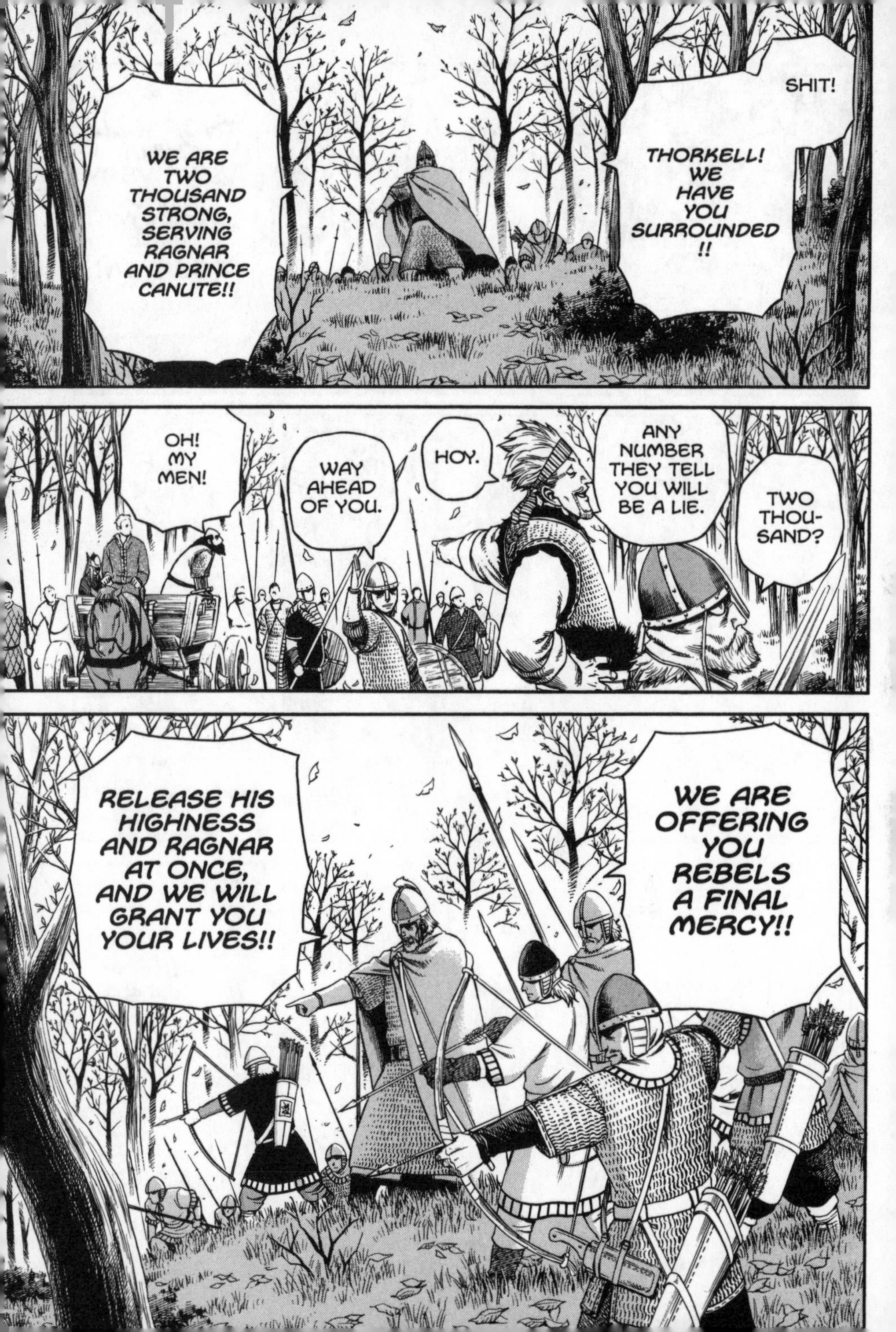
SHIT!
THORKELL! WE HAVE YOU SURROUNDED!!
WE ARE TWO THOUSAND STRONG, SERVING RAGNAR AND PRINCE CANUTE!!
TWO THOU-SAND?
ANY NUMBER THEY TELL YOU WILL BE A LIE.
HOY.
WAY AHEAD OF YOU.
OH! MY MEN!
WE ARE OFFERING YOU REBELS A FINAL MERCY!!
RELEASE HIS HIGHNESS AND RAGNAR AT ONCE, AND WE WILL GRANT YOU YOUR LIVES!!

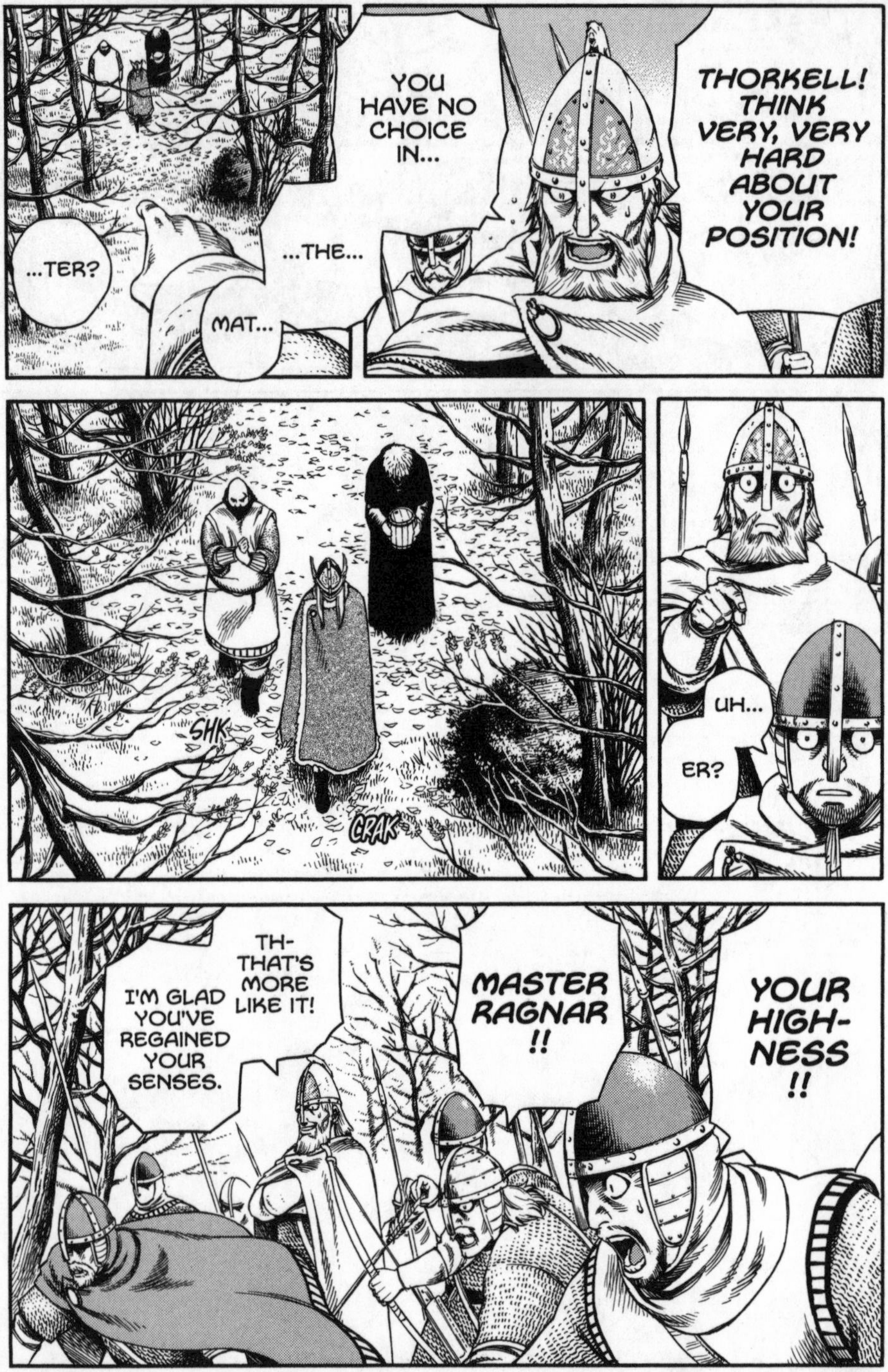
THORKELL! THINK VERY, VERY HARD ABOUT YOUR POSITION!
YOU HAVE NO CHOICE IN...
...THE...
MAT...
...TER?
UH...
ER?
SHK
GRAK
YOUR HIGH-NESS !!
MASTER RAGNAR !!
TH-THAT'S MORE LIKE IT!
I'M GLAD YOU'VE REGAINED YOUR SENSES.

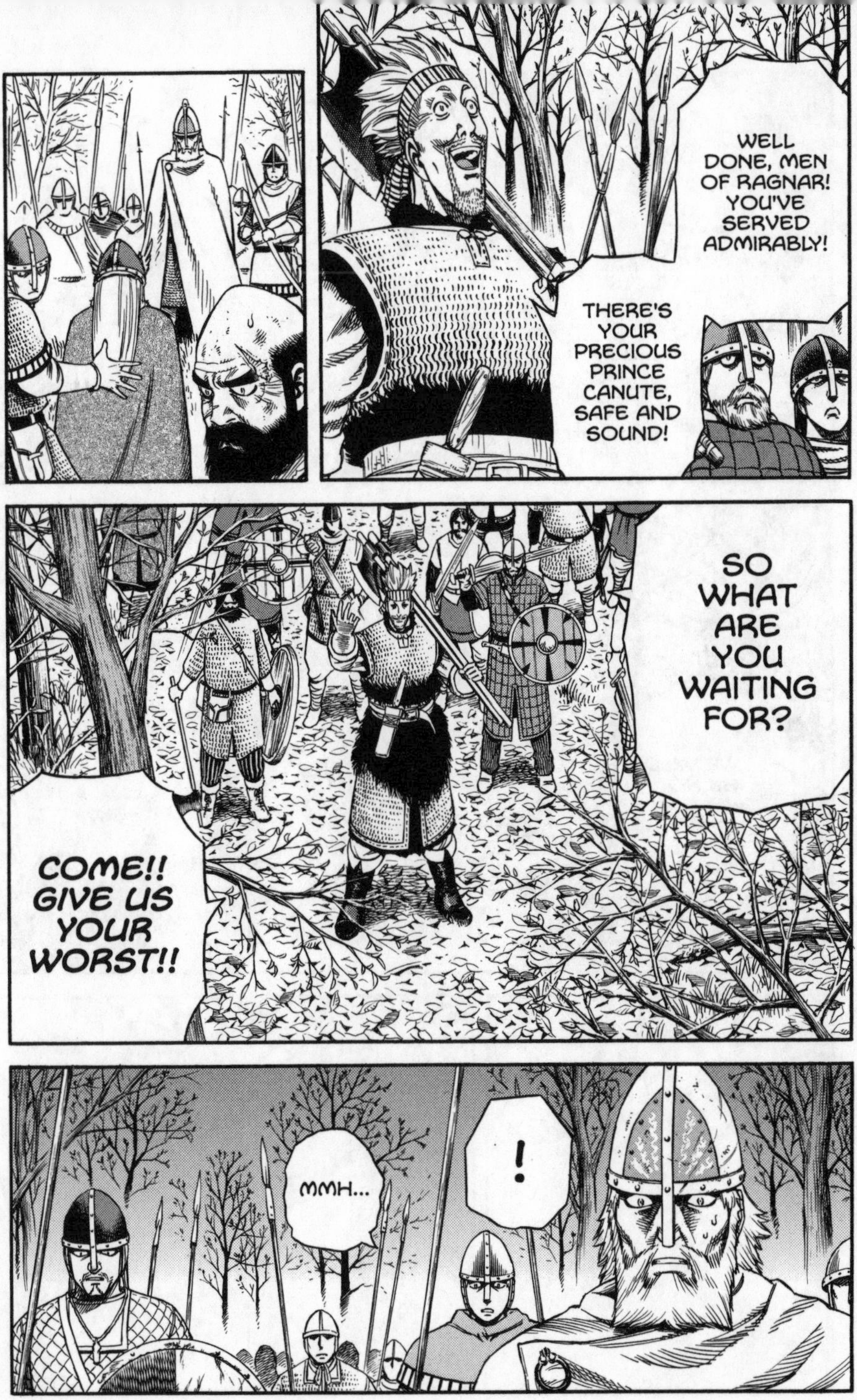
WELL DONE, MEN OF RAGNAR! YOU'VE SERVED ADMIRABLY!
THERE'S YOUR PRECIOUS PRINCE CANUTE, SAFE AND SOUND!
SO WHAT ARE YOU WAITING FOR?
COME!! GIVE US YOUR WORST!!
!
MMH...

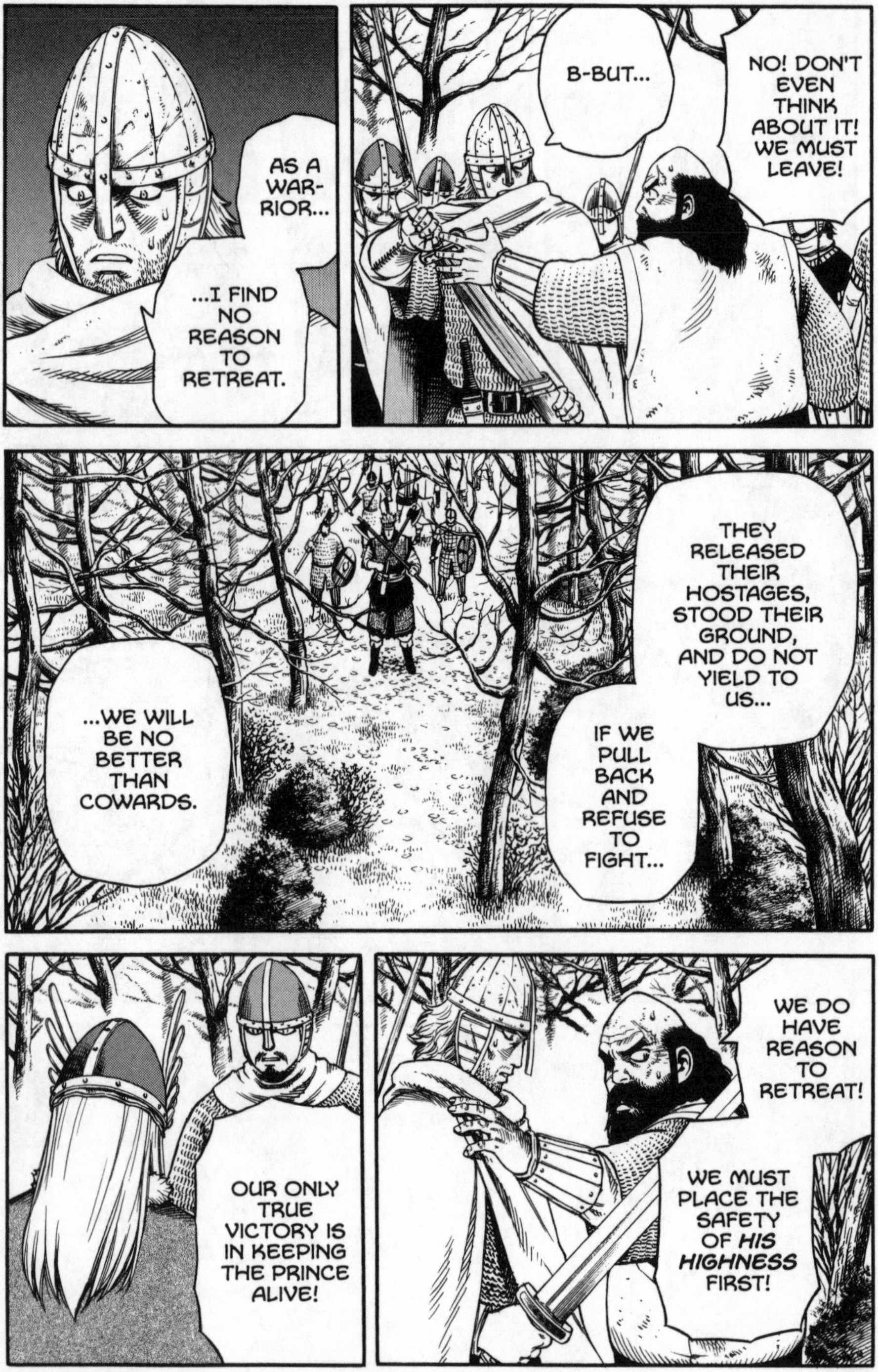
NO! DON'T EVEN THINK ABOUT IT! WE MUST LEAVE!
B-BUT...
AS A WAR-RIOR...
...I FIND NO REASON TO RETREAT.
THEY RELEASED THEIR HOSTAGES, STOOD THEIR GROUND, AND DO NOT YIELD TO US...
IF WE PULL BACK AND REFUSE TO FIGHT...
...WE WILL BE NO BETTER THAN COWARDS.
WE DO HAVE REASON TO RETREAT!
WE MUST PLACE THE SAFETY OF *HIS HIGHNESS* FIRST!
OUR ONLY TRUE VICTORY IS IN KEEPING THE PRINCE ALIVE!

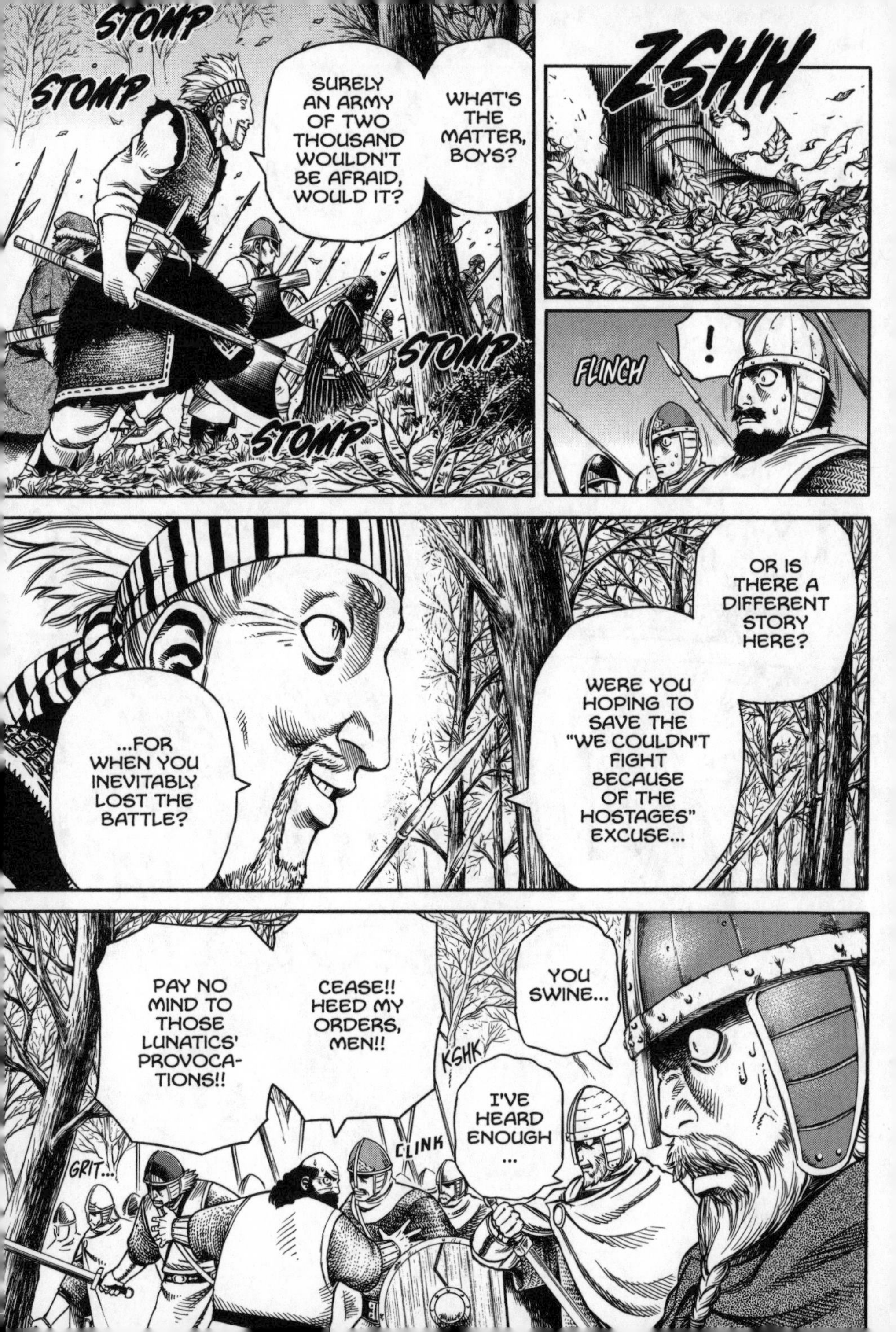
ZSHH
!
FLINCH
WHAT'S THE MATTER, BOYS?
SURELY AN ARMY OF TWO THOUSAND WOULDN'T BE AFRAID, WOULD IT?
STOMP
STOMP
STOMP
STOMP
OR IS THERE A DIFFERENT STORY HERE?
WERE YOU HOPING TO SAVE THE "WE COULDN'T FIGHT BECAUSE OF THE HOSTAGES" EXCUSE...
...FOR WHEN YOU INEVITABLY LOST THE BATTLE?
YOU SWINE...
KSHK
I'VE HEARD ENOUGH ...
CEASE!! HEED MY ORDERS, MEN!!
PAY NO MIND TO THOSE LUNATICS' PROVOCA-TIONS!!
CLINK
GRIT...

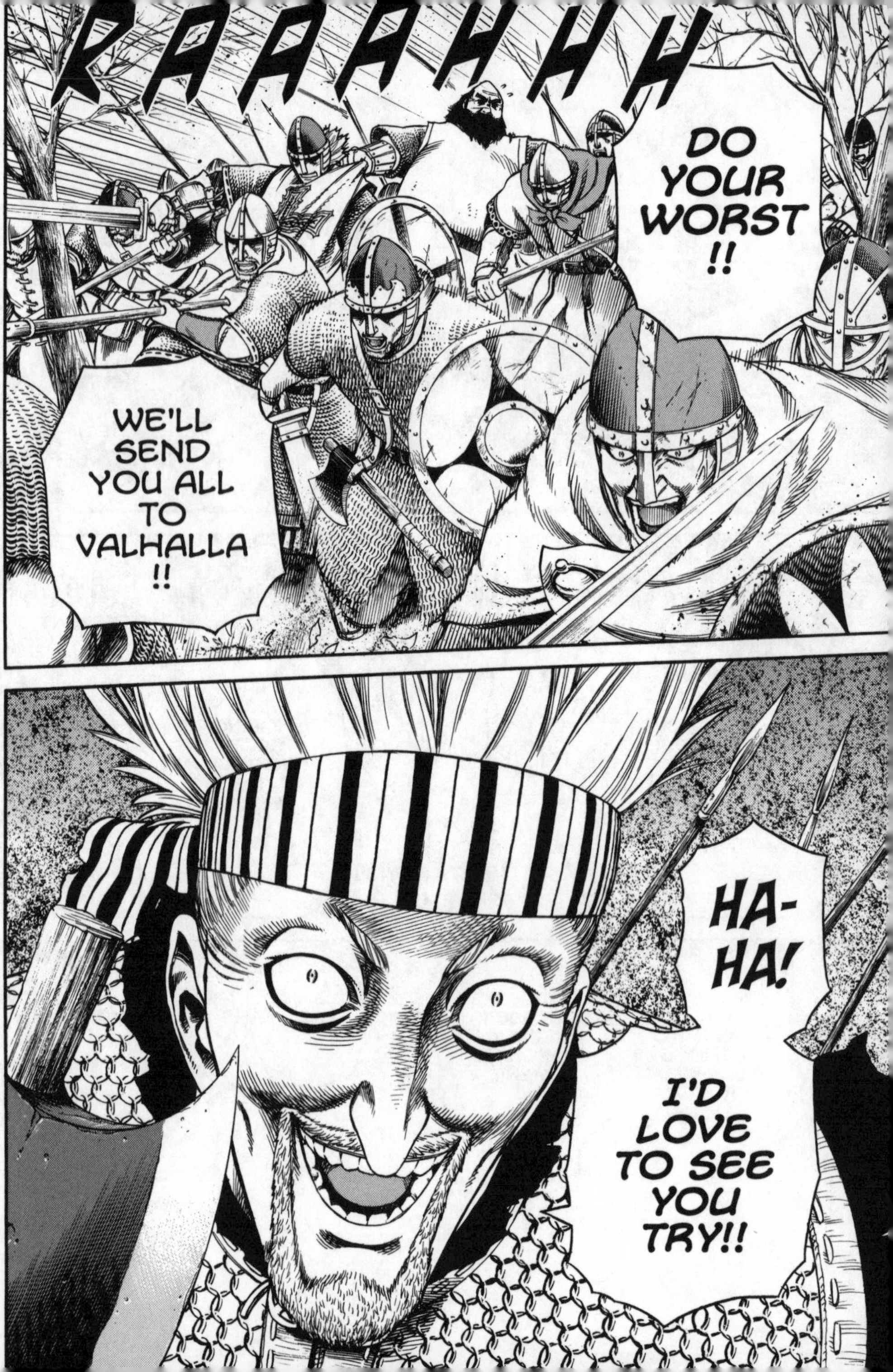
RAAAHHH
DO YOUR WORST!!
WE'LL SEND YOU ALL TO VALHALLA!!
HA-HA!
I'D LOVE TO SEE YOU TRY!!

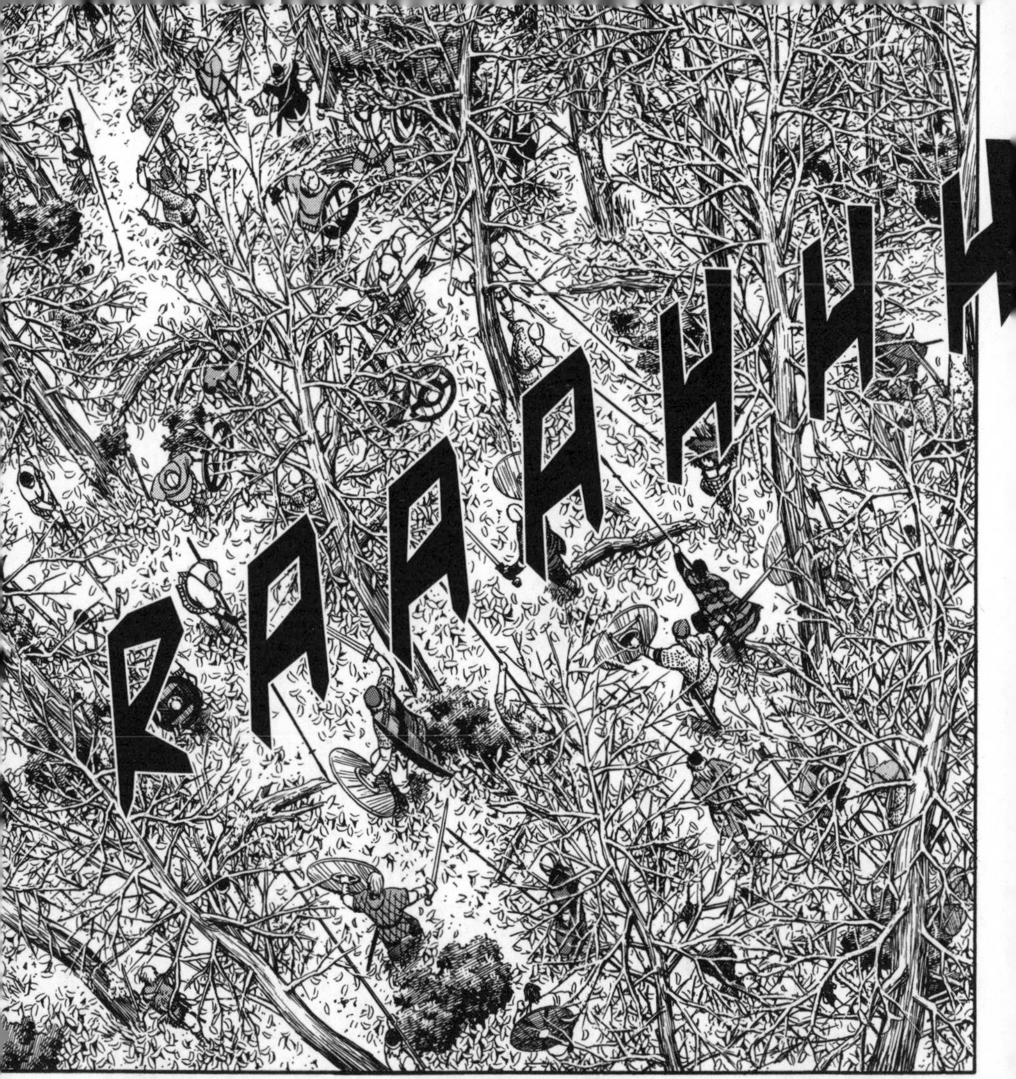
RAAAHHHHK
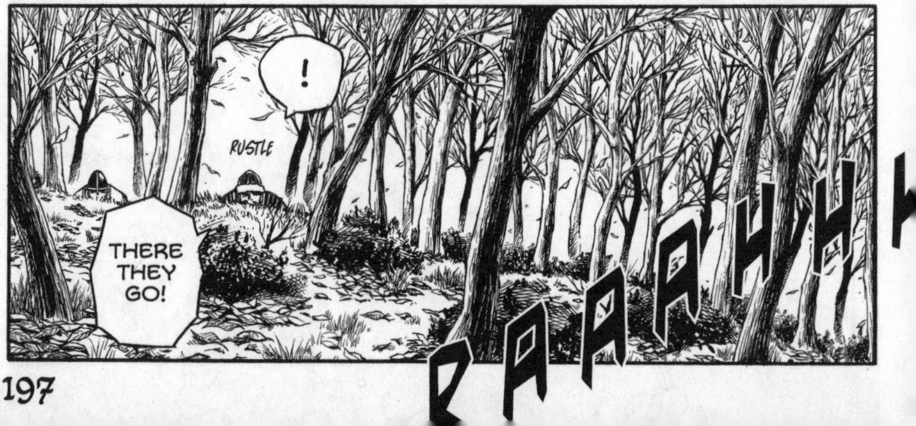
!
RUSTLE
THERE THEY GO!
RAAAAHHHK

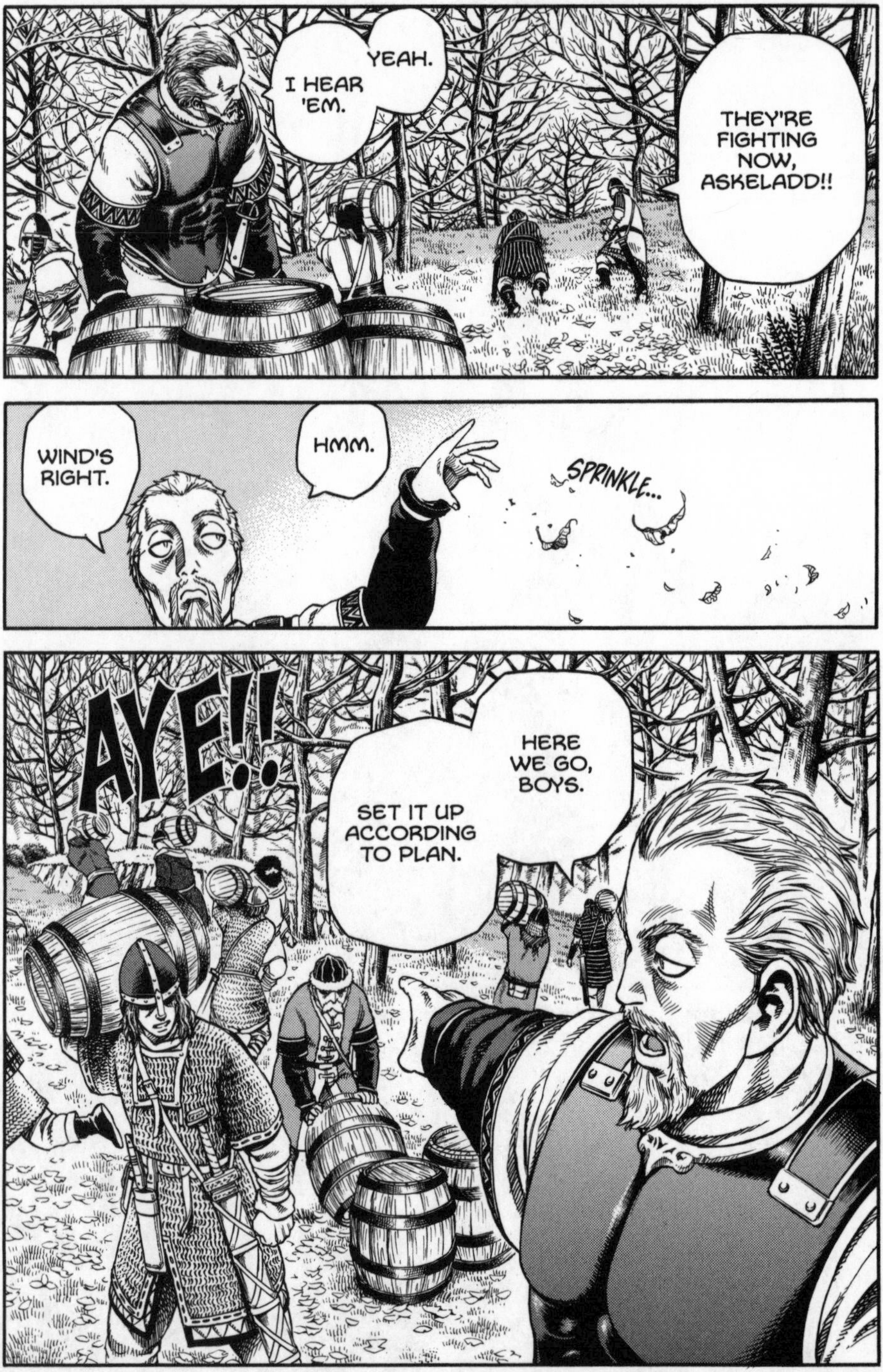
THEY'RE FIGHTING NOW, ASKELADD!!
YEAH. I HEAR 'EM.
SPRINKLE...
HMM.
WIND'S RIGHT.
HERE WE GO, BOYS.
SET IT UP ACCORDING TO PLAN.
AYE!!

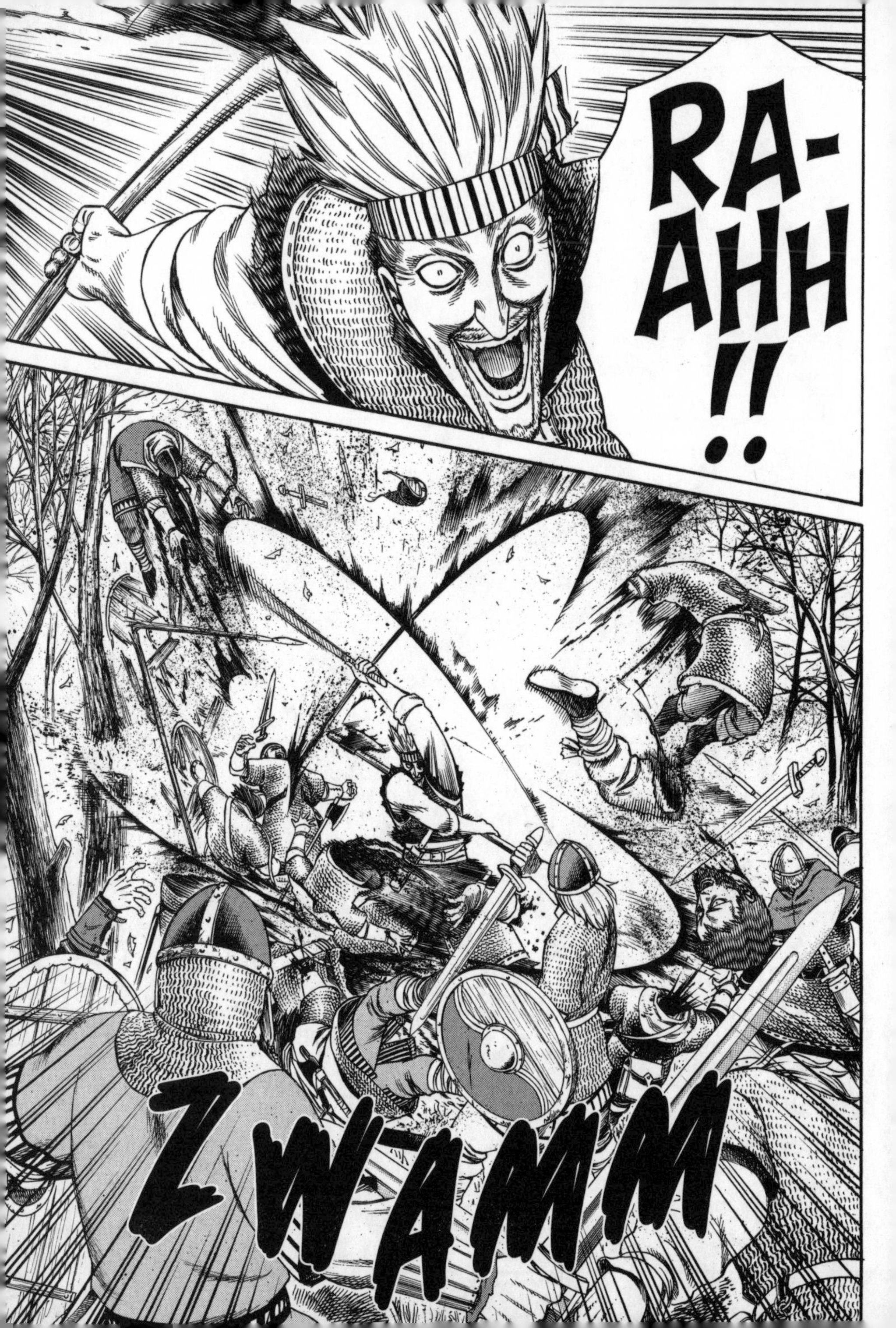
RA-
AHH
!!
ZWAMM

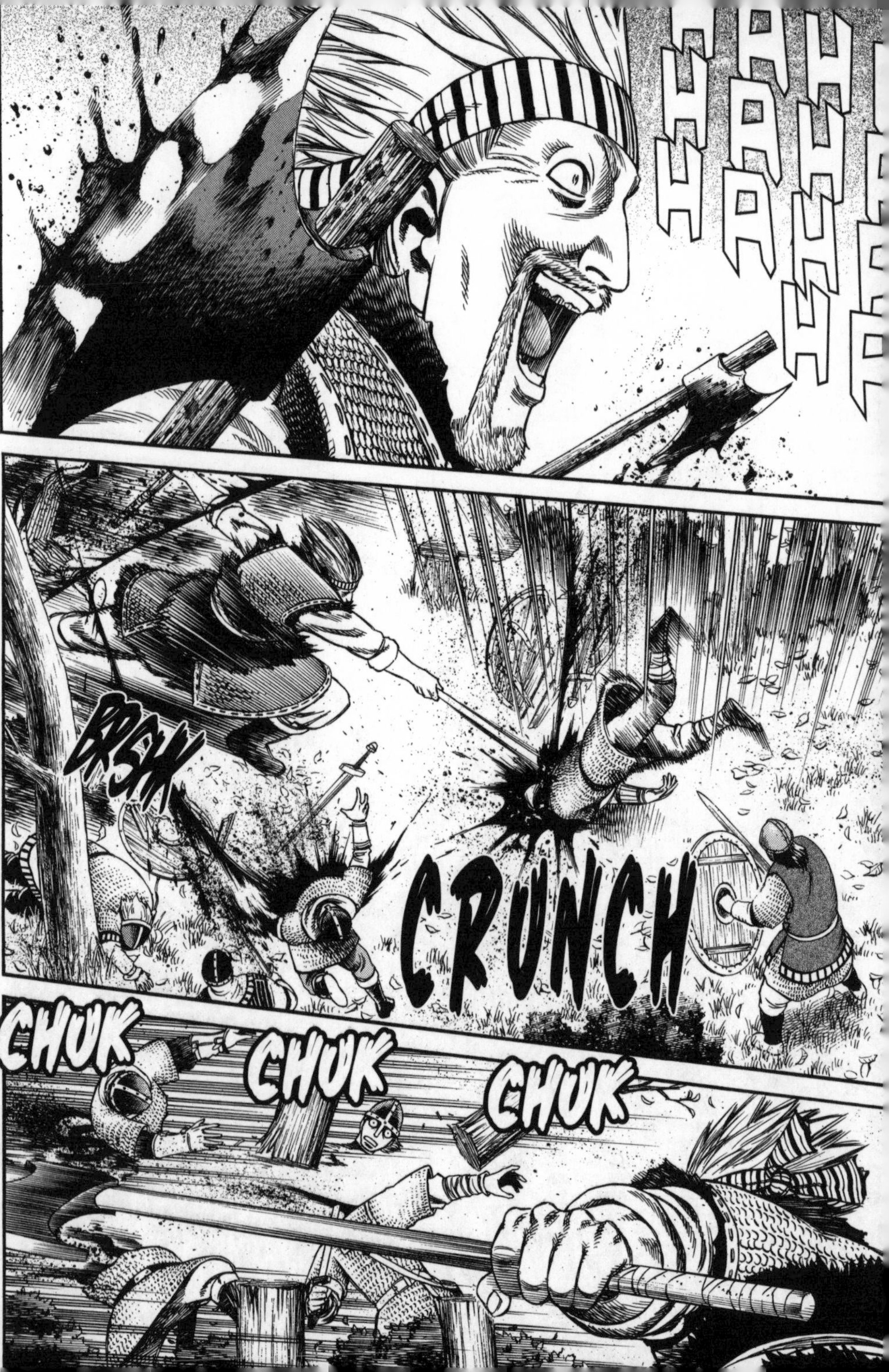
HAHAHAHAHAHA
BRSHK
CRUNCH
CHUK
CHUK
CHUK

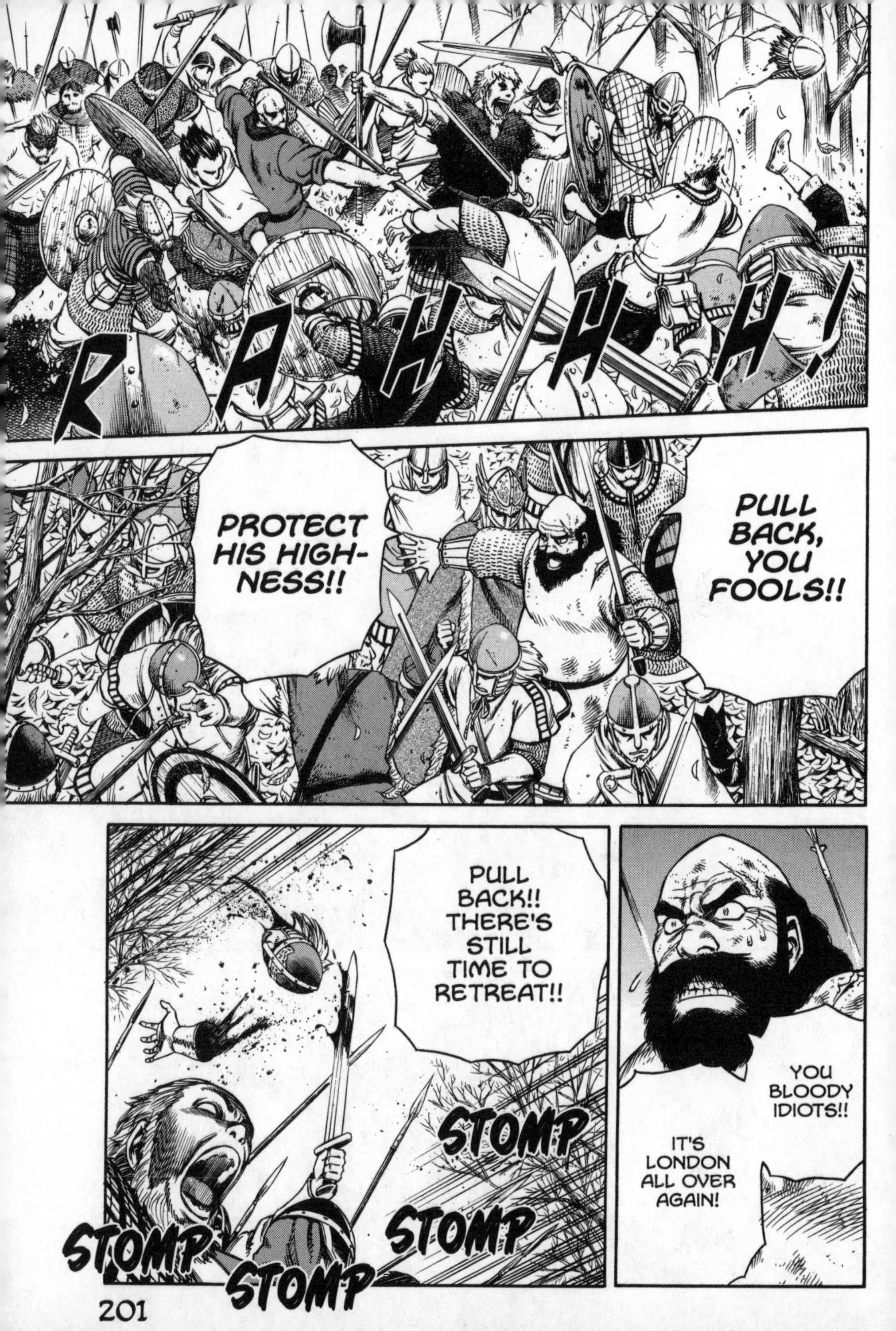
RAHHHH!
PULL BACK, YOU FOOLS!!
PROTECT HIS HIGHNESS!!
YOU BLOODY IDIOTS!!
IT'S LONDON ALL OVER AGAIN!
PULL BACK!! THERE'S STILL TIME TO RETREAT!!
STOMP
STOMP
STOMP
STOMP

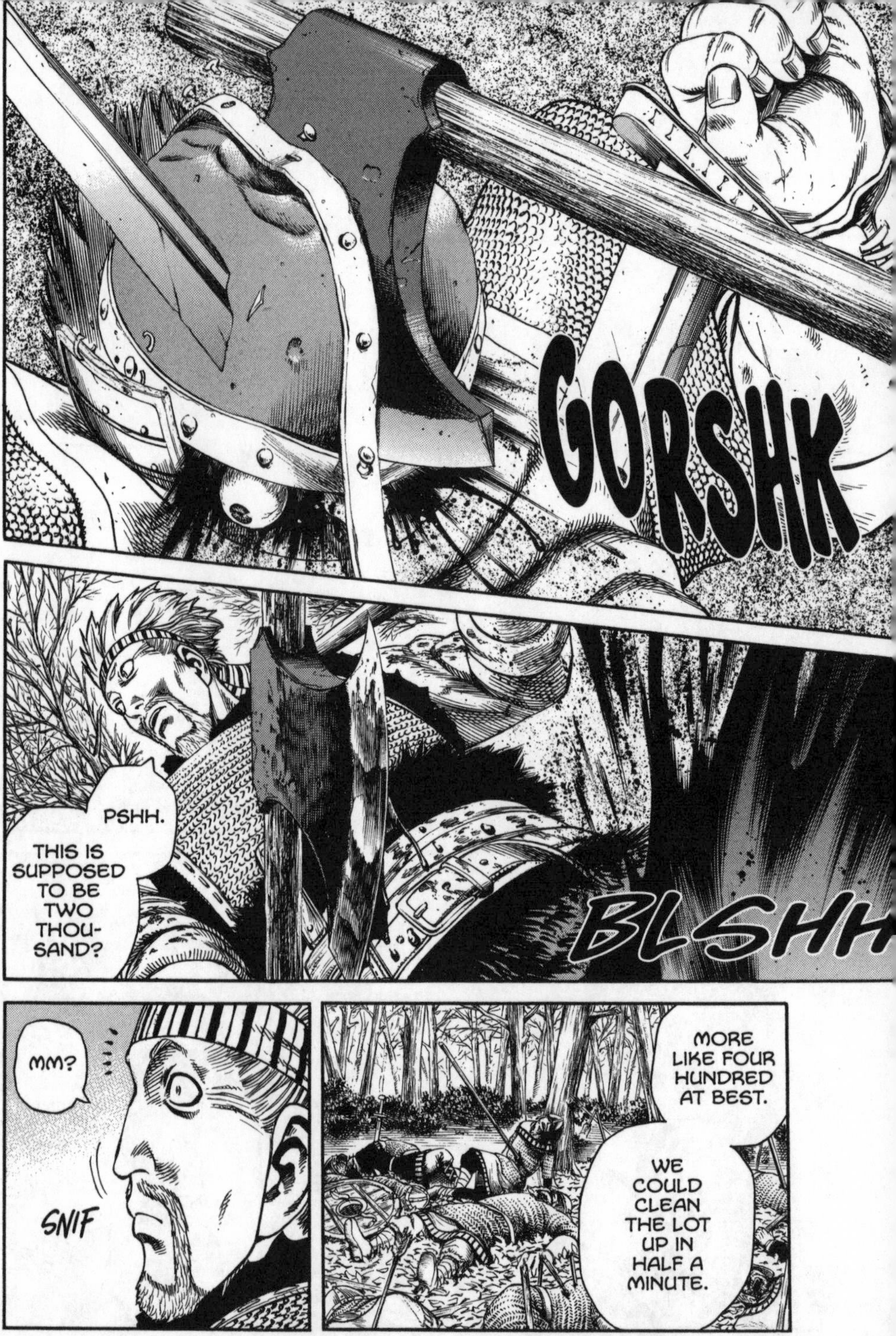
GORSHK
BLSHH
PSHH.
THIS IS SUPPOSED TO BE TWO THOUSAND?
MORE LIKE FOUR HUNDRED AT BEST.
WE COULD CLEAN THE LOT UP IN HALF A MINUTE.
MM?
SNIF

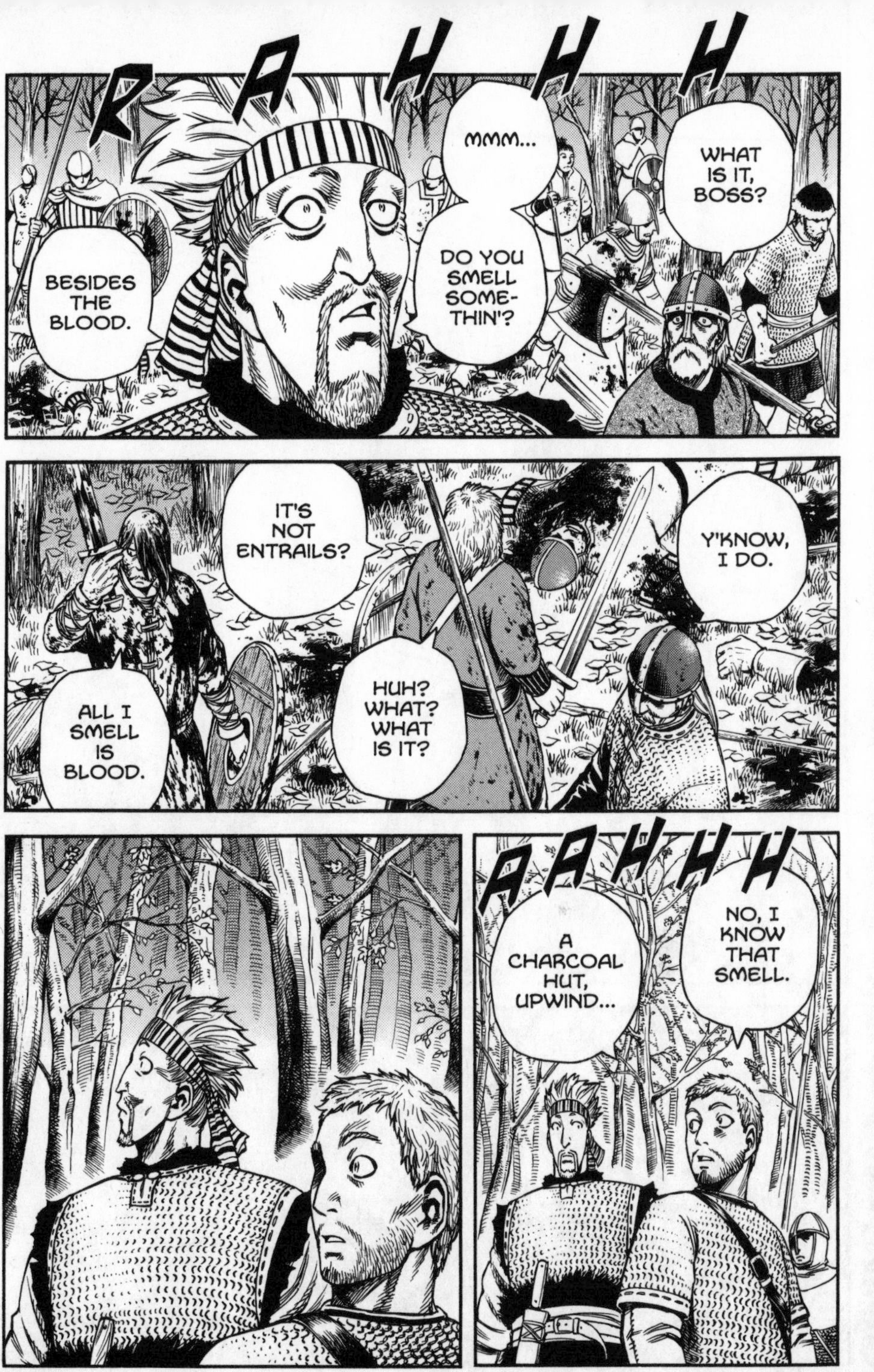
RAHHHH
WHAT IS IT, BOSS?
MMM...
DO YOU SMELL SOME-THIN'?
BESIDES THE BLOOD.
Y'KNOW, I DO.
IT'S NOT ENTRAILS?
HUH? WHAT? WHAT IS IT?
ALL I SMELL IS BLOOD.
AAHHHH
NO, I KNOW THAT SMELL.
A CHARCOAL HUT, UPWIND...

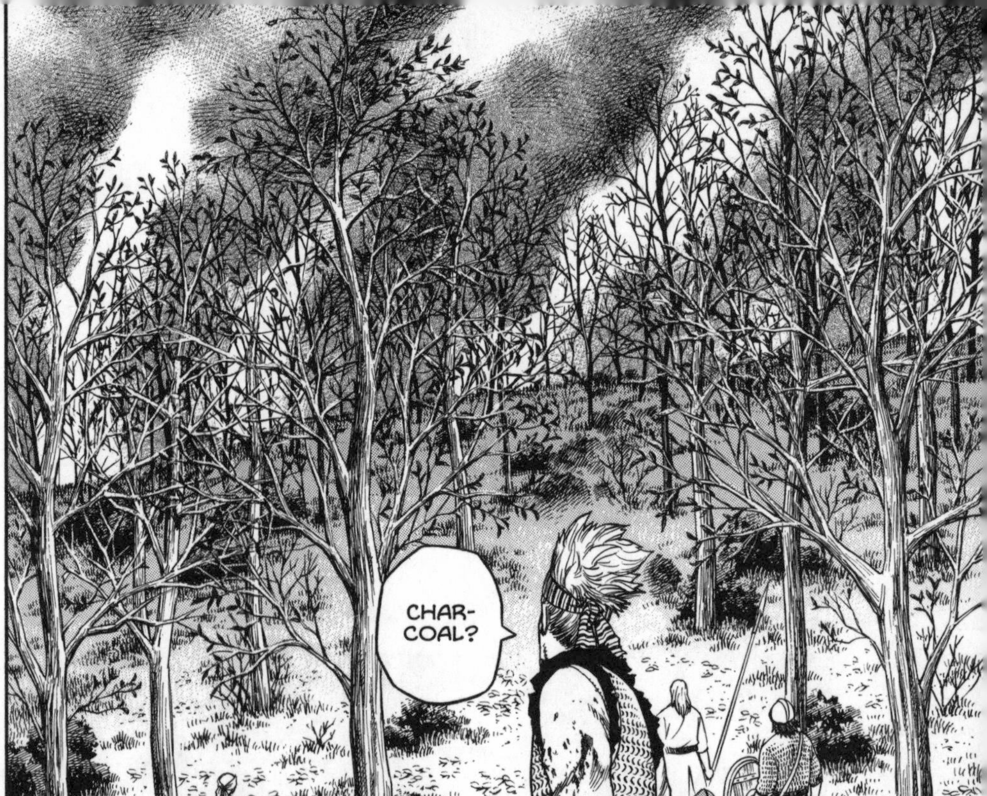
CHAR-
COAL?

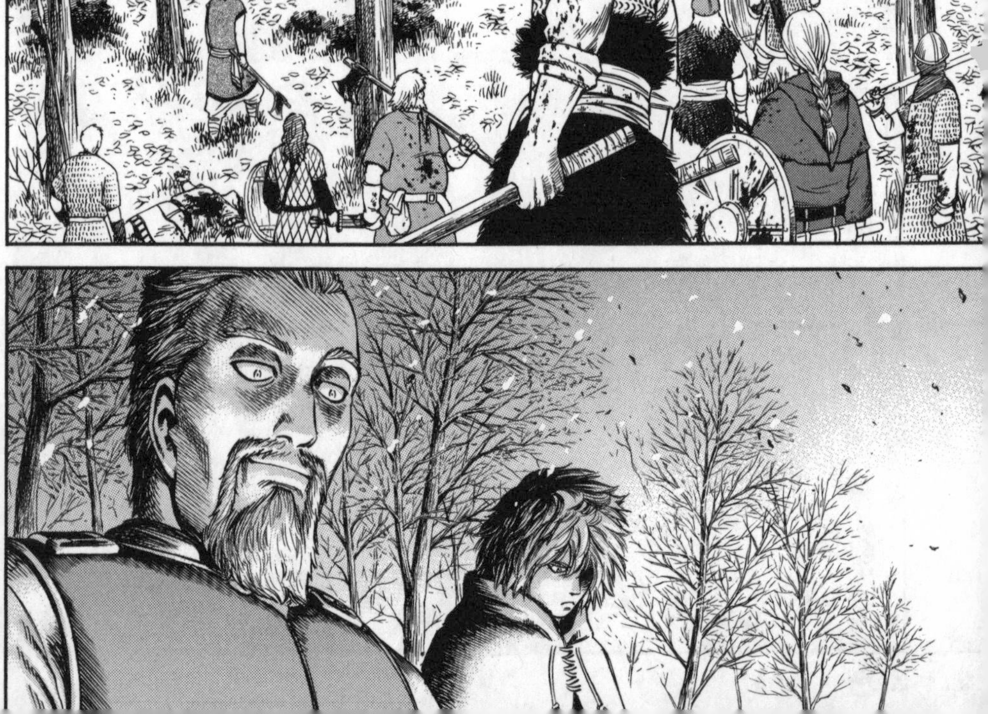

CHAPTER 21 • END

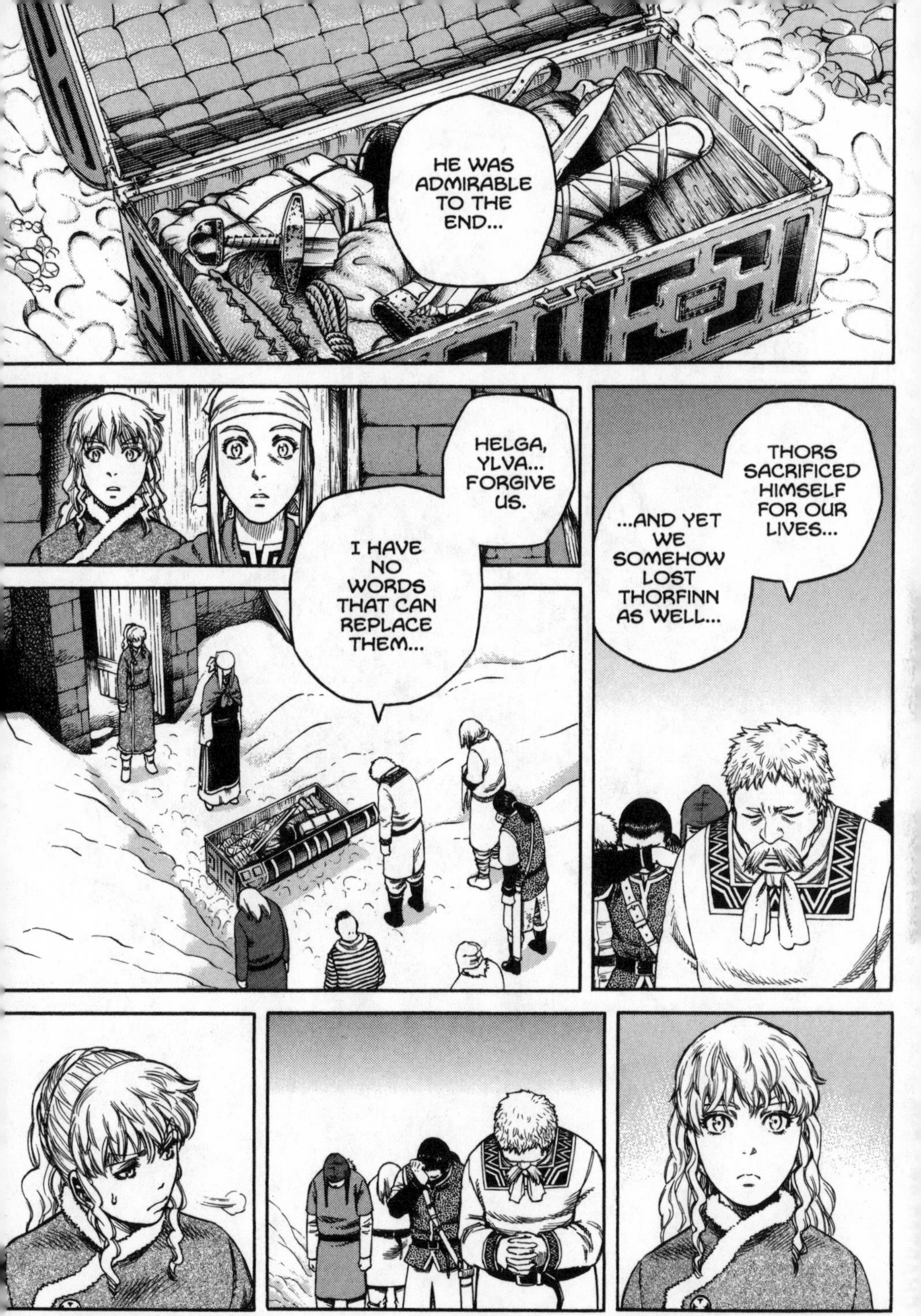
HE WAS ADMIRABLE TO THE END...
THORS SACRIFICED HIMSELF FOR OUR LIVES...
...AND YET WE SOMEHOW LOST THORFINN AS WELL...
HELGA, YLVA... FORGIVE US.
I HAVE NO WORDS THAT CAN REPLACE THEM...

BONUS STORY: YLVA AT WORK

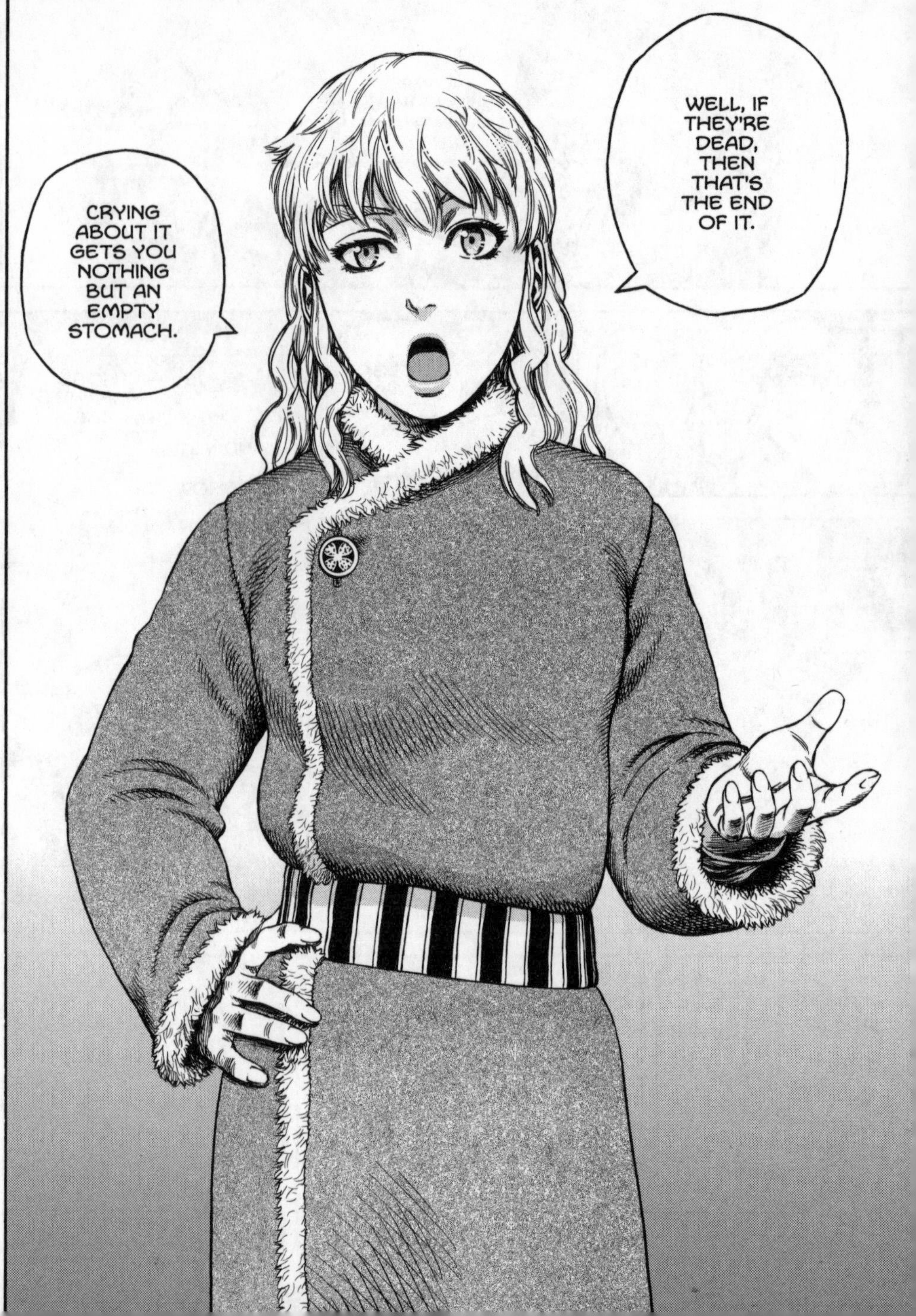
WELL, IF THEY'RE DEAD, THEN THAT'S THE END OF IT.
CRYING ABOUT IT GETS YOU NOTHING BUT AN EMPTY STOMACH.

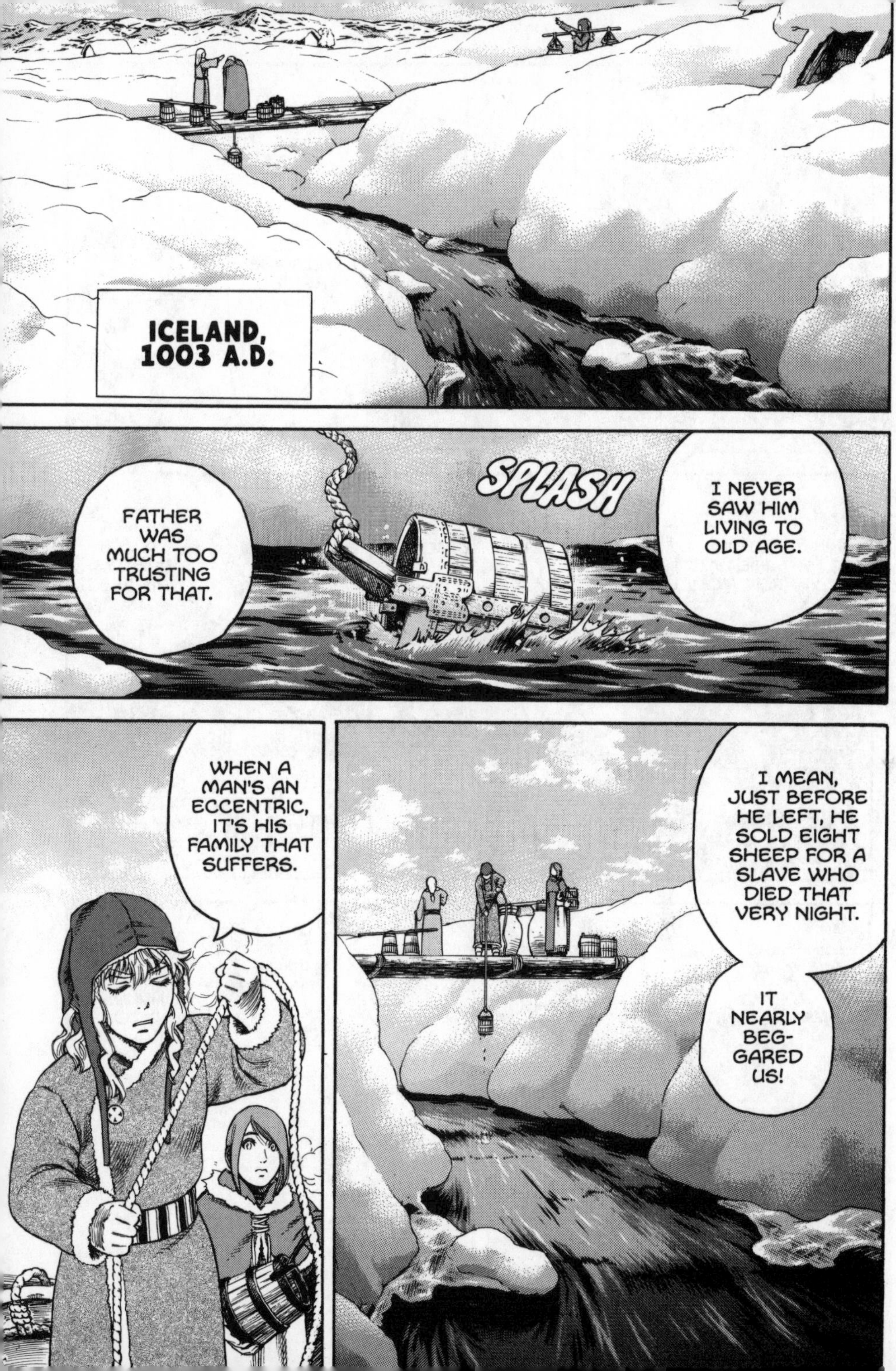
ICELAND, 1003 A.D.
I NEVER SAW HIM LIVING TO OLD AGE.
SPLASH
FATHER WAS MUCH TOO TRUSTING FOR THAT.
I MEAN, JUST BEFORE HE LEFT, HE SOLD EIGHT SHEEP FOR A SLAVE WHO DIED THAT VERY NIGHT.
IT NEARLY BEG-GARED US!
WHEN A MAN'S AN ECCENTRIC, IT'S HIS FAMILY THAT SUFFERS.

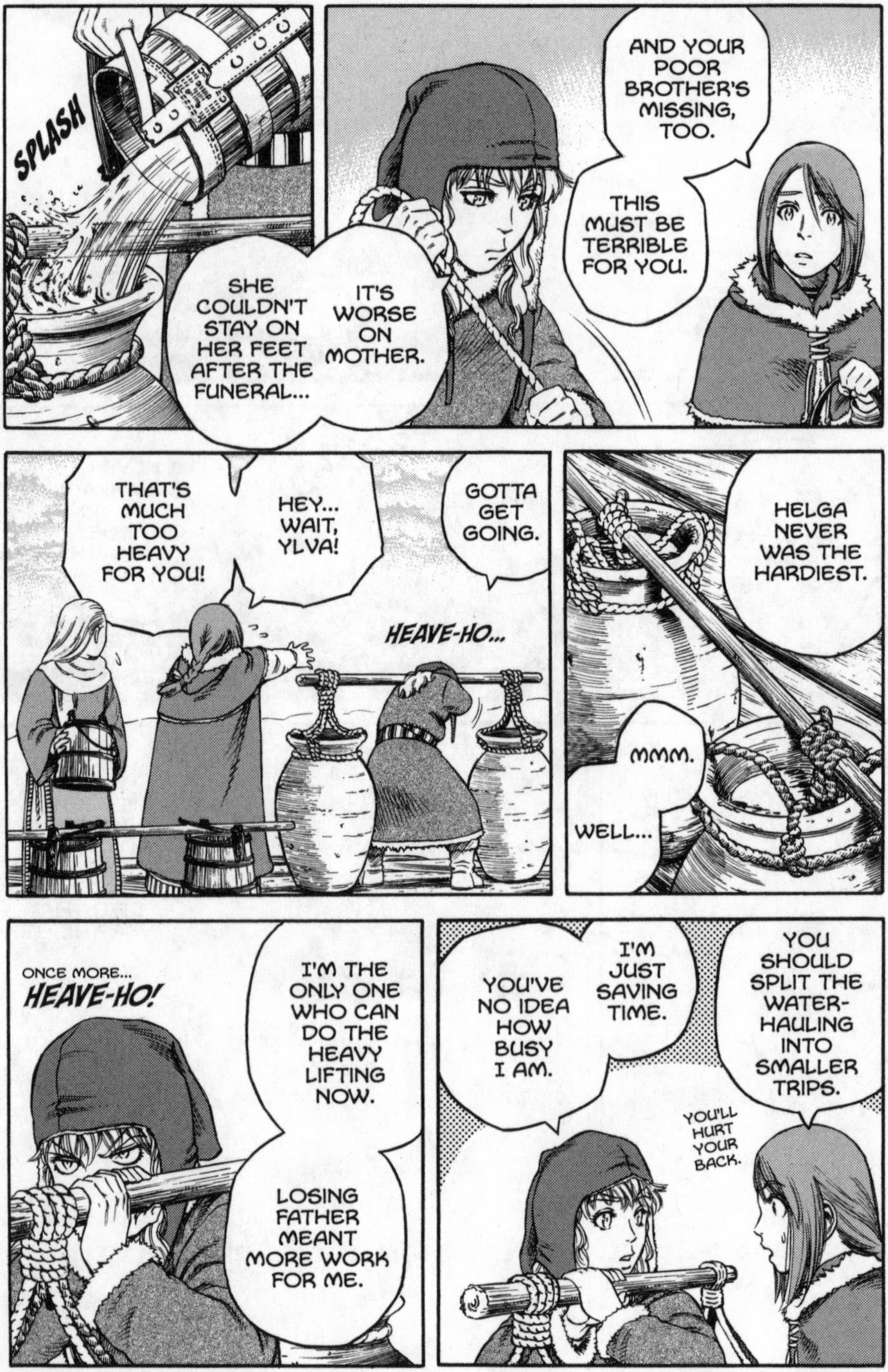
AND YOUR POOR BROTHER'S MISSING, TOO.
THIS MUST BE TERRIBLE FOR YOU.
IT'S WORSE ON MOTHER.
SHE COULDN'T STAY ON HER FEET AFTER THE FUNERAL...
SPLASH
HELGA NEVER WAS THE HARDIEST.
MMM.
WELL...
GOTTA GET GOING.
HEAVE-HO...
HEY... WAIT, YLVA!
THAT'S MUCH TOO HEAVY FOR YOU!
YOU SHOULD SPLIT THE WATER-HAULING INTO SMALLER TRIPS.
YOU'LL HURT YOUR BACK.
I'M JUST SAVING TIME.
YOU'VE NO IDEA HOW BUSY I AM.
ONCE MORE... HEAVE-HO!
I'M THE ONLY ONE WHO CAN DO THE HEAVY LIFTING NOW.
LOSING FATHER MEANT MORE WORK FOR ME.

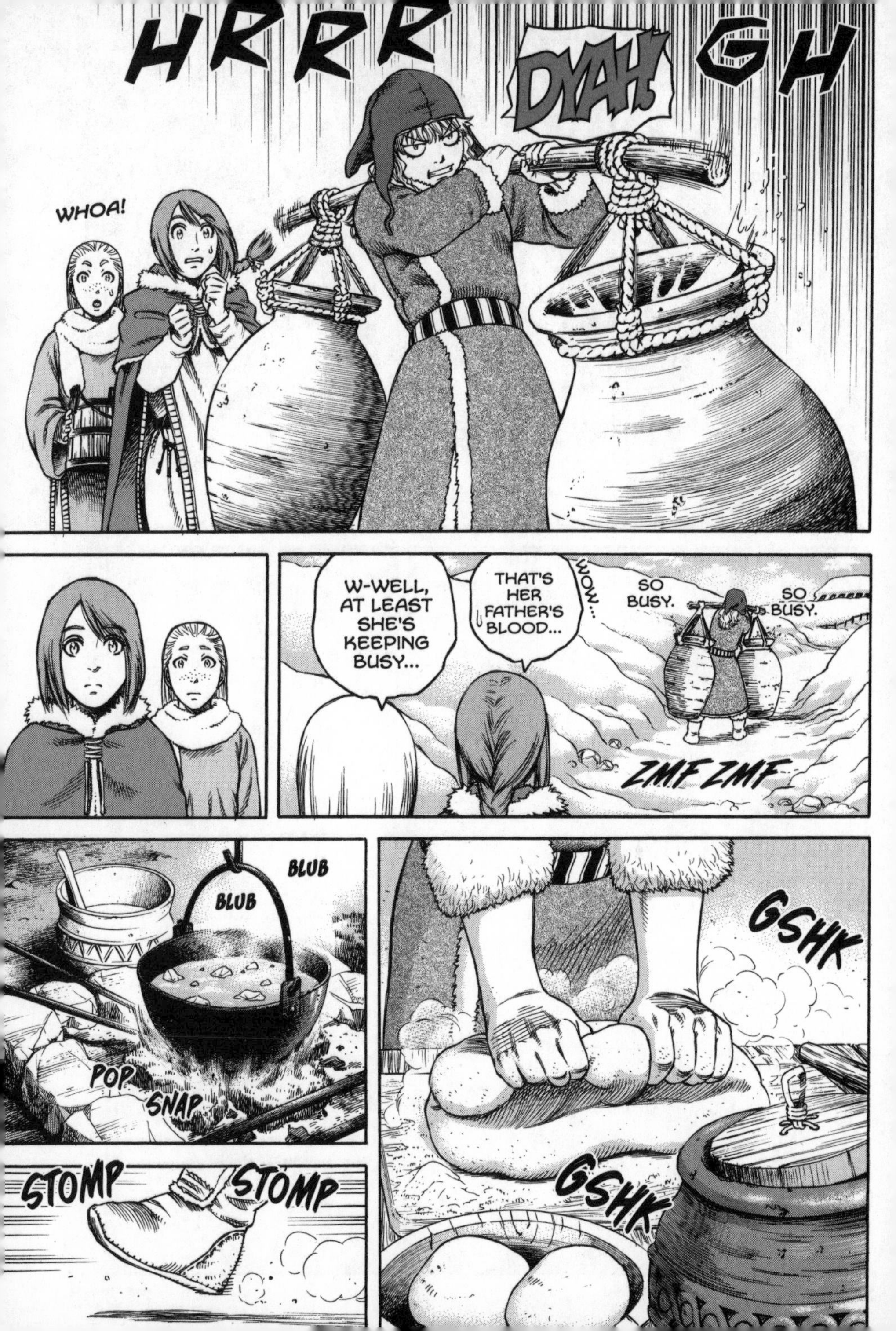
HRRR
DYAH!
GH
WHOA!
SO BUSY.
SO BUSY.
WOW...
THAT'S HER FATHER'S BLOOD...
W-WELL, AT LEAST SHE'S KEEPING BUSY...
ZMF ZMF
GSHK
GSHK
BLUB
BLUB
POP
SNAP
STOMP
STOMP

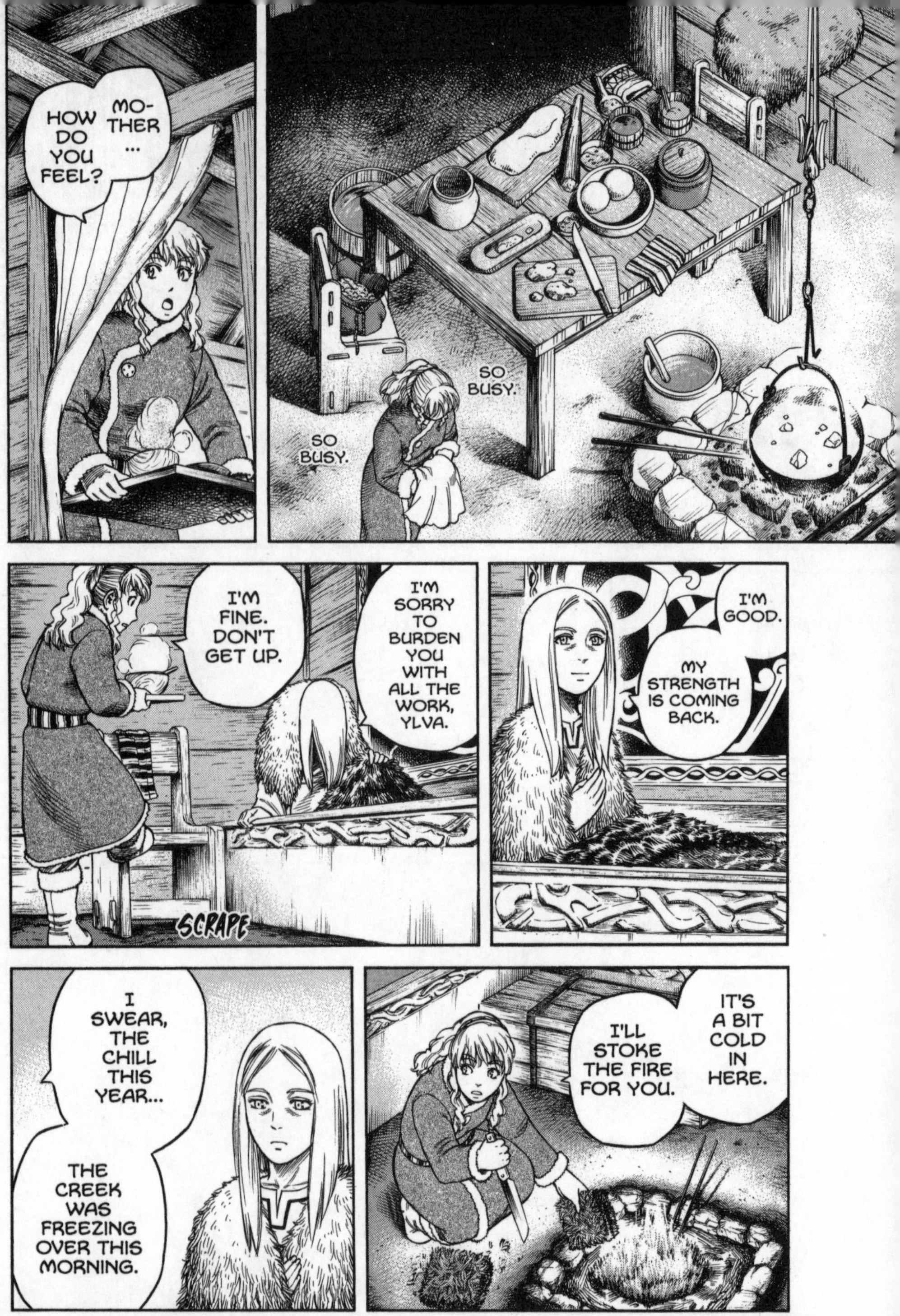
SO BUSY.
SO BUSY.
MO-THER ...
HOW DO YOU FEEL?
I'M GOOD.
MY STRENGTH IS COMING BACK.
I'M SORRY TO BURDEN YOU WITH ALL THE WORK, YLVA.
I'M FINE. DON'T GET UP.
SCRAPE
IT'S A BIT COLD IN HERE.
I'LL STOKE THE FIRE FOR YOU.
I SWEAR, THE CHILL THIS YEAR...
THE CREEK WAS FREEZING OVER THIS MORNING.

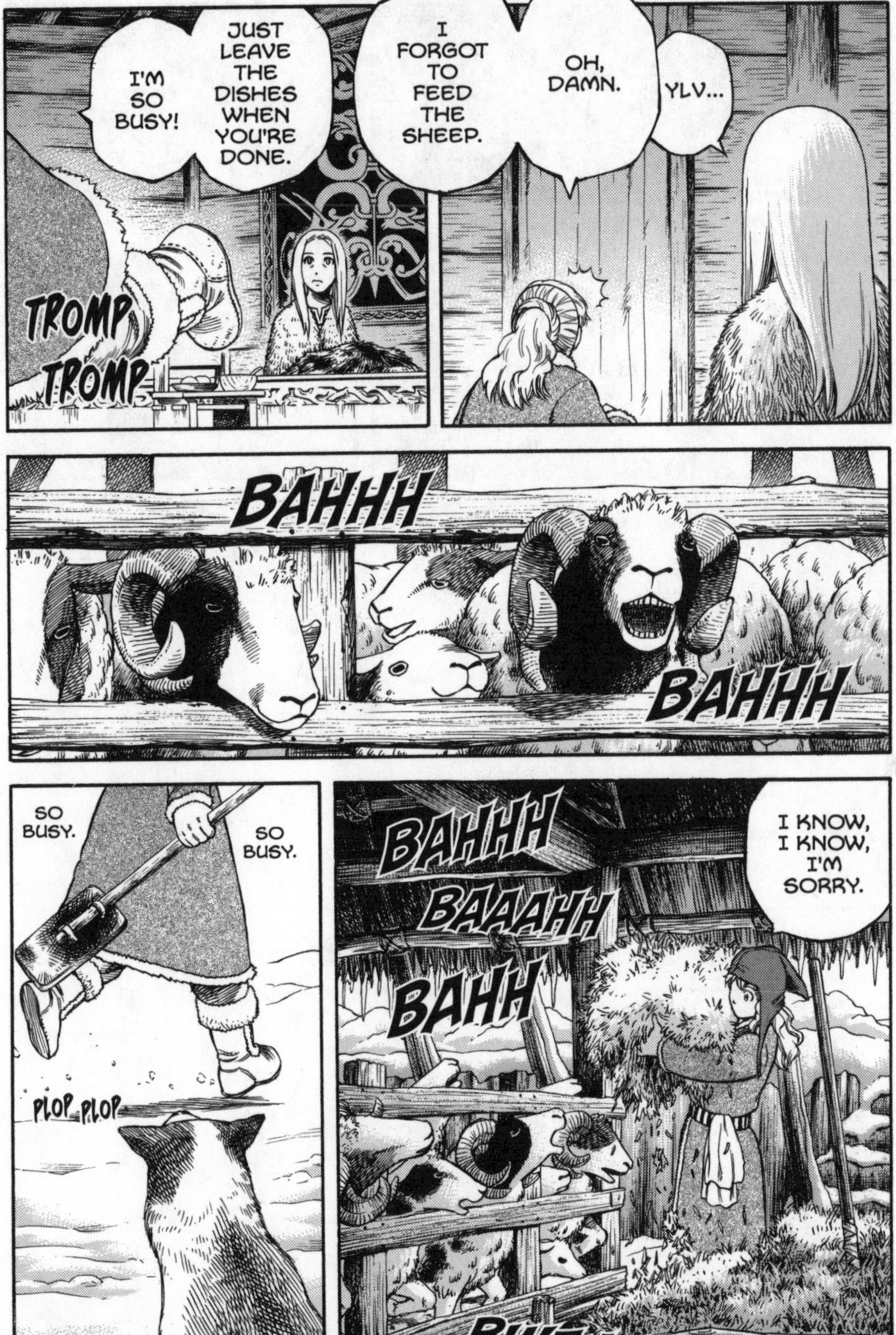
YLV...
OH, DAMN.
I FORGOT TO FEED THE SHEEP.
JUST LEAVE THE DISHES WHEN YOU'RE DONE.
I'M SO BUSY!
TROMP TROMP
BAHHH
BAHHH
I KNOW, I KNOW, I'M SORRY.
BAHHH
BAAAHH
BAHH
BWEHH
SO BUSY.
SO BUSY.
PLOP PLOP

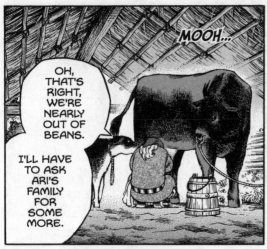

TSST
MOOH...
OH, THAT'S RIGHT, WE'RE NEARLY OUT OF BEANS.
I'LL HAVE TO ASK ARI'S FAMILY FOR SOME MORE.
AND I'LL NEED HELP SHEARING THE SHEEP COME THE SPRING.
SHK
SHK
IT'S FAR TOO MUCH FOR MOTHER AND ME TO HANDLE OURSELVES.
THIS LABOR SHORTAGE IS A CRISIS.
RAHHH
WHAT CAN I DO? TAKE A HUSBAND?
MEN! GET THE MEN!
GRAB YOUR HARPOONS AND GET TO THE WATER! HURRY!!
RAHH

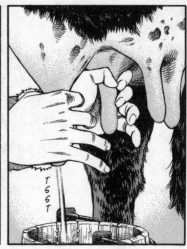

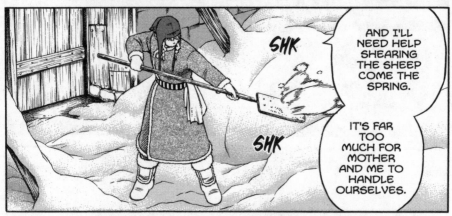

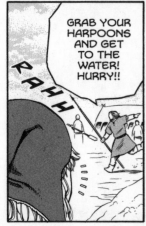

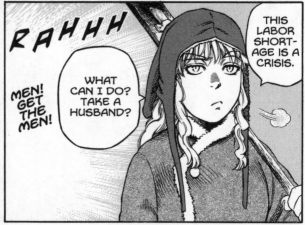

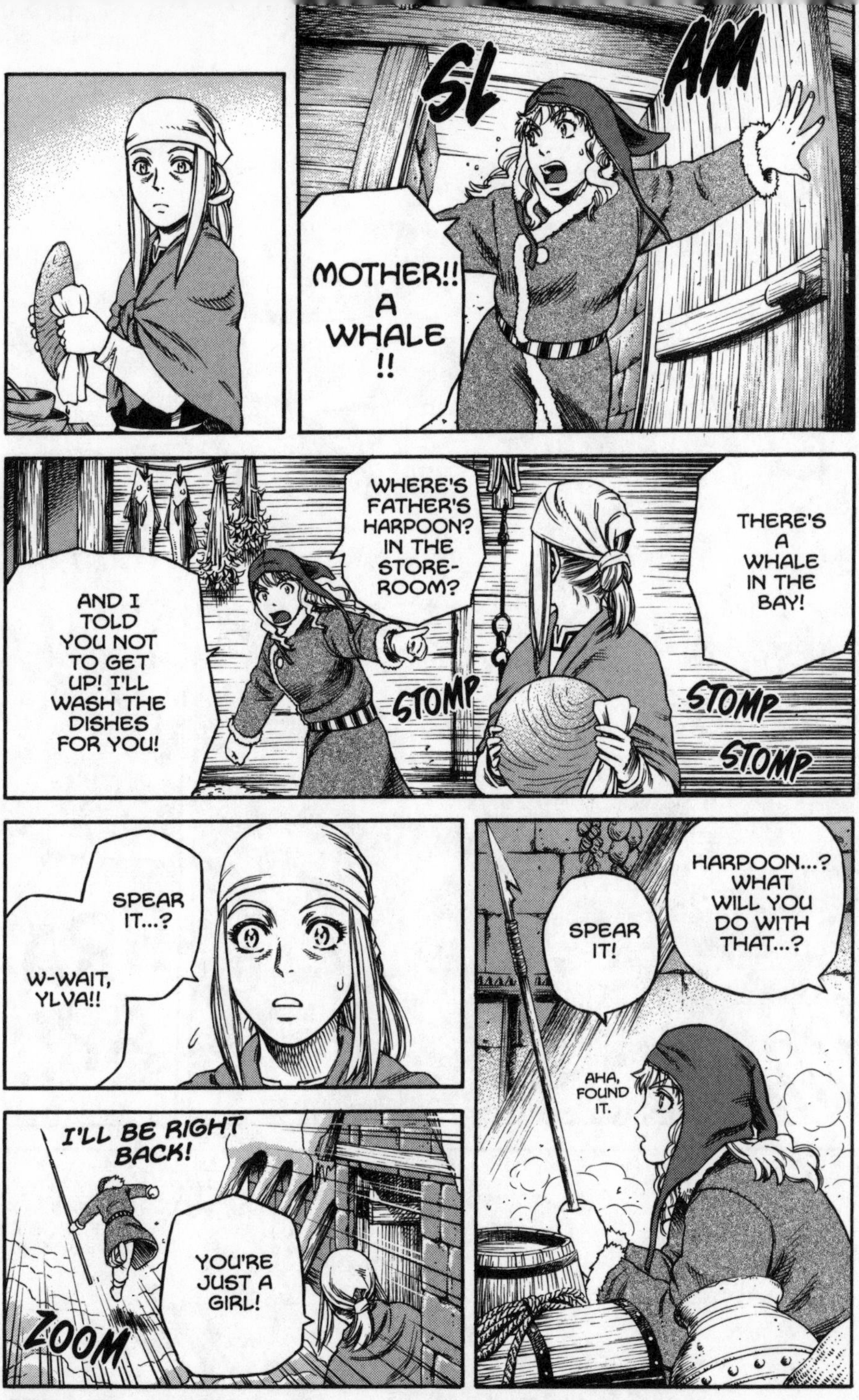
SLAM
MOTHER!! A WHALE !!
THERE'S A WHALE IN THE BAY!
STOMP
STOMP
WHERE'S FATHER'S HARPOON? IN THE STORE-ROOM?
STOMP
AND I TOLD YOU NOT TO GET UP! I'LL WASH THE DISHES FOR YOU!
HARPOON...? WHAT WILL YOU DO WITH THAT...?
SPEAR IT!
AHA, FOUND IT.
SPEAR IT...?
W-WAIT, YLVA!!
I'LL BE RIGHT BACK!
YOU'RE JUST A GIRL!
ZOOM

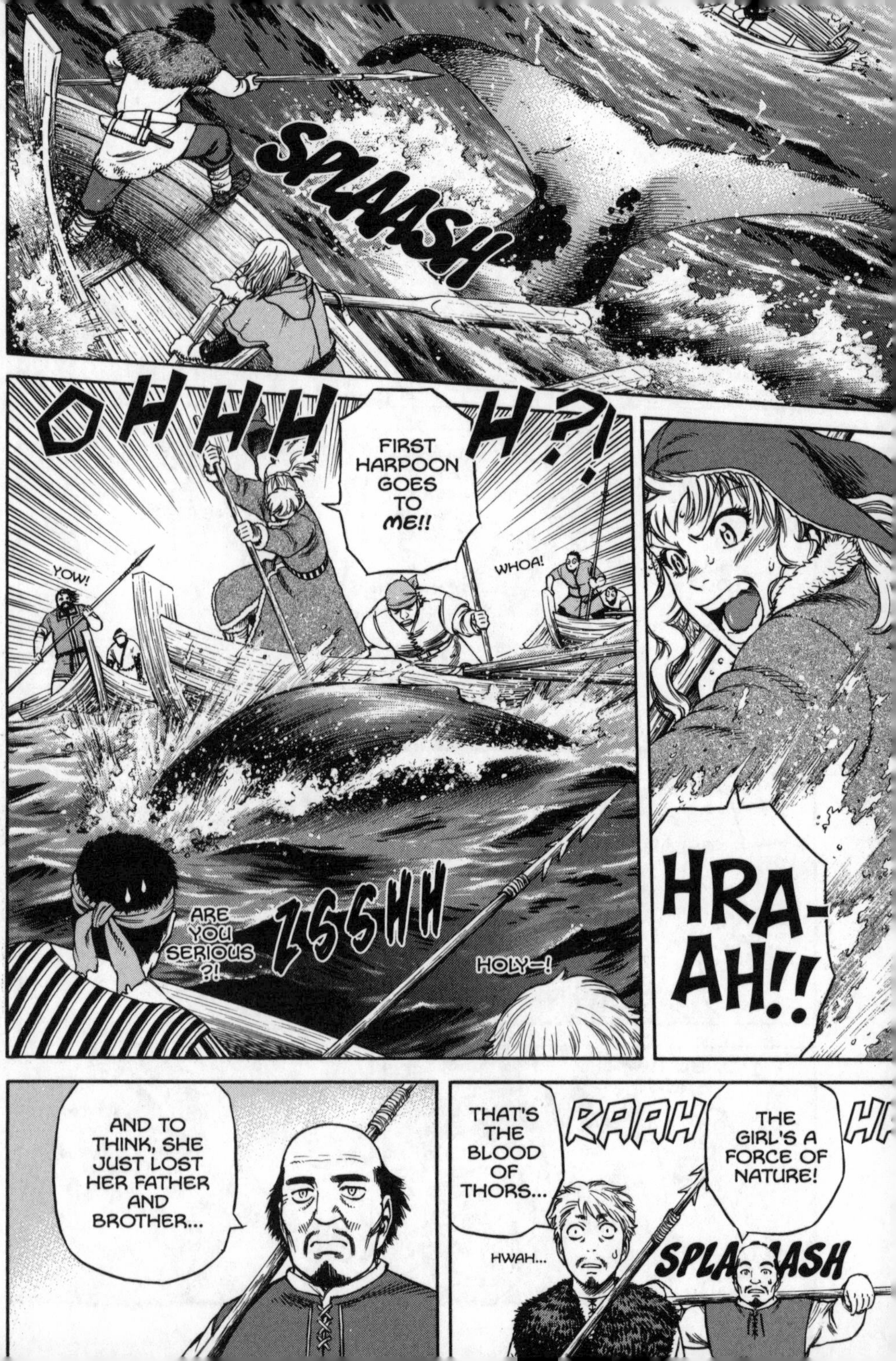
SPLAASH
HRA-AH!!
OHHHH H?!
FIRST HARPOON GOES TO ME!!
WHOA!
YOW!
HOLY—!
ZSSHH
ARE YOU SERIOUS ?!
RAAH
THE GIRL'S A FORCE OF NATURE!
THAT'S THE BLOOD OF THORS...
HWAH...
SPLA ASH
AND TO THINK, SHE JUST LOST HER FATHER AND BROTHER...

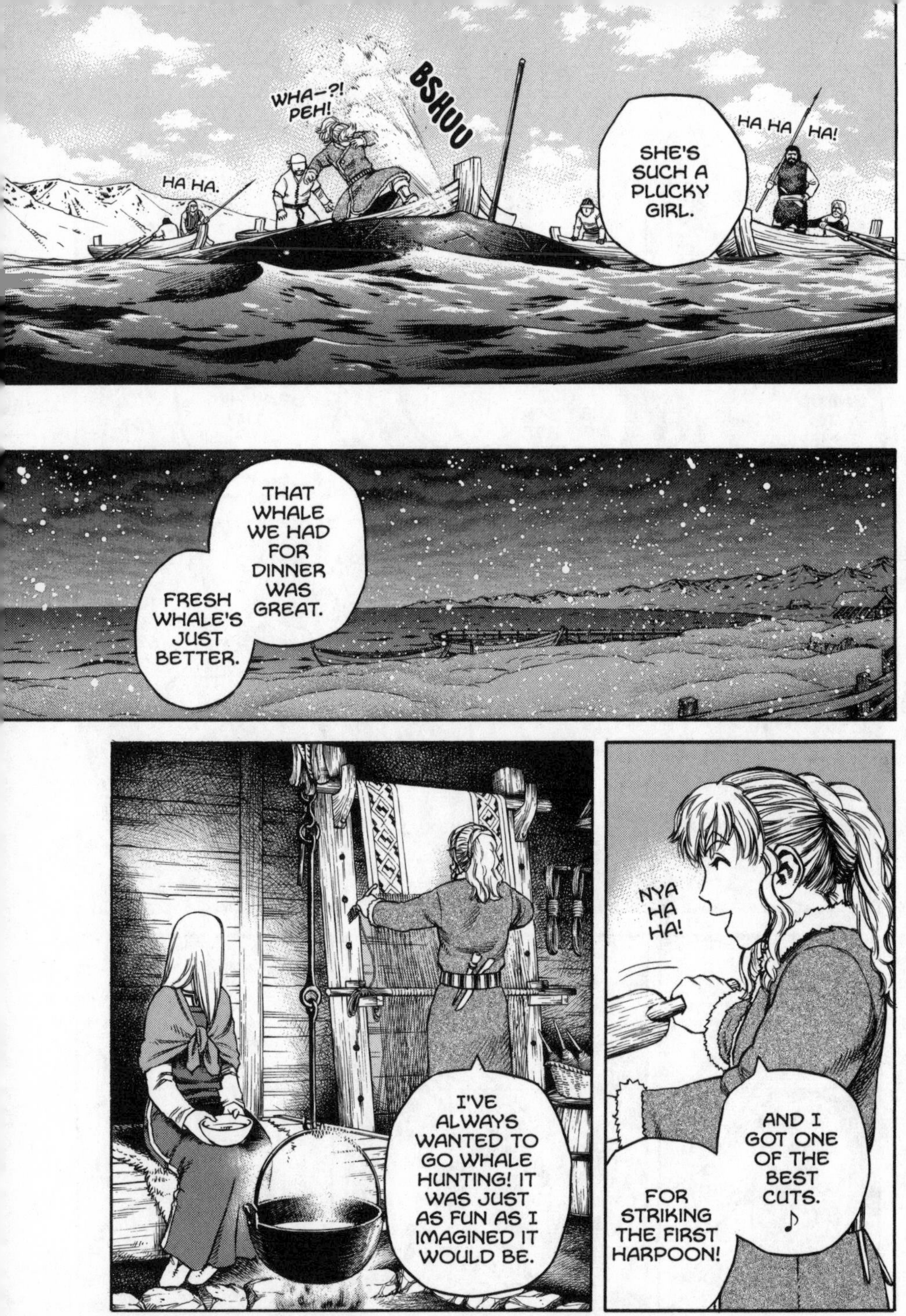
HA HA HA!
SHE'S SUCH A PLUCKY GIRL.
BSHUU
WHA—?! PEH!
HA HA.
THAT WHALE WE HAD FOR DINNER WAS GREAT.
FRESH WHALE'S JUST BETTER.
NYA HA HA!
AND I GOT ONE OF THE BEST CUTS. ♪
FOR STRIKING THE FIRST HARPOON!
I'VE ALWAYS WANTED TO GO WHALE HUNTING! IT WAS JUST AS FUN AS I IMAGINED IT WOULD BE.

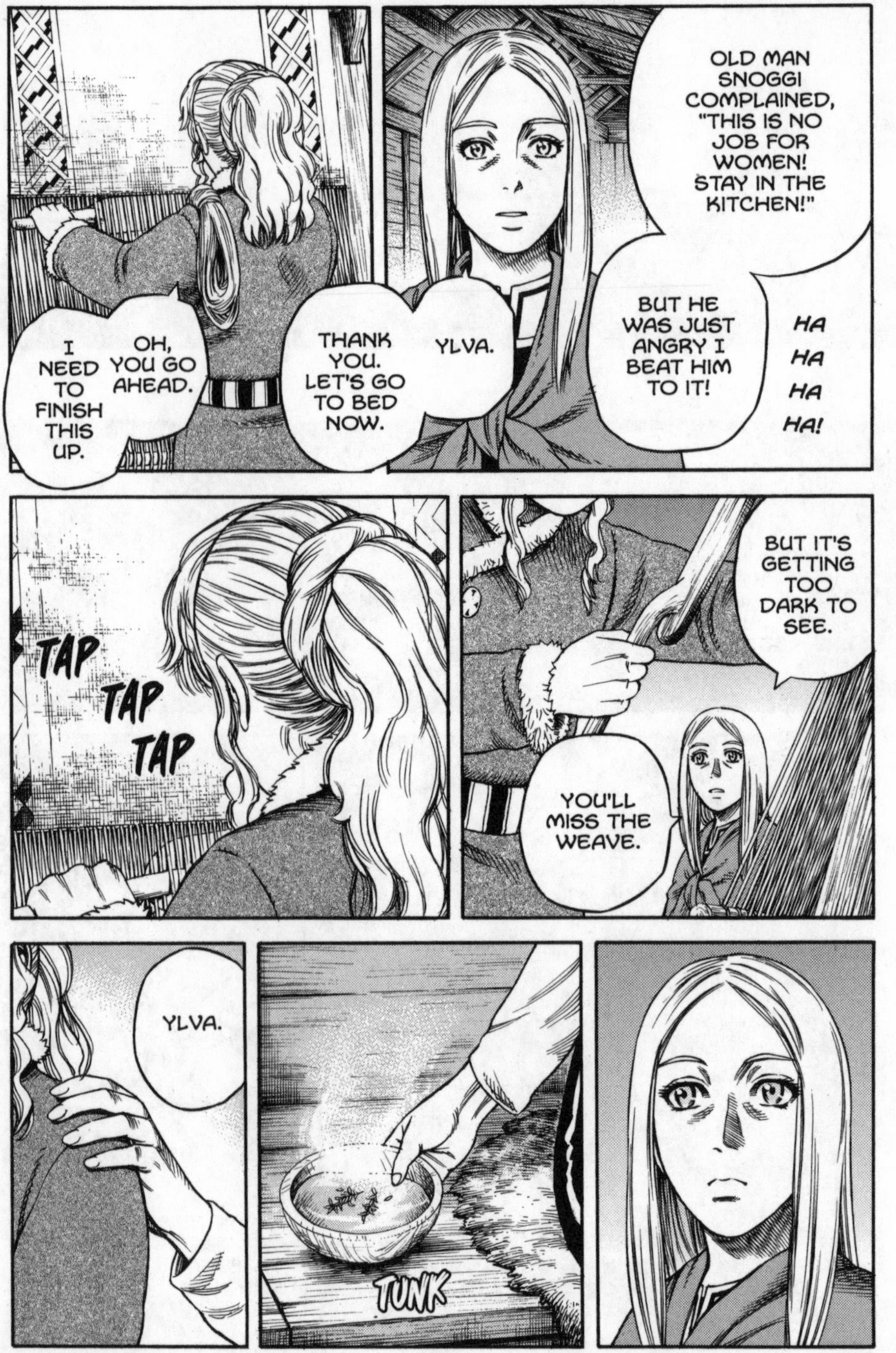
OLD MAN SNOGGI COMPLAINED, "THIS IS NO JOB FOR WOMEN! STAY IN THE KITCHEN!"
BUT HE WAS JUST ANGRY I BEAT HIM TO IT!
HA HA HA HA!
YLVA.
THANK YOU. LET'S GO TO BED NOW.
OH, YOU GO AHEAD.
I NEED TO FINISH THIS UP.
BUT IT'S GETTING TOO DARK TO SEE.
YOU'LL MISS THE WEAVE.
TAP TAP TAP
TUNK
YLVA.

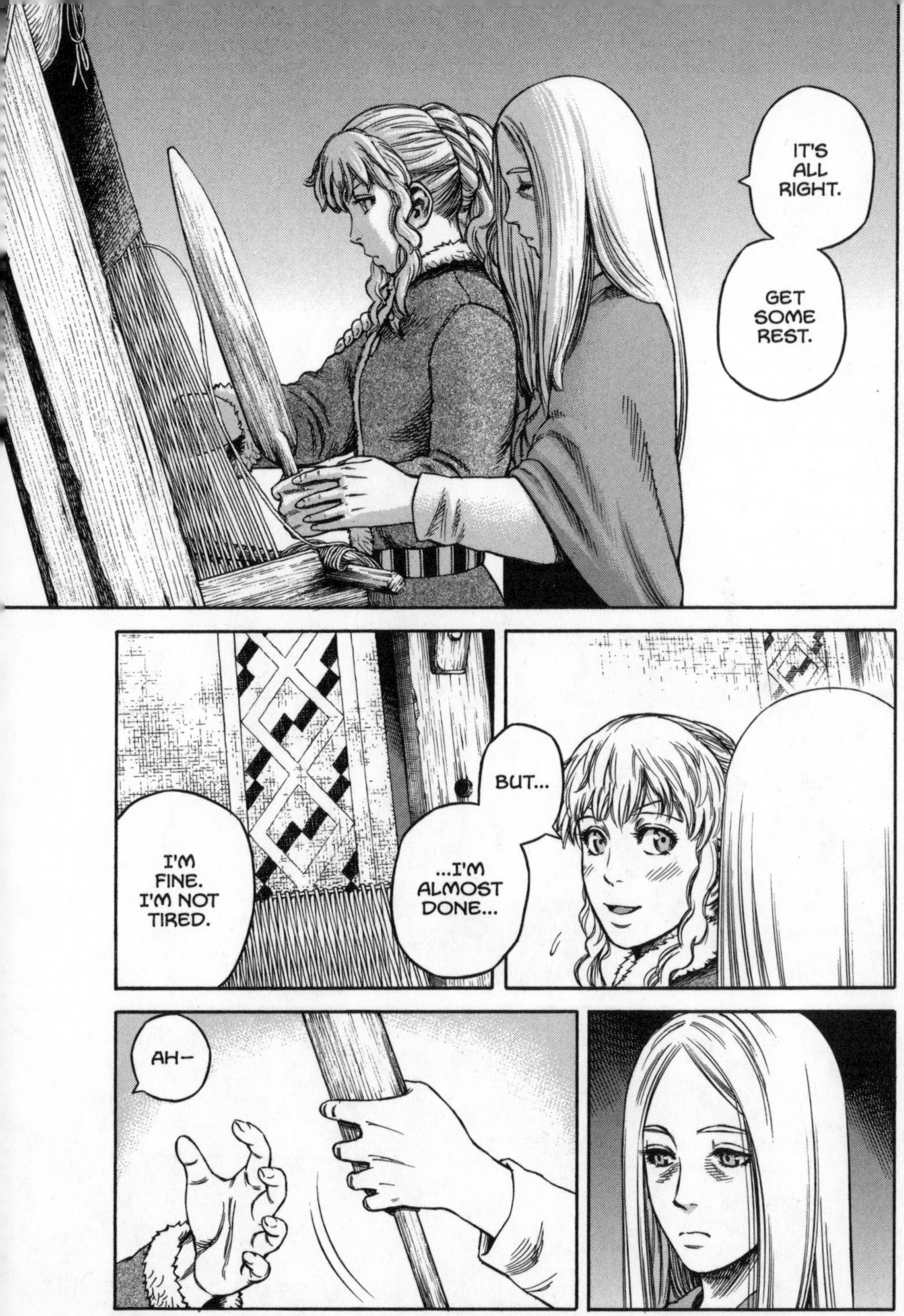
IT'S ALL RIGHT.
GET SOME REST.
BUT...
...I'M ALMOST DONE...
I'M FINE. I'M NOT TIRED.
AH–

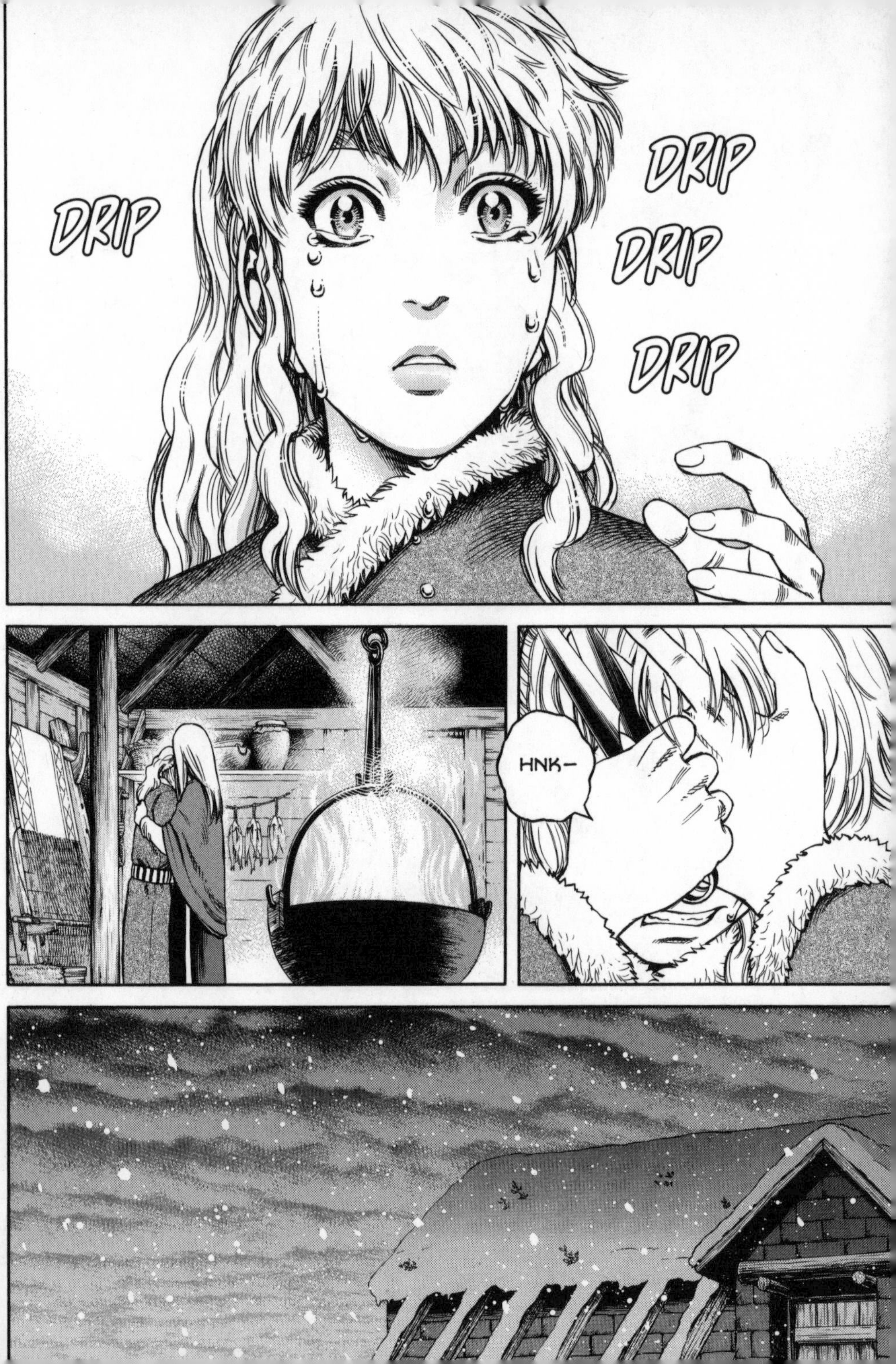
DRIP
DRIP
DRIP
DRIP
HNK–

BONUS STORY 1 • END

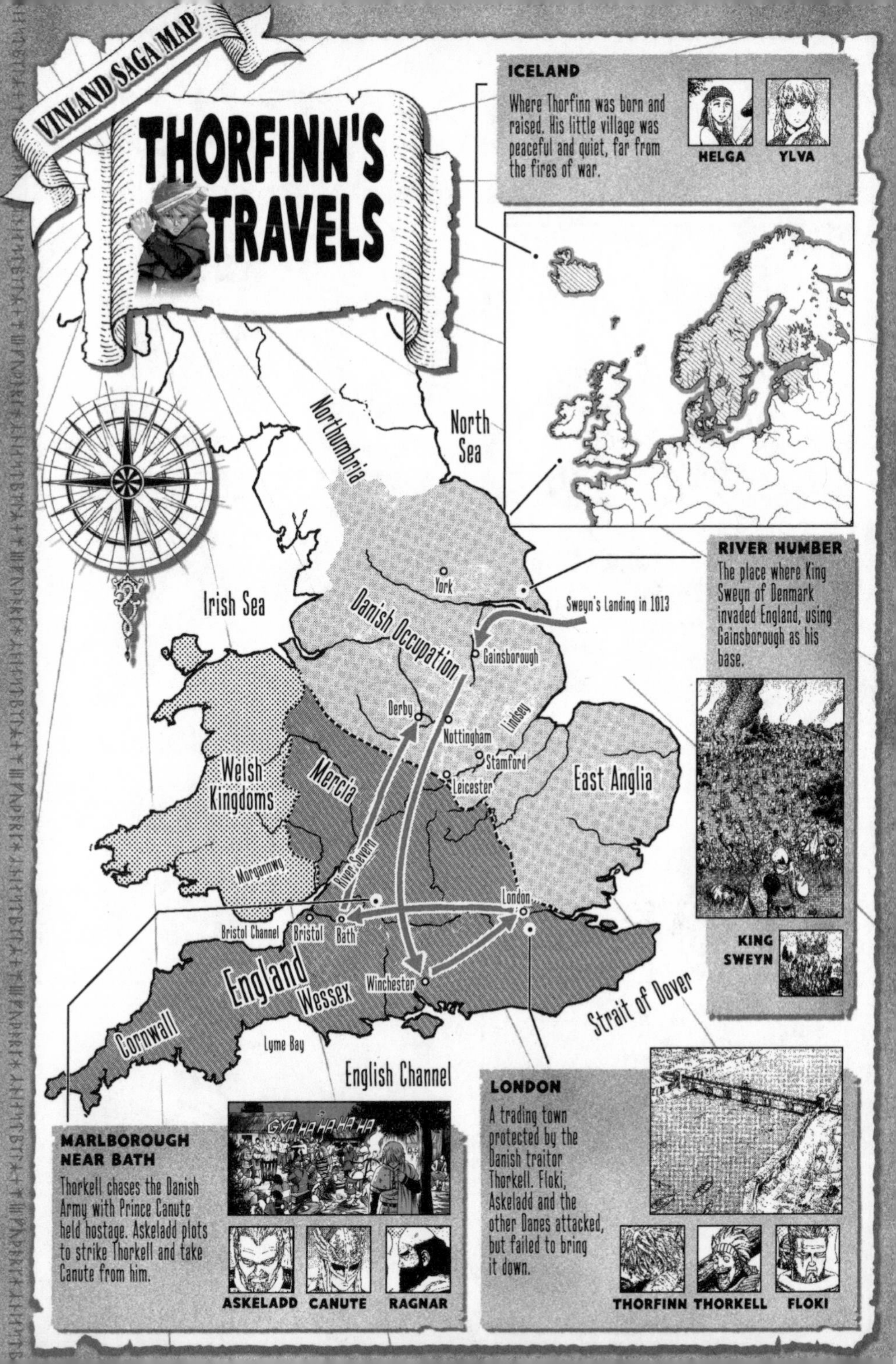

VINLAND SAGA MAP
THORFINN'S TRAVELS
ICELAND
Where Thorfinn was born and raised. His little village was peaceful and quiet, far from the fires of war.
HELGA
YLVA
North Sea
Northumbria
RIVER HUMBER
The place where King Sweyn of Denmark invaded England, using Gainsborough as his base.
York
Irish Sea
Danish Occupation
Sweyn's Landing in 1013
Gainsborough
Derby
Nottingham
Lindsey
Stamford
Leicester
Welsh Kingdoms
Mercia
East Anglia
River Severn
Morgannwg
London
Bristol Channel
Bristol
Bath
KING SWEYN
England
Wessex
Winchester
Strait of Dover
Cornwall
Lyme Bay
English Channel
LONDON
A trading town protected by the Danish traitor Thorkell. Floki, Askeladd and the other Danes attacked, but failed to bring it down.
GYA HA HA HA HA
MARLBOROUGH NEAR BATH
Thorkell chases the Danish Army with Prince Canute held hostage. Askeladd plots to strike Thorkell and take Canute from him.
ASKELADD
CANUTE
RAGNAR
THORFINN
THORKELL
FLOKI

ARTIST INTRODUCTIONS

WE MADE THIS.

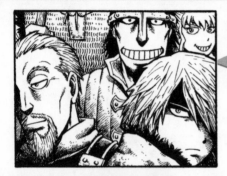

HAITO KUMAGAI

SENSEI'S KARAOKE IS AMAZING. YOUR LOCAL PUNK BAND HAS NOTHING ON THIS GUY.

HE'S FAST, TALENTED, AND DOES THE WORK OF THREE. GREAT FOR GORY SCENES.

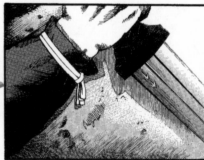

KAZUOKI SUZUKI

YUKIMURA-SENSEI IS A GREAT ARTIST WHO PROVIDES GENTLE GUIDANCE FOR EVEN A ROOKIE SUCH AS MYSELF. HOWEVER, I HAVE TO ASK YOU TO STOP TOUCHING MY BUTT.

NO WAY. I'LL NEVER STOP. I'D LIKE TO SEE YOU TRY TO SUE ME.

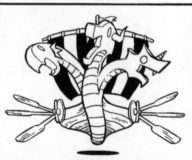

TOMOYUKI TAKAMI

I MAKE DOJINSHI SOMETIMES. MY CIRCLE'S NAME IS "GENKAI TSUSHINSHA." IF YOU SEE ONE ANYWHERE, PICK IT UP.

THEY'RE REALLY WELL-MADE DOJINSHI. 500 YEN IS A STEAL!

HOORAY! VINLAND SAGA VOLUME 3
IS OUT NOW !!
WAIT, THAT'S NOT THREE FINGERS!
AW, CRAP.

DAIJU WATANABE

I HAVE A ONE-SHOT MANGA IN "TALES OF WARLORDS," OCTOBER 2006. I'VE USED ALL THE TRICKS YUKIMURA-SENSEI TAUGHT ME, SO CHECK IT OUT.

HE'S GREAT AT MARIO KART AND KARAOKE. I'LL BEAT HIM SOMEDAY, THOUGH.

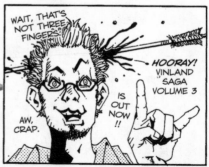

AFTERWORD

The more I draw Vikings, the more questions I have. What did they use to cut their toenails? Scissors? Did they get cavities without toothbrushes? Did they clean their ears out? What did they use? They sound like silly, pointless questions, but if one is to depict the Vikings' daily lives in art, that makes them very important, in my opinion. After all, they didn't spend every waking moment at war. I guess I find these topics much more interesting than stuffy chronologies and historical accounts. By the way, I have yet to find any reference to the Vikings' post-toilet wiping habits in my reference materials. I mean, not that I'm considering that to be the final say in the matter...yet...

MAKOTO YUKIMURA

VINLAND SAGA

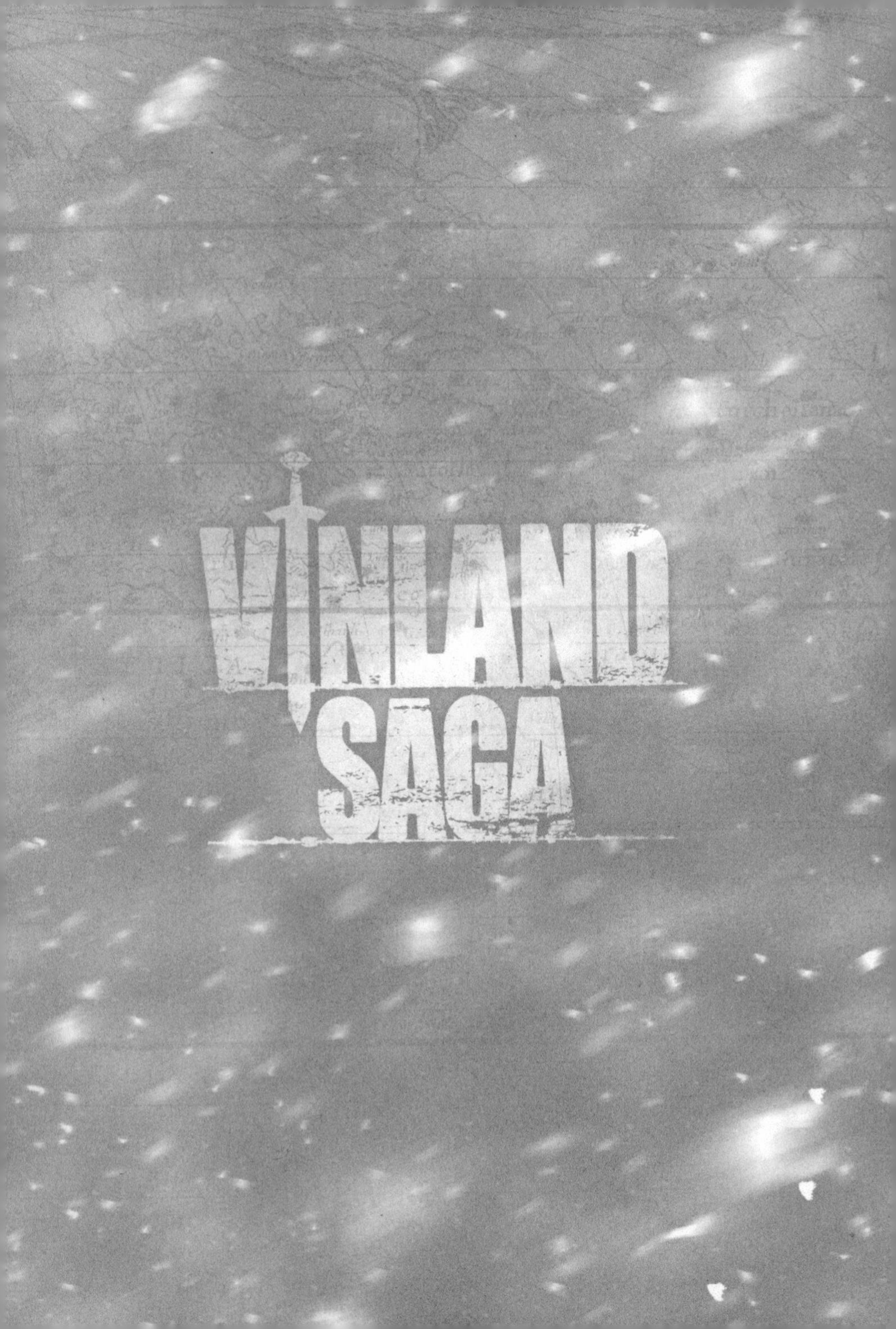
VINLAND
SAGA

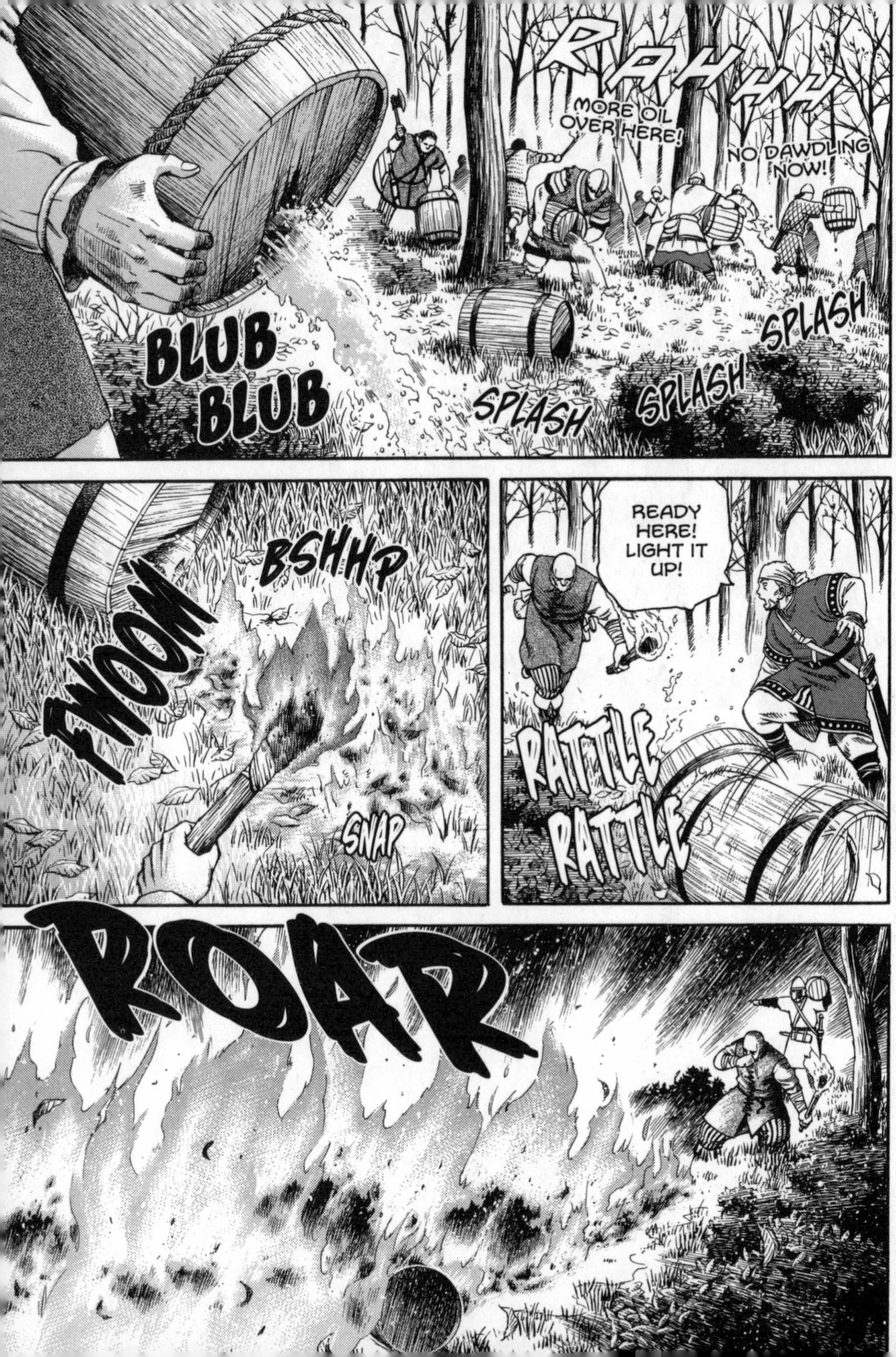
RAHHH
NO DAWDLING NOW!
MORE OIL OVER HERE!
SPLASH
SPLASH
SPLASH
BLUB BLUB
READY HERE! LIGHT IT UP!
RATTLE RATTLE
BSHHP
FWOOM
SNAP
ROAR

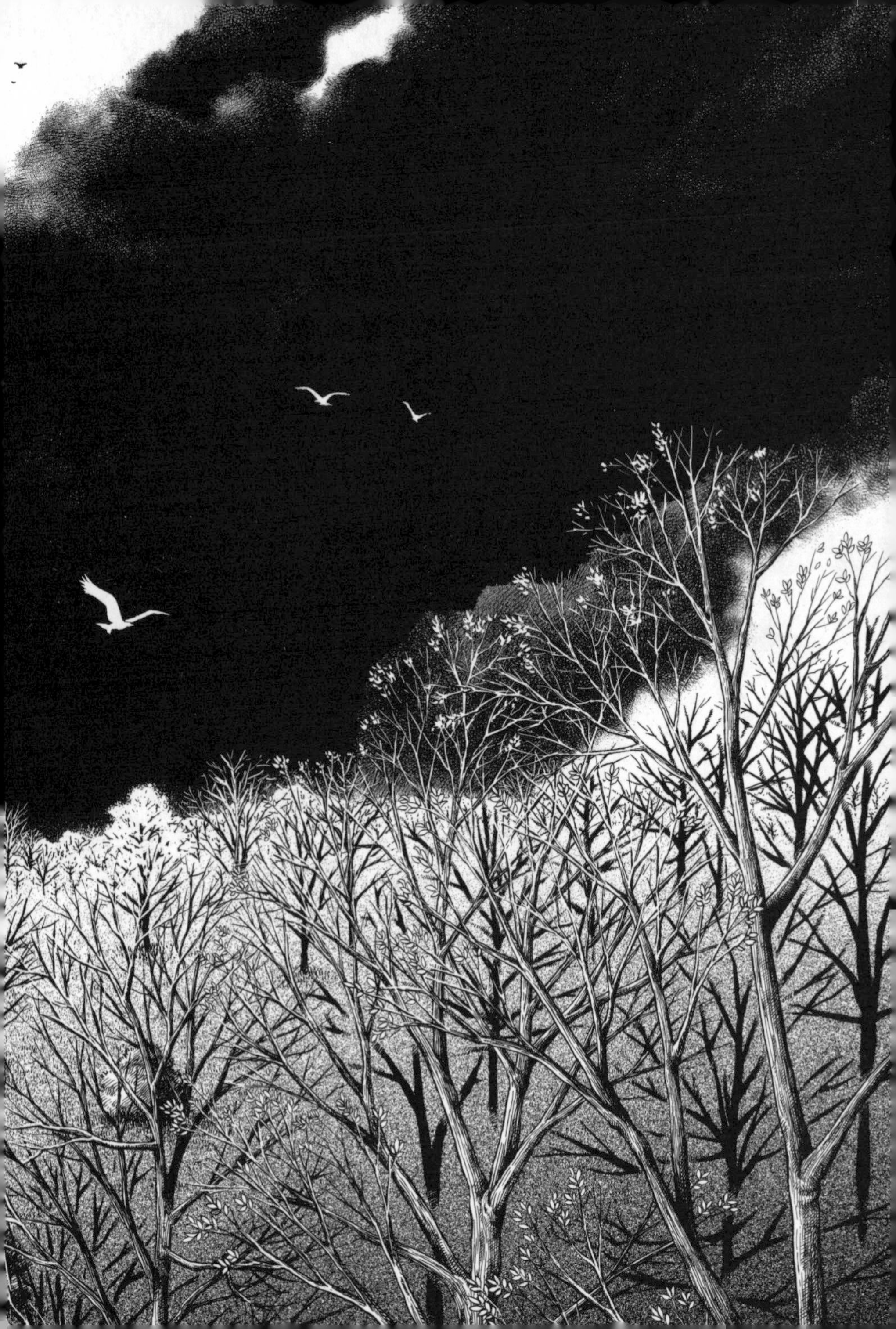

CHAPTER 22: THE TROLL'S SON

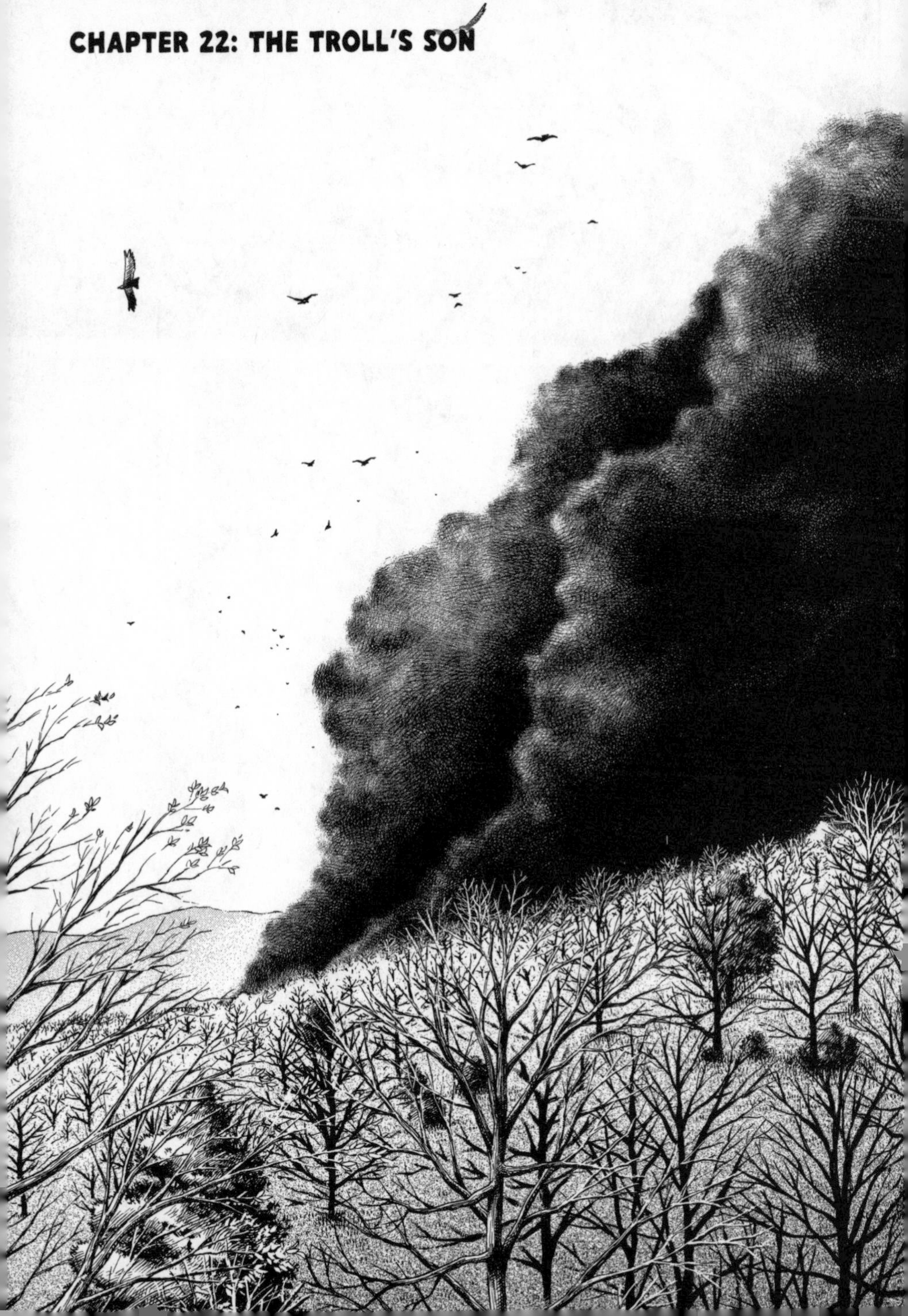

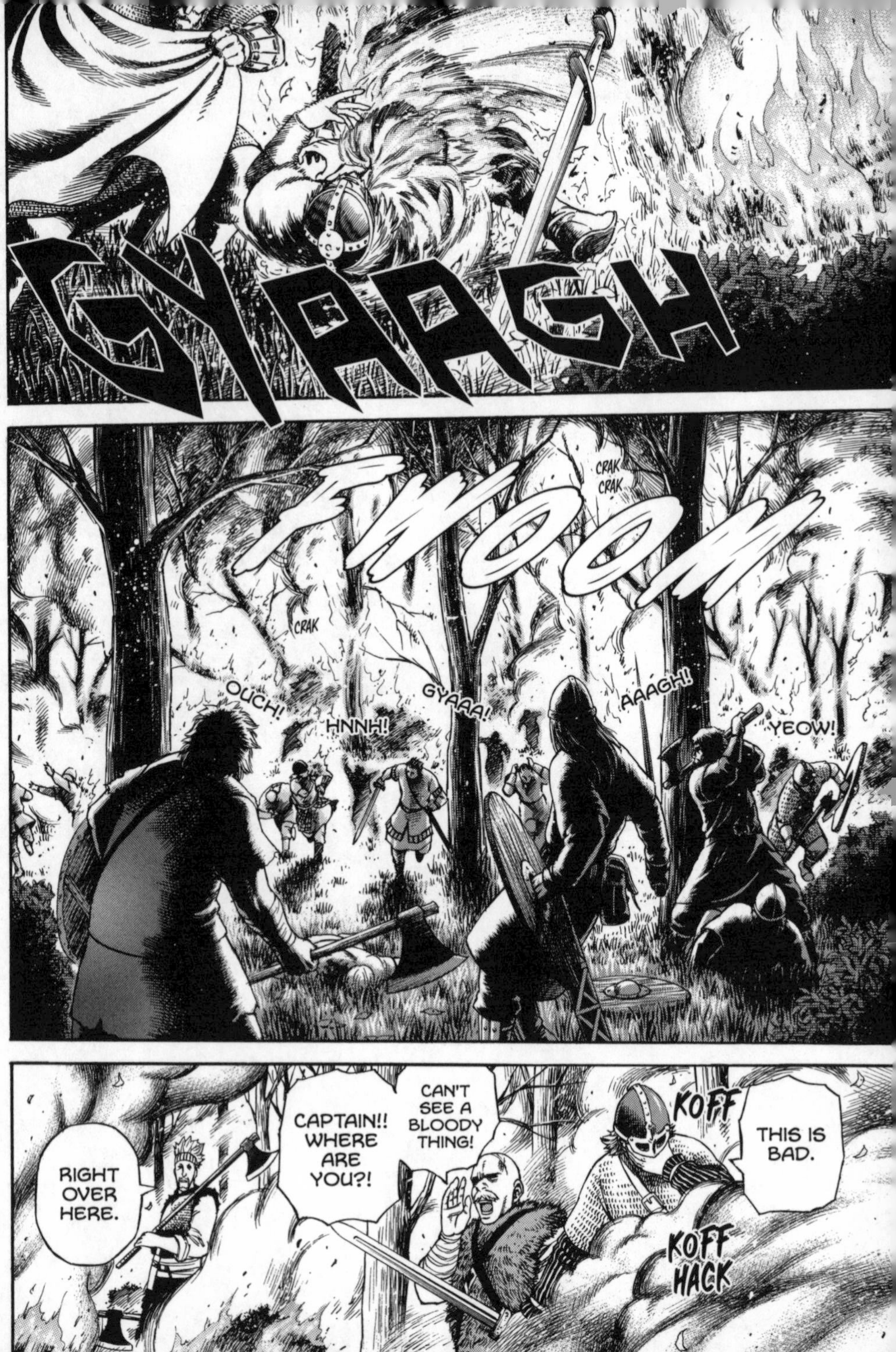
GYAAGH
FWOOM
CRAK CRAK
CRAK
YEOW!
AAAGH!
GYAAA!
HNNH!
OUCH!
KOFF
THIS IS BAD.
KOFF HACK
CAN'T SEE A BLOODY THING!
CAPTAIN!! WHERE ARE YOU?!
RIGHT OVER HERE.

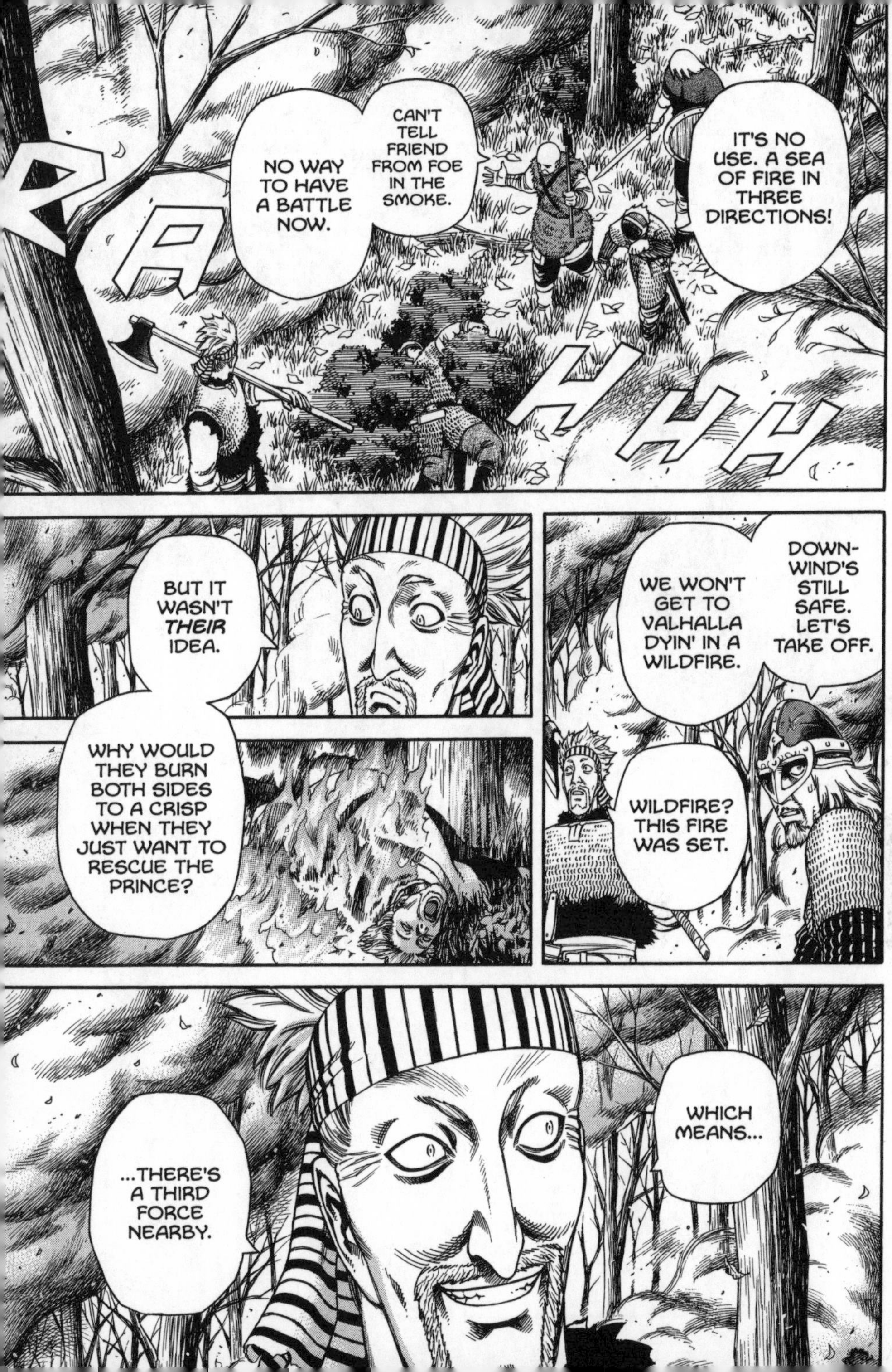
IT'S NO USE. A SEA OF FIRE IN THREE DIRECTIONS!
CAN'T TELL FRIEND FROM FOE IN THE SMOKE.
NO WAY TO HAVE A BATTLE NOW.
RAHHH
DOWN-WIND'S STILL SAFE. LET'S TAKE OFF.
WE WON'T GET TO VALHALLA DYIN' IN A WILDFIRE.
WILDFIRE? THIS FIRE WAS SET.
BUT IT WASN'T *THEIR* IDEA.
WHY WOULD THEY BURN BOTH SIDES TO A CRISP WHEN THEY JUST WANT TO RESCUE THE PRINCE?
WHICH MEANS...
...THERE'S A THIRD FORCE NEARBY.

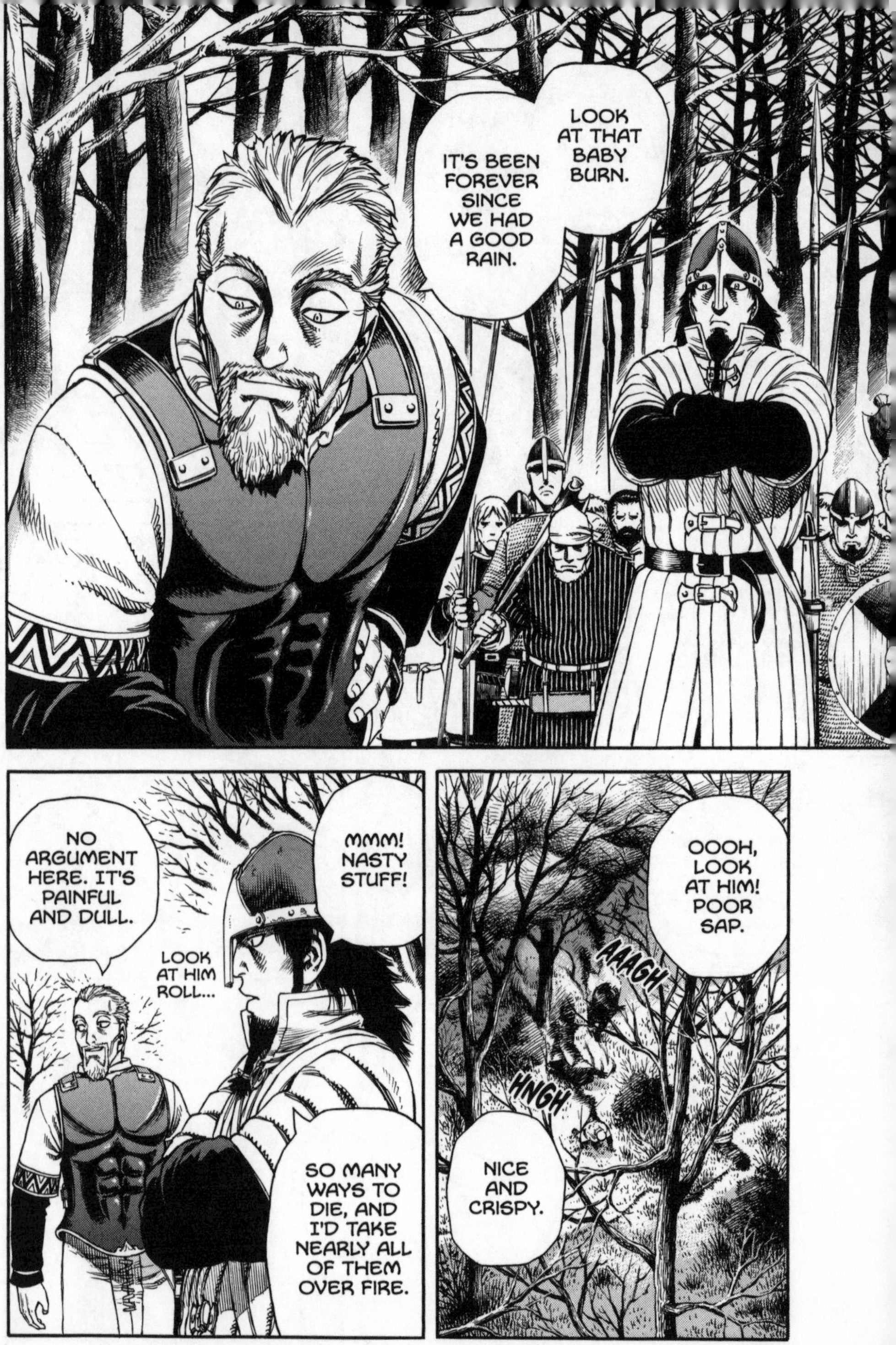
LOOK AT THAT BABY BURN.
IT'S BEEN FOREVER SINCE WE HAD A GOOD RAIN.
OOOH, LOOK AT HIM! POOR SAP.
AAAGH
HNGH
NICE AND CRISPY.
MMM! NASTY STUFF!
NO ARGUMENT HERE. IT'S PAINFUL AND DULL.
LOOK AT HIM ROLL...
SO MANY WAYS TO DIE, AND I'D TAKE NEARLY ALL OF THEM OVER FIRE.

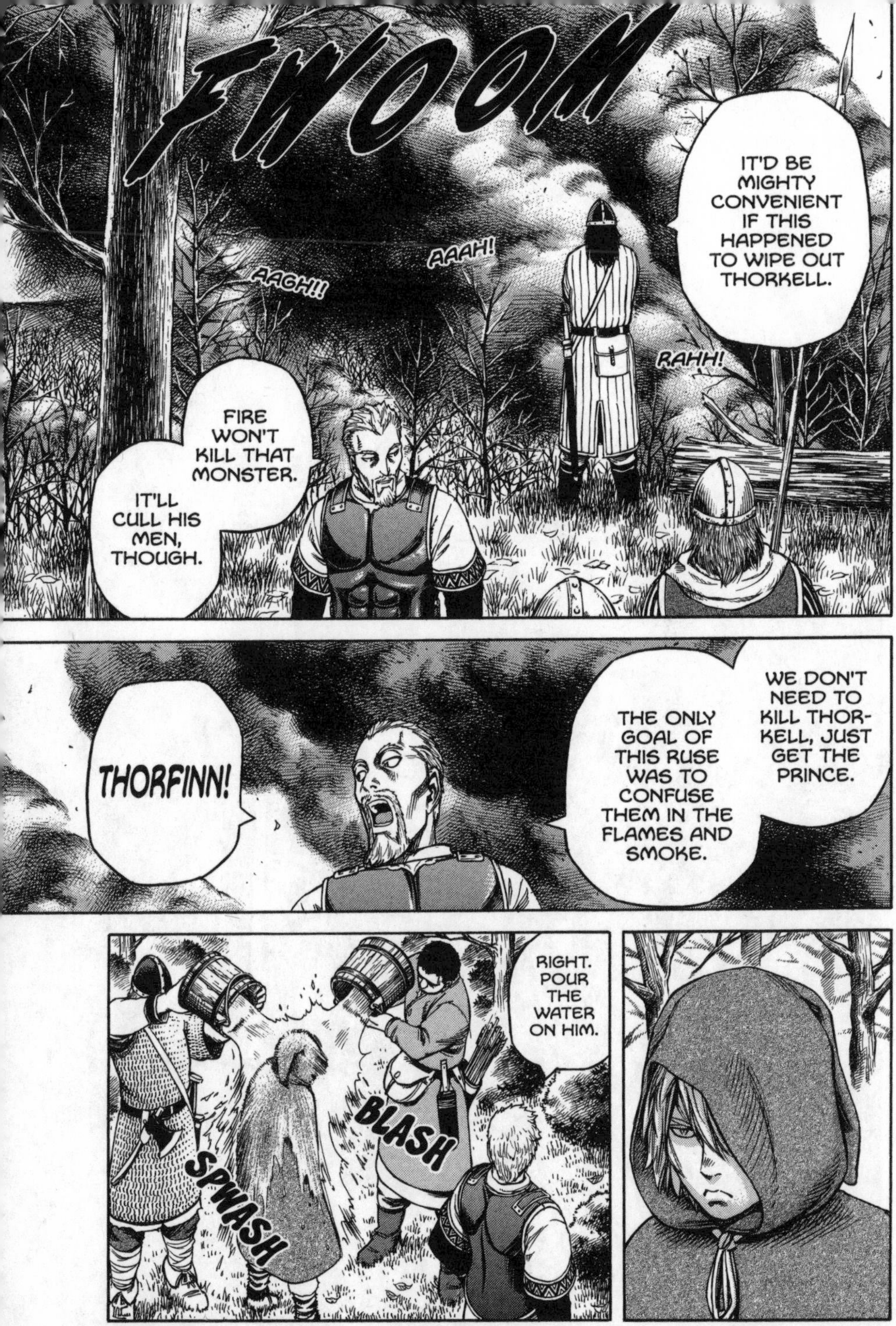
FWOOM
IT'D BE MIGHTY CONVENIENT IF THIS HAPPENED TO WIPE OUT THORKELL.
AAAH!
AAGH!!
RAHH!
FIRE WON'T KILL THAT MONSTER.
IT'LL CULL HIS MEN, THOUGH.
WE DON'T NEED TO KILL THOR-KELL, JUST GET THE PRINCE.
THE ONLY GOAL OF THIS RUSE WAS TO CONFUSE THEM IN THE FLAMES AND SMOKE.
THORFINN!
RIGHT. POUR THE WATER ON HIM.
BLASH
SPWASH

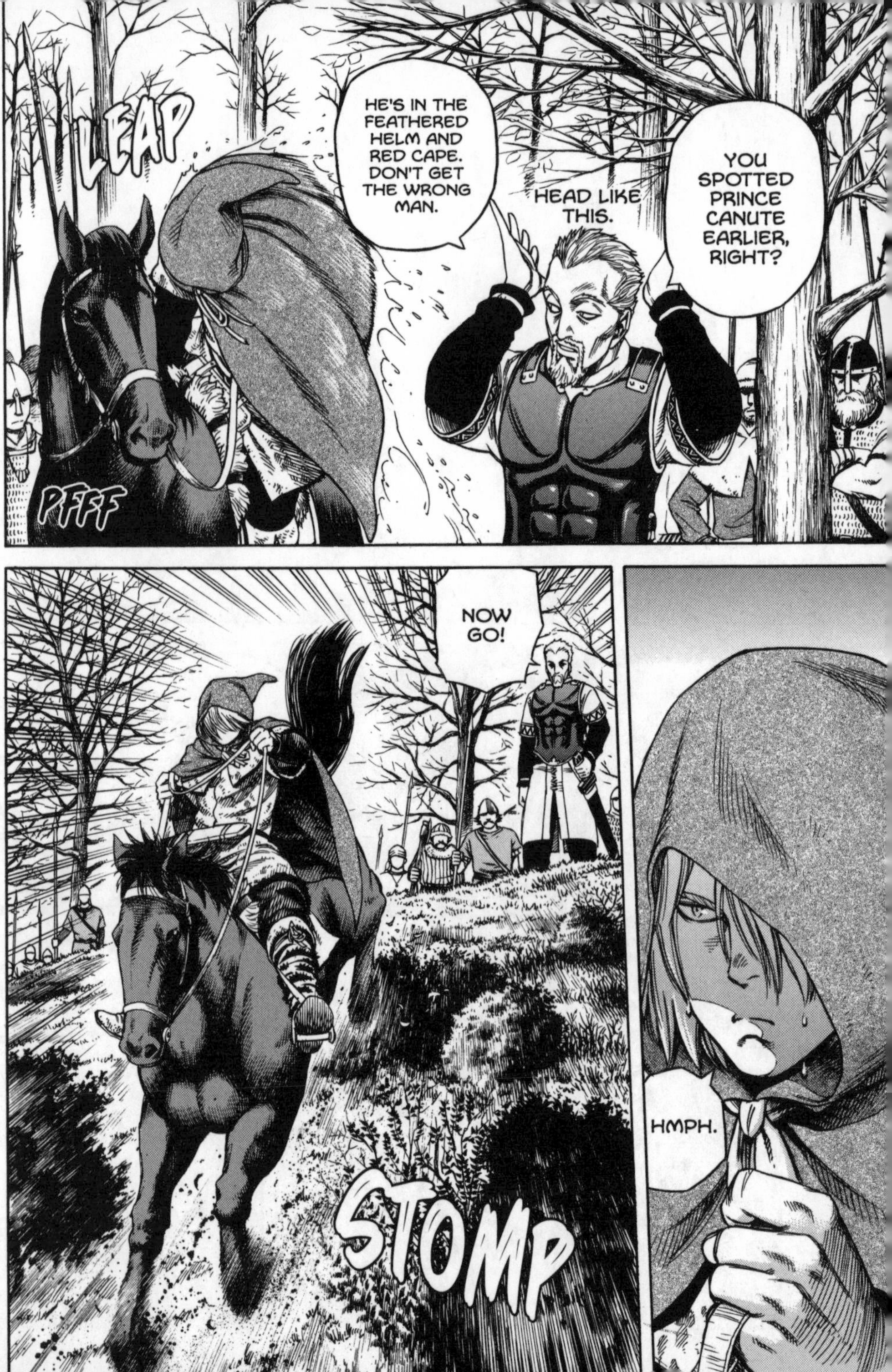
YOU SPOTTED PRINCE CANUTE EARLIER, RIGHT?
HEAD LIKE THIS.
HE'S IN THE FEATHERED HELM AND RED CAPE. DON'T GET THE WRONG MAN.
LEAP
PFFF
HMPH.
NOW GO!
STOMP

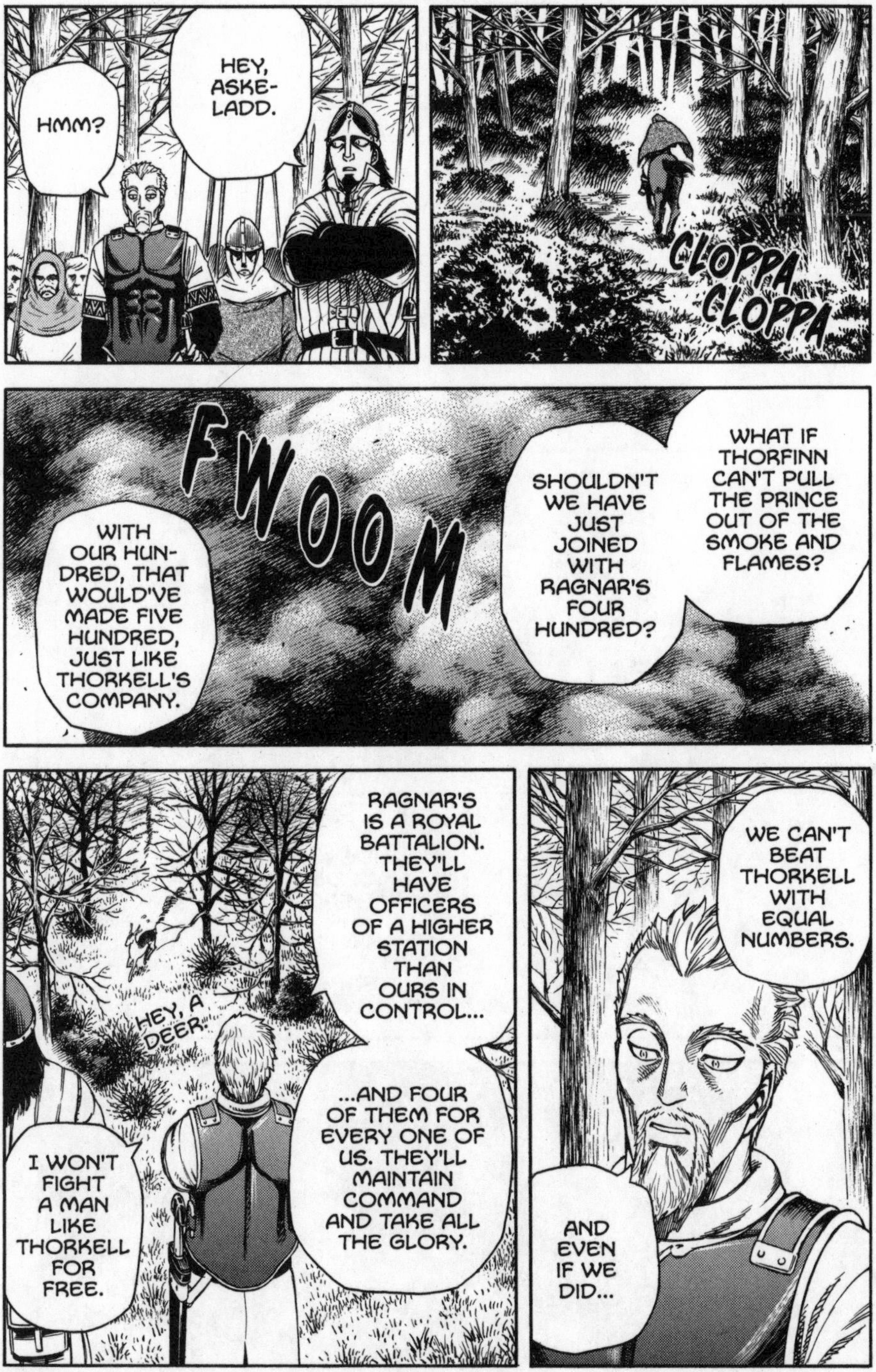
CLOPPA CLOPPA
HEY, ASKE-LADD.
HMM?
WHAT IF THORFINN CAN'T PULL THE PRINCE OUT OF THE SMOKE AND FLAMES?
SHOULDN'T WE HAVE JUST JOINED WITH RAGNAR'S FOUR HUNDRED?
FWOOM
WITH OUR HUN-DRED, THAT WOULD'VE MADE FIVE HUNDRED, JUST LIKE THORKELL'S COMPANY.
WE CAN'T BEAT THORKELL WITH EQUAL NUMBERS.
AND EVEN IF WE DID...
RAGNAR'S IS A ROYAL BATTALION. THEY'LL HAVE OFFICERS OF A HIGHER STATION THAN OURS IN CONTROL...
...AND FOUR OF THEM FOR EVERY ONE OF US. THEY'LL MAINTAIN COMMAND AND TAKE ALL THE GLORY.
HEY, A DEER.
I WON'T FIGHT A MAN LIKE THORKELL FOR FREE.

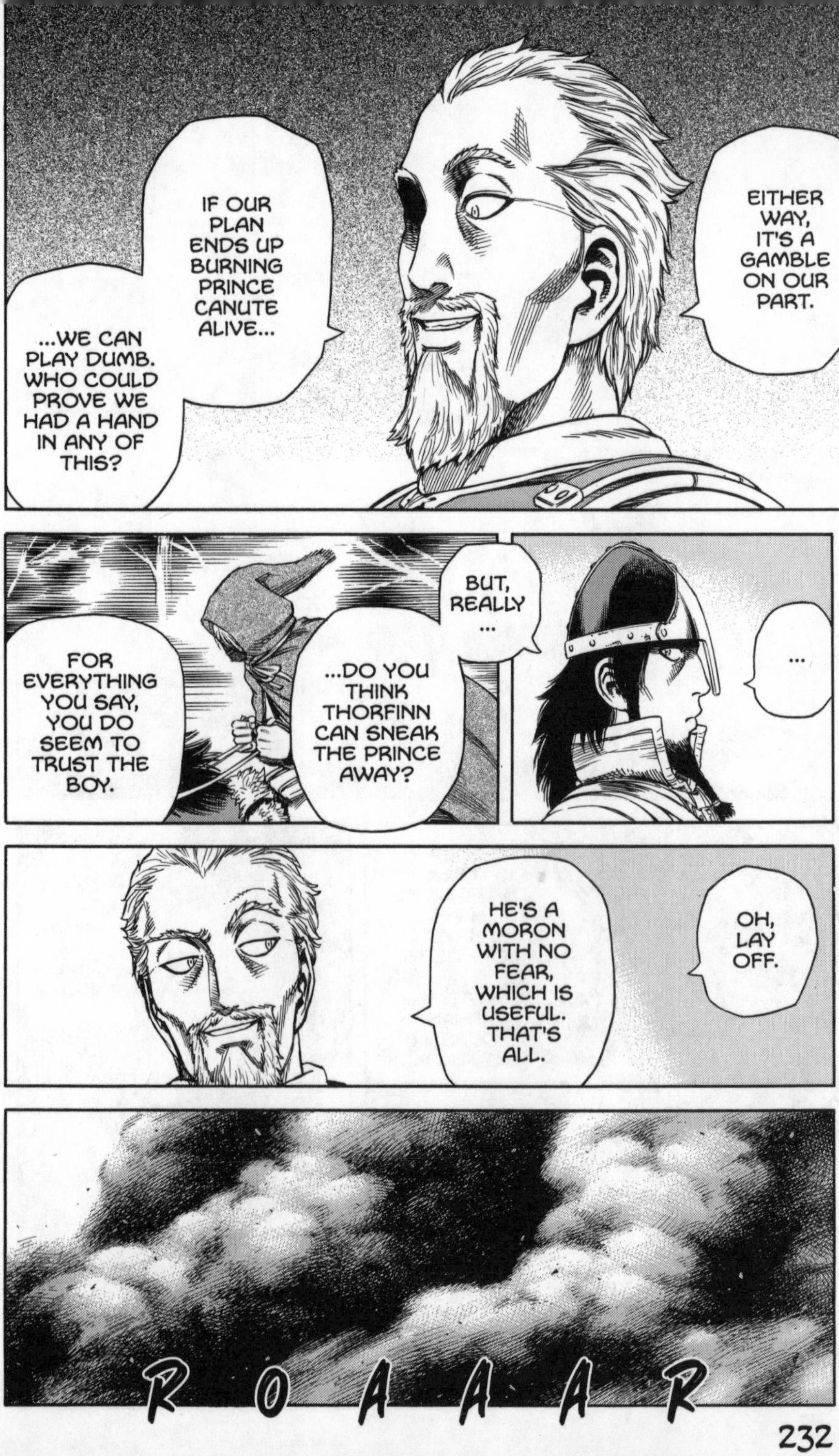
EITHER WAY, IT'S A GAMBLE ON OUR PART.
IF OUR PLAN ENDS UP BURNING PRINCE CANUTE ALIVE...
...WE CAN PLAY DUMB. WHO COULD PROVE WE HAD A HAND IN ANY OF THIS?
...
BUT, REALLY ...
...DO YOU THINK THORFINN CAN SNEAK THE PRINCE AWAY?
FOR EVERYTHING YOU SAY, YOU DO SEEM TO TRUST THE BOY.
OH, LAY OFF.
HE'S A MORON WITH NO FEAR, WHICH IS USEFUL. THAT'S ALL.
ROAAAR

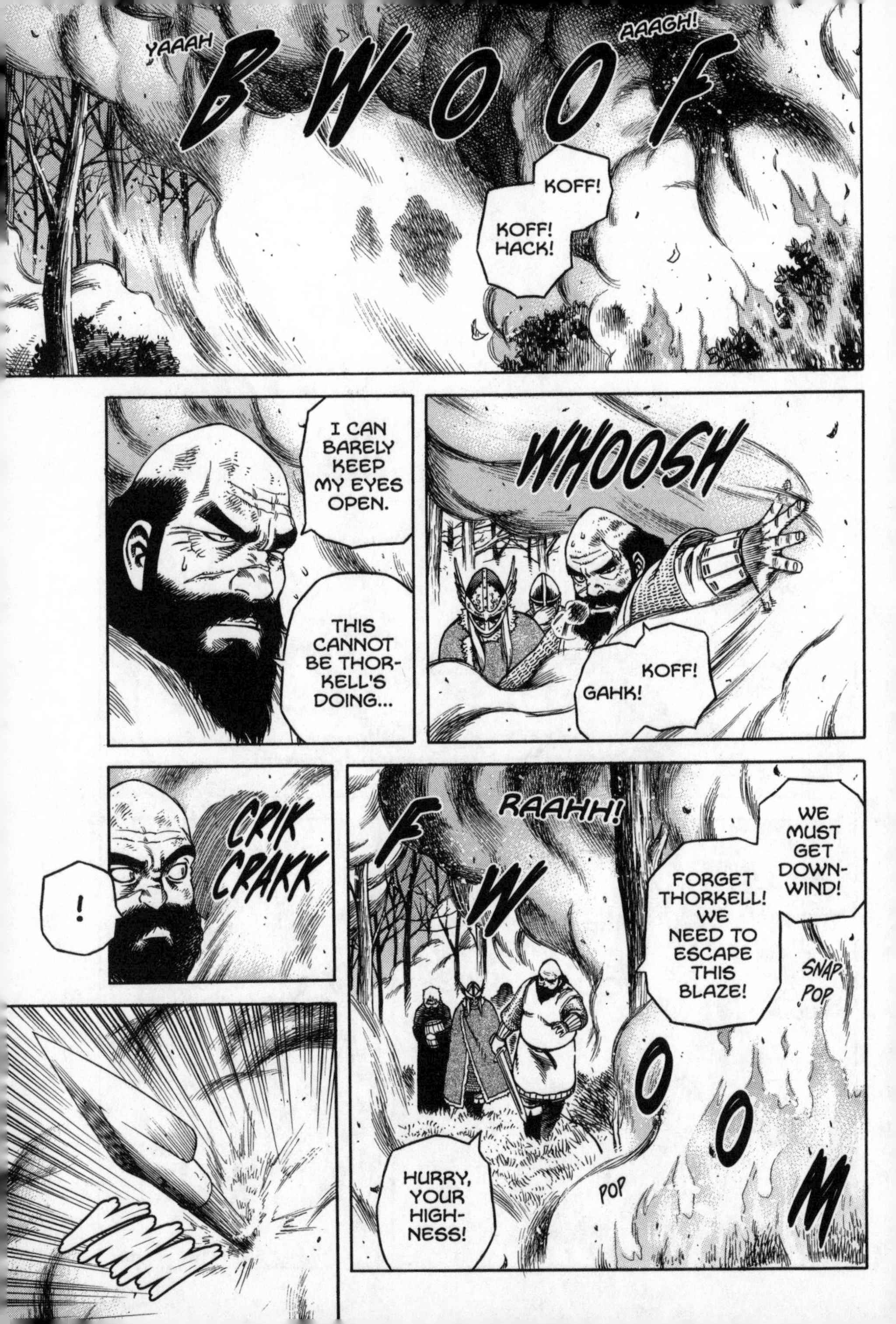
AAAGH!
BWOOF
YAAAH
KOFF!
KOFF! HACK!
WHOOSH
KOFF! GAHK!
I CAN BARELY KEEP MY EYES OPEN.
THIS CANNOT BE THORKELL'S DOING...
WE MUST GET DOWN-WIND!
FORGET THORKELL! WE NEED TO ESCAPE THIS BLAZE!
RAAHH!
FWOOOM
SNAP POP
POP
HURRY, YOUR HIGH-NESS!
CRIK CRAKK
!

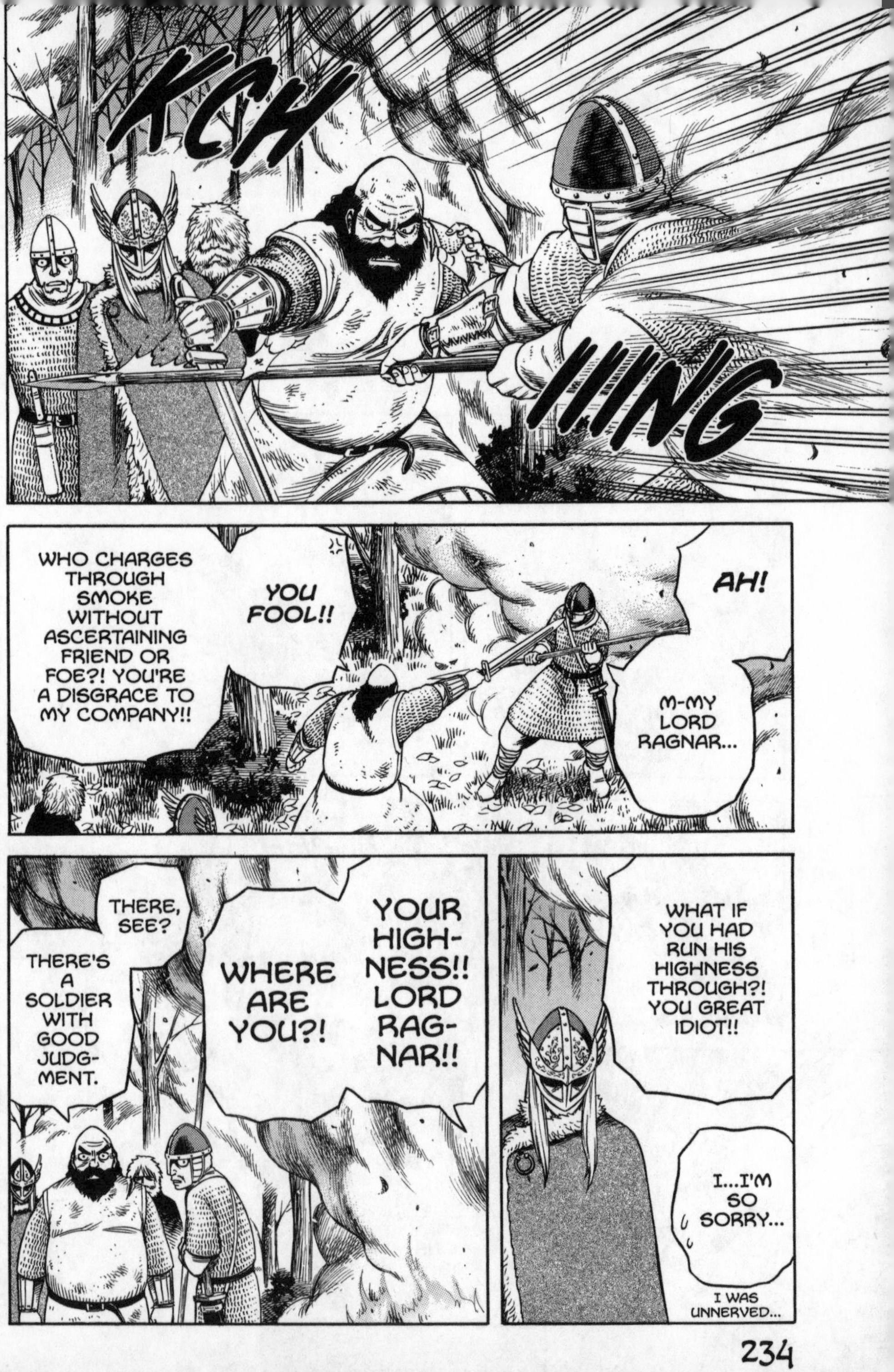
KCH
IIING
AH!
M-MY LORD RAGNAR...
YOU FOOL!!
WHO CHARGES THROUGH SMOKE WITHOUT ASCERTAINING FRIEND OR FOE?! YOU'RE A DISGRACE TO MY COMPANY!!
WHAT IF YOU HAD RUN HIS HIGHNESS THROUGH?! YOU GREAT IDIOT!!
I...I'M SO SORRY...
I WAS UNNERVED...
YOUR HIGH-NESS!! LORD RAG-NAR!!
WHERE ARE YOU?!
THERE, SEE?
THERE'S A SOLDIER WITH GOOD JUDG-MENT.

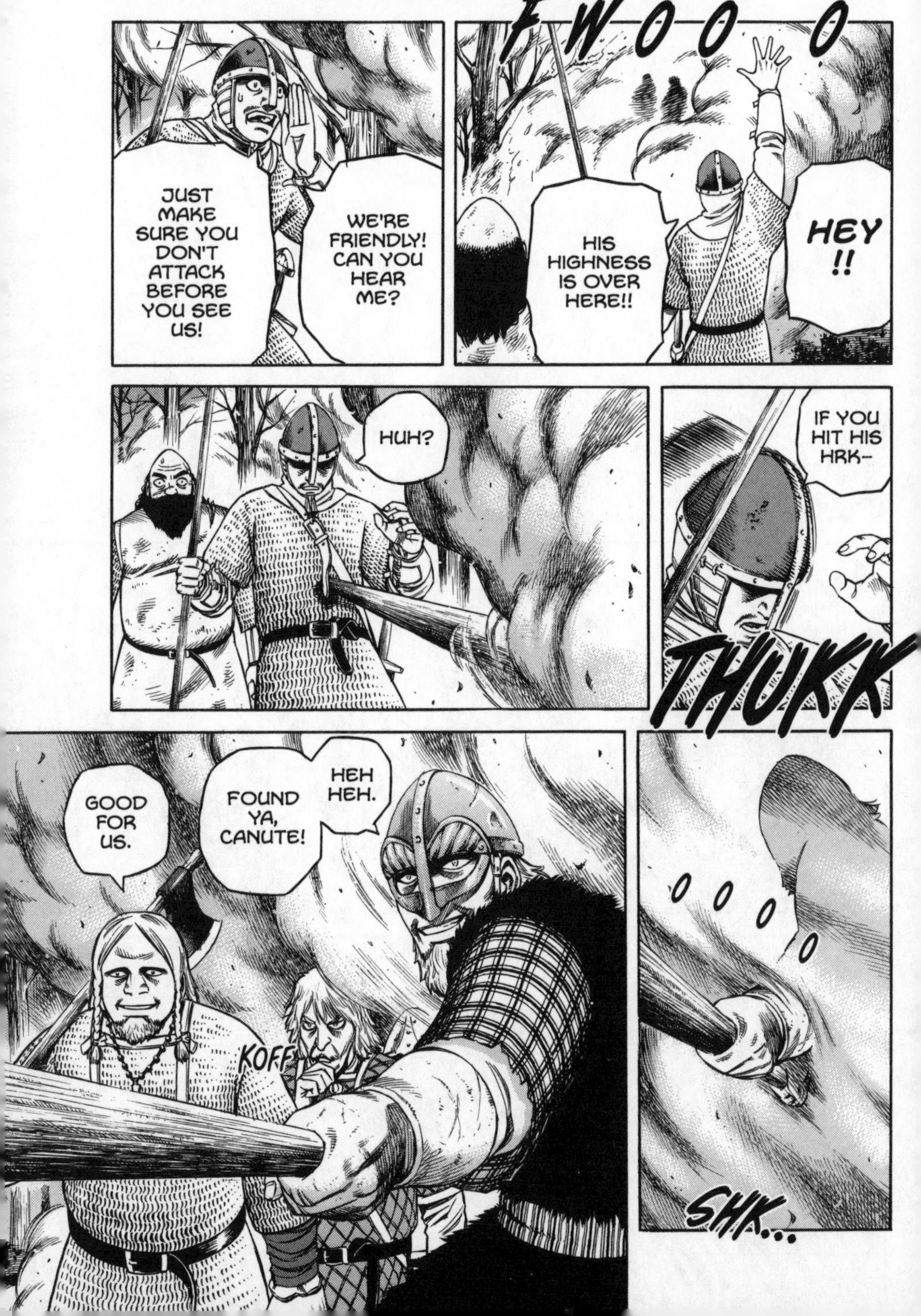
FWOOOO
HEY!!
HIS HIGHNESS IS OVER HERE!!
WE'RE FRIENDLY! CAN YOU HEAR ME?
JUST MAKE SURE YOU DON'T ATTACK BEFORE YOU SEE US!
IF YOU HIT HIS HRK-
THUKK
HUH?
OOOO
SHK...
HEH HEH.
FOUND YA, CANUTE!
GOOD FOR US.
KOFF

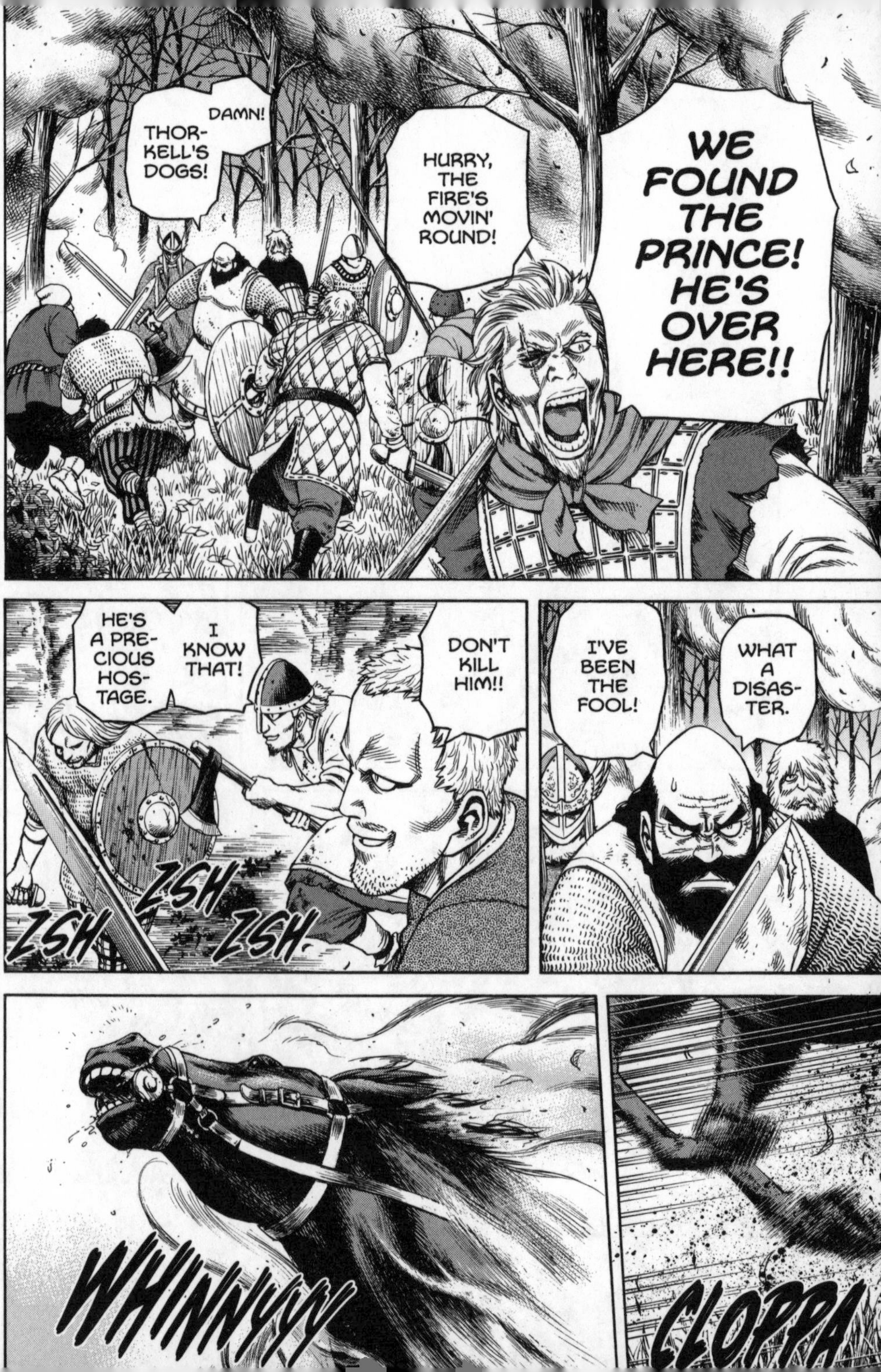
WE FOUND THE PRINCE! HE'S OVER HERE!!
HURRY, THE FIRE'S MOVIN' ROUND!
DAMN! THOR-KELL'S DOGS!
WHAT A DISAS-TER.
I'VE BEEN THE FOOL!
DON'T KILL HIM!!
I KNOW THAT!
HE'S A PRE-CIOUS HOS-TAGE.
ZSH
ZSH
ZSH
ZSH
CLOPPA
WHINNYYY

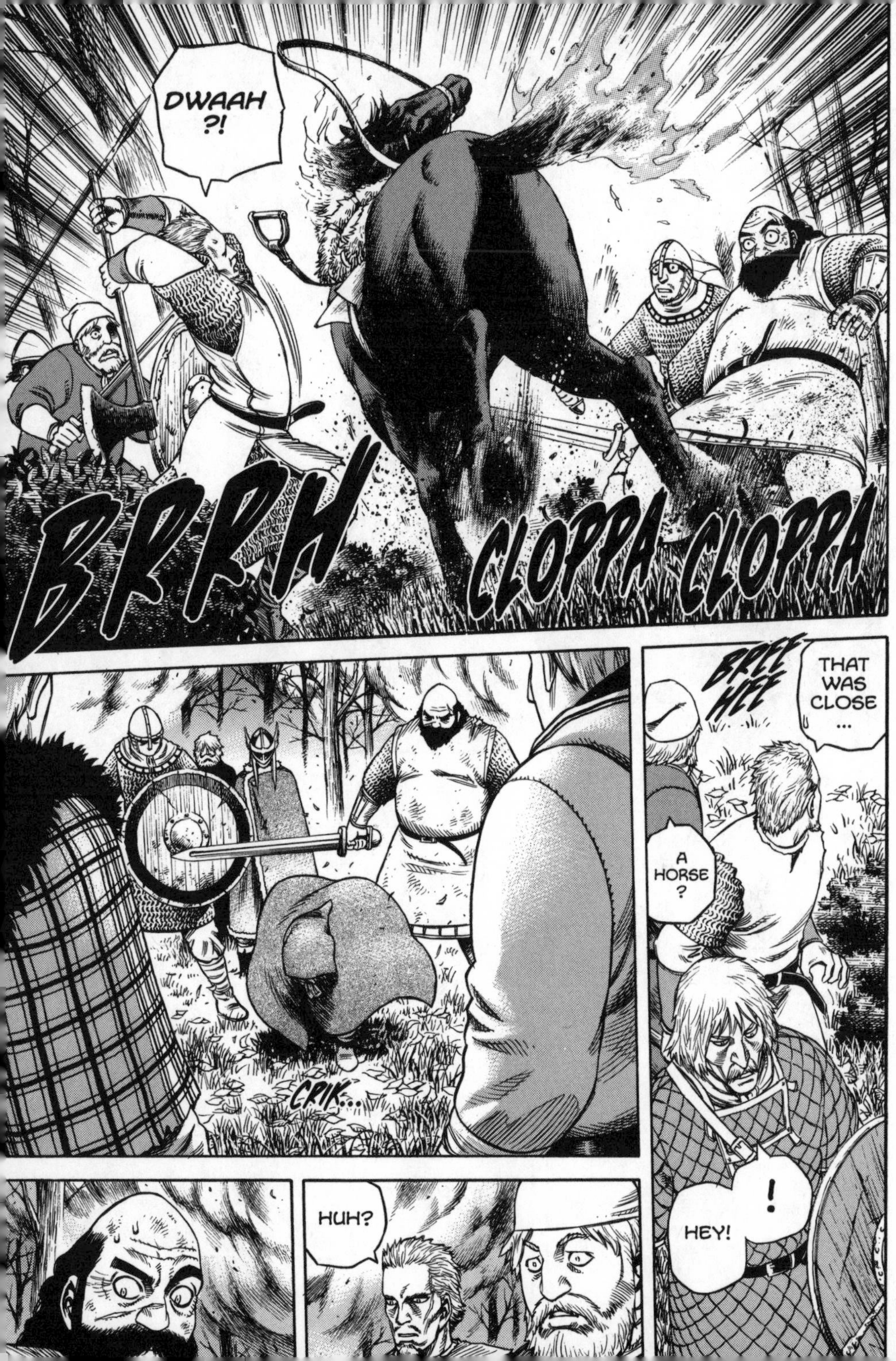
DWAAH ?!
CLOPPA CLOPPA
BRRRH
BREE HEE
THAT WAS CLOSE ...
A HORSE ?
!
HEY!
CRIK...
HUH?

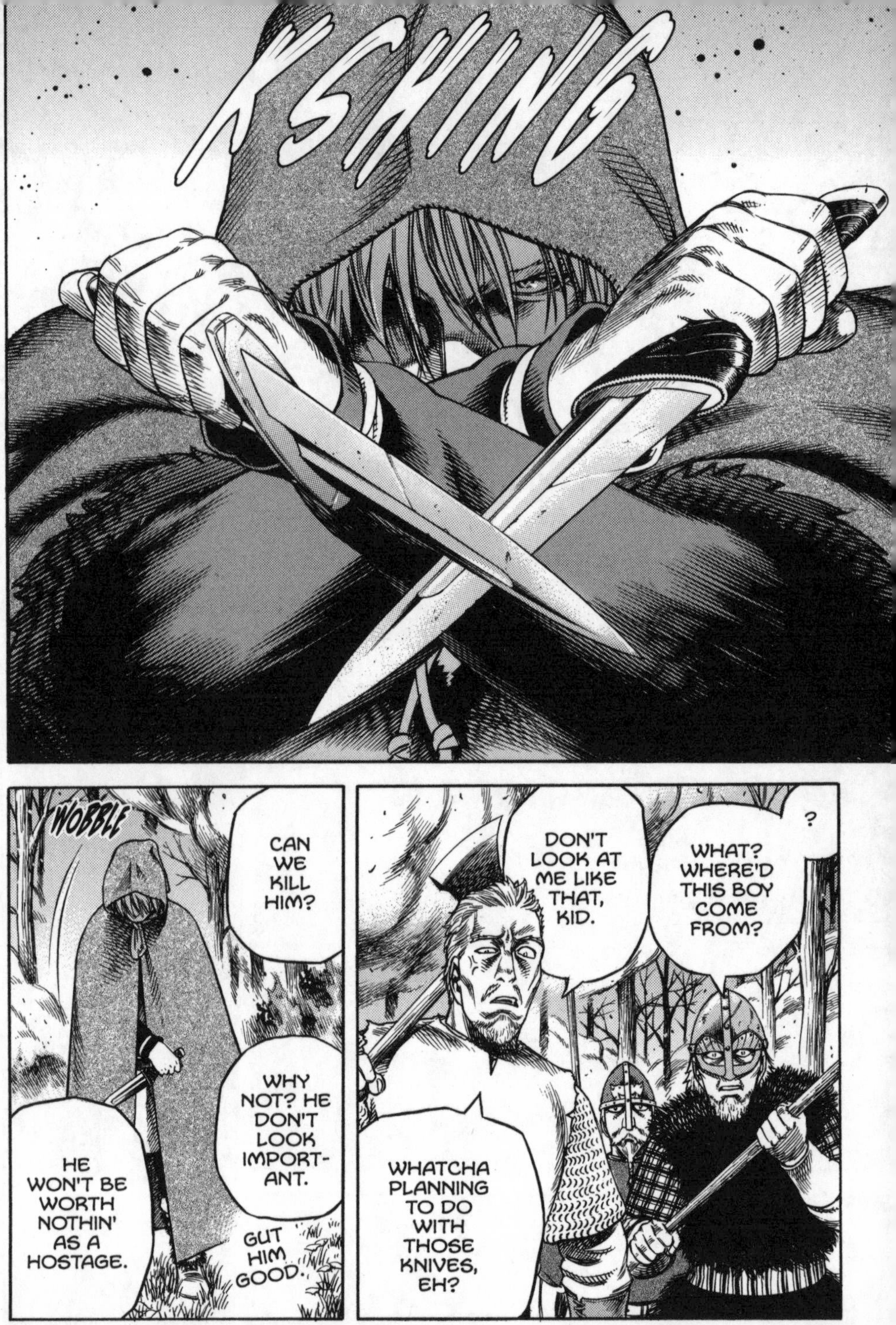
K'SHING
?
WHAT? WHERE'D THIS BOY COME FROM?
DON'T LOOK AT ME LIKE THAT, KID.
WHATCHA PLANNING TO DO WITH THOSE KNIVES, EH?
CAN WE KILL HIM?
WOBBLE
WHY NOT? HE DON'T LOOK IMPORT-ANT.
GUT HIM GOOD.
HE WON'T BE WORTH NOTHIN' AS A HOSTAGE.

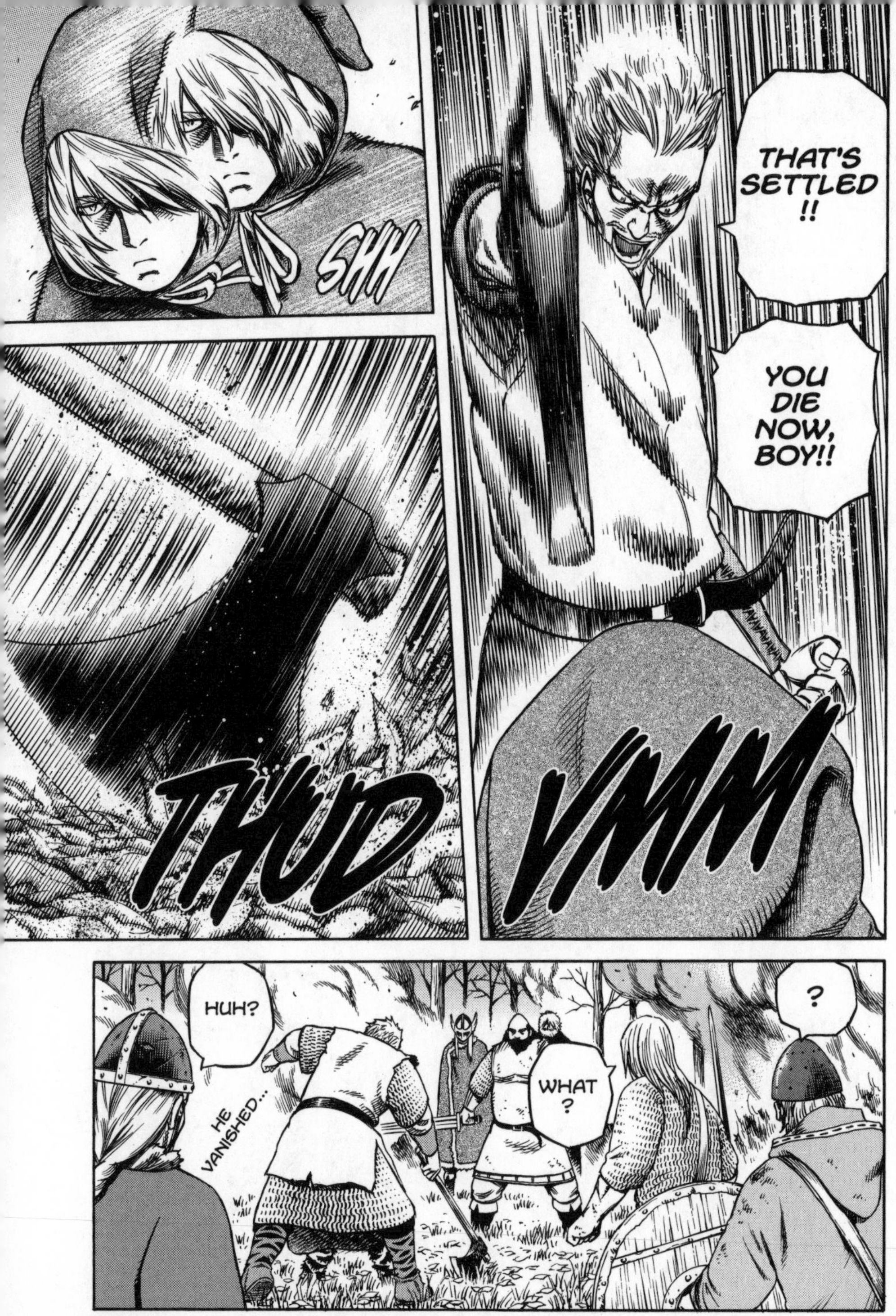
THAT'S SETTLED !!
YOU DIE NOW, BOY!!
VMM
SHH
THUD
?
WHAT ?
HUH?
HE VANISHED...

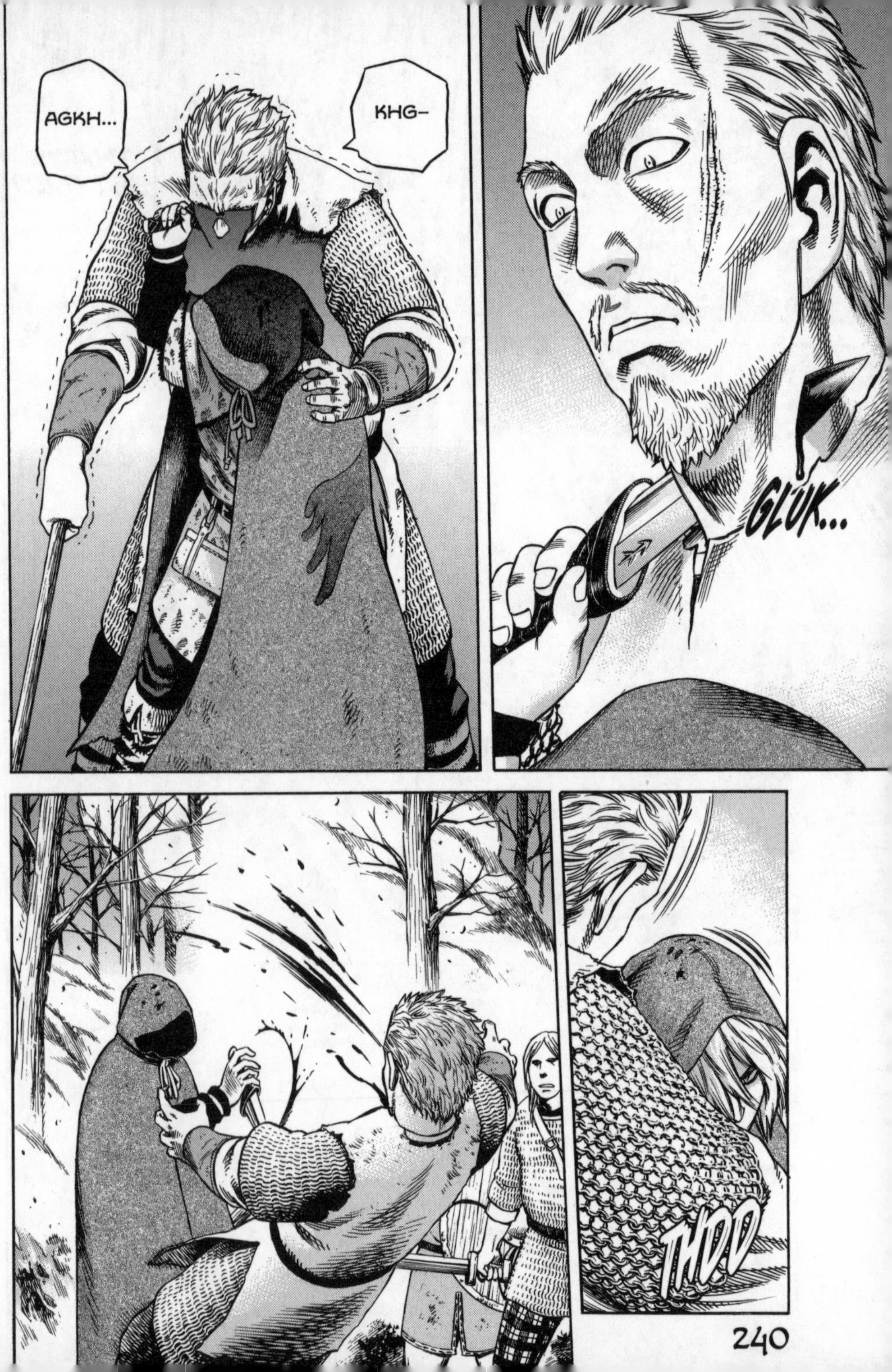
GLUK...
KHG-
AGKH...
THUD

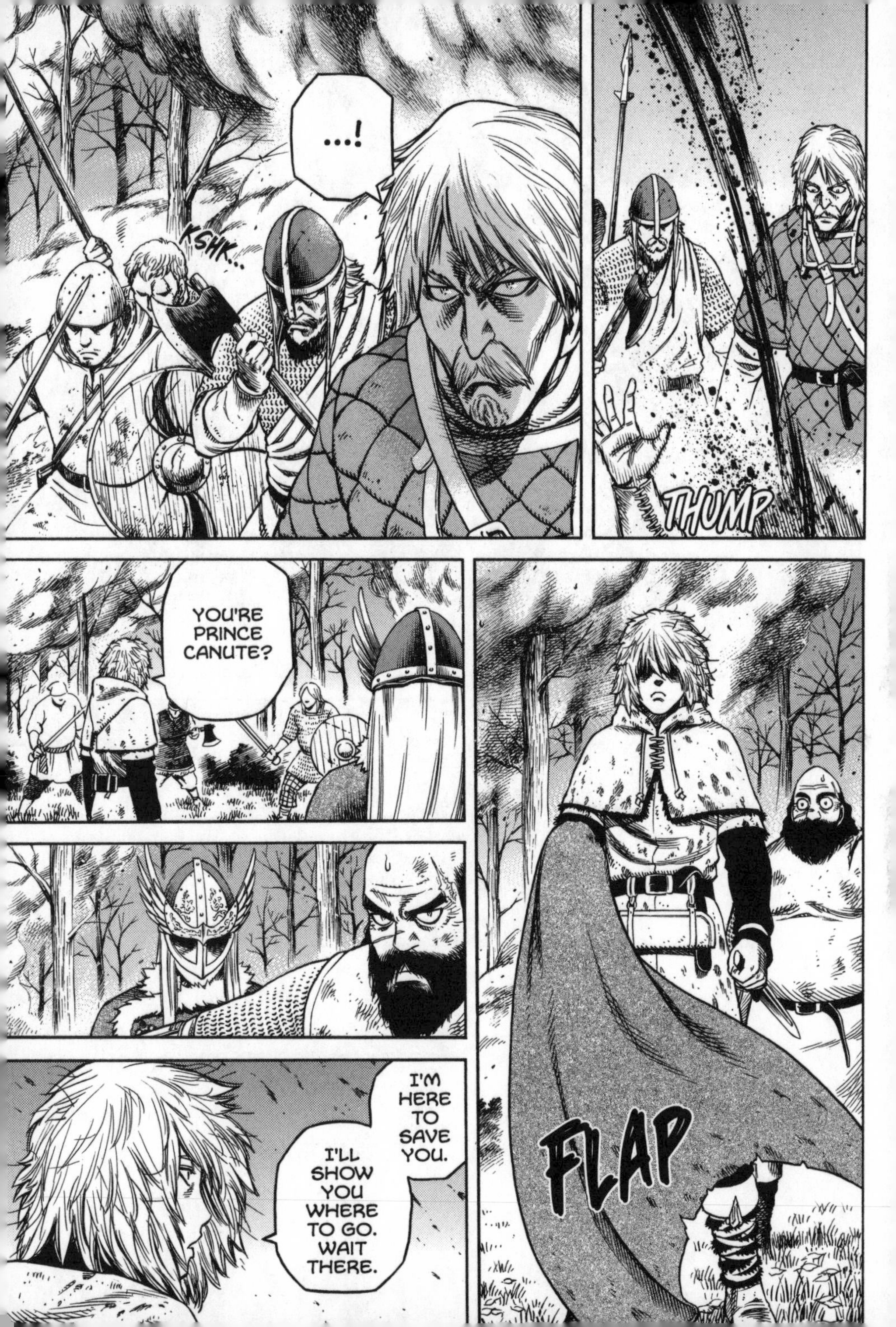
THUMP
...!
KSHK...
FLAP
YOU'RE PRINCE CANUTE?
I'M HERE TO SAVE YOU.
I'LL SHOW YOU WHERE TO GO. WAIT THERE.

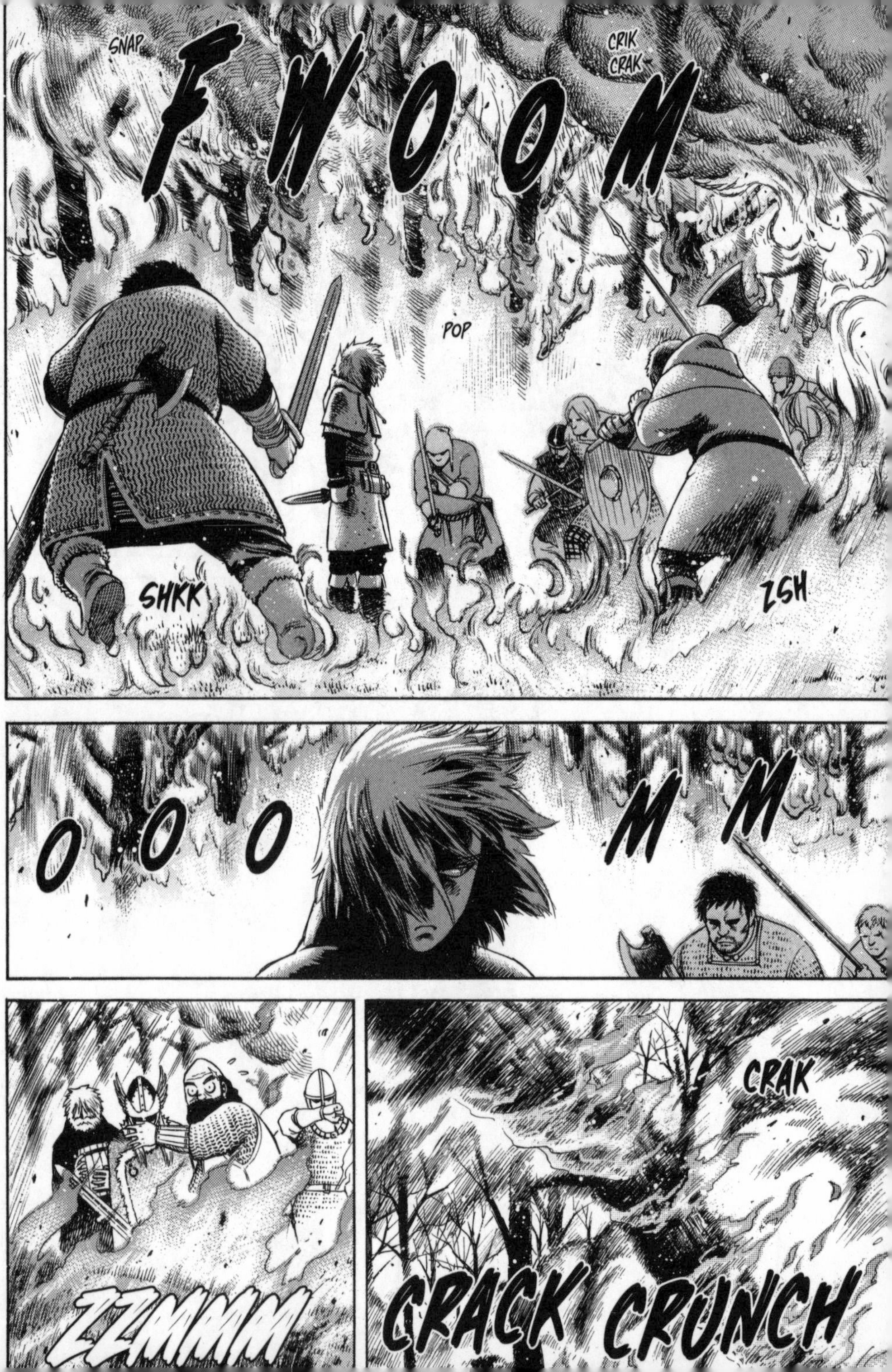
CRIK CRAK
FWOOM
SNAP
POP
ZSH
SHKK
OOOMM
CRAK
CRACK CRUNCH
ZZMMMM

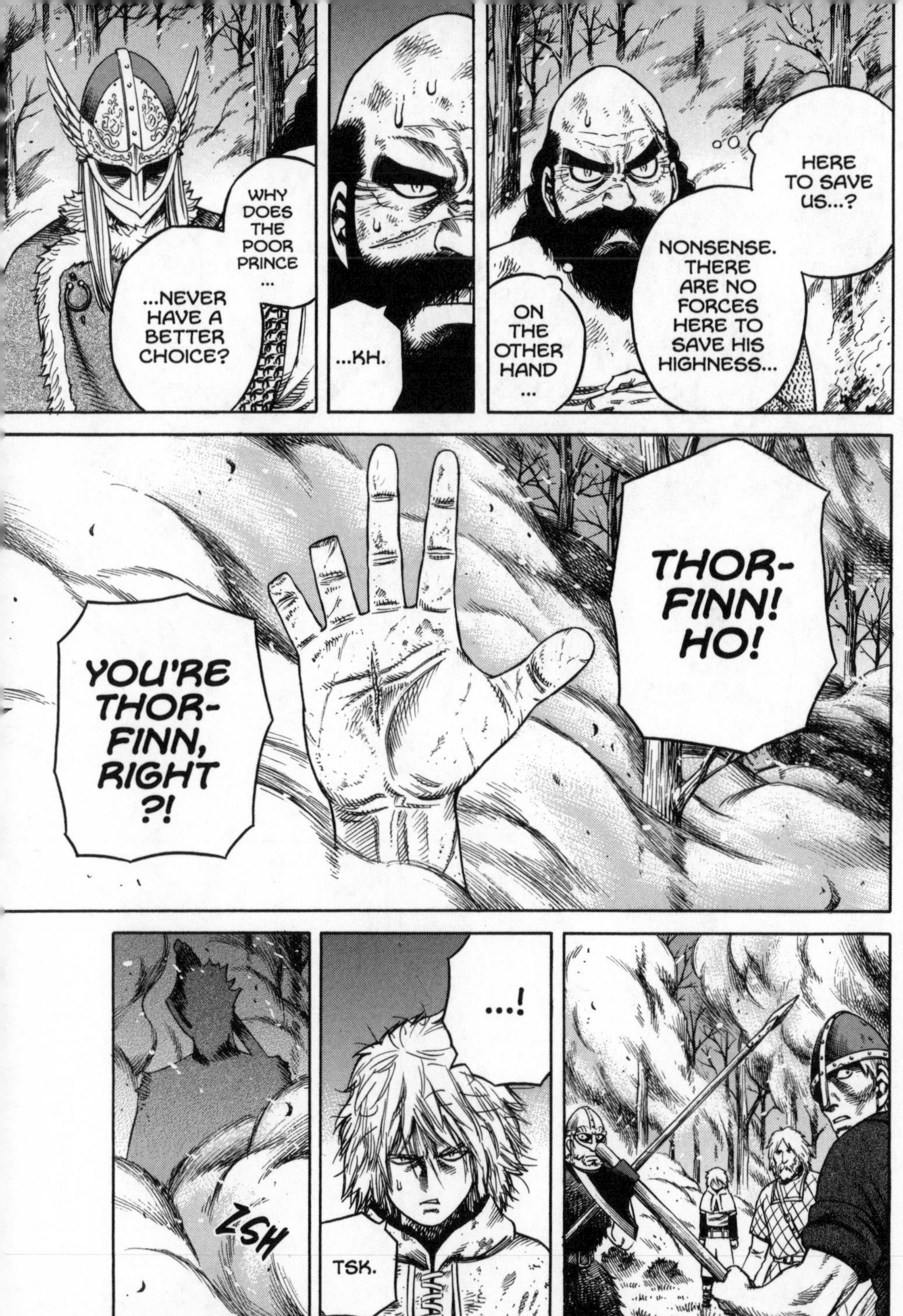
HERE TO SAVE US...?
NONSENSE. THERE ARE NO FORCES HERE TO SAVE HIS HIGHNESS...
ON THE OTHER HAND ...
...KH.
WHY DOES THE POOR PRINCE ...
...NEVER HAVE A BETTER CHOICE?
THOR-FINN! HO!
YOU'RE THOR-FINN, RIGHT ?!
...!
TSK.
ZSH

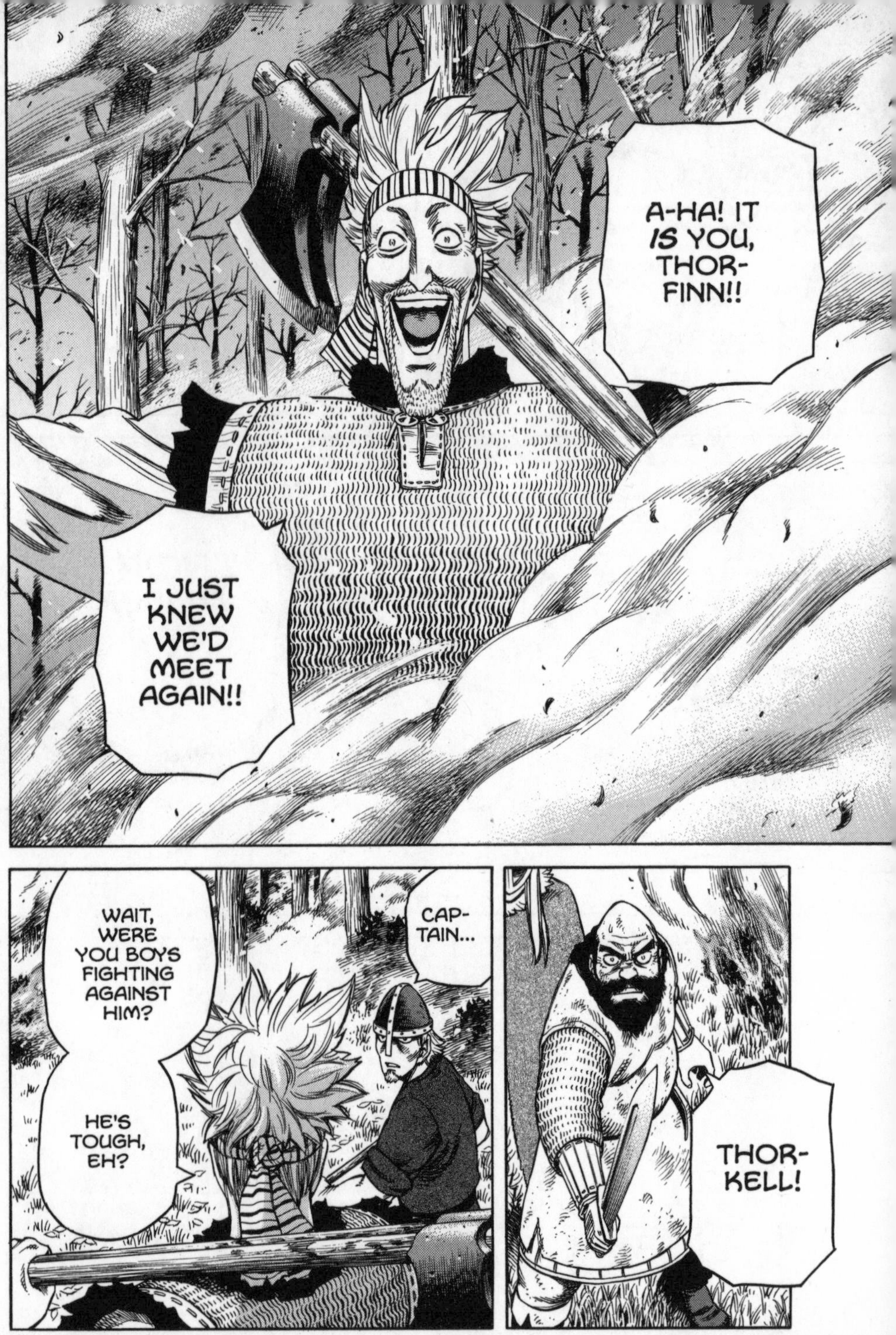
A-HA! IT *IS* YOU, THOR-FINN!!
I JUST KNEW WE'D MEET AGAIN!!
THOR-KELL!
CAP-TAIN...
WAIT, WERE YOU BOYS FIGHTING AGAINST HIM?
HE'S TOUGH, EH?

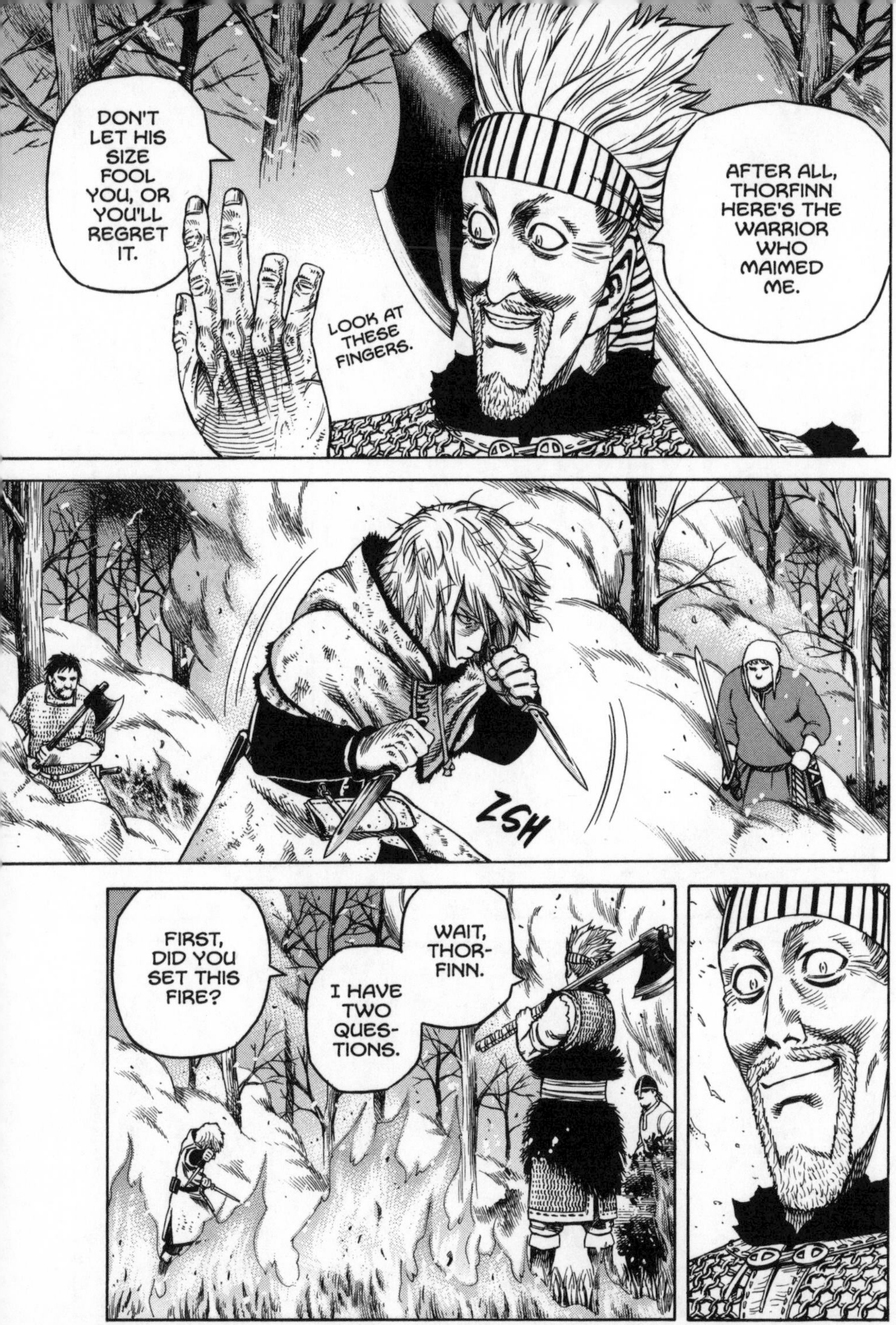
AFTER ALL, THORFINN HERE'S THE WARRIOR WHO MAIMED ME.
LOOK AT THESE FINGERS.
DON'T LET HIS SIZE FOOL YOU, OR YOU'LL REGRET IT.
ZSH
WAIT, THOR-FINN.
I HAVE TWO QUES-TIONS.
FIRST, DID YOU SET THIS FIRE?

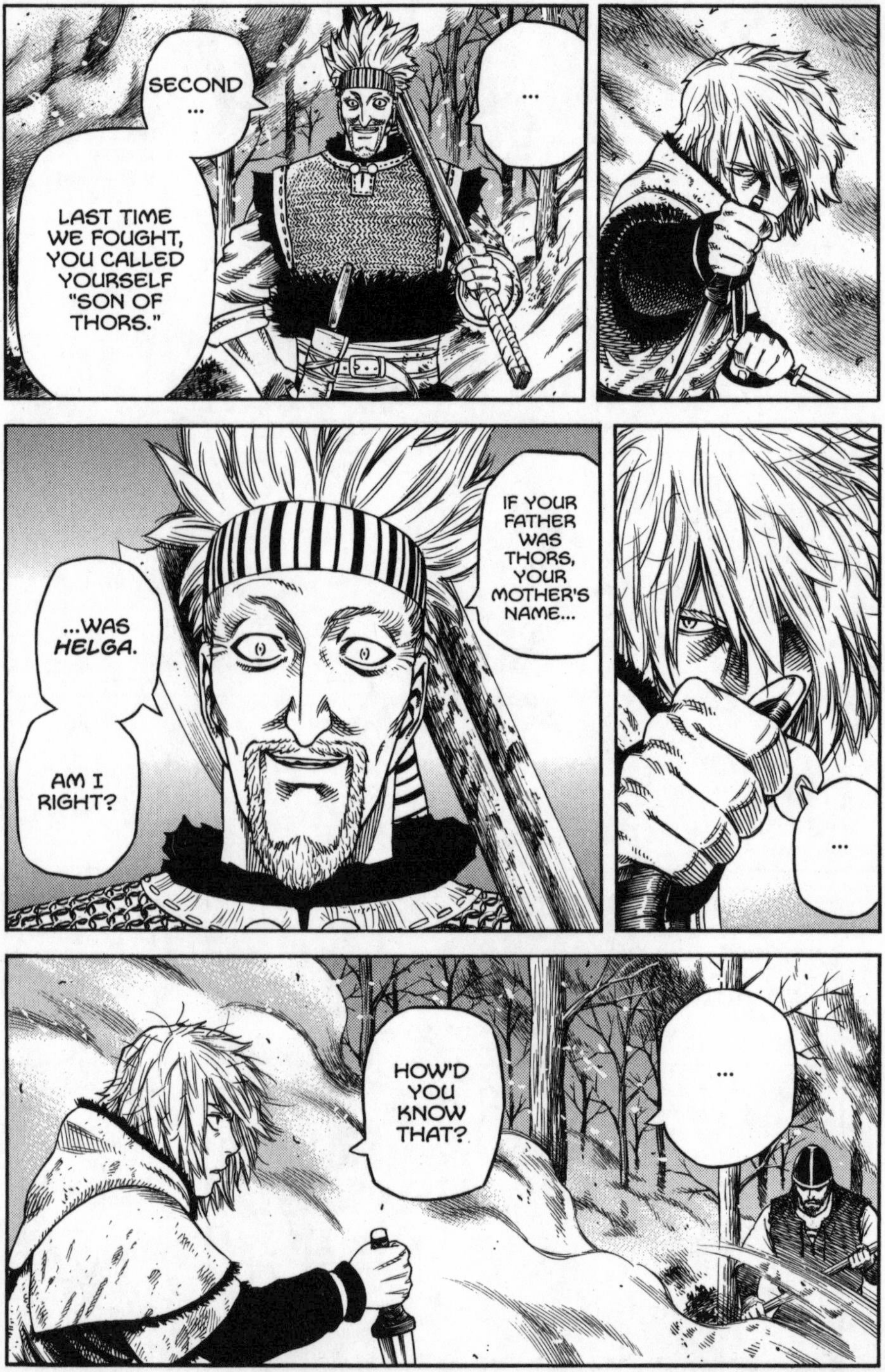
...
SECOND ...
LAST TIME WE FOUGHT, YOU CALLED YOURSELF "SON OF THORS."
...
IF YOUR FATHER WAS THORS, YOUR MOTHER'S NAME...
...WAS HELGA.
AM I RIGHT?
...
HOW'D YOU KNOW THAT?

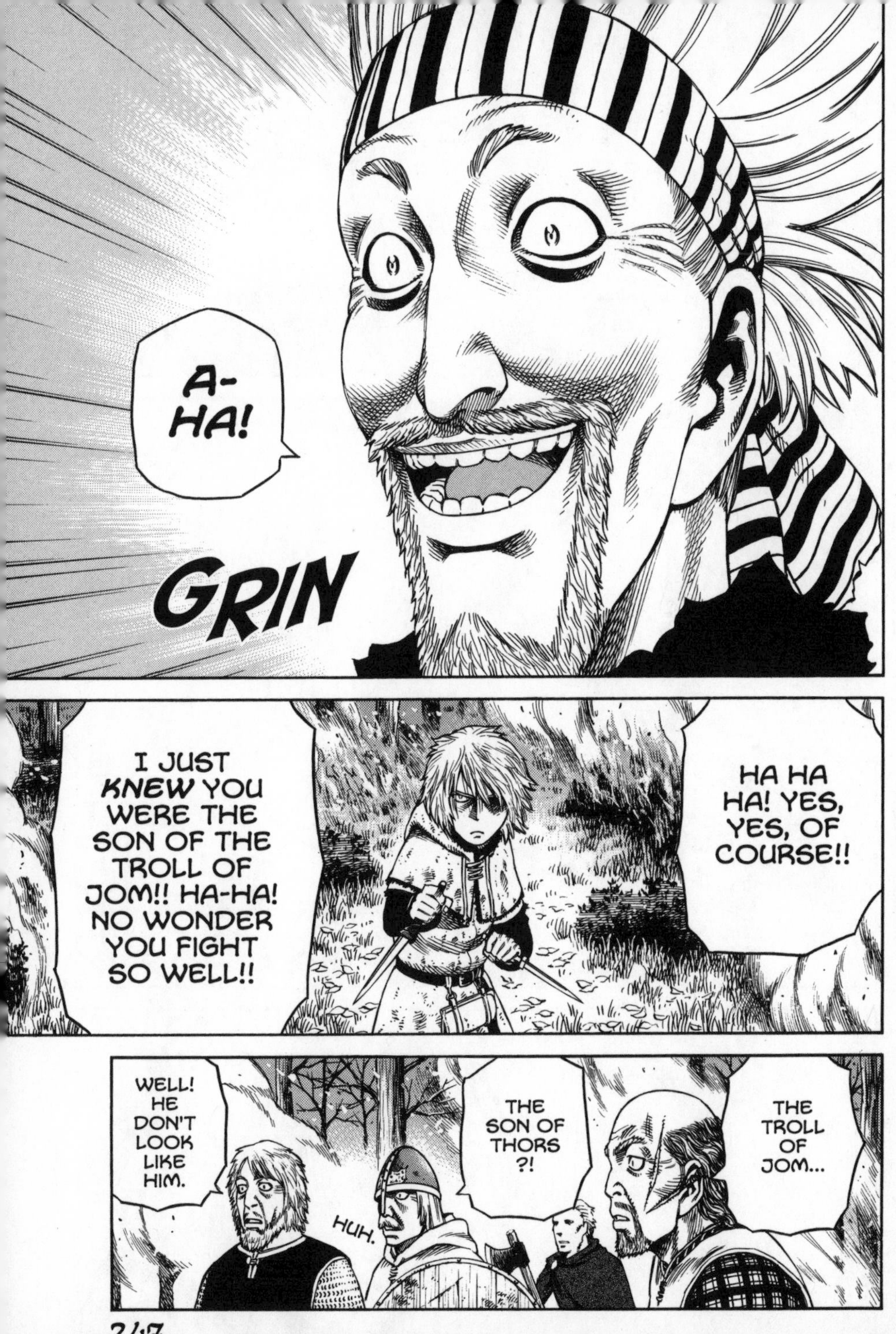
A-HA!
GRIN
HA HA HA! YES, YES, OF COURSE!!
I JUST KNEW YOU WERE THE SON OF THE TROLL OF JOM!! HA-HA! NO WONDER YOU FIGHT SO WELL!!
THE TROLL OF JOM...
THE SON OF THORS ?!
HUH.
WELL! HE DON'T LOOK LIKE HIM.

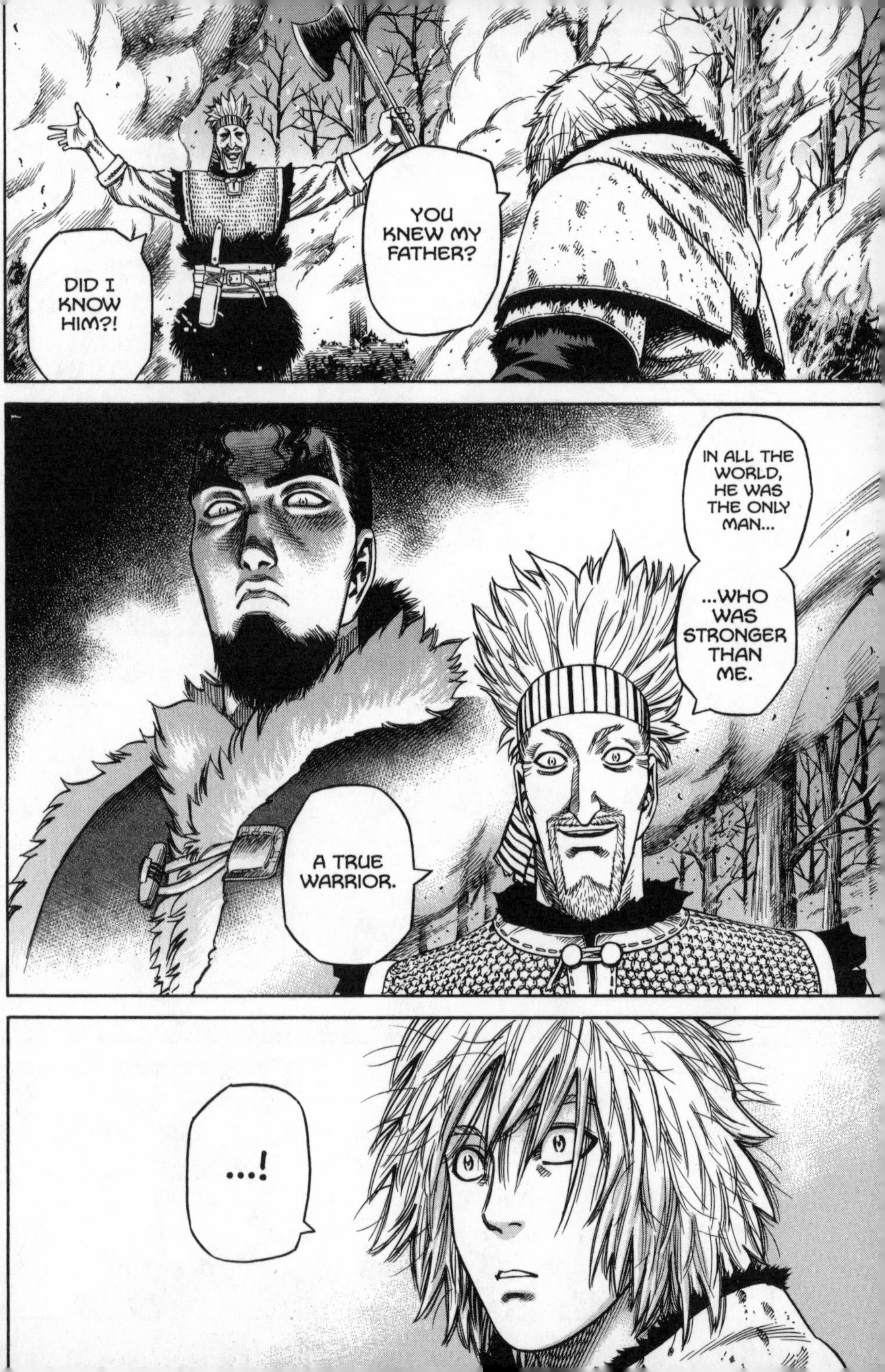
YOU KNEW MY FATHER?
DID I KNOW HIM?!
IN ALL THE WORLD, HE WAS THE ONLY MAN...
...WHO WAS STRONGER THAN ME.
A TRUE WARRIOR.
...!

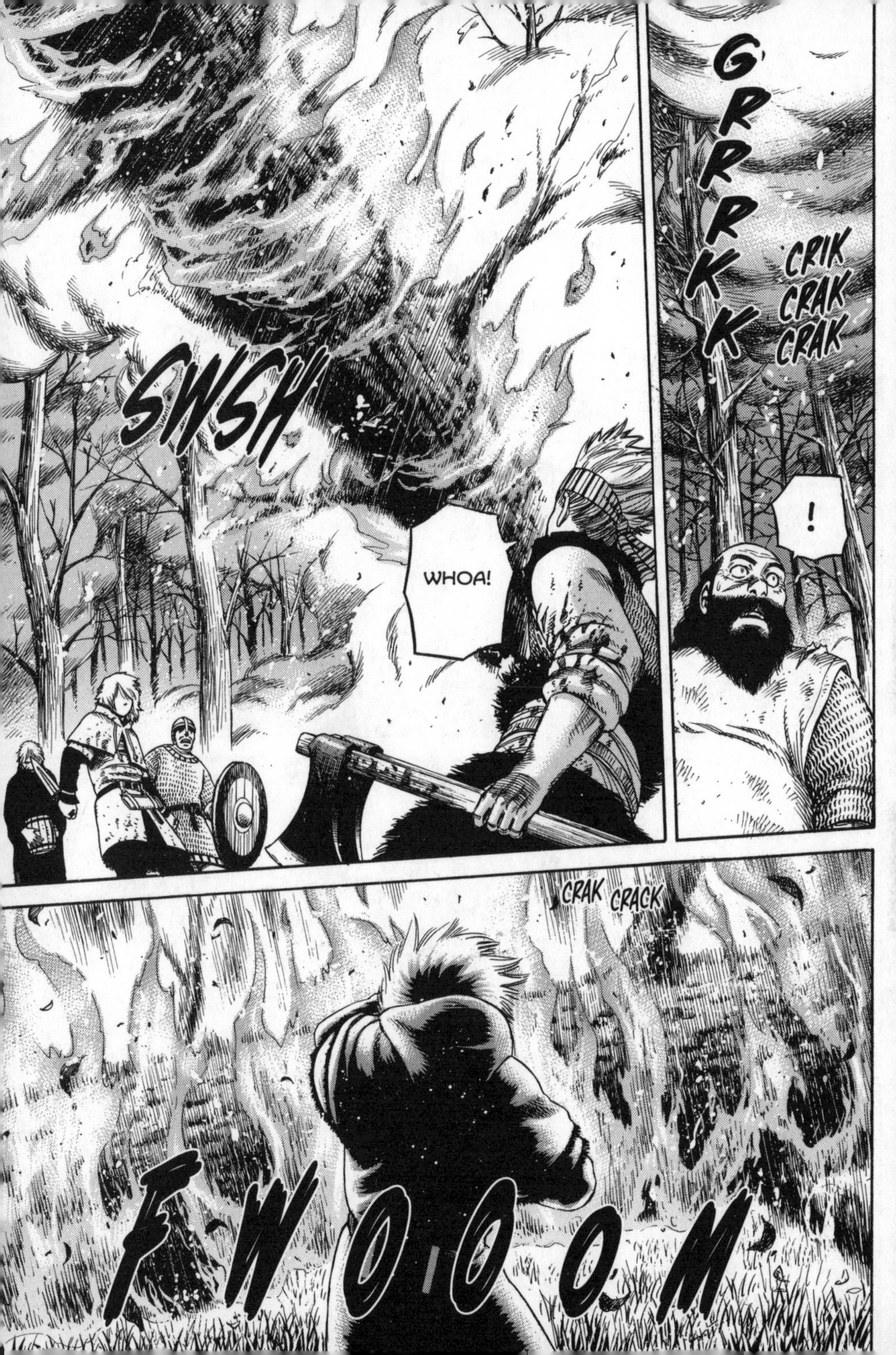
GRRRKK
CRIK CRAK CRAK
!
SWSH
WHOA!
CRAK CRACK
FWOOOM

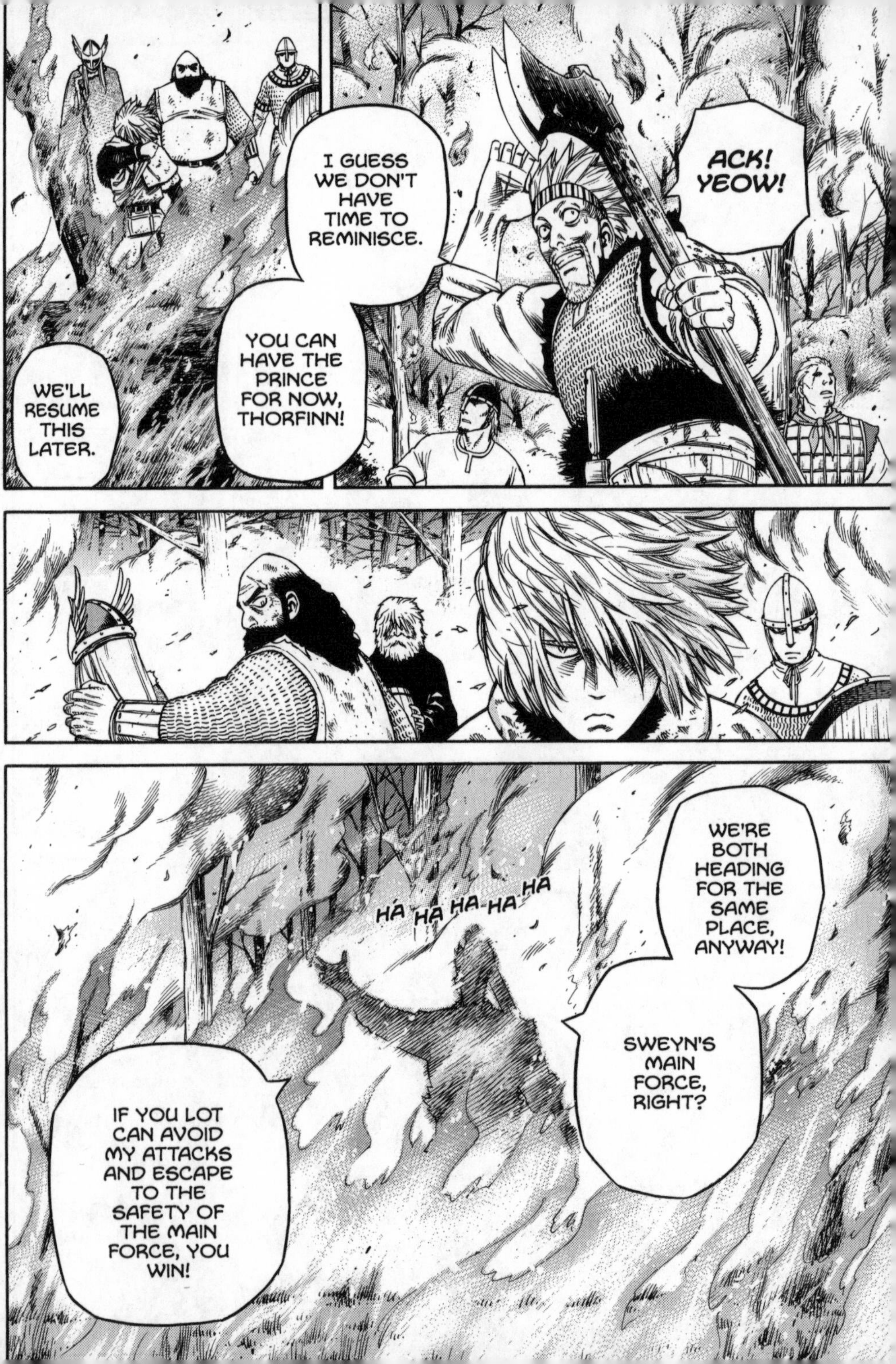
ACK! YEOW!
I GUESS WE DON'T HAVE TIME TO REMINISCE.
YOU CAN HAVE THE PRINCE FOR NOW, THORFINN!
WE'LL RESUME THIS LATER.
WE'RE BOTH HEADING FOR THE SAME PLACE, ANYWAY!
HA HA HA HA HA
SWEYN'S MAIN FORCE, RIGHT?
IF YOU LOT CAN AVOID MY ATTACKS AND ESCAPE TO THE SAFETY OF THE MAIN FORCE, YOU WIN!

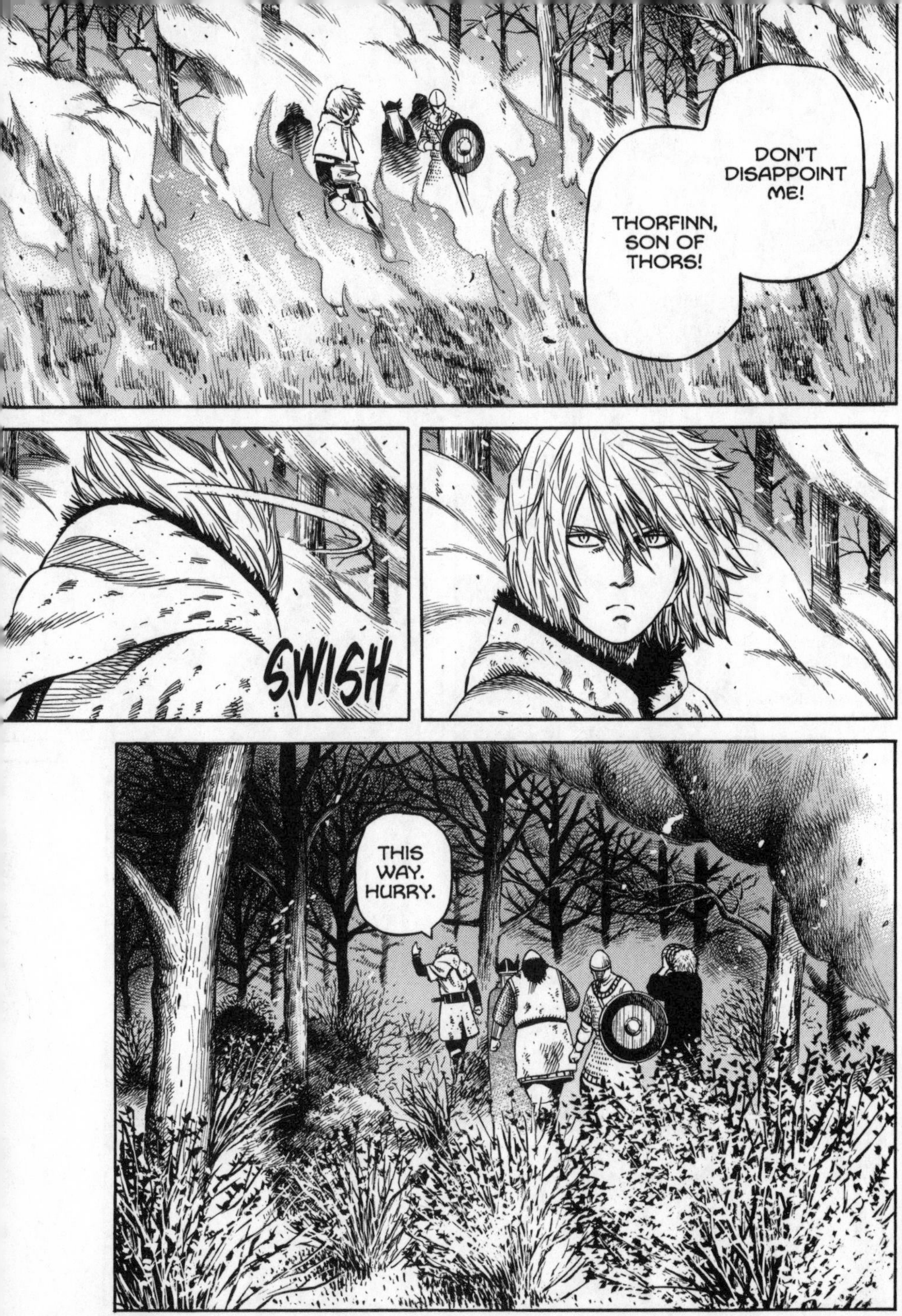
DON'T DISAPPOINT ME!
THORFINN, SON OF THORS!
SWISH
THIS WAY. HURRY.

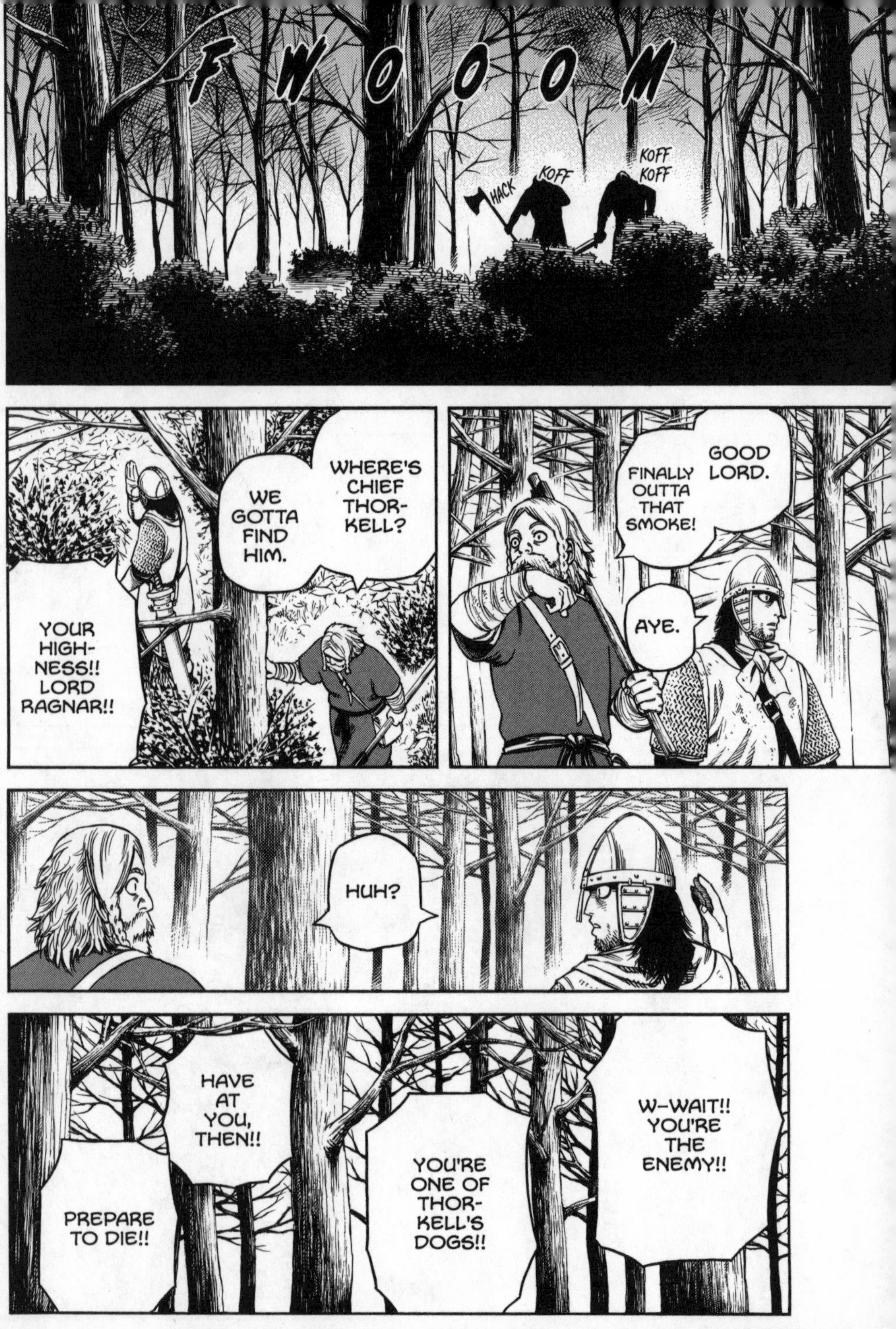
FWOOOM
KOFF KOFF
HACK KOFF
GOOD LORD.
FINALLY OUTTA THAT SMOKE!
AYE.
WHERE'S CHIEF THOR-KELL?
WE GOTTA FIND HIM.
YOUR HIGH-NESS!! LORD RAGNAR!!
HUH?
W-WAIT!! YOU'RE THE ENEMY!!
YOU'RE ONE OF THOR-KELL'S DOGS!!
HAVE AT YOU, THEN!!
PREPARE TO DIE!!

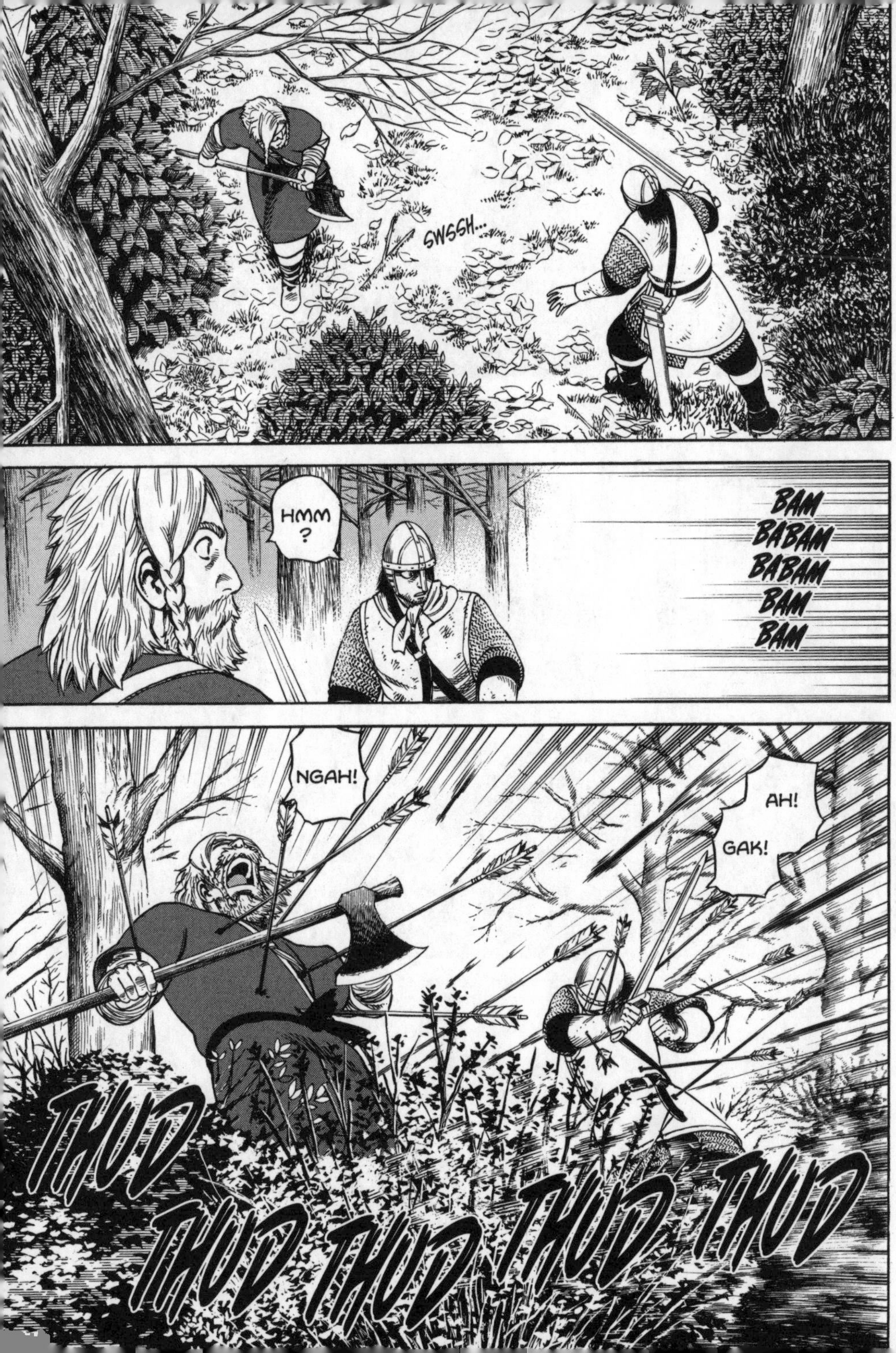
SWSSH...
BAM BABAM BABAM BAM BAM
HMM?
AH!
GAK!
NGAH!
THUD THUD THUD THUD THUD

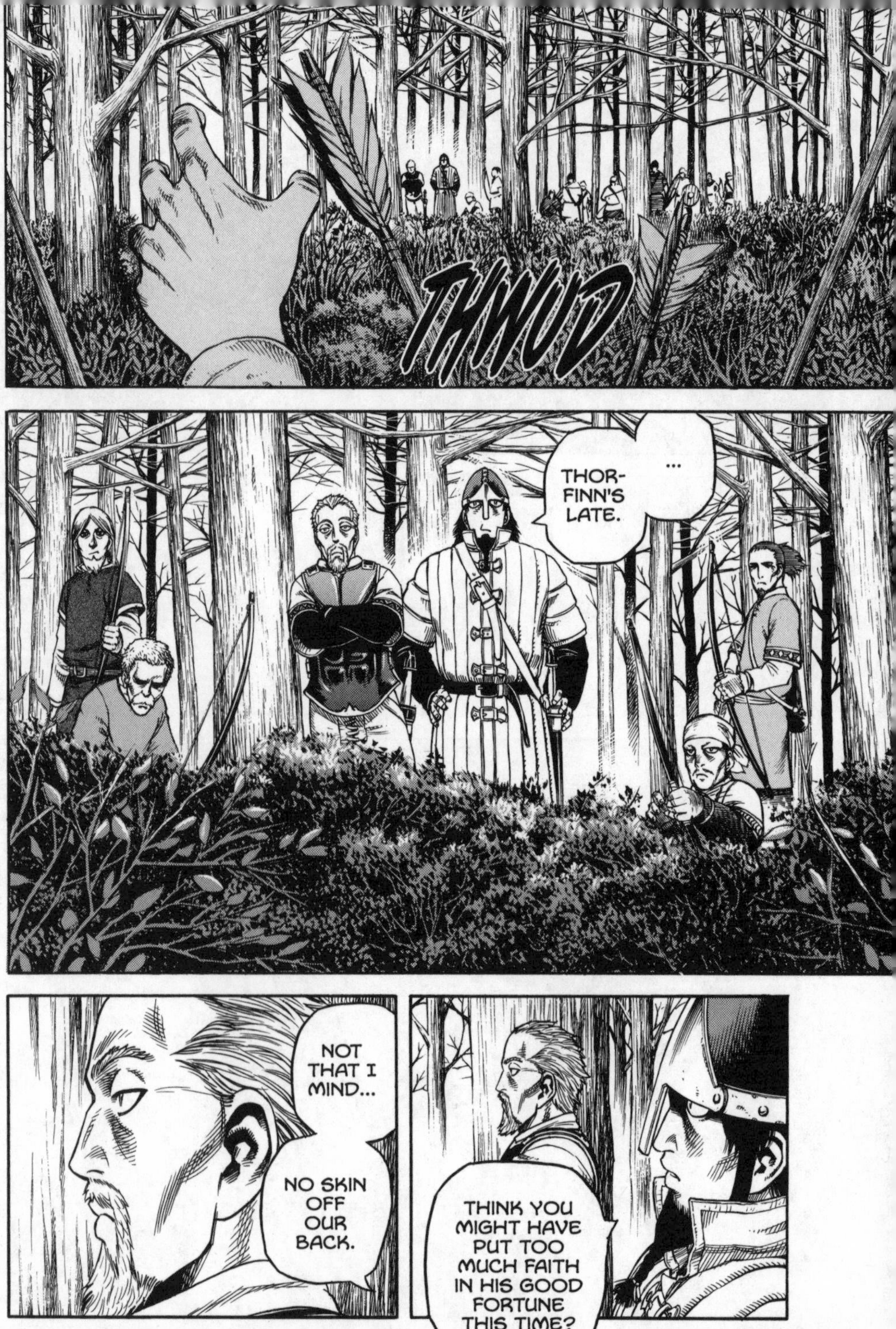
THWUD
...
THOR-FINN'S LATE.
THINK YOU MIGHT HAVE PUT TOO MUCH FAITH IN HIS GOOD FORTUNE THIS TIME?
NOT THAT I MIND...
NO SKIN OFF OUR BACK.

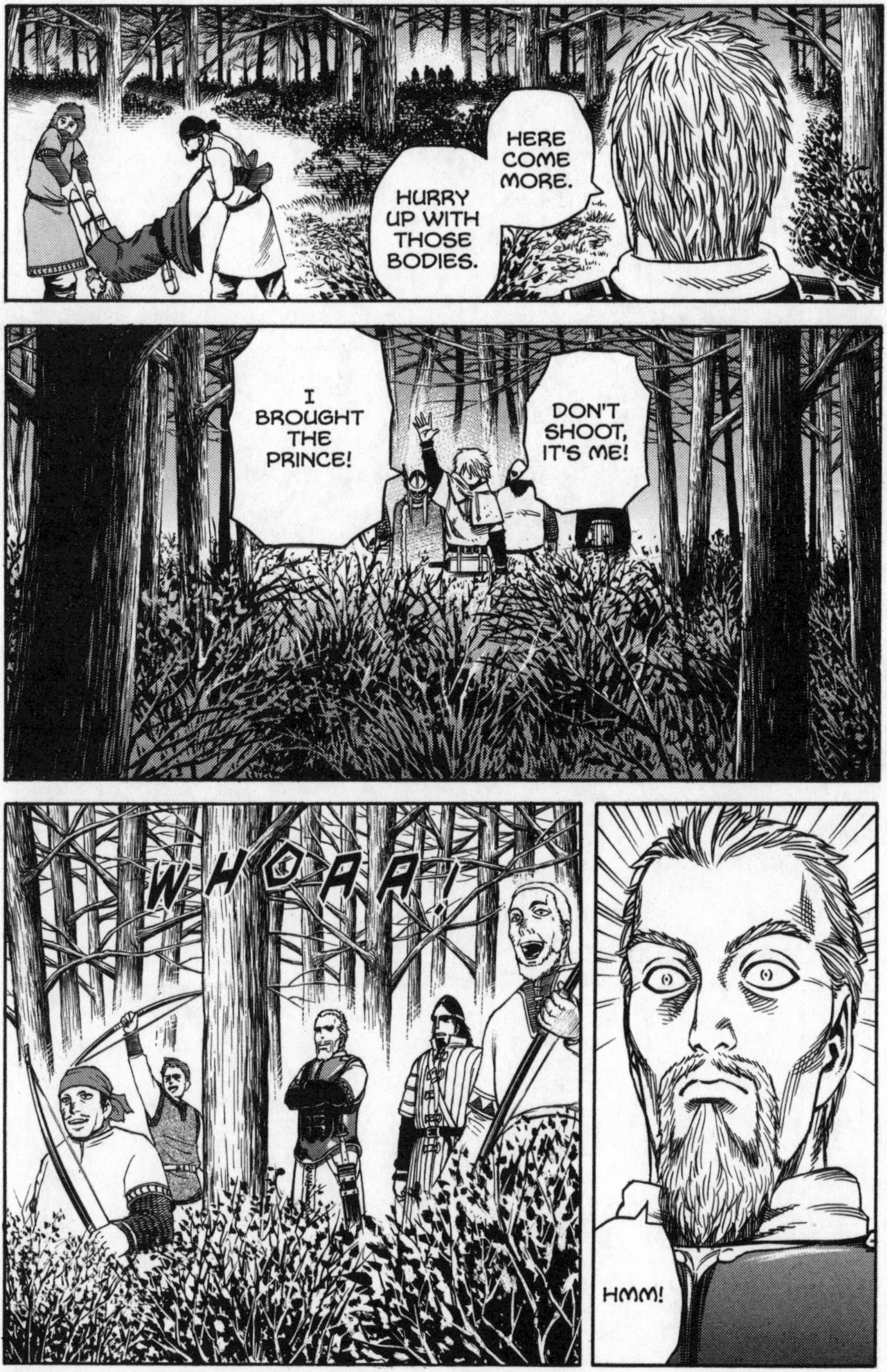
HERE COME MORE.
HURRY UP WITH THOSE BODIES.
DON'T SHOOT, IT'S ME!
I BROUGHT THE PRINCE!
HMM!
WHOAA!

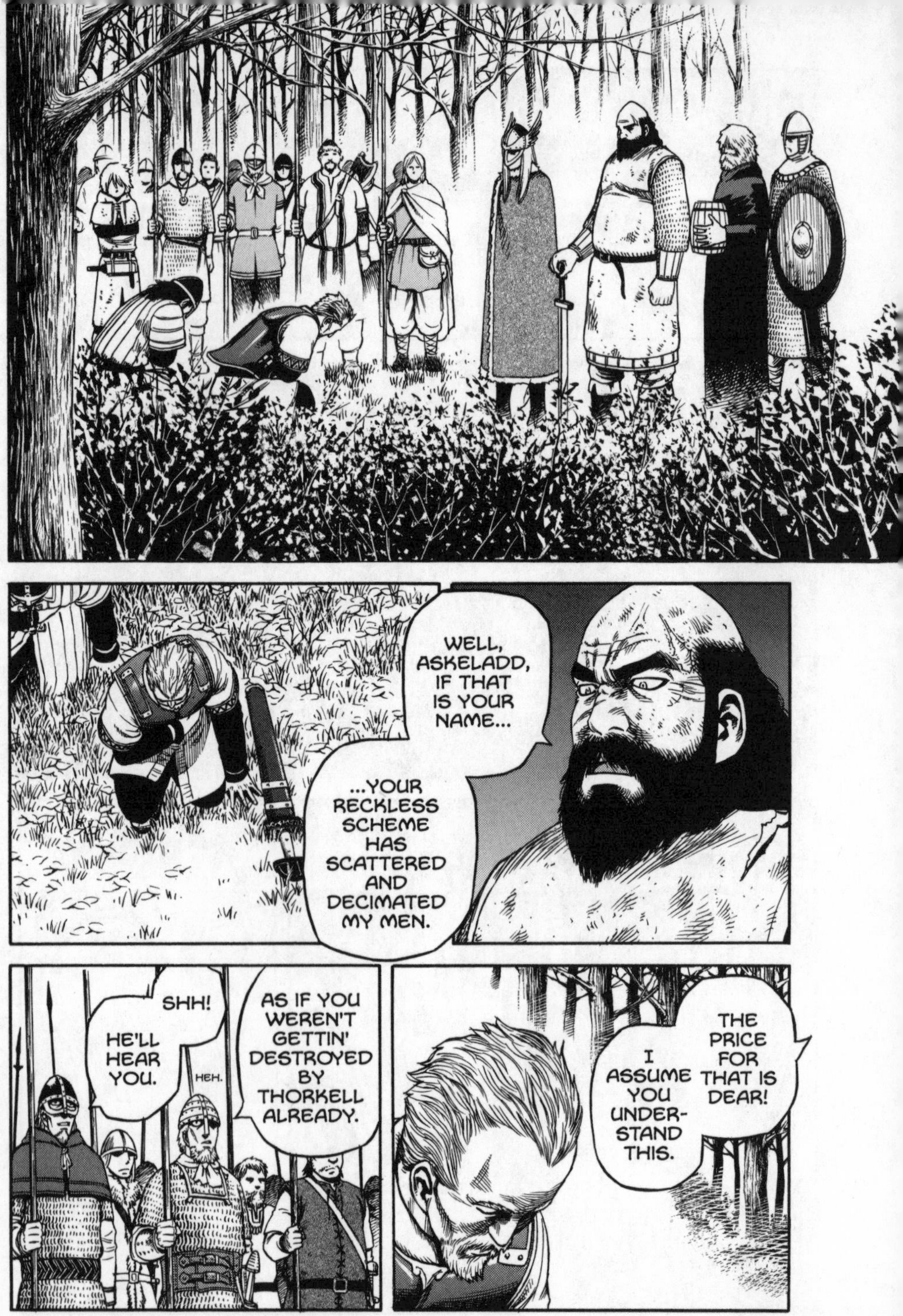
WELL, ASKELADD, IF THAT IS YOUR NAME...
...YOUR RECKLESS SCHEME HAS SCATTERED AND DECIMATED MY MEN.
THE PRICE FOR THAT IS DEAR!
I ASSUME YOU UNDER-STAND THIS.
AS IF YOU WEREN'T GETTIN' DESTROYED BY THORKELL ALREADY.
HEH.
SHH!
HE'LL HEAR YOU.

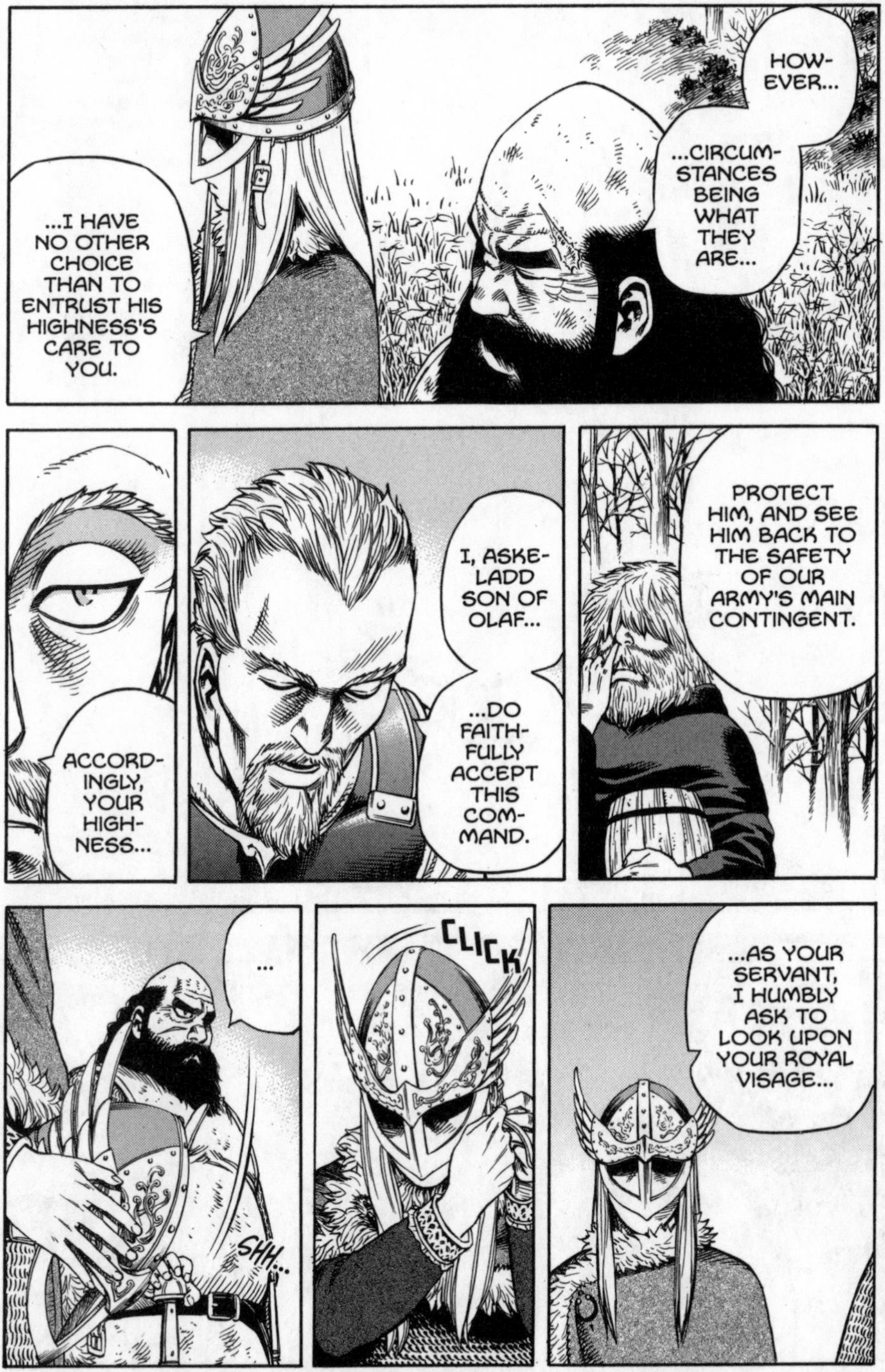
HOW-EVER...
...CIRCUM-STANCES BEING WHAT THEY ARE...
...I HAVE NO OTHER CHOICE THAN TO ENTRUST HIS HIGHNESS'S CARE TO YOU.
PROTECT HIM, AND SEE HIM BACK TO THE SAFETY OF OUR ARMY'S MAIN CONTINGENT.
I, ASKE-LADD SON OF OLAF...
...DO FAITH-FULLY ACCEPT THIS COM-MAND.
ACCORD-INGLY, YOUR HIGH-NESS...
...AS YOUR SERVANT, I HUMBLY ASK TO LOOK UPON YOUR ROYAL VISAGE...
CLICK
...
SHH...

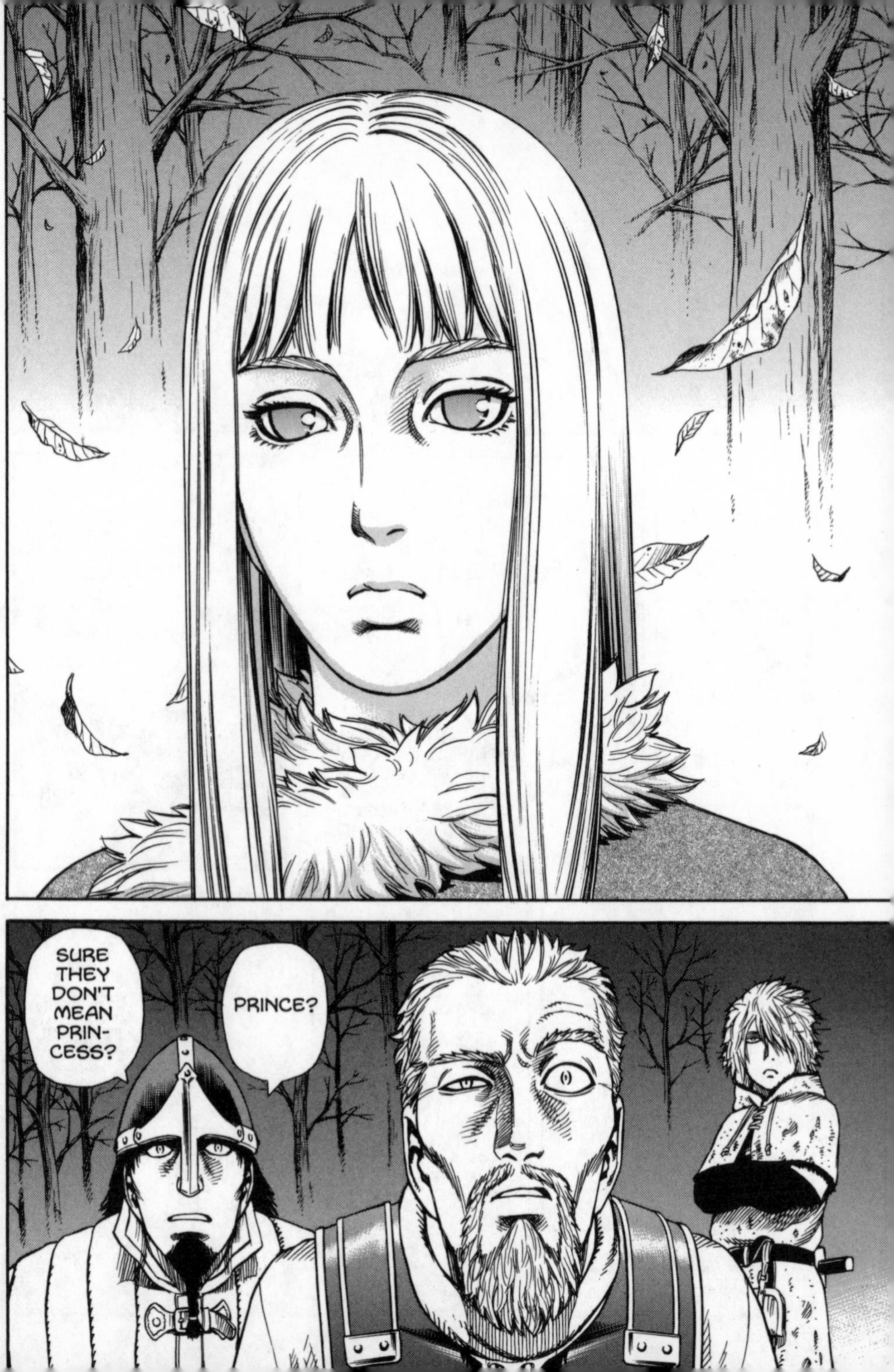
PRINCE?
SURE THEY DON'T MEAN PRIN-CESS?

CHAPTER 22 - END

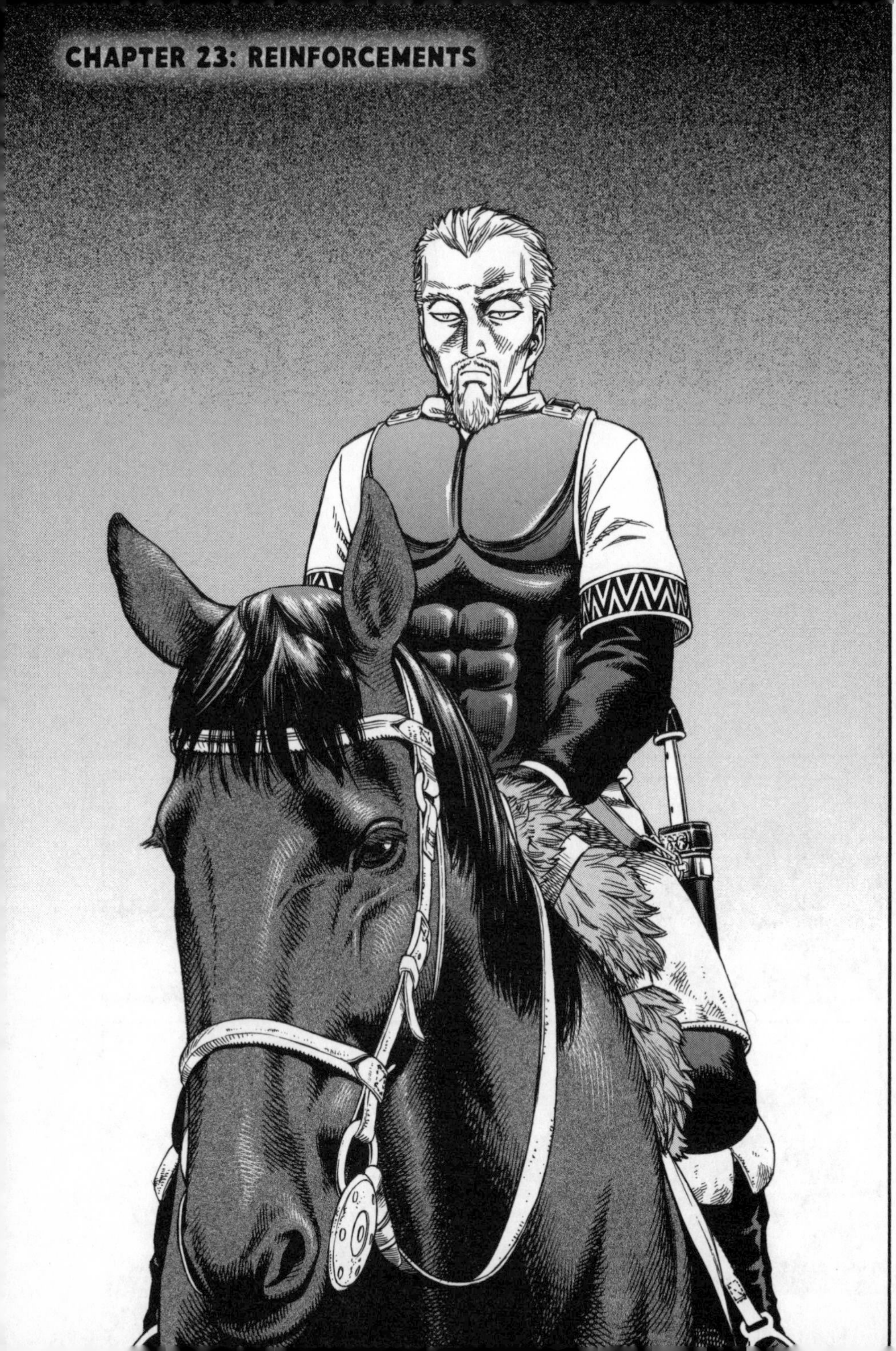
CHAPTER 23: REINFORCEMENTS

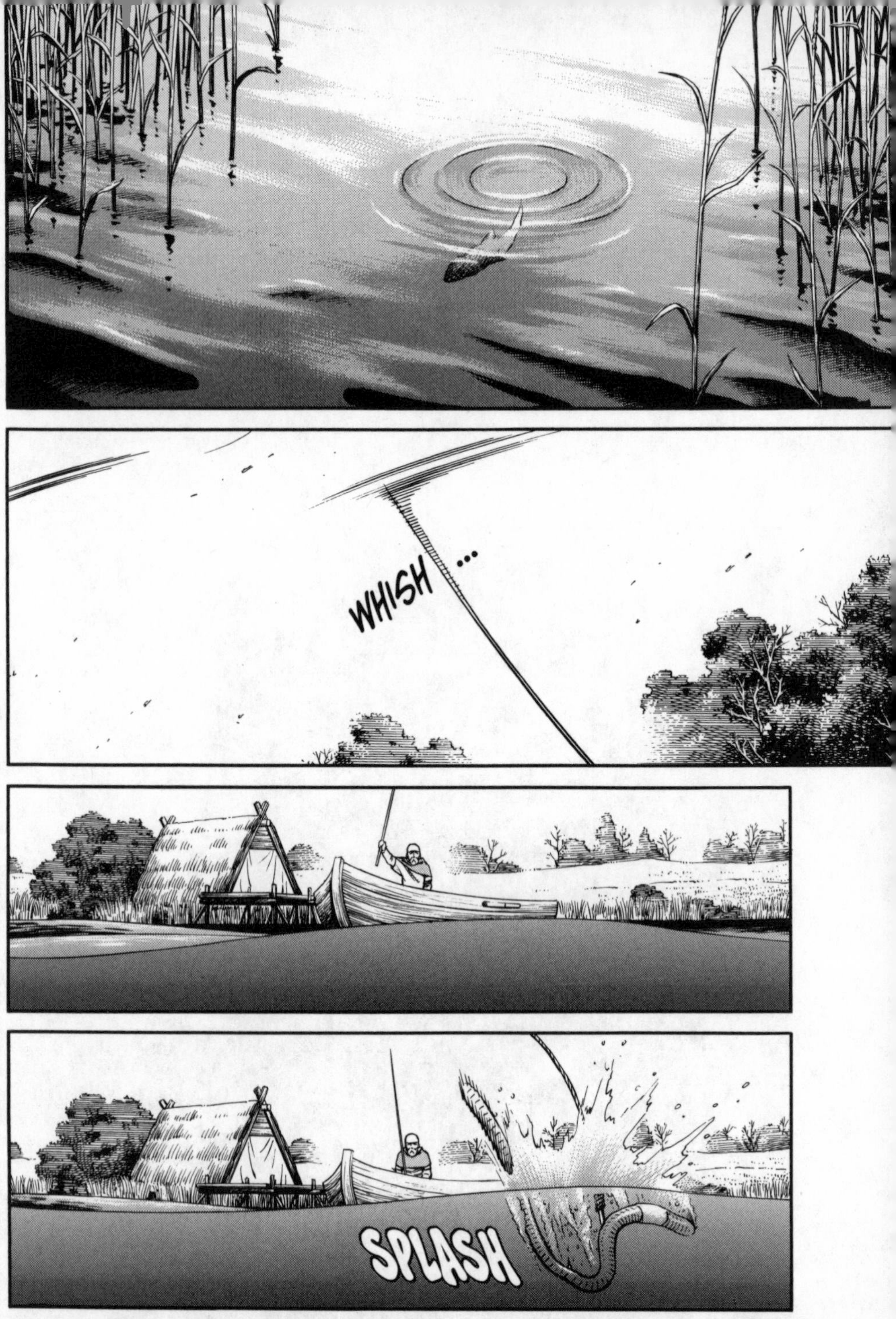
WHISH...
SPLASH

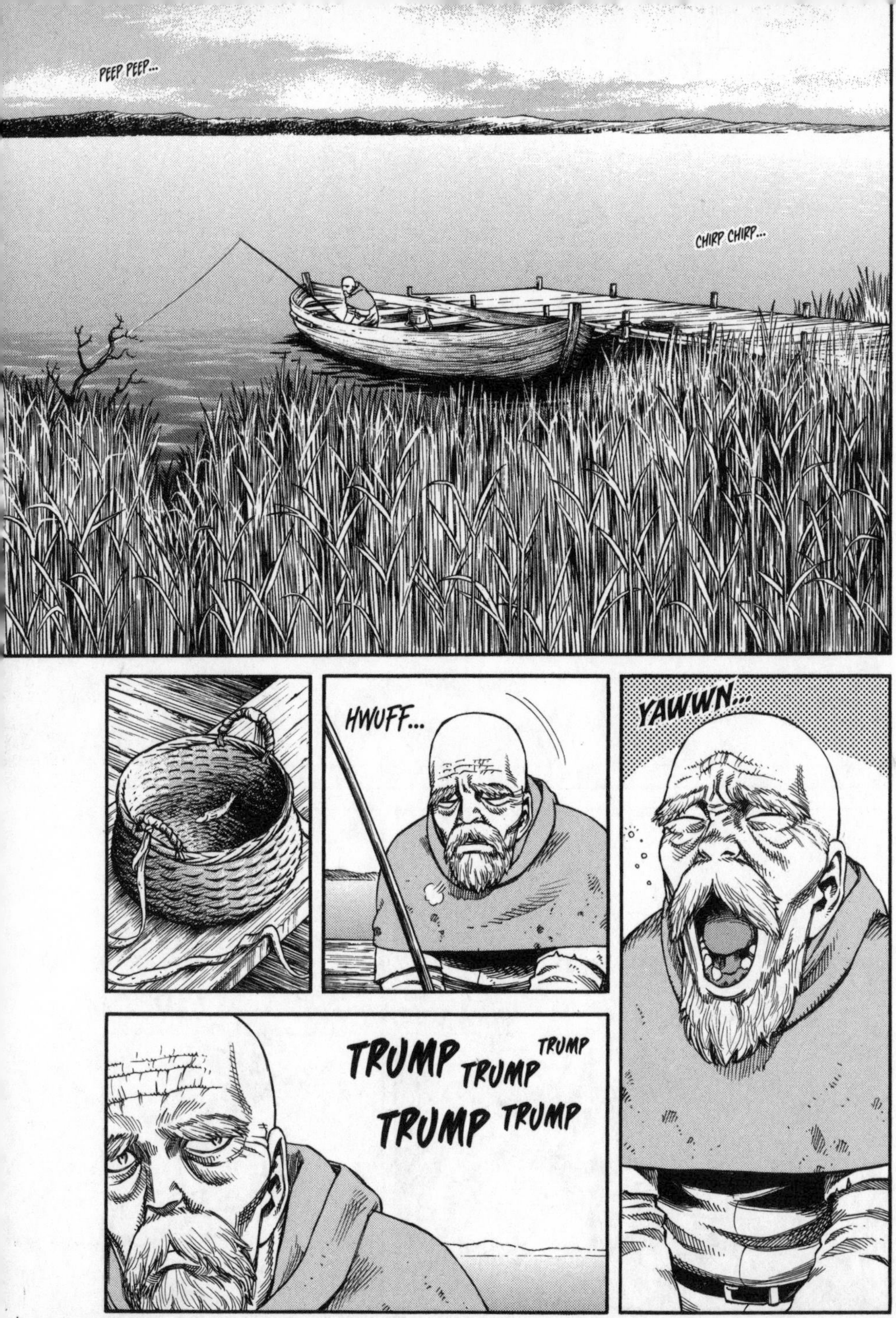
PEEP PEEP...
CHIRP CHIRP...
YAWWN...
HWUFF...
TRUMP TRUMP TRUMP
TRUMP TRUMP

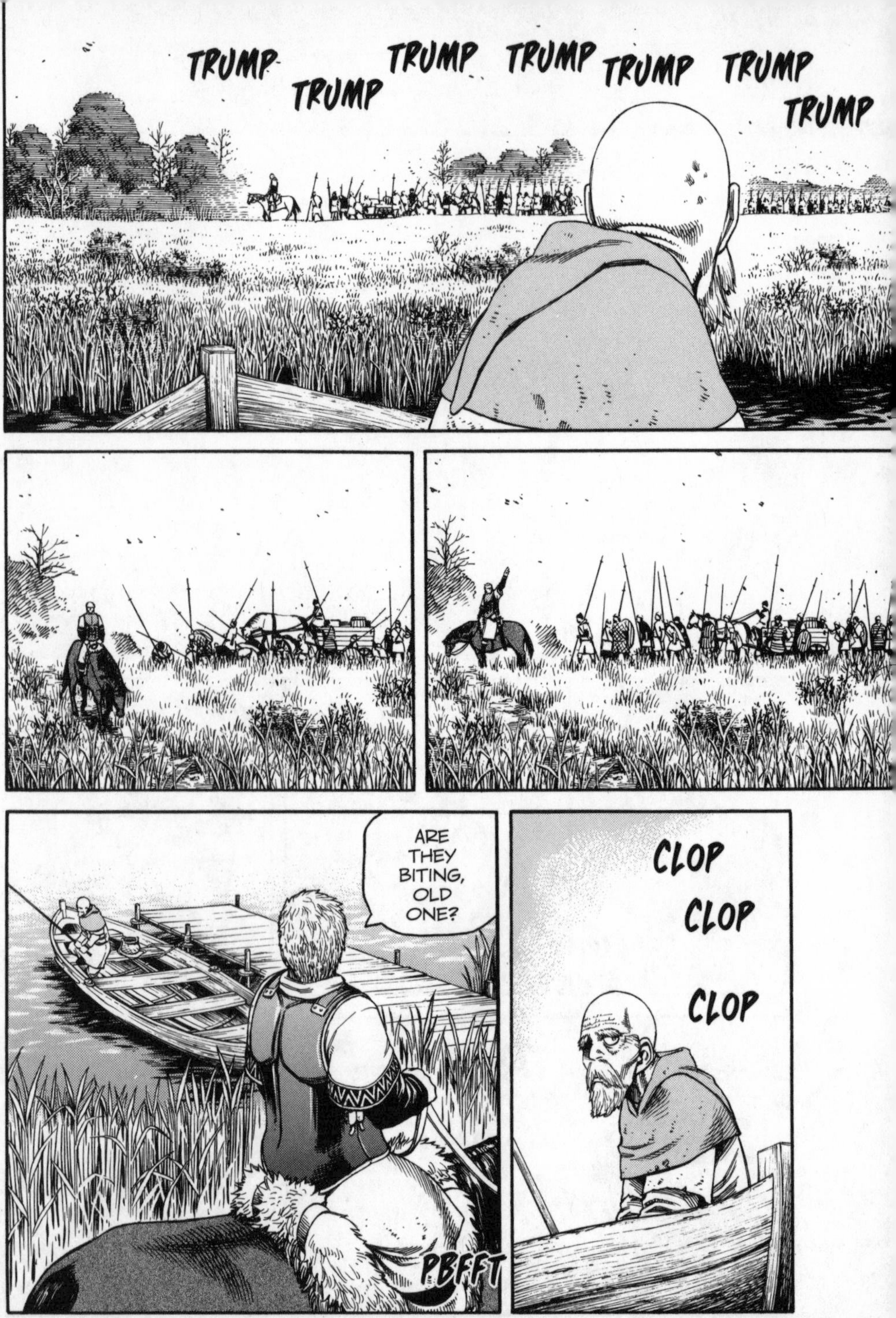
TRUMP
TRUMP
TRUMP
TRUMP
TRUMP
TRUMP
TRUMP
CLOP
CLOP
CLOP
ARE THEY BITING, OLD ONE?
PBFFT

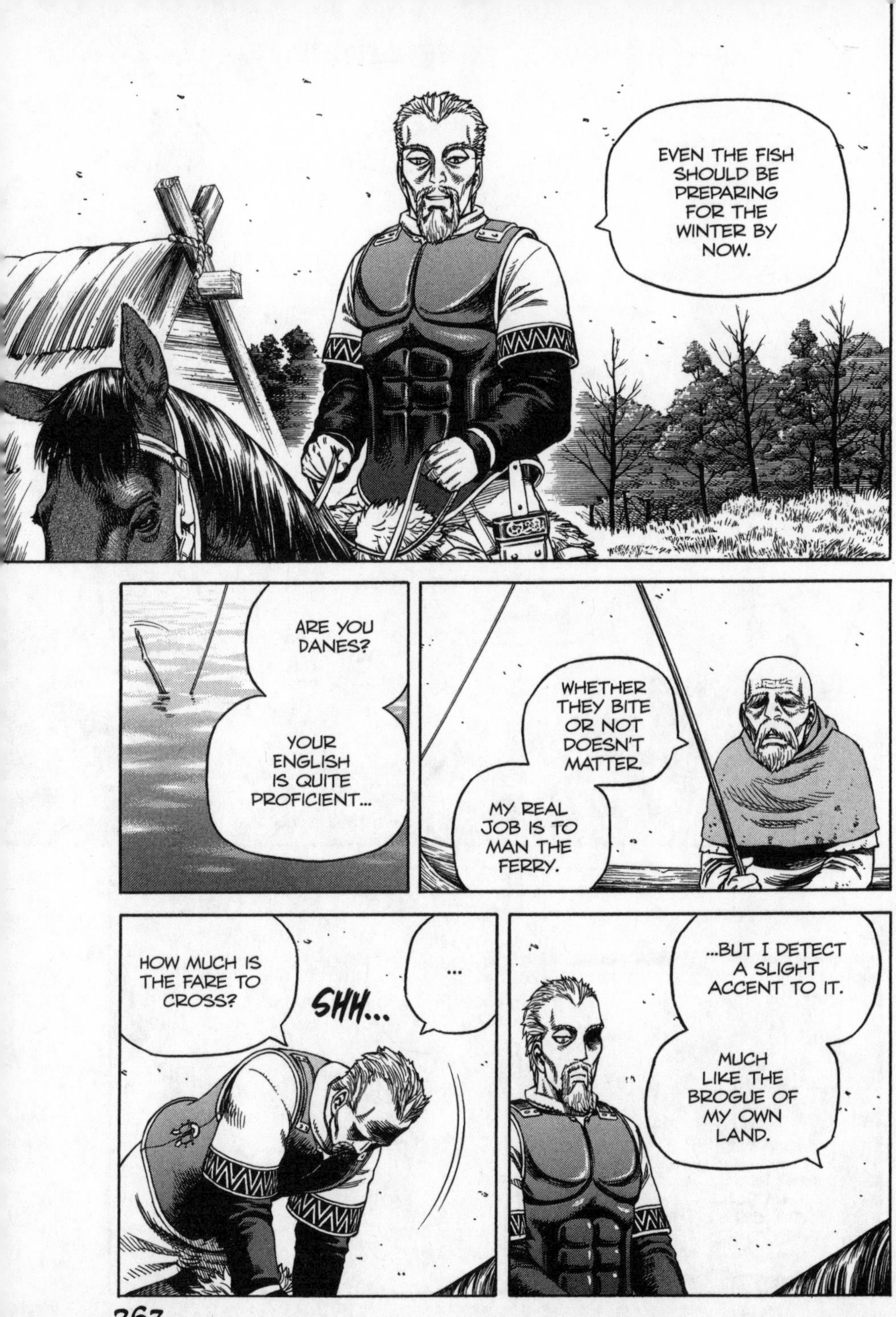
EVEN THE FISH SHOULD BE PREPARING FOR THE WINTER BY NOW.
WHETHER THEY BITE OR NOT DOESN'T MATTER.
MY REAL JOB IS TO MAN THE FERRY.
ARE YOU DANES?
YOUR ENGLISH IS QUITE PROFICIENT...
...BUT I DETECT A SLIGHT ACCENT TO IT.
MUCH LIKE THE BROGUE OF MY OWN LAND.
...
HOW MUCH IS THE FARE TO CROSS?
SHH...

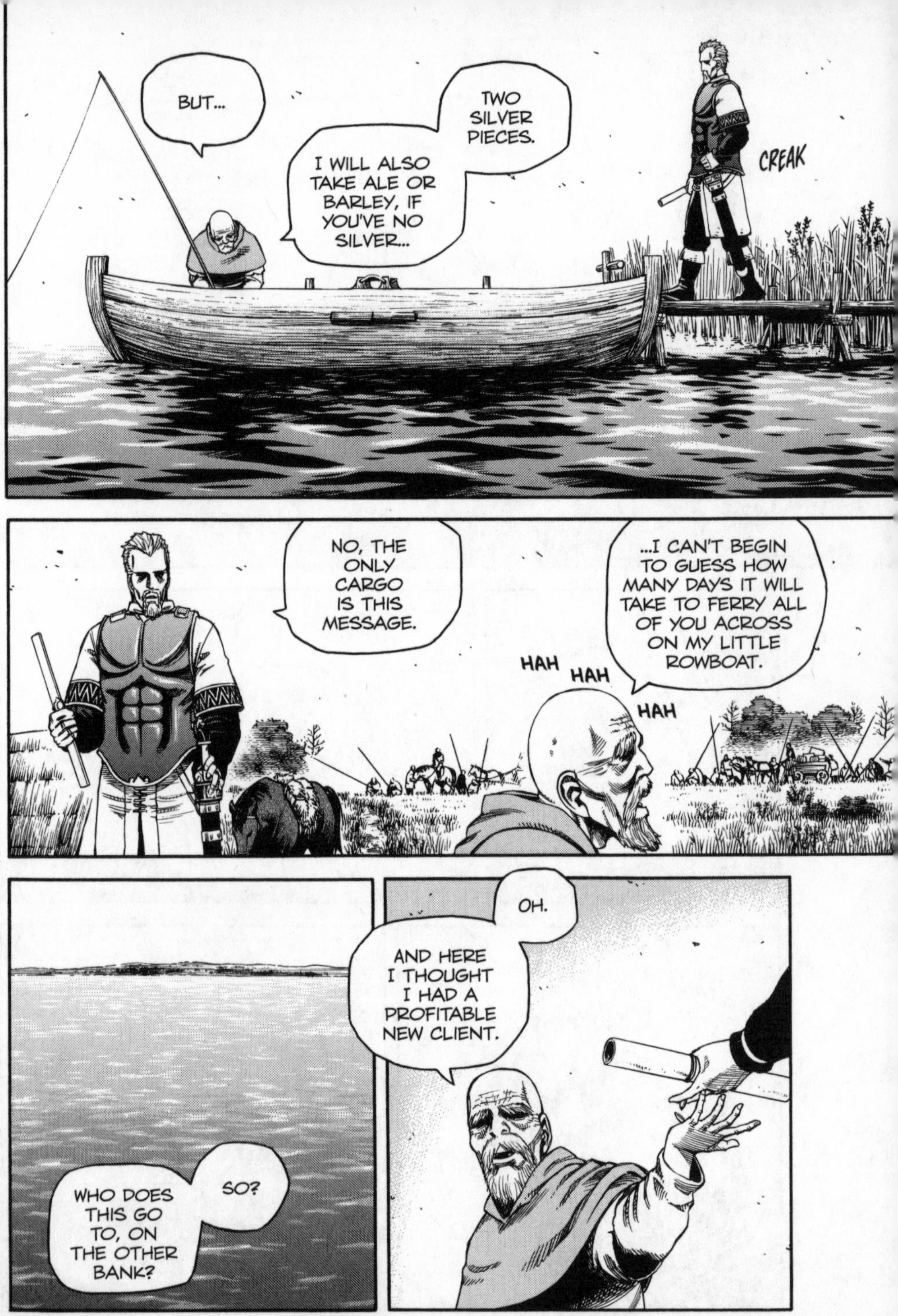
TWO SILVER PIECES.
CREAK
I WILL ALSO TAKE ALE OR BARLEY, IF YOU'VE NO SILVER...
BUT...
...I CAN'T BEGIN TO GUESS HOW MANY DAYS IT WILL TAKE TO FERRY ALL OF YOU ACROSS ON MY LITTLE ROWBOAT.
HAH HAH HAH
NO, THE ONLY CARGO IS THIS MESSAGE.
OH.
AND HERE I THOUGHT I HAD A PROFITABLE NEW CLIENT.
SO?
WHO DOES THIS GO TO, ON THE OTHER BANK?

TO ANYONE WITH AUTHORITY.

AT ONCE.

TELL THEM IT IS A MESSAGE FROM ASKELADD, SON OF LYDIA.

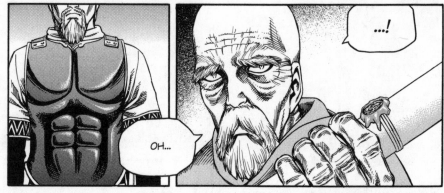

...!

OH...

IT SHALL BE DONE.

AT ONCE.

ZSH...

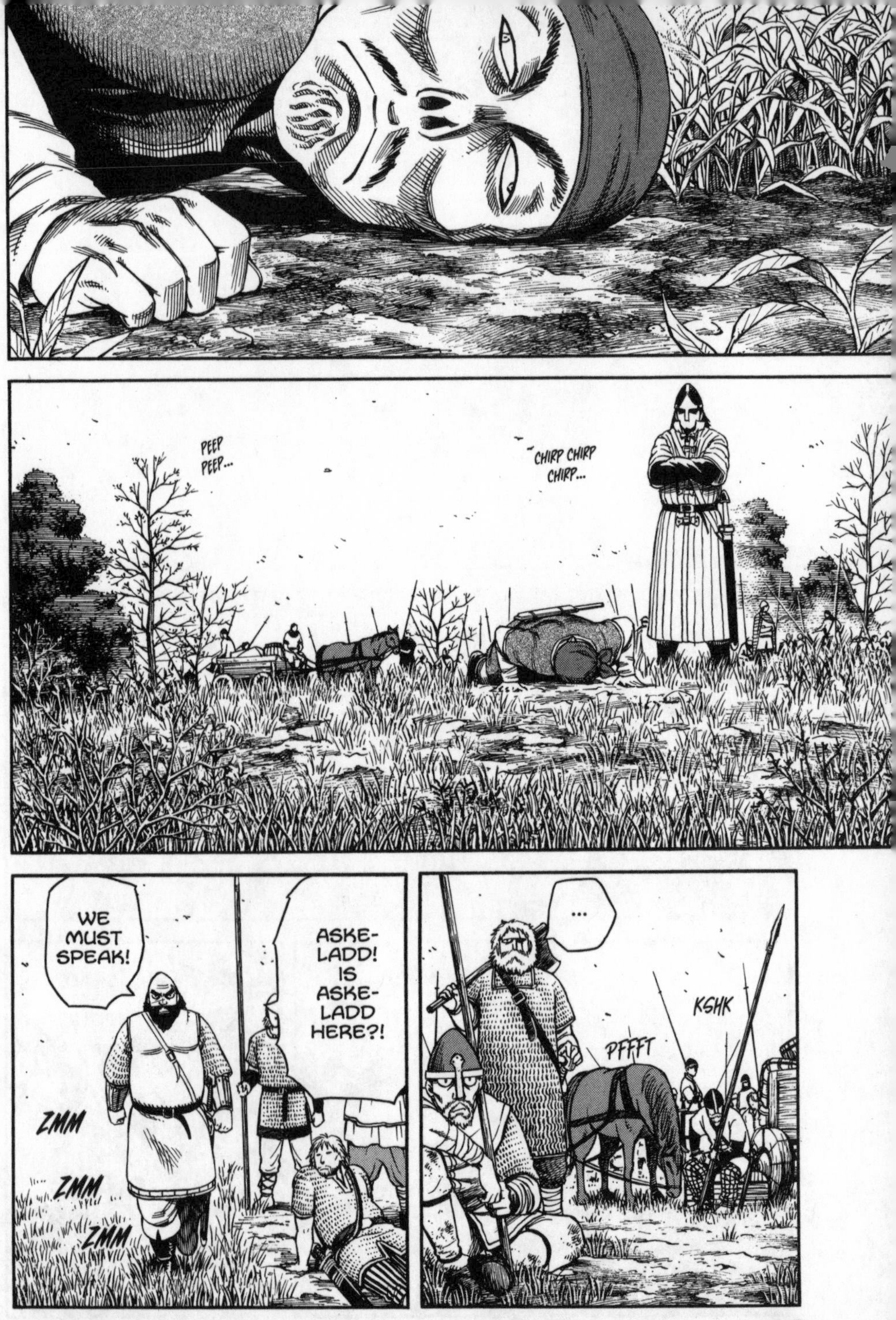
CHIRP CHIRP CHIRP...
PEEP PEEP...
...
KSHK
PFFFT
ASKE-LADD! IS ASKE-LADD HERE?!
WE MUST SPEAK!
ZMM
ZMM
ZMM

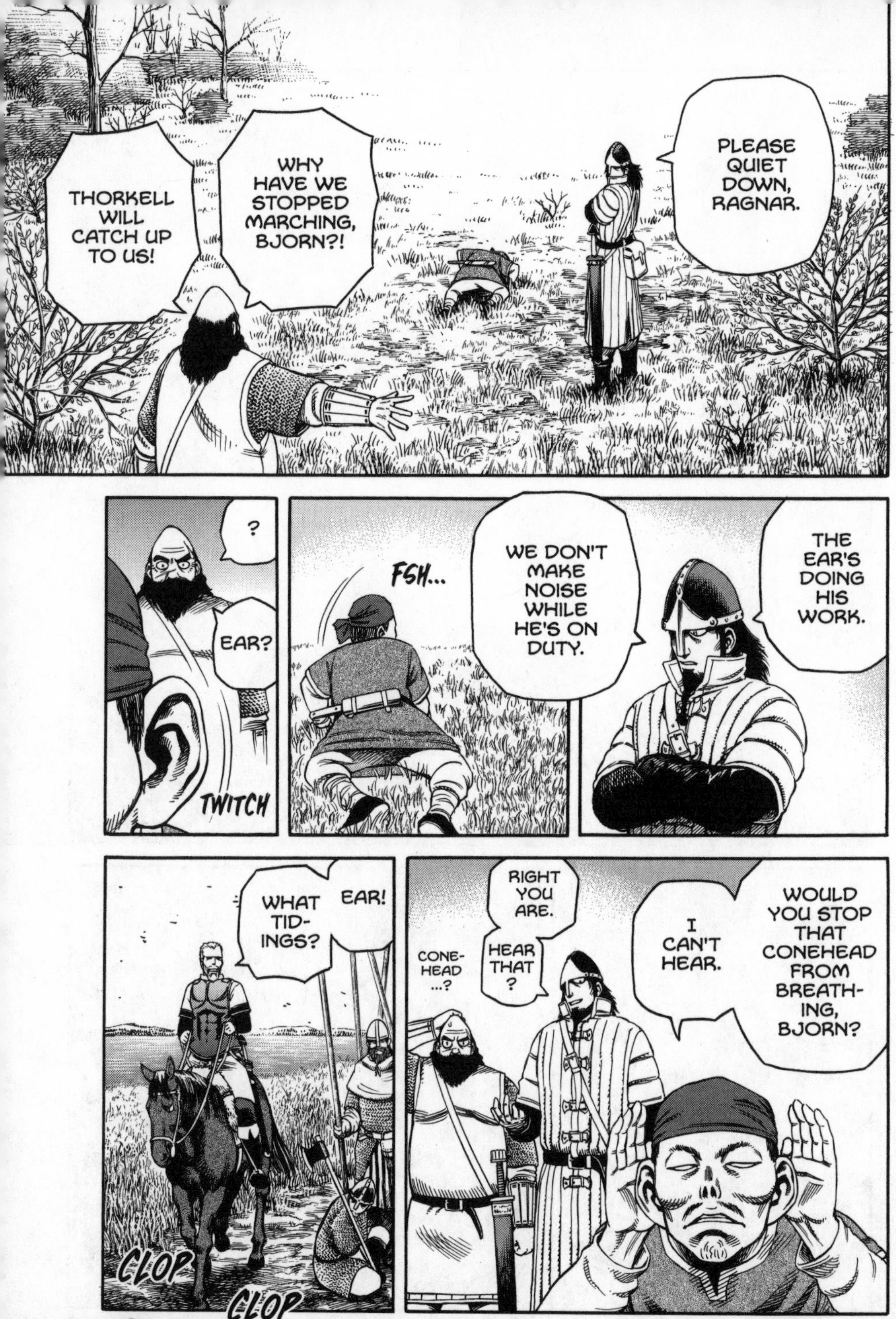
PLEASE QUIET DOWN, RAGNAR.
WHY HAVE WE STOPPED MARCHING, BJORN?!
THORKELL WILL CATCH UP TO US!
THE EAR'S DOING HIS WORK.
WE DON'T MAKE NOISE WHILE HE'S ON DUTY.
FSH...
?
EAR?
TWITCH
WOULD YOU STOP THAT CONEHEAD FROM BREATHING, BJORN?
I CAN'T HEAR.
RIGHT YOU ARE.
HEAR THAT?
CONE-HEAD ...?
EAR!
WHAT TIDINGS?
CLOP
CLOP

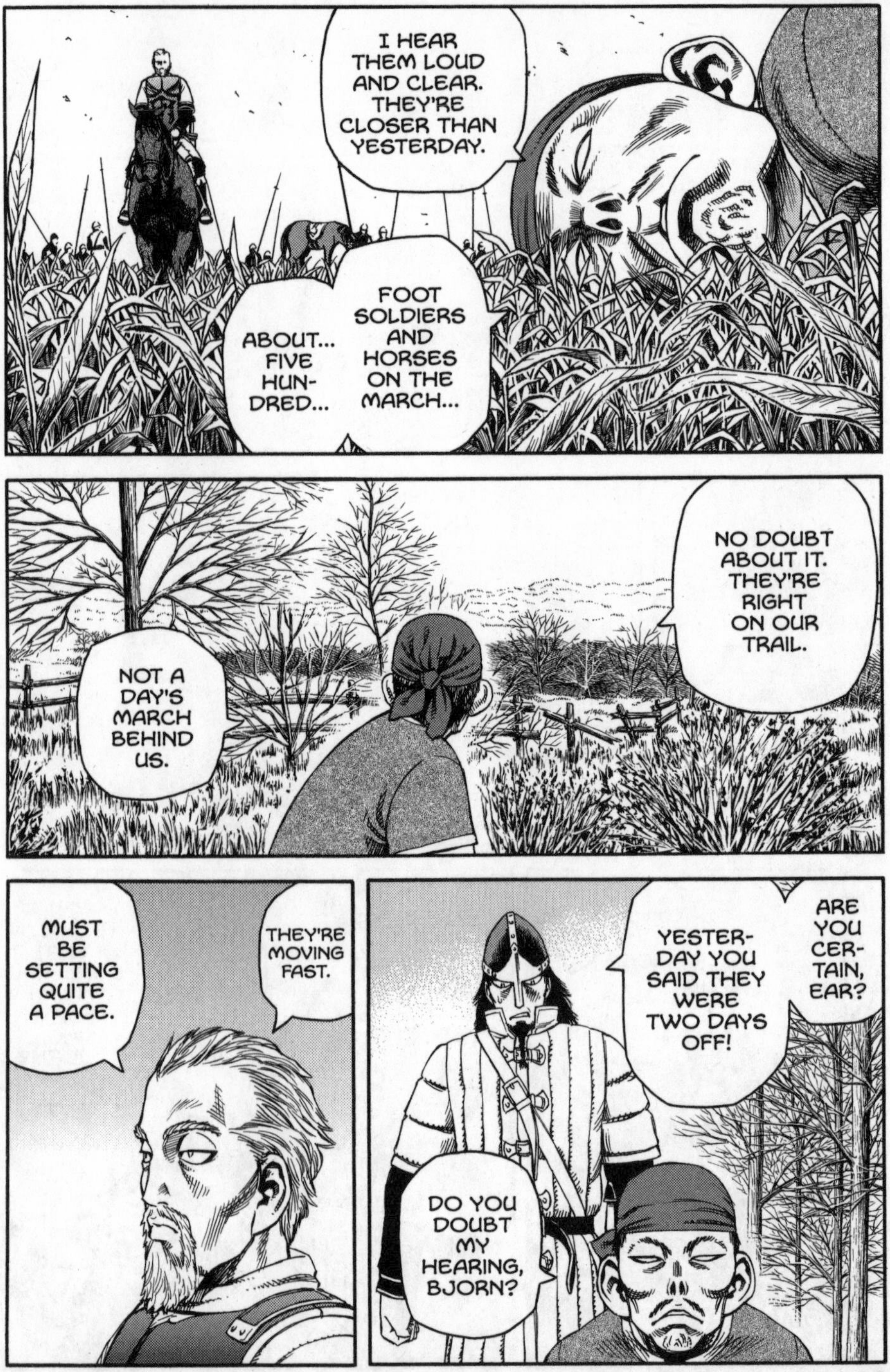
I HEAR THEM LOUD AND CLEAR. THEY'RE CLOSER THAN YESTERDAY.
FOOT SOLDIERS AND HORSES ON THE MARCH...
ABOUT... FIVE HUNDRED...
NO DOUBT ABOUT IT. THEY'RE RIGHT ON OUR TRAIL.
NOT A DAY'S MARCH BEHIND US.
ARE YOU CERTAIN, EAR?
YESTERDAY YOU SAID THEY WERE TWO DAYS OFF!
DO YOU DOUBT MY HEARING, BJORN?
THEY'RE MOVING FAST.
MUST BE SETTING QUITE A PACE.

AT THIS RATE, THORKELL WILL LIKELY CATCH US...

...WITHIN A FEW DAYS.

NO TALKING!

QUIET!!

TWITCH

!

ZIP

HORSES!

ON THE HILL! TWO!

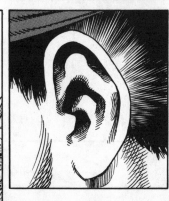

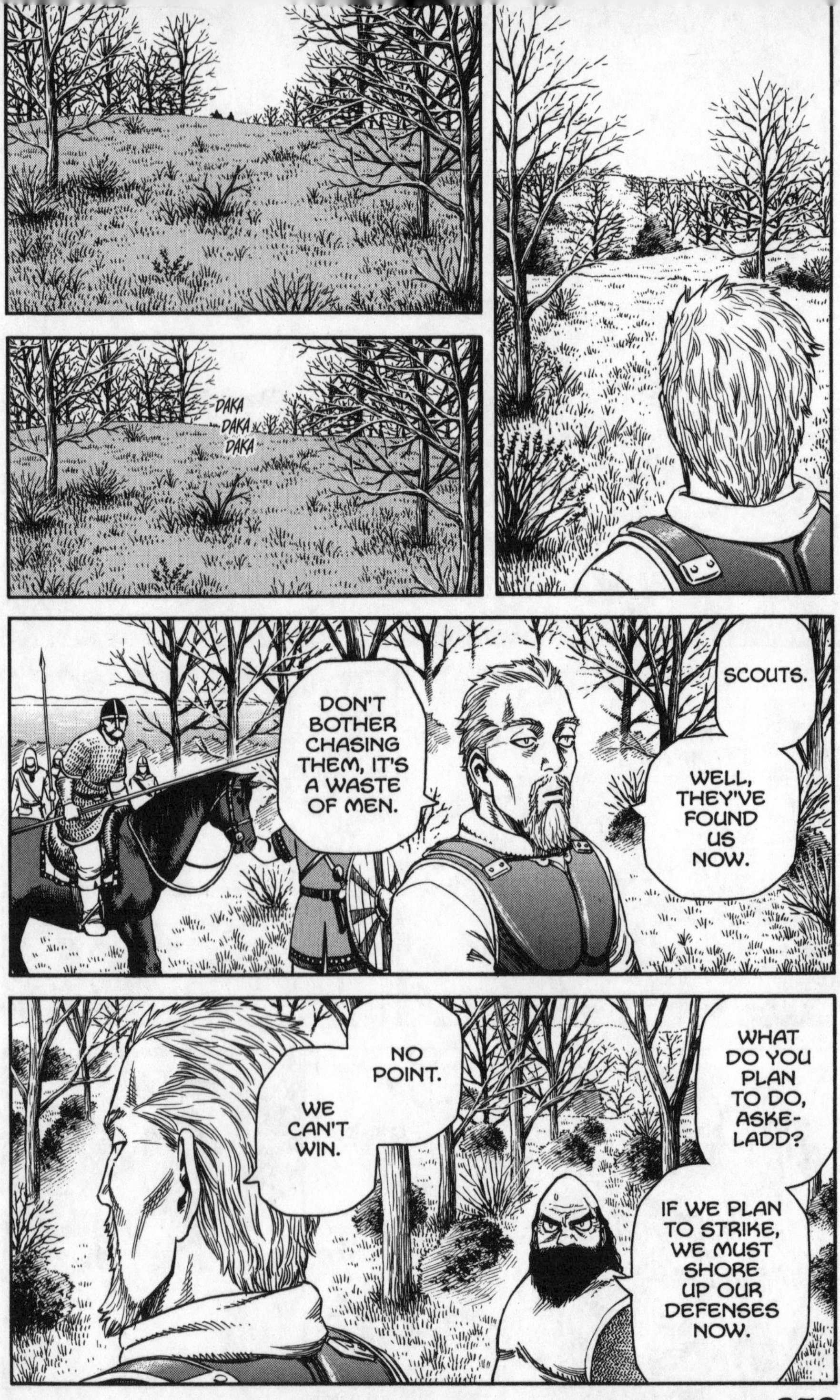
DAKA DAKA DAKA
SCOUTS.
WELL, THEY'VE FOUND US NOW.
DON'T BOTHER CHASING THEM, IT'S A WASTE OF MEN.
WHAT DO YOU PLAN TO DO, ASKE-LADD?
IF WE PLAN TO STRIKE, WE MUST SHORE UP OUR DEFENSES NOW.
NO POINT.
WE CAN'T WIN.

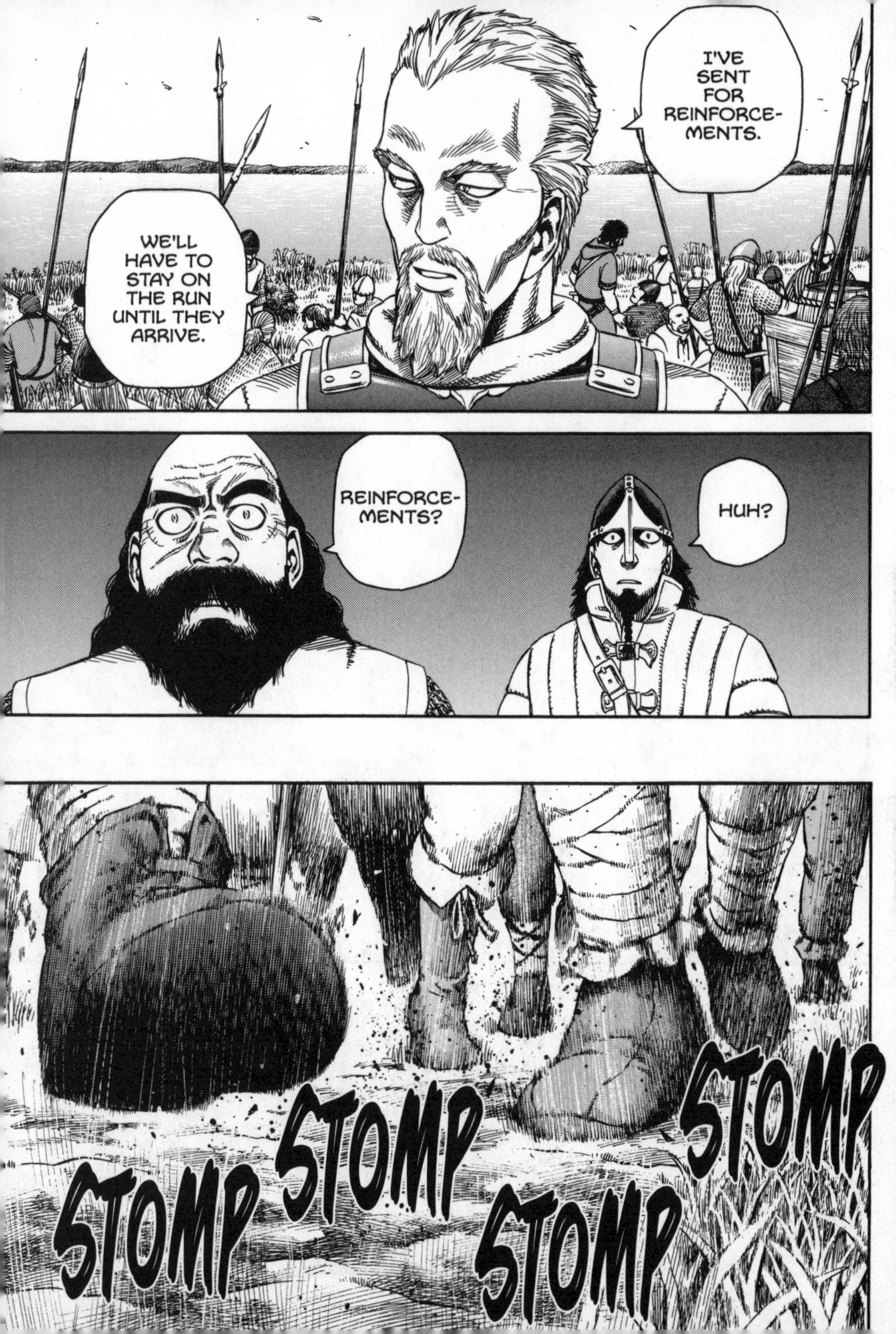
I'VE SENT FOR REINFORCE-MENTS.
WE'LL HAVE TO STAY ON THE RUN UNTIL THEY ARRIVE.
HUH?
REINFORCE-MENTS?
STOMP
STOMP
STOMP
STOMP

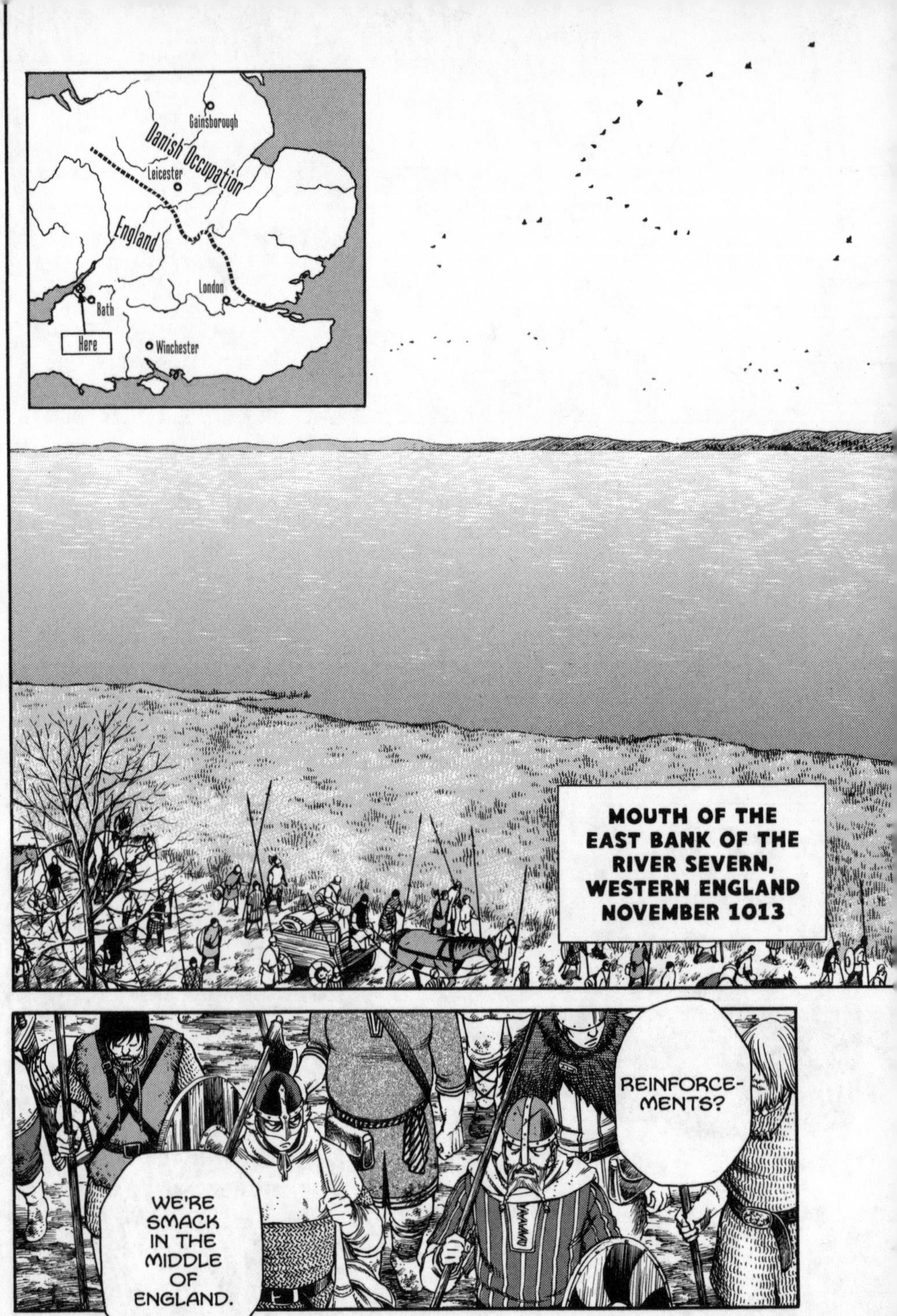
Gainsborough
Danish Occupation
Leicester
England
London
Bath
Here
Winchester
MOUTH OF THE EAST BANK OF THE RIVER SEVERN, WESTERN ENGLAND NOVEMBER 1013
REINFORCE-MENTS?
WE'RE SMACK IN THE MIDDLE OF ENGLAND.

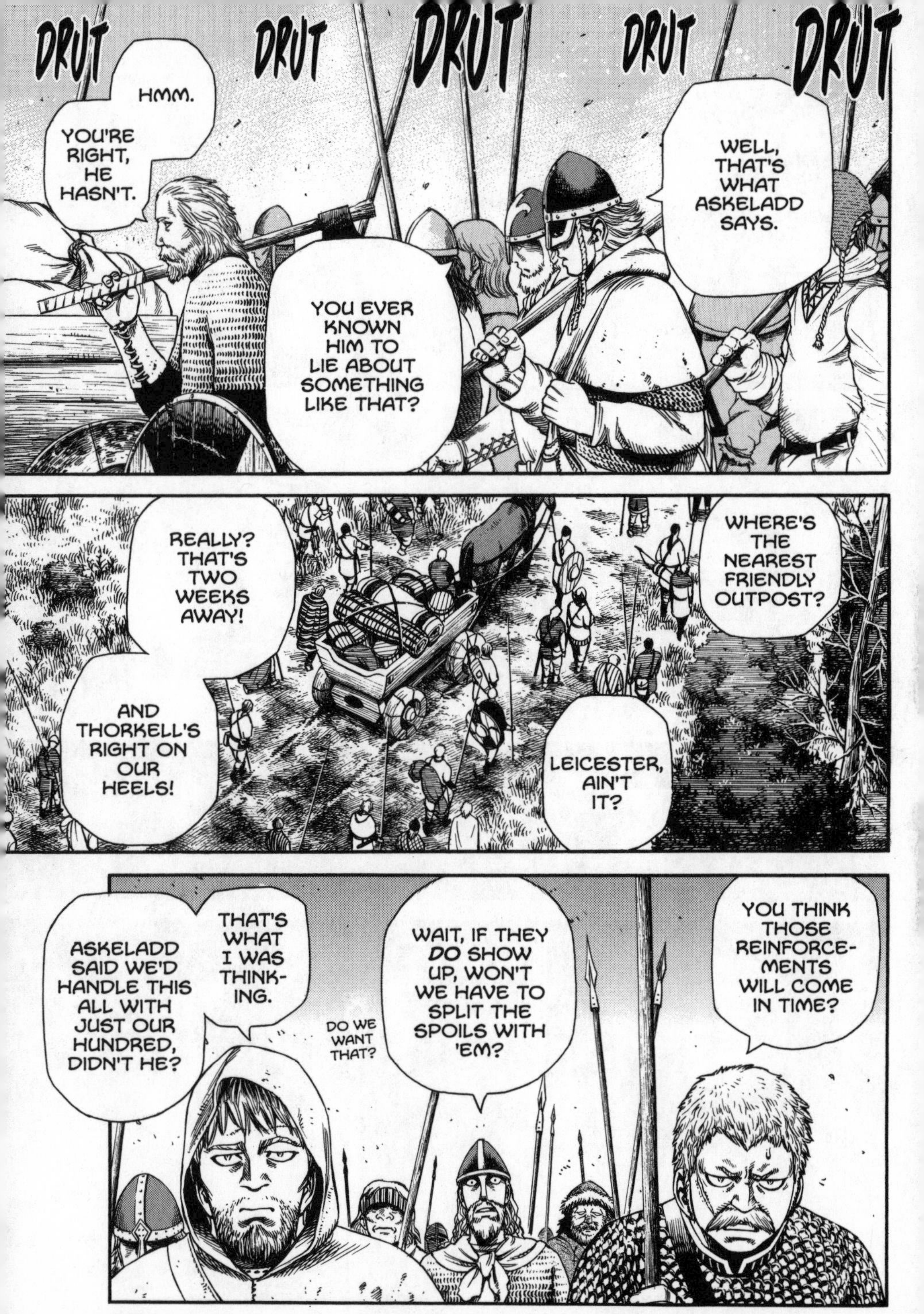
DRUT
DRUT
DRUT
DRUT
DRUT
WELL, THAT'S WHAT ASKELADD SAYS.
YOU EVER KNOWN HIM TO LIE ABOUT SOMETHING LIKE THAT?
HMM.
YOU'RE RIGHT, HE HASN'T.
WHERE'S THE NEAREST FRIENDLY OUTPOST?
LEICESTER, AIN'T IT?
REALLY? THAT'S TWO WEEKS AWAY!
AND THORKELL'S RIGHT ON OUR HEELS!
YOU THINK THOSE REINFORCEMENTS WILL COME IN TIME?
WAIT, IF THEY *DO* SHOW UP, WON'T WE HAVE TO SPLIT THE SPOILS WITH 'EM?
DO WE WANT THAT?
THAT'S WHAT I WAS THINKING.
ASKELADD SAID WE'D HANDLE THIS ALL WITH JUST OUR HUNDRED, DIDN'T HE?

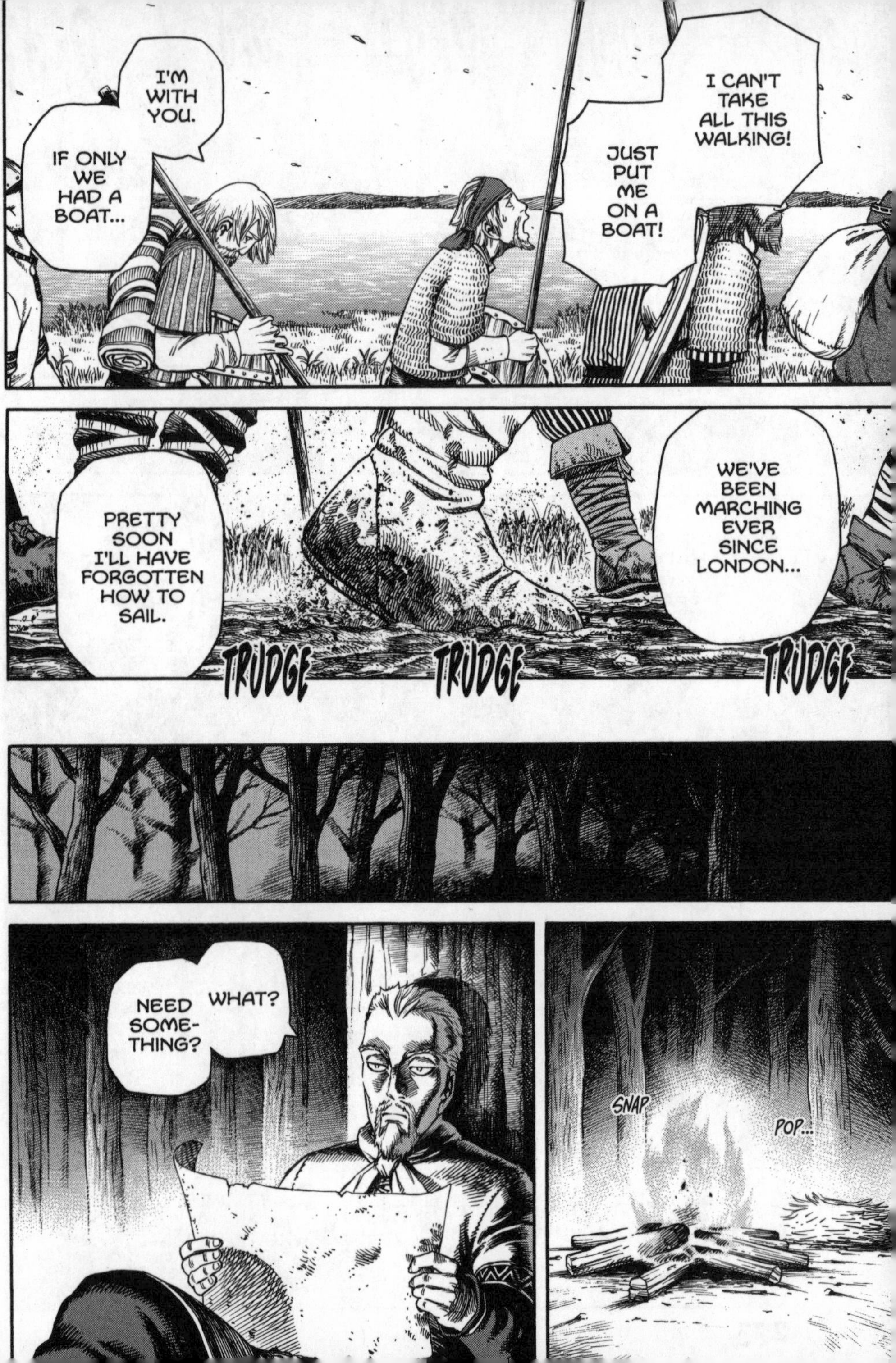
I CAN'T TAKE ALL THIS WALKING!
JUST PUT ME ON A BOAT!
I'M WITH YOU.
IF ONLY WE HAD A BOAT...
WE'VE BEEN MARCHING EVER SINCE LONDON...
PRETTY SOON I'LL HAVE FORGOTTEN HOW TO SAIL.
TRUDGE
TRUDGE
TRUDGE
SNAP
POP...
WHAT?
NEED SOME-THING?

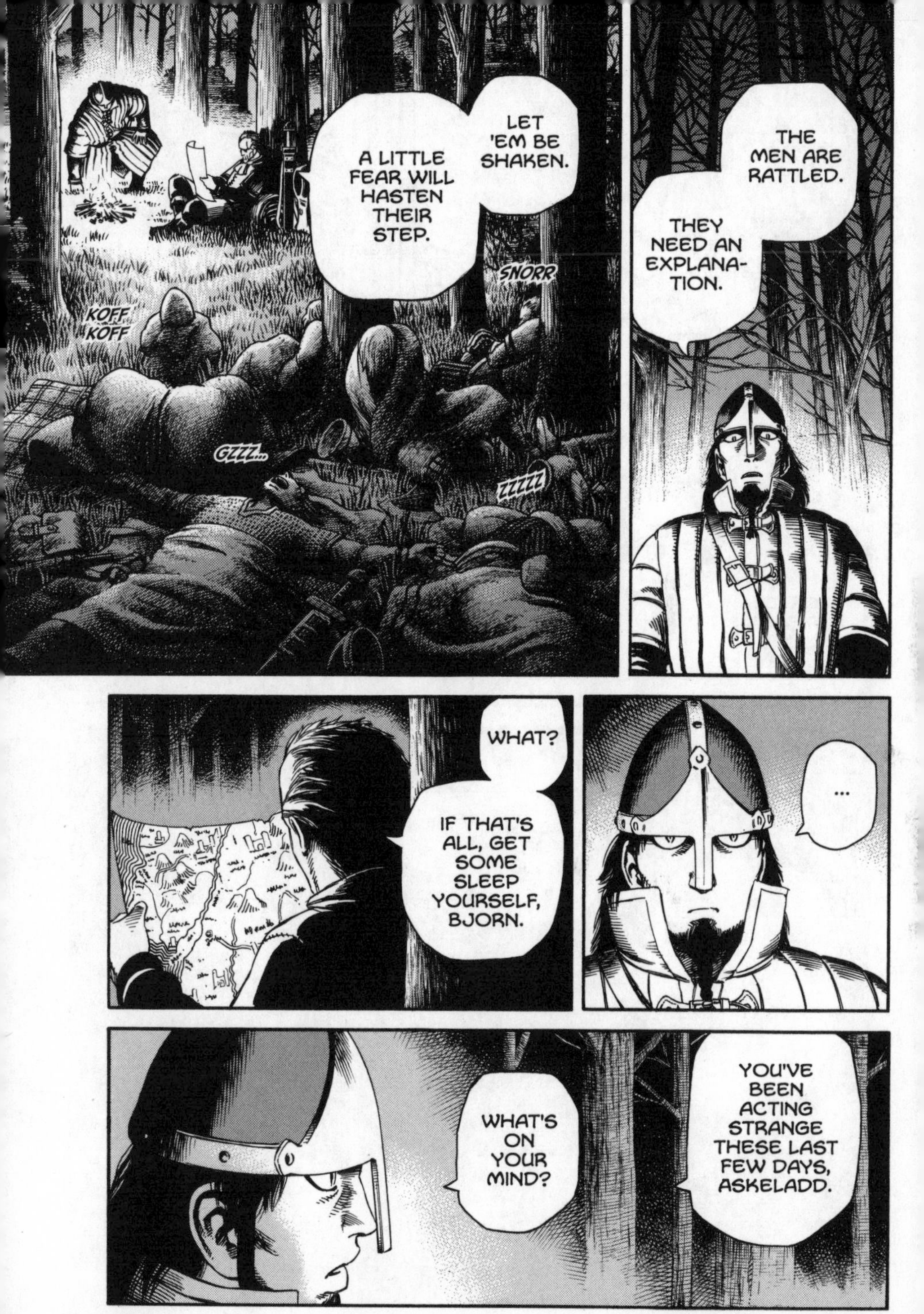
THE MEN ARE RATTLED.
THEY NEED AN EXPLANATION.
LET 'EM BE SHAKEN.
A LITTLE FEAR WILL HASTEN THEIR STEP.
SNORR
KOFF KOFF
GZZZ...
ZZZZZ
...
WHAT?
IF THAT'S ALL, GET SOME SLEEP YOURSELF, BJORN.
YOU'VE BEEN ACTING STRANGE THESE LAST FEW DAYS, ASKELADD.
WHAT'S ON YOUR MIND?

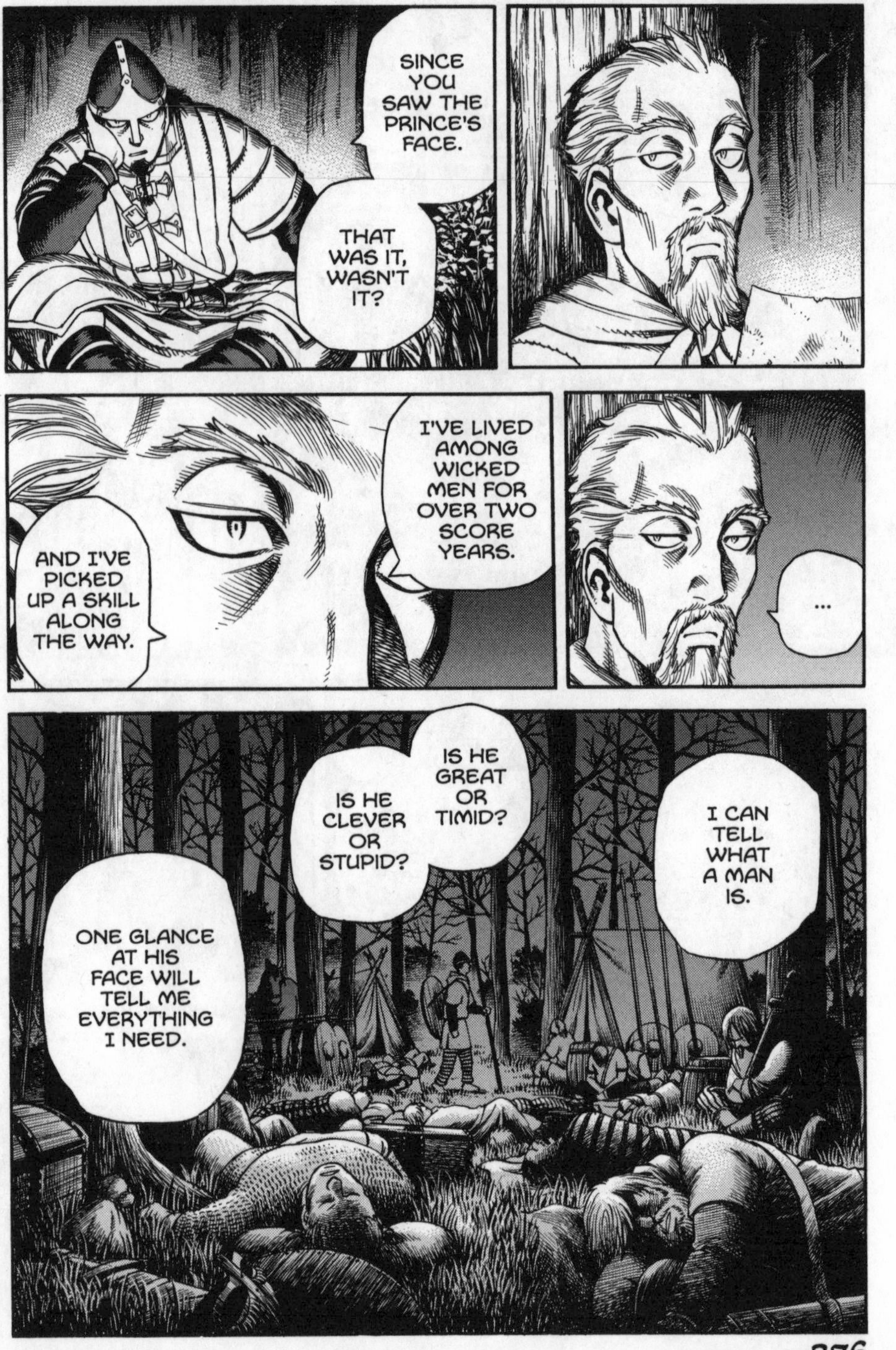

SINCE YOU SAW THE PRINCE'S FACE.
THAT WAS IT, WASN'T IT?
...
I'VE LIVED AMONG WICKED MEN FOR OVER TWO SCORE YEARS.
AND I'VE PICKED UP A SKILL ALONG THE WAY.
I CAN TELL WHAT A MAN IS.
IS HE GREAT OR TIMID?
IS HE CLEVER OR STUPID?
ONE GLANCE AT HIS FACE WILL TELL ME EVERYTHING I NEED.

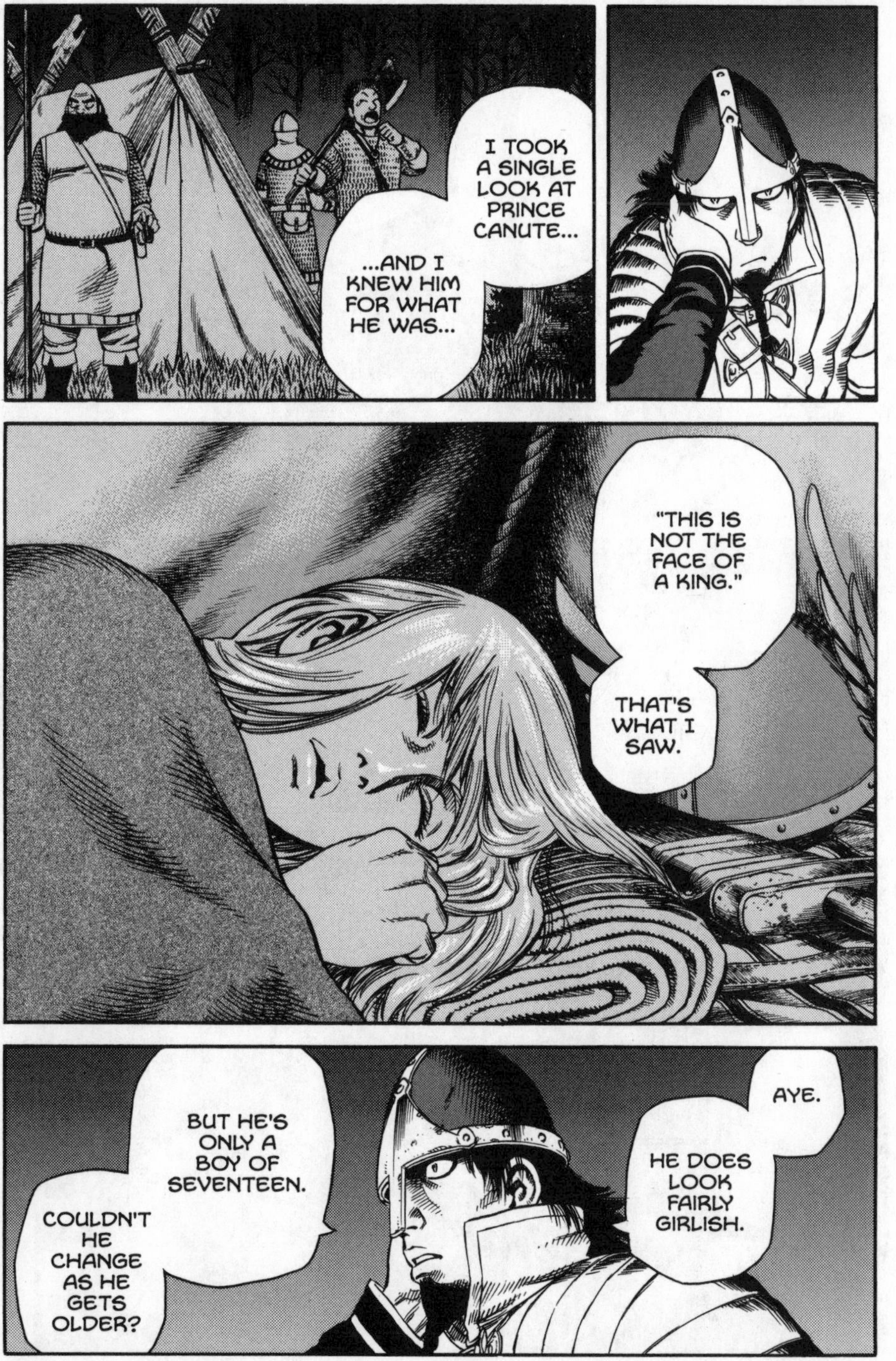
I TOOK A SINGLE LOOK AT PRINCE CANUTE...
...AND I KNEW HIM FOR WHAT HE WAS...
"THIS IS NOT THE FACE OF A KING."
THAT'S WHAT I SAW.
AYE.
HE DOES LOOK FAIRLY GIRLISH.
BUT HE'S ONLY A BOY OF SEVENTEEN.
COULDN'T HE CHANGE AS HE GETS OLDER?

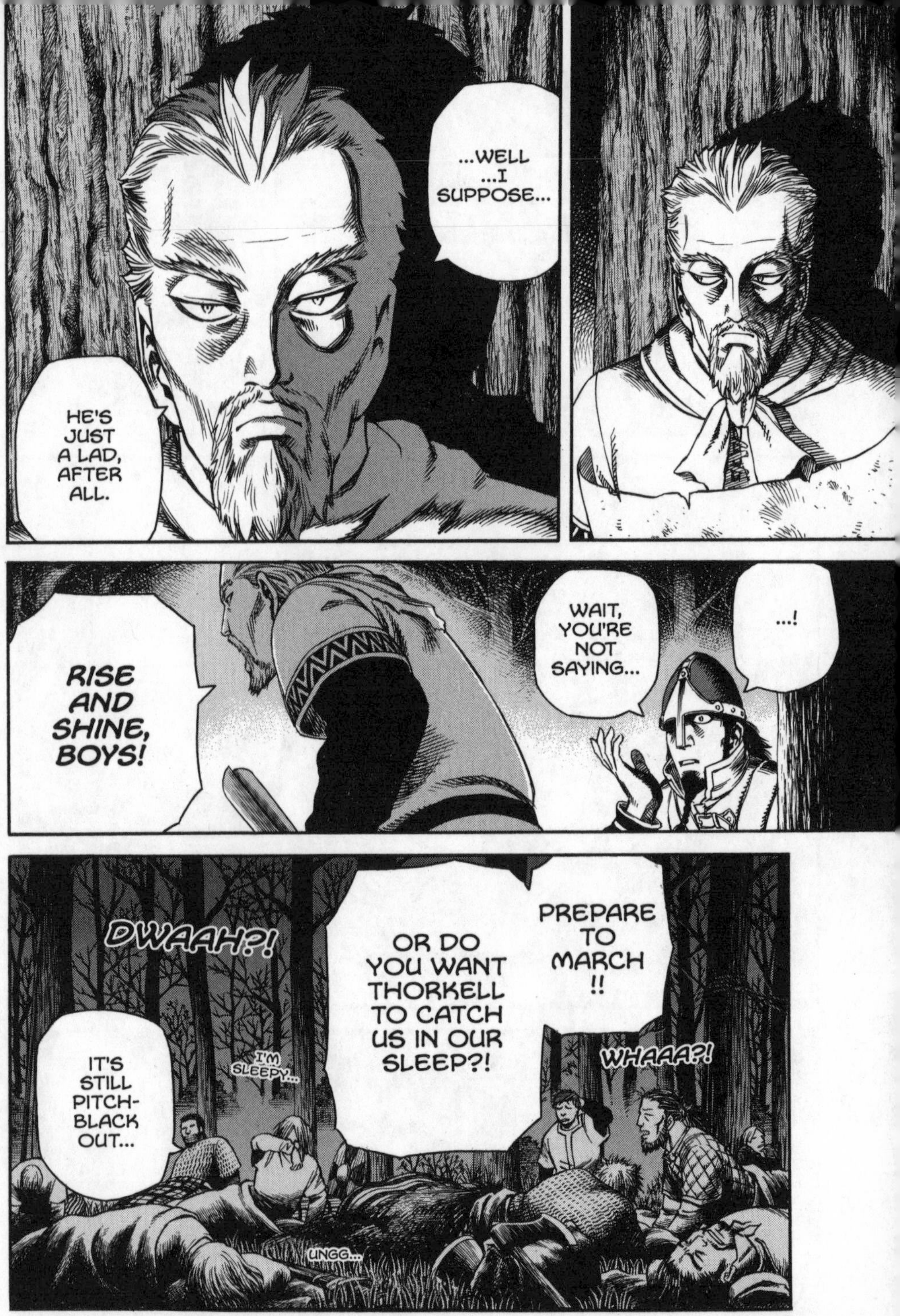

...WELL ...I SUPPOSE...
HE'S JUST A LAD, AFTER ALL.
...!
WAIT, YOU'RE NOT SAYING...
RISE AND SHINE, BOYS!
PREPARE TO MARCH !!
OR DO YOU WANT THORKELL TO CATCH US IN OUR SLEEP?!
WHAAA?!
DWAAH?!
I'M SLEEPY...
IT'S STILL PITCH-BLACK OUT...
UNGG...

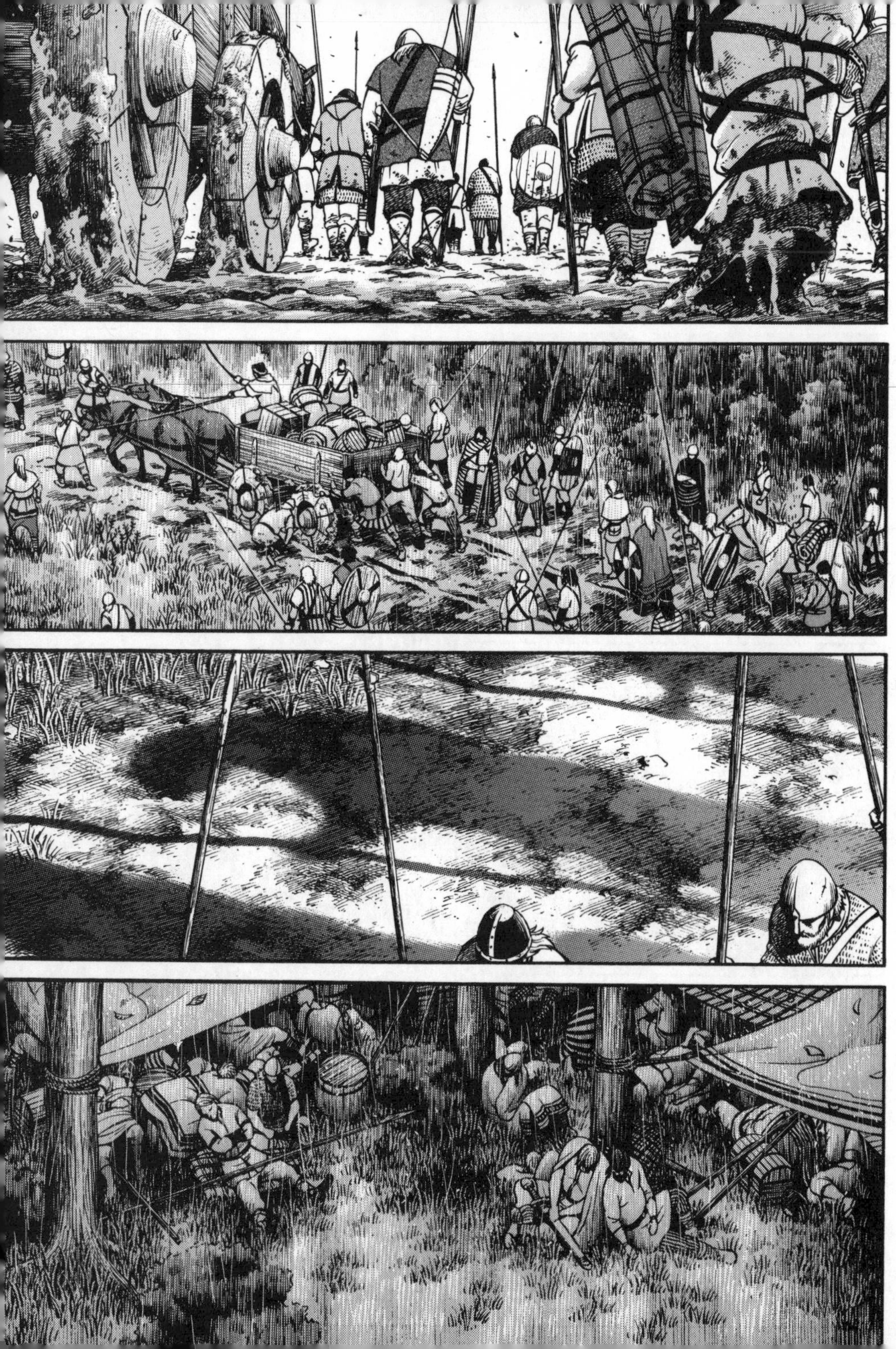

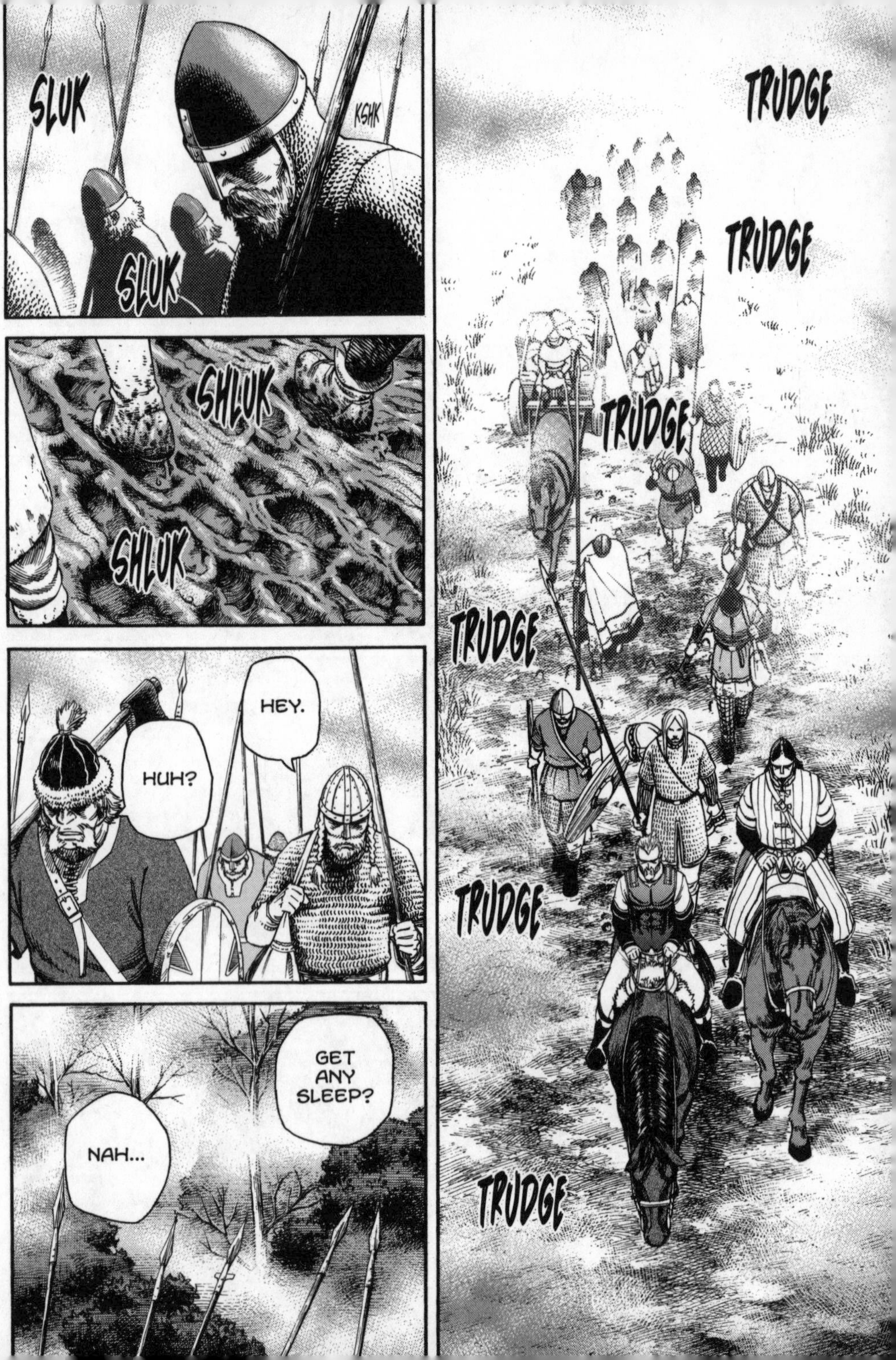
TRUDGE
TRUDGE
TRUDGE
TRUDGE
TRUDGE
TRUDGE
SLUK
KSHK
SLUK
SHLUK
SHLUK
HEY.
HUH?
GET ANY SLEEP?
NAH...

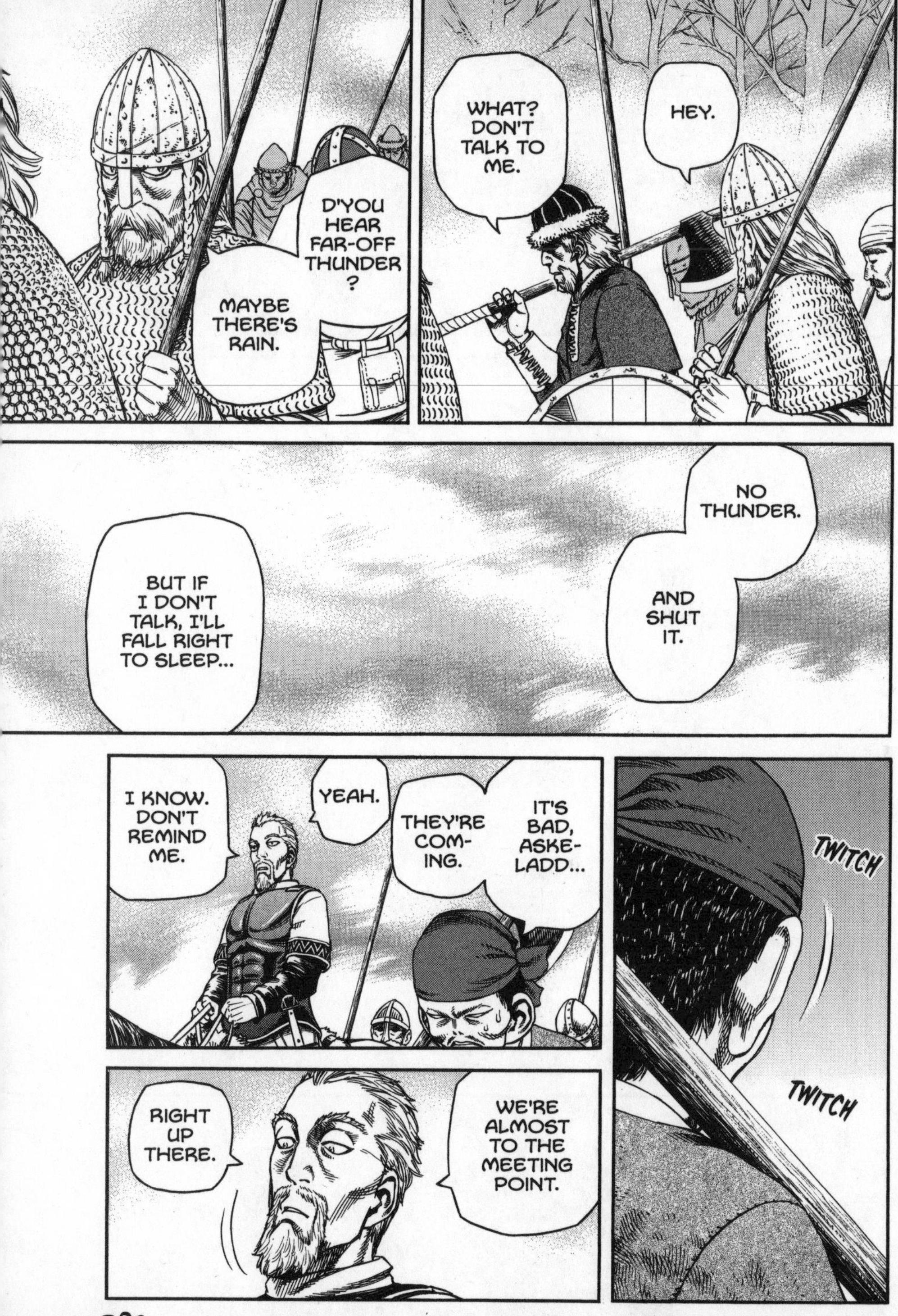
HEY.
WHAT? DON'T TALK TO ME.
D'YOU HEAR FAR-OFF THUNDER?
MAYBE THERE'S RAIN.
NO THUNDER.
AND SHUT IT.
BUT IF I DON'T TALK, I'LL FALL RIGHT TO SLEEP...
TWITCH
TWITCH
IT'S BAD, ASKE-LADD...
THEY'RE COM-ING.
YEAH.
I KNOW. DON'T REMIND ME.
WE'RE ALMOST TO THE MEETING POINT.
RIGHT UP THERE.

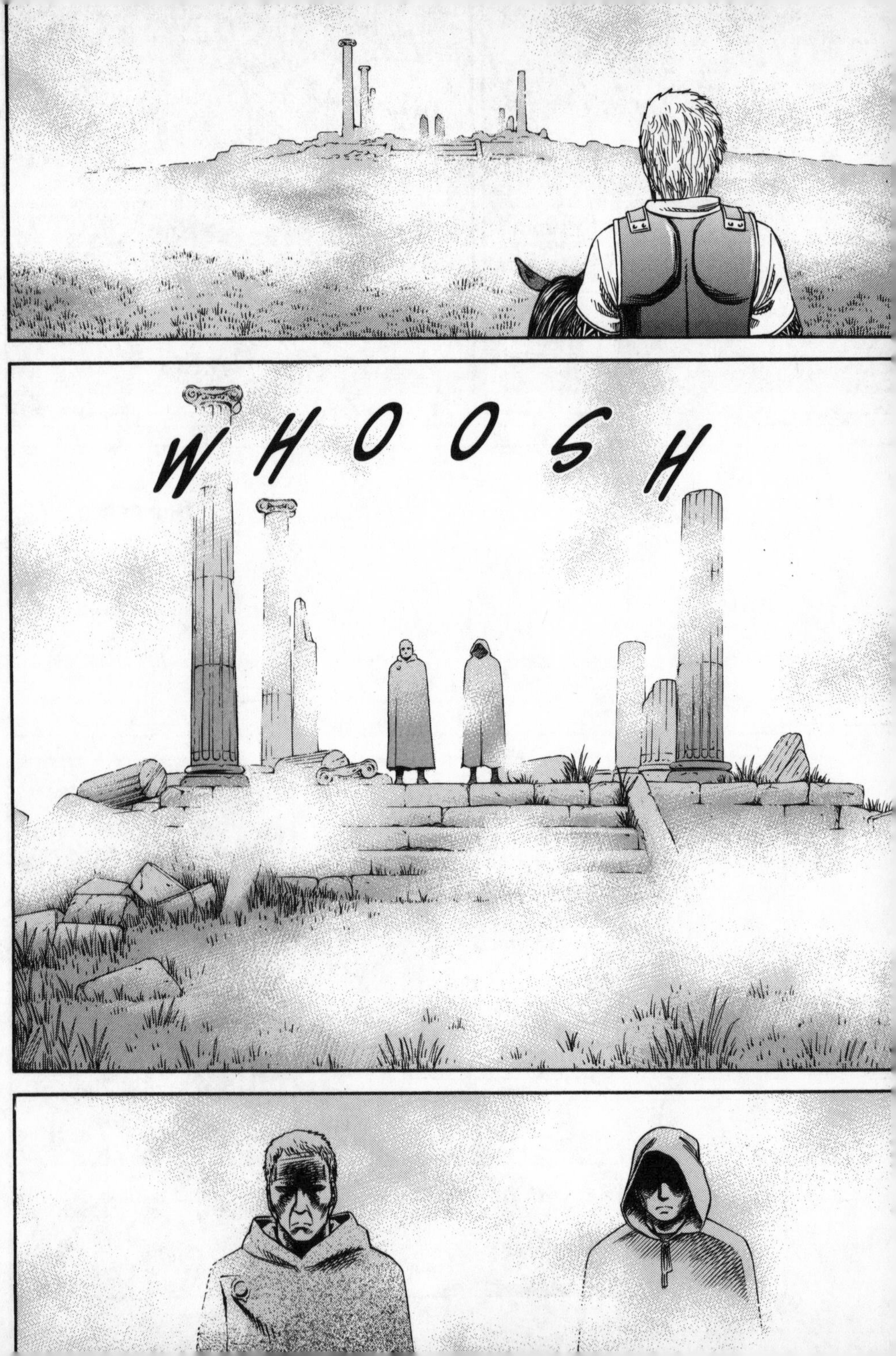
WHOOSH

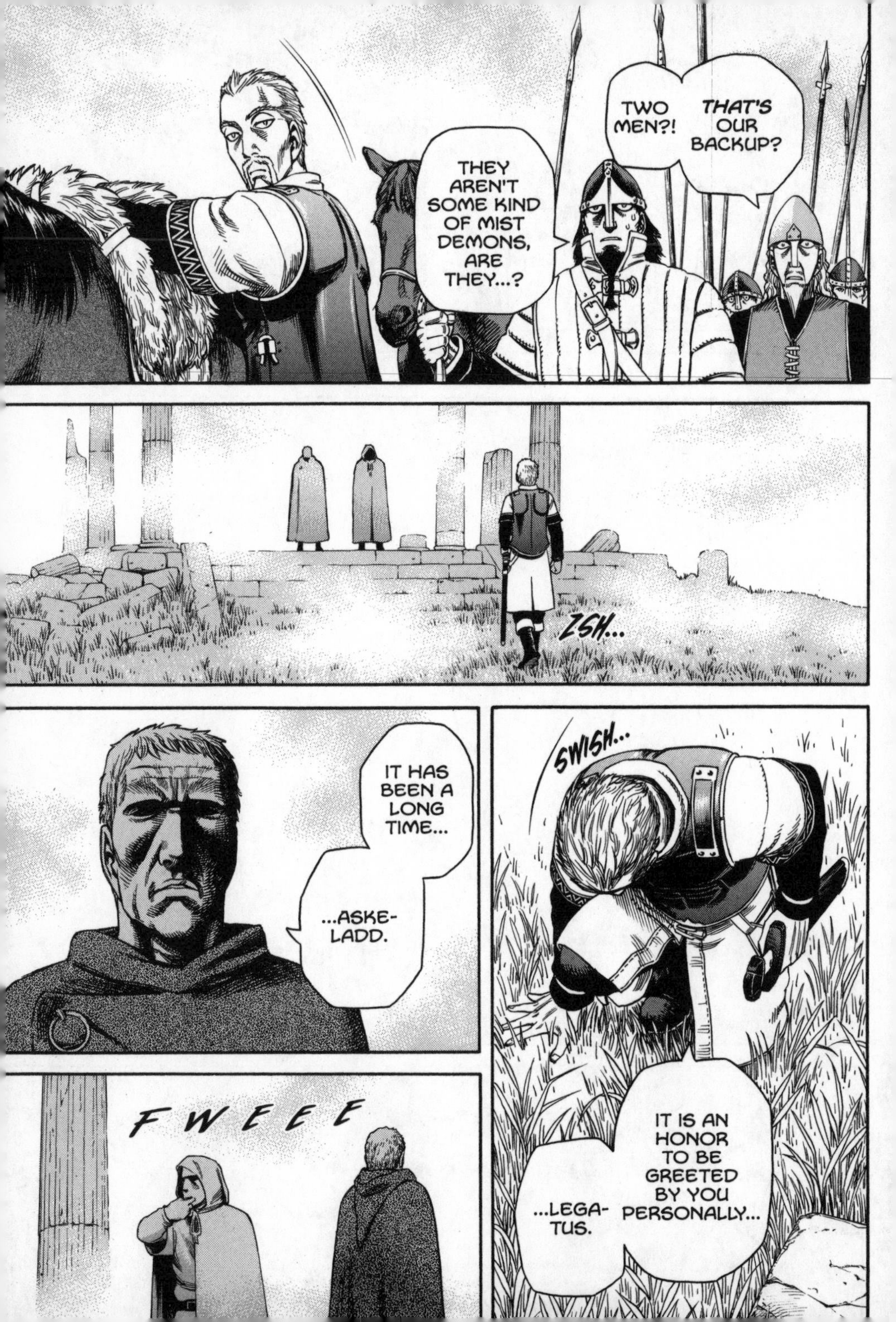
TWO MEN?! THAT'S OUR BACKUP?
THEY AREN'T SOME KIND OF MIST DEMONS, ARE THEY...?
ZSH...
SWISH...
IT IS AN HONOR TO BE GREETED BY YOU PERSONALLY...
...LEGATUS.
IT HAS BEEN A LONG TIME...
...ASKELADD.
FWEEE

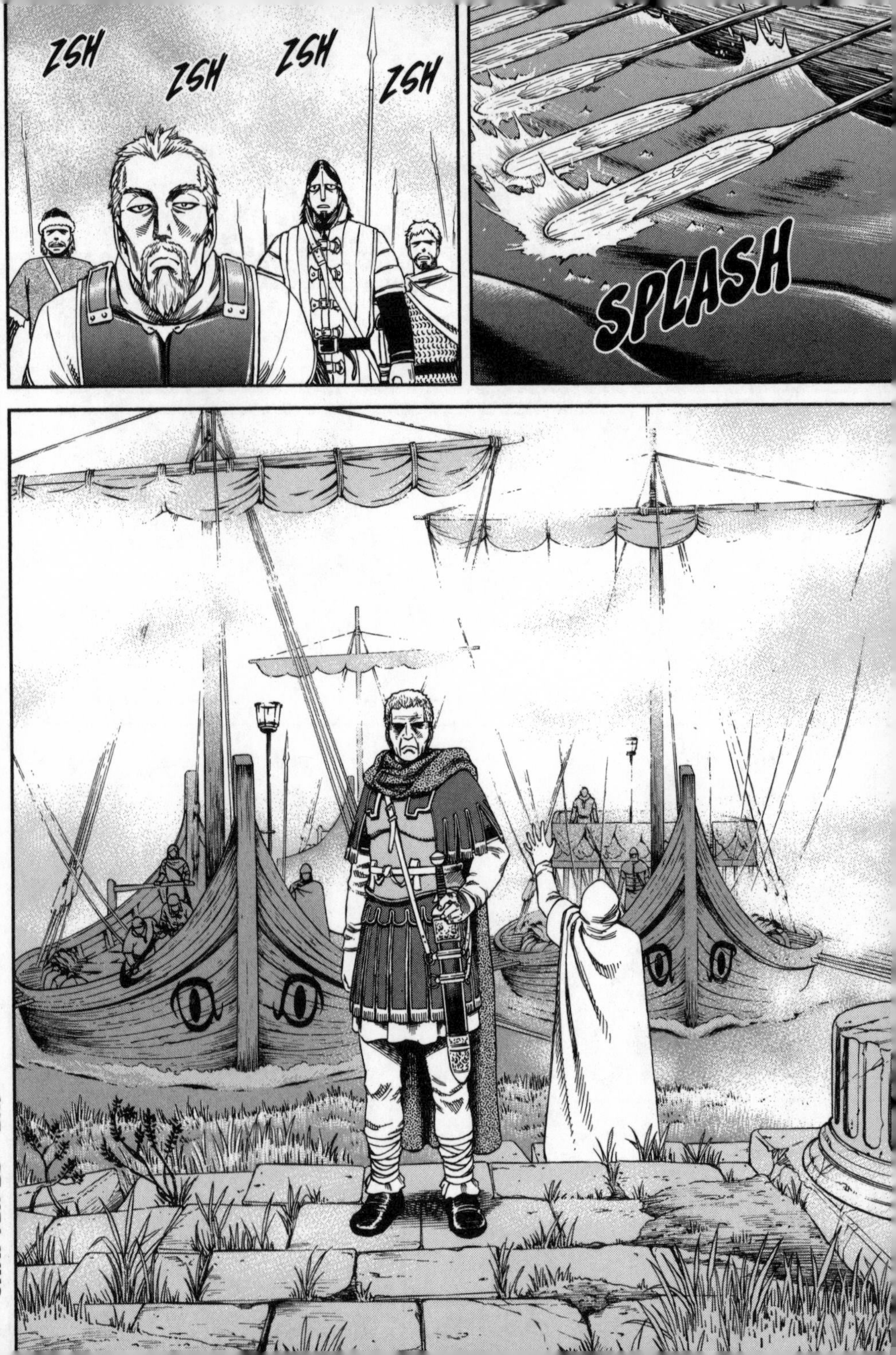
SPLASH
ZSH
ZSH
ZSH
ZSH

CHAPTER 23 - END

CHAPTER 24: THE LAND ON THE FAR BANK

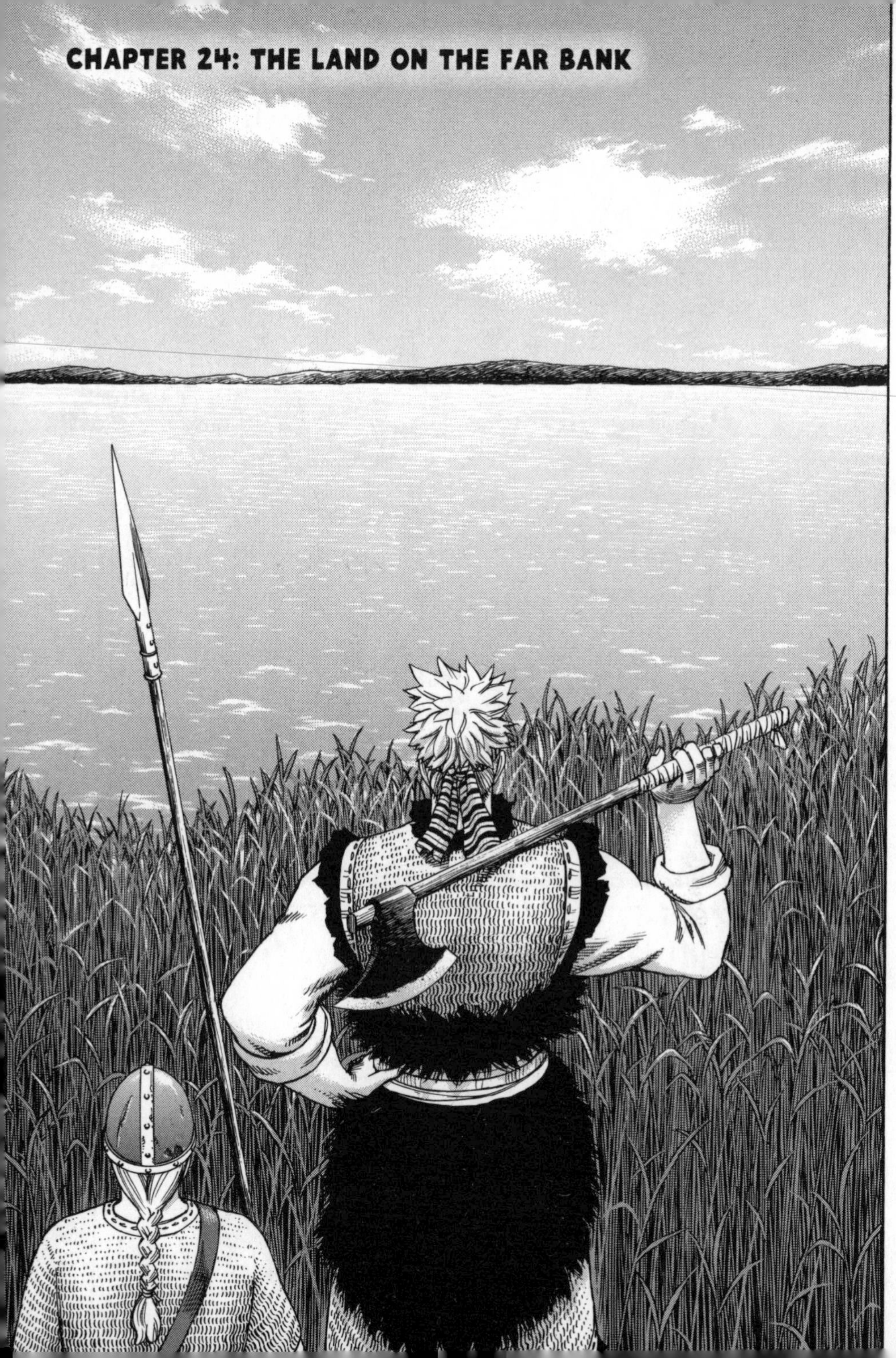

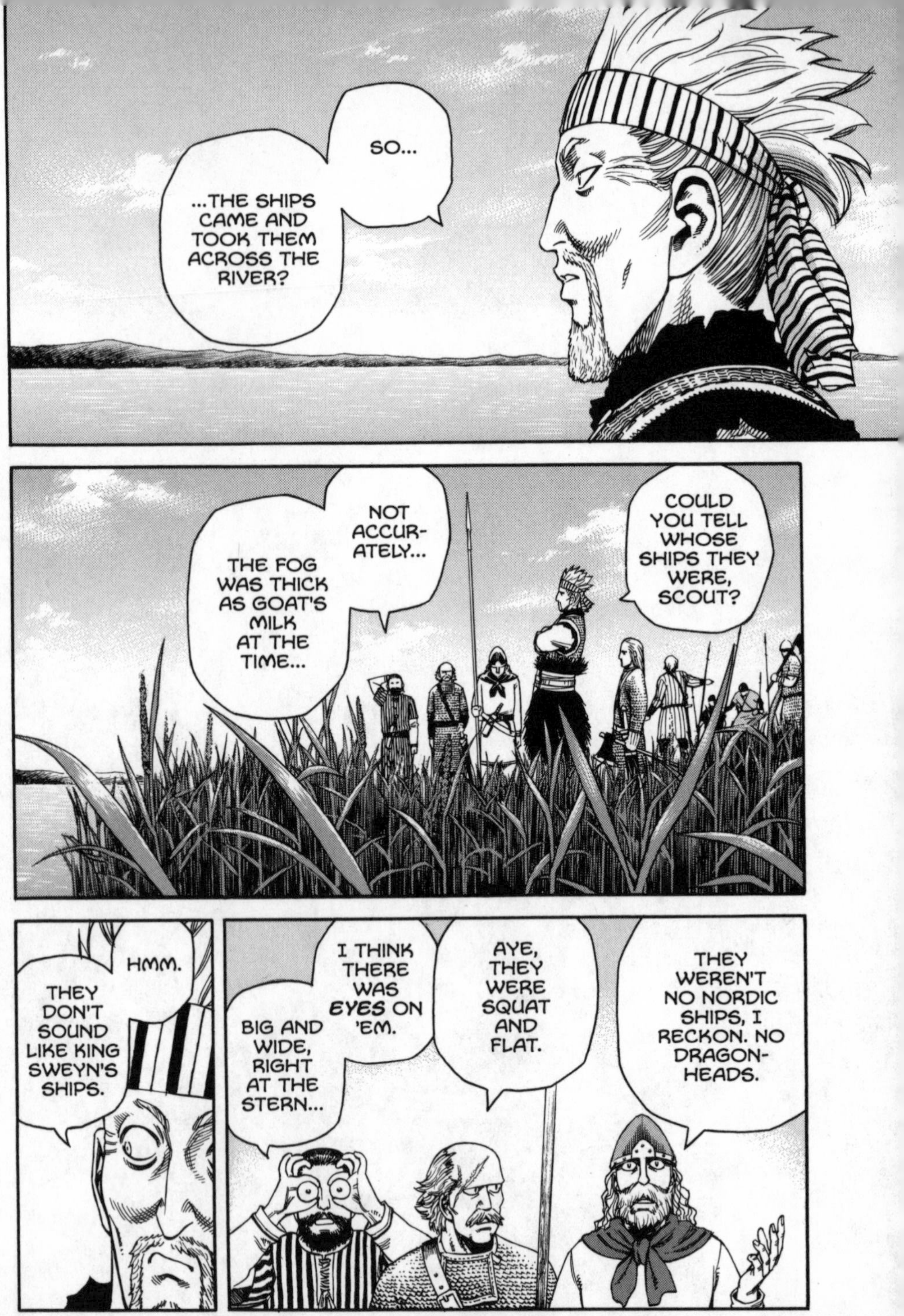
SO...
...THE SHIPS CAME AND TOOK THEM ACROSS THE RIVER?
COULD YOU TELL WHOSE SHIPS THEY WERE, SCOUT?
NOT ACCUR-ATELY...
THE FOG WAS THICK AS GOAT'S MILK AT THE TIME...
THEY WEREN'T NO NORDIC SHIPS, I RECKON. NO DRAGON-HEADS.
AYE, THEY WERE SQUAT AND FLAT.
I THINK THERE WAS *EYES* ON 'EM.
BIG AND WIDE, RIGHT AT THE STERN...
HMM.
THEY DON'T SOUND LIKE KING SWEYN'S SHIPS.

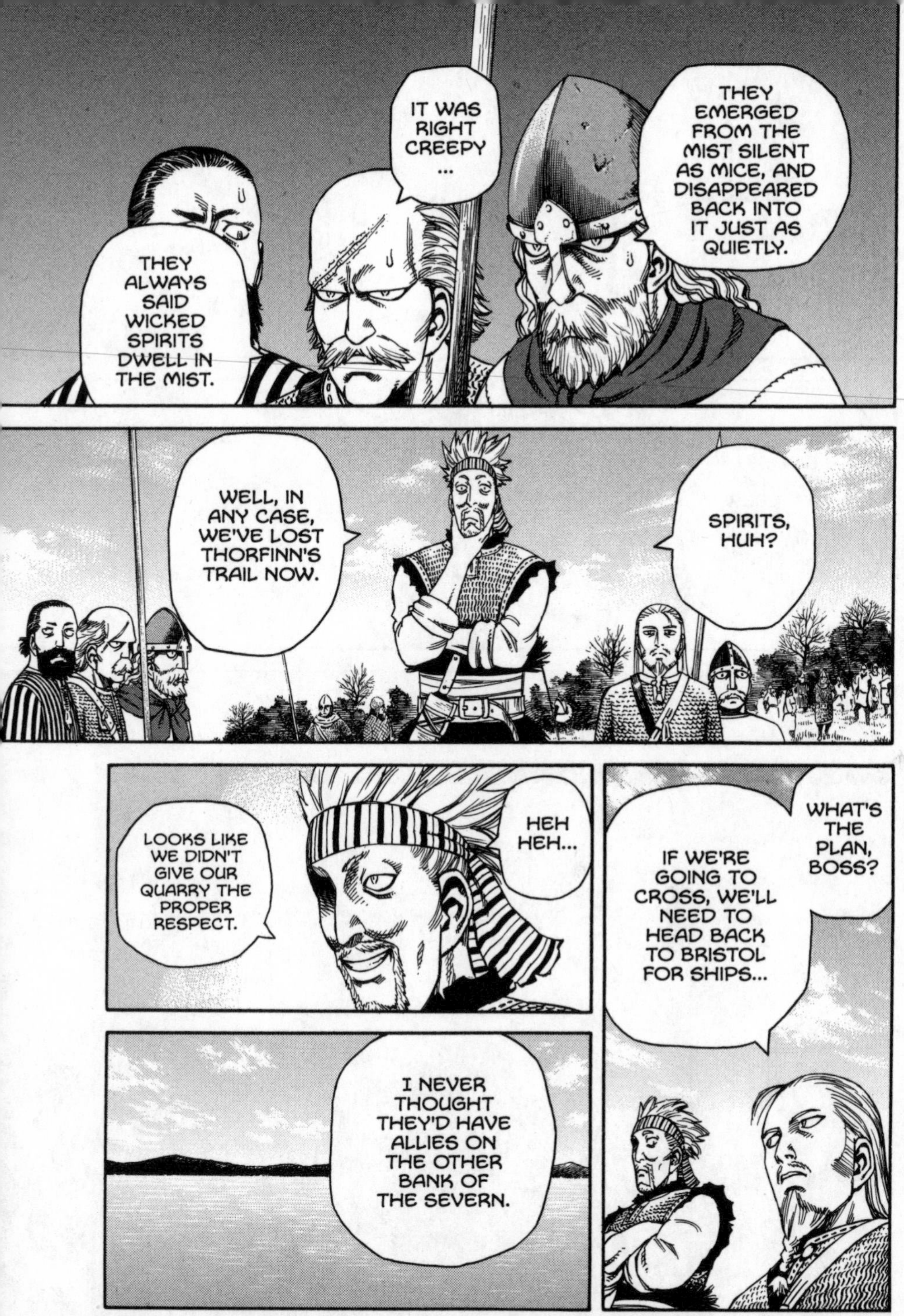
THEY EMERGED FROM THE MIST SILENT AS MICE, AND DISAPPEARED BACK INTO IT JUST AS QUIETLY.
IT WAS RIGHT CREEPY ...
THEY ALWAYS SAID WICKED SPIRITS DWELL IN THE MIST.
SPIRITS, HUH?
WELL, IN ANY CASE, WE'VE LOST THORFINN'S TRAIL NOW.
WHAT'S THE PLAN, BOSS?
IF WE'RE GOING TO CROSS, WE'LL NEED TO HEAD BACK TO BRISTOL FOR SHIPS...
HEH HEH...
LOOKS LIKE WE DIDN'T GIVE OUR QUARRY THE PROPER RESPECT.
I NEVER THOUGHT THEY'D HAVE ALLIES ON THE OTHER BANK OF THE SEVERN.

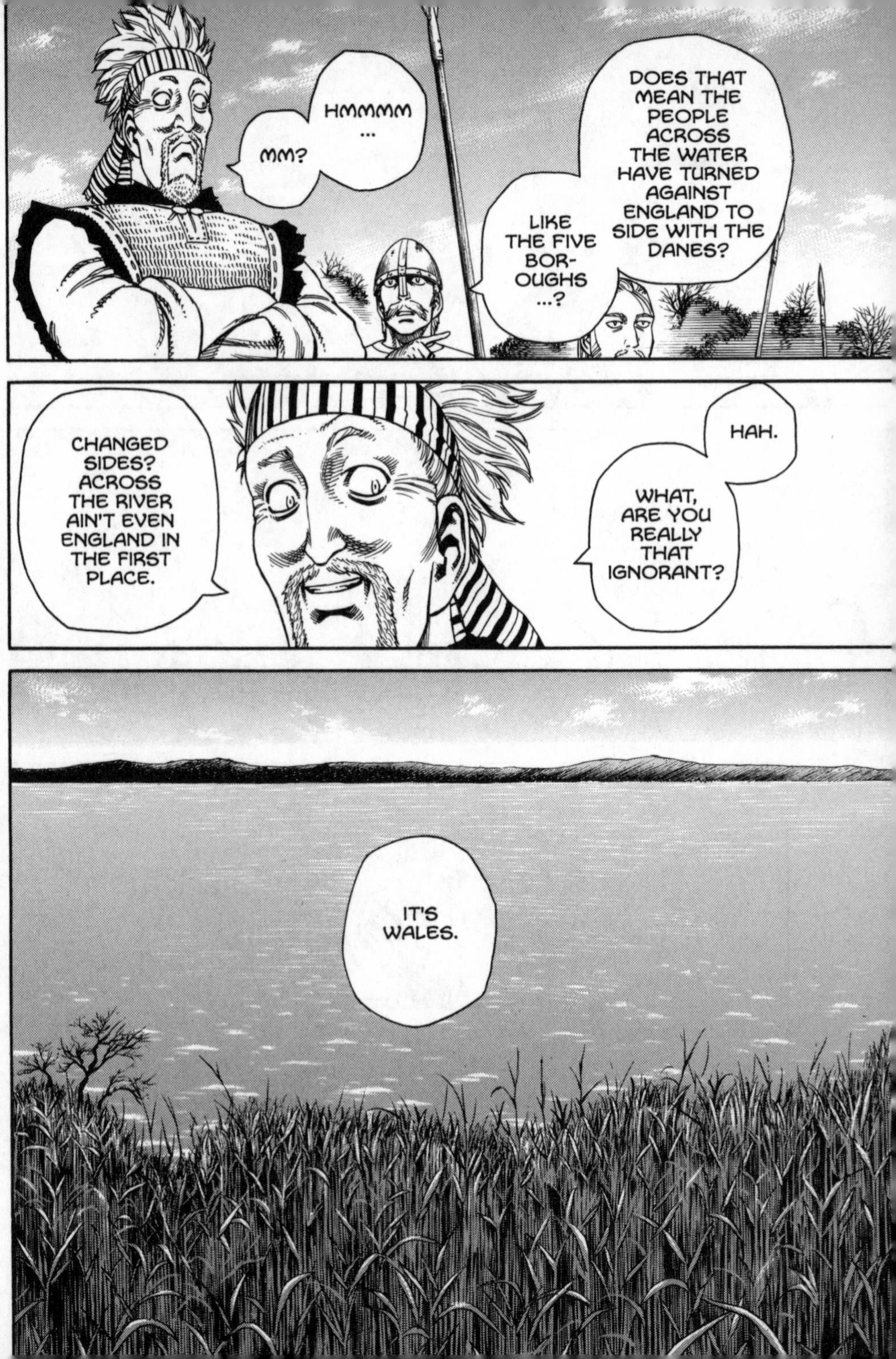
DOES THAT MEAN THE PEOPLE ACROSS THE WATER HAVE TURNED AGAINST ENGLAND TO SIDE WITH THE DANES?
LIKE THE FIVE BOR-OUGHS ...?
HMMMM ...
MM?
HAH.
WHAT, ARE YOU REALLY THAT IGNORANT?
CHANGED SIDES? ACROSS THE RIVER AIN'T EVEN ENGLAND IN THE FIRST PLACE.
IT'S WALES.

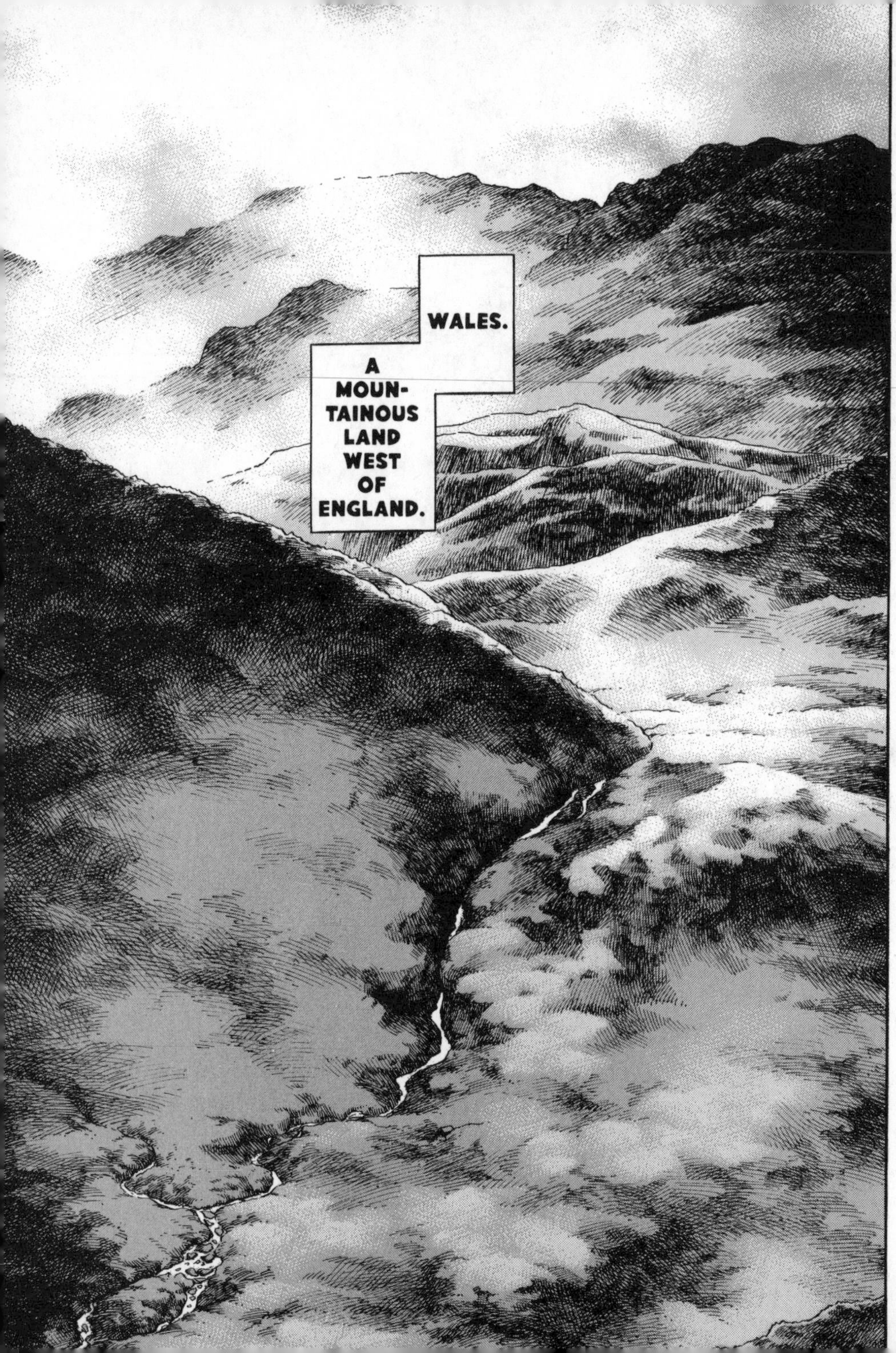
WALES.
A MOUNTAINOUS LAND WEST OF ENGLAND.

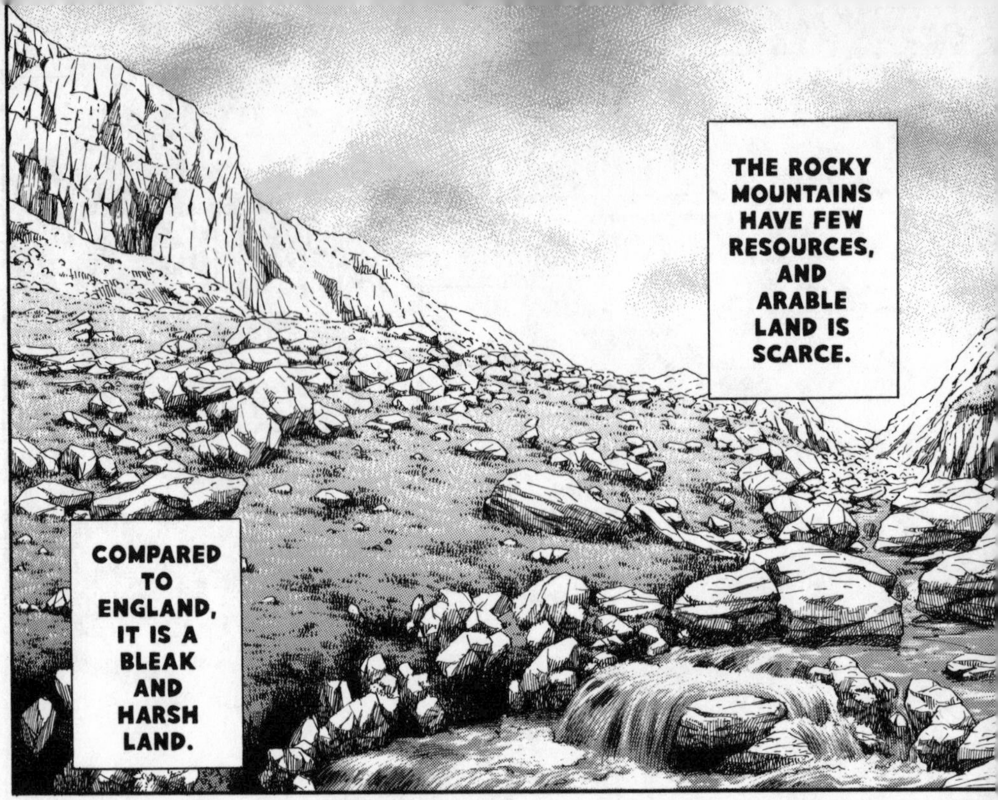
THE ROCKY MOUNTAINS HAVE FEW RESOURCES, AND ARABLE LAND IS SCARCE.
COMPARED TO ENGLAND, IT IS A BLEAK AND HARSH LAND.

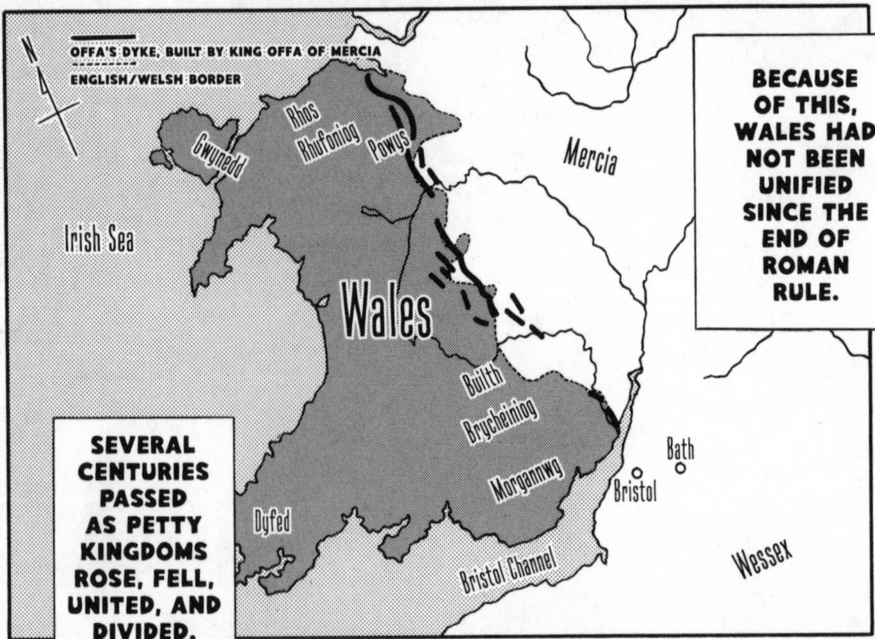
BECAUSE OF THIS, WALES HAD NOT BEEN UNIFIED SINCE THE END OF ROMAN RULE.
OFFA'S DYKE, BUILT BY KING OFFA OF MERCIA
ENGLISH/WELSH BORDER
Rhos
Rhufoniog
Gwynedd
Powys
Mercia
Irish Sea
Wales
Builth
Brycheiniog
Morgannwg
Bath
Bristol
Dyfed
Bristol Channel
Wessex
SEVERAL CENTURIES PASSED AS PETTY KINGDOMS ROSE, FELL, UNITED, AND DIVIDED.

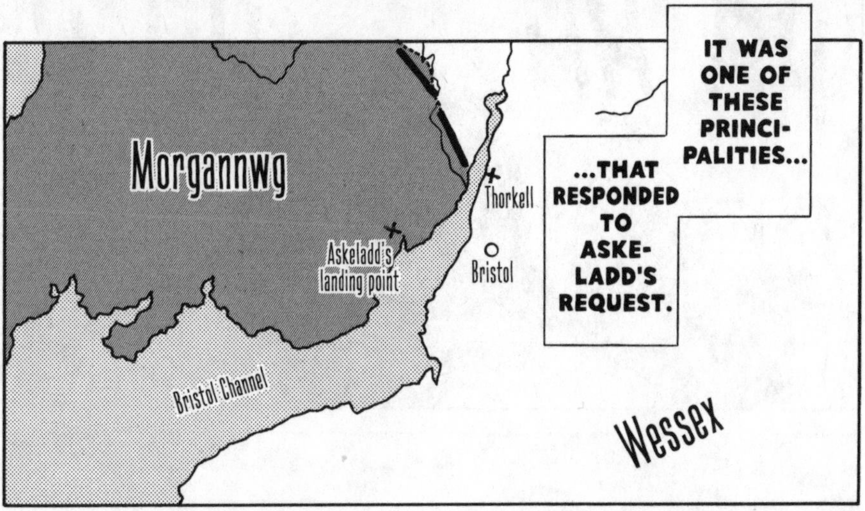
IT WAS ONE OF THESE PRINCI-PALITIES...
...THAT RESPONDED TO ASKE-LADD'S REQUEST.
Morgannwg
Thorkell
Askeladd's landing point
Bristol
Bristol Channel
Wessex

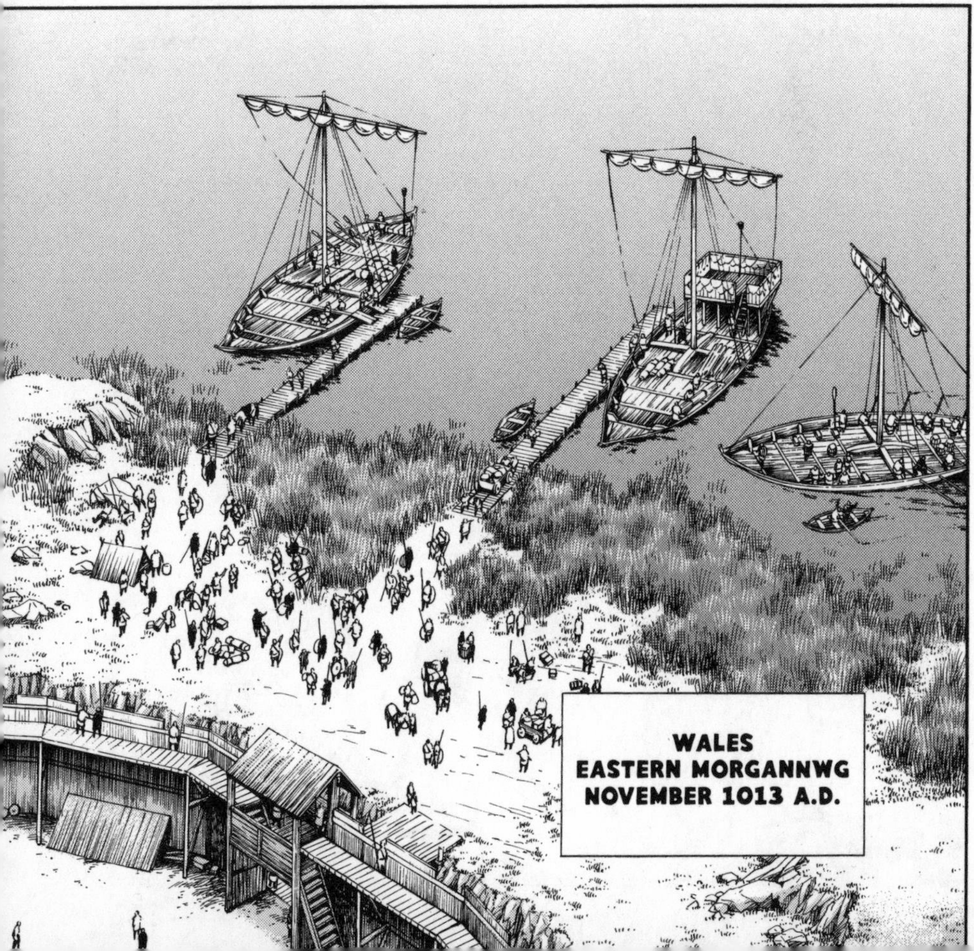
WALES
EASTERN MORGANNWG
NOVEMBER 1013 A.D.

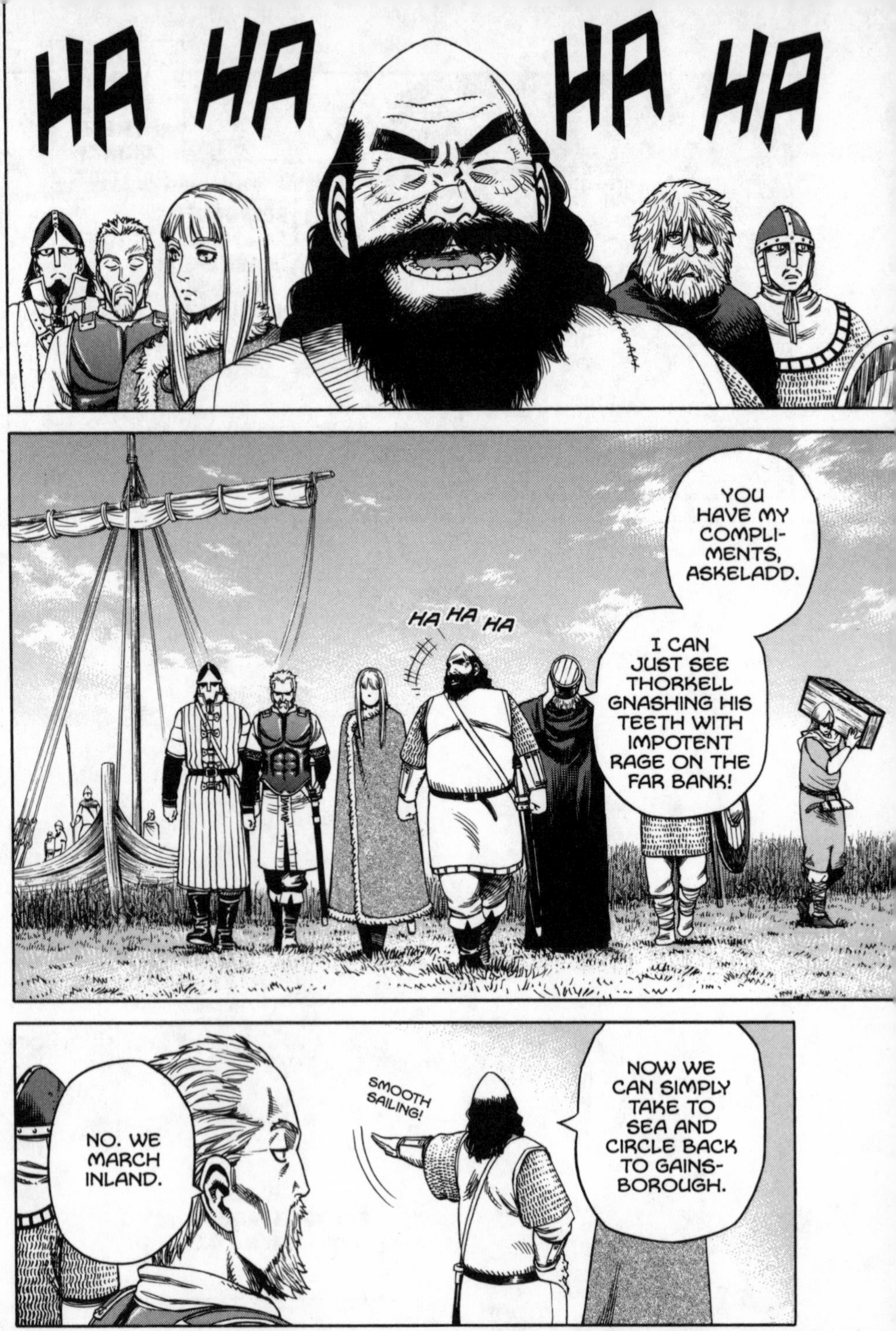
HA HA HA HA
YOU HAVE MY COMPLIMENTS, ASKELADD.
I CAN JUST SEE THORKELL GNASHING HIS TEETH WITH IMPOTENT RAGE ON THE FAR BANK!
HA HA HA
NOW WE CAN SIMPLY TAKE TO SEA AND CIRCLE BACK TO GAINS-BOROUGH.
SMOOTH SAILING!
NO. WE MARCH INLAND.

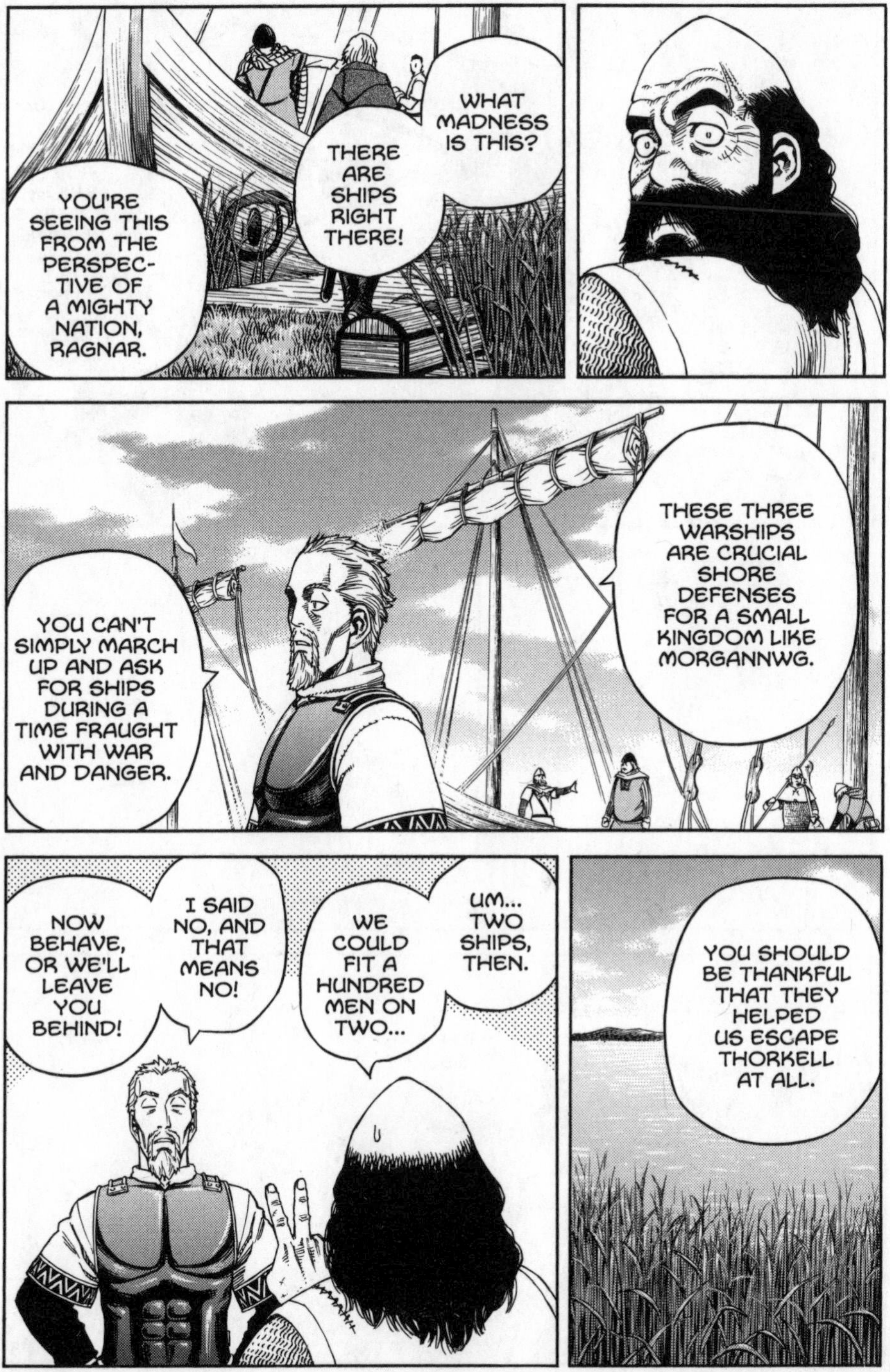
WHAT MADNESS IS THIS?
THERE ARE SHIPS RIGHT THERE!
YOU'RE SEEING THIS FROM THE PERSPEC-TIVE OF A MIGHTY NATION, RAGNAR.
THESE THREE WARSHIPS ARE CRUCIAL SHORE DEFENSES FOR A SMALL KINGDOM LIKE MORGANNWG.
YOU CAN'T SIMPLY MARCH UP AND ASK FOR SHIPS DURING A TIME FRAUGHT WITH WAR AND DANGER.
YOU SHOULD BE THANKFUL THAT THEY HELPED US ESCAPE THORKELL AT ALL.
UM... TWO SHIPS, THEN.
WE COULD FIT A HUNDRED MEN ON TWO...
I SAID NO, AND THAT MEANS NO!
NOW BEHAVE, OR WE'LL LEAVE YOU BEHIND!

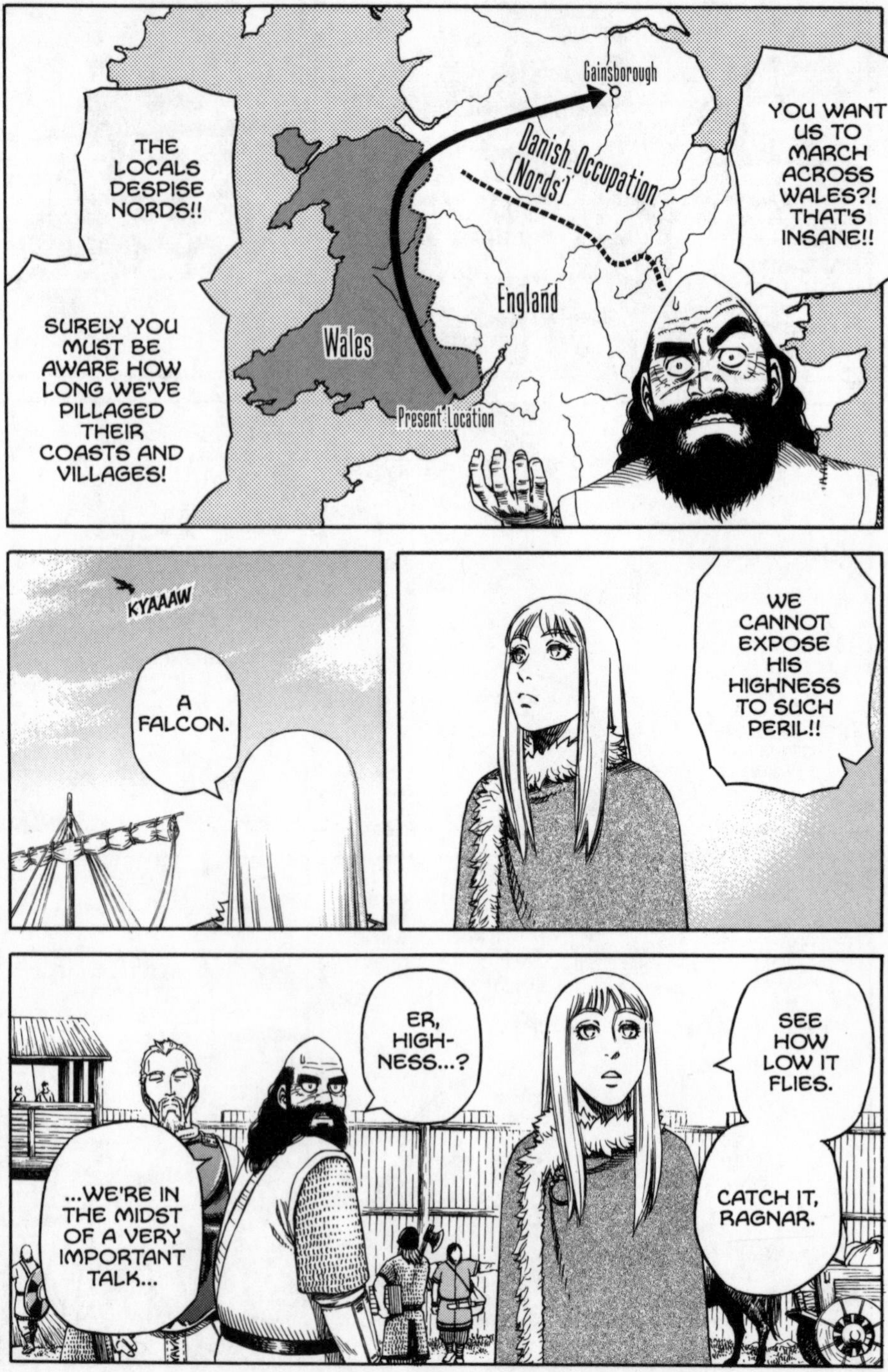

YOU WANT US TO MARCH ACROSS WALES?! THAT'S INSANE!!
Gainsborough
Danish Occupation (Nords)
England
Wales
Present Location
THE LOCALS DESPISE NORDS!!
SURELY YOU MUST BE AWARE HOW LONG WE'VE PILLAGED THEIR COASTS AND VILLAGES!
WE CANNOT EXPOSE HIS HIGHNESS TO SUCH PERIL!!
KYAAAW
A FALCON.
SEE HOW LOW IT FLIES.
ER, HIGH-NESS...?
...WE'RE IN THE MIDST OF A VERY IMPORTANT TALK...
CATCH IT, RAGNAR.

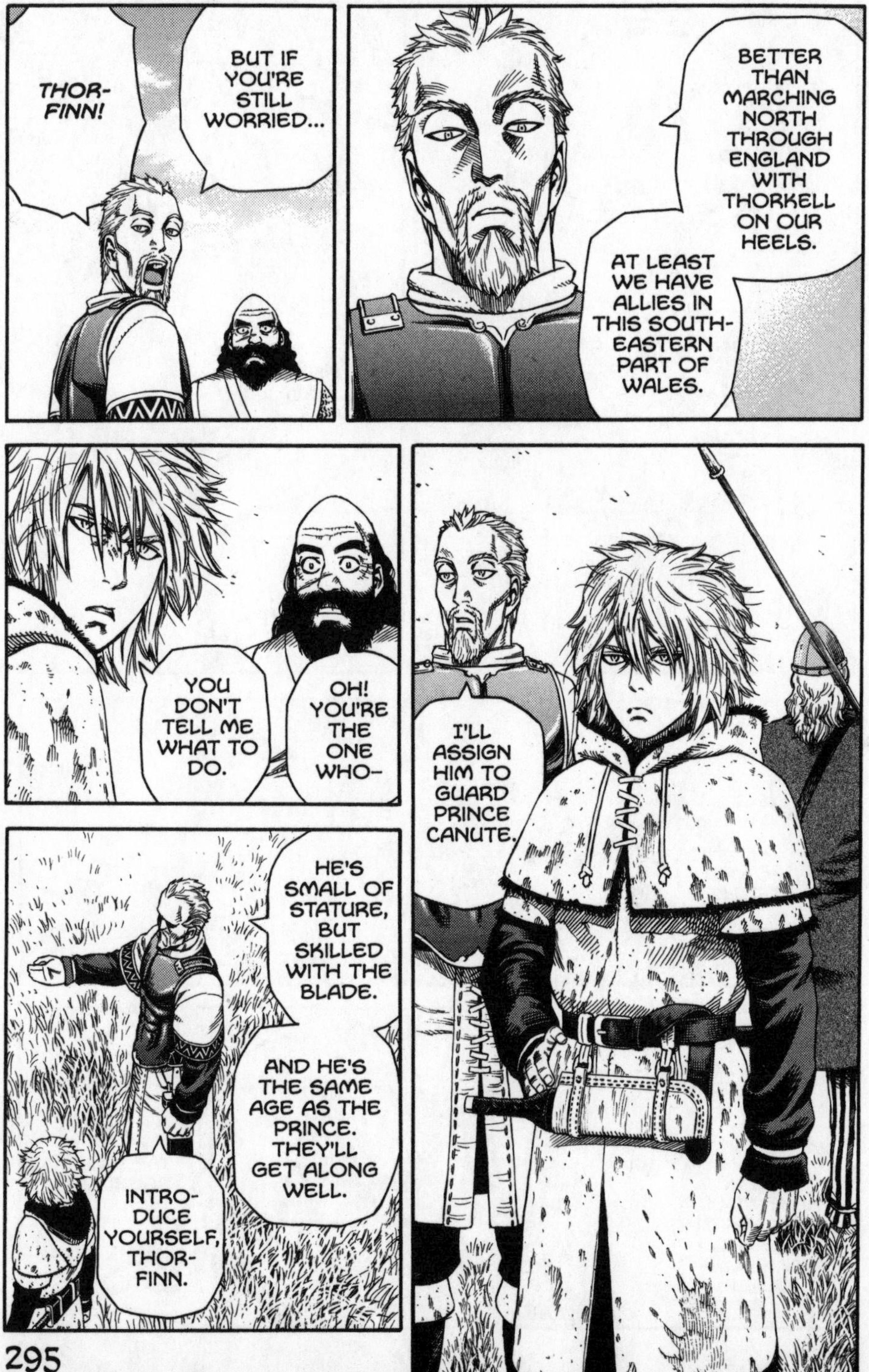

BETTER THAN MARCHING NORTH THROUGH ENGLAND WITH THORKELL ON OUR HEELS.
AT LEAST WE HAVE ALLIES IN THIS SOUTH-EASTERN PART OF WALES.
BUT IF YOU'RE STILL WORRIED...
THOR-FINN!
I'LL ASSIGN HIM TO GUARD PRINCE CANUTE.
OH! YOU'RE THE ONE WHO-
YOU DON'T TELL ME WHAT TO DO.
HE'S SMALL OF STATURE, BUT SKILLED WITH THE BLADE.
AND HE'S THE SAME AGE AS THE PRINCE. THEY'LL GET ALONG WELL.
INTRO-DUCE YOURSELF, THOR-FINN.

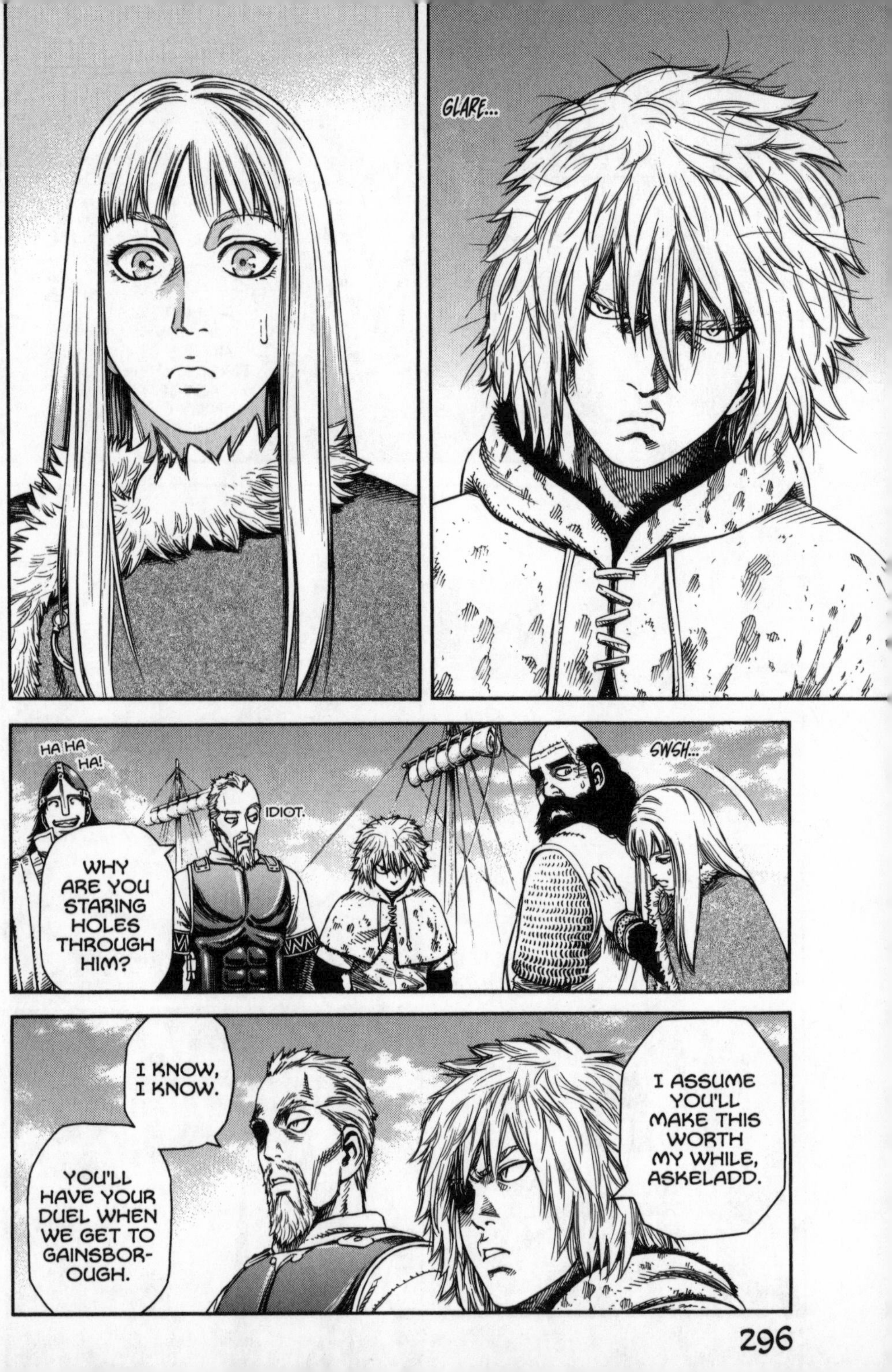
GLARE...
SWSH...
HA HA HA!
IDIOT.
WHY ARE YOU STARING HOLES THROUGH HIM?
I ASSUME YOU'LL MAKE THIS WORTH MY WHILE, ASKELADD.
I KNOW, I KNOW.
YOU'LL HAVE YOUR DUEL WHEN WE GET TO GAINSBOR-OUGH.

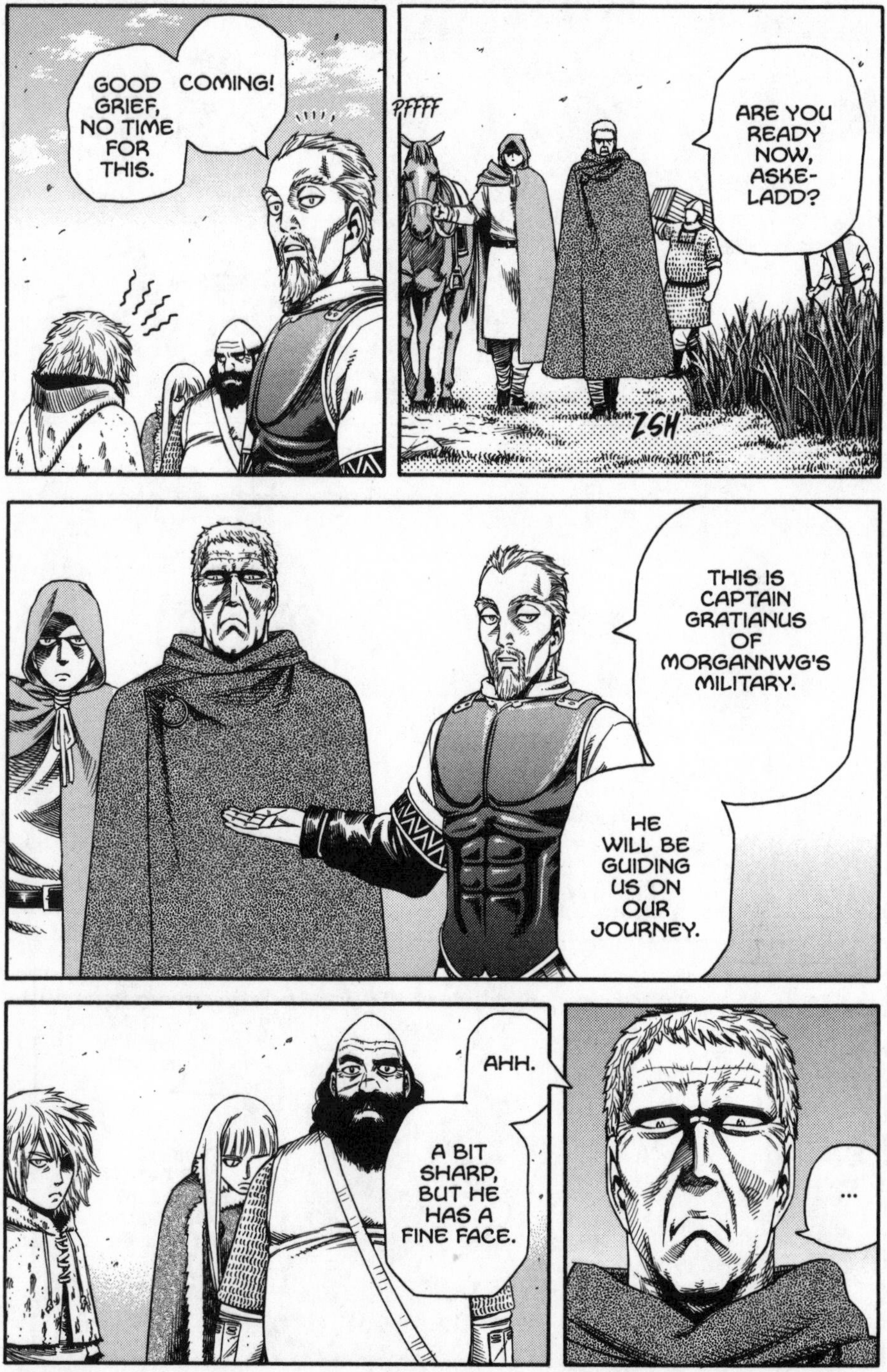
ARE YOU READY NOW, ASKE-LADD?
PFFFF
ZSH
COMING!
GOOD GRIEF, NO TIME FOR THIS.
THIS IS CAPTAIN GRATIANUS OF MORGANNWG'S MILITARY.
HE WILL BE GUIDING US ON OUR JOURNEY.
...
AHH.
A BIT SHARP, BUT HE HAS A FINE FACE.

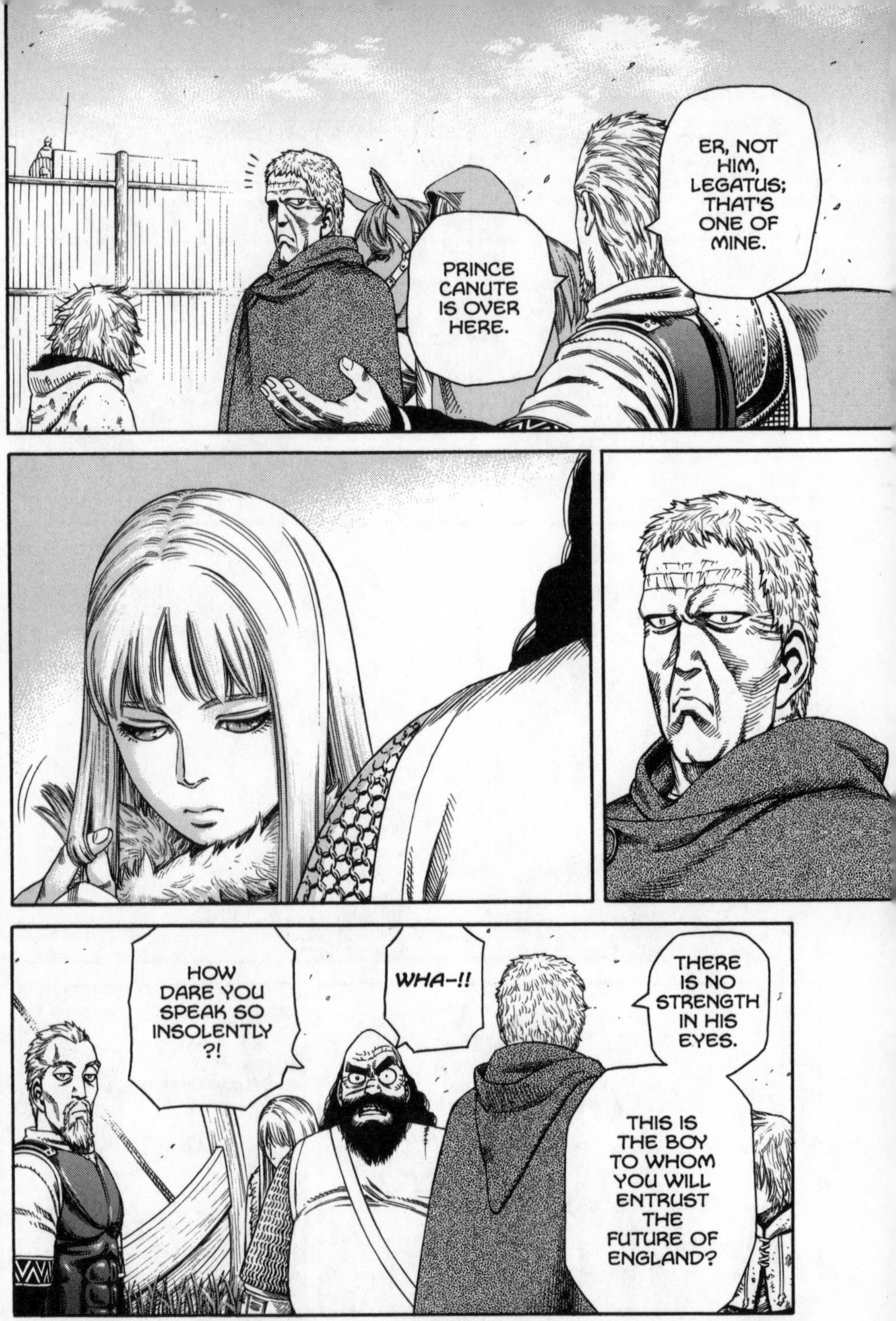
ER, NOT HIM, LEGATUS; THAT'S ONE OF MINE.
PRINCE CANUTE IS OVER HERE.
THERE IS NO STRENGTH IN HIS EYES.
THIS IS THE BOY TO WHOM YOU WILL ENTRUST THE FUTURE OF ENGLAND?
WHA-!!
HOW DARE YOU SPEAK SO INSOLENTLY ?!

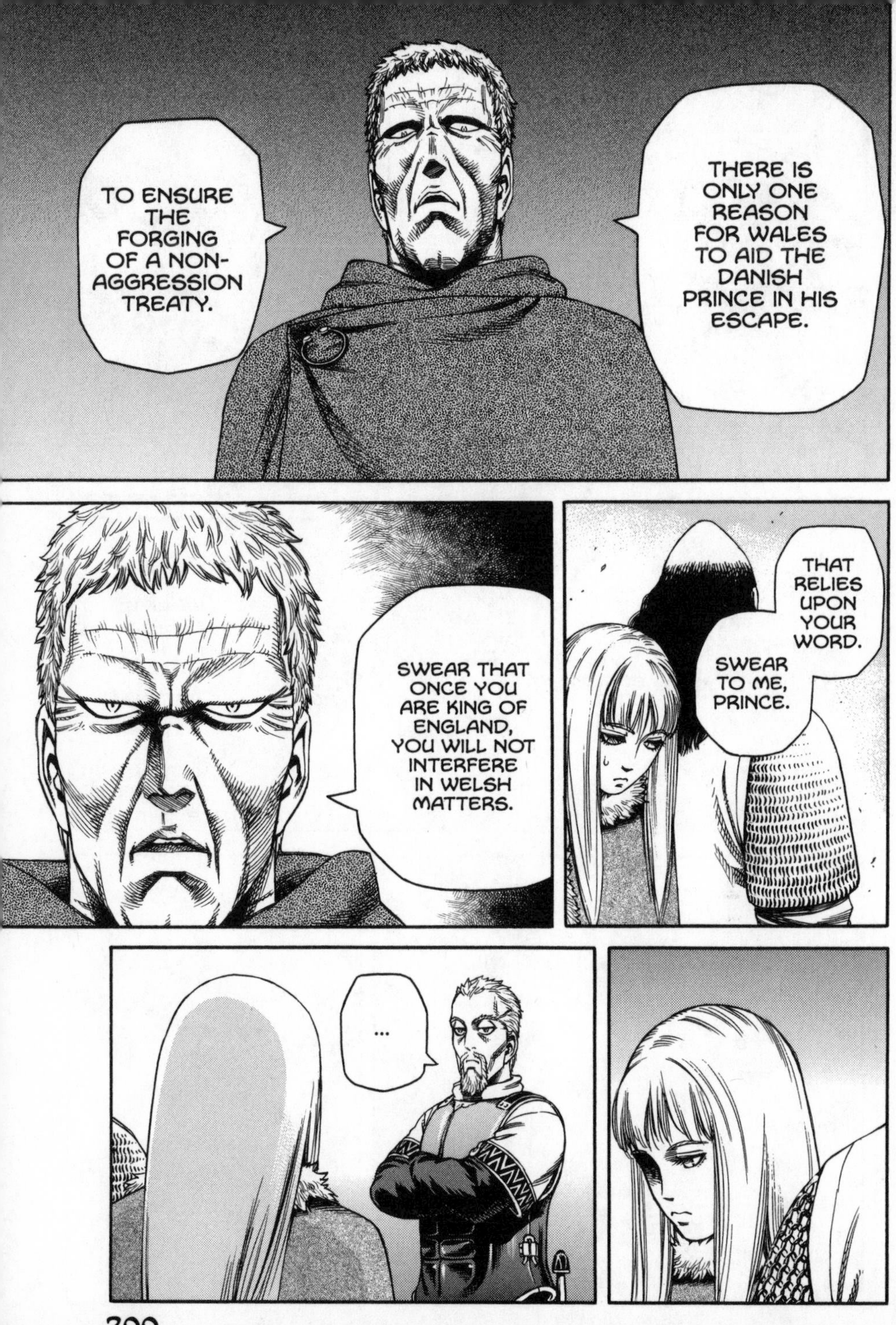
THERE IS ONLY ONE REASON FOR WALES TO AID THE DANISH PRINCE IN HIS ESCAPE.
TO ENSURE THE FORGING OF A NON-AGGRESSION TREATY.
THAT RELIES UPON YOUR WORD.
SWEAR TO ME, PRINCE.
SWEAR THAT ONCE YOU ARE KING OF ENGLAND, YOU WILL NOT INTERFERE IN WELSH MATTERS.
...

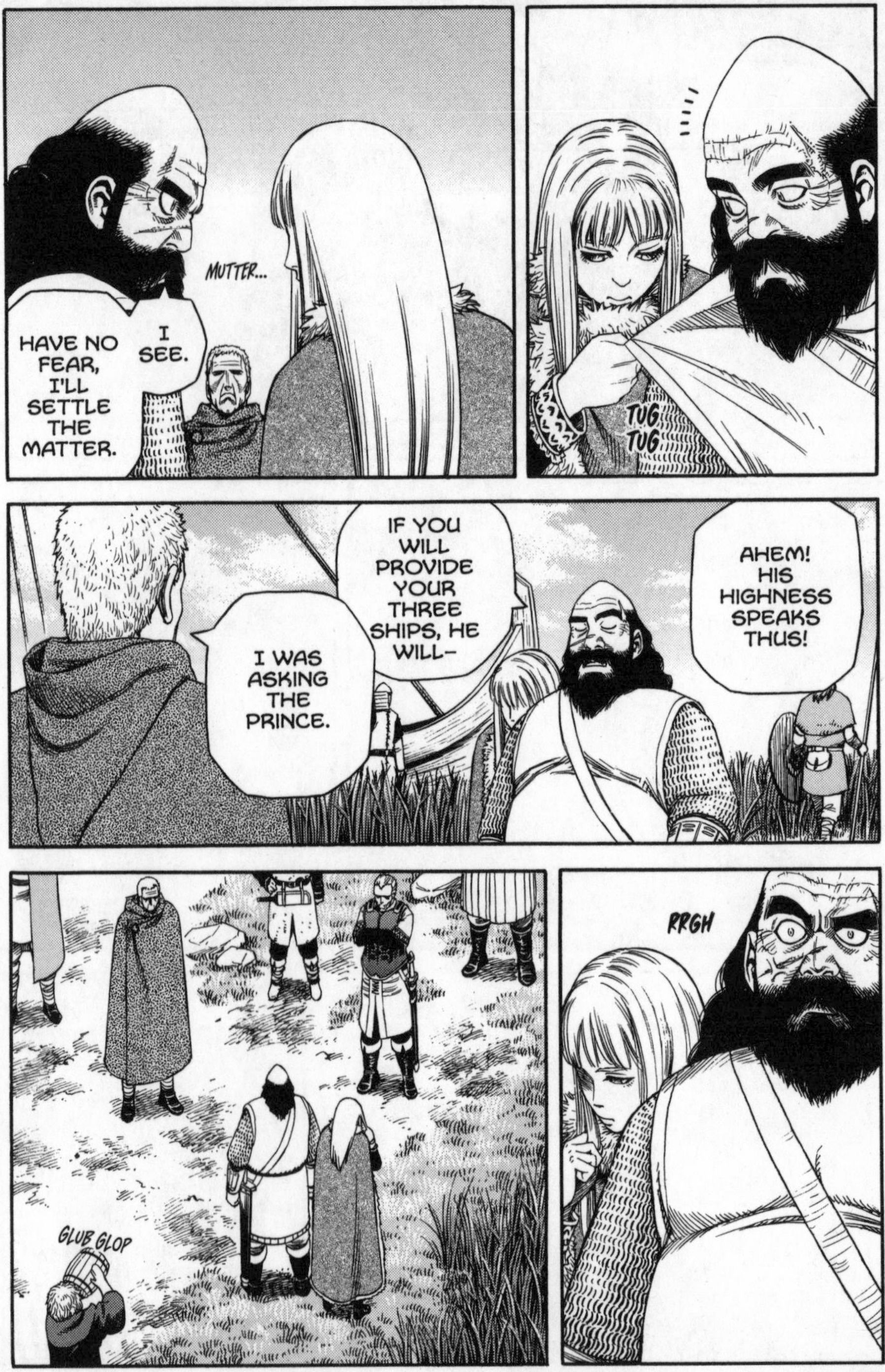
...
TUG TUG
MUTTER...
I SEE.
HAVE NO FEAR, I'LL SETTLE THE MATTER.
AHEM! HIS HIGHNESS SPEAKS THUS!
IF YOU WILL PROVIDE YOUR THREE SHIPS, HE WILL–
I WAS ASKING THE PRINCE.
RRGH
GLUB GLOP

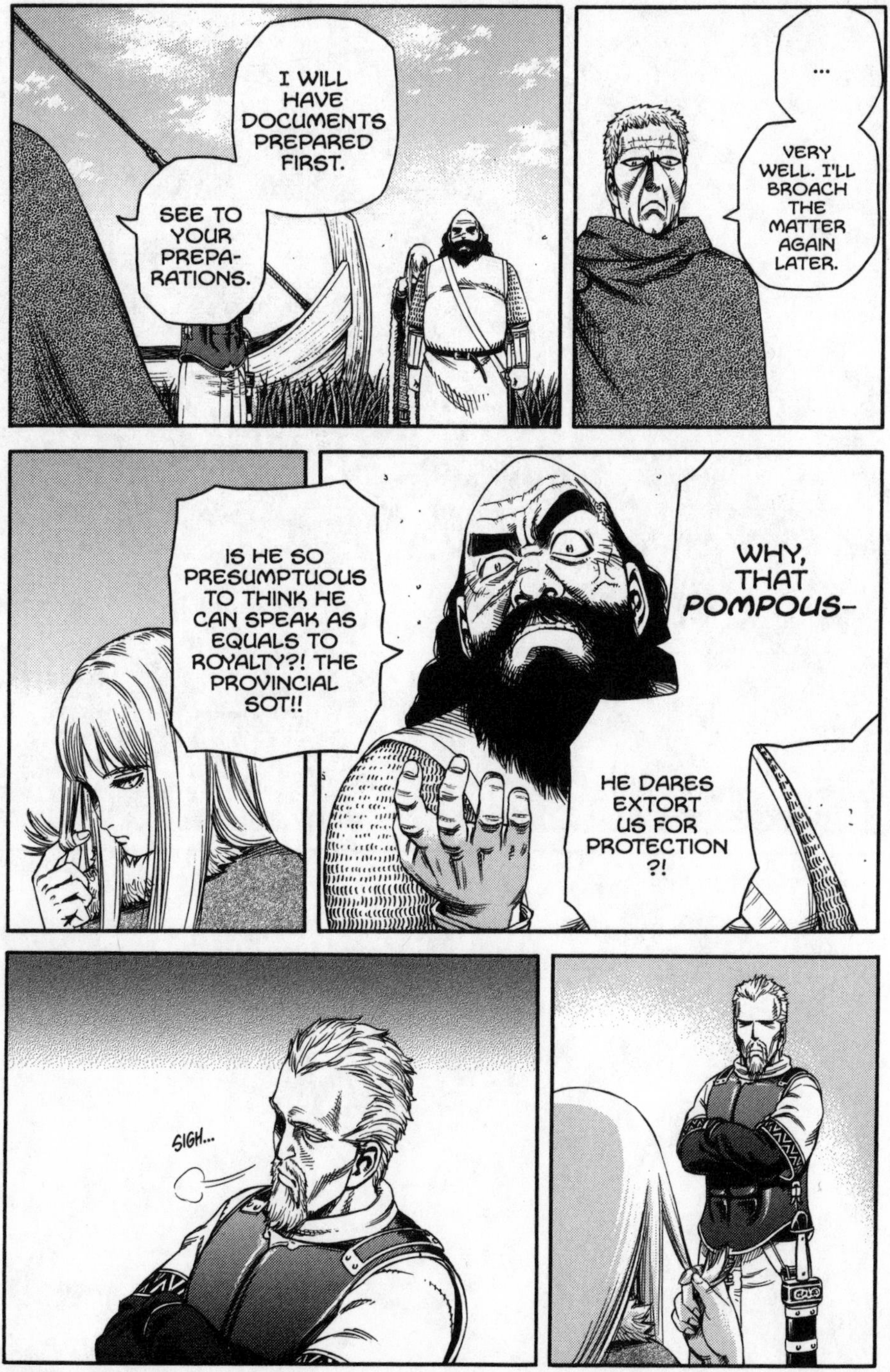
...
VERY WELL. I'LL BROACH THE MATTER AGAIN LATER.
I WILL HAVE DOCUMENTS PREPARED FIRST.
SEE TO YOUR PREPARATIONS.
WHY, THAT *POMPOUS*-
HE DARES EXTORT US FOR PROTECTION ?!
IS HE SO PRESUMPTUOUS TO THINK HE CAN SPEAK AS EQUALS TO ROYALTY?! THE PROVINCIAL SOT!!
SIGH...

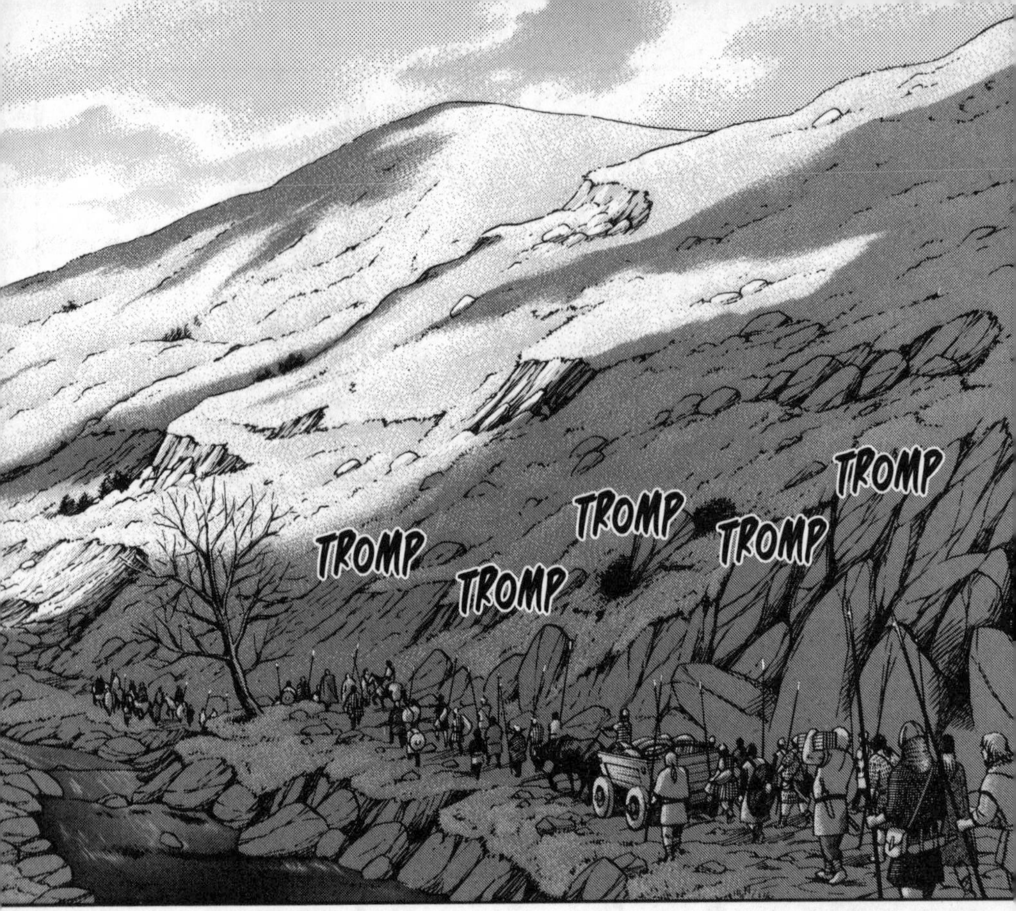
TROMP
TROMP
TROMP
TROMP
TROMP

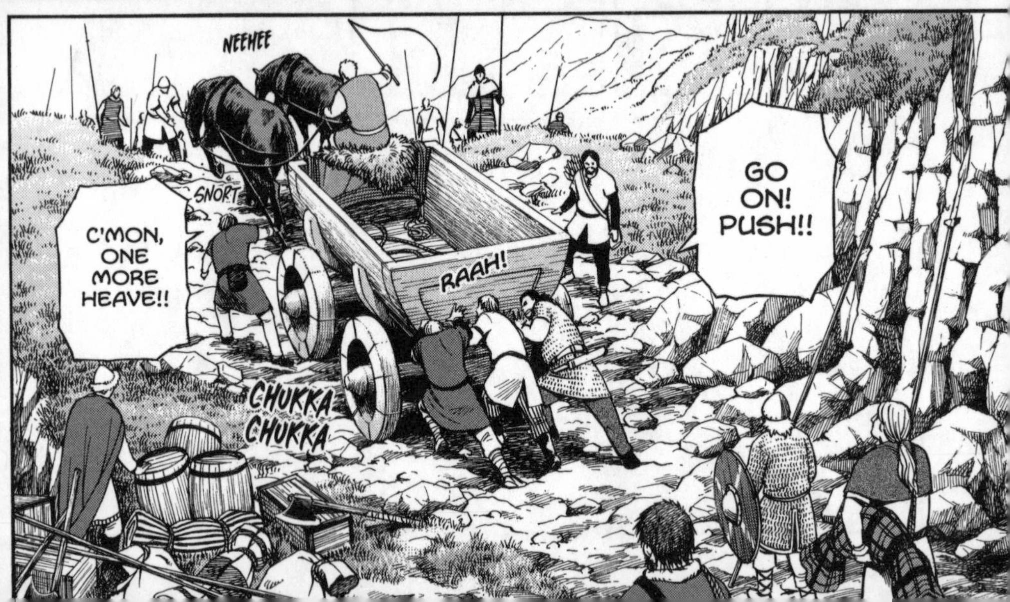
GO ON! PUSH!!
NEEHEE
SNORT
C'MON, ONE MORE HEAVE!!
RAAH!
CHUKKA CHUKKA

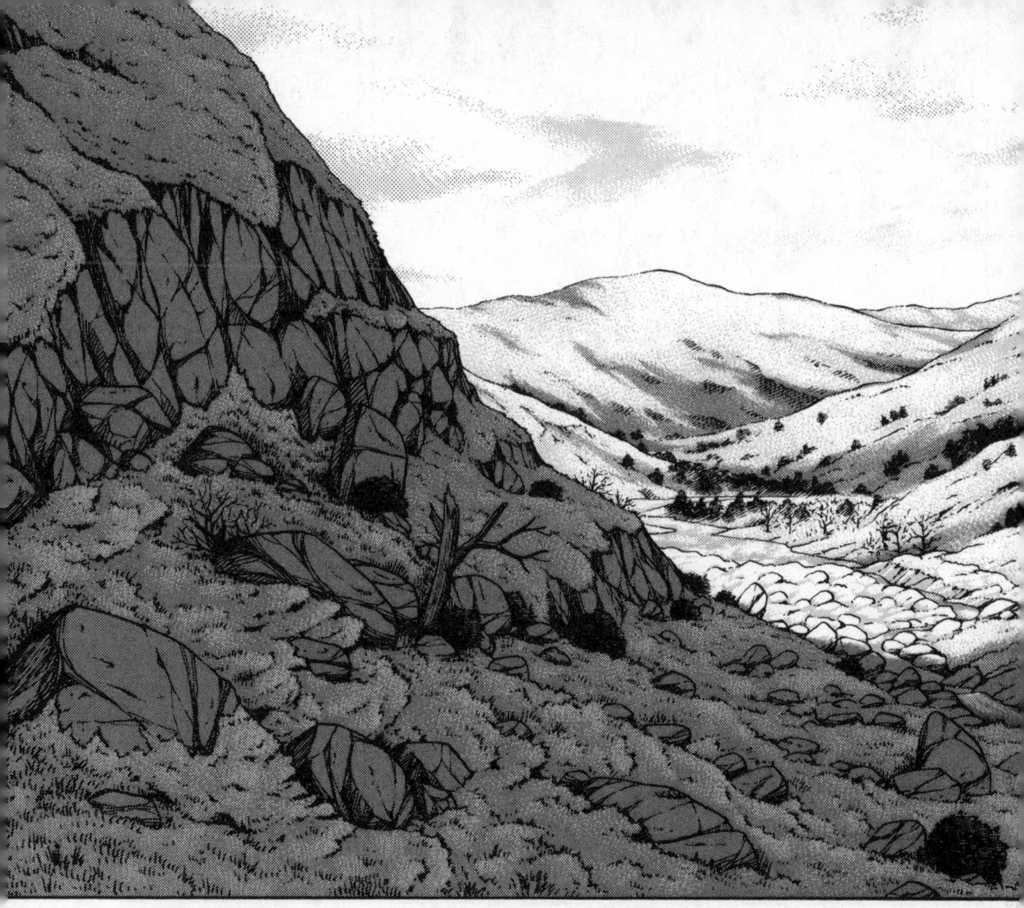

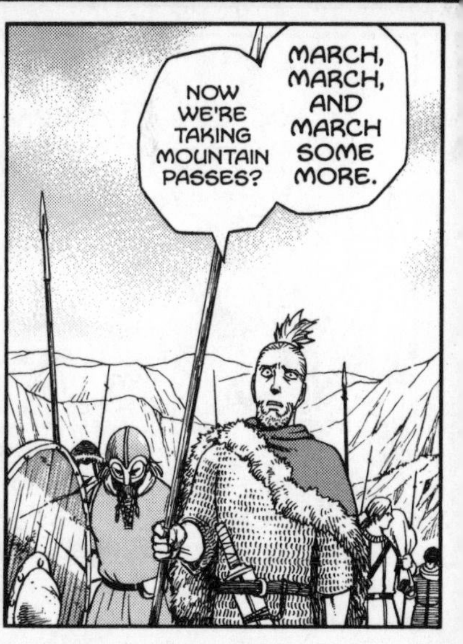
MARCH, MARCH, AND MARCH SOME MORE.
NOW WE'RE TAKING MOUNTAIN PASSES?

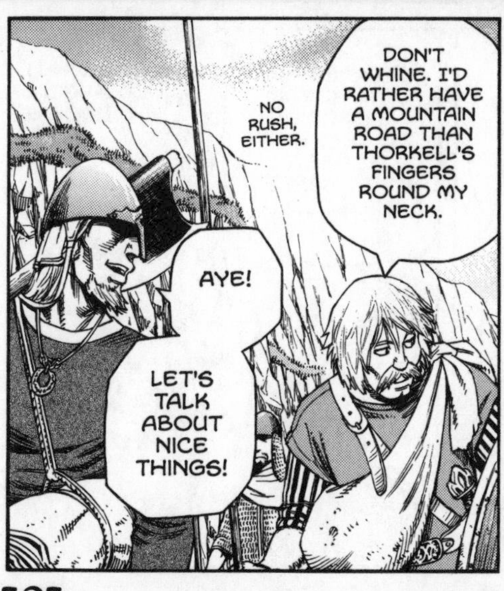
DON'T WHINE. I'D RATHER HAVE A MOUNTAIN ROAD THAN THORKELL'S FINGERS ROUND MY NECK.
NO RUSH, EITHER.
AYE!
LET'S TALK ABOUT NICE THINGS!

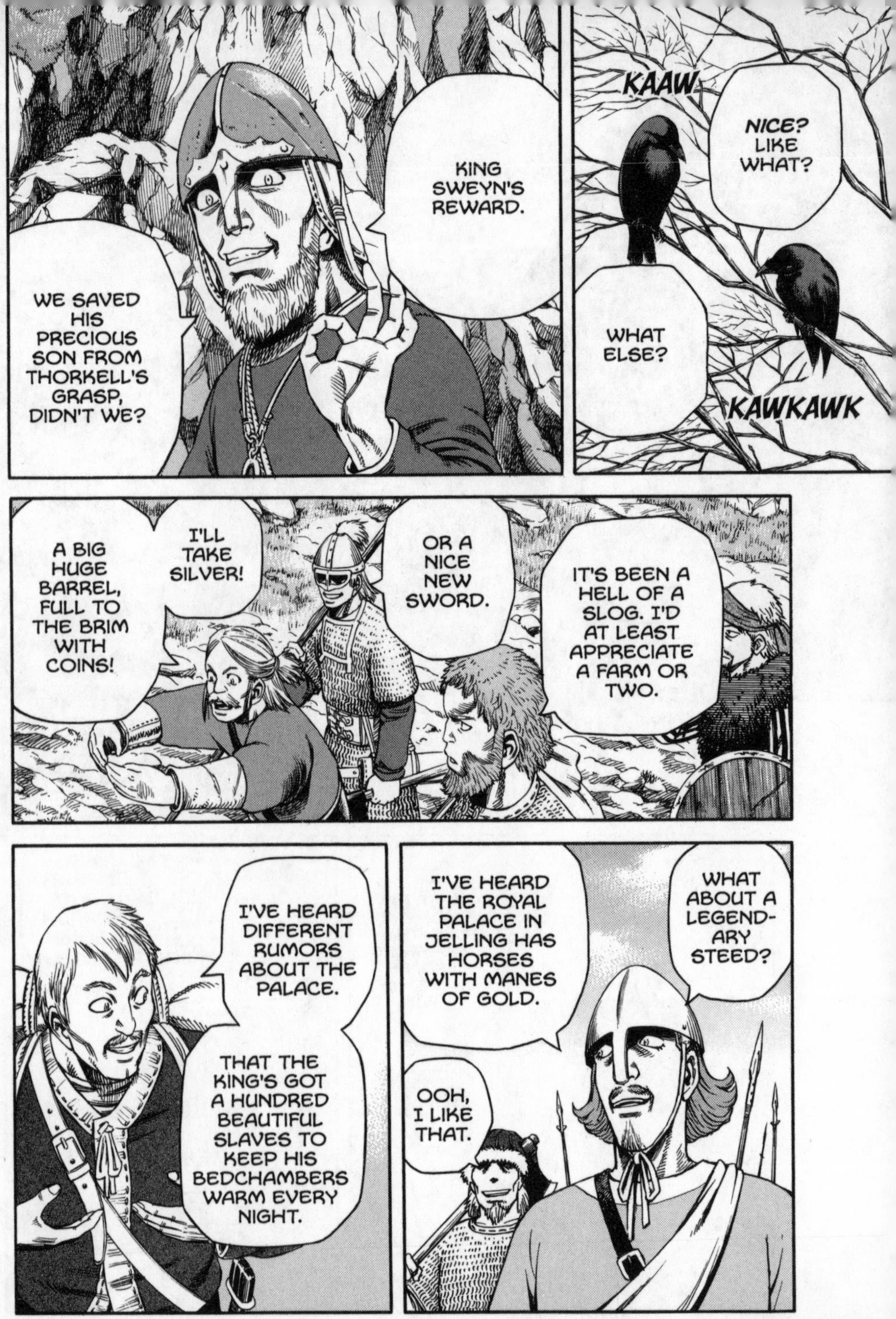
KAAW
NICE? LIKE WHAT?
WHAT ELSE?
KAWKAWK
KING SWEYN'S REWARD.
WE SAVED HIS PRECIOUS SON FROM THORKELL'S GRASP, DIDN'T WE?
IT'S BEEN A HELL OF A SLOG. I'D AT LEAST APPRECIATE A FARM OR TWO.
OR A NICE NEW SWORD.
I'LL TAKE SILVER!
A BIG HUGE BARREL, FULL TO THE BRIM WITH COINS!
WHAT ABOUT A LEGEND-ARY STEED?
I'VE HEARD THE ROYAL PALACE IN JELLING HAS HORSES WITH MANES OF GOLD.
OOH, I LIKE THAT.
I'VE HEARD DIFFERENT RUMORS ABOUT THE PALACE.
THAT THE KING'S GOT A HUNDRED BEAUTIFUL SLAVES TO KEEP HIS BEDCHAMBERS WARM EVERY NIGHT.

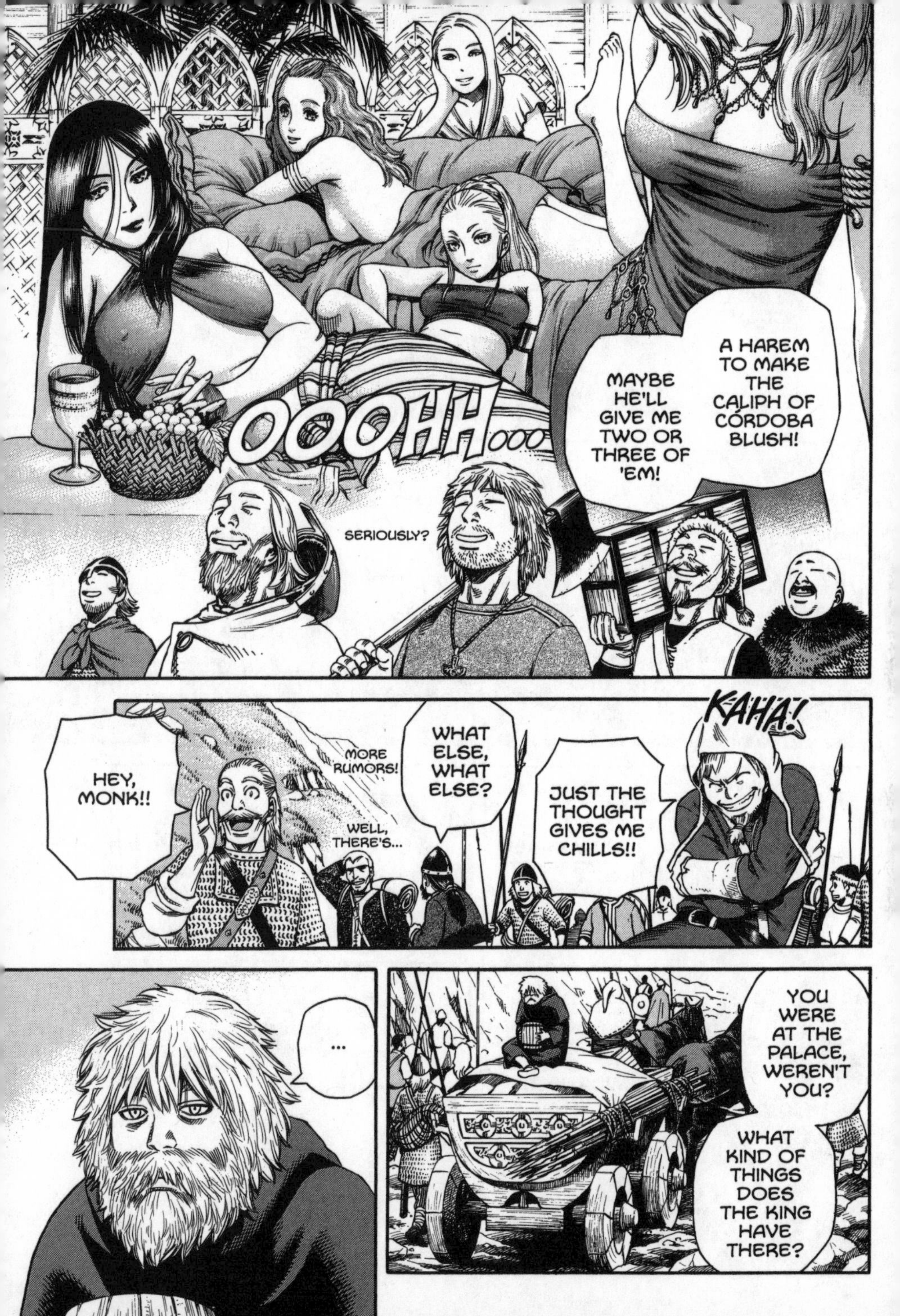
A HAREM TO MAKE THE CALIPH OF CÓRDOBA BLUSH!
MAYBE HE'LL GIVE ME TWO OR THREE OF 'EM!
OOOHHOOO
SERIOUSLY?
KAHA!
JUST THE THOUGHT GIVES ME CHILLS!!
WHAT ELSE, WHAT ELSE?
WELL, THERE'S...
MORE RUMORS!
HEY, MONK!!
YOU WERE AT THE PALACE, WEREN'T YOU?
WHAT KIND OF THINGS DOES THE KING HAVE THERE?
...

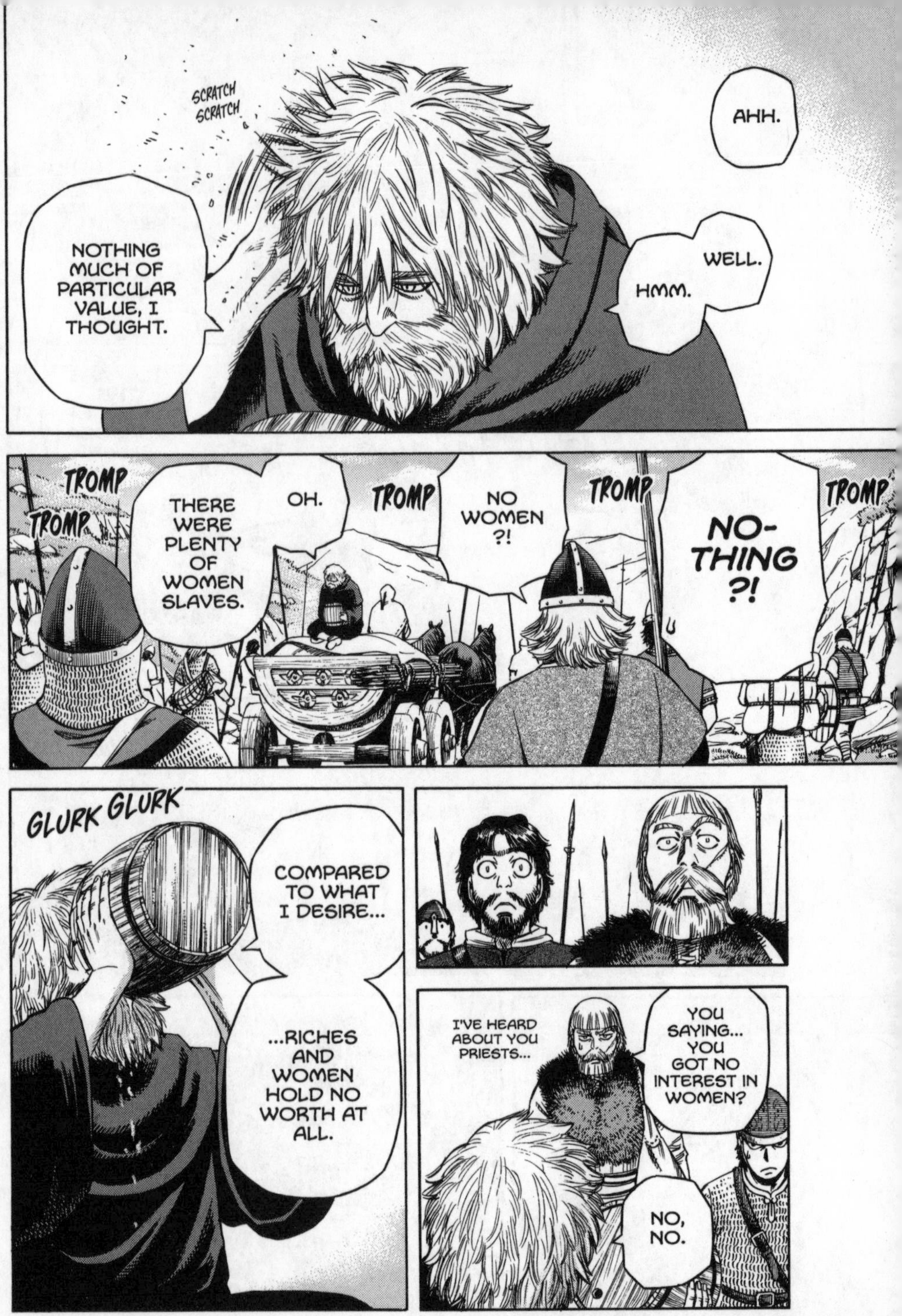
AHH.
WELL.
HMM.
SCRATCH SCRATCH
NOTHING MUCH OF PARTICULAR VALUE, I THOUGHT.
TROMP
NO-THING?!
TROMP
NO WOMEN?!
TROMP
OH.
THERE WERE PLENTY OF WOMEN SLAVES.
TROMP
TROMP
YOU SAYING... YOU GOT NO INTEREST IN WOMEN?
I'VE HEARD ABOUT YOU PRIESTS...
NO, NO.
GLURK GLURK
COMPARED TO WHAT I DESIRE...
...RICHES AND WOMEN HOLD NO WORTH AT ALL.

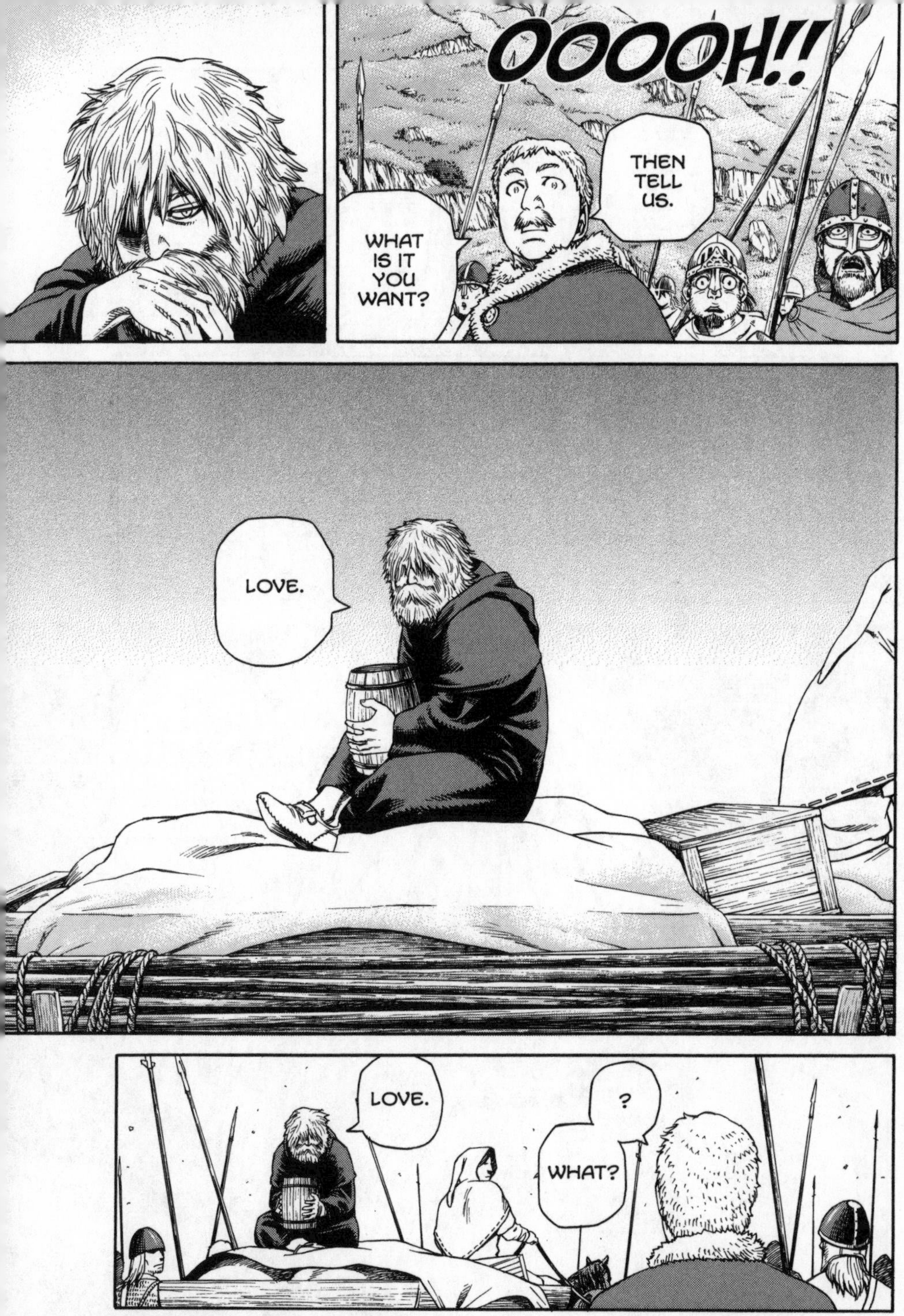
OOOOH!!
THEN TELL US.
WHAT IS IT YOU WANT?
LOVE.
? WHAT?
LOVE.

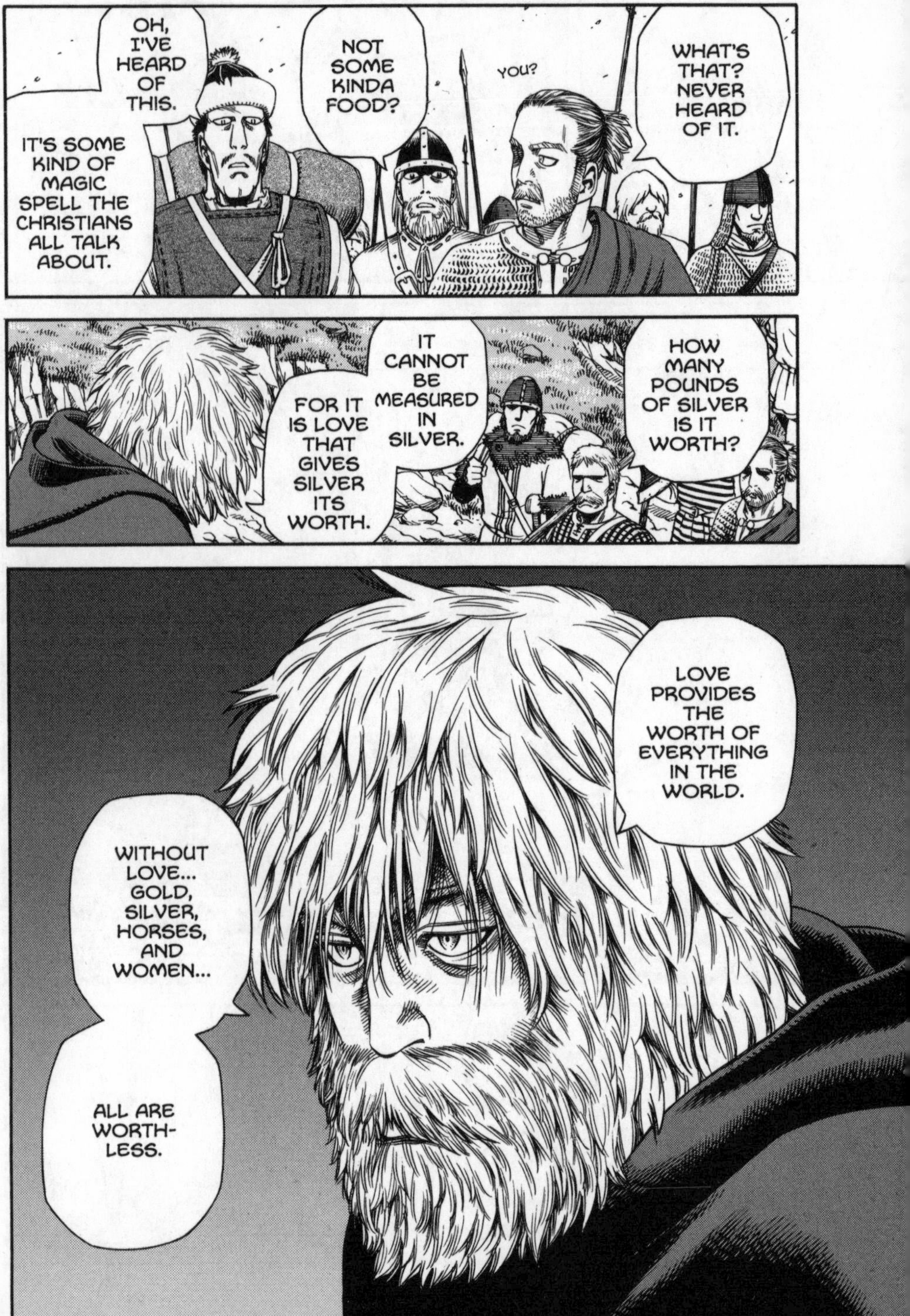
WHAT'S THAT? NEVER HEARD OF IT.
YOU?
NOT SOME KINDA FOOD?
OH, I'VE HEARD OF THIS.
IT'S SOME KIND OF MAGIC SPELL THE CHRISTIANS ALL TALK ABOUT.
HOW MANY POUNDS OF SILVER IS IT WORTH?
IT CANNOT BE MEASURED IN SILVER.
FOR IT IS LOVE THAT GIVES SILVER ITS WORTH.
LOVE PROVIDES THE WORTH OF EVERYTHING IN THE WORLD.
WITHOUT LOVE... GOLD, SILVER, HORSES, AND WOMEN...
ALL ARE WORTH-LESS.

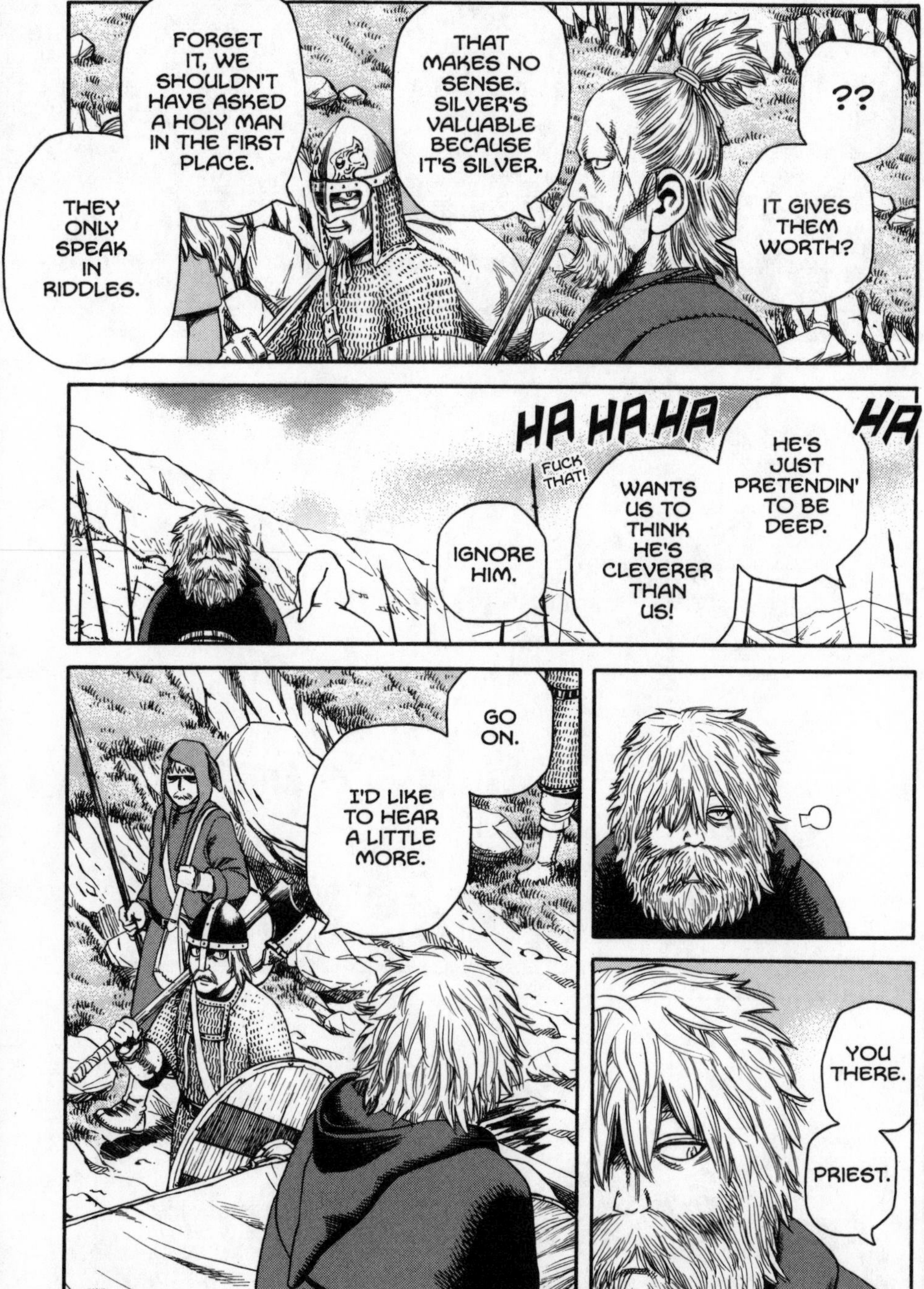
??
IT GIVES THEM WORTH?
THAT MAKES NO SENSE. SILVER'S VALUABLE BECAUSE IT'S SILVER.
FORGET IT, WE SHOULDN'T HAVE ASKED A HOLY MAN IN THE FIRST PLACE.
THEY ONLY SPEAK IN RIDDLES.
HA
HE'S JUST PRETENDIN' TO BE DEEP.
HA HA HA
WANTS US TO THINK HE'S CLEVERER THAN US!
FUCK THAT!
IGNORE HIM.
YOU THERE.
PRIEST.
GO ON.
I'D LIKE TO HEAR A LITTLE MORE.

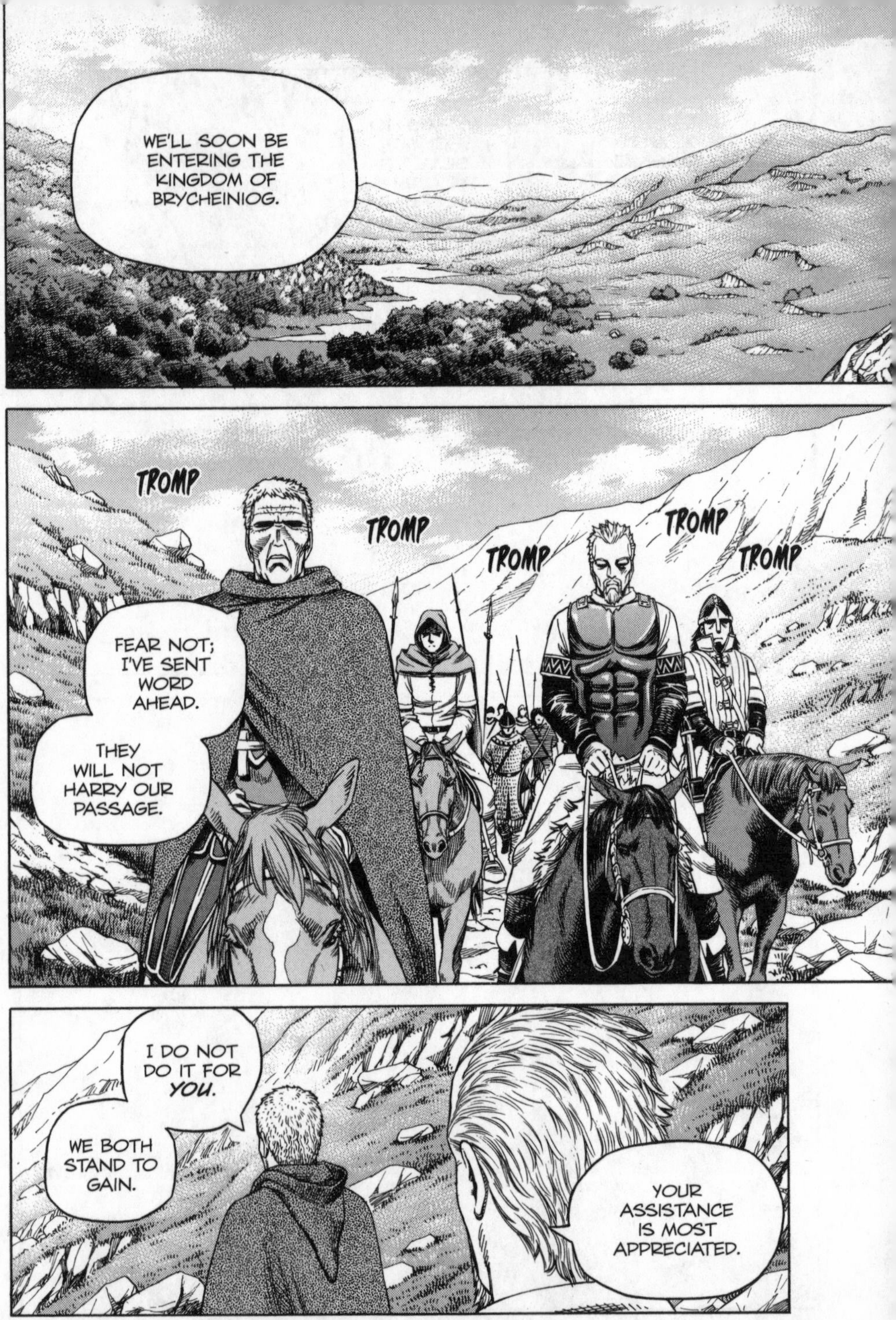
WE'LL SOON BE ENTERING THE KINGDOM OF BRYCHEINIOG.
TROMP
TROMP
TROMP
TROMP
TROMP
FEAR NOT; I'VE SENT WORD AHEAD.
THEY WILL NOT HARRY OUR PASSAGE.
YOUR ASSISTANCE IS MOST APPRECIATED.
I DO NOT DO IT FOR *YOU*.
WE BOTH STAND TO GAIN.

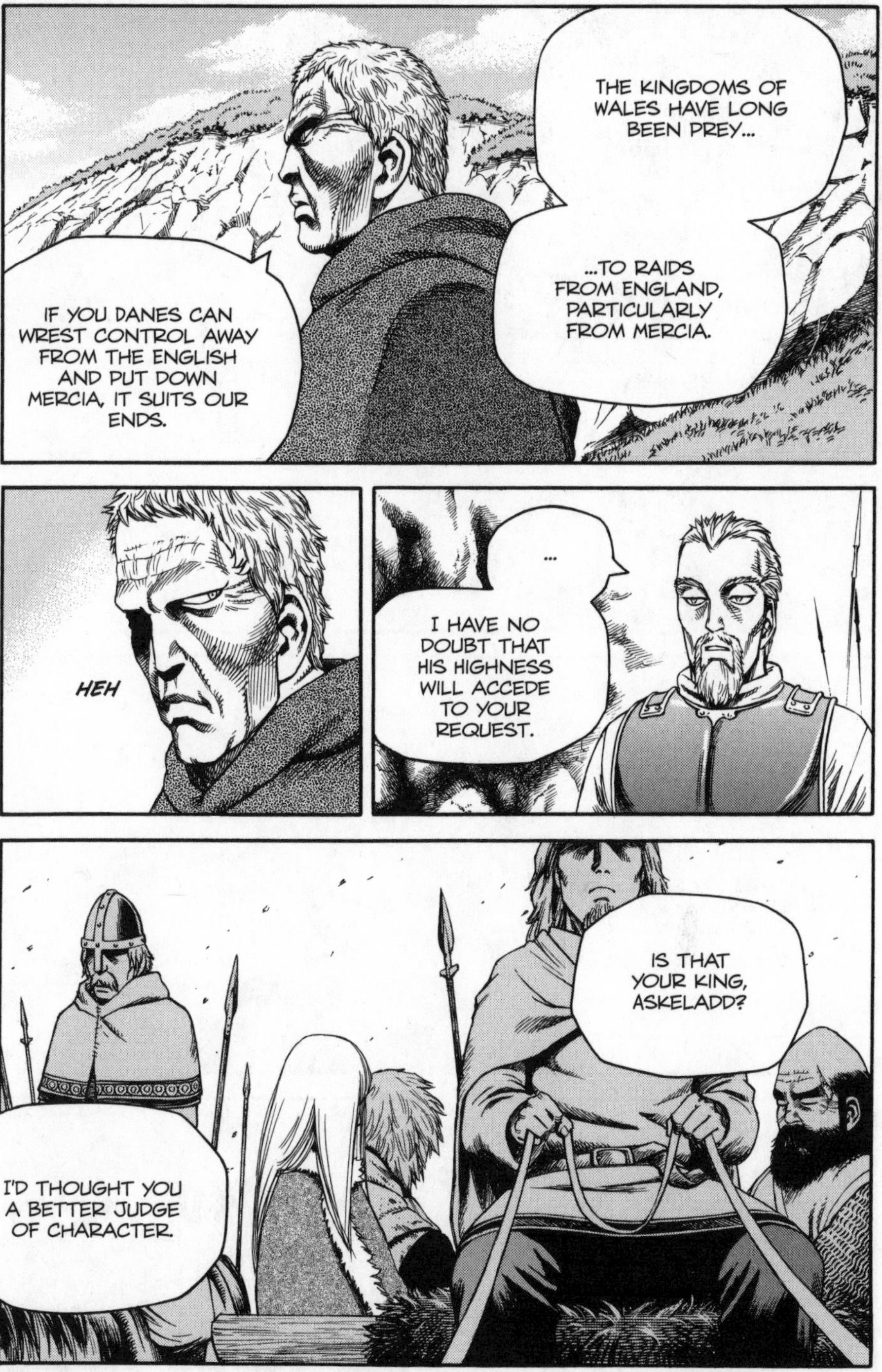
THE KINGDOMS OF WALES HAVE LONG BEEN PREY...
...TO RAIDS FROM ENGLAND, PARTICULARLY FROM MERCIA.
IF YOU DANES CAN WREST CONTROL AWAY FROM THE ENGLISH AND PUT DOWN MERCIA, IT SUITS OUR ENDS.
...
I HAVE NO DOUBT THAT HIS HIGHNESS WILL ACCEDE TO YOUR REQUEST.
HEH
IS THAT YOUR KING, ASKELADD?
I'D THOUGHT YOU A BETTER JUDGE OF CHARACTER.

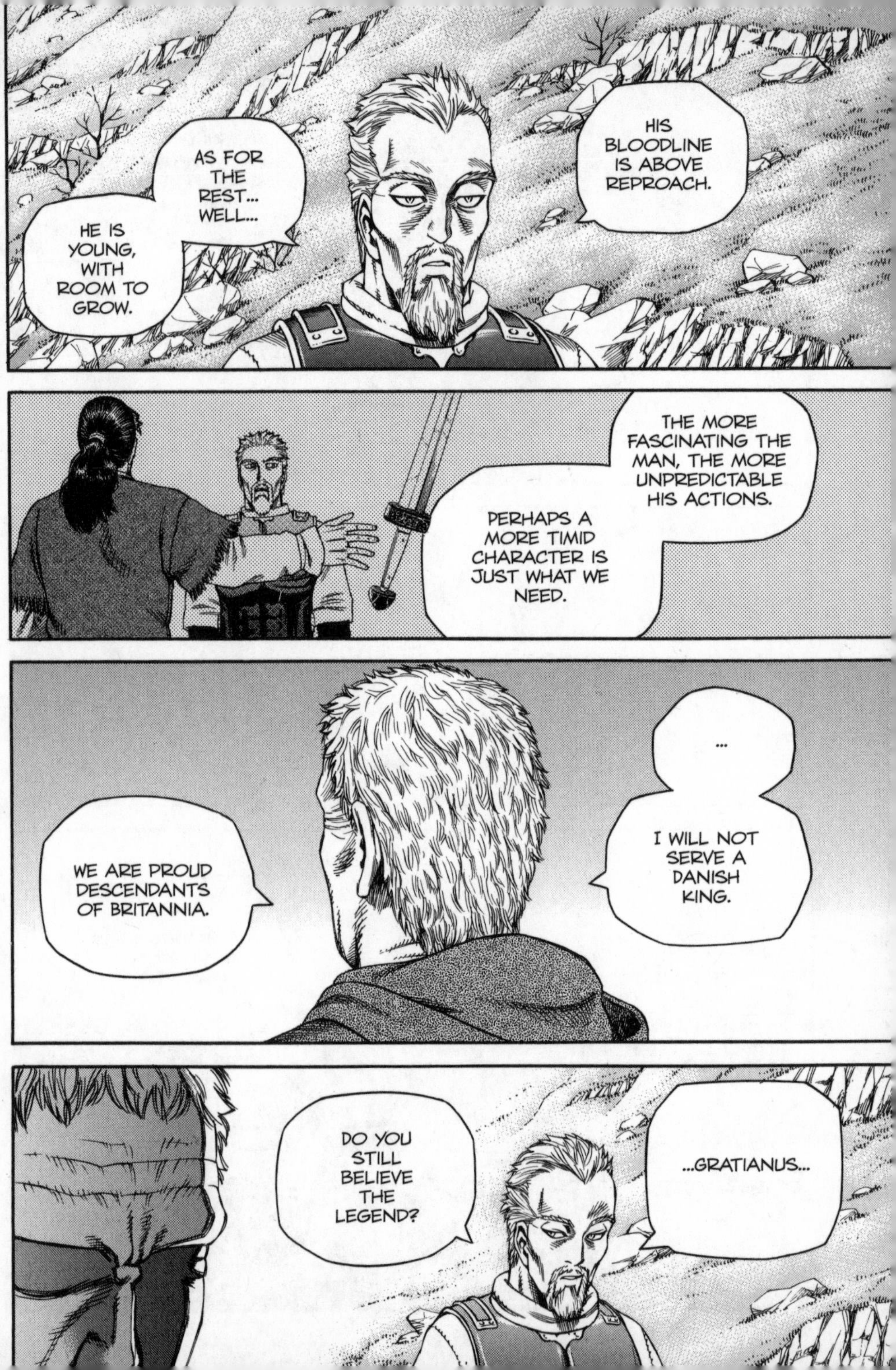
HIS BLOODLINE IS ABOVE REPROACH.
AS FOR THE REST... WELL...
HE IS YOUNG, WITH ROOM TO GROW.
THE MORE FASCINATING THE MAN, THE MORE UNPREDICTABLE HIS ACTIONS.
PERHAPS A MORE TIMID CHARACTER IS JUST WHAT WE NEED.
...
I WILL NOT SERVE A DANISH KING.
WE ARE PROUD DESCENDANTS OF BRITANNIA.
...GRATIANUS...
DO YOU STILL BELIEVE THE LEGEND?

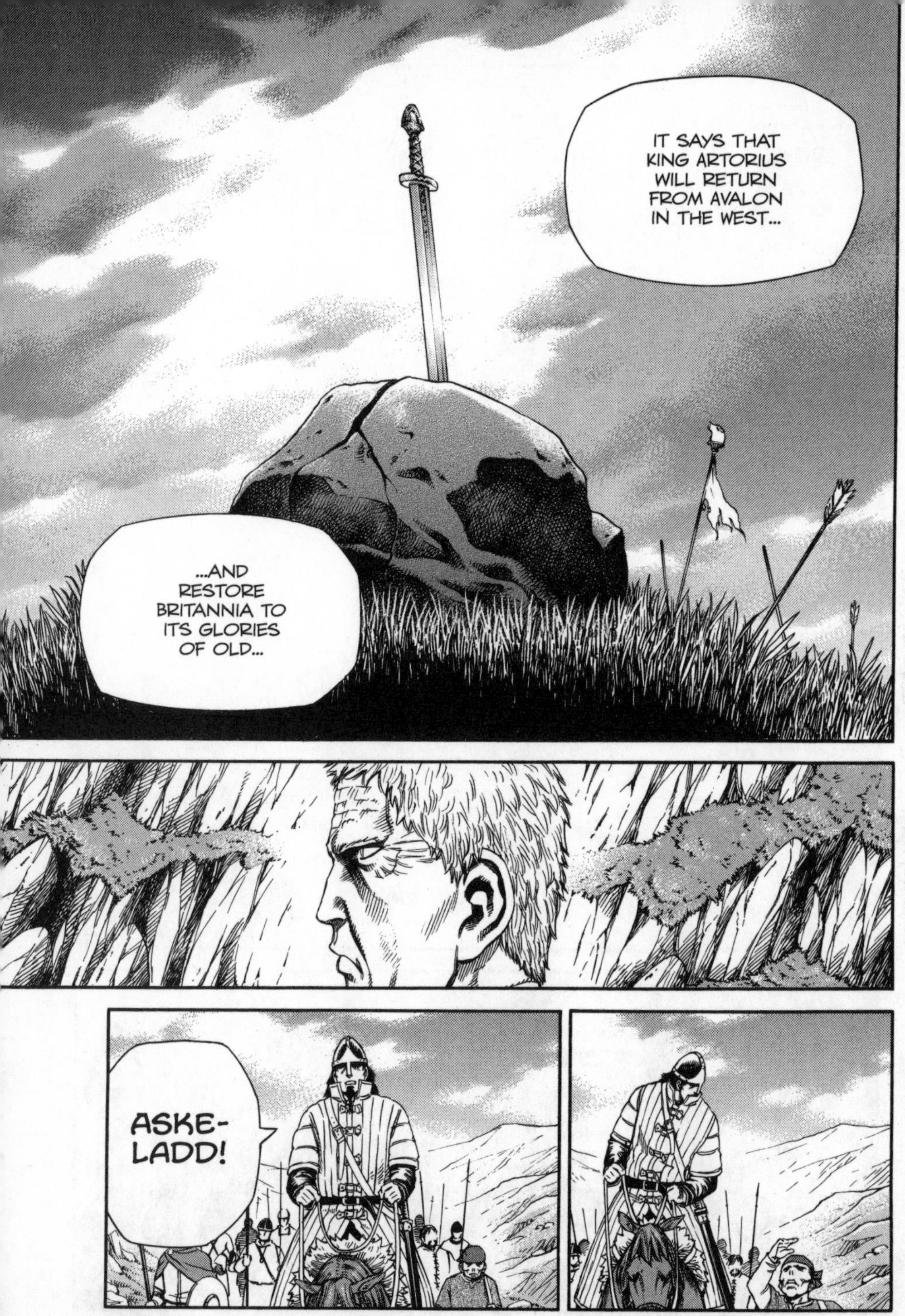
IT SAYS THAT KING ARTORIUS WILL RETURN FROM AVALON IN THE WEST...
...AND RESTORE BRITANNIA TO ITS GLORIES OF OLD...
ASKE-LADD!

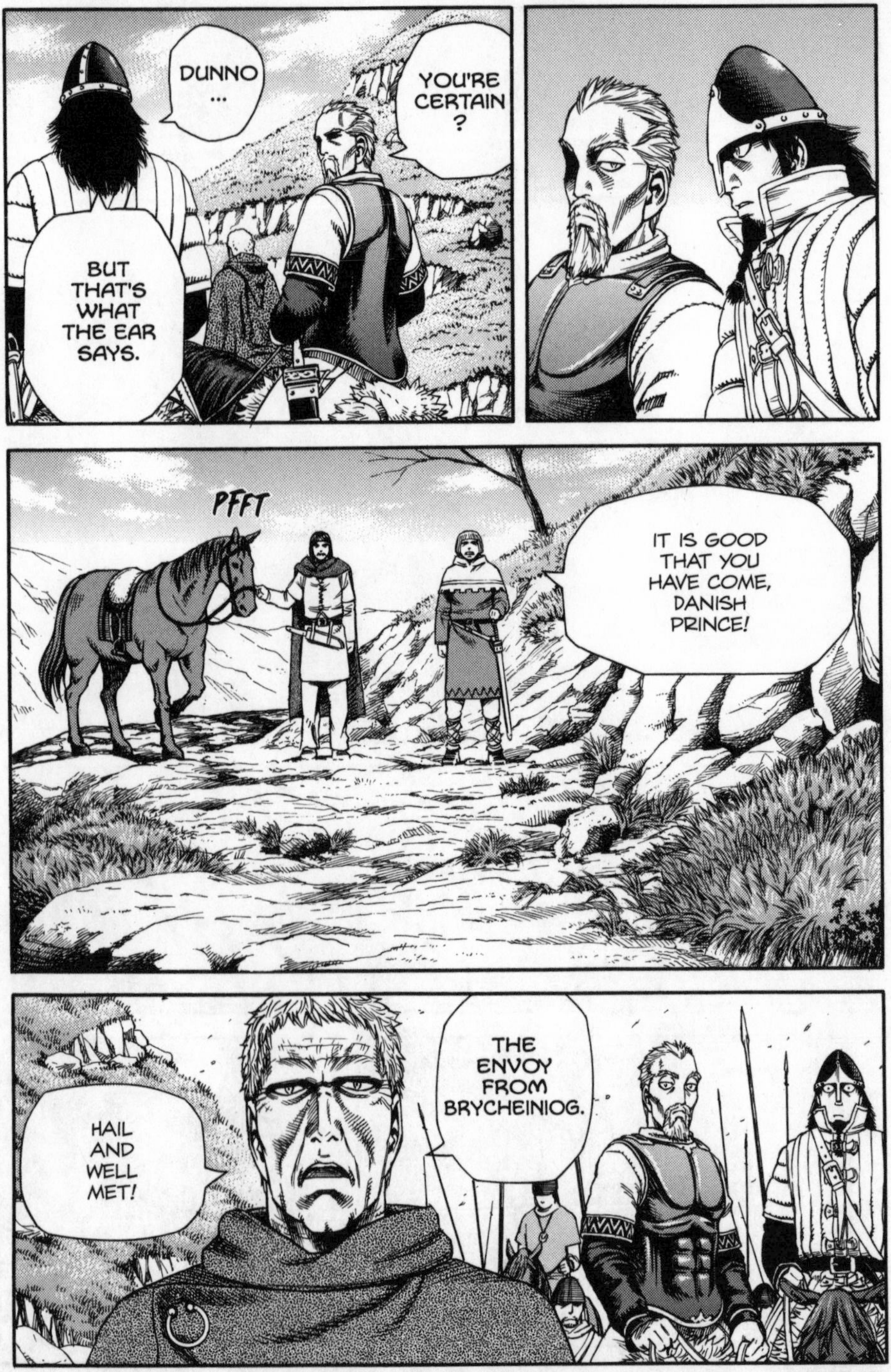
YOU'RE CERTAIN ?
DUNNO ...
BUT THAT'S WHAT THE EAR SAYS.
IT IS GOOD THAT YOU HAVE COME, DANISH PRINCE!
PFFT
THE ENVOY FROM BRYCHEINIOG.
HAIL AND WELL MET!

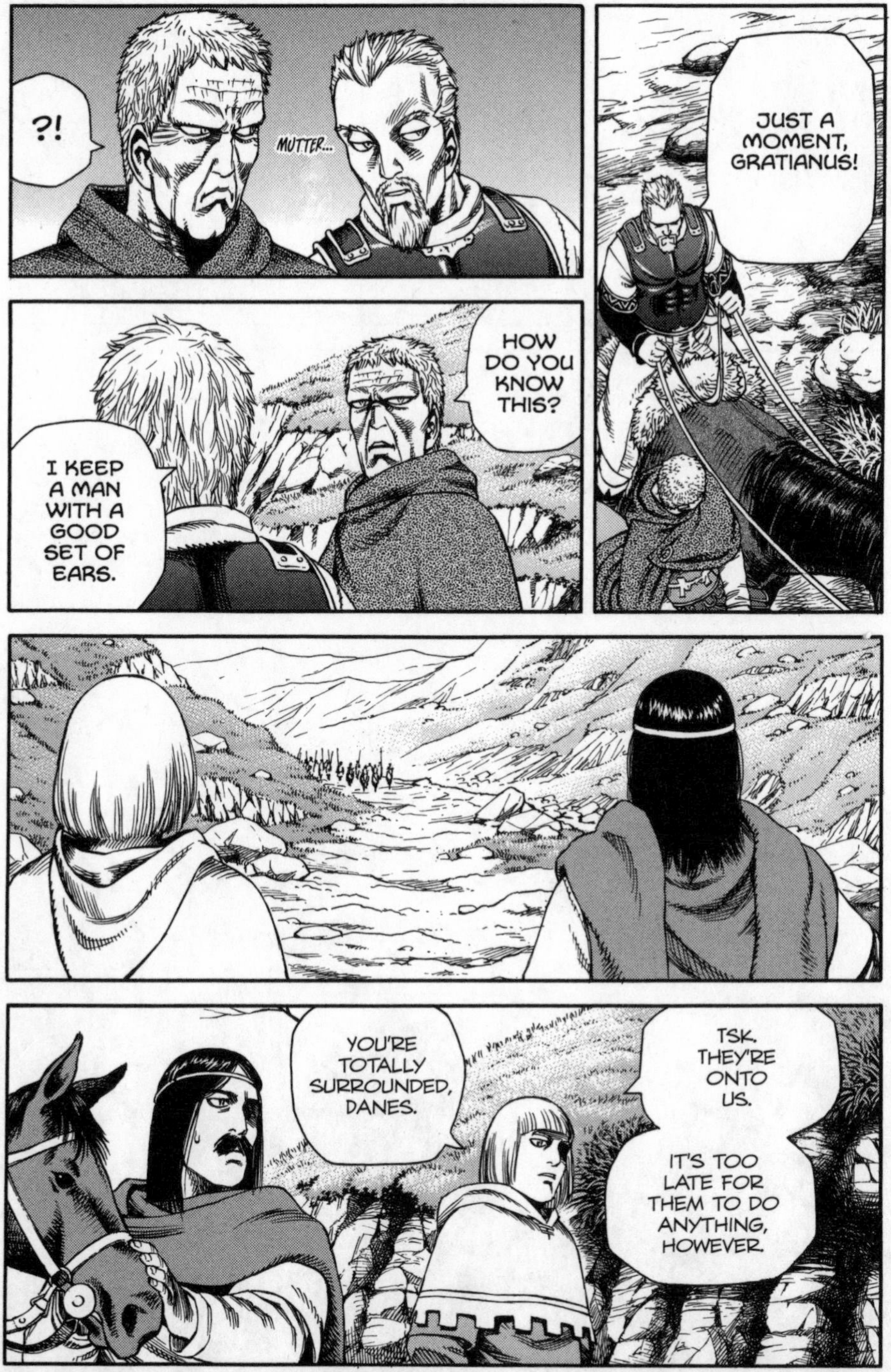
JUST A MOMENT, GRATIANUS!
MUTTER...
?!
HOW DO YOU KNOW THIS?
I KEEP A MAN WITH A GOOD SET OF EARS.
TSK. THEY'RE ONTO US.
IT'S TOO LATE FOR THEM TO DO ANYTHING, HOWEVER.
YOU'RE TOTALLY SURROUNDED, DANES.

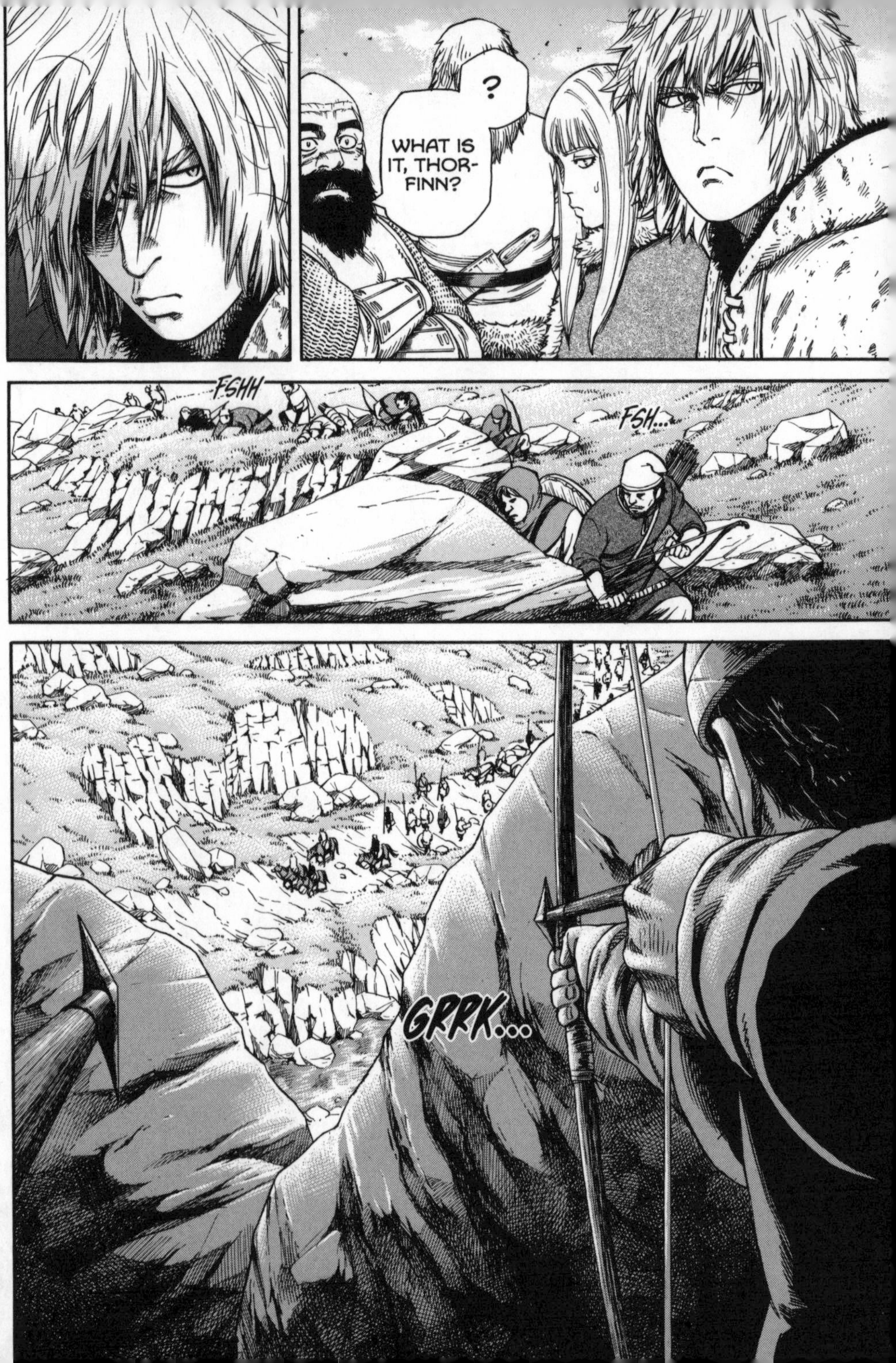
?
WHAT IS IT, THORFINN?
FSHH
FSH...
GRRK...

CHAPTER 24 - END

CHAPTER 25: BLUFF

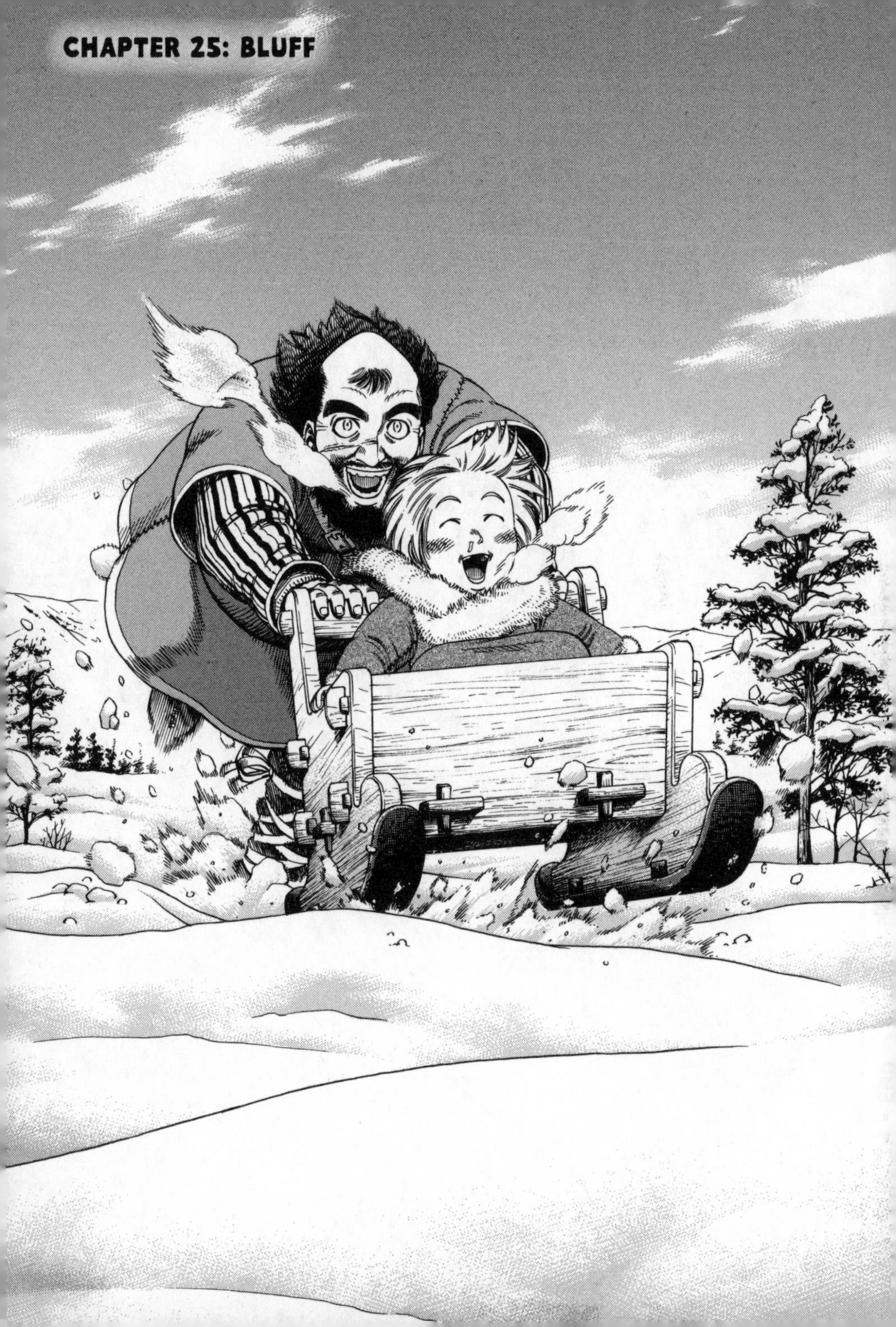

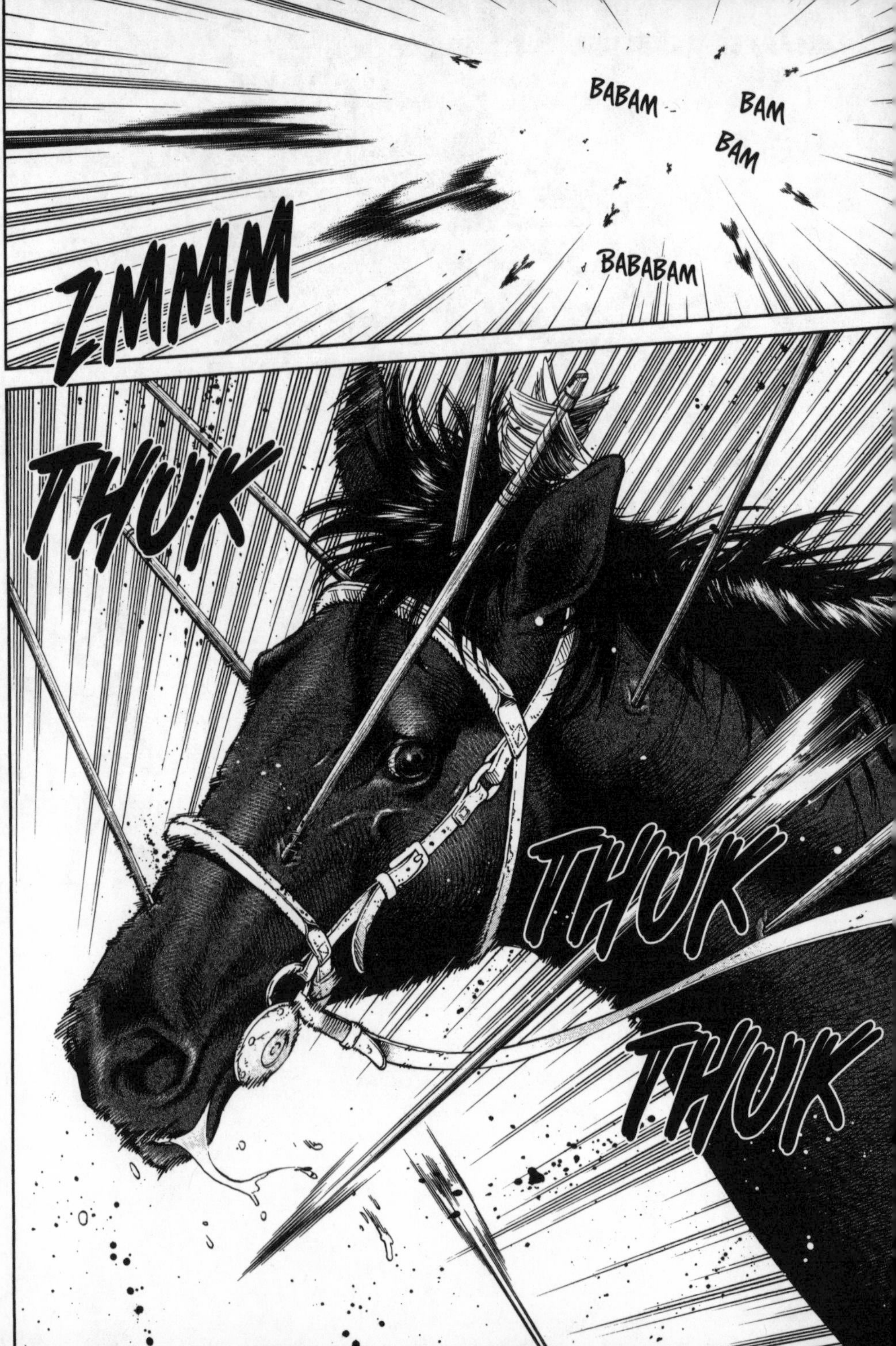
BAM
BAM
BABAM
BABABAM
ZMMMM
THUK
THUK
THUK

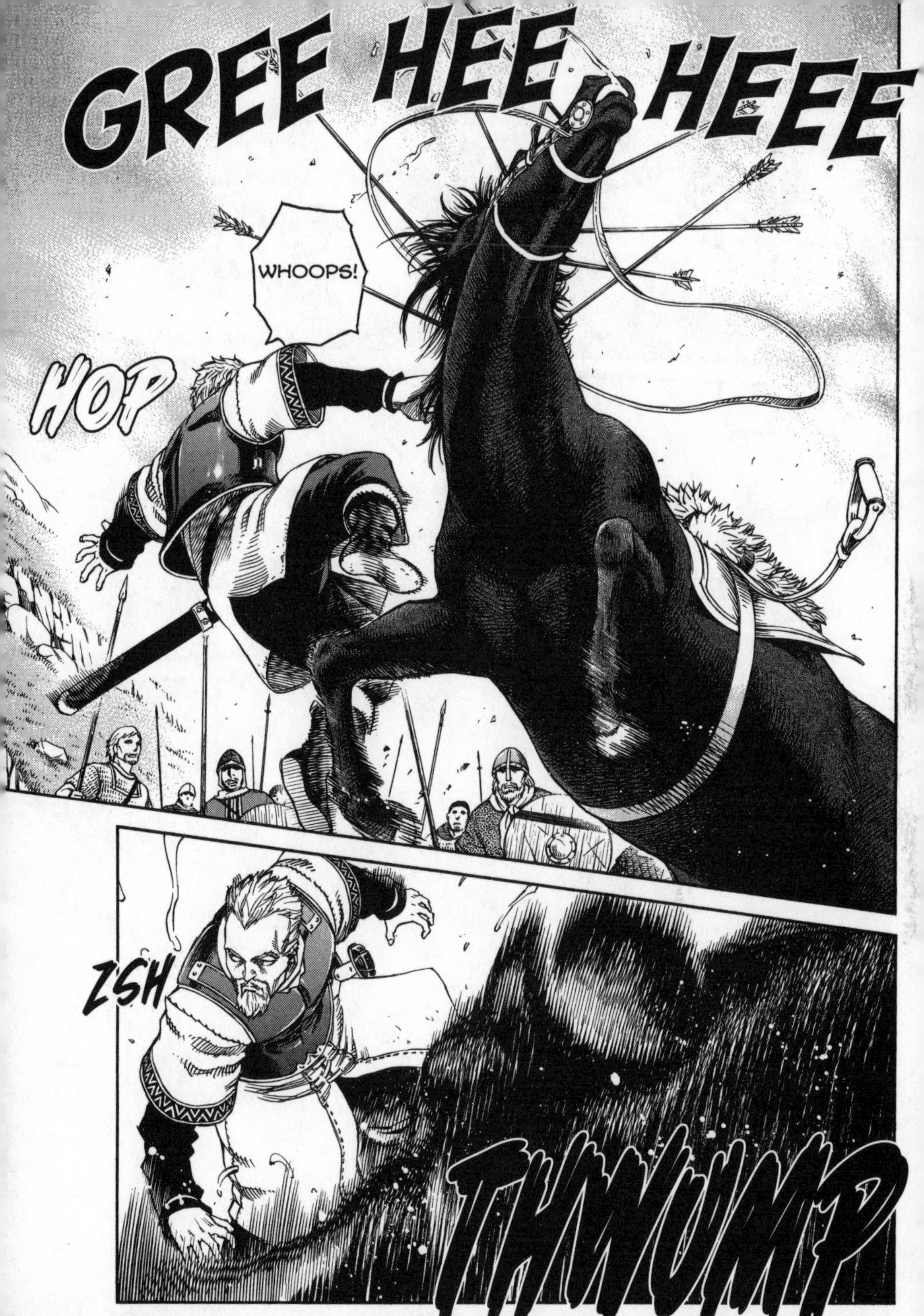
GREE HEE HEEE
WHOOPS!
HOP
ZSH
THWUMP

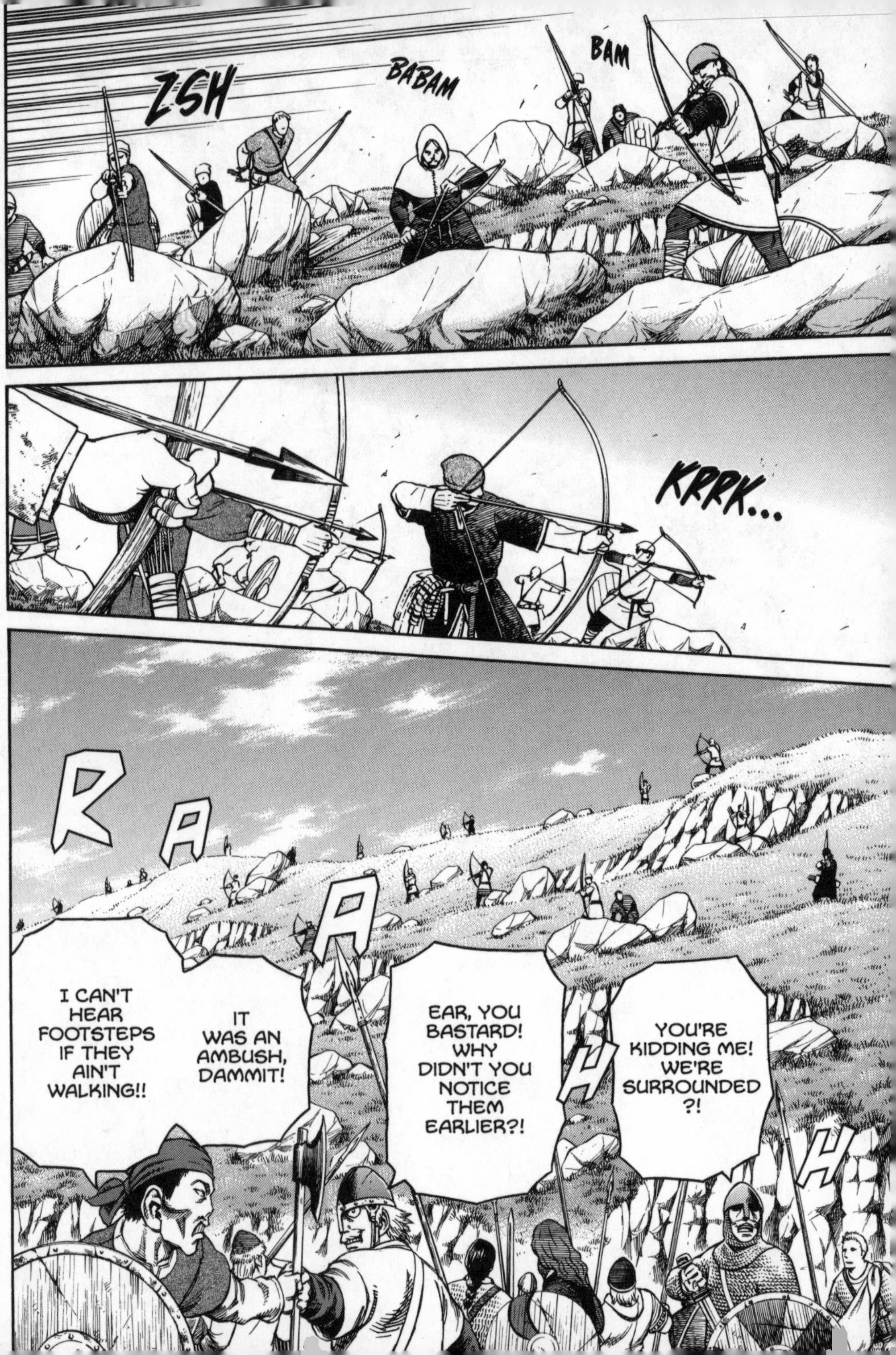
BAM
BABAM
ZSH
KRRK...
RAAHH
YOU'RE KIDDING ME! WE'RE SURROUNDED?!
EAR, YOU BASTARD! WHY DIDN'T YOU NOTICE THEM EARLIER?!
IT WAS AN AMBUSH, DAMMIT!
I CAN'T HEAR FOOTSTEPS IF THEY AIN'T WALKING!!

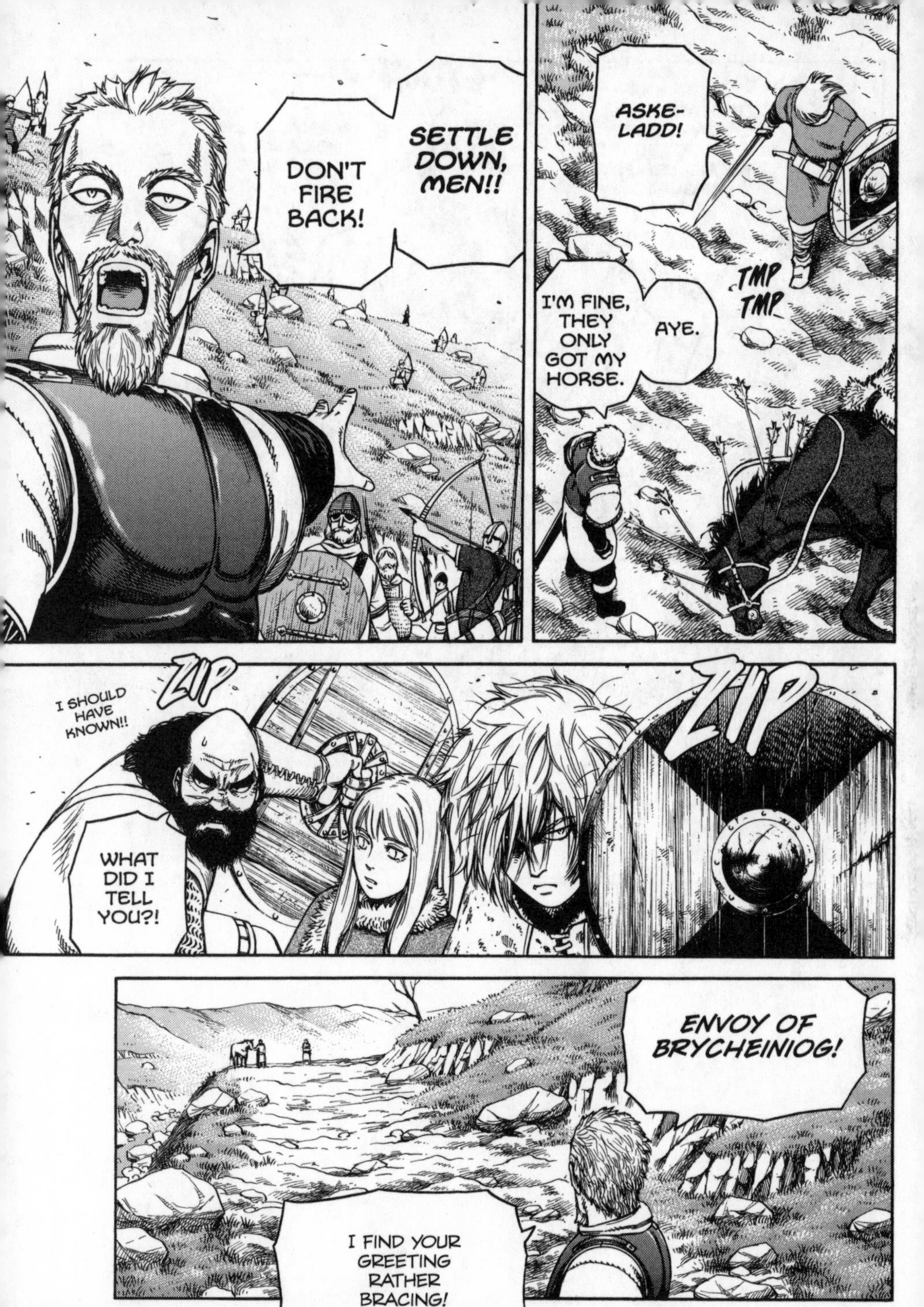
ASKE-LADD!
TMP TMP
AYE.
I'M FINE, THEY ONLY GOT MY HORSE.
SETTLE DOWN, MEN!!
DON'T FIRE BACK!
ZIP
ZIP
I SHOULD HAVE KNOWN!!
WHAT DID I TELL YOU?!
ENVOY OF BRYCHEINIOG!
I FIND YOUR GREETING RATHER BRACING!

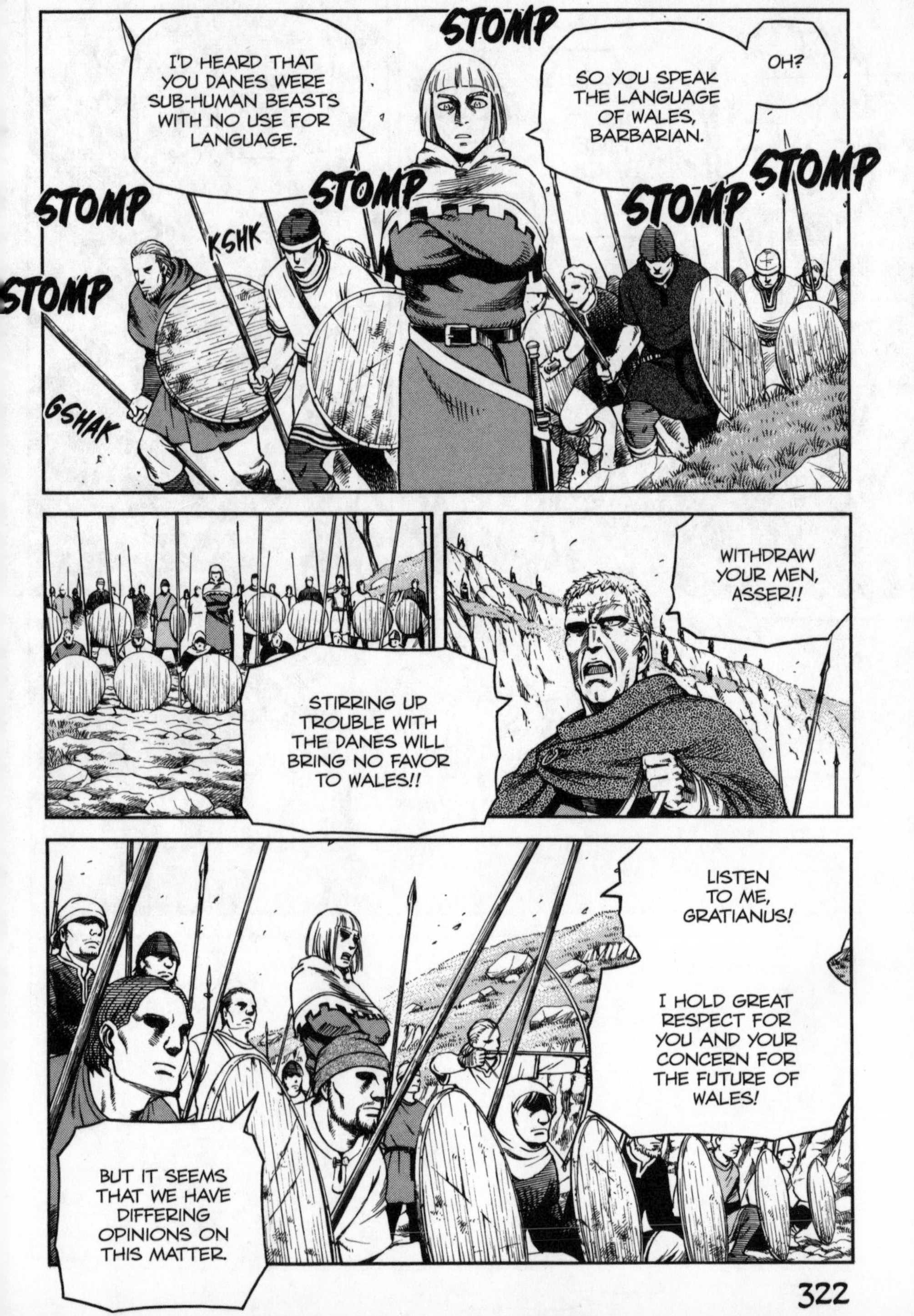
STOMP
OH?
SO YOU SPEAK THE LANGUAGE OF WALES, BARBARIAN.
I'D HEARD THAT YOU DANES WERE SUB-HUMAN BEASTS WITH NO USE FOR LANGUAGE.
STOMP
STOMP
STOMP
KSHK
STOMP
STOMP
GSHAK
WITHDRAW YOUR MEN, ASSER!!
STIRRING UP TROUBLE WITH THE DANES WILL BRING NO FAVOR TO WALES!!
LISTEN TO ME, GRATIANUS!
I HOLD GREAT RESPECT FOR YOU AND YOUR CONCERN FOR THE FUTURE OF WALES!
BUT IT SEEMS THAT WE HAVE DIFFERING OPINIONS ON THIS MATTER.

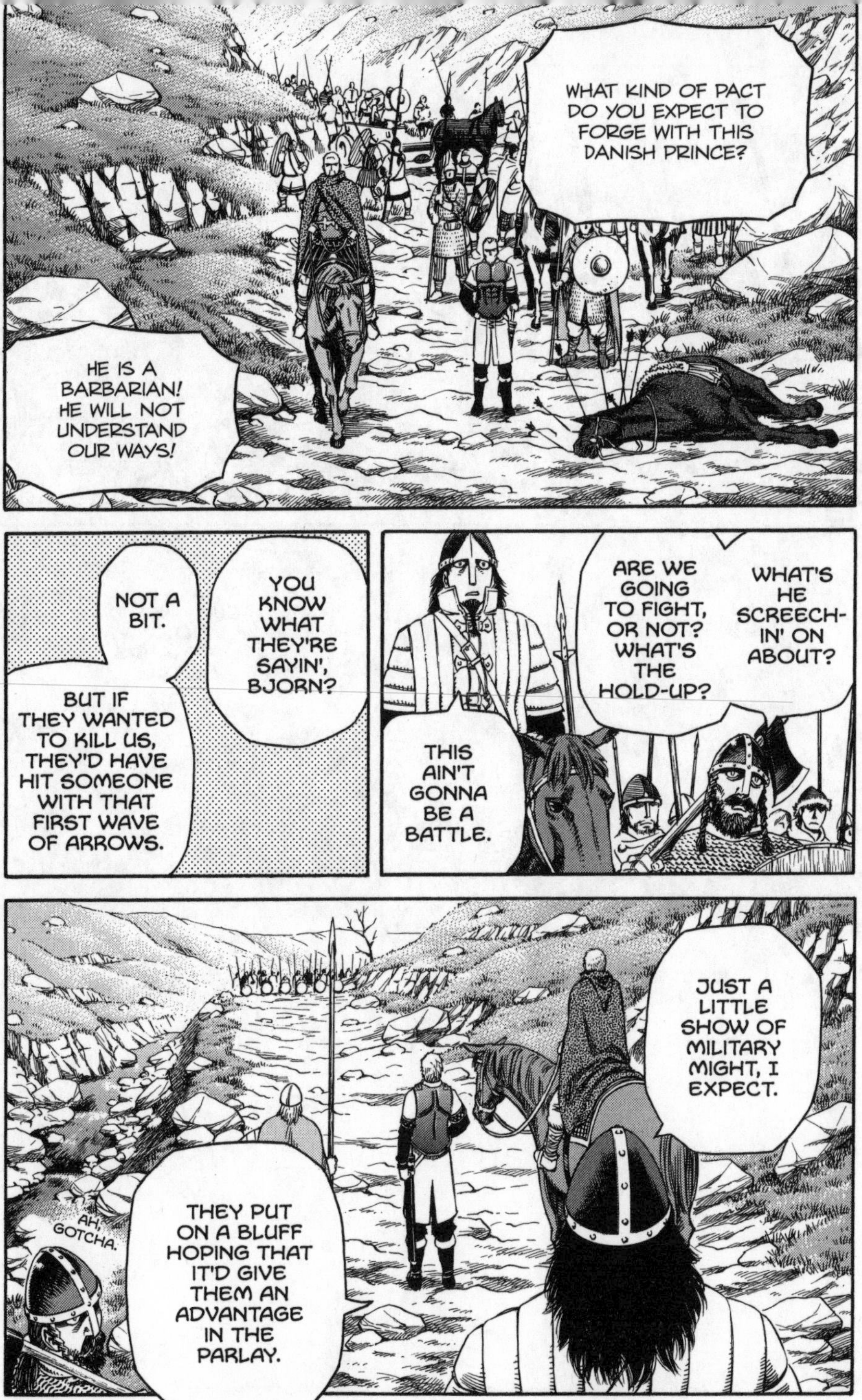
WHAT KIND OF PACT DO YOU EXPECT TO FORGE WITH THIS DANISH PRINCE?
HE IS A BARBARIAN! HE WILL NOT UNDERSTAND OUR WAYS!
WHAT'S HE SCREECH-IN' ON ABOUT?
ARE WE GOING TO FIGHT, OR NOT? WHAT'S THE HOLD-UP?
THIS AIN'T GONNA BE A BATTLE.
YOU KNOW WHAT THEY'RE SAYIN', BJORN?
NOT A BIT.
BUT IF THEY WANTED TO KILL US, THEY'D HAVE HIT SOMEONE WITH THAT FIRST WAVE OF ARROWS.
JUST A LITTLE SHOW OF MILITARY MIGHT, I EXPECT.
THEY PUT ON A BLUFF HOPING THAT IT'D GIVE THEM AN ADVANTAGE IN THE PARLAY.
AH, GOTCHA.

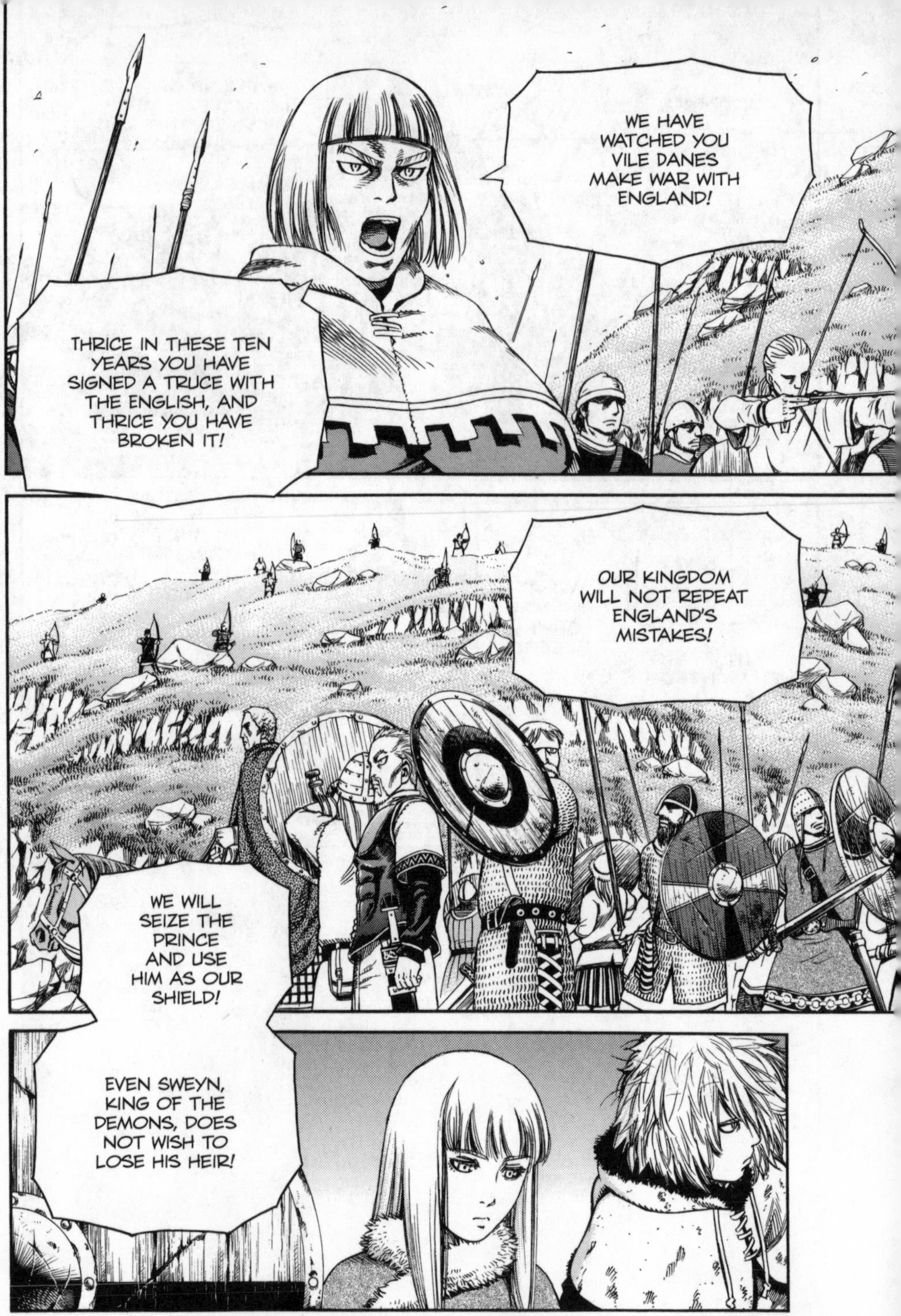
WE HAVE WATCHED YOU VILE DANES MAKE WAR WITH ENGLAND!
THRICE IN THESE TEN YEARS YOU HAVE SIGNED A TRUCE WITH THE ENGLISH, AND THRICE YOU HAVE BROKEN IT!
OUR KINGDOM WILL NOT REPEAT ENGLAND'S MISTAKES!
WE WILL SEIZE THE PRINCE AND USE HIM AS OUR SHIELD!
EVEN SWEYN, KING OF THE DEMONS, DOES NOT WISH TO LOSE HIS HEIR!

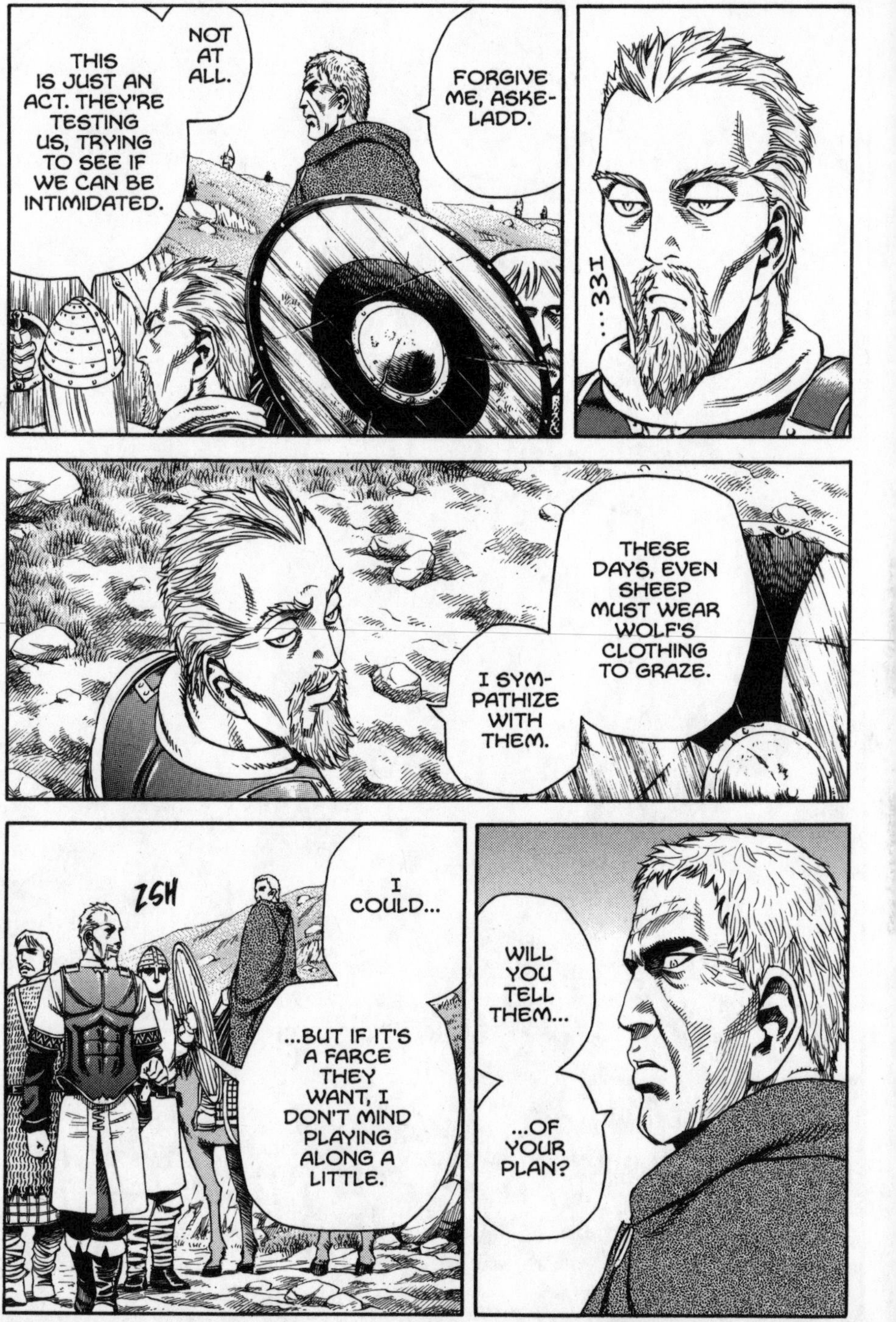
HEE...
FORGIVE ME, ASKE-LADD.
NOT AT ALL.
THIS IS JUST AN ACT. THEY'RE TESTING US, TRYING TO SEE IF WE CAN BE INTIMIDATED.
THESE DAYS, EVEN SHEEP MUST WEAR WOLF'S CLOTHING TO GRAZE.
I SYMPATHIZE WITH THEM.
WILL YOU TELL THEM...
...OF YOUR PLAN?
I COULD...
...BUT IF IT'S A FARCE THEY WANT, I DON'T MIND PLAYING ALONG A LITTLE.
ZSH

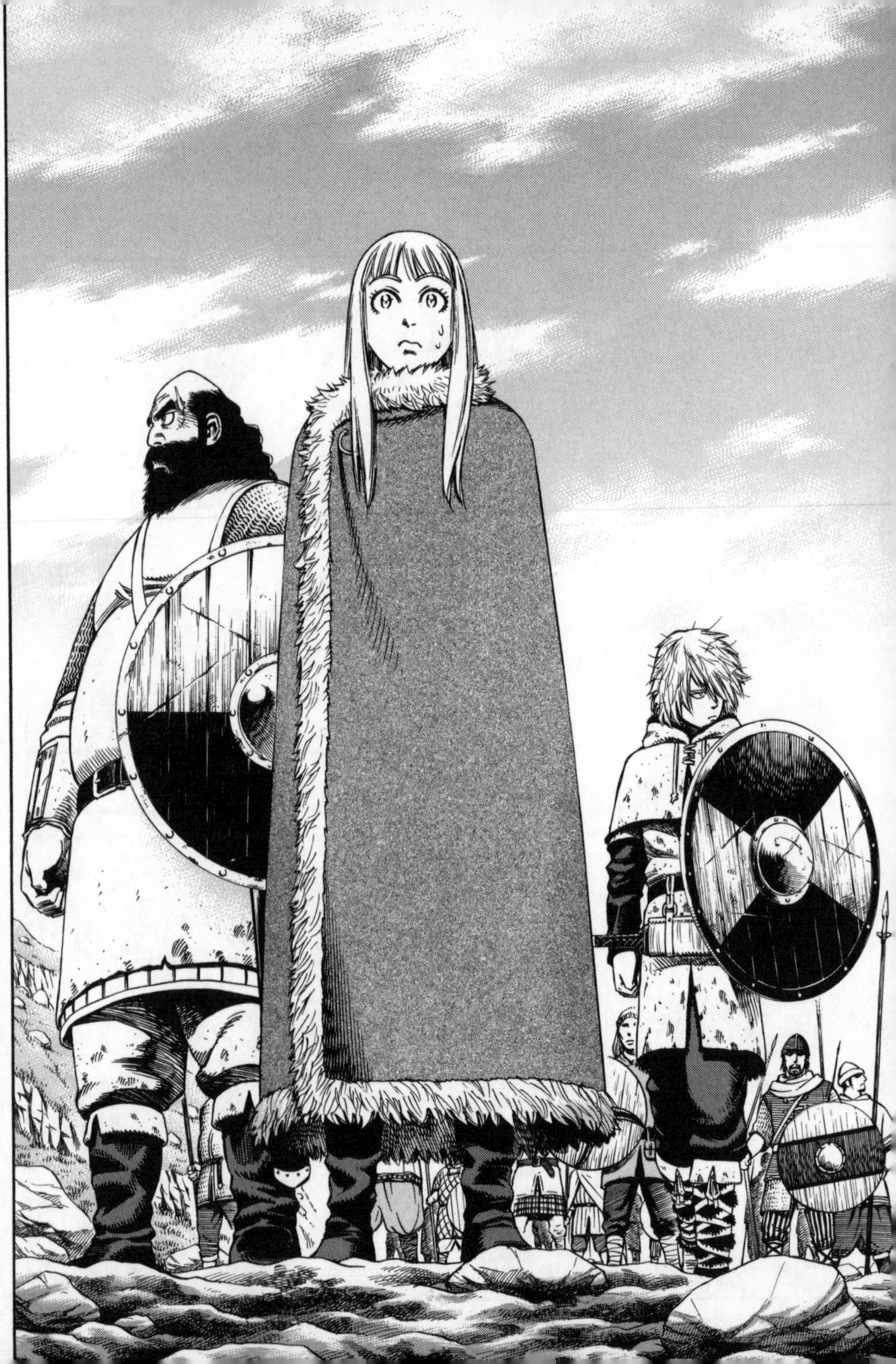

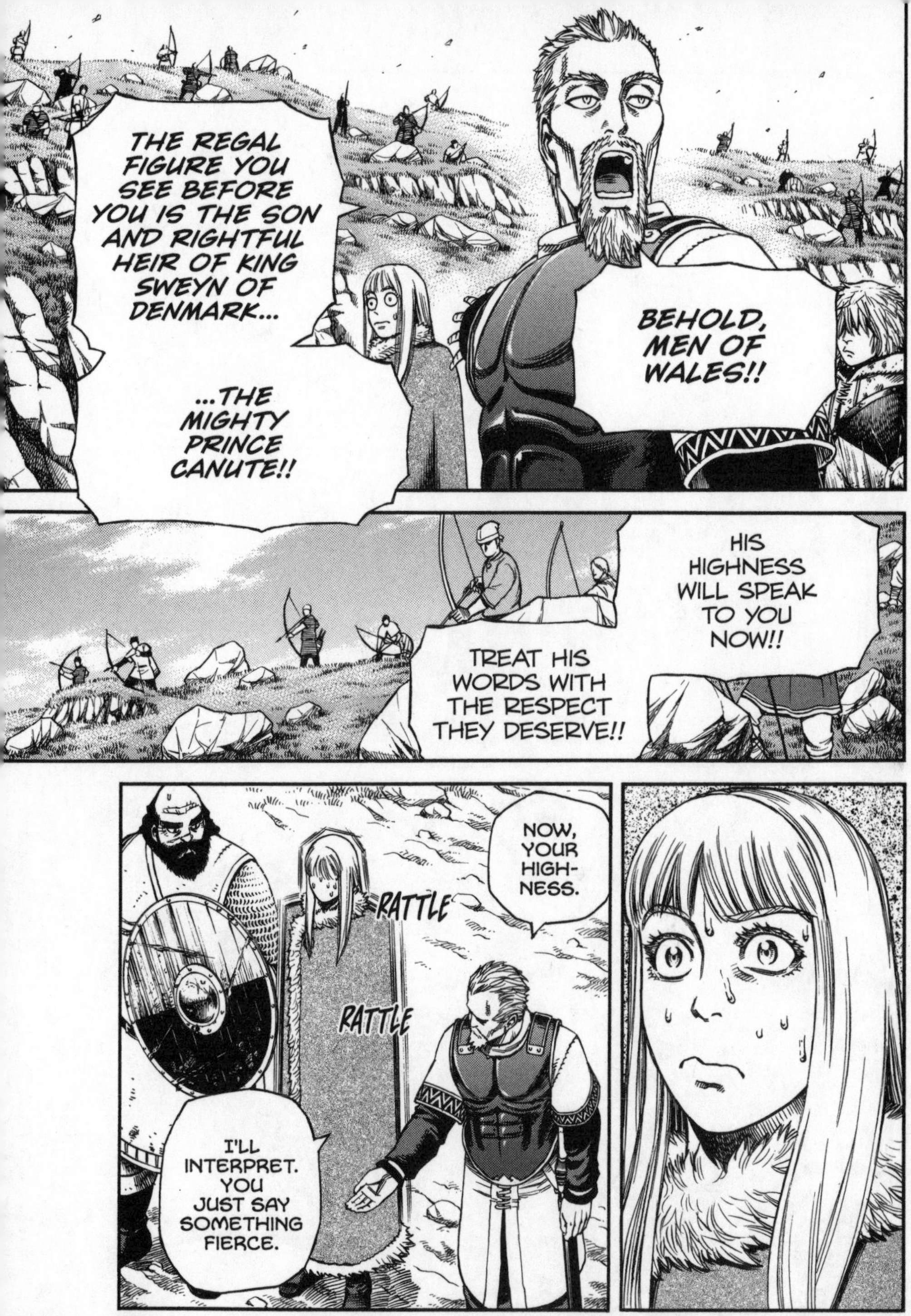
BEHOLD, MEN OF WALES!!
THE REGAL FIGURE YOU SEE BEFORE YOU IS THE SON AND RIGHTFUL HEIR OF KING SWEYN OF DENMARK...
...THE MIGHTY PRINCE CANUTE!!
HIS HIGHNESS WILL SPEAK TO YOU NOW!!
TREAT HIS WORDS WITH THE RESPECT THEY DESERVE!!
NOW, YOUR HIGH-NESS.
RATTLE
RATTLE
I'LL INTERPRET. YOU JUST SAY SOMETHING FIERCE.

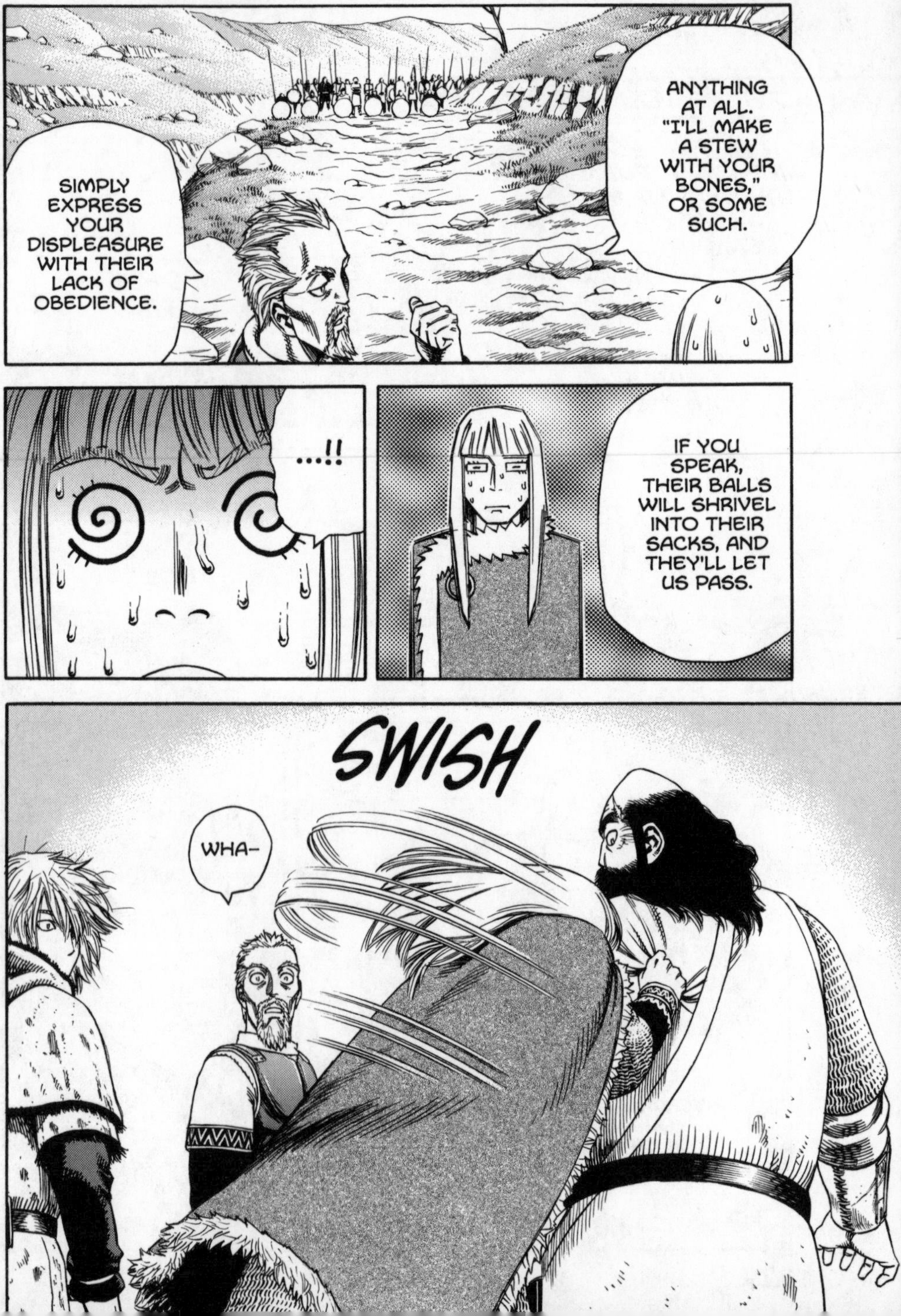
ANYTHING AT ALL. "I'LL MAKE A STEW WITH YOUR BONES," OR SOME SUCH.
SIMPLY EXPRESS YOUR DISPLEASURE WITH THEIR LACK OF OBEDIENCE.
IF YOU SPEAK, THEIR BALLS WILL SHRIVEL INTO THEIR SACKS, AND THEY'LL LET US PASS.
...!!
SWISH
WHA-

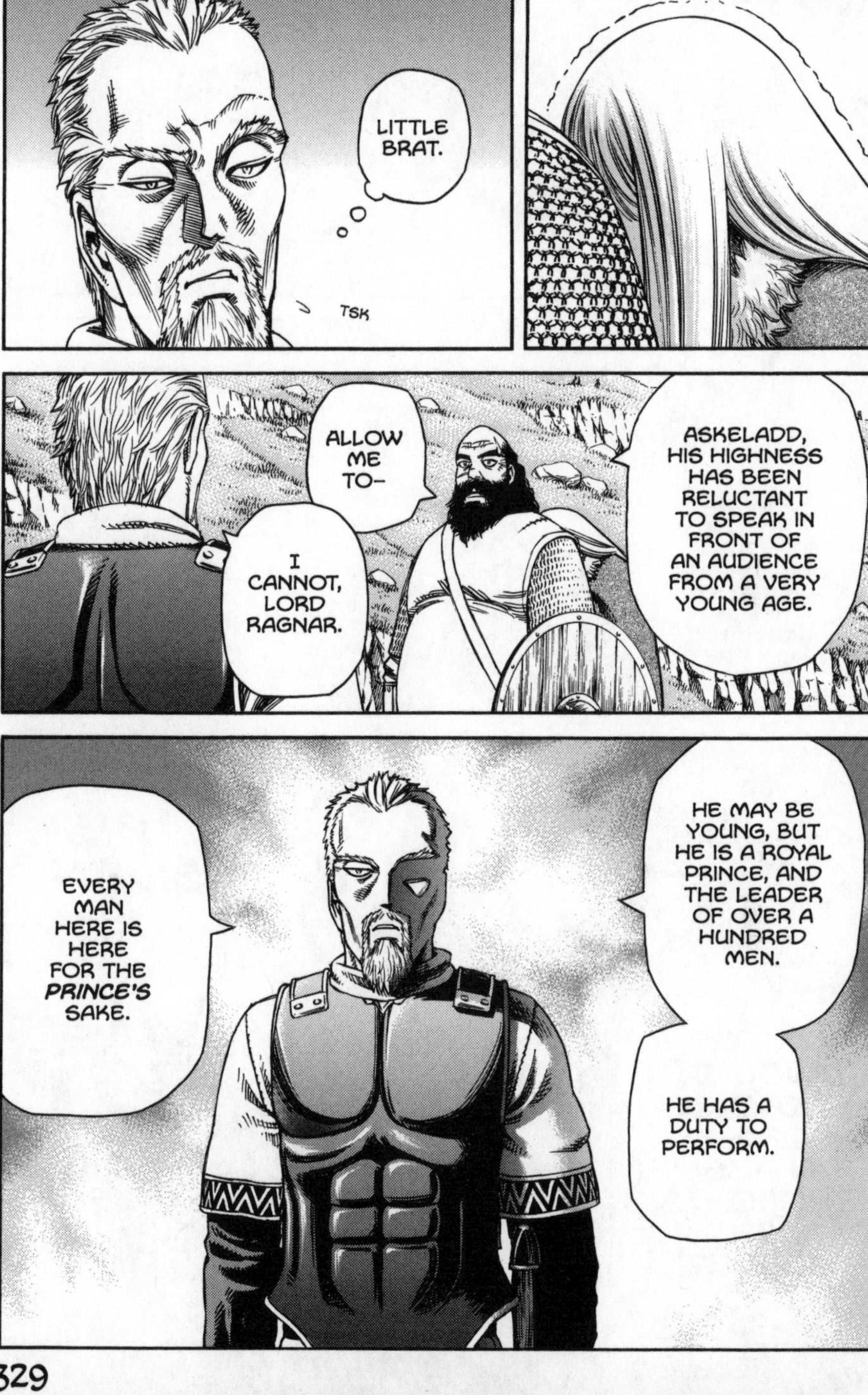
LITTLE BRAT.
TSK
ASKELADD, HIS HIGHNESS HAS BEEN RELUCTANT TO SPEAK IN FRONT OF AN AUDIENCE FROM A VERY YOUNG AGE.
ALLOW ME TO-
I CANNOT, LORD RAGNAR.
HE MAY BE YOUNG, BUT HE IS A ROYAL PRINCE, AND THE LEADER OF OVER A HUNDRED MEN.
HE HAS A DUTY TO PERFORM.
EVERY MAN HERE IS HERE FOR THE *PRINCE'S* SAKE.

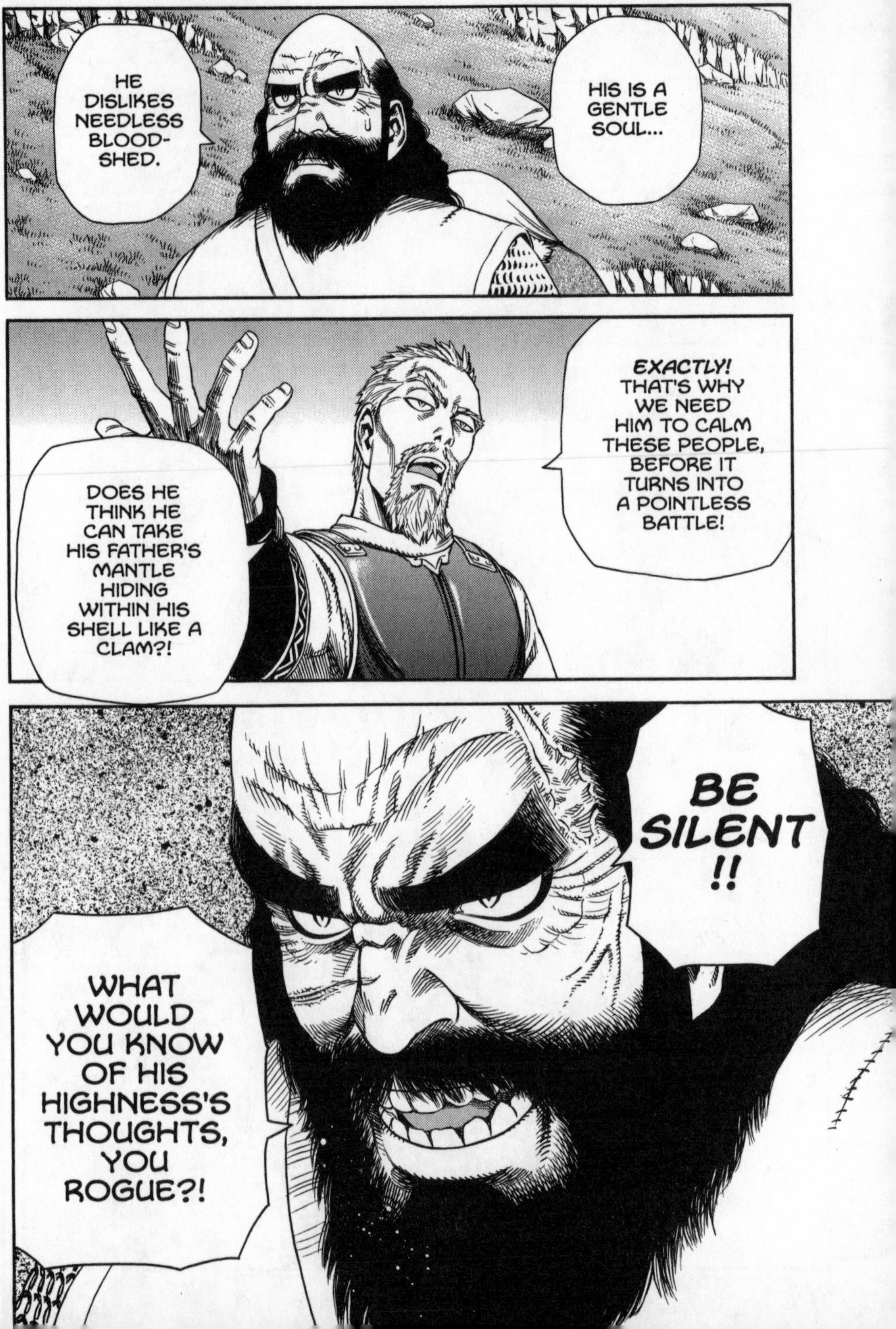
HIS IS A GENTLE SOUL...
HE DISLIKES NEEDLESS BLOOD-SHED.
EXACTLY! THAT'S WHY WE NEED HIM TO CALM THESE PEOPLE, BEFORE IT TURNS INTO A POINTLESS BATTLE!
DOES HE THINK HE CAN TAKE HIS FATHER'S MANTLE HIDING WITHIN HIS SHELL LIKE A CLAM?!
BE SILENT !!
WHAT WOULD YOU KNOW OF HIS HIGHNESS'S THOUGHTS, YOU ROGUE?!

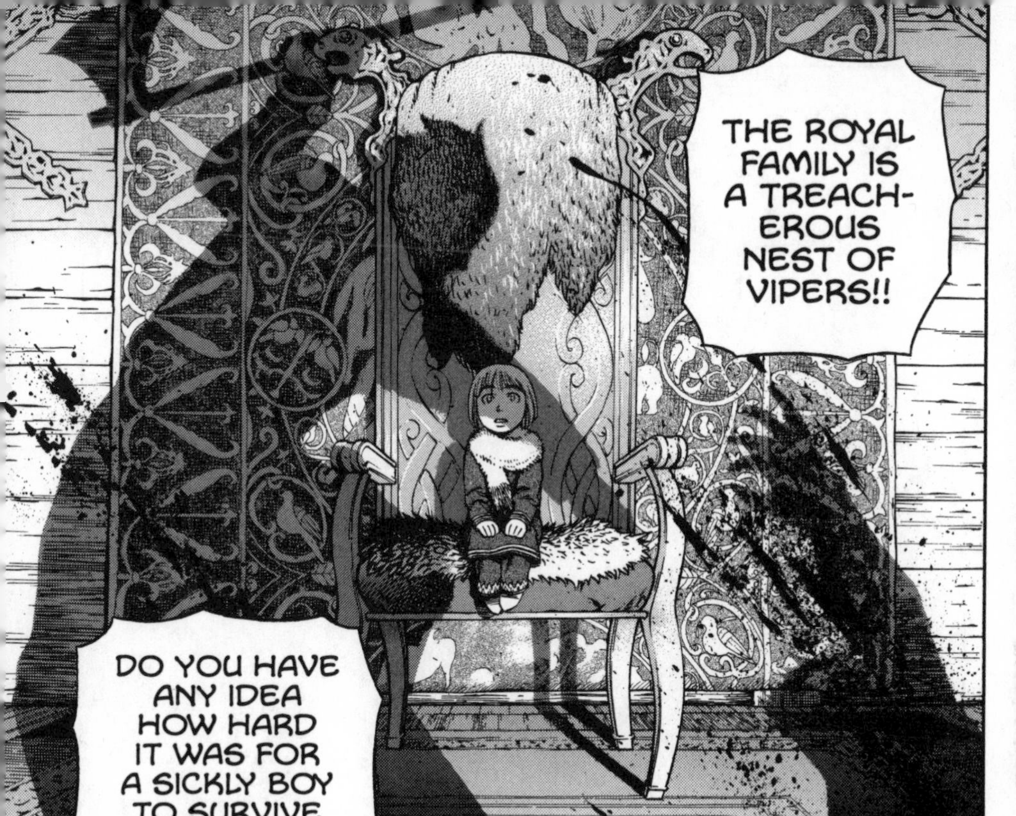
THE ROYAL FAMILY IS A TREACH-EROUS NEST OF VIPERS!!
DO YOU HAVE ANY IDEA HOW HARD IT WAS FOR A SICKLY BOY TO SURVIVE IN THEIR MIDST?!

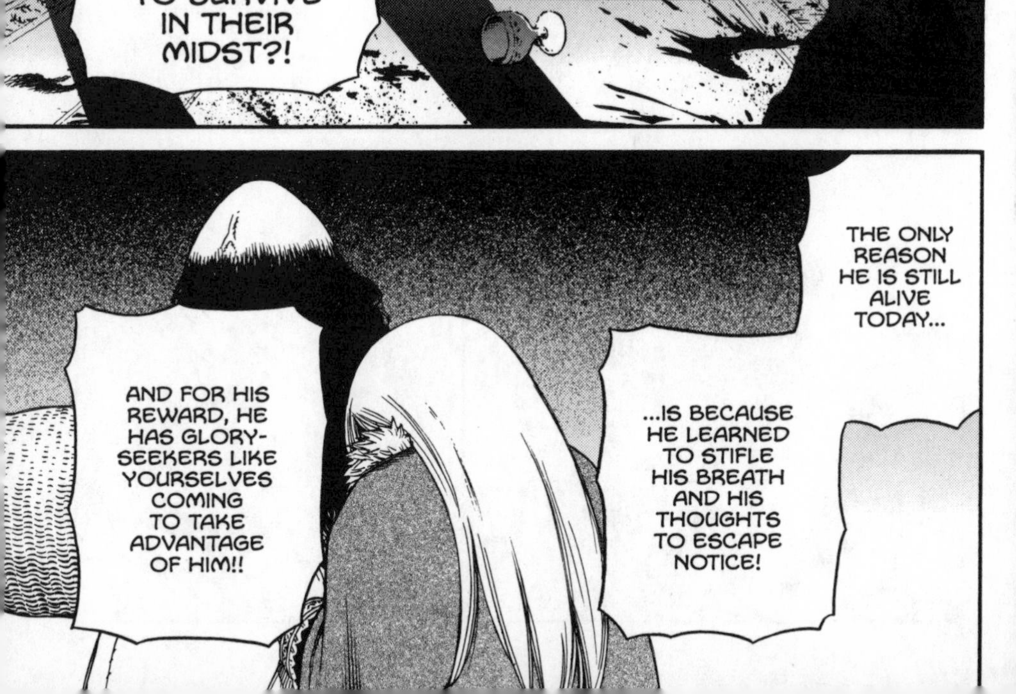
THE ONLY REASON HE IS STILL ALIVE TODAY...
...IS BECAUSE HE LEARNED TO STIFLE HIS BREATH AND HIS THOUGHTS TO ESCAPE NOTICE!
AND FOR HIS REWARD, HE HAS GLORY-SEEKERS LIKE YOURSELVES COMING TO TAKE ADVANTAGE OF HIM!!

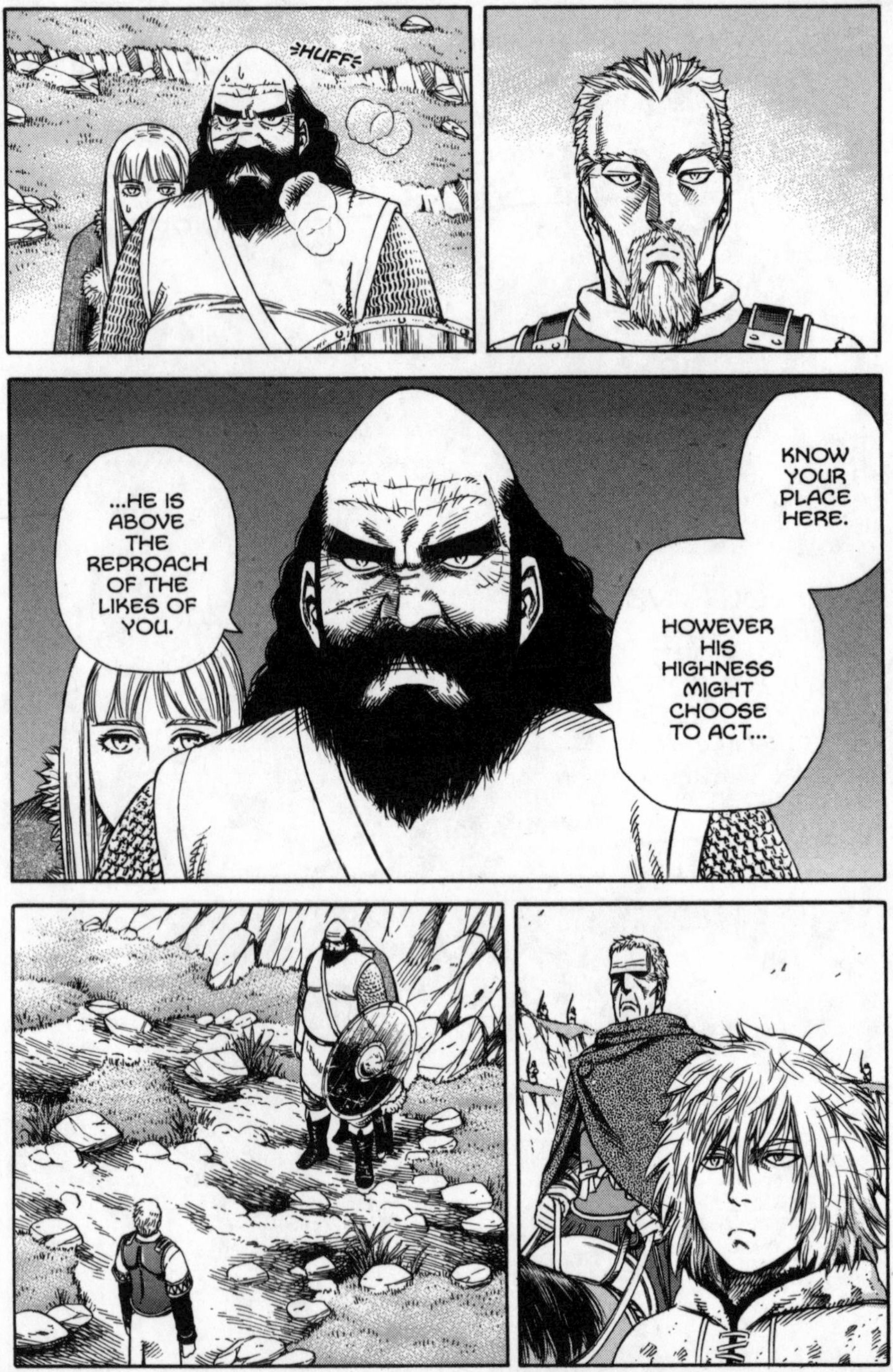
HUFF
KNOW YOUR PLACE HERE.
HOWEVER HIS HIGHNESS MIGHT CHOOSE TO ACT...
...HE IS ABOVE THE REPROACH OF THE LIKES OF YOU.

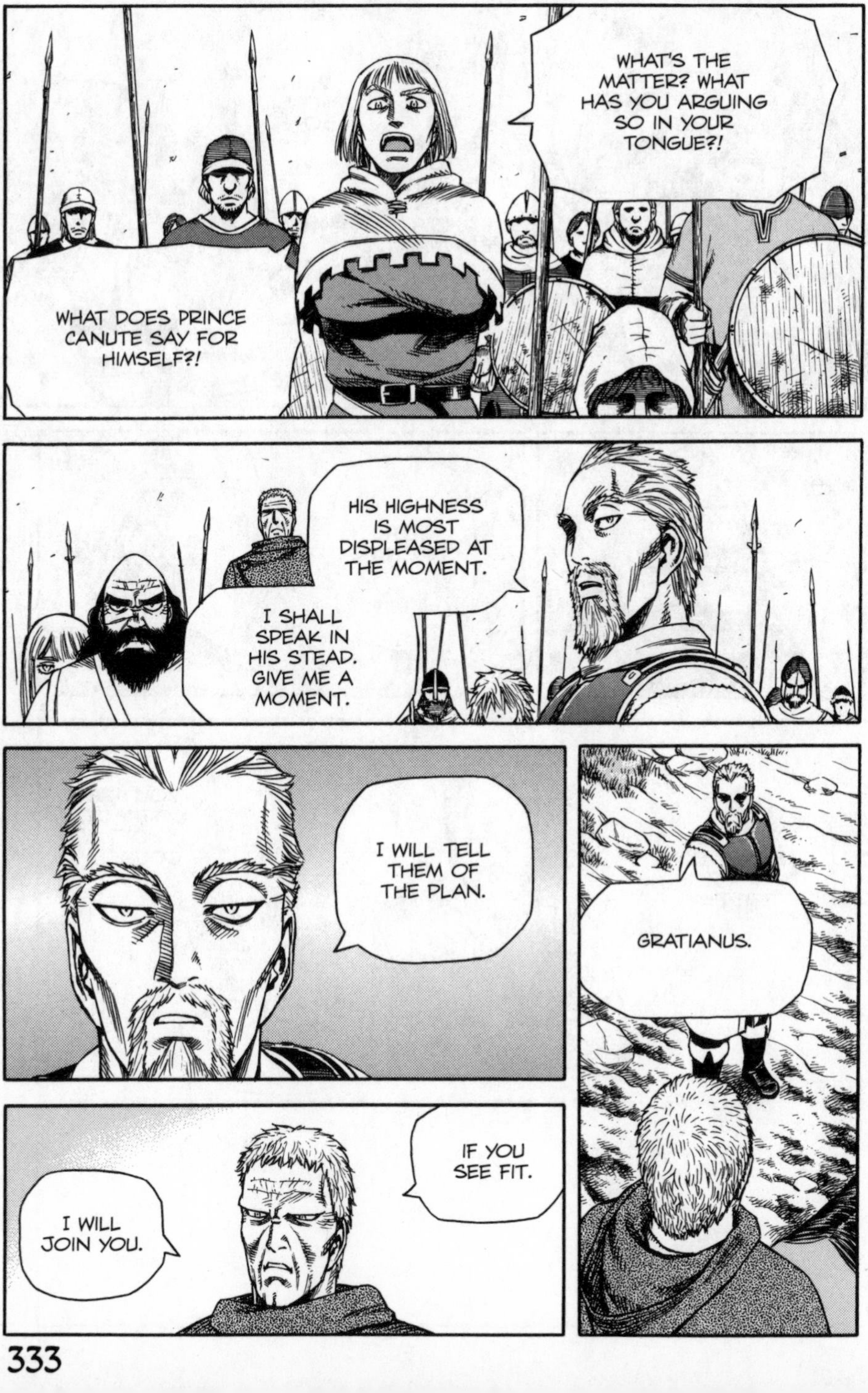
WHAT'S THE MATTER? WHAT HAS YOU ARGUING SO IN YOUR TONGUE?!
WHAT DOES PRINCE CANUTE SAY FOR HIMSELF?!
HIS HIGHNESS IS MOST DISPLEASED AT THE MOMENT.
I SHALL SPEAK IN HIS STEAD. GIVE ME A MOMENT.
GRATIANUS.
I WILL TELL THEM OF THE PLAN.
IF YOU SEE FIT.
I WILL JOIN YOU.

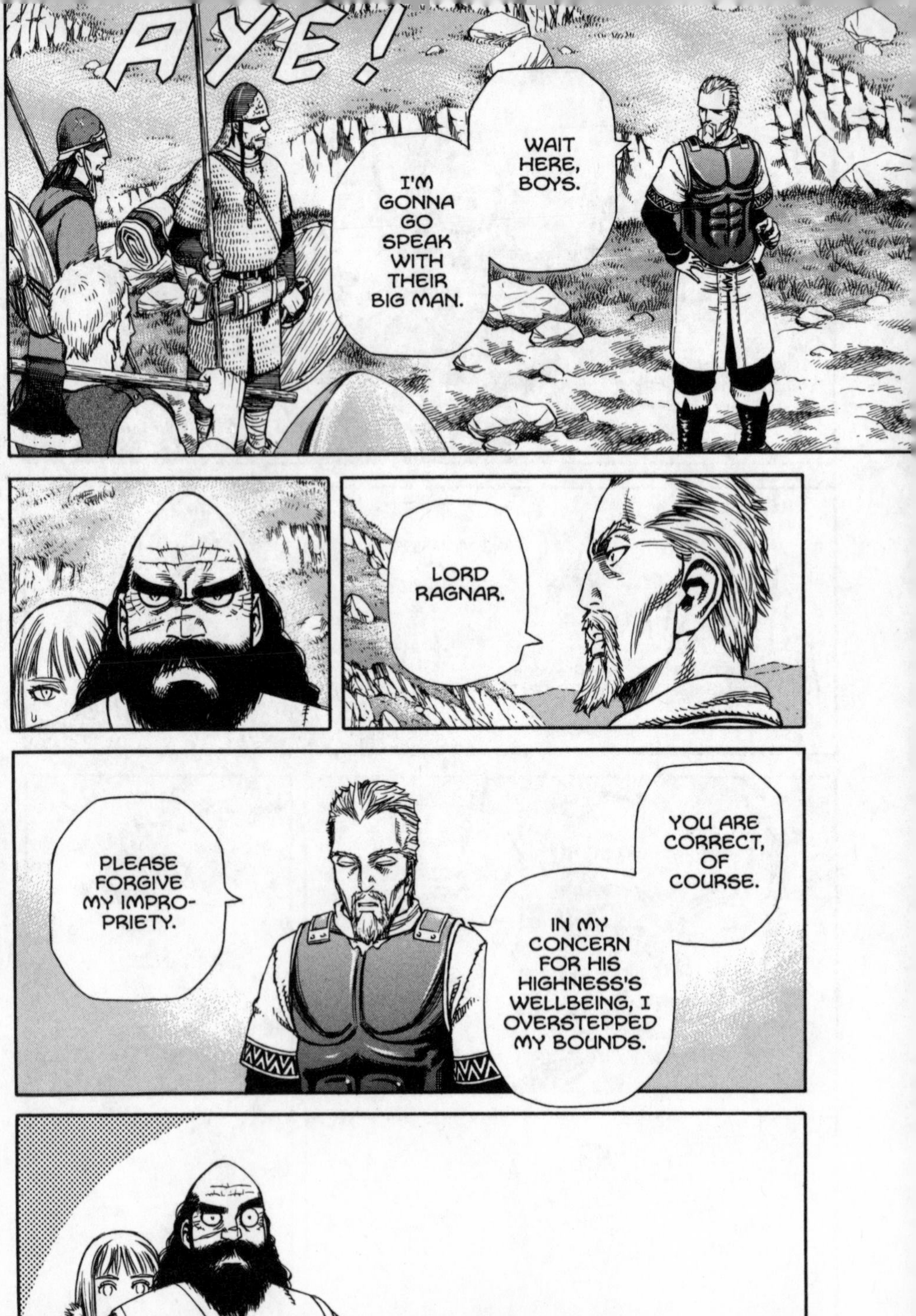
WAIT HERE, BOYS.
I'M GONNA GO SPEAK WITH THEIR BIG MAN.
AYE!
LORD RAGNAR.
YOU ARE CORRECT, OF COURSE.
IN MY CONCERN FOR HIS HIGHNESS'S WELLBEING, I OVERSTEPPED MY BOUNDS.
PLEASE FORGIVE MY IMPRO-PRIETY.

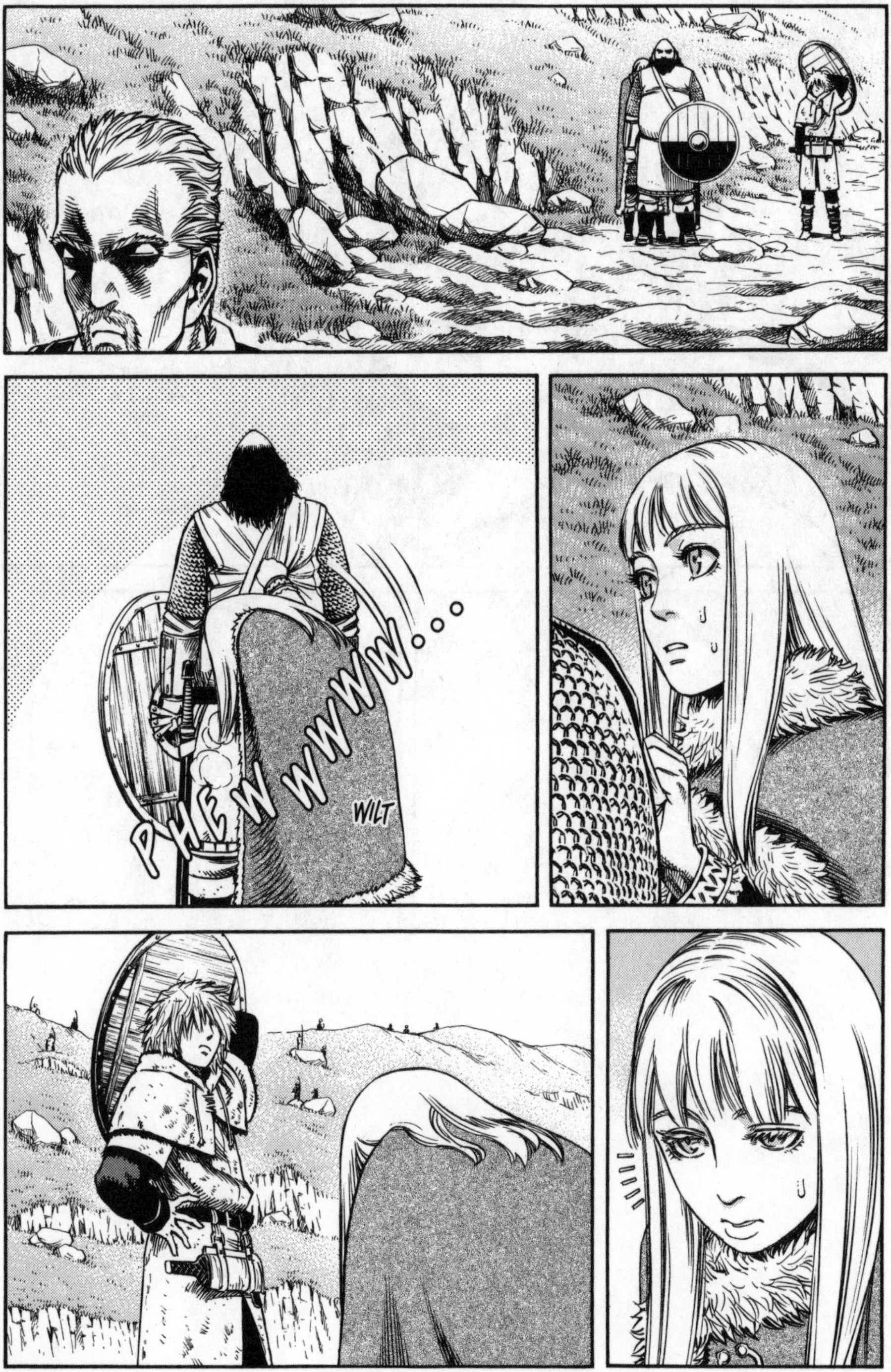
PHEWWWWWW...
WILT

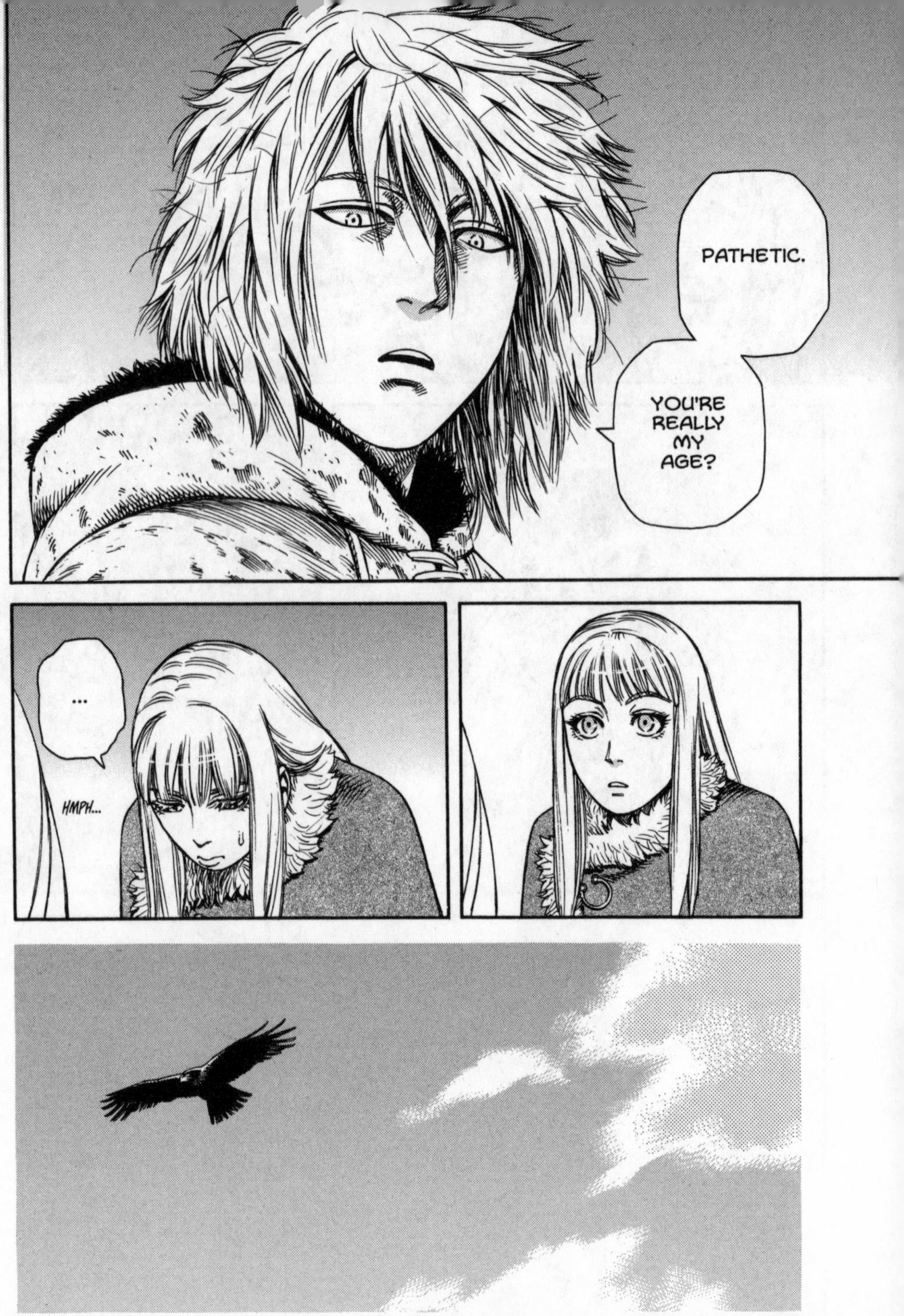
PATHETIC.
YOU'RE REALLY MY AGE?
...
HMPH...

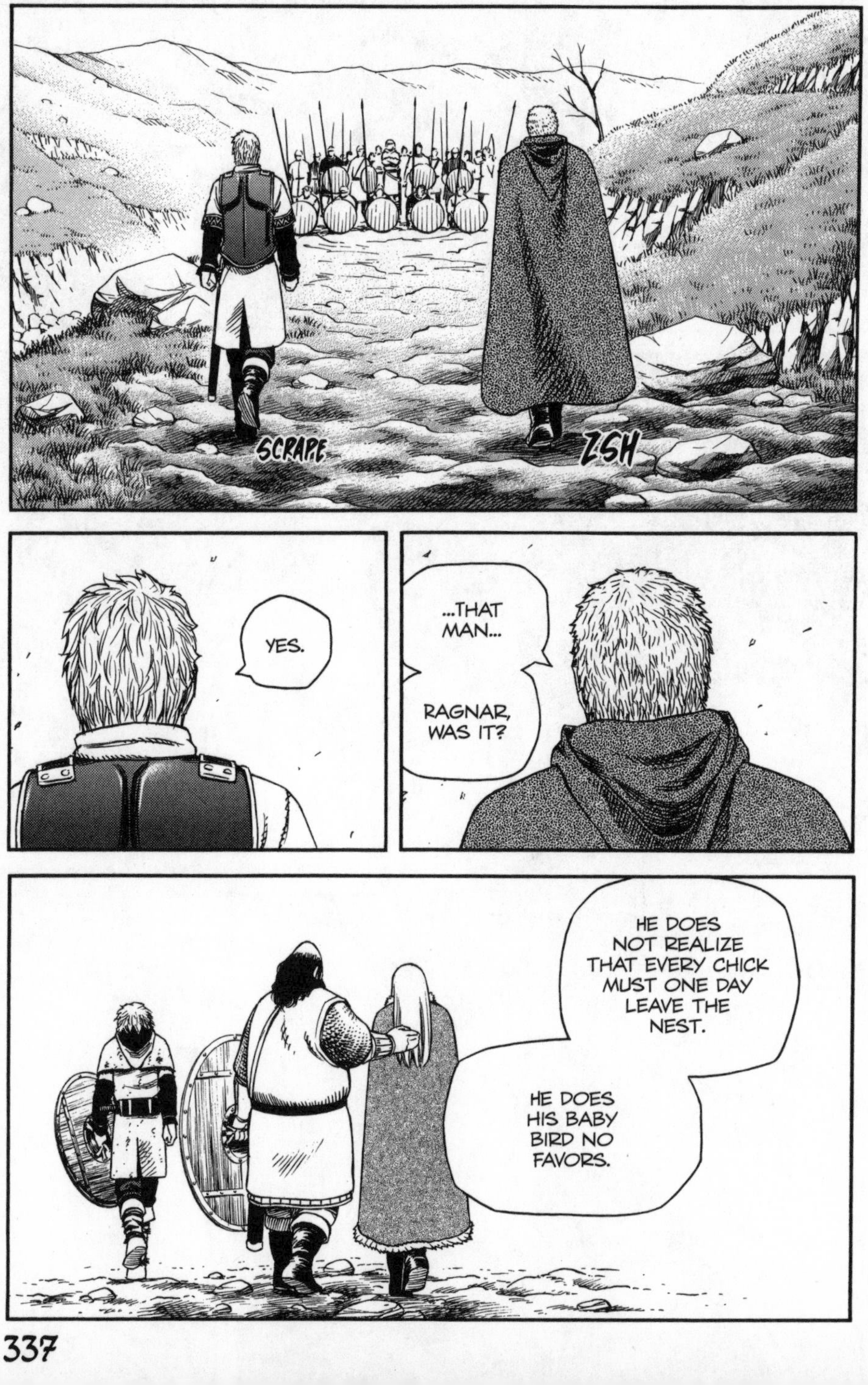
ZSH
SCRAPE
...THAT MAN...
RAGNAR, WAS IT?
YES.
HE DOES NOT REALIZE THAT EVERY CHICK MUST ONE DAY LEAVE THE NEST.
HE DOES HIS BABY BIRD NO FAVORS.

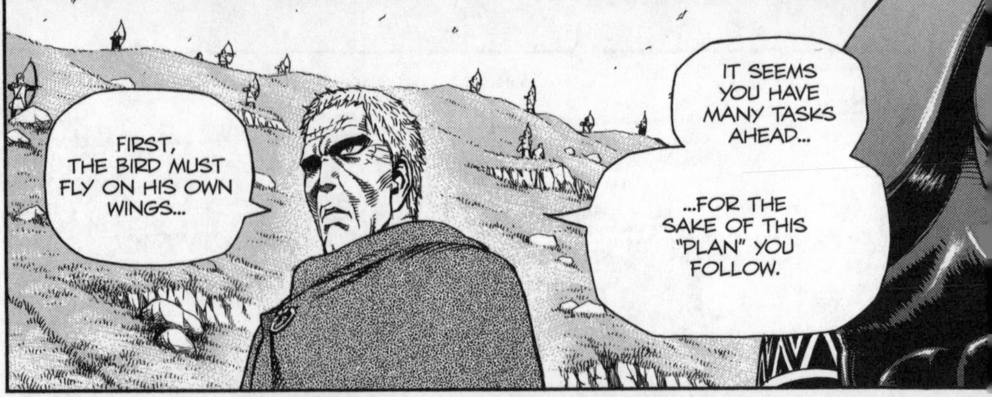
IT SEEMS YOU HAVE MANY TASKS AHEAD...
...FOR THE SAKE OF THIS "PLAN" YOU FOLLOW.
FIRST, THE BIRD MUST FLY ON HIS OWN WINGS...

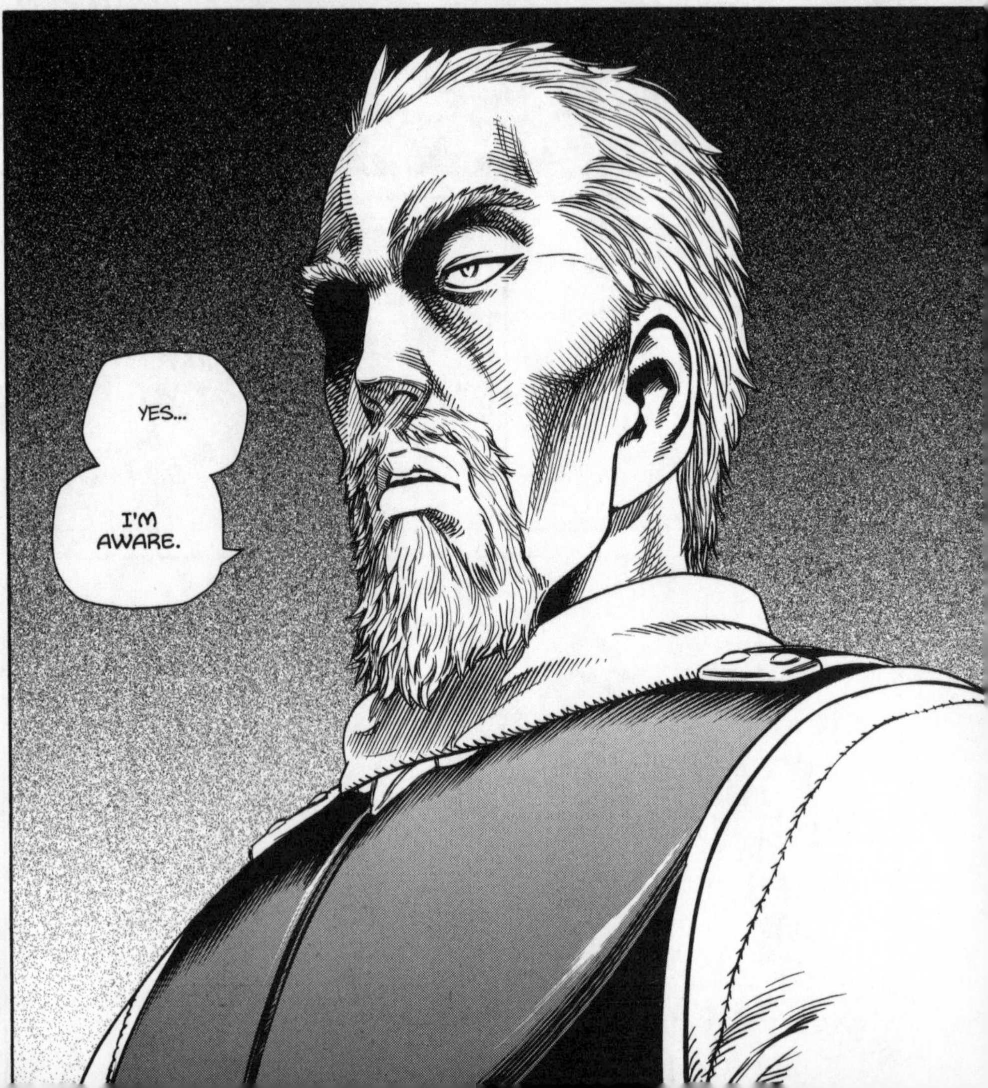
YES...
I'M AWARE.

CHAPTER 25 - END

CHAPTER 26: ARTORIUS

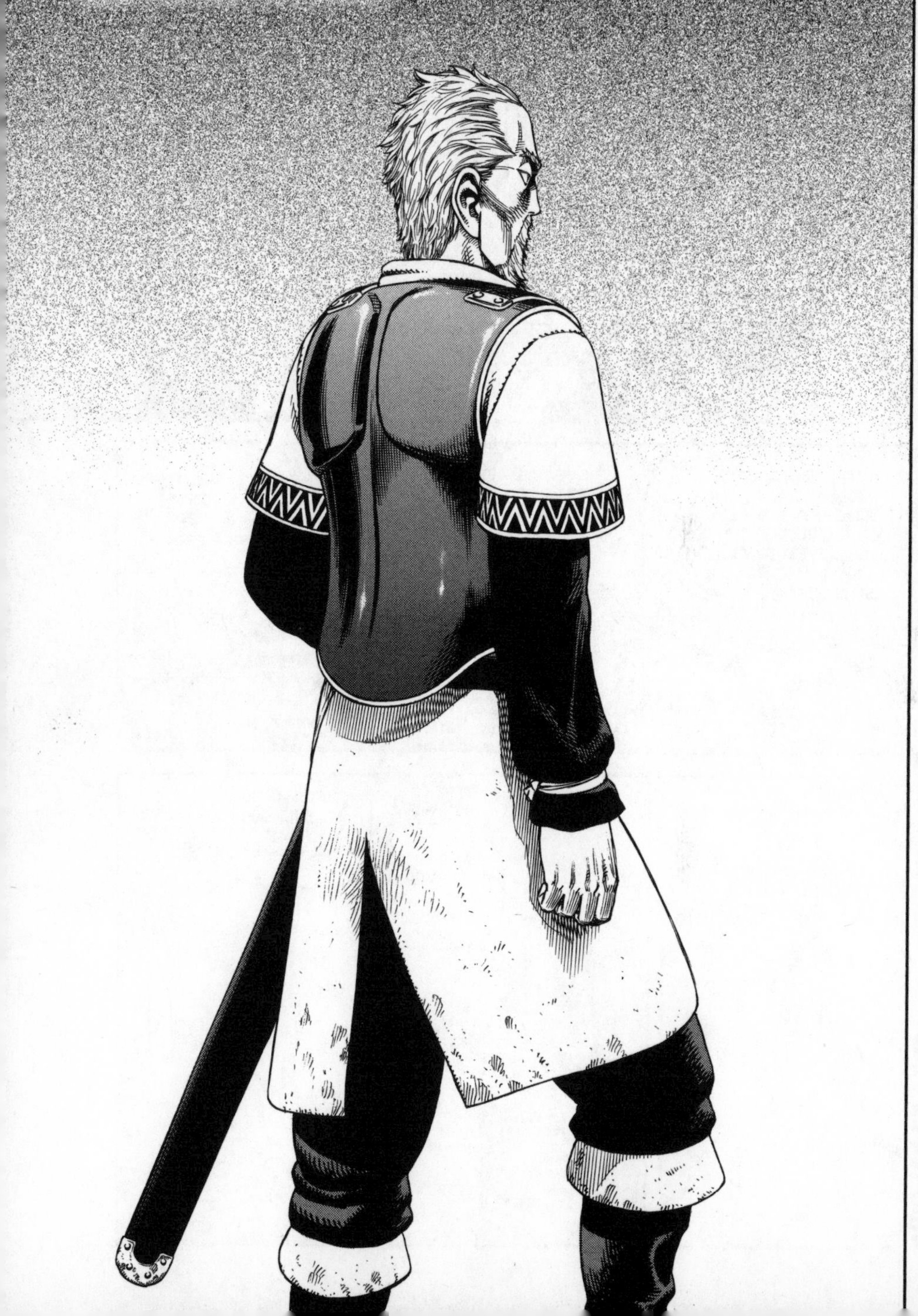

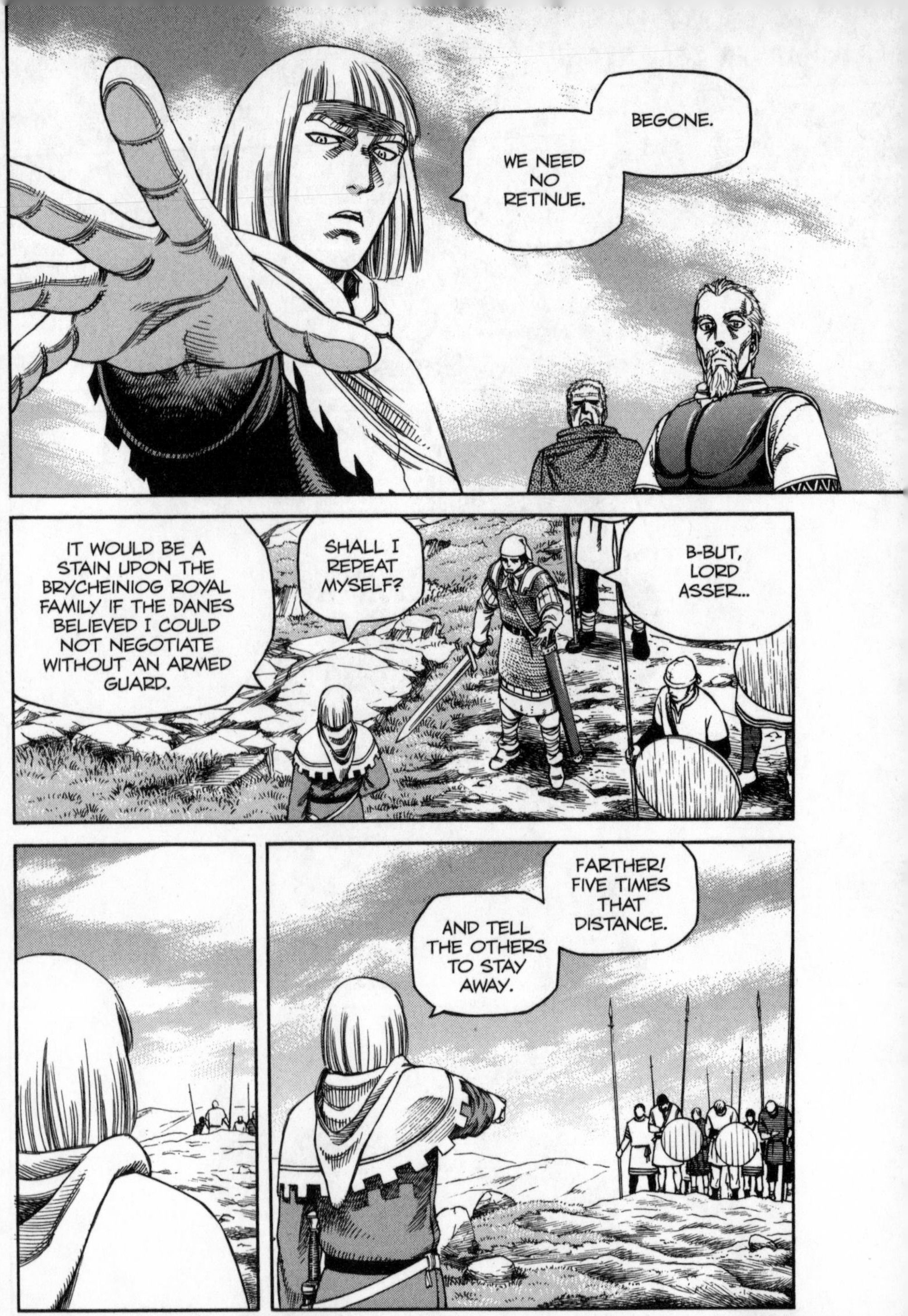
BEGONE. WE NEED NO RETINUE.
B-BUT, LORD ASSER...
SHALL I REPEAT MYSELF?
IT WOULD BE A STAIN UPON THE BRYCHEINIOG ROYAL FAMILY IF THE DANES BELIEVED I COULD NOT NEGOTIATE WITHOUT AN ARMED GUARD.
FARTHER! FIVE TIMES THAT DISTANCE.
AND TELL THE OTHERS TO STAY AWAY.

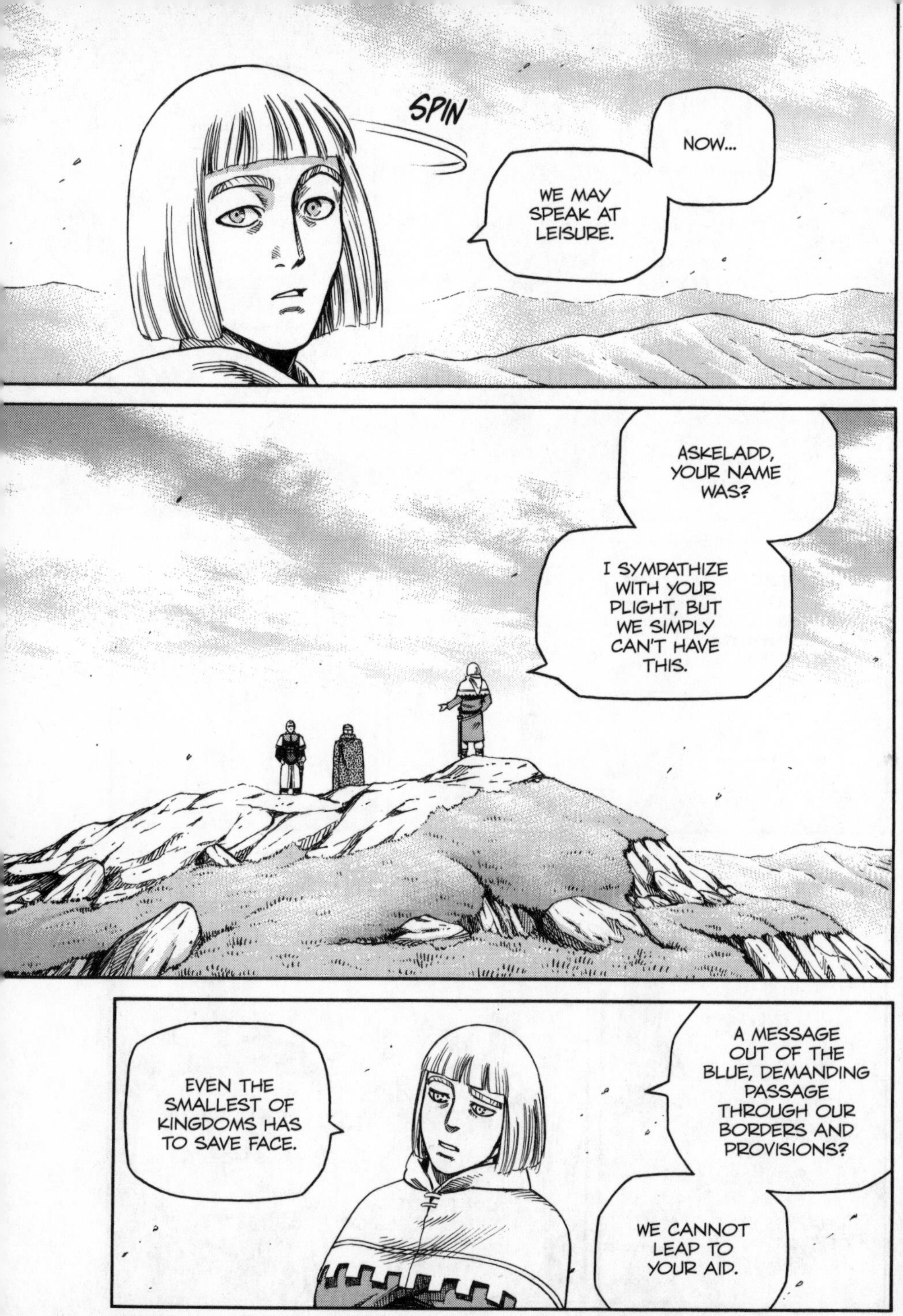
SPIN
NOW...
WE MAY SPEAK AT LEISURE.
ASKELADD, YOUR NAME WAS?
I SYMPATHIZE WITH YOUR PLIGHT, BUT WE SIMPLY CAN'T HAVE THIS.
A MESSAGE OUT OF THE BLUE, DEMANDING PASSAGE THROUGH OUR BORDERS AND PROVISIONS?
WE CANNOT LEAP TO YOUR AID.
EVEN THE SMALLEST OF KINGDOMS HAS TO SAVE FACE.

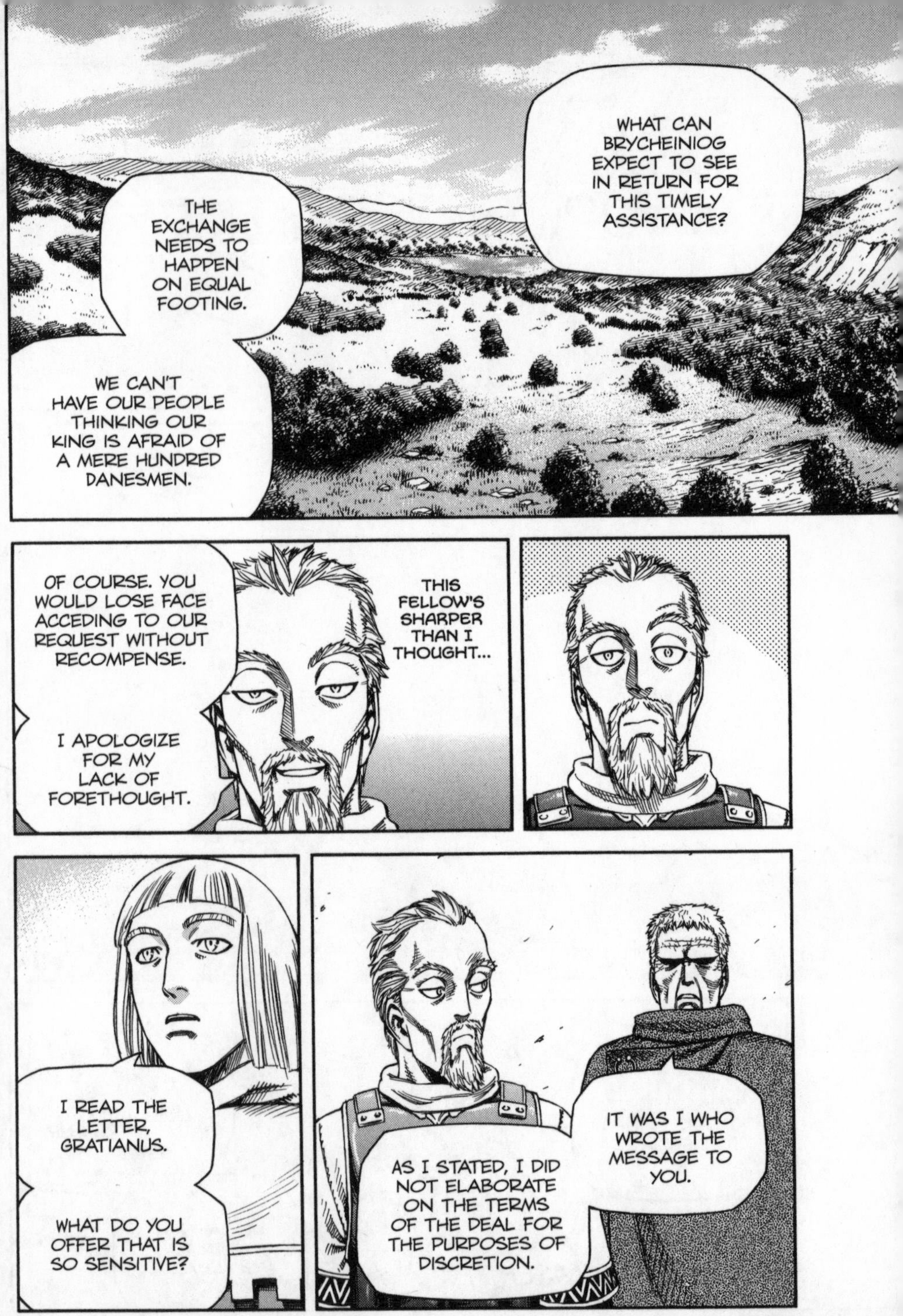
WHAT CAN BRYCHEINIOG EXPECT TO SEE IN RETURN FOR THIS TIMELY ASSISTANCE?
THE EXCHANGE NEEDS TO HAPPEN ON EQUAL FOOTING.
WE CAN'T HAVE OUR PEOPLE THINKING OUR KING IS AFRAID OF A MERE HUNDRED DANESMEN.
THIS FELLOW'S SHARPER THAN I THOUGHT...
OF COURSE. YOU WOULD LOSE FACE ACCEDING TO OUR REQUEST WITHOUT RECOMPENSE.
I APOLOGIZE FOR MY LACK OF FORETHOUGHT.
IT WAS I WHO WROTE THE MESSAGE TO YOU.
AS I STATED, I DID NOT ELABORATE ON THE TERMS OF THE DEAL FOR THE PURPOSES OF DISCRETION.
I READ THE LETTER, GRATIANUS.
WHAT DO YOU OFFER THAT IS SO SENSITIVE?

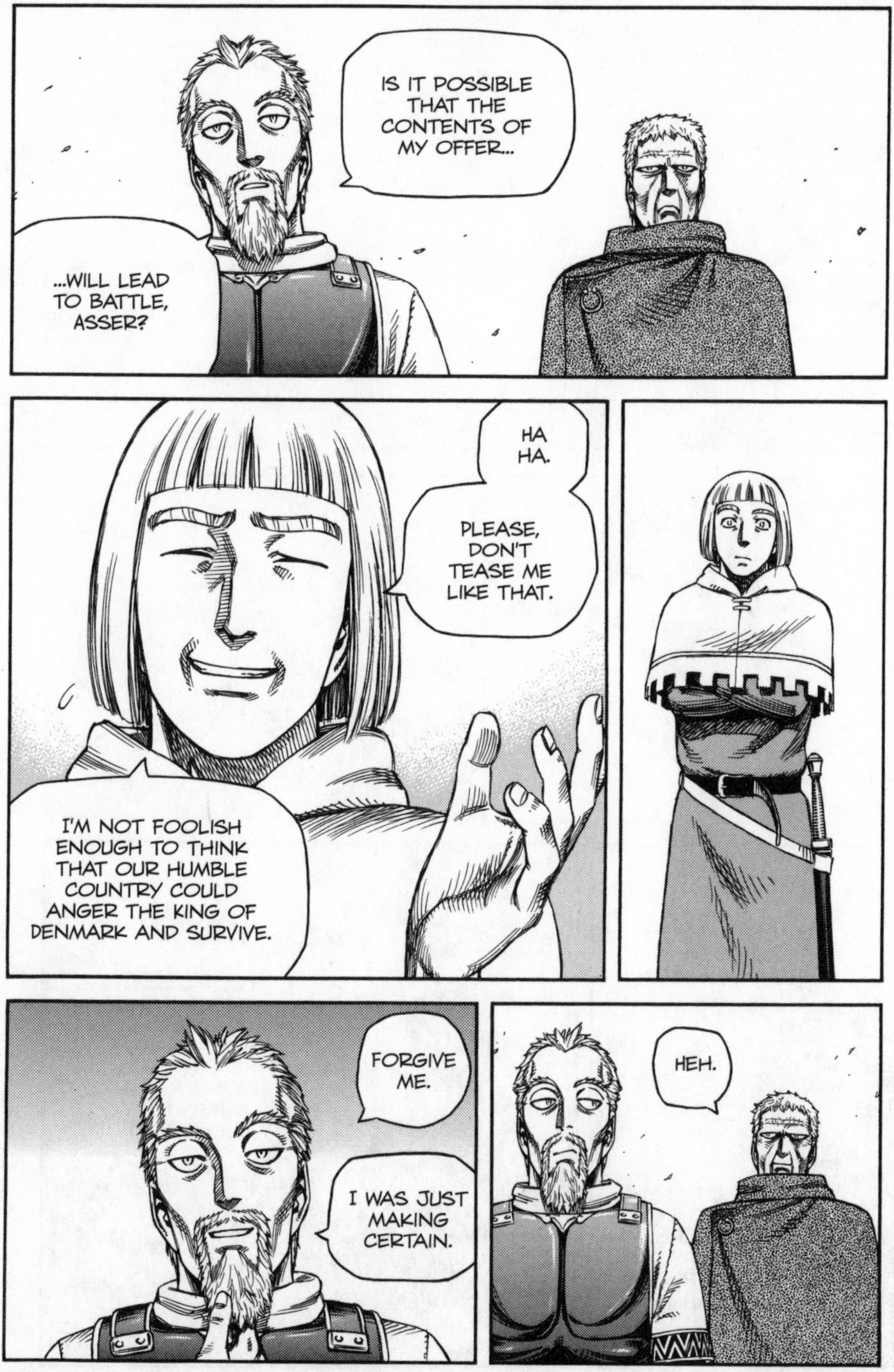
IS IT POSSIBLE THAT THE CONTENTS OF MY OFFER...
...WILL LEAD TO BATTLE, ASSER?
HA HA.
PLEASE, DON'T TEASE ME LIKE THAT.
I'M NOT FOOLISH ENOUGH TO THINK THAT OUR HUMBLE COUNTRY COULD ANGER THE KING OF DENMARK AND SURVIVE.
HEH.
FORGIVE ME.
I WAS JUST MAKING CERTAIN.

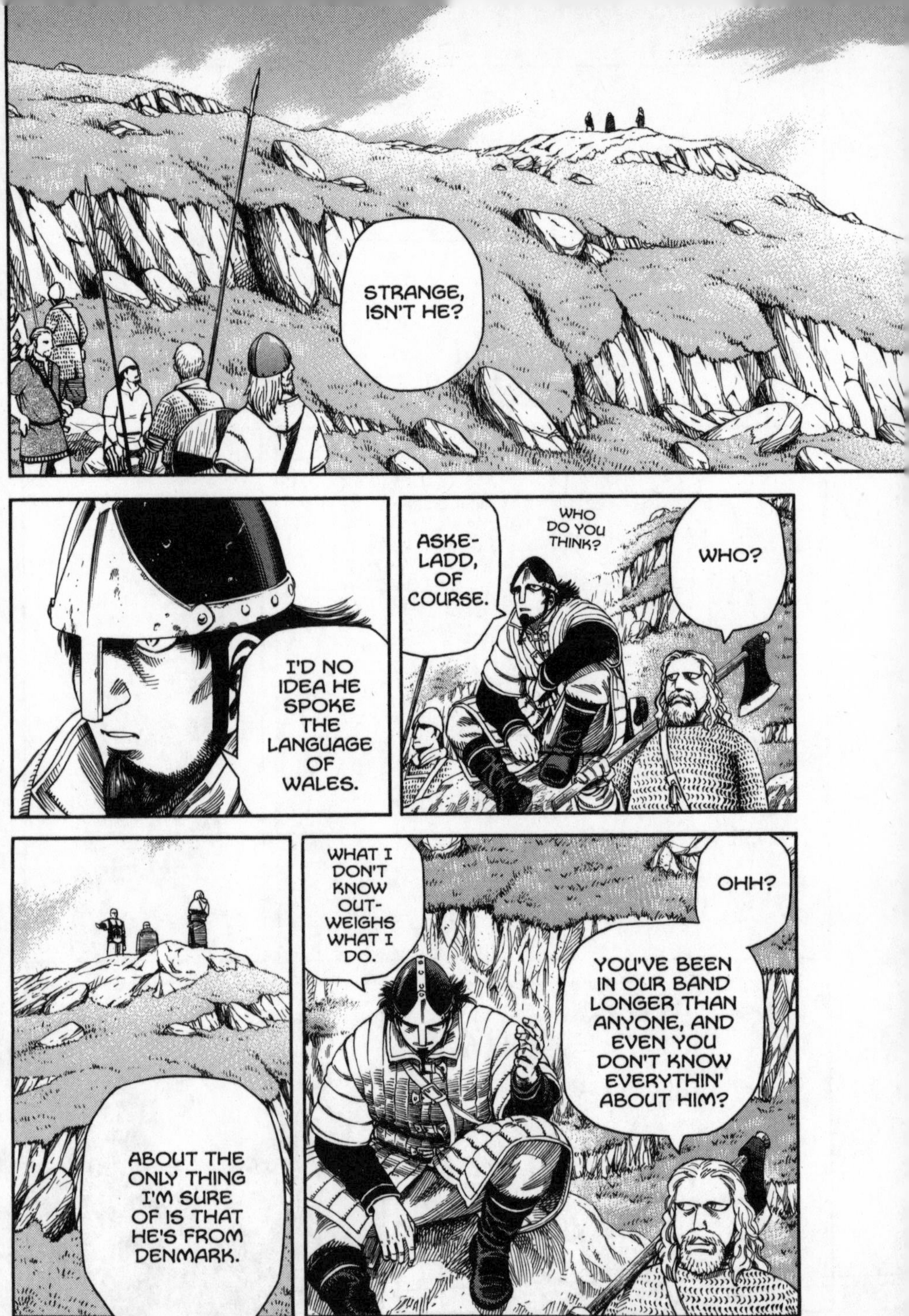
STRANGE, ISN'T HE?
WHO?
WHO DO YOU THINK?
ASKE-LADD, OF COURSE.
I'D NO IDEA HE SPOKE THE LANGUAGE OF WALES.
OHH?
WHAT I DON'T KNOW OUT-WEIGHS WHAT I DO.
YOU'VE BEEN IN OUR BAND LONGER THAN ANYONE, AND EVEN YOU DON'T KNOW EVERYTHIN' ABOUT HIM?
ABOUT THE ONLY THING I'M SURE OF IS THAT HE'S FROM DENMARK.

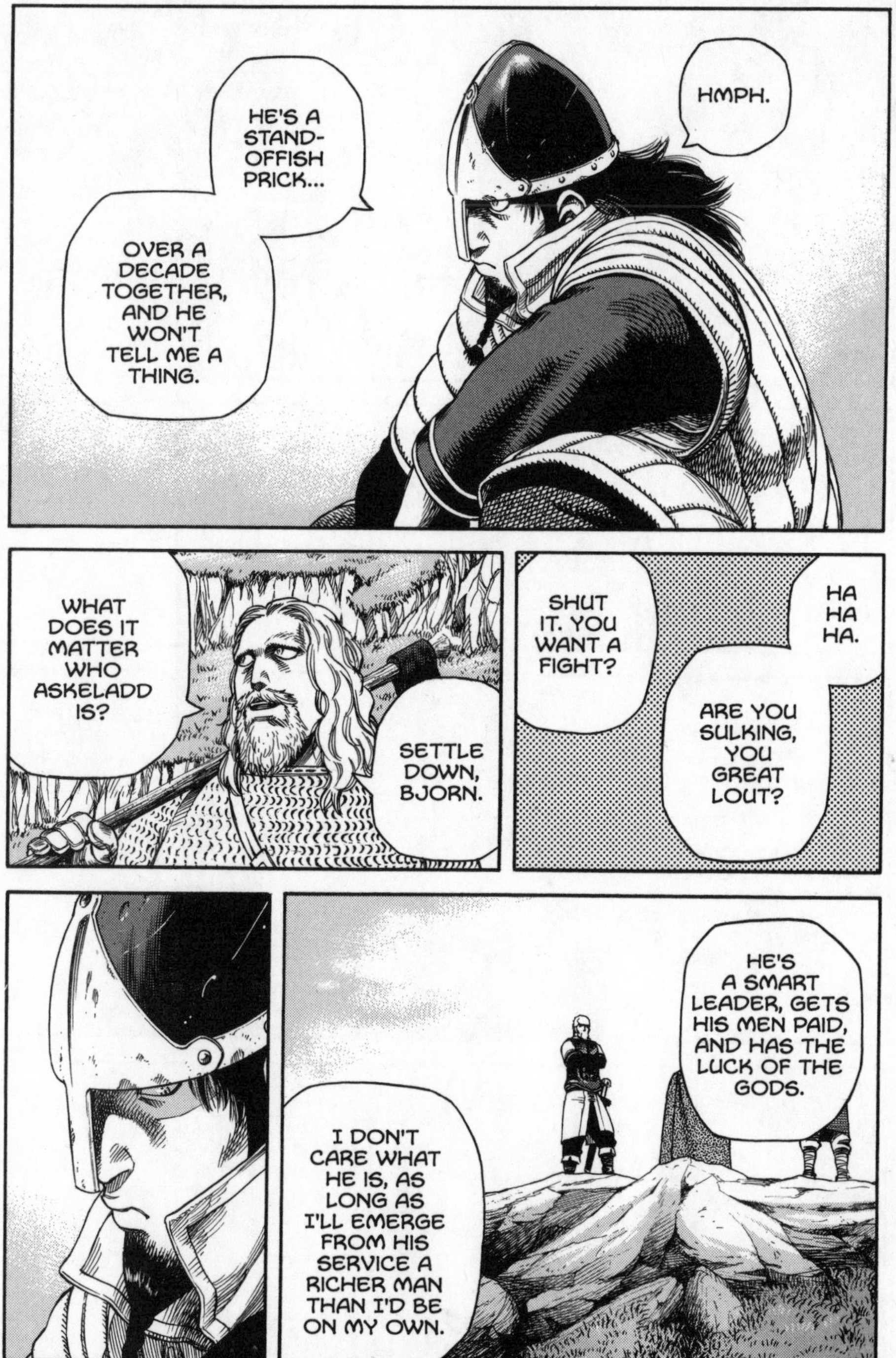
HMPH.
HE'S A STAND-OFFISH PRICK...
OVER A DECADE TOGETHER, AND HE WON'T TELL ME A THING.
HA HA HA.
SHUT IT. YOU WANT A FIGHT?
ARE YOU SULKING, YOU GREAT LOUT?
SETTLE DOWN, BJORN.
WHAT DOES IT MATTER WHO ASKELADD IS?
HE'S A SMART LEADER, GETS HIS MEN PAID, AND HAS THE LUCK OF THE GODS.
I DON'T CARE WHAT HE IS, AS LONG AS I'LL EMERGE FROM HIS SERVICE A RICHER MAN THAN I'D BE ON MY OWN.

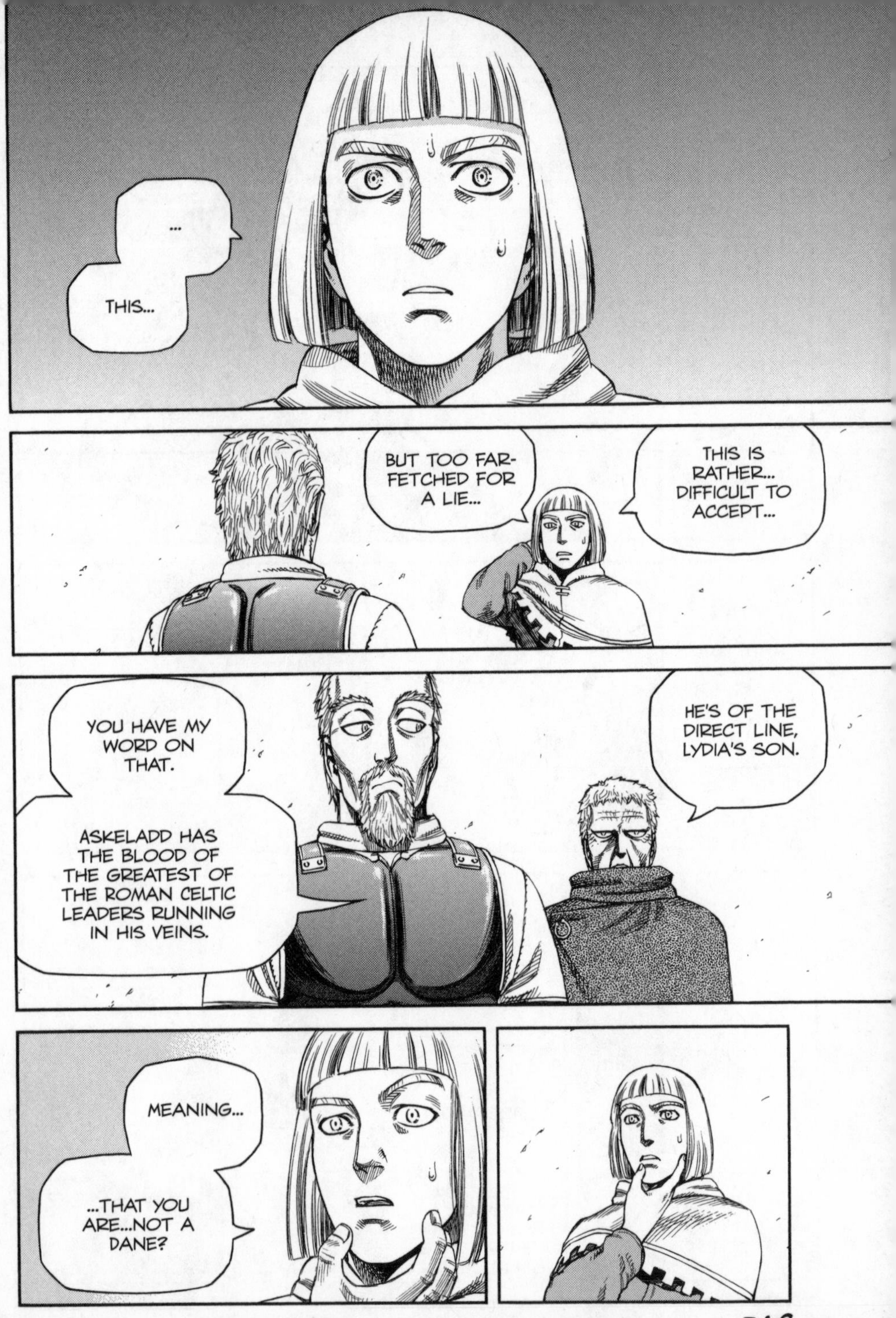
...
THIS...
THIS IS RATHER... DIFFICULT TO ACCEPT...
BUT TOO FAR-FETCHED FOR A LIE...
HE'S OF THE DIRECT LINE, LYDIA'S SON.
YOU HAVE MY WORD ON THAT.
ASKELADD HAS THE BLOOD OF THE GREATEST OF THE ROMAN CELTIC LEADERS RUNNING IN HIS VEINS.
MEANING...
...THAT YOU ARE...NOT A DANE?

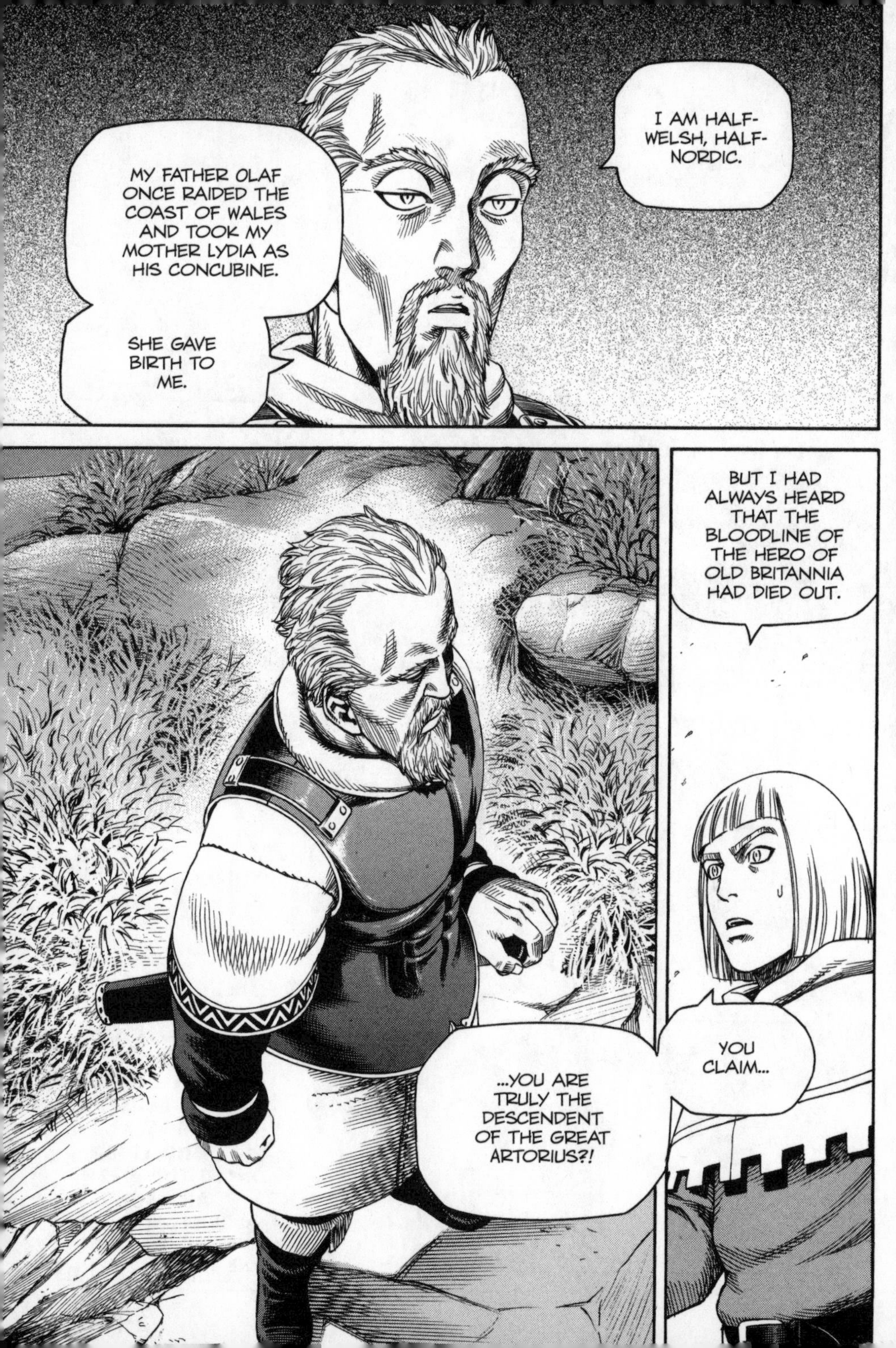
I AM HALF-WELSH, HALF-NORDIC.
MY FATHER OLAF ONCE RAIDED THE COAST OF WALES AND TOOK MY MOTHER LYDIA AS HIS CONCUBINE.
SHE GAVE BIRTH TO ME.
BUT I HAD ALWAYS HEARD THAT THE BLOODLINE OF THE HERO OF OLD BRITANNIA HAD DIED OUT.
YOU CLAIM...
...YOU ARE TRULY THE DESCENDENT OF THE GREAT ARTORIUS?!

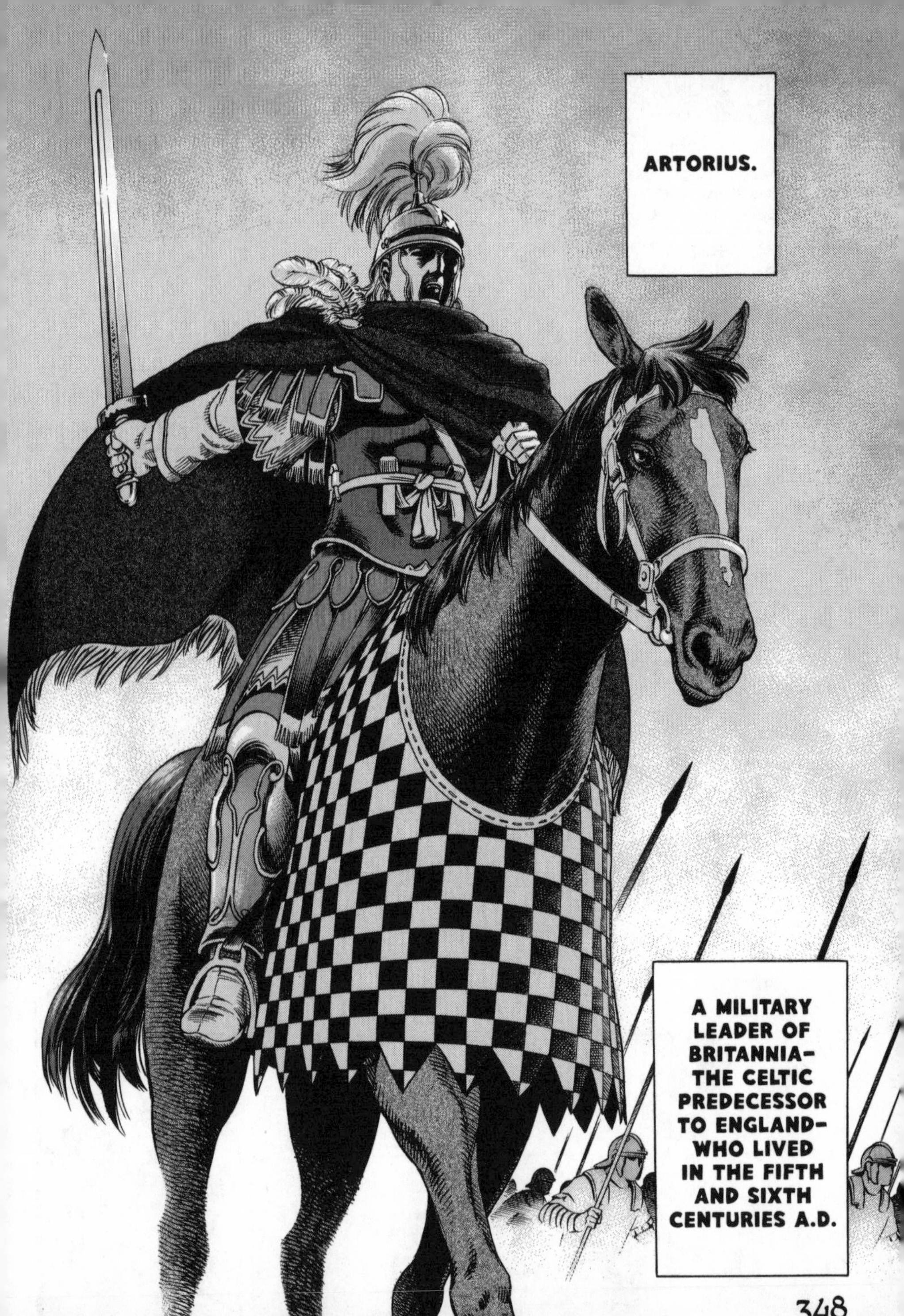
ARTORIUS.
A MILITARY LEADER OF BRITANNIA—THE CELTIC PREDECESSOR TO ENGLAND—WHO LIVED IN THE FIFTH AND SIXTH CENTURIES A.D.

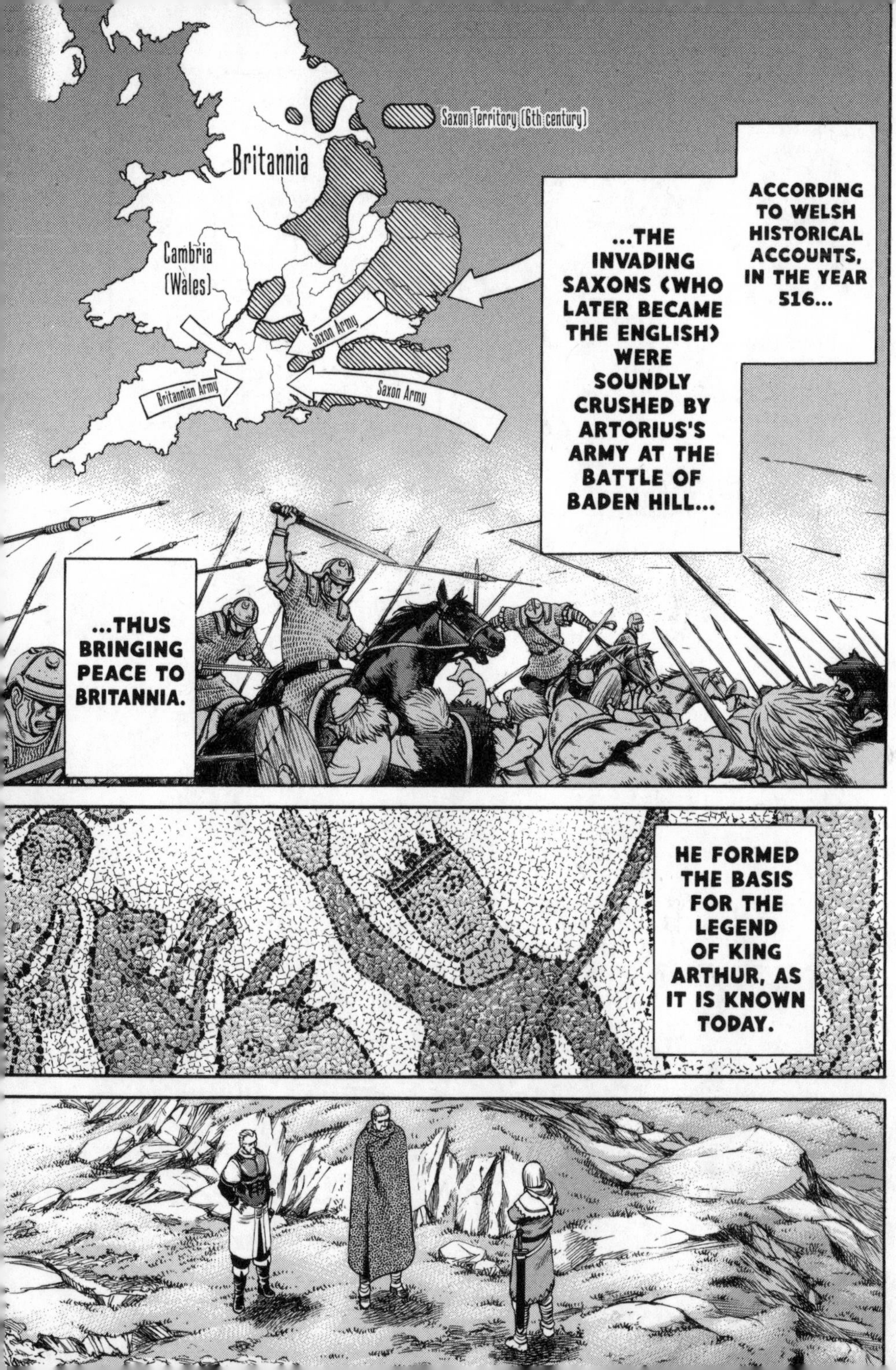
ACCORDING TO WELSH HISTORICAL ACCOUNTS, IN THE YEAR 516...
...THE INVADING SAXONS (WHO LATER BECAME THE ENGLISH) WERE SOUNDLY CRUSHED BY ARTORIUS'S ARMY AT THE BATTLE OF BADEN HILL...
Saxon Territory (6th century)
Britannia
Cambria (Wales)
Saxon Army
Britannian Army
Saxon Army
...THUS BRINGING PEACE TO BRITANNIA.
HE FORMED THE BASIS FOR THE LEGEND OF KING ARTHUR, AS IT IS KNOWN TODAY.

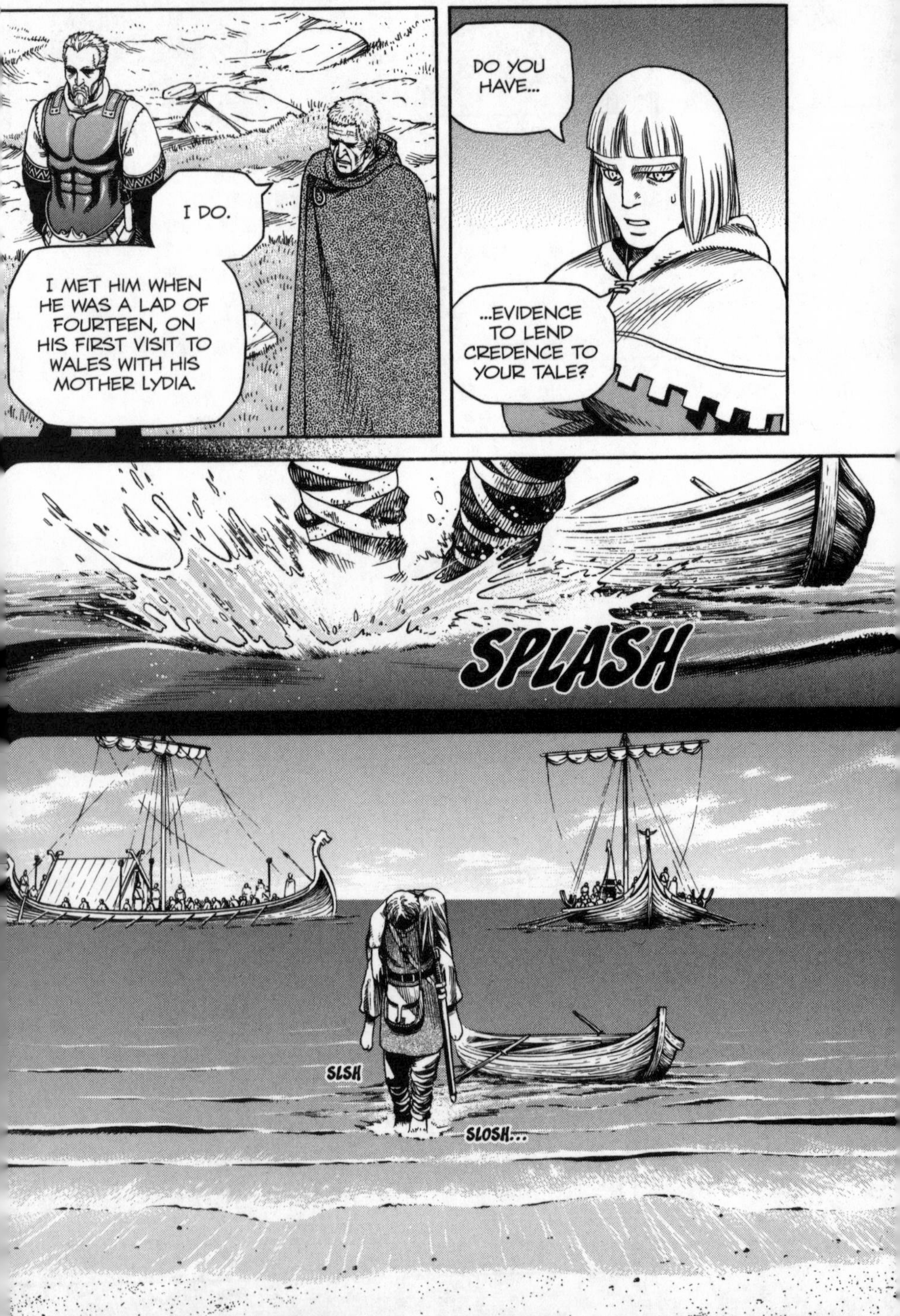
DO YOU HAVE...
...EVIDENCE TO LEND CREDENCE TO YOUR TALE?
I DO.
I MET HIM WHEN HE WAS A LAD OF FOURTEEN, ON HIS FIRST VISIT TO WALES WITH HIS MOTHER LYDIA.
SPLASH
SLSH
SLOSH...

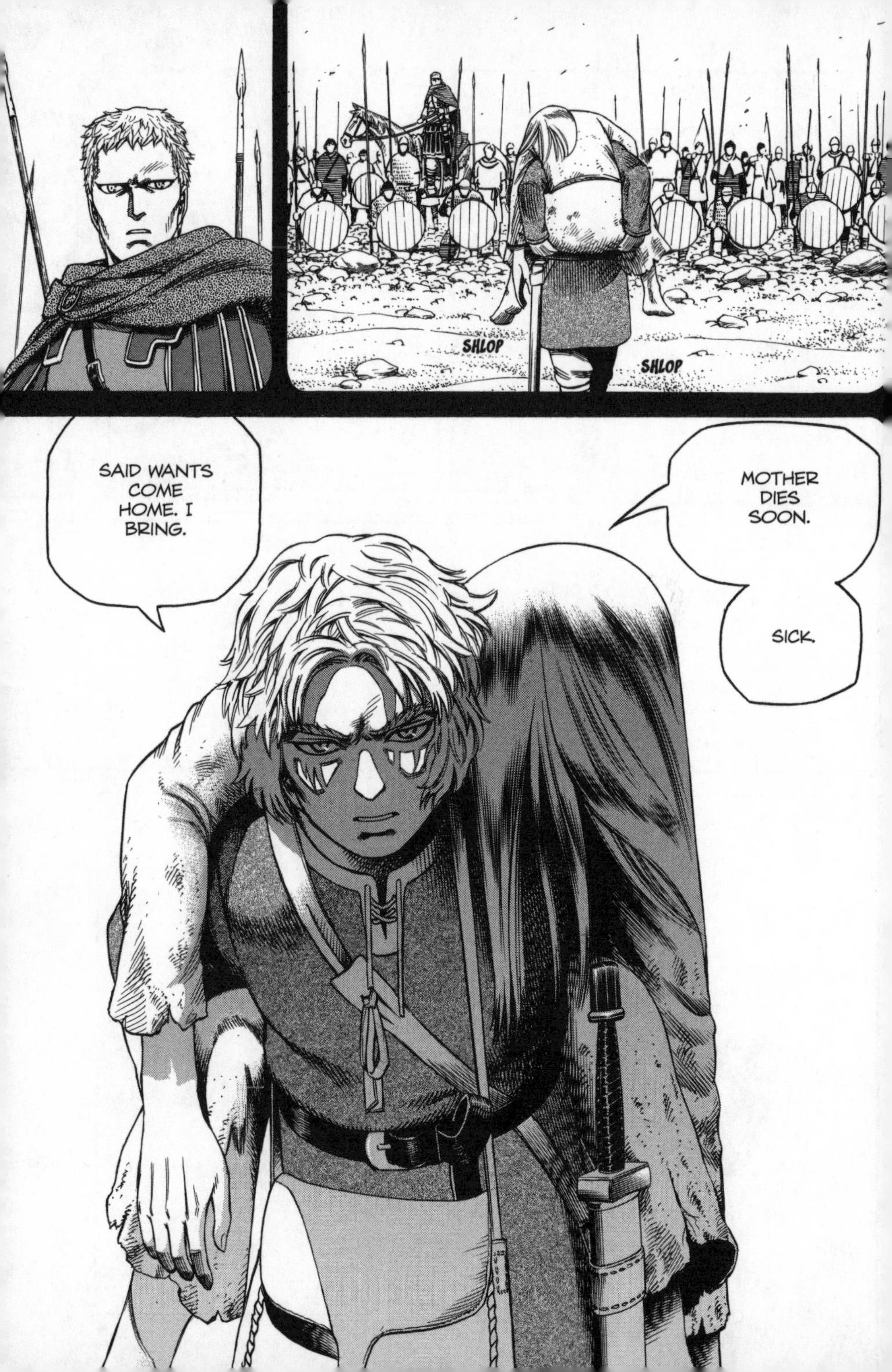
SHLOP
SHLOP
MOTHER DIES SOON.
SICK.
SAID WANTS COME HOME. I BRING.

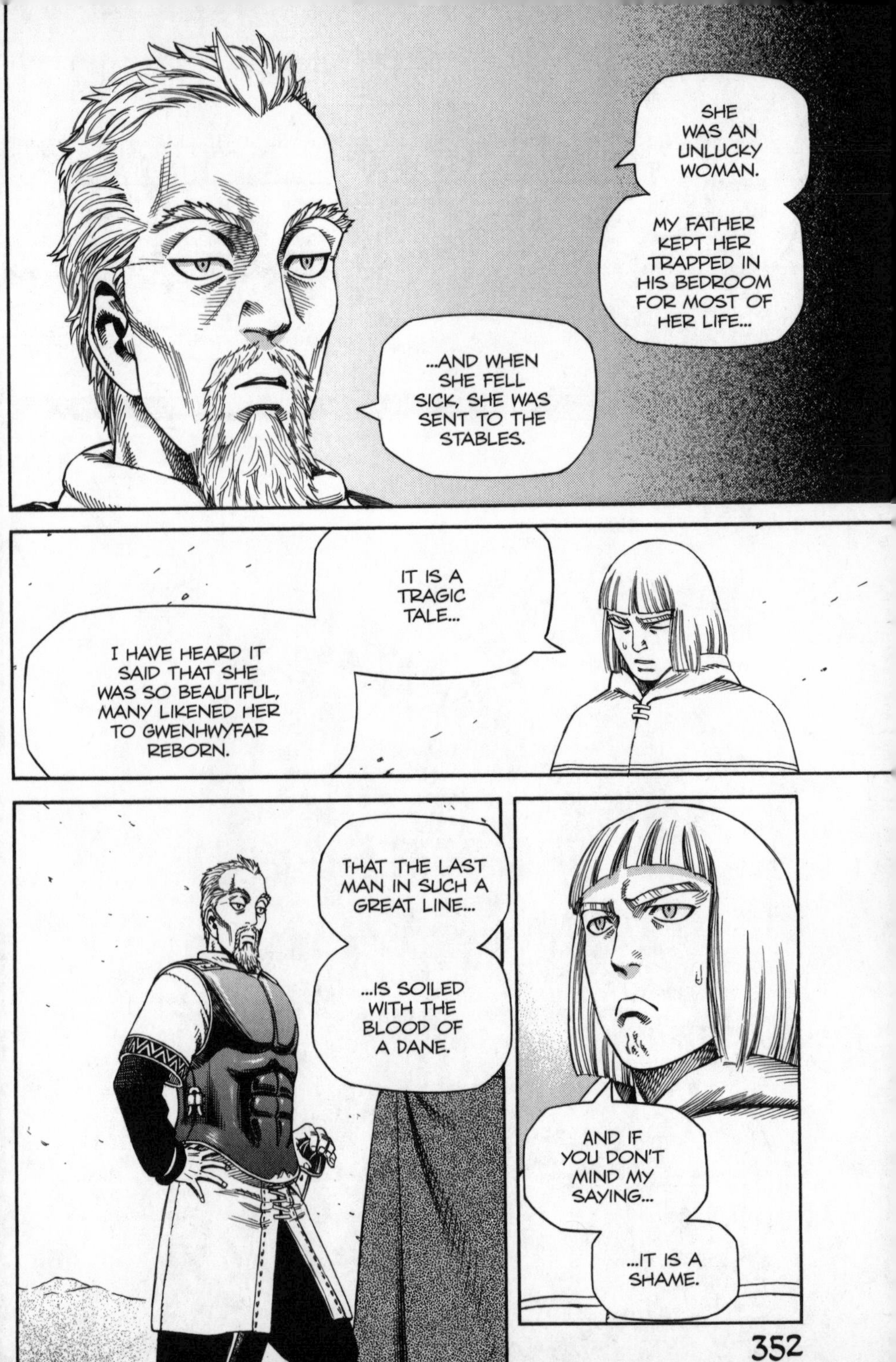
SHE WAS AN UNLUCKY WOMAN.
MY FATHER KEPT HER TRAPPED IN HIS BEDROOM FOR MOST OF HER LIFE...
...AND WHEN SHE FELL SICK, SHE WAS SENT TO THE STABLES.
IT IS A TRAGIC TALE...
I HAVE HEARD IT SAID THAT SHE WAS SO BEAUTIFUL, MANY LIKENED HER TO GWENHWYFAR REBORN.
AND IF YOU DON'T MIND MY SAYING...
...IT IS A SHAME.
THAT THE LAST MAN IN SUCH A GREAT LINE...
...IS SOILED WITH THE BLOOD OF A DANE.

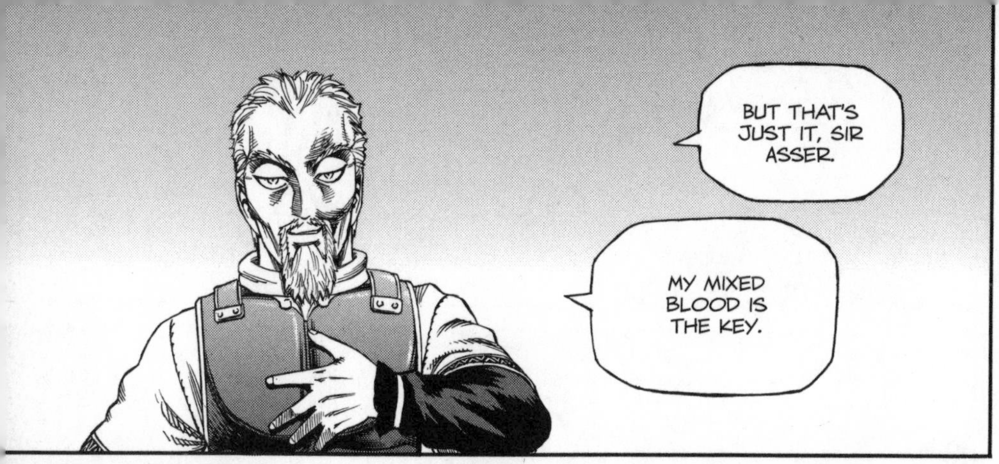
BUT THAT'S JUST IT, SIR ASSER.
MY MIXED BLOOD IS THE KEY.
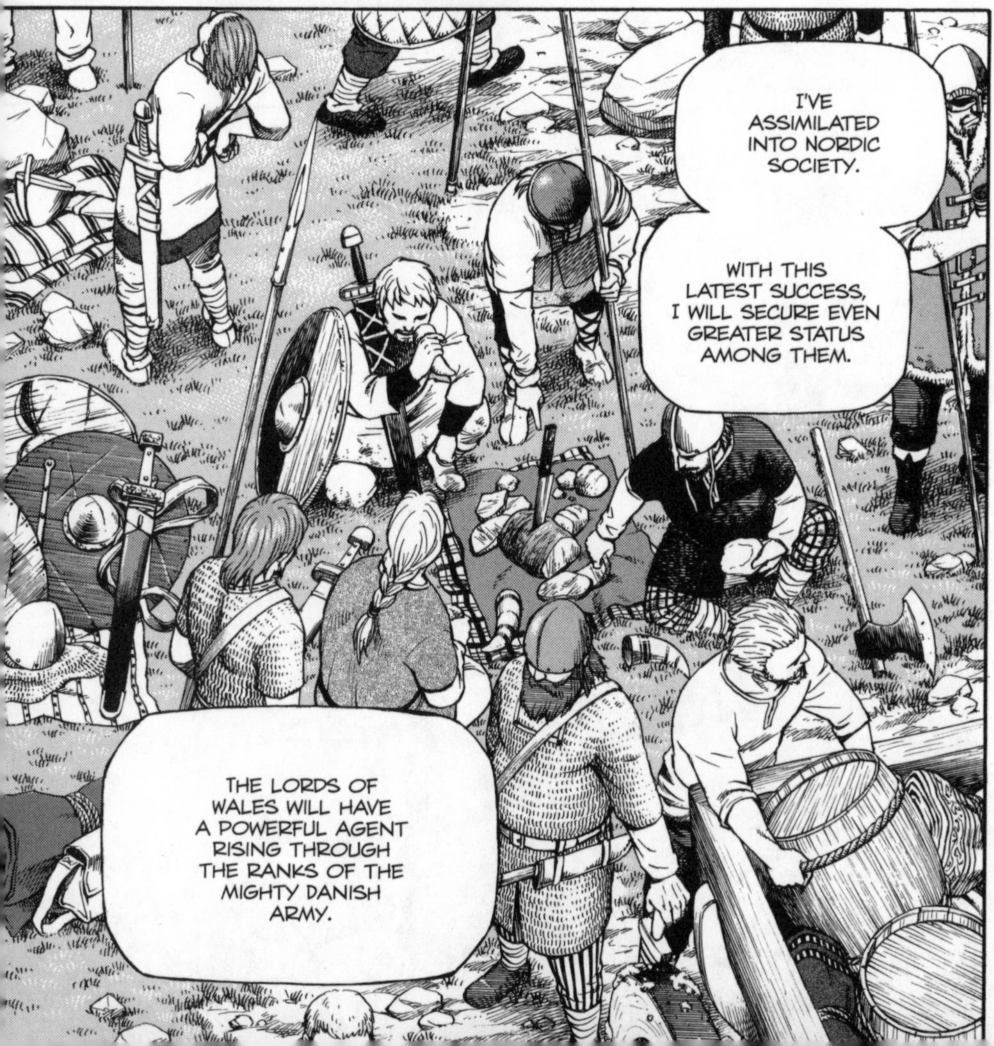
I'VE ASSIMILATED INTO NORDIC SOCIETY.
WITH THIS LATEST SUCCESS, I WILL SECURE EVEN GREATER STATUS AMONG THEM.
THE LORDS OF WALES WILL HAVE A POWERFUL AGENT RISING THROUGH THE RANKS OF THE MIGHTY DANISH ARMY.

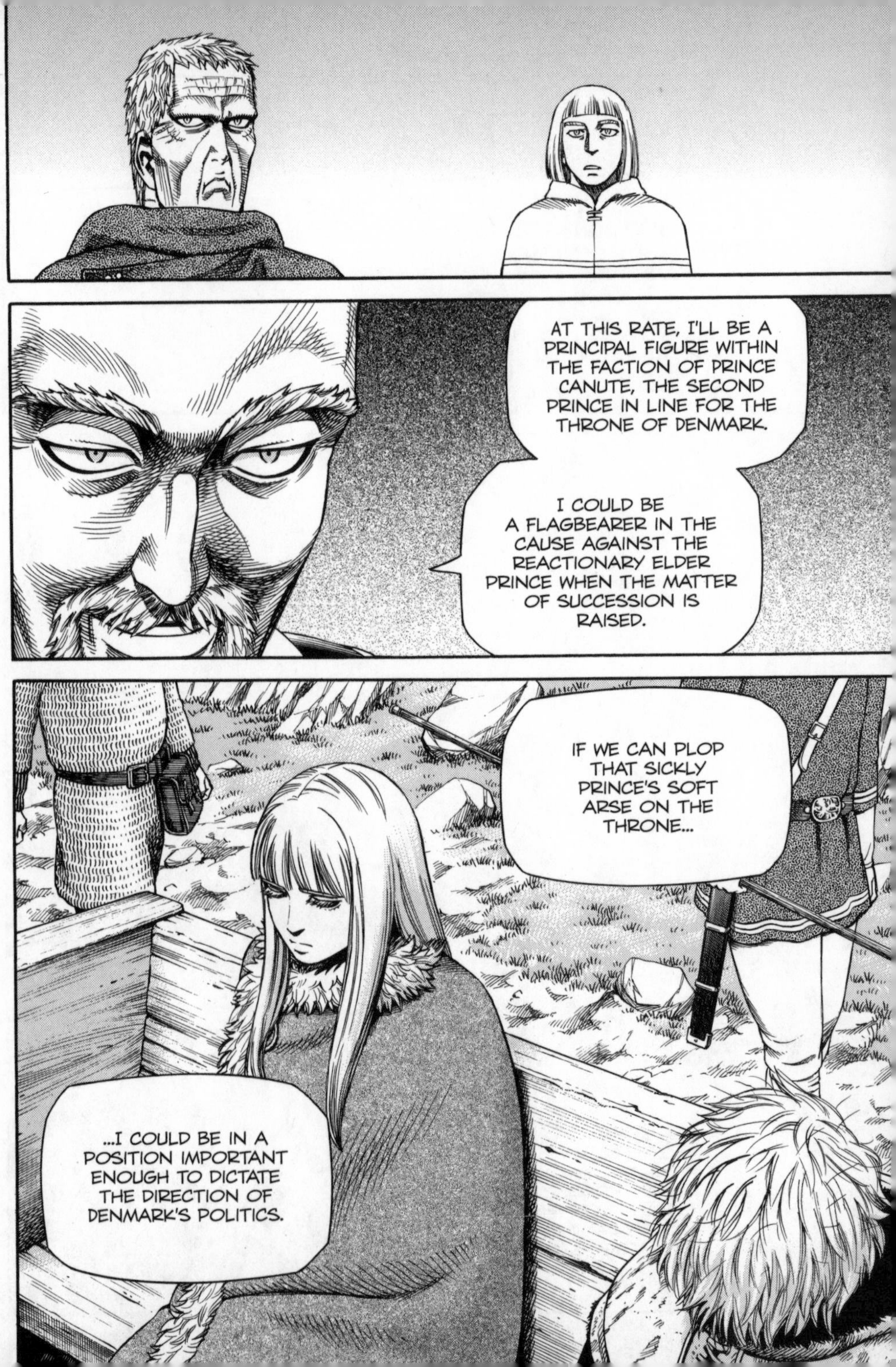
AT THIS RATE, I'LL BE A PRINCIPAL FIGURE WITHIN THE FACTION OF PRINCE CANUTE, THE SECOND PRINCE IN LINE FOR THE THRONE OF DENMARK.
I COULD BE A FLAGBEARER IN THE CAUSE AGAINST THE REACTIONARY ELDER PRINCE WHEN THE MATTER OF SUCCESSION IS RAISED.
IF WE CAN PLOP THAT SICKLY PRINCE'S SOFT ARSE ON THE THRONE...
...I COULD BE IN A POSITION IMPORTANT ENOUGH TO DICTATE THE DIRECTION OF DENMARK'S POLITICS.

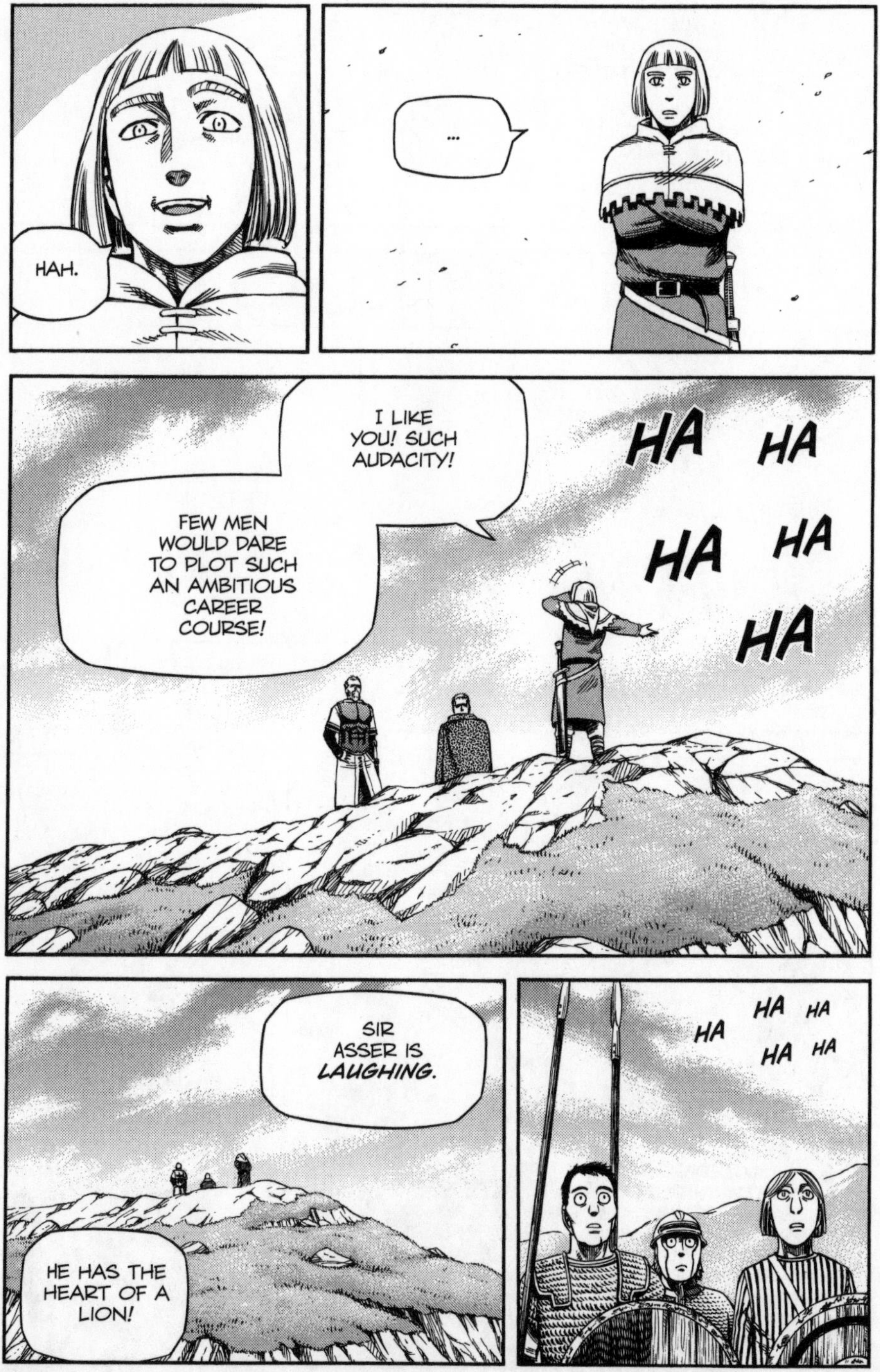
...
HAH.
I LIKE YOU! SUCH AUDACITY!
FEW MEN WOULD DARE TO PLOT SUCH AN AMBITIOUS CAREER COURSE!
HA HA HA HA HA
HA HA HA HA HA HA
SIR ASSER IS *LAUGHING.*
HE HAS THE HEART OF A LION!

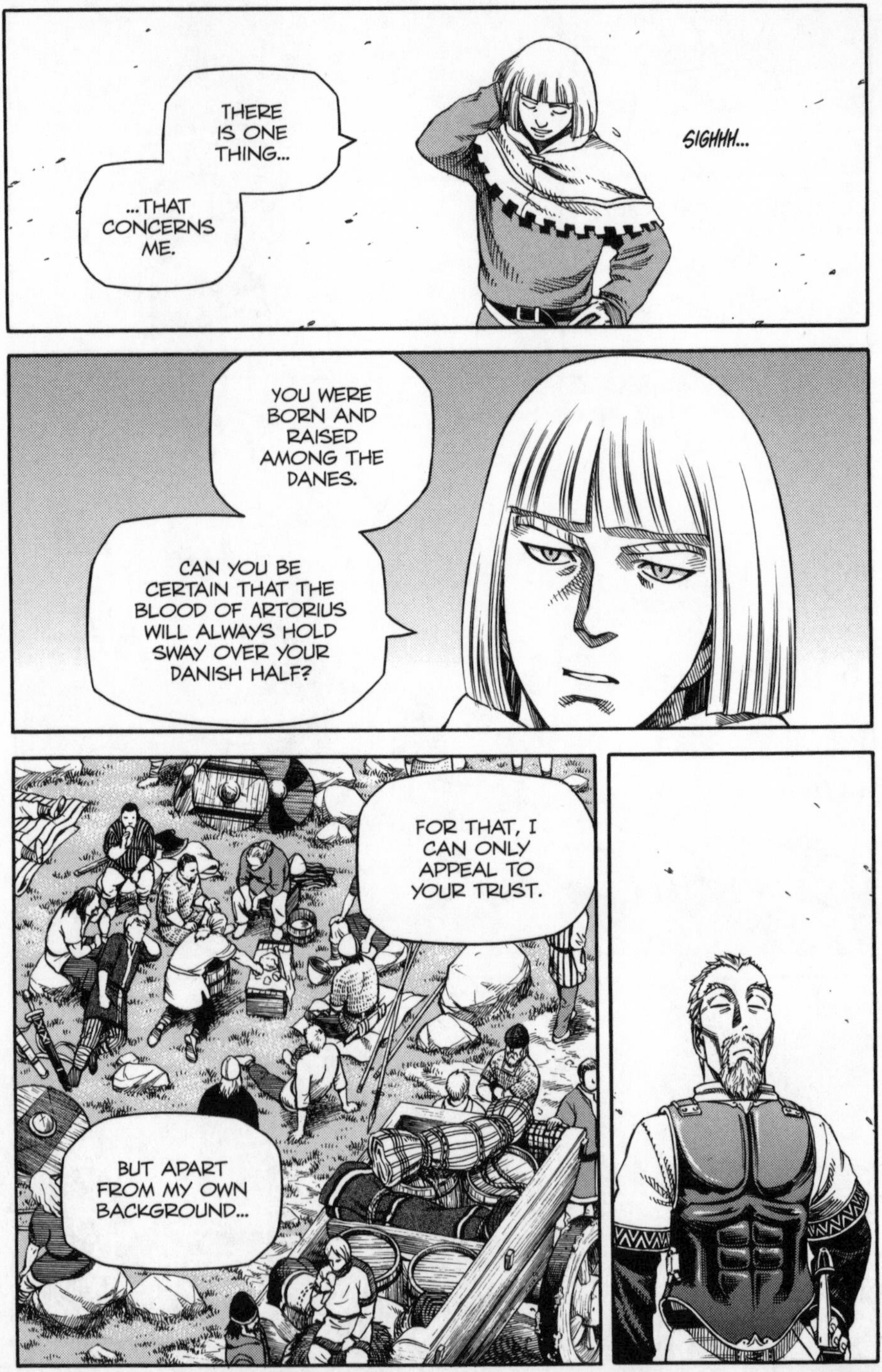
SIGHHH...
THERE IS ONE THING...
...THAT CONCERNS ME.
YOU WERE BORN AND RAISED AMONG THE DANES.
CAN YOU BE CERTAIN THAT THE BLOOD OF ARTORIUS WILL ALWAYS HOLD SWAY OVER YOUR DANISH HALF?
FOR THAT, I CAN ONLY APPEAL TO YOUR TRUST.
BUT APART FROM MY OWN BACKGROUND...

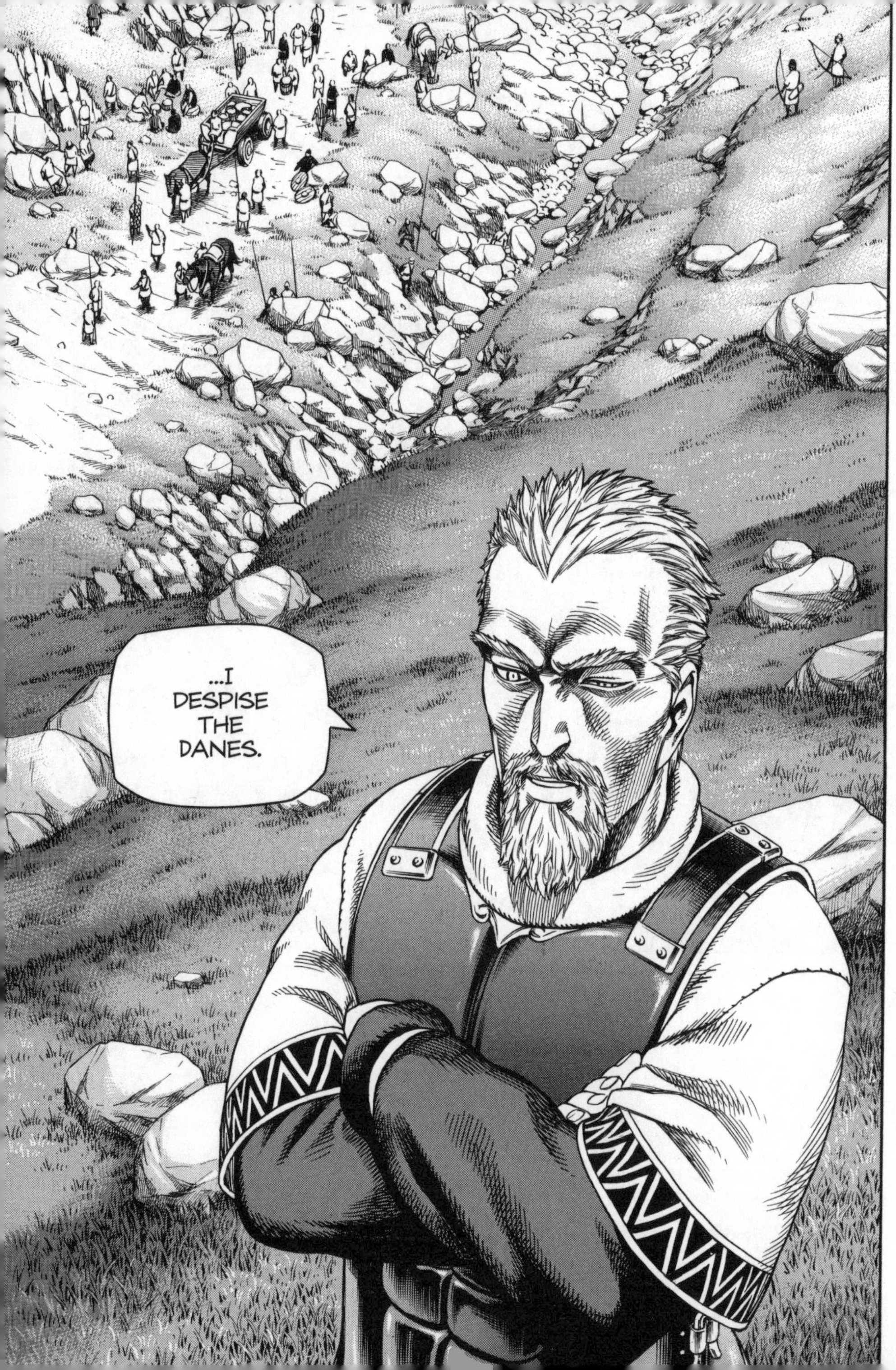
...I DESPISE THE DANES.

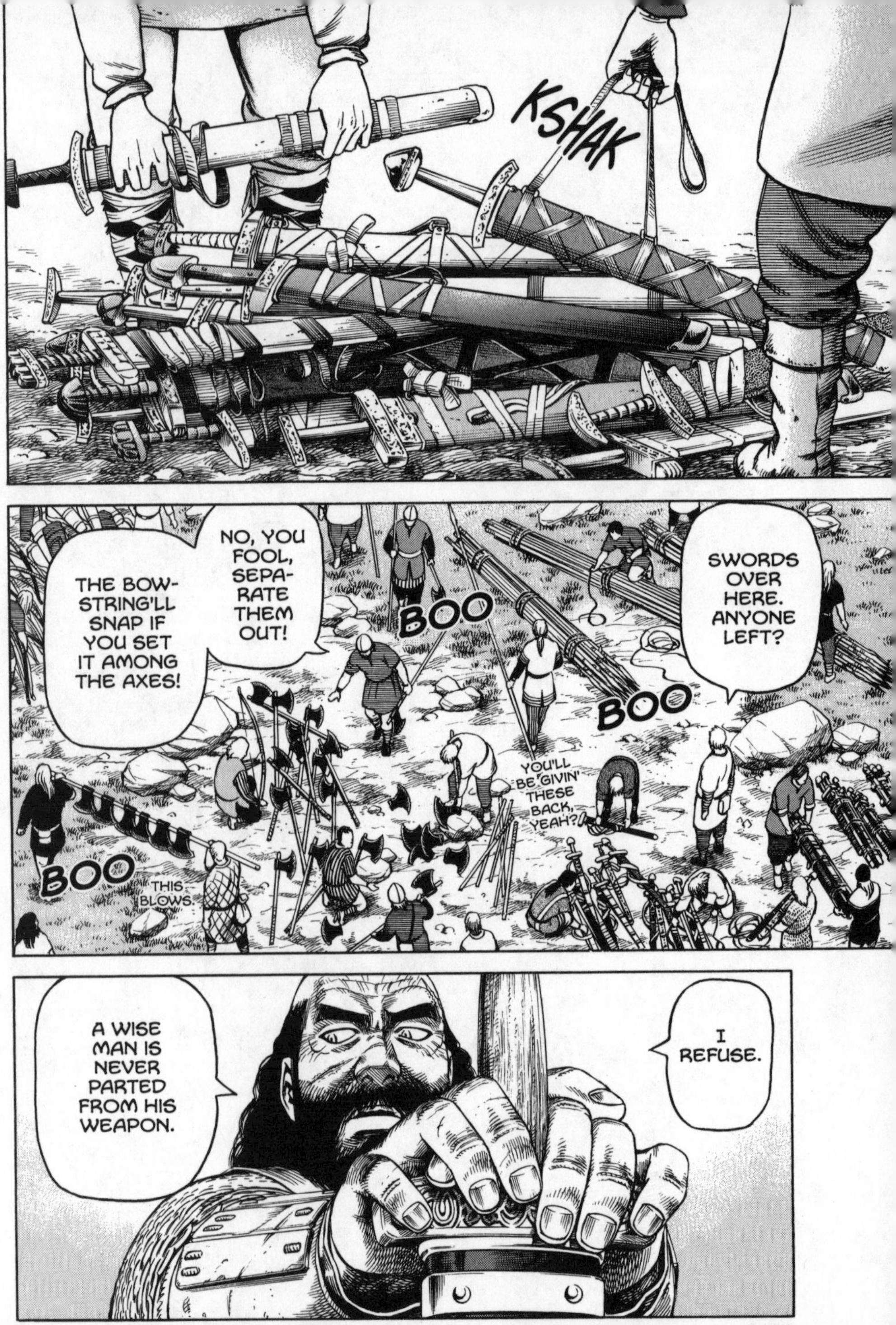
KSHAK
SWORDS OVER HERE. ANYONE LEFT?
BOO
YOU'LL BE GIVIN' THESE BACK, YEAH?
BOO
NO, YOU FOOL, SEPA-RATE THEM OUT!
THE BOW-STRING'LL SNAP IF YOU SET IT AMONG THE AXES!
BOO
THIS BLOWS.
I REFUSE.
A WISE MAN IS NEVER PARTED FROM HIS WEAPON.

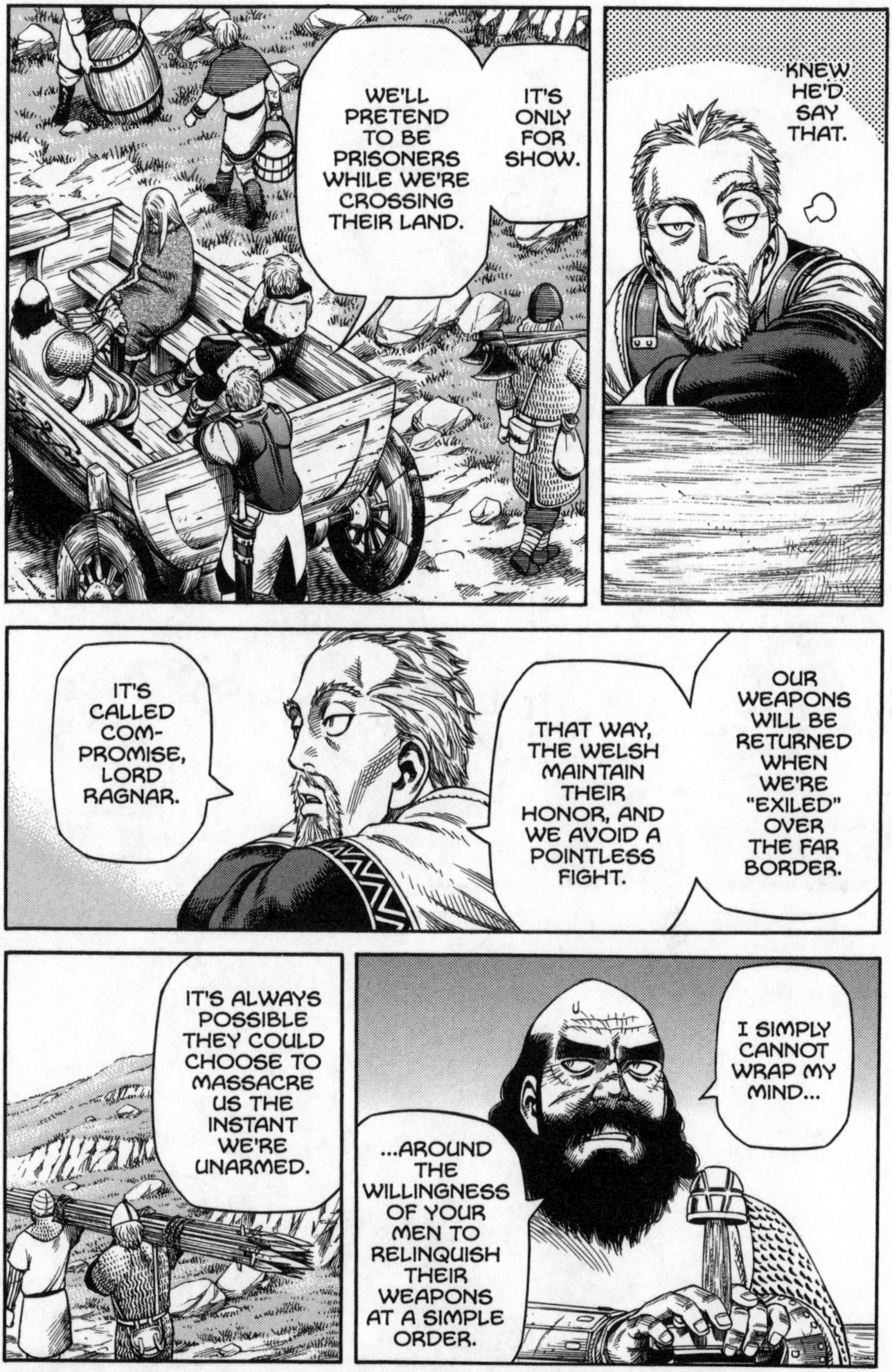
KNEW HE'D SAY THAT.
IT'S ONLY FOR SHOW.
WE'LL PRETEND TO BE PRISONERS WHILE WE'RE CROSSING THEIR LAND.
OUR WEAPONS WILL BE RETURNED WHEN WE'RE "EXILED" OVER THE FAR BORDER.
THAT WAY, THE WELSH MAINTAIN THEIR HONOR, AND WE AVOID A POINTLESS FIGHT.
IT'S CALLED COM-PROMISE, LORD RAGNAR.
I SIMPLY CANNOT WRAP MY MIND...
...AROUND THE WILLINGNESS OF YOUR MEN TO RELINQUISH THEIR WEAPONS AT A SIMPLE ORDER.
IT'S ALWAYS POSSIBLE THEY COULD CHOOSE TO MASSACRE US THE INSTANT WE'RE UNARMED.

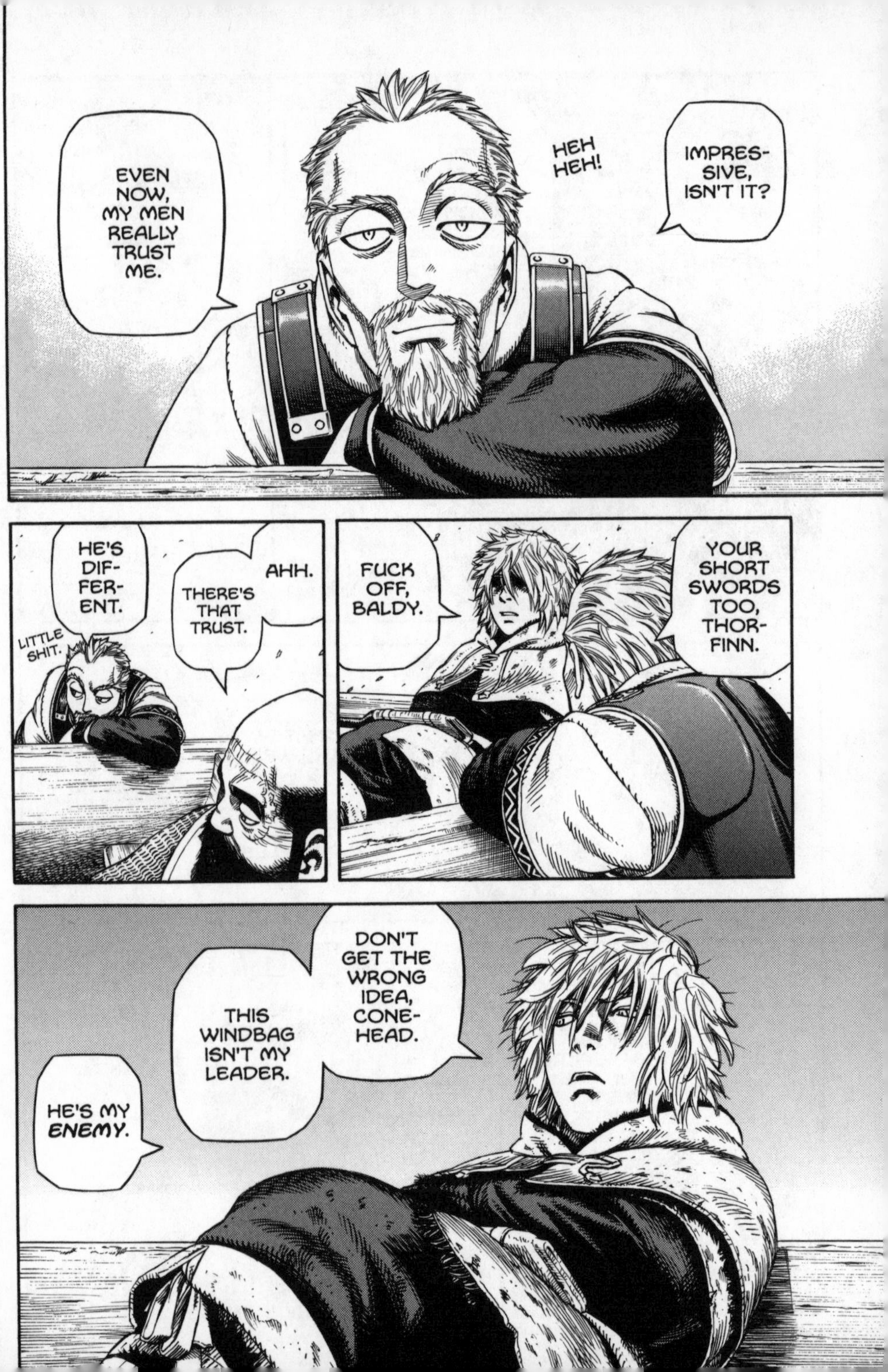
IMPRES-SIVE, ISN'T IT?
HEH HEH!
EVEN NOW, MY MEN REALLY TRUST ME.
YOUR SHORT SWORDS TOO, THORFINN.
FUCK OFF, BALDY.
AHH.
THERE'S THAT TRUST.
HE'S DIF-FER-ENT.
LITTLE SHIT.
DON'T GET THE WRONG IDEA, CONE-HEAD.
THIS WINDBAG ISN'T MY LEADER.
HE'S MY *ENEMY*.

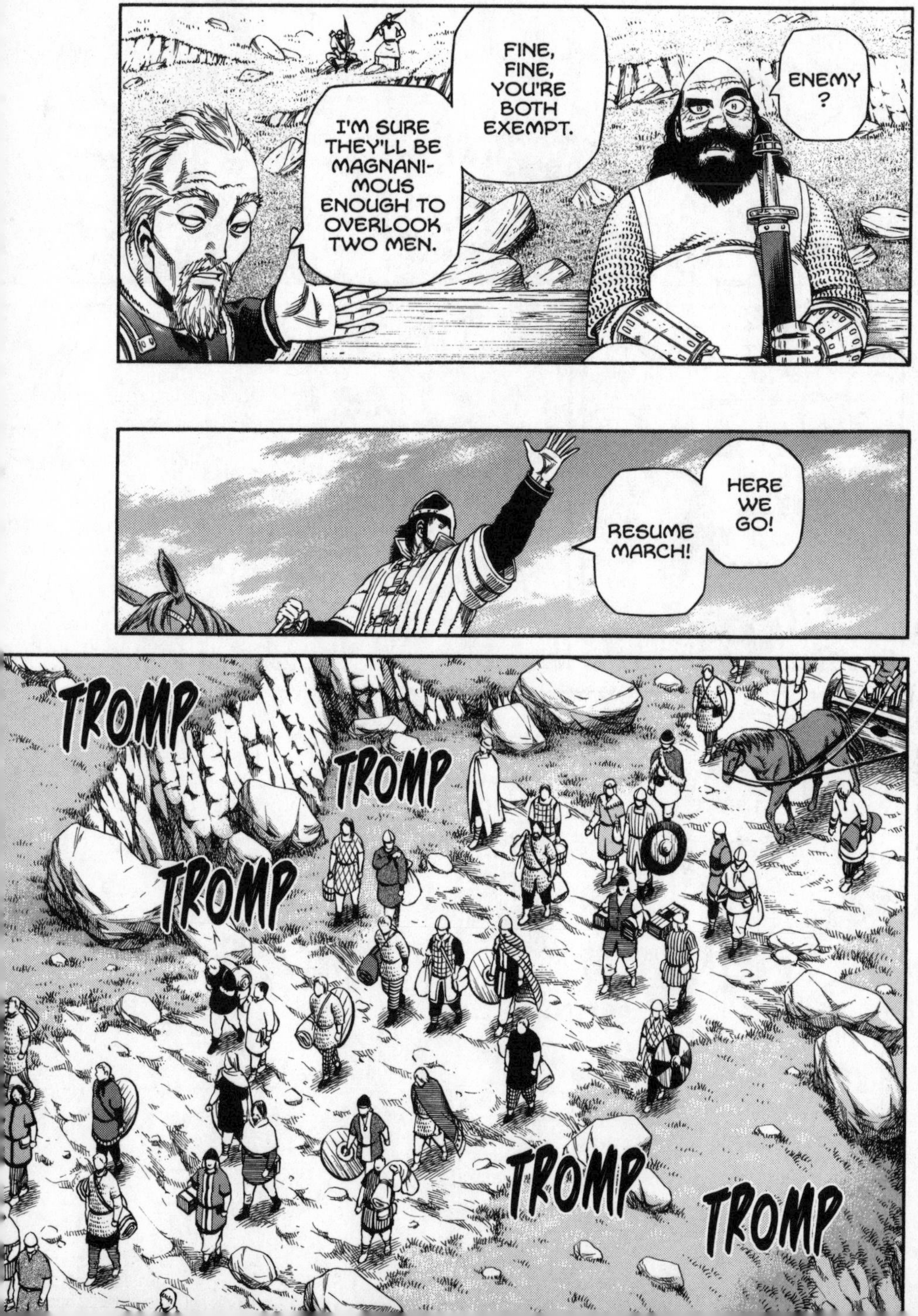
ENEMY?
FINE, FINE, YOU'RE BOTH EXEMPT.
I'M SURE THEY'LL BE MAGNANI-MOUS ENOUGH TO OVERLOOK TWO MEN.
HERE WE GO!
RESUME MARCH!
TROMP
TROMP
TROMP
TROMP
TROMP

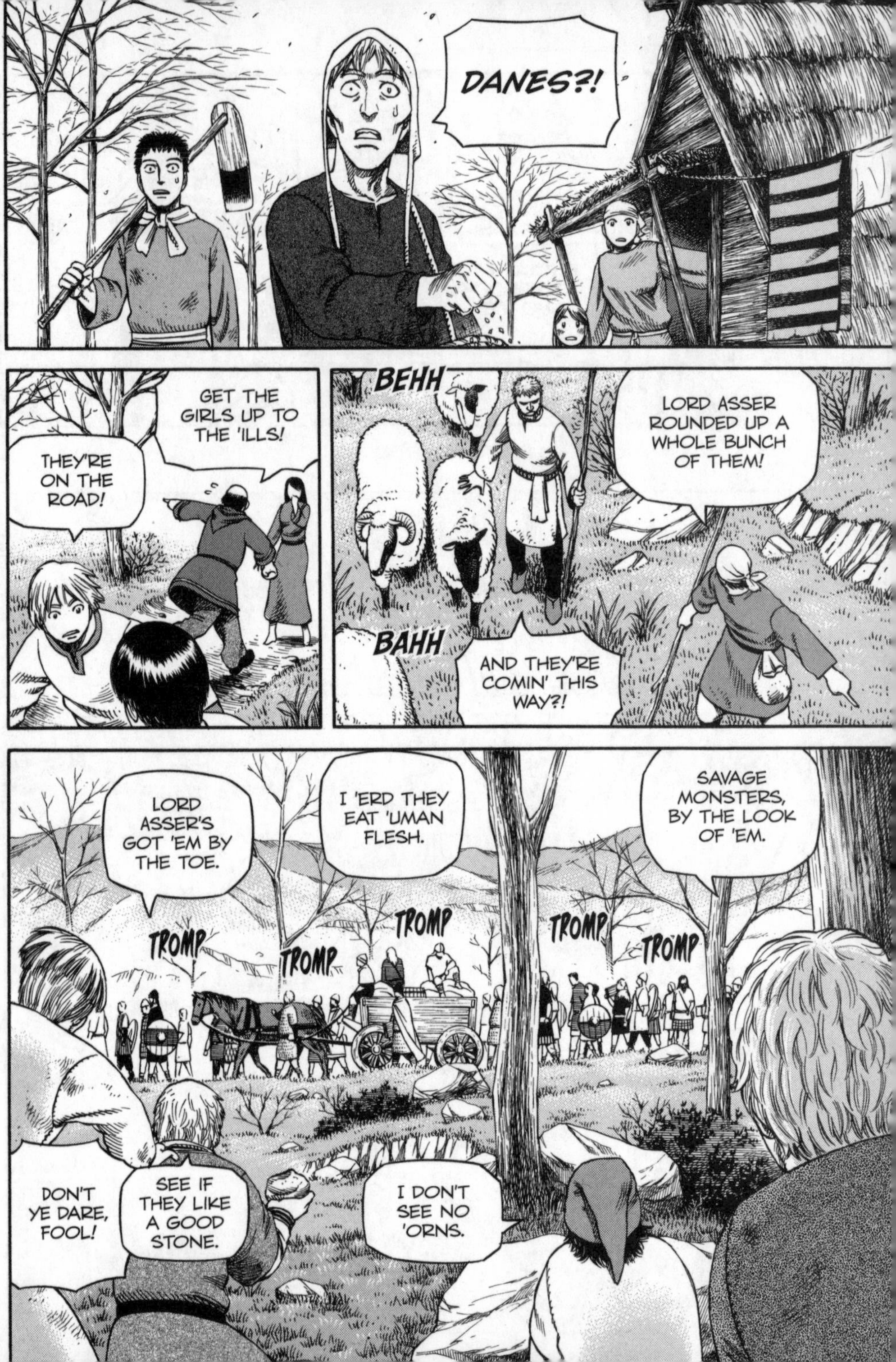
DANES?!
BEHH
LORD ASSER ROUNDED UP A WHOLE BUNCH OF THEM!
BAHH
AND THEY'RE COMIN' THIS WAY?!
GET THE GIRLS UP TO THE 'ILLS!
THEY'RE ON THE ROAD!
SAVAGE MONSTERS, BY THE LOOK OF 'EM.
I 'ERD THEY EAT 'UMAN FLESH.
LORD ASSER'S GOT 'EM BY THE TOE.
TROMP
TROMP
TROMP
TROMP
TROMP
I DON'T SEE NO 'ORNS.
SEE IF THEY LIKE A GOOD STONE.
DON'T YE DARE, FOOL!

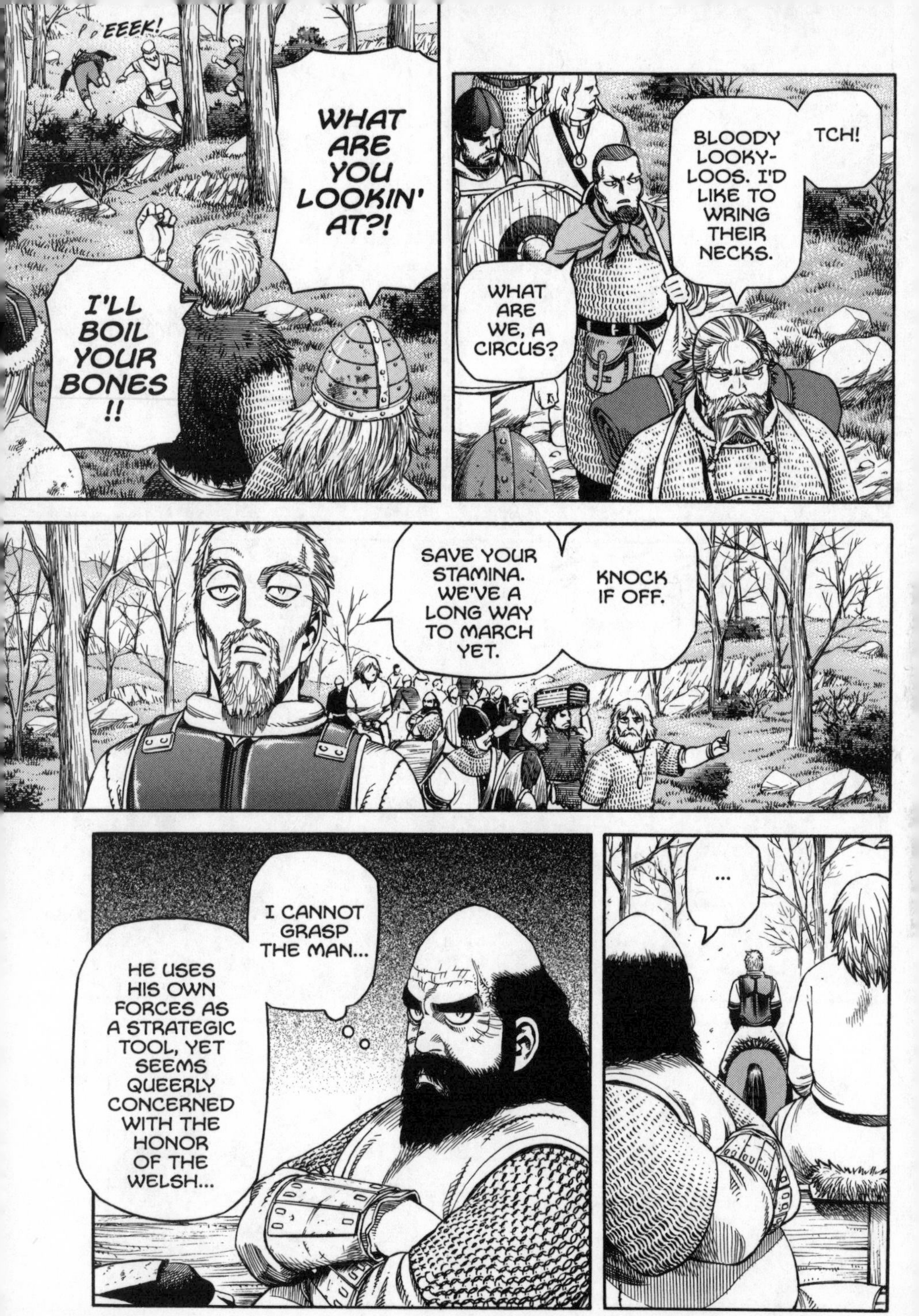
TCH!
BLOODY LOOKY-LOOS. I'D LIKE TO WRING THEIR NECKS.
WHAT ARE WE, A CIRCUS?
EEEK!
WHAT ARE YOU LOOKIN' AT?!
I'LL BOIL YOUR BONES!!
KNOCK IF OFF.
SAVE YOUR STAMINA. WE'VE A LONG WAY TO MARCH YET.
...
I CANNOT GRASP THE MAN...
HE USES HIS OWN FORCES AS A STRATEGIC TOOL, YET SEEMS QUEERLY CONCERNED WITH THE HONOR OF THE WELSH...

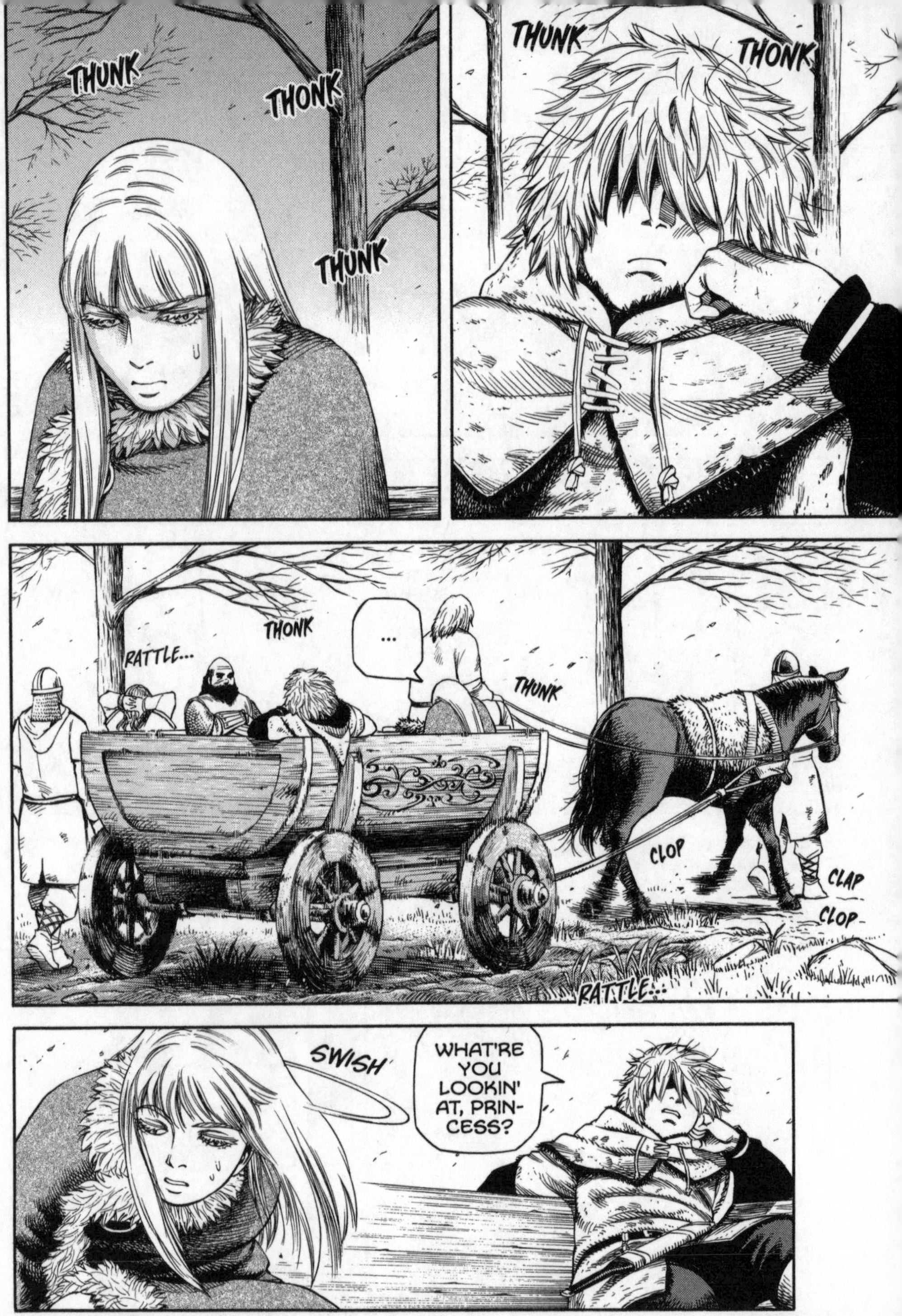
THUNK
THONK
THUNK
THONK
THUNK
THUNK
CLAP
CLOP
CLOP
...
THONK
RATTLE...
RATTLE...
WHAT'RE YOU LOOKIN' AT, PRIN-CESS?
SWISH

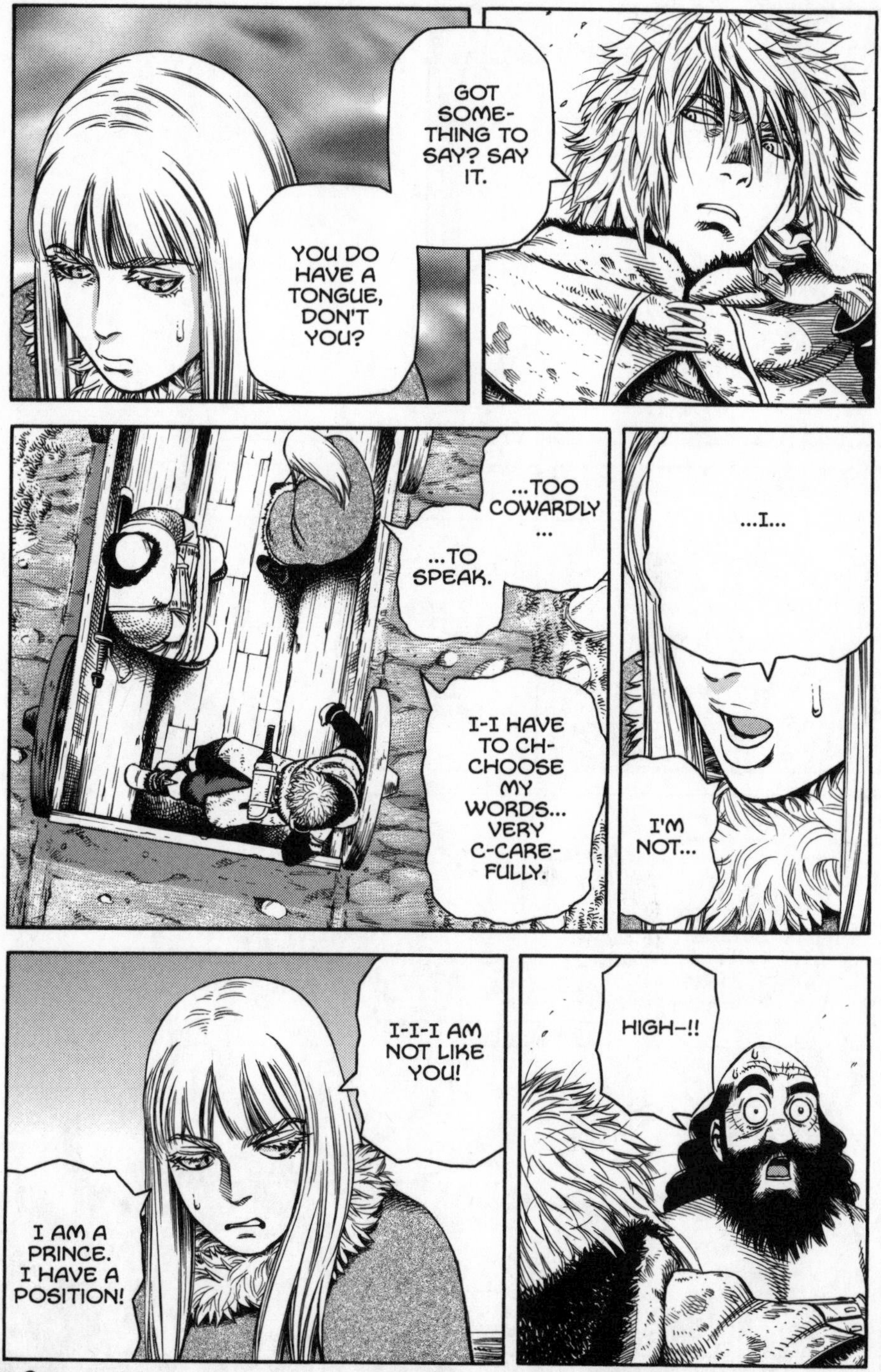
GOT SOME-THING TO SAY? SAY IT.
YOU DO HAVE A TONGUE, DON'T YOU?
...I...
I'M NOT...
...TOO COWARDLY ...
...TO SPEAK.
I-I HAVE TO CH-CHOOSE MY WORDS... VERY C-CARE-FULLY.
HIGH-!!
I-I-I AM NOT LIKE YOU!
I AM A PRINCE. I HAVE A POSITION!

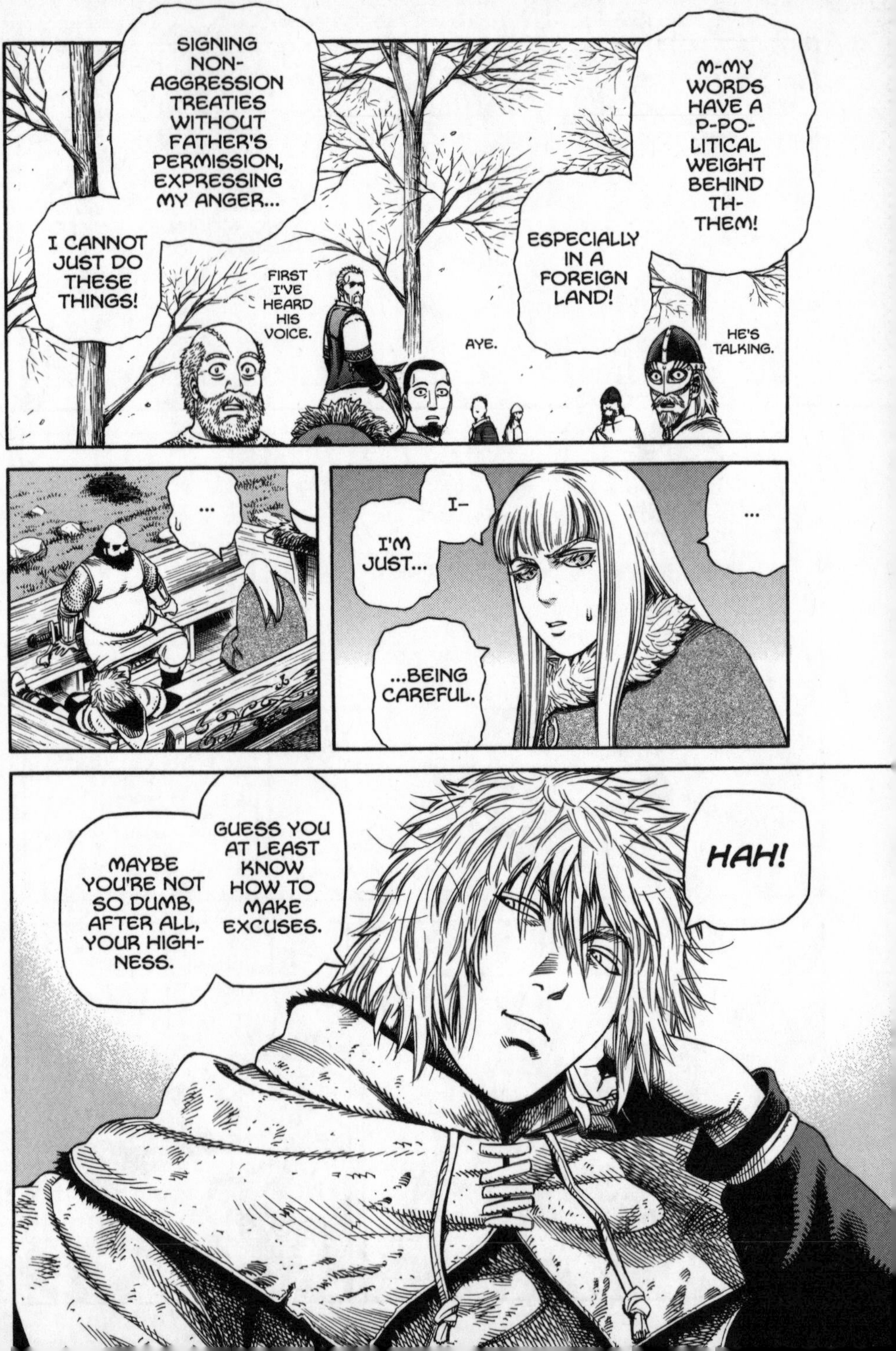
M-MY WORDS HAVE A P-POLITICAL WEIGHT BEHIND TH- THEM!
ESPECIALLY IN A FOREIGN LAND!
HE'S TALKING.
AYE.
SIGNING NON-AGGRESSION TREATIES WITHOUT FATHER'S PERMISSION, EXPRESSING MY ANGER...
FIRST I'VE HEARD HIS VOICE.
I CANNOT JUST DO THESE THINGS!
...
I-
I'M JUST...
...BEING CAREFUL.
...
HAH!
GUESS YOU AT LEAST KNOW HOW TO MAKE EXCUSES.
MAYBE YOU'RE NOT SO DUMB, AFTER ALL, YOUR HIGHNESS.

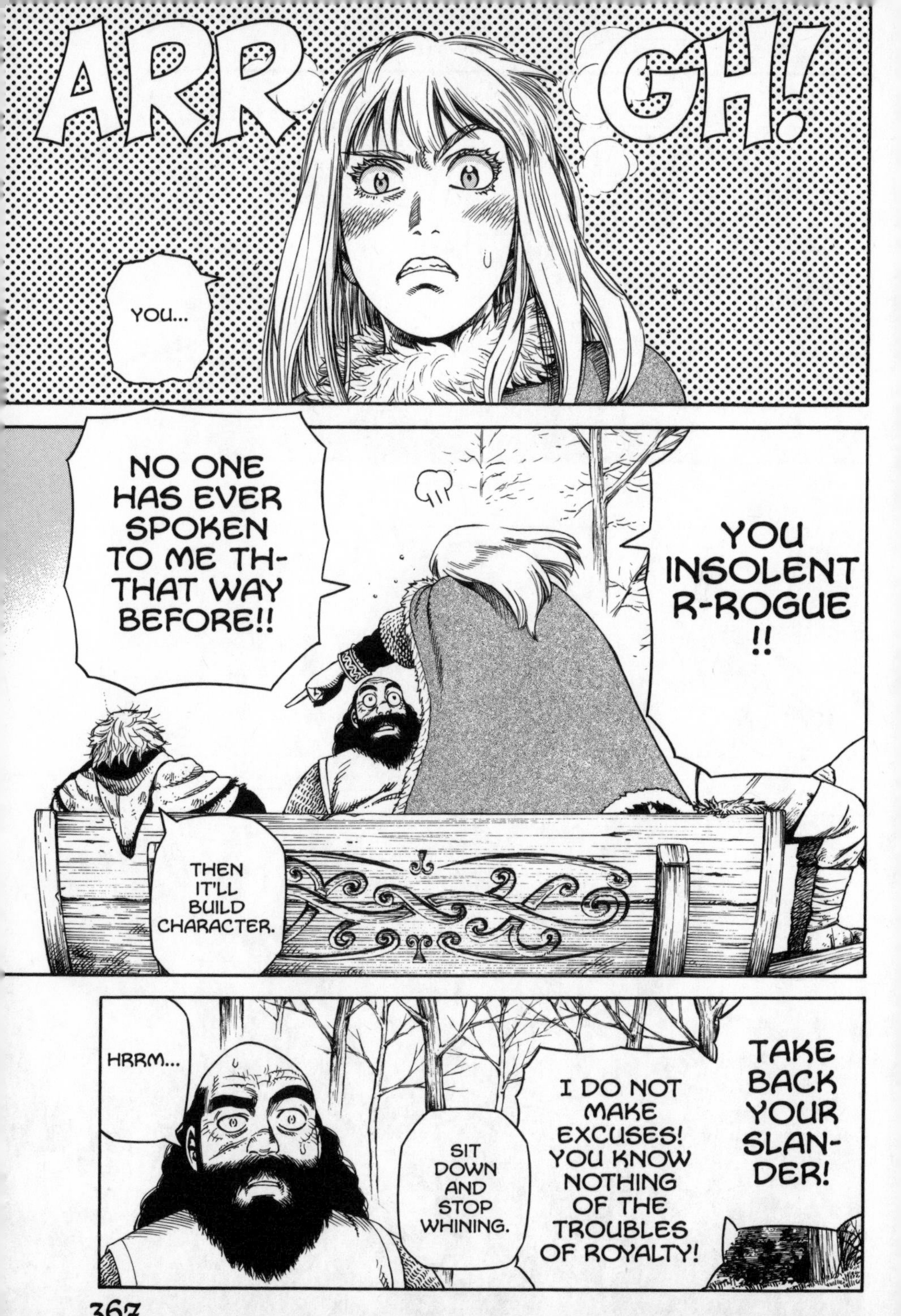
ARRGH!
YOU...
YOU INSOLENT R-ROGUE!!
NO ONE HAS EVER SPOKEN TO ME TH-THAT WAY BEFORE!!
THEN IT'LL BUILD CHARACTER.
TAKE BACK YOUR SLAN-DER!
I DO NOT MAKE EXCUSES! YOU KNOW NOTHING OF THE TROUBLES OF ROYALTY!
SIT DOWN AND STOP WHINING.
HRRM...

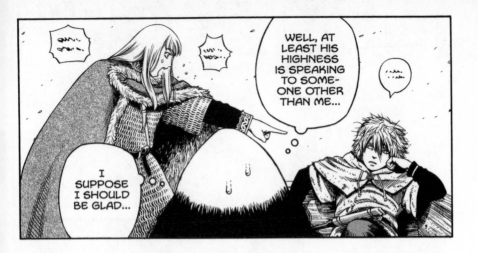

WELL, AT LEAST HIS HIGHNESS IS SPEAKING TO SOMEONE OTHER THAN ME...

I SUPPOSE I SHOULD BE GLAD...

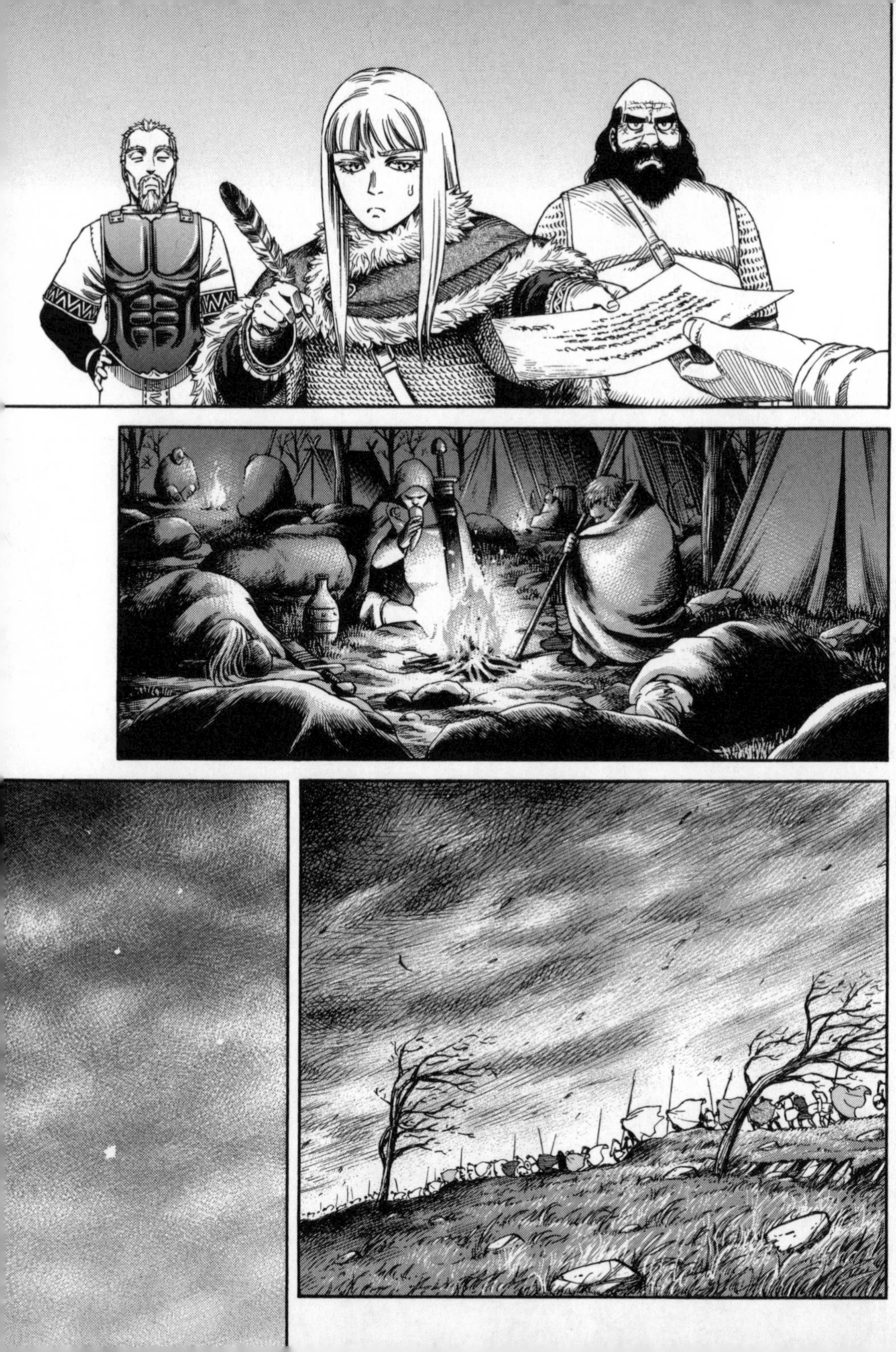

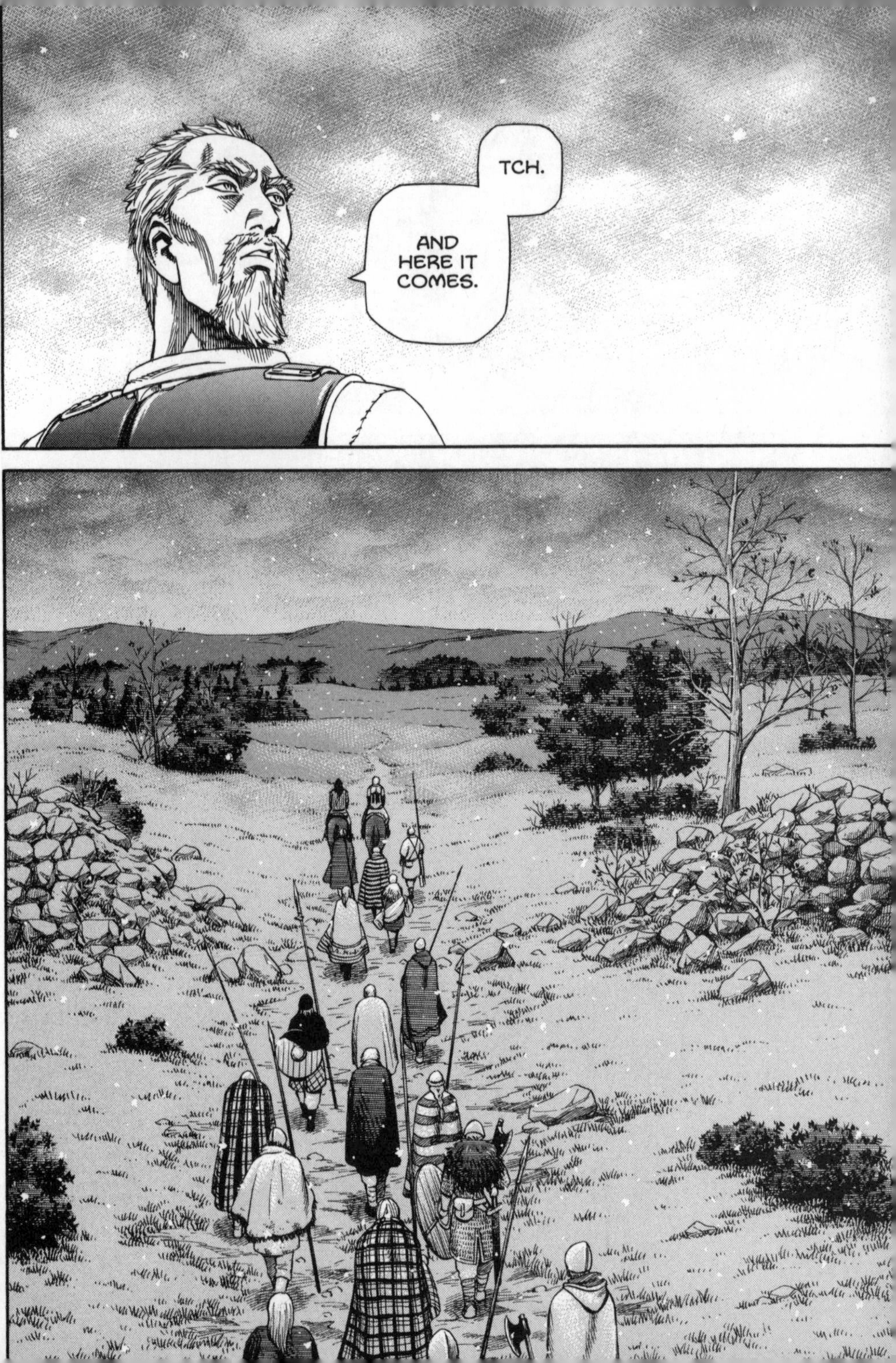
TCH.
AND HERE IT COMES.

CHAPTER 26 • END

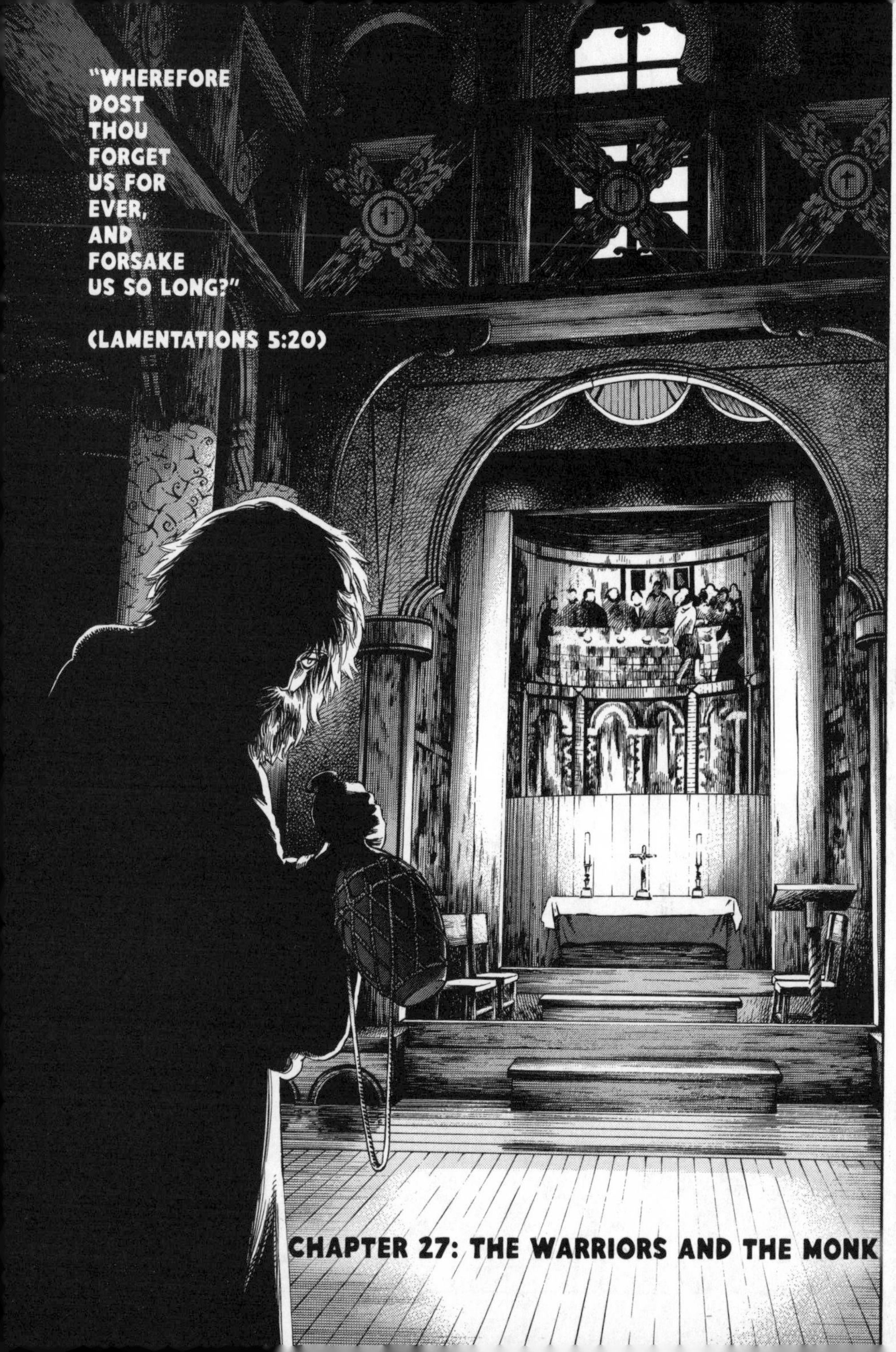
"WHEREFORE DOST THOU FORGET US FOR EVER, AND FORSAKE US SO LONG?"
(LAMENTATIONS 5:20)
CHAPTER 27: THE WARRIORS AND THE MONK

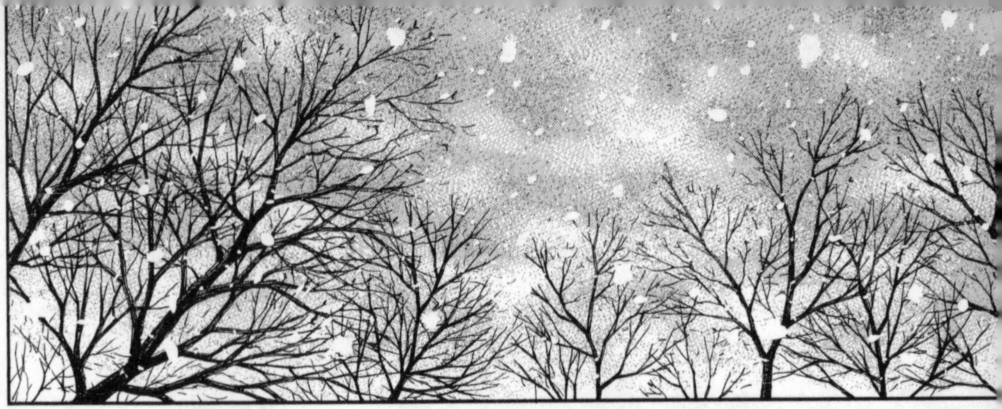

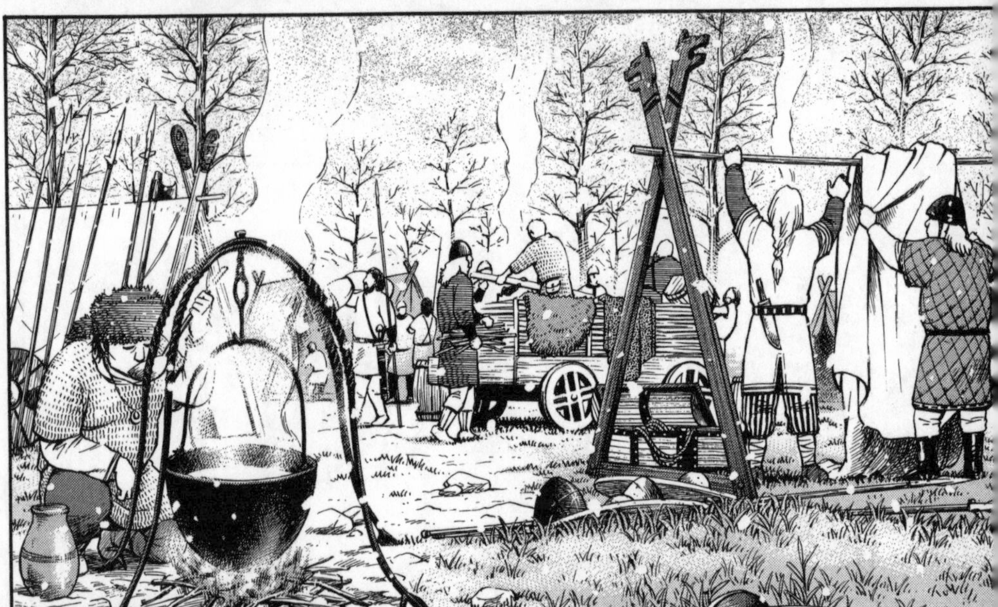

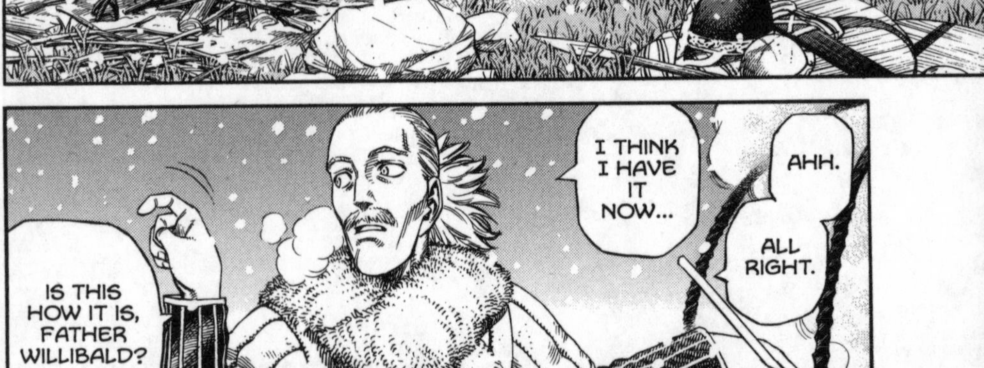
AHH.
ALL RIGHT.
I THINK I HAVE IT NOW...
IS THIS HOW IT IS, FATHER WILLIBALD?

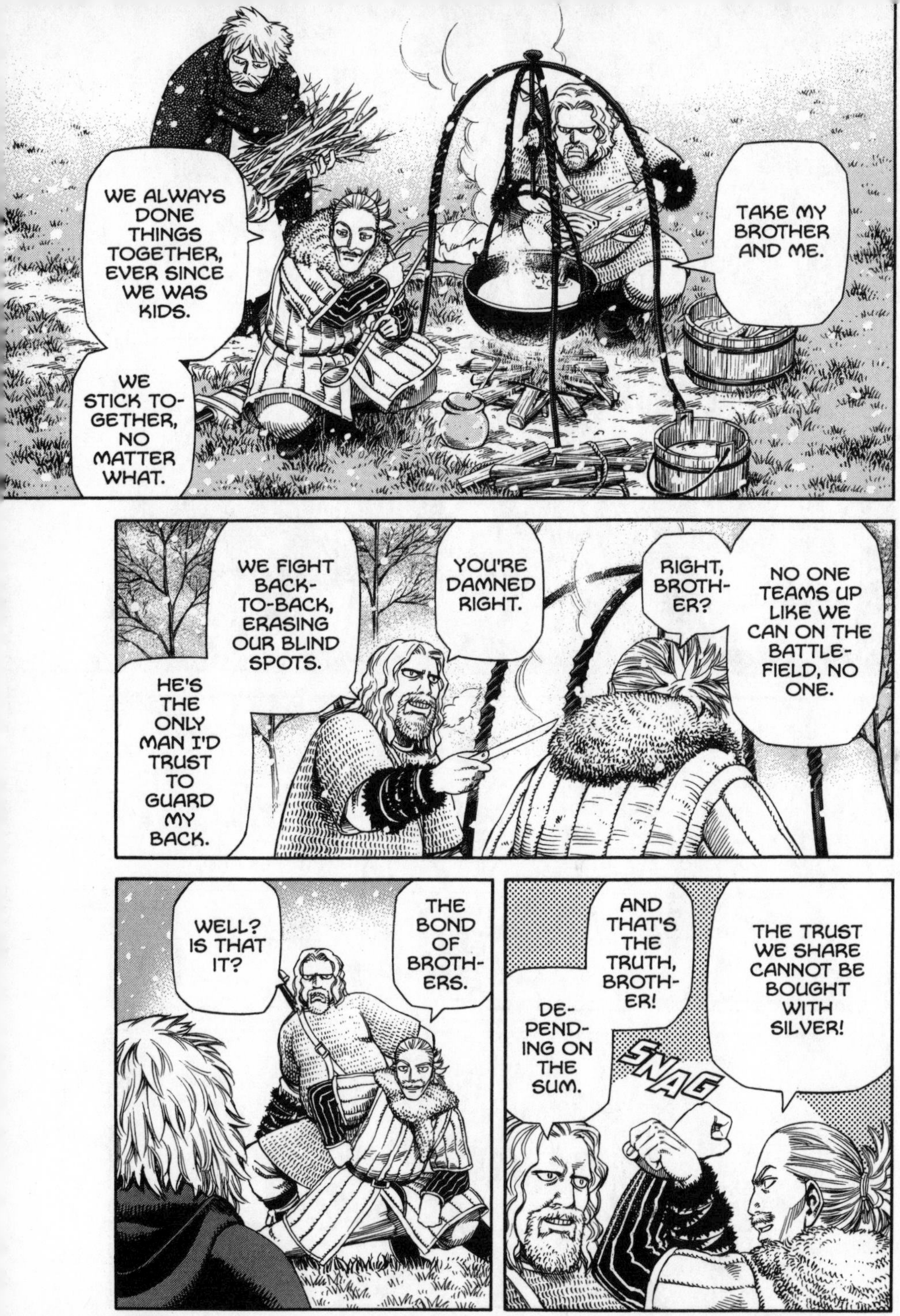
TAKE MY BROTHER AND ME.
WE ALWAYS DONE THINGS TOGETHER, EVER SINCE WE WAS KIDS.
WE STICK TOGETHER, NO MATTER WHAT.
NO ONE TEAMS UP LIKE WE CAN ON THE BATTLEFIELD, NO ONE.
RIGHT, BROTHER?
YOU'RE DAMNED RIGHT.
WE FIGHT BACK-TO-BACK, ERASING OUR BLIND SPOTS.
HE'S THE ONLY MAN I'D TRUST TO GUARD MY BACK.
THE TRUST WE SHARE CANNOT BE BOUGHT WITH SILVER!
AND THAT'S THE TRUTH, BROTHER!
SNAG
DEPENDING ON THE SUM.
THE BOND OF BROTHERS.
WELL? IS THAT IT?

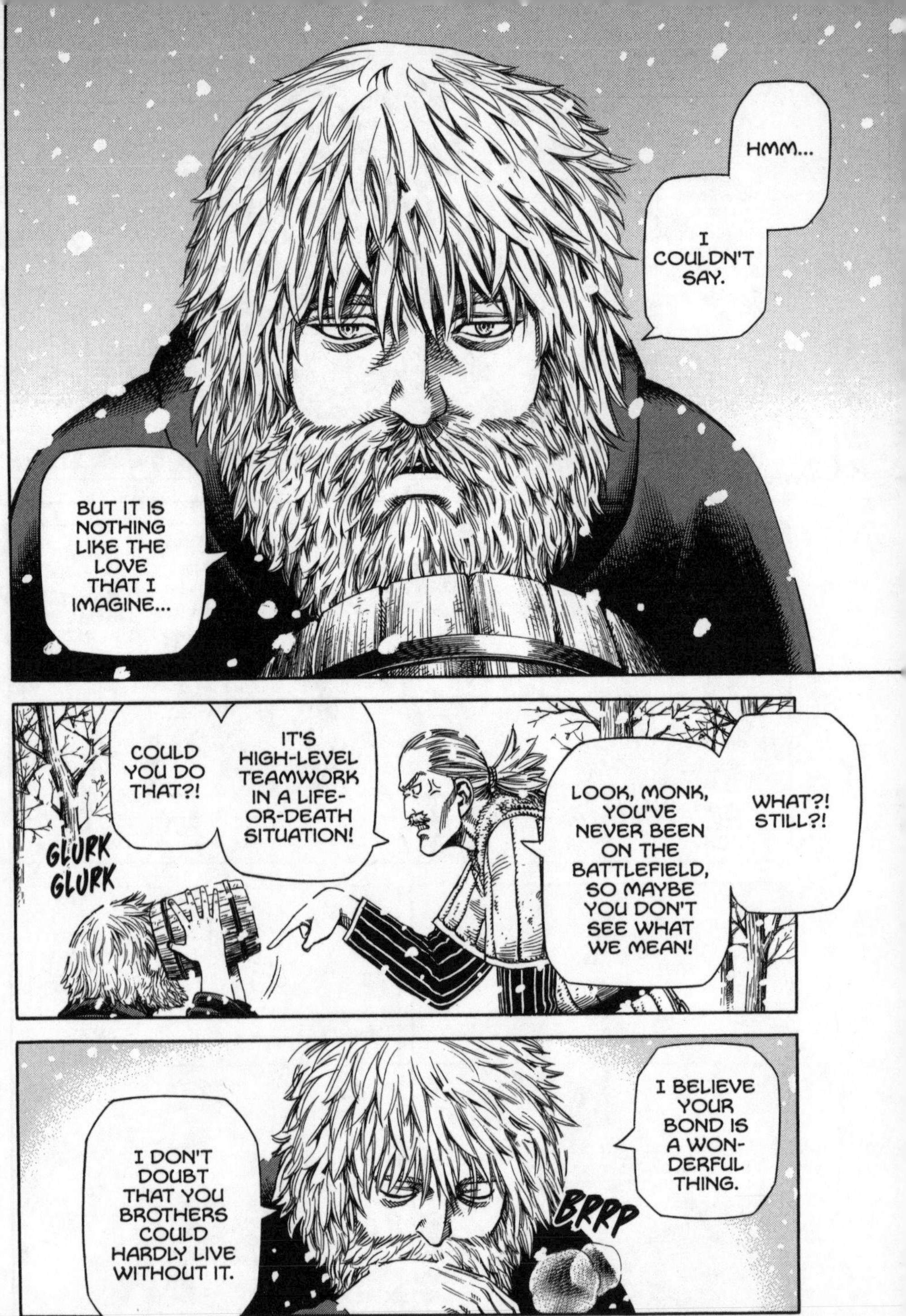
HMM...
I COULDN'T SAY.
BUT IT IS NOTHING LIKE THE LOVE THAT I IMAGINE...
WHAT?! STILL?!
LOOK, MONK, YOU'VE NEVER BEEN ON THE BATTLEFIELD, SO MAYBE YOU DON'T SEE WHAT WE MEAN!
IT'S HIGH-LEVEL TEAMWORK IN A LIFE-OR-DEATH SITUATION!
COULD YOU DO THAT?!
GLURK GLURK
I BELIEVE YOUR BOND IS A WON-DERFUL THING.
BRRP
I DON'T DOUBT THAT YOU BROTHERS COULD HARDLY LIVE WITHOUT IT.

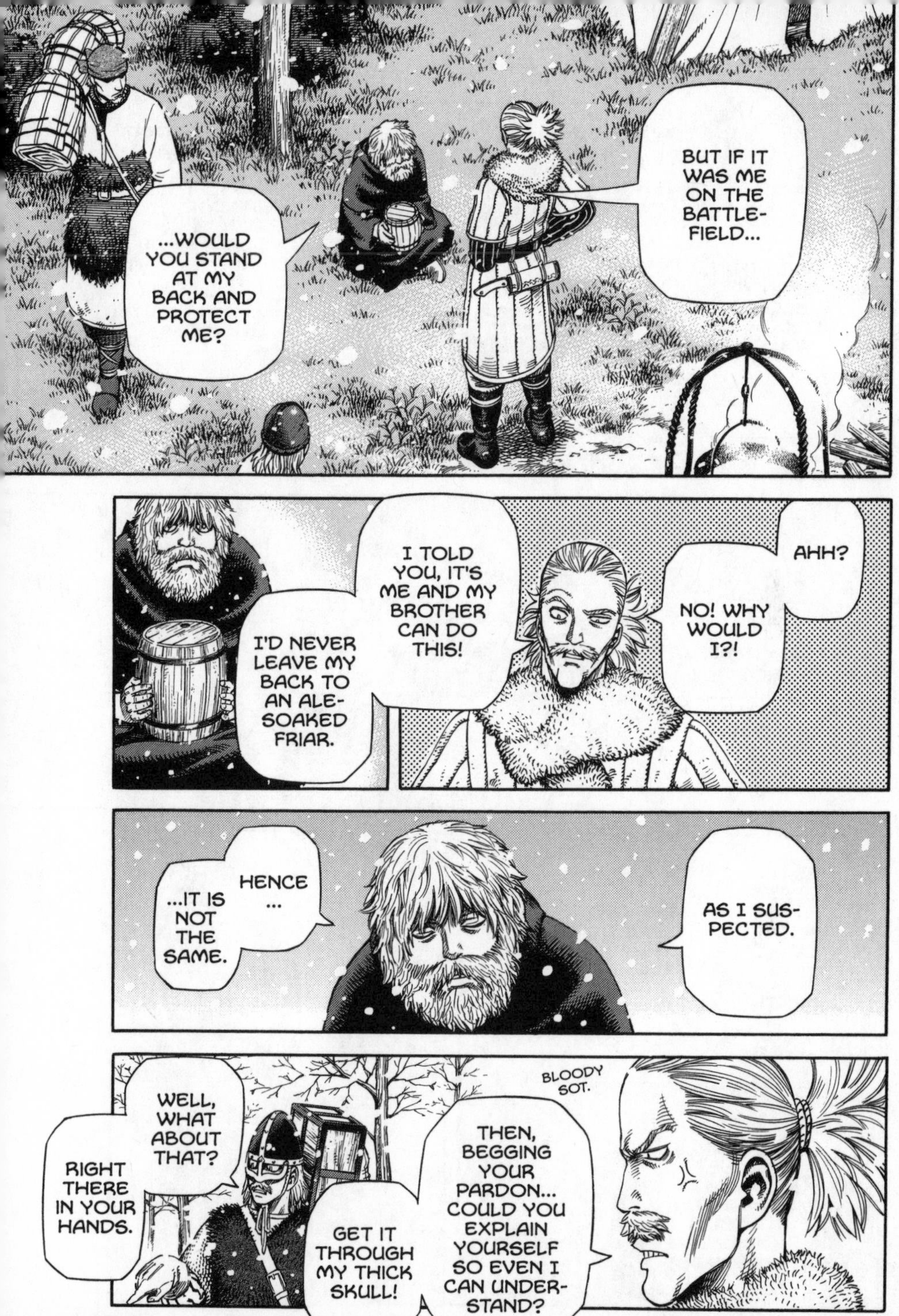
BUT IF IT WAS ME ON THE BATTLEFIELD...
...WOULD YOU STAND AT MY BACK AND PROTECT ME?
AHH?
NO! WHY WOULD I?!
I TOLD YOU, IT'S ME AND MY BROTHER CAN DO THIS!
I'D NEVER LEAVE MY BACK TO AN ALE-SOAKED FRIAR.
AS I SUSPECTED.
HENCE...
...IT IS NOT THE SAME.
BLOODY SOT.
THEN, BEGGING YOUR PARDON... COULD YOU EXPLAIN YOURSELF SO EVEN I CAN UNDERSTAND?
GET IT THROUGH MY THICK SKULL!
WELL, WHAT ABOUT THAT?
RIGHT THERE IN YOUR HANDS.

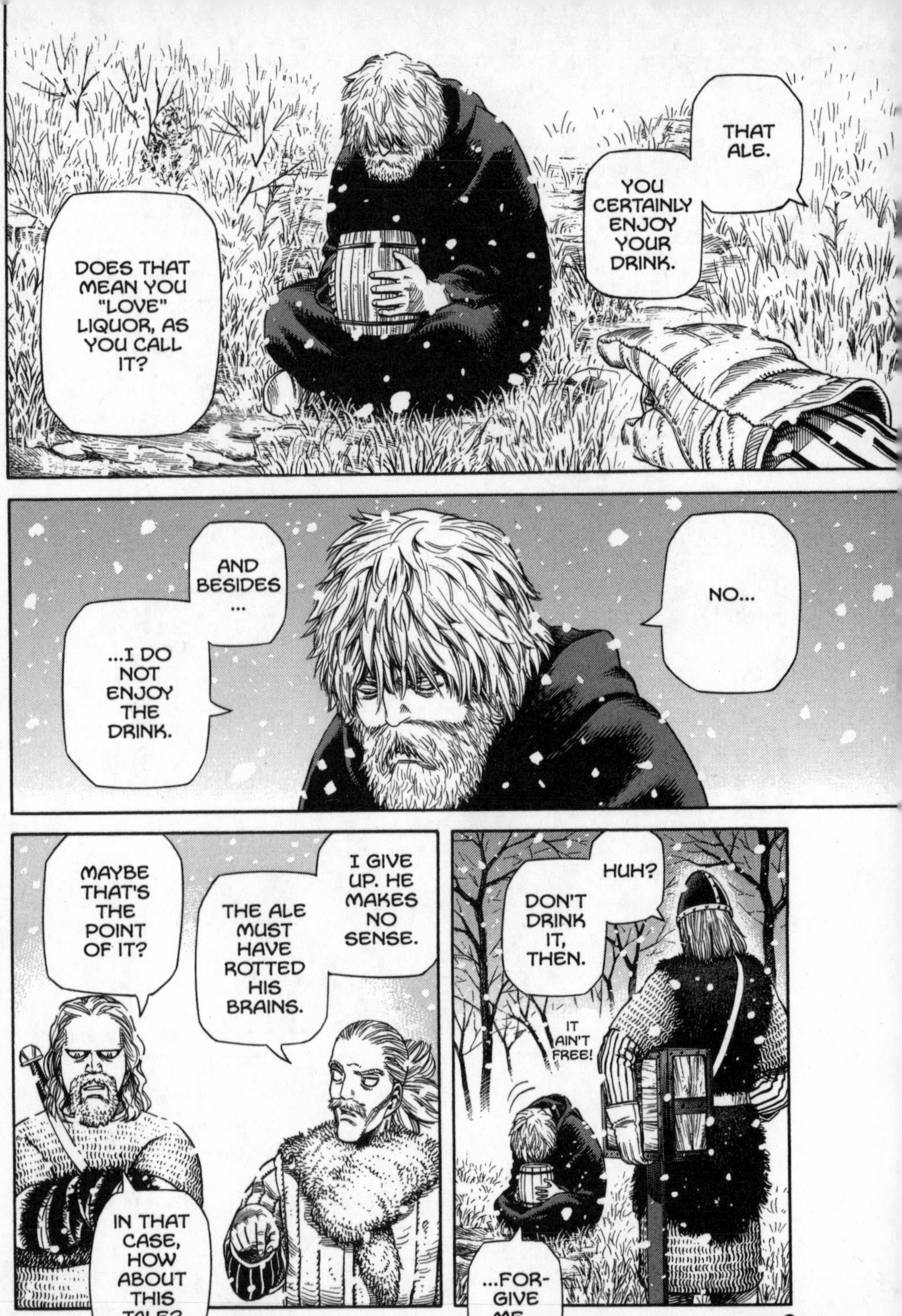
THAT ALE.
YOU CERTAINLY ENJOY YOUR DRINK.
DOES THAT MEAN YOU "LOVE" LIQUOR, AS YOU CALL IT?
NO...
AND BESIDES...
...I DO NOT ENJOY THE DRINK.
HUH?
DON'T DRINK IT, THEN.
IT AIN'T FREE!
...FOR-GIVE ME...
I GIVE UP. HE MAKES NO SENSE.
THE ALE MUST HAVE ROTTED HIS BRAINS.
MAYBE THAT'S THE POINT OF IT?
IN THAT CASE, HOW ABOUT THIS TALE?

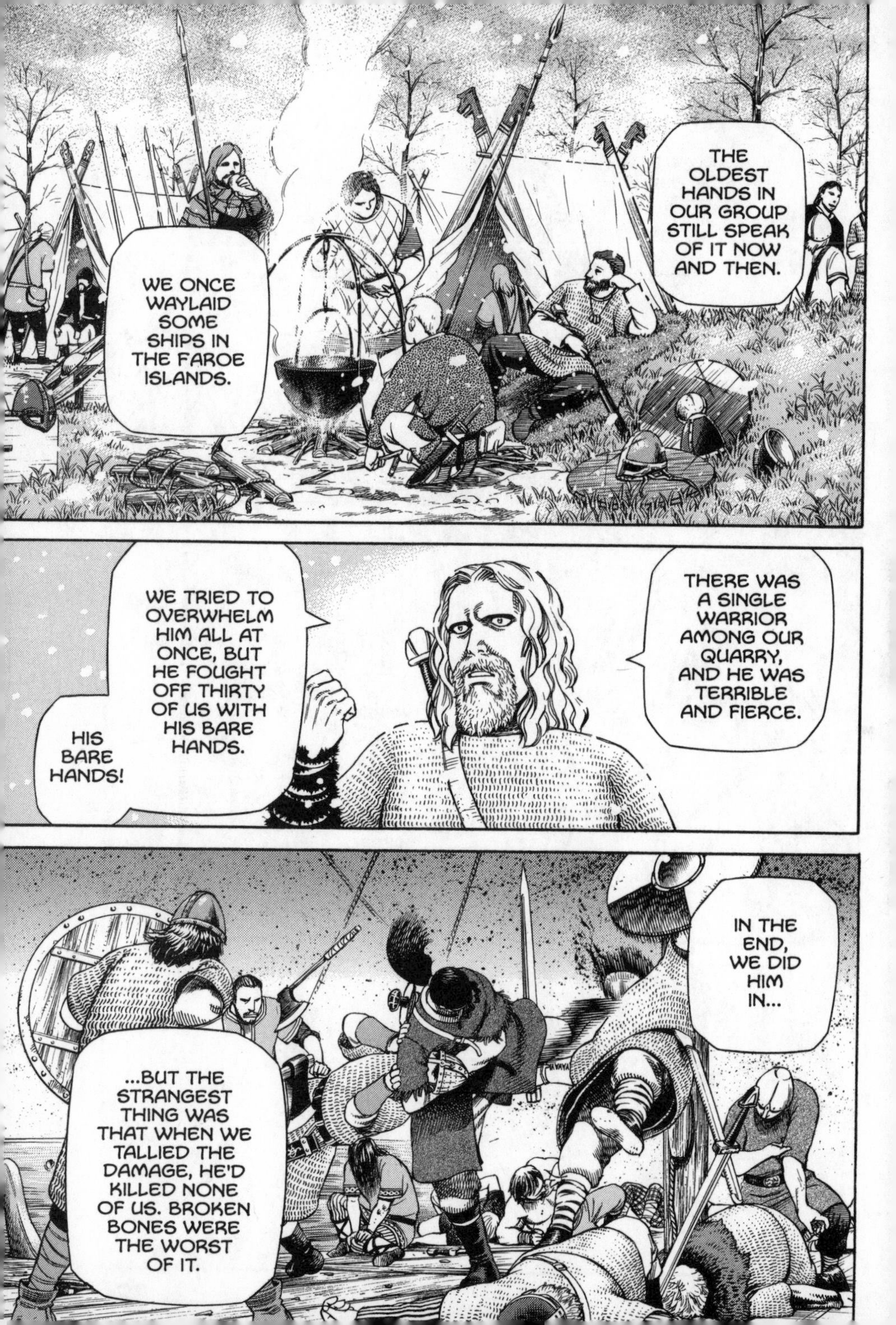
THE OLDEST HANDS IN OUR GROUP STILL SPEAK OF IT NOW AND THEN.
WE ONCE WAYLAID SOME SHIPS IN THE FAROE ISLANDS.
THERE WAS A SINGLE WARRIOR AMONG OUR QUARRY, AND HE WAS TERRIBLE AND FIERCE.
WE TRIED TO OVERWHELM HIM ALL AT ONCE, BUT HE FOUGHT OFF THIRTY OF US WITH HIS BARE HANDS.
HIS BARE HANDS!
IN THE END, WE DID HIM IN...
...BUT THE STRANGEST THING WAS THAT WHEN WE TALLIED THE DAMAGE, HE'D KILLED NONE OF US. BROKEN BONES WERE THE WORST OF IT.

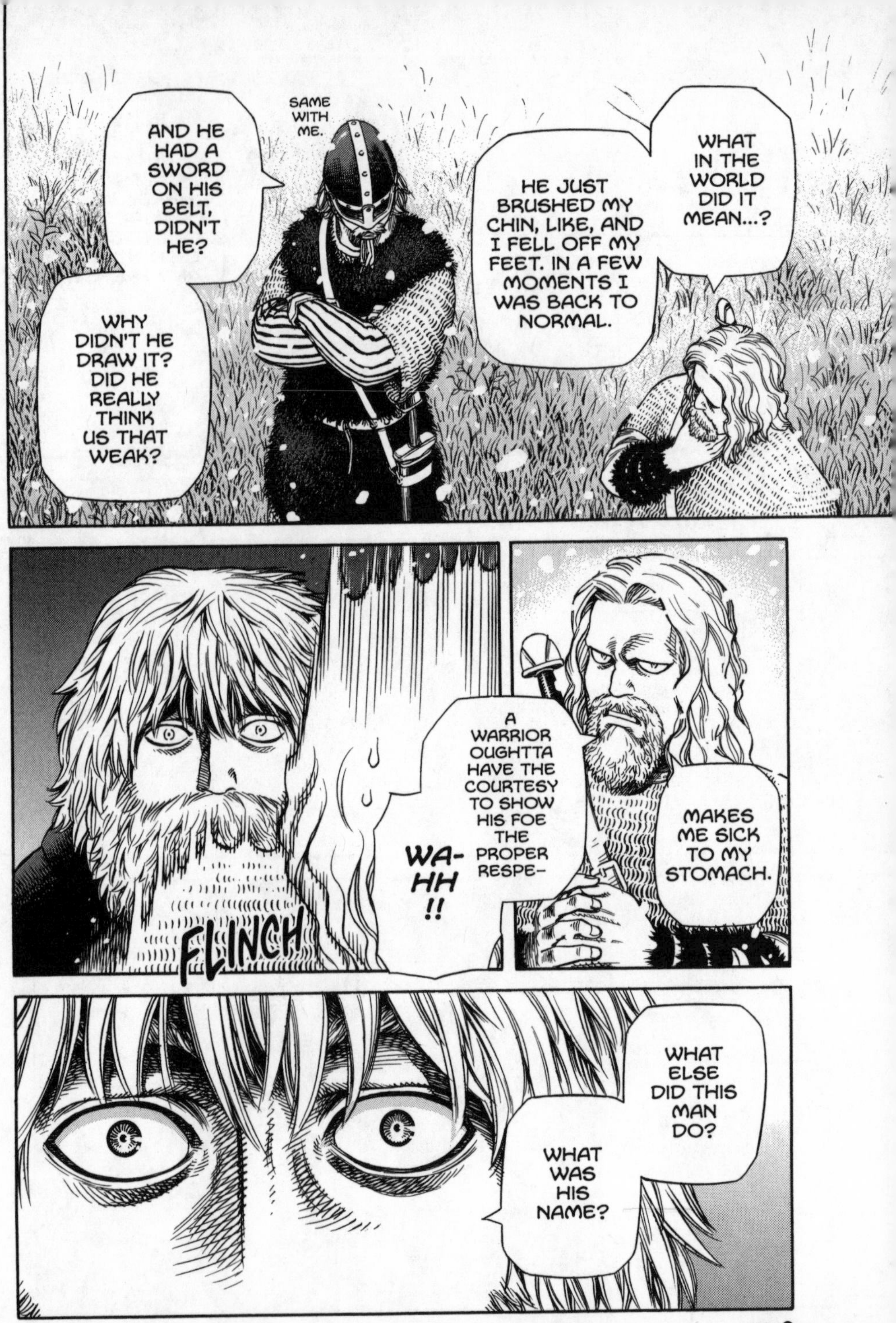
WHAT IN THE WORLD DID IT MEAN...?
HE JUST BRUSHED MY CHIN, LIKE, AND I FELL OFF MY FEET. IN A FEW MOMENTS I WAS BACK TO NORMAL.
SAME WITH ME.
AND HE HAD A SWORD ON HIS BELT, DIDN'T HE?
WHY DIDN'T HE DRAW IT? DID HE REALLY THINK US THAT WEAK?
MAKES ME SICK TO MY STOMACH.
A WARRIOR OUGHTTA HAVE THE COURTESY TO SHOW HIS FOE THE PROPER RESPE-
WA-HH !!
FLINCH
WHAT ELSE DID THIS MAN DO?
WHAT WAS HIS NAME?

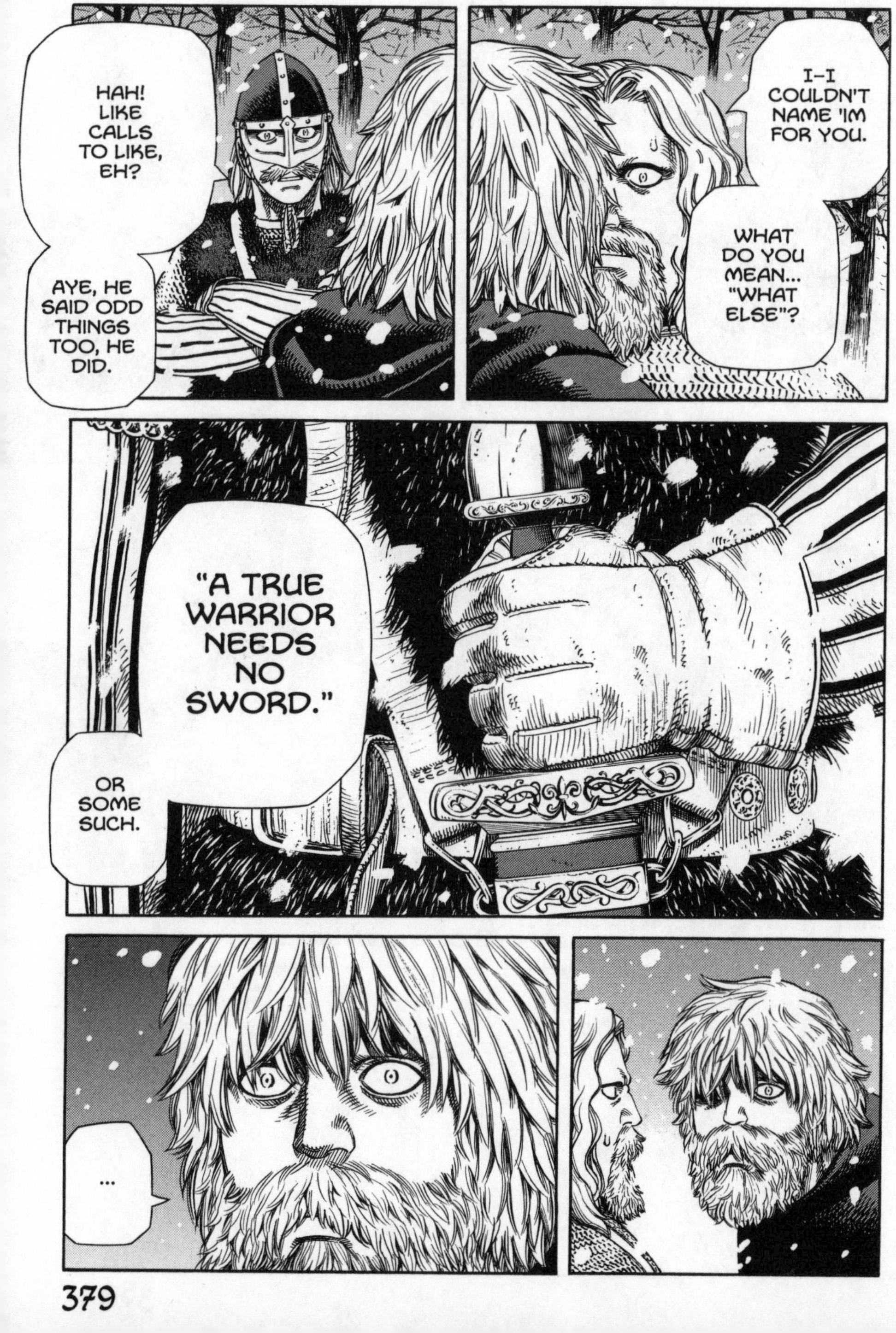
I–I COULDN'T NAME 'IM FOR YOU.
WHAT DO YOU MEAN... "WHAT ELSE"?
HAH! LIKE CALLS TO LIKE, EH?
AYE, HE SAID ODD THINGS TOO, HE DID.
"A TRUE WARRIOR NEEDS NO SWORD."
OR SOME SUCH.
...

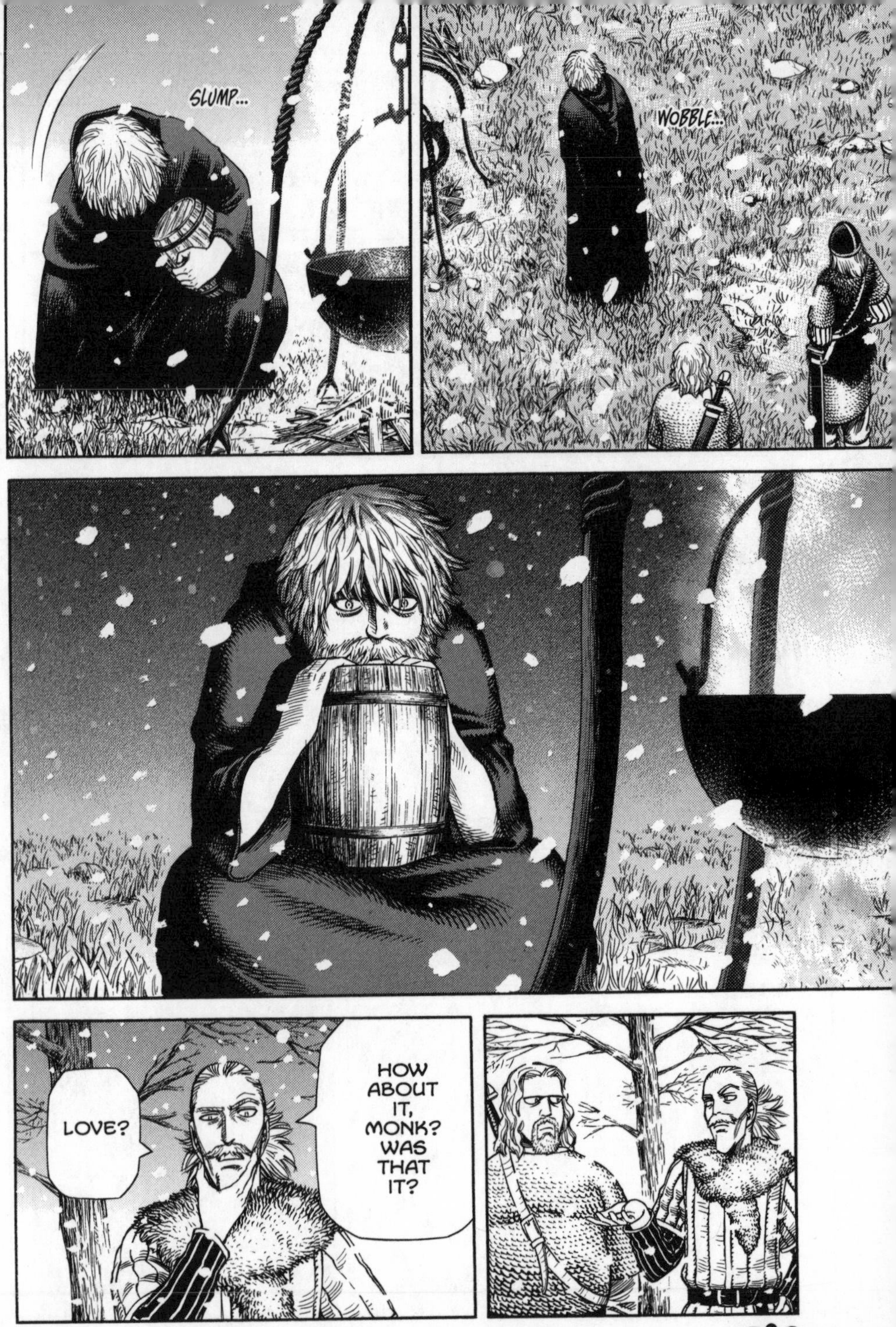
WOBBLE...
SLUMP...
HOW ABOUT IT, MONK? WAS THAT IT?
LOVE?

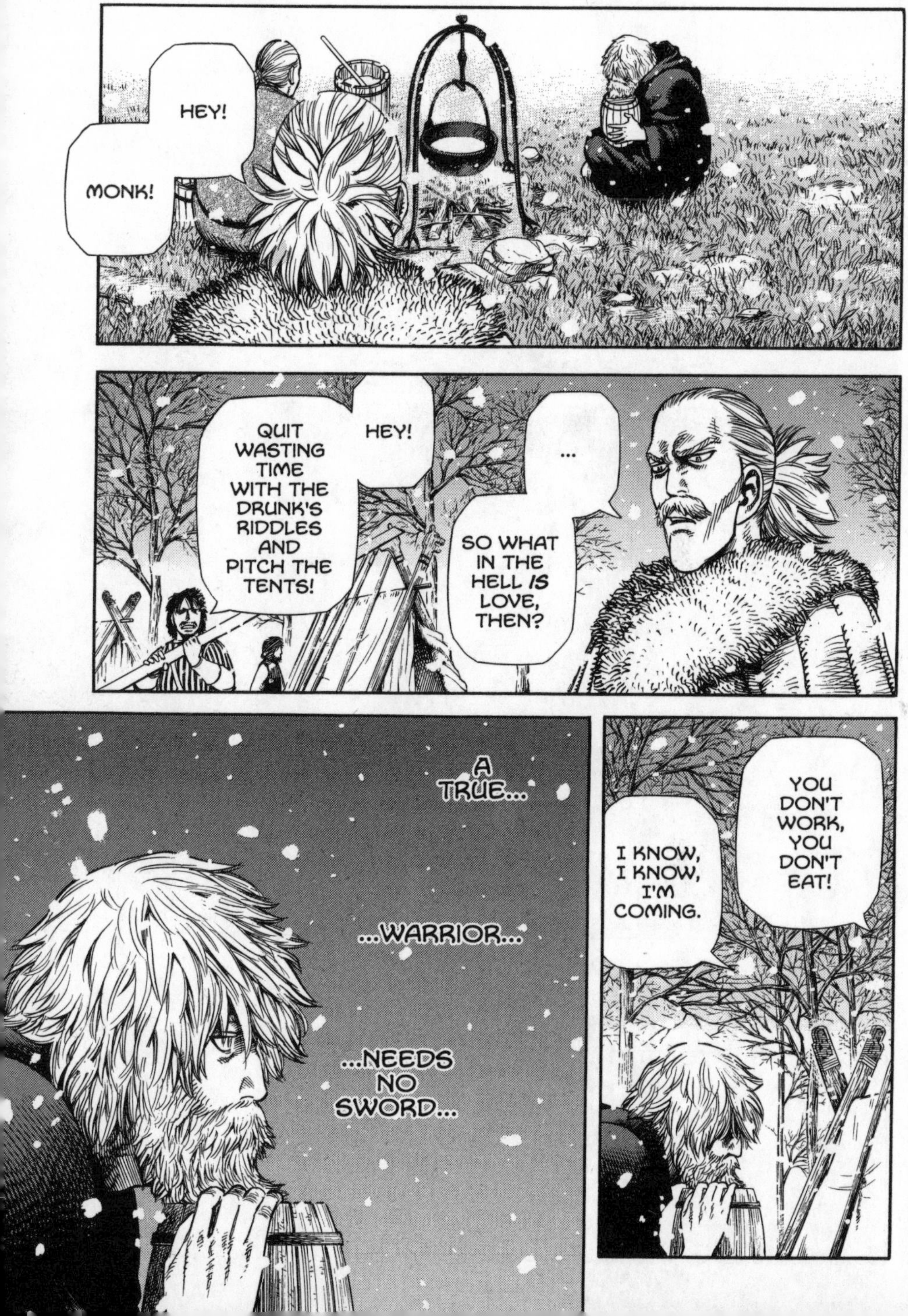
HEY!
MONK!
...
SO WHAT IN THE HELL *IS* LOVE, THEN?
HEY!
QUIT WASTING TIME WITH THE DRUNK'S RIDDLES AND PITCH THE TENTS!
YOU DON'T WORK, YOU DON'T EAT!
I KNOW, I KNOW, I'M COMING.
A TRUE...
...WARRIOR...
...NEEDS NO SWORD...

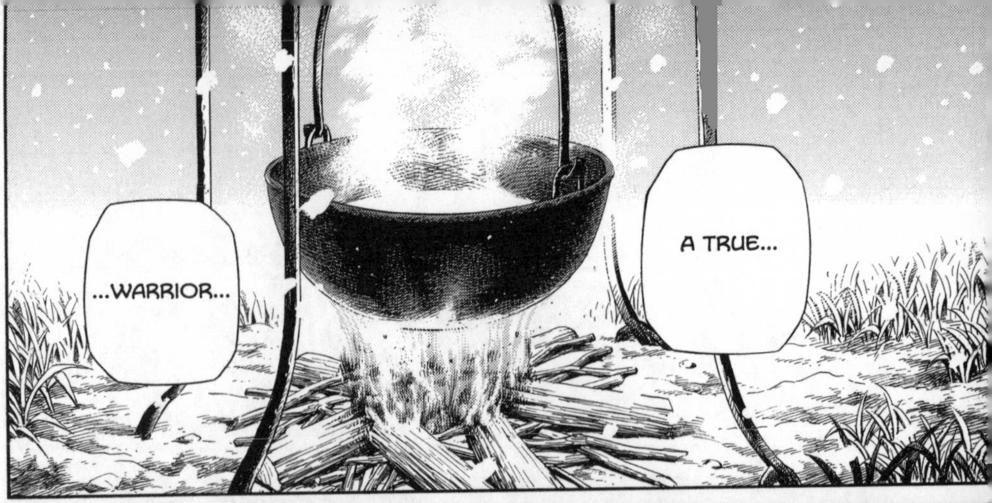
A TRUE...
...WARRIOR...

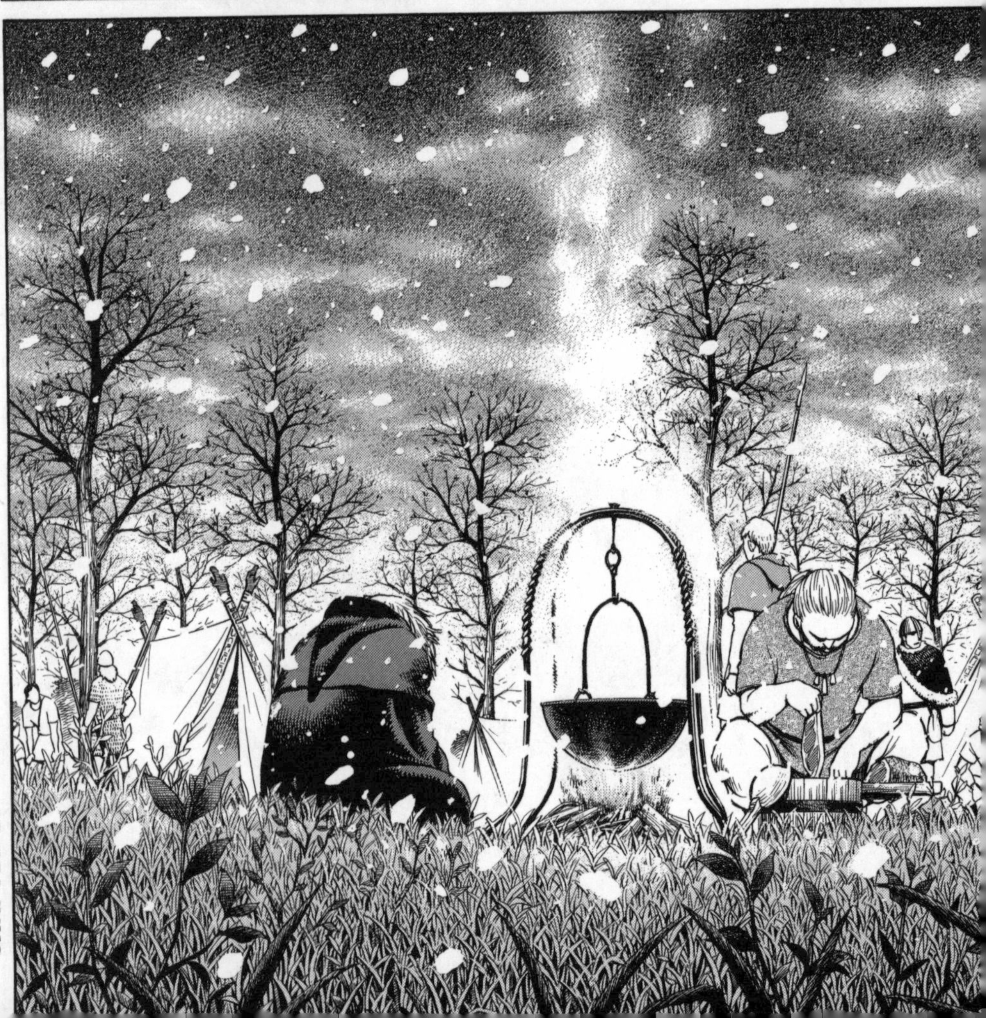

CHAPTER 27 - END

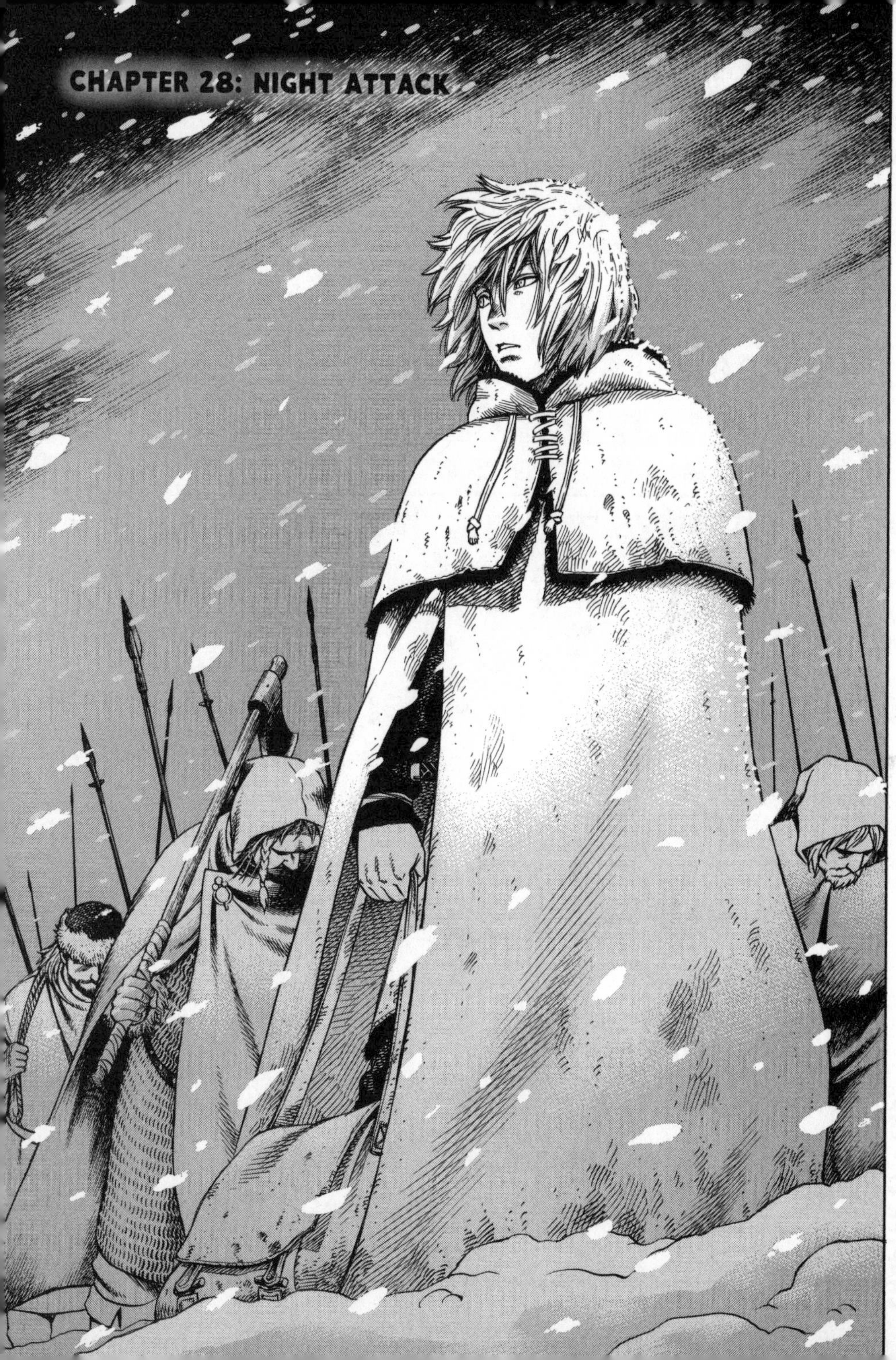
CHAPTER 28: NIGHT ATTACK

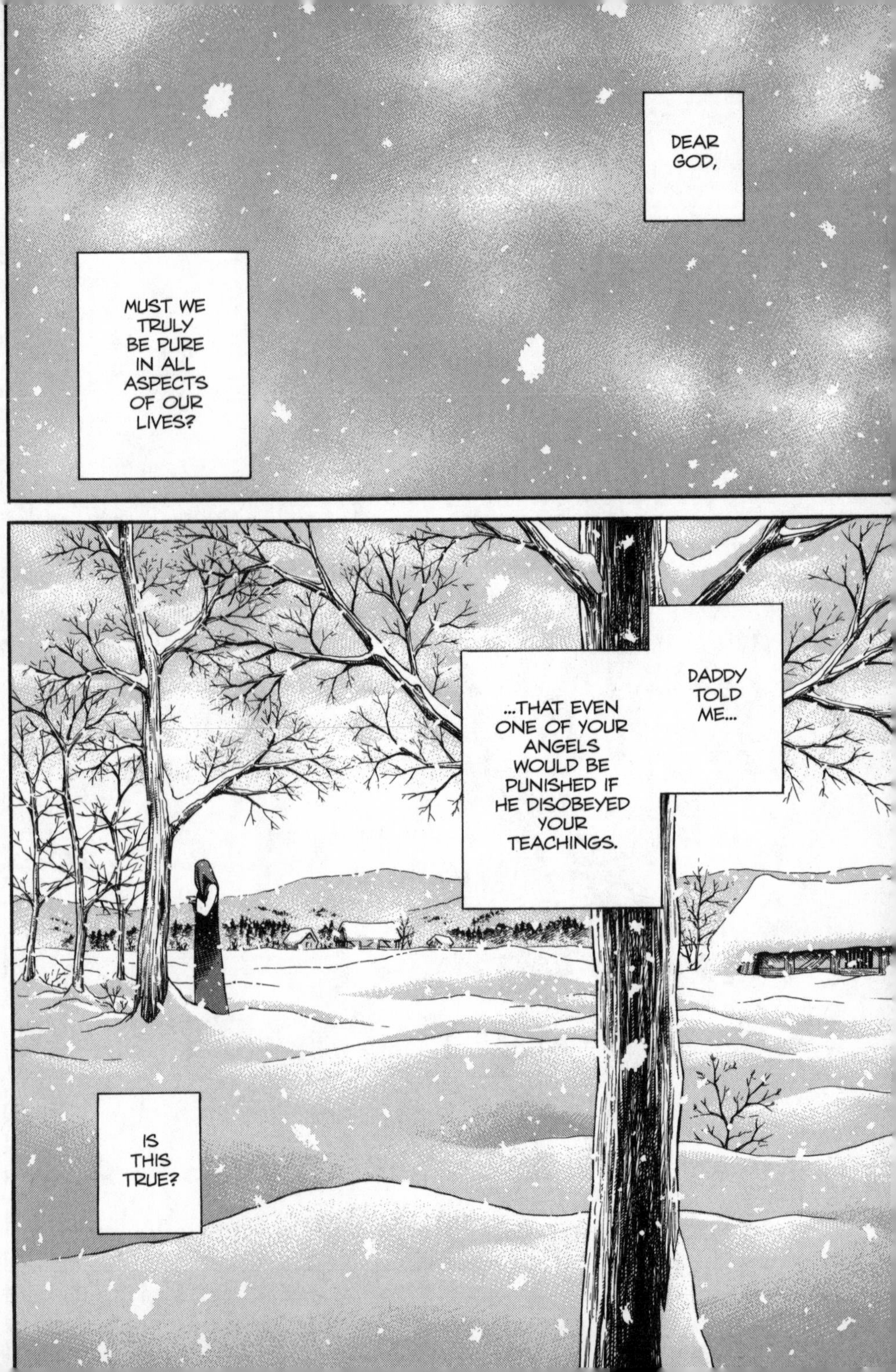
DEAR GOD,
MUST WE TRULY BE PURE IN ALL ASPECTS OF OUR LIVES?
DADDY TOLD ME...
...THAT EVEN ONE OF YOUR ANGELS WOULD BE PUNISHED IF HE DISOBEYED YOUR TEACHINGS.
IS THIS TRUE?

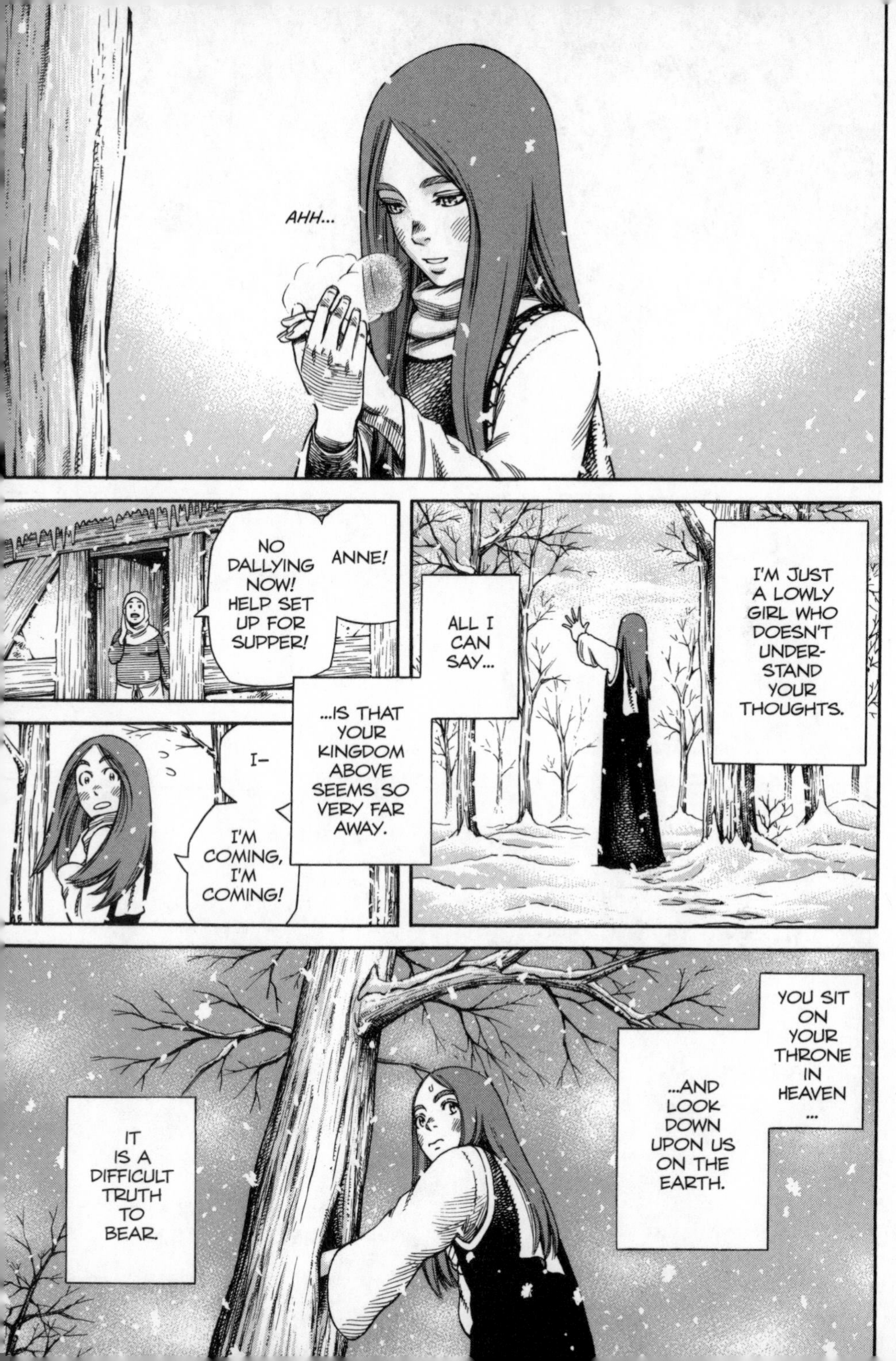
AHH...
I'M JUST A LOWLY GIRL WHO DOESN'T UNDER-STAND YOUR THOUGHTS.
ALL I CAN SAY...
...IS THAT YOUR KINGDOM ABOVE SEEMS SO VERY FAR AWAY.
ANNE!
NO DALLYING NOW! HELP SET UP FOR SUPPER!
I–
I'M COMING, I'M COMING!
YOU SIT ON YOUR THRONE IN HEAVEN ...
...AND LOOK DOWN UPON US ON THE EARTH.
IT IS A DIFFICULT TRUTH TO BEAR.

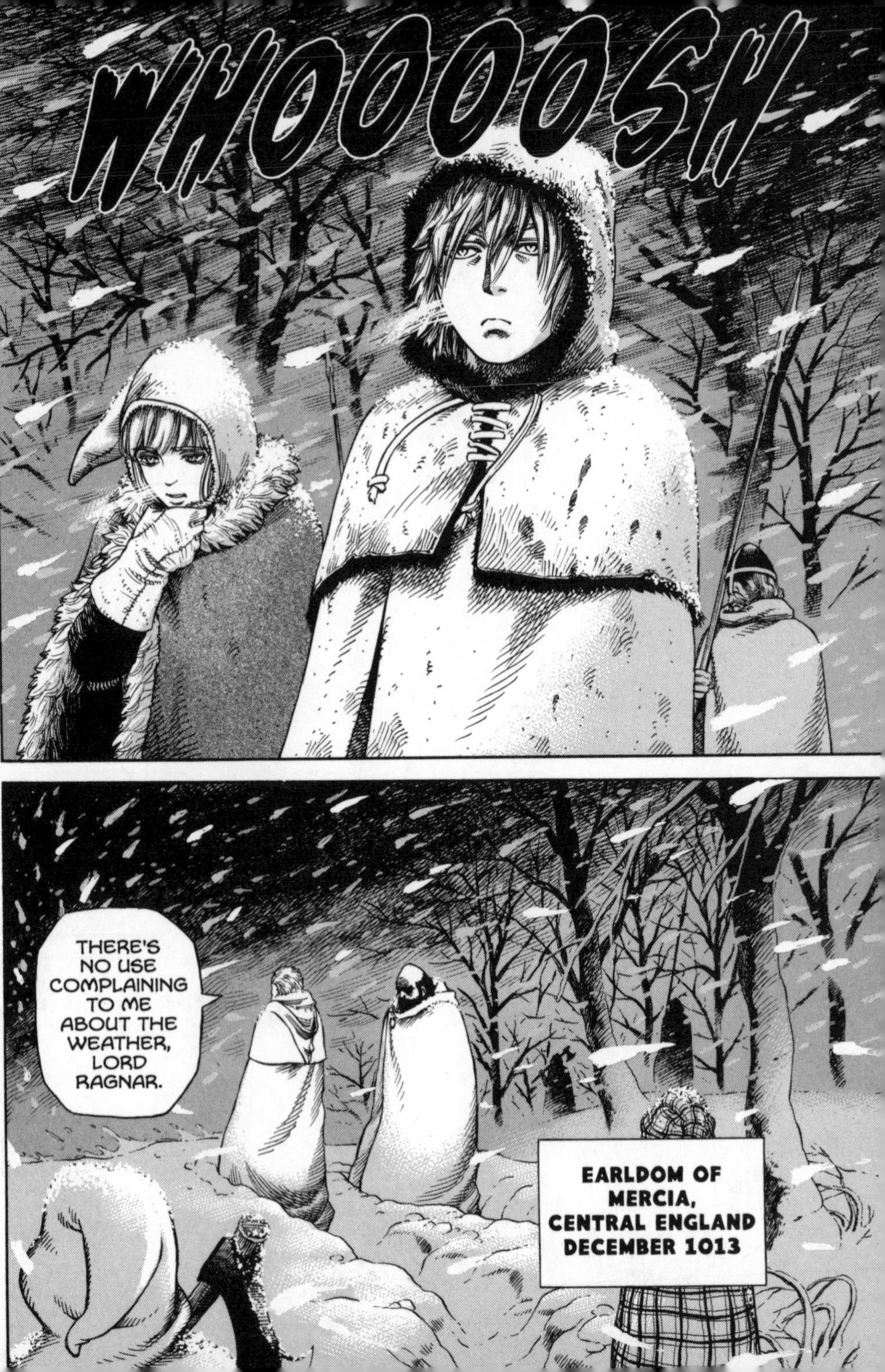
WHOOOOSH
EARLDOM OF MERCIA, CENTRAL ENGLAND DECEMBER 1013
THERE'S NO USE COMPLAINING TO ME ABOUT THE WEATHER, LORD RAGNAR.

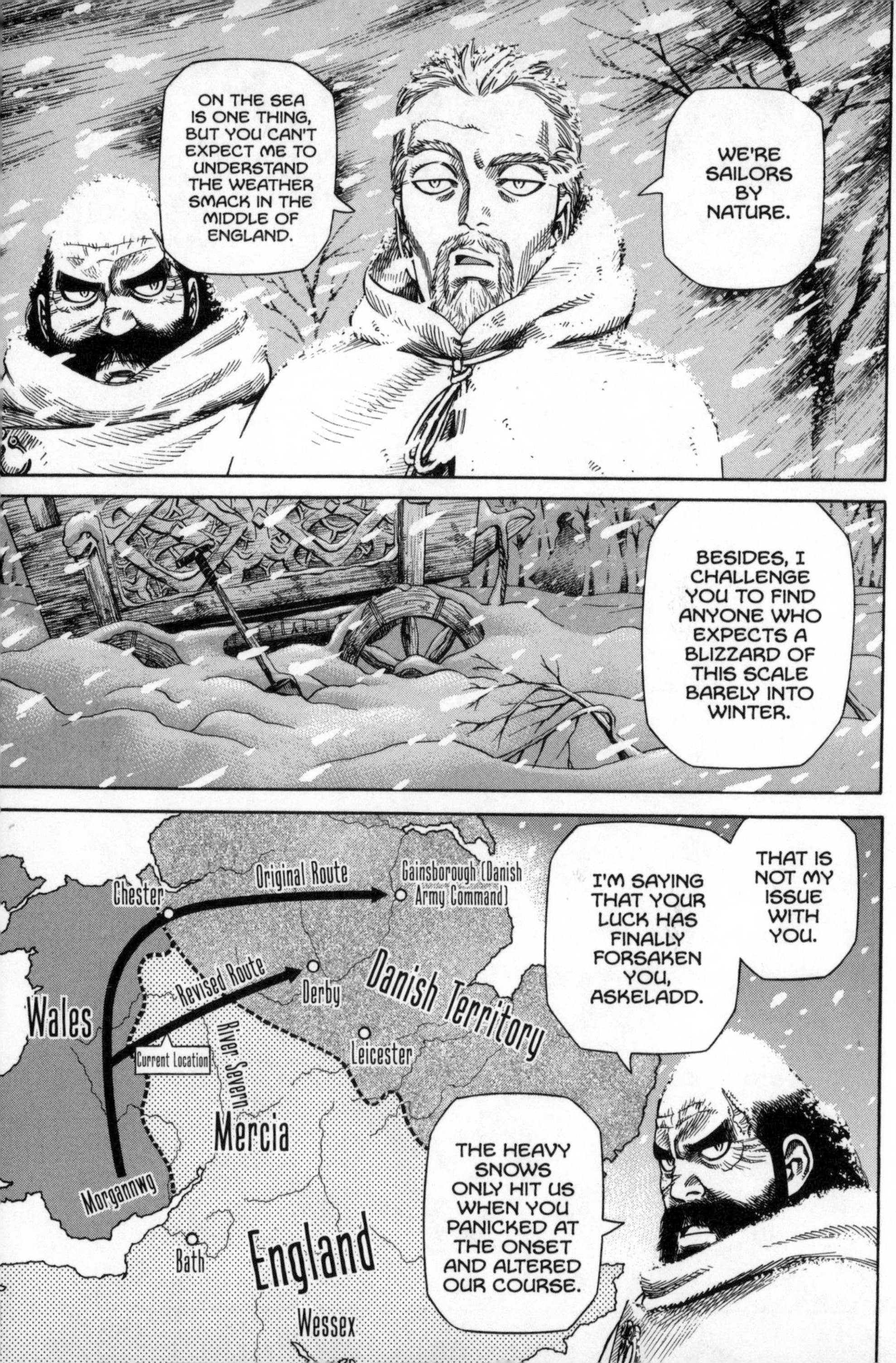
WE'RE SAILORS BY NATURE.
ON THE SEA IS ONE THING, BUT YOU CAN'T EXPECT ME TO UNDERSTAND THE WEATHER SMACK IN THE MIDDLE OF ENGLAND.
BESIDES, I CHALLENGE YOU TO FIND ANYONE WHO EXPECTS A BLIZZARD OF THIS SCALE BARELY INTO WINTER.
THAT IS NOT MY ISSUE WITH YOU.
I'M SAYING THAT YOUR LUCK HAS FINALLY FORSAKEN YOU, ASKELADD.
THE HEAVY SNOWS ONLY HIT US WHEN YOU PANICKED AT THE ONSET AND ALTERED OUR COURSE.
Gainsborough (Danish Army Command)
Original Route
Chester
Revised Route
Derby
Danish Territory
Wales
Current Location
River Severn
Leicester
Mercia
Morgannwg
Bath
England
Wessex

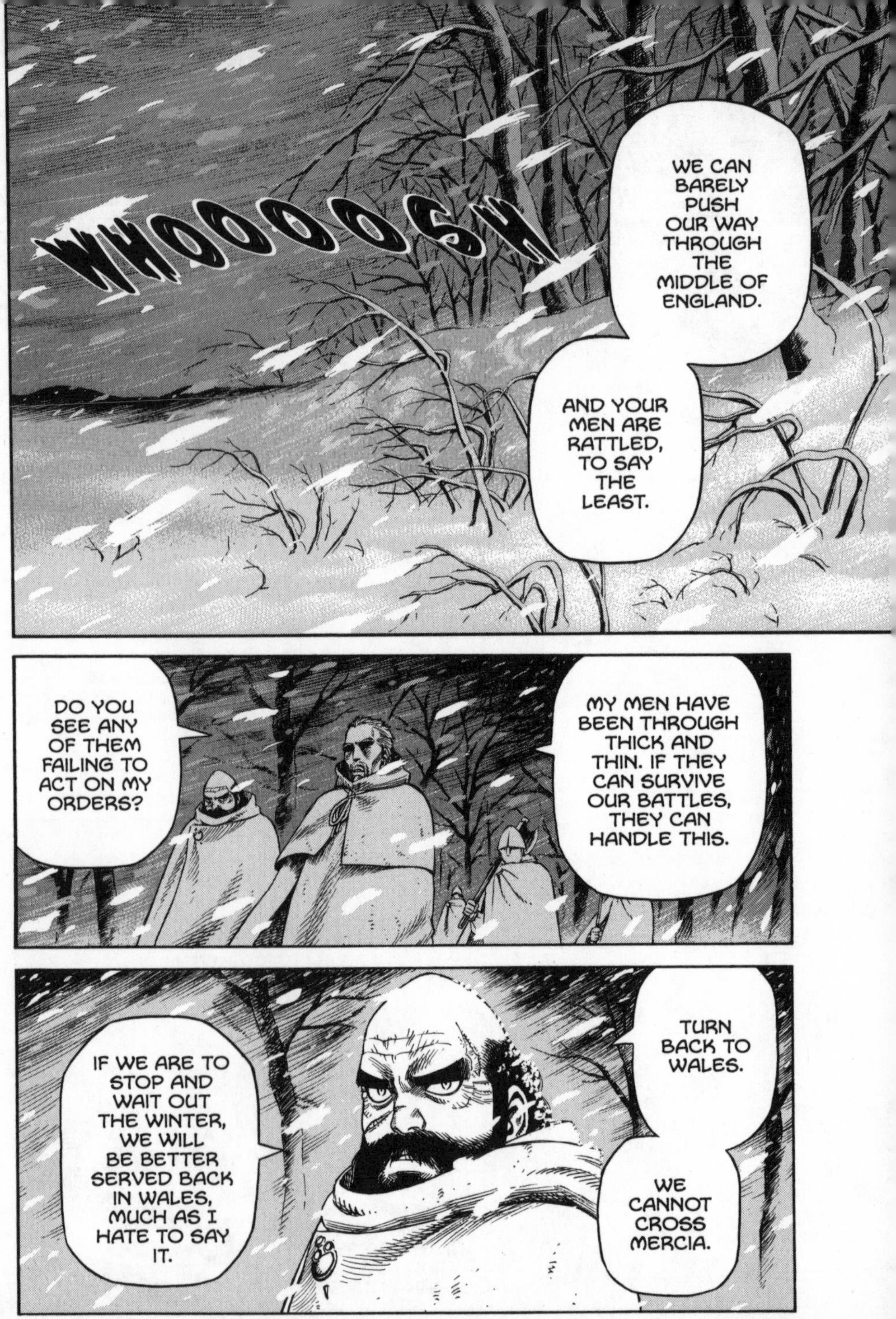
WE CAN BARELY PUSH OUR WAY THROUGH THE MIDDLE OF ENGLAND.
AND YOUR MEN ARE RATTLED, TO SAY THE LEAST.
WHOOOOSH
MY MEN HAVE BEEN THROUGH THICK AND THIN. IF THEY CAN SURVIVE OUR BATTLES, THEY CAN HANDLE THIS.
DO YOU SEE ANY OF THEM FAILING TO ACT ON MY ORDERS?
TURN BACK TO WALES.
WE CANNOT CROSS MERCIA.
IF WE ARE TO STOP AND WAIT OUT THE WINTER, WE WILL BE BETTER SERVED BACK IN WALES, MUCH AS I HATE TO SAY IT.

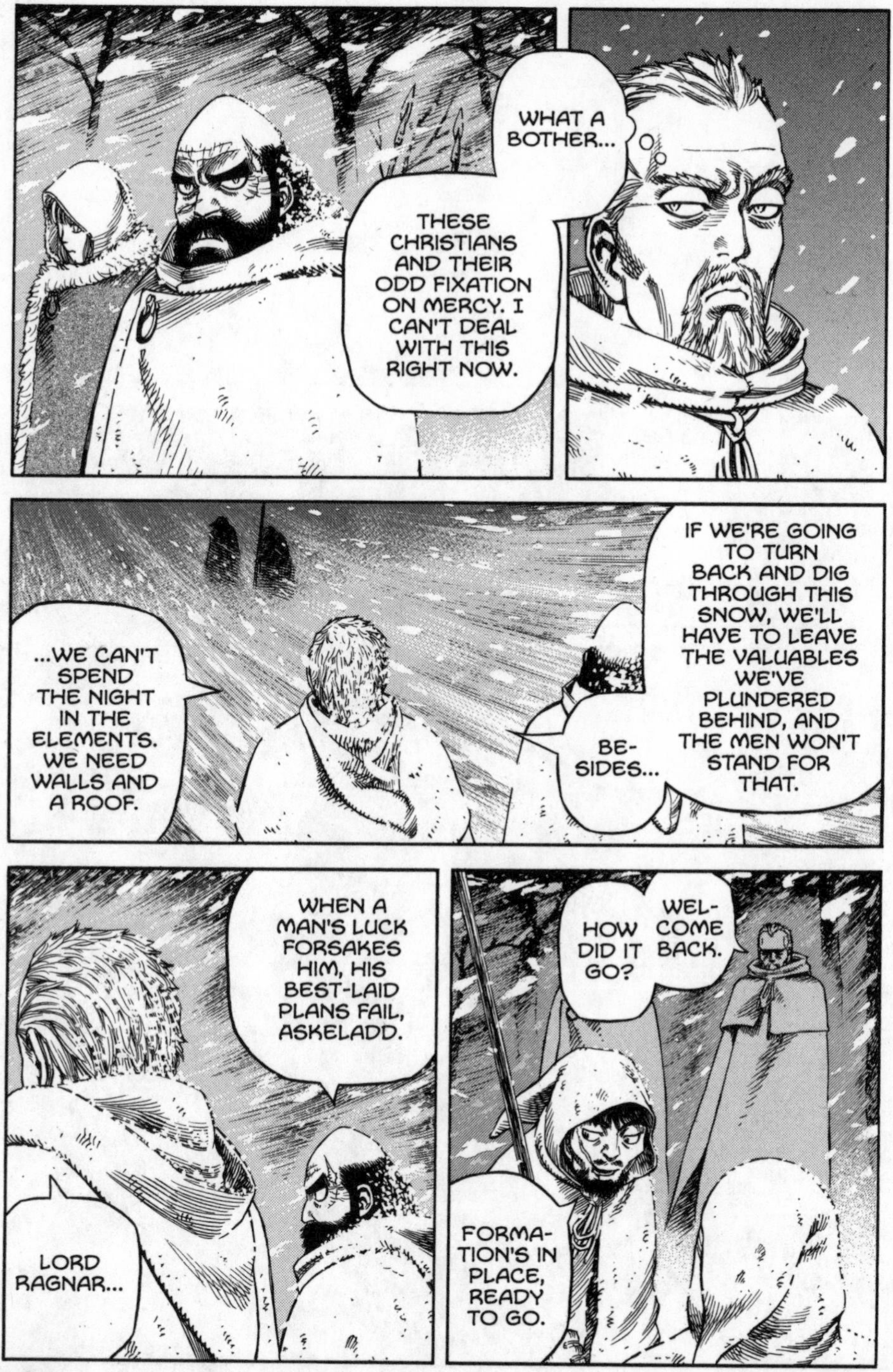
WHAT A BOTHER...
THESE CHRISTIANS AND THEIR ODD FIXATION ON MERCY. I CAN'T DEAL WITH THIS RIGHT NOW.
IF WE'RE GOING TO TURN BACK AND DIG THROUGH THIS SNOW, WE'LL HAVE TO LEAVE THE VALUABLES WE'VE PLUNDERED BEHIND, AND THE MEN WON'T STAND FOR THAT.
BE-SIDES...
...WE CAN'T SPEND THE NIGHT IN THE ELEMENTS. WE NEED WALLS AND A ROOF.
WEL-COME BACK.
HOW DID IT GO?
FORMA-TION'S IN PLACE, READY TO GO.
WHEN A MAN'S LUCK FORSAKES HIM, HIS BEST-LAID PLANS FAIL, ASKELADD.
LORD RAGNAR...

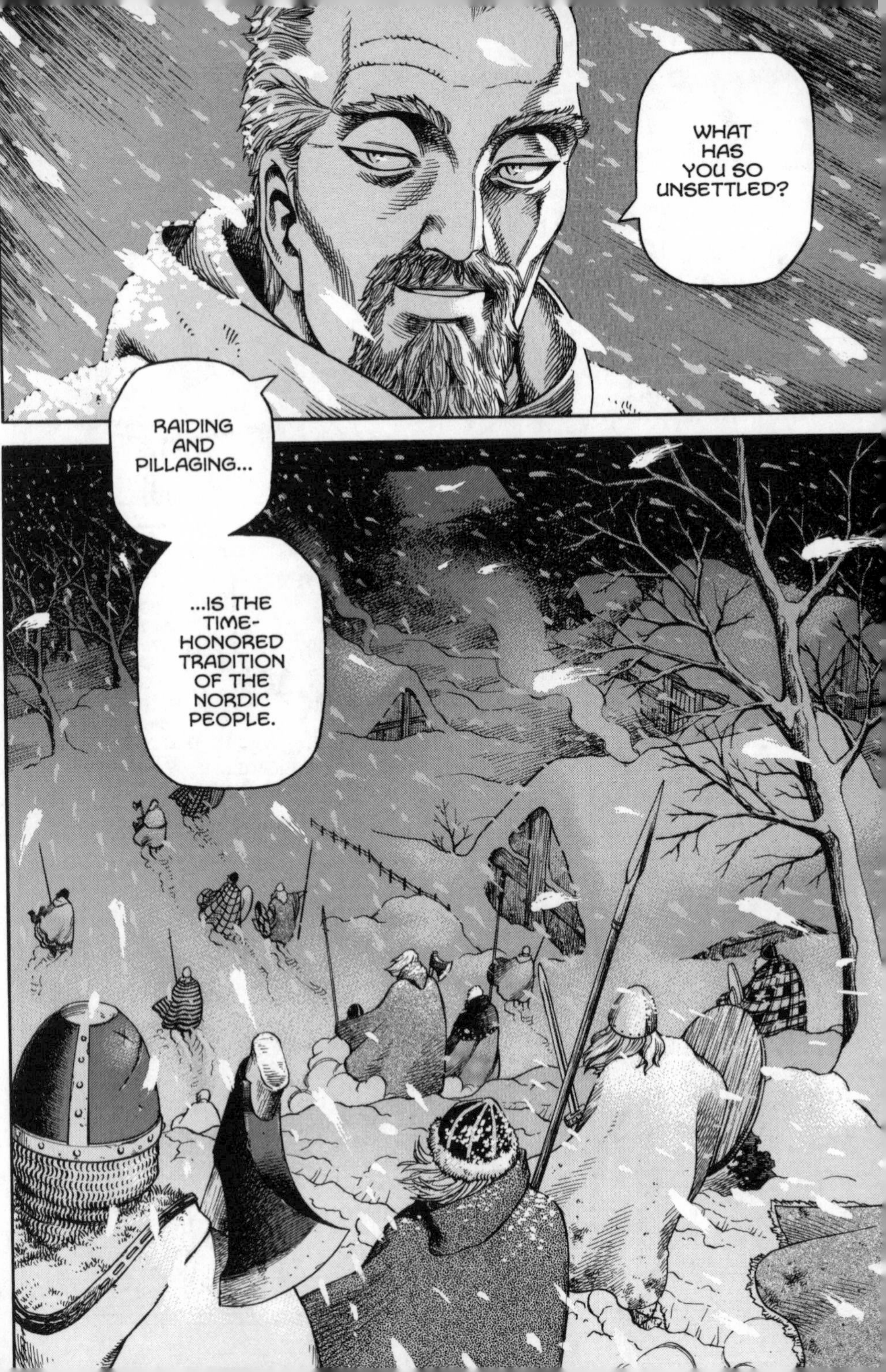
WHAT HAS YOU SO UNSETTLED?
RAIDING AND PILLAGING...
...IS THE TIME-HONORED TRADITION OF THE NORDIC PEOPLE.

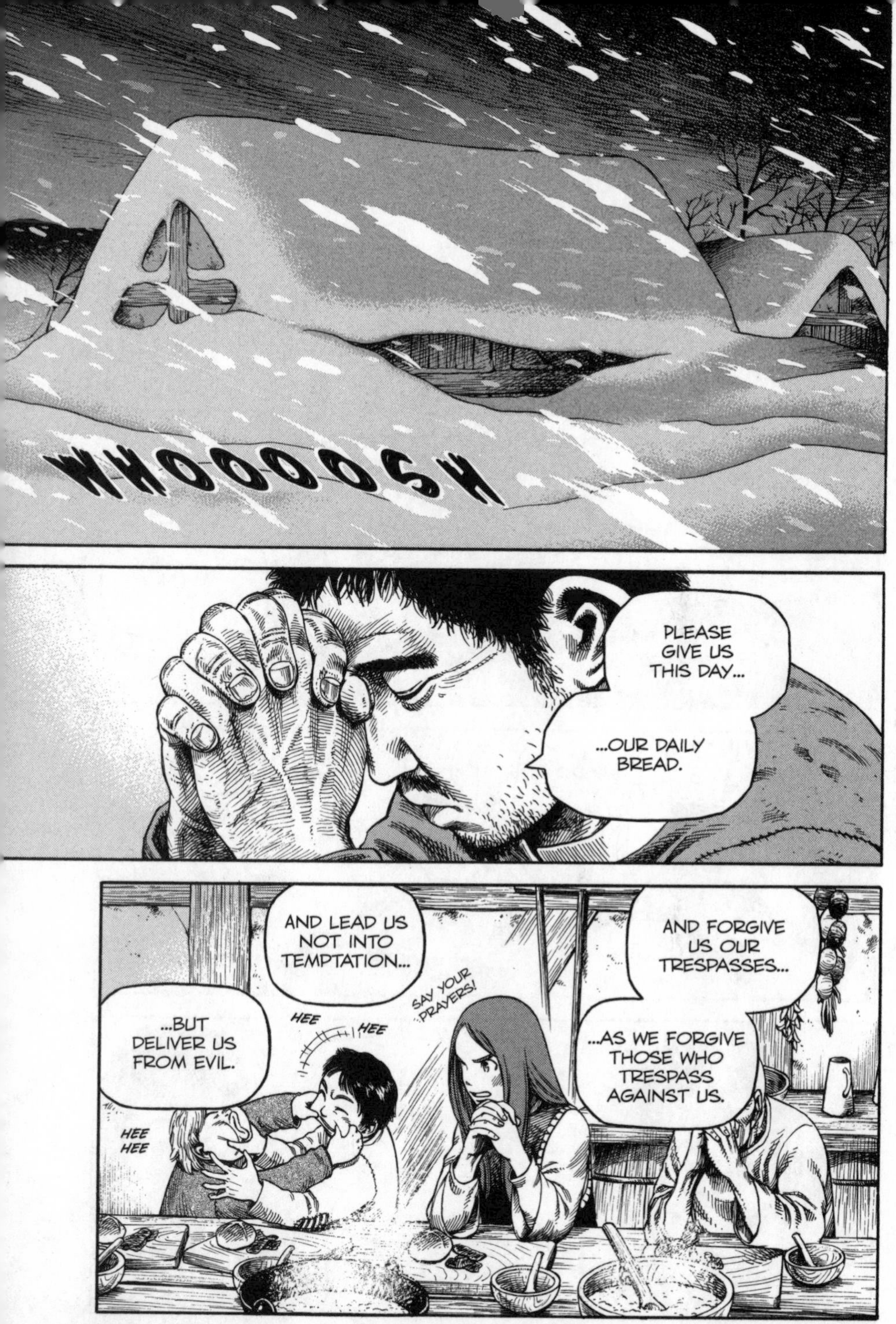
WHOOOOSH
PLEASE GIVE US THIS DAY...
...OUR DAILY BREAD.
AND FORGIVE US OUR TRESPASSES...
...AS WE FORGIVE THOSE WHO TRESPASS AGAINST US.
SAY YOUR PRAYERS!
AND LEAD US NOT INTO TEMPTATION...
HEE HEE
...BUT DELIVER US FROM EVIL.
HEE HEE

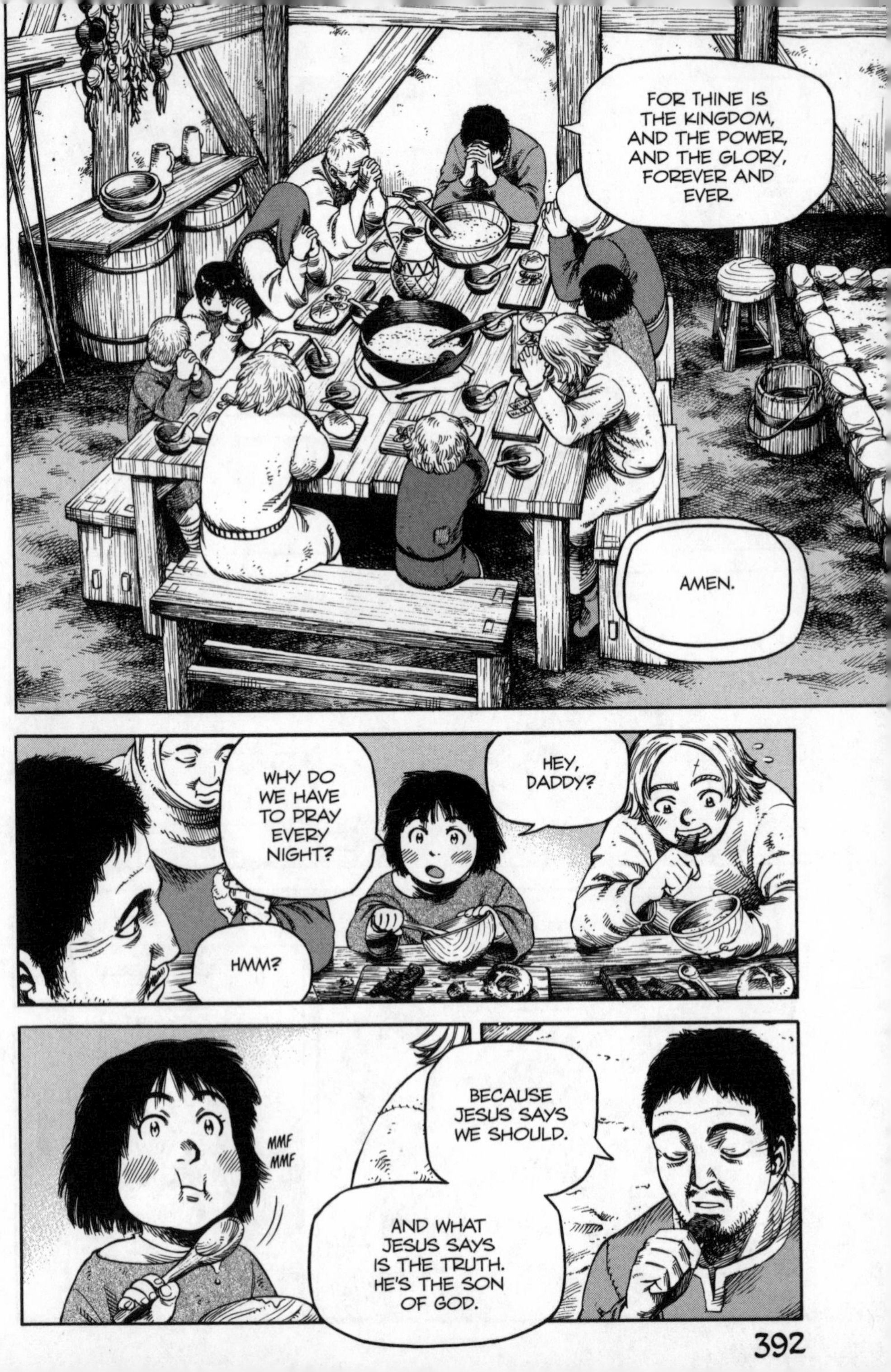
FOR THINE IS THE KINGDOM, AND THE POWER, AND THE GLORY, FOREVER AND EVER.
AMEN.
HEY, DADDY?
WHY DO WE HAVE TO PRAY EVERY NIGHT?
HMM?
BECAUSE JESUS SAYS WE SHOULD.
AND WHAT JESUS SAYS IS THE TRUTH. HE'S THE SON OF GOD.
MMF MMF

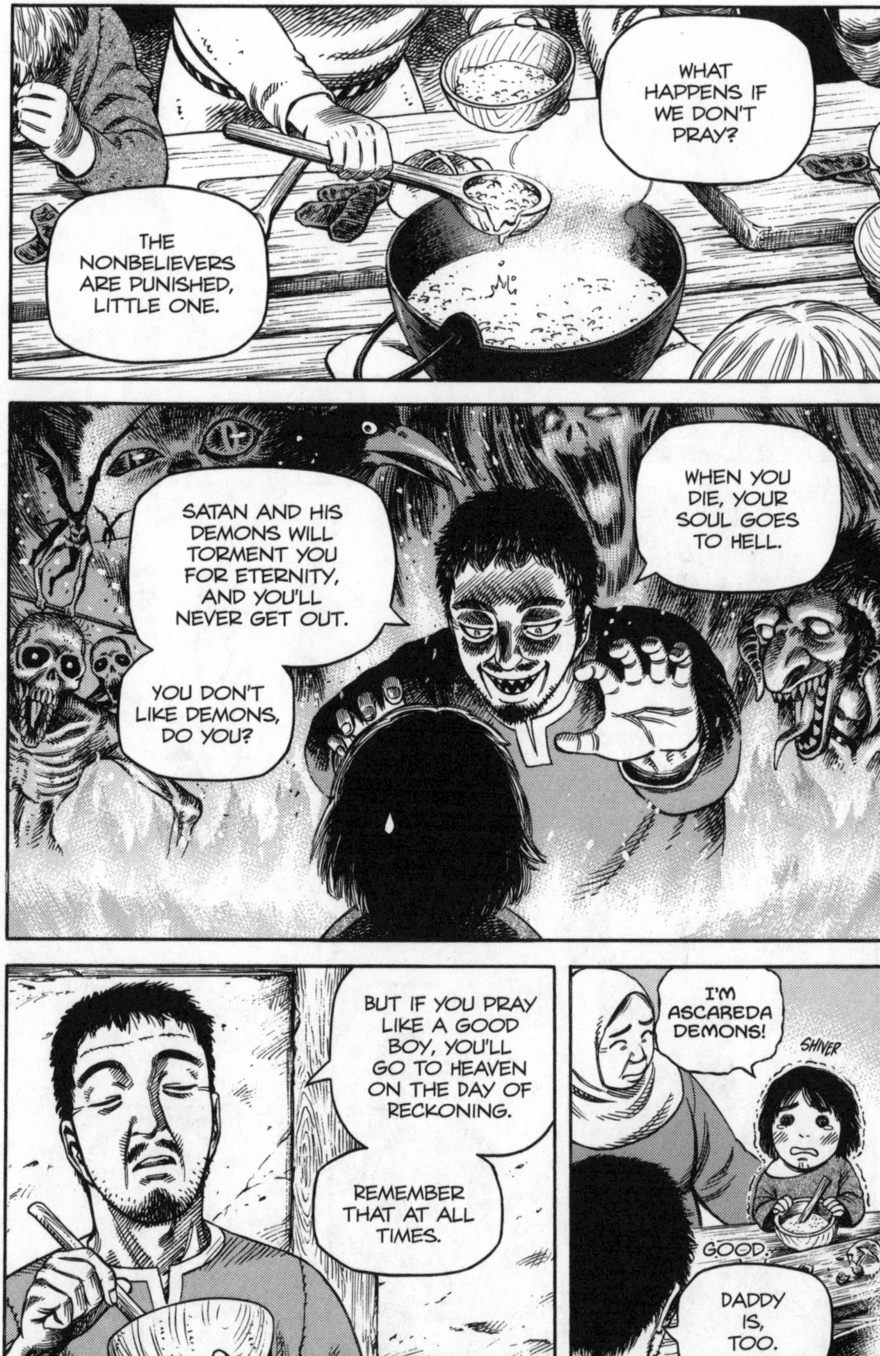
WHAT HAPPENS IF WE DON'T PRAY?
THE NONBELIEVERS ARE PUNISHED, LITTLE ONE.
WHEN YOU DIE, YOUR SOUL GOES TO HELL.
SATAN AND HIS DEMONS WILL TORMENT YOU FOR ETERNITY, AND YOU'LL NEVER GET OUT.
YOU DON'T LIKE DEMONS, DO YOU?
I'M ASCAREDA DEMONS!
SHIVER
GOOD.
DADDY IS, TOO.
BUT IF YOU PRAY LIKE A GOOD BOY, YOU'LL GO TO HEAVEN ON THE DAY OF RECKONING.
REMEMBER THAT AT ALL TIMES.

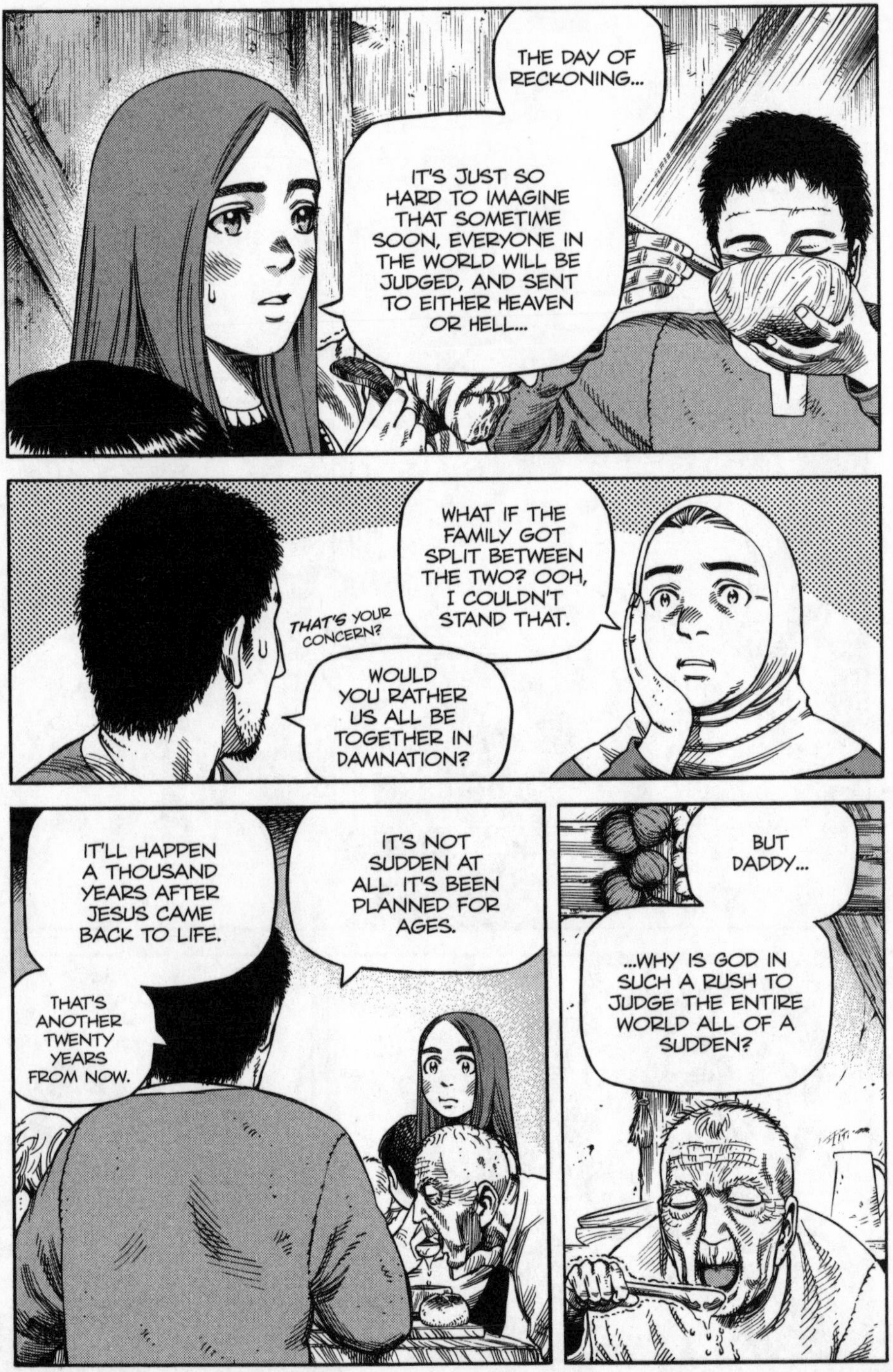
THE DAY OF RECKONING...
IT'S JUST SO HARD TO IMAGINE THAT SOMETIME SOON, EVERYONE IN THE WORLD WILL BE JUDGED, AND SENT TO EITHER HEAVEN OR HELL...
WHAT IF THE FAMILY GOT SPLIT BETWEEN THE TWO? OOH, I COULDN'T STAND THAT.
THAT'S YOUR CONCERN?
WOULD YOU RATHER US ALL BE TOGETHER IN DAMNATION?
BUT DADDY...
...WHY IS GOD IN SUCH A RUSH TO JUDGE THE ENTIRE WORLD ALL OF A SUDDEN?
IT'S NOT SUDDEN AT ALL. IT'S BEEN PLANNED FOR AGES.
IT'LL HAPPEN A THOUSAND YEARS AFTER JESUS CAME BACK TO LIFE.
THAT'S ANOTHER TWENTY YEARS FROM NOW.

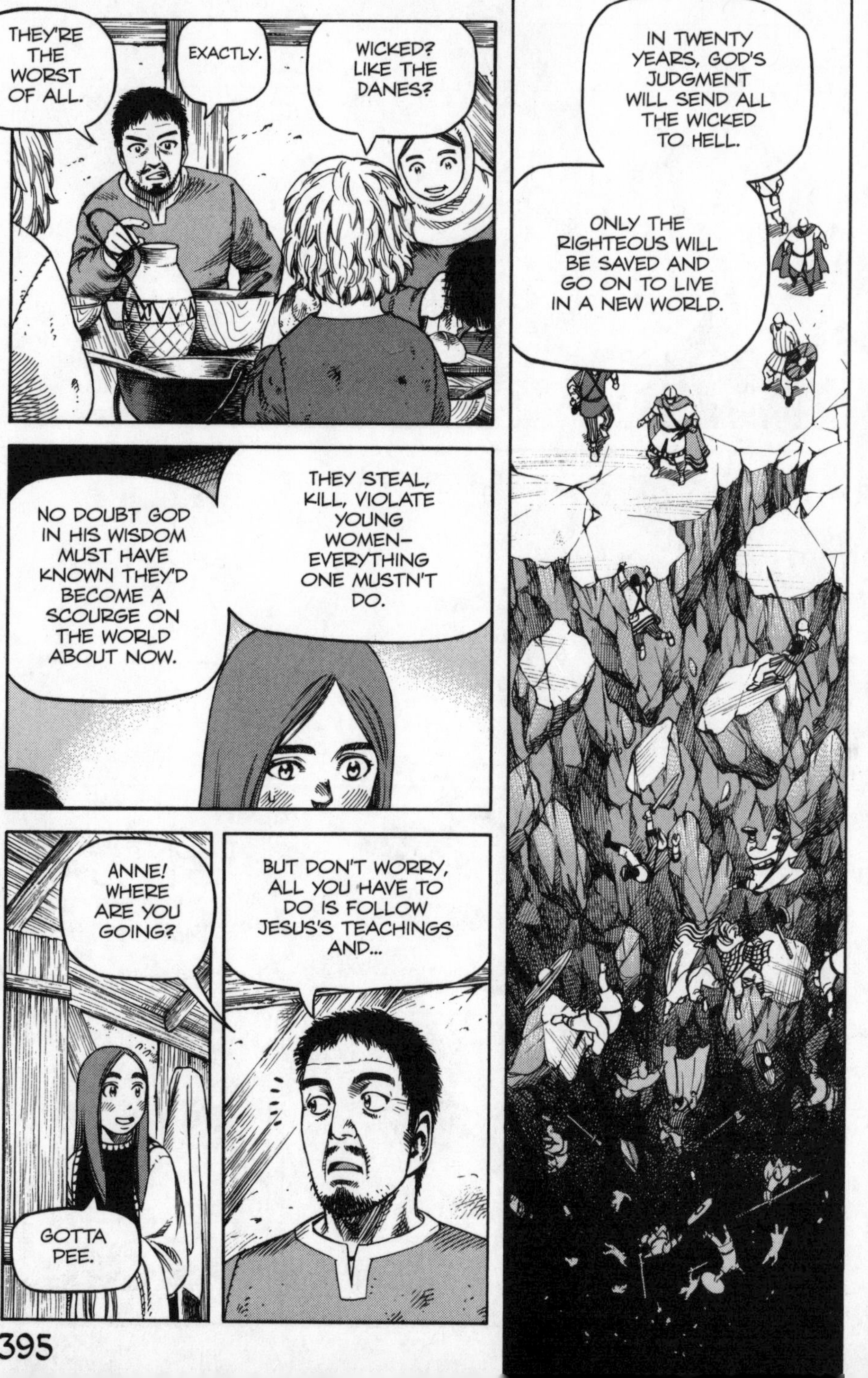
IN TWENTY YEARS, GOD'S JUDGMENT WILL SEND ALL THE WICKED TO HELL.
ONLY THE RIGHTEOUS WILL BE SAVED AND GO ON TO LIVE IN A NEW WORLD.
WICKED? LIKE THE DANES?
EXACTLY.
THEY'RE THE WORST OF ALL.
THEY STEAL, KILL, VIOLATE YOUNG WOMEN— EVERYTHING ONE MUSTN'T DO.
NO DOUBT GOD IN HIS WISDOM MUST HAVE KNOWN THEY'D BECOME A SCOURGE ON THE WORLD ABOUT NOW.
BUT DON'T WORRY, ALL YOU HAVE TO DO IS FOLLOW JESUS'S TEACHINGS AND...
ANNE! WHERE ARE YOU GOING?
GOTTA PEE.

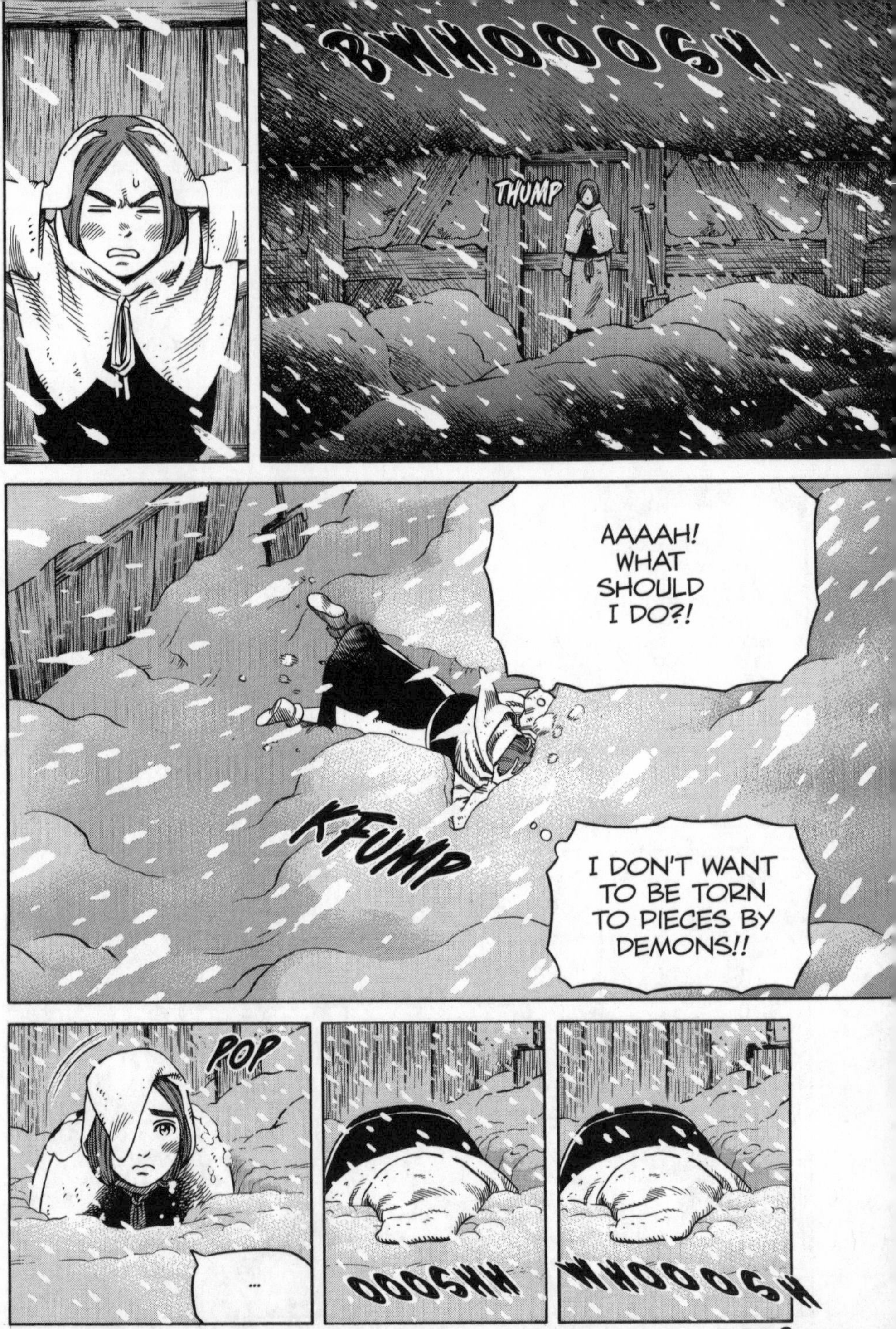
BWHOOOSH
THUMP
AAAAH! WHAT SHOULD I DO?!
I DON'T WANT TO BE TORN TO PIECES BY DEMONS!!
KFUMP
WHOOOSH
OOOSHH
POP
...

SHINK

FSHUP
FSHUP

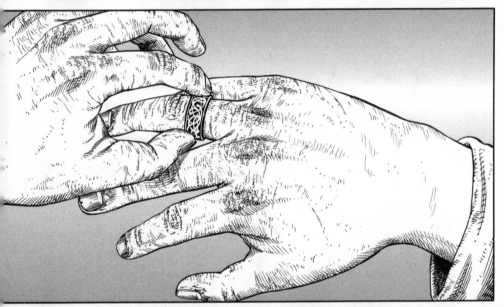

OH,
BUT...

...IT'S SO
BEAUTIFUL...

WHOOOSH

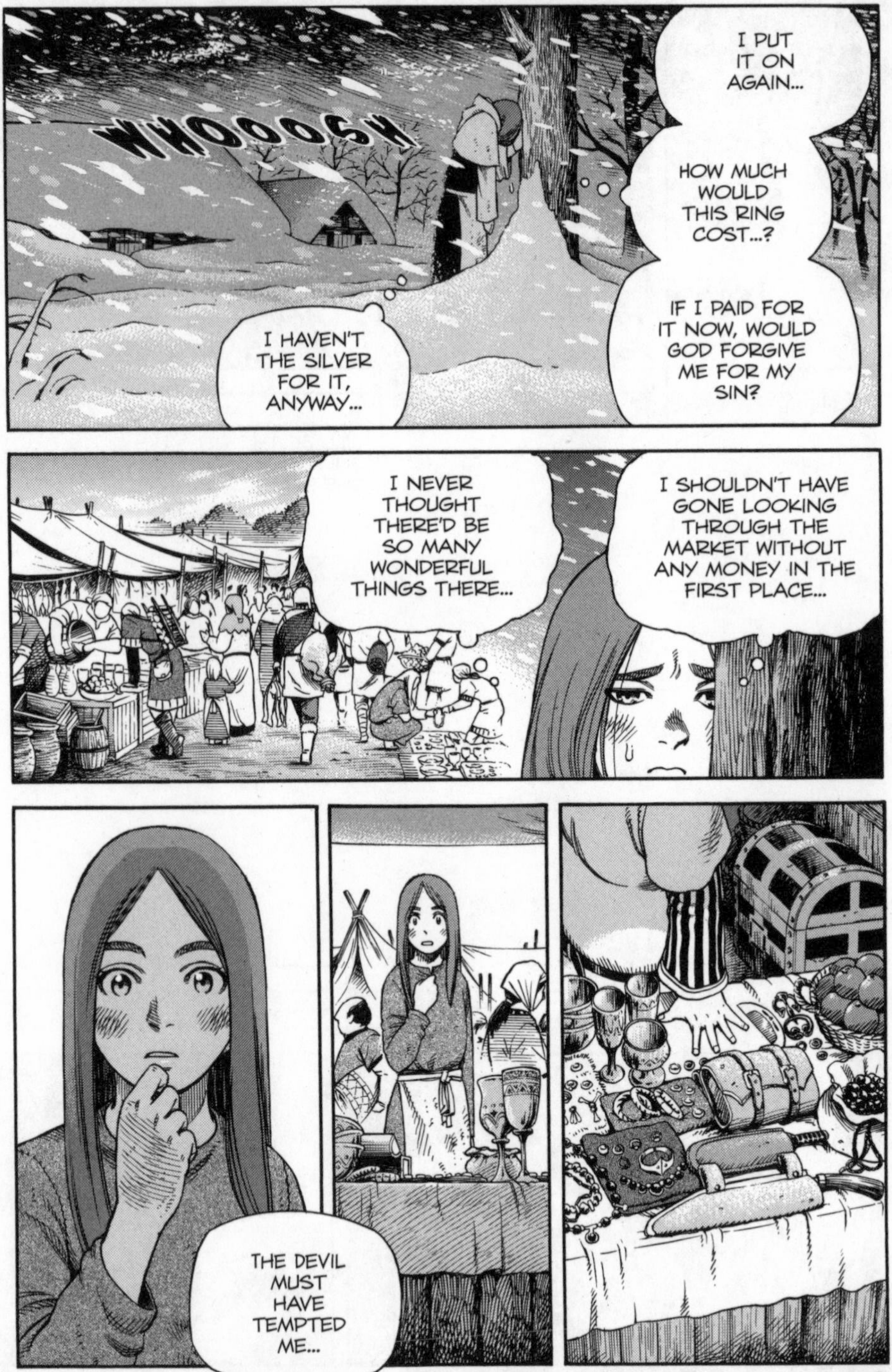
I PUT IT ON AGAIN...
WHOOOSH
HOW MUCH WOULD THIS RING COST...?
IF I PAID FOR IT NOW, WOULD GOD FORGIVE ME FOR MY SIN?
I HAVEN'T THE SILVER FOR IT, ANYWAY...
I SHOULDN'T HAVE GONE LOOKING THROUGH THE MARKET WITHOUT ANY MONEY IN THE FIRST PLACE...
I NEVER THOUGHT THERE'D BE SO MANY WONDERFUL THINGS THERE...
THE DEVIL MUST HAVE TEMPTED ME...

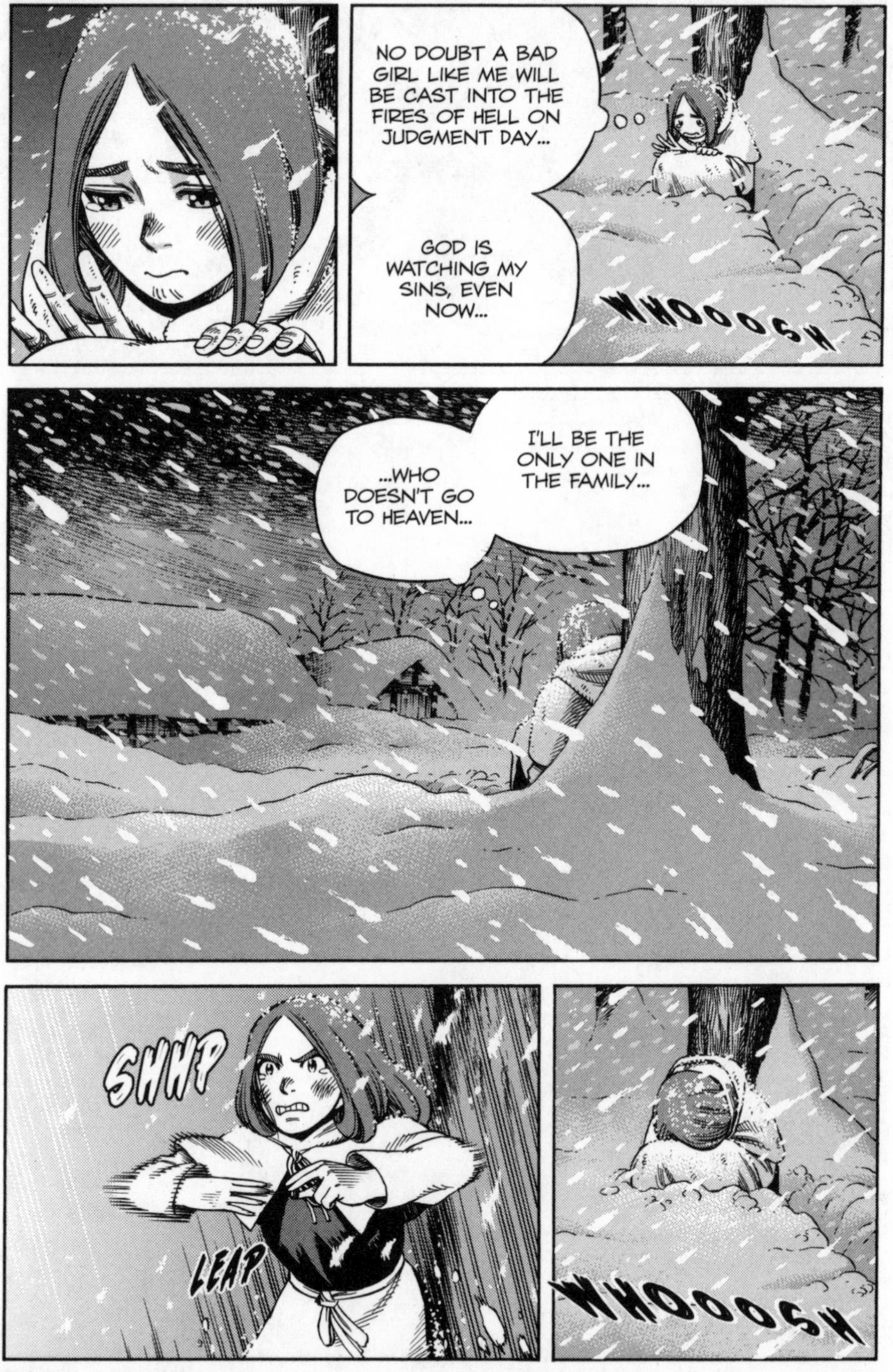
NO DOUBT A BAD GIRL LIKE ME WILL BE CAST INTO THE FIRES OF HELL ON JUDGMENT DAY...
GOD IS WATCHING MY SINS, EVEN NOW...
WHOOOOSH
I'LL BE THE ONLY ONE IN THE FAMILY...
...WHO DOESN'T GO TO HEAVEN...
WHOOOOSH
SHHP
LEAP

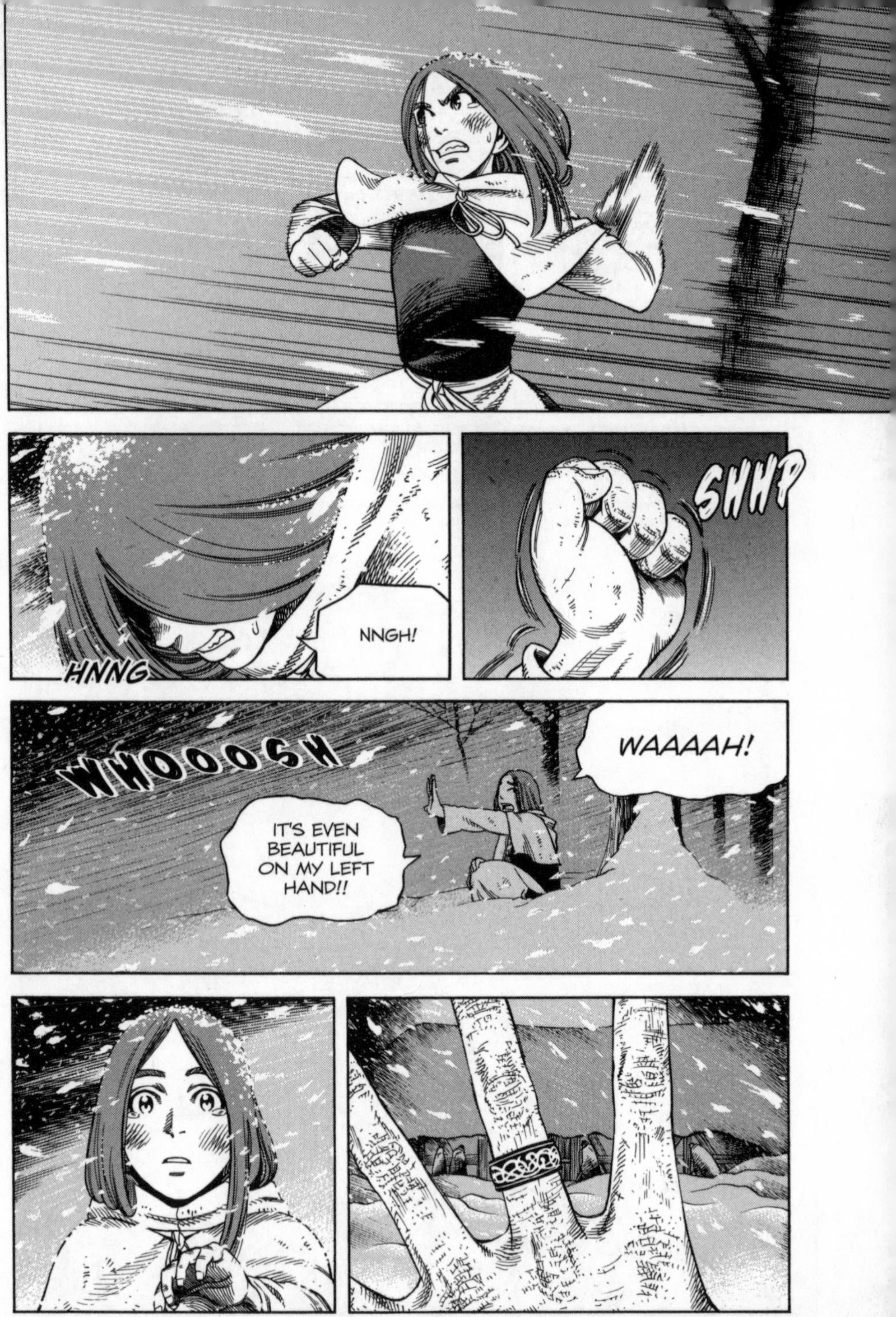
SHHP
NNGH!
HNNG
WAAAAH!
WHOOOSH
IT'S EVEN BEAUTIFUL ON MY LEFT HAND!!

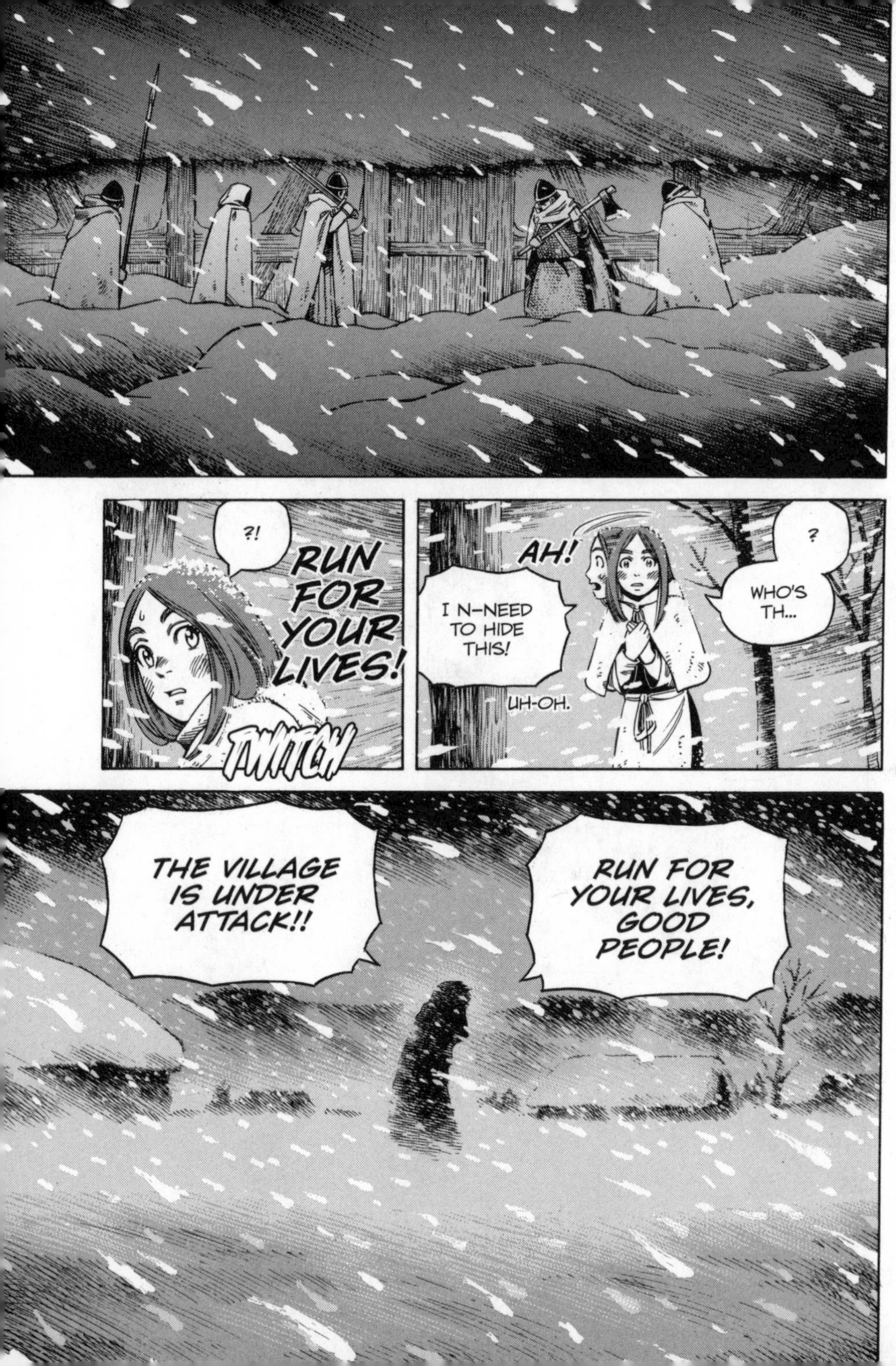
?
WHO'S TH...
AH!
I N-NEED TO HIDE THIS!
UH-OH.
?!
RUN FOR YOUR LIVES!
TWITCH
RUN FOR YOUR LIVES, GOOD PEOPLE!
THE VILLAGE IS UNDER ATTACK!!

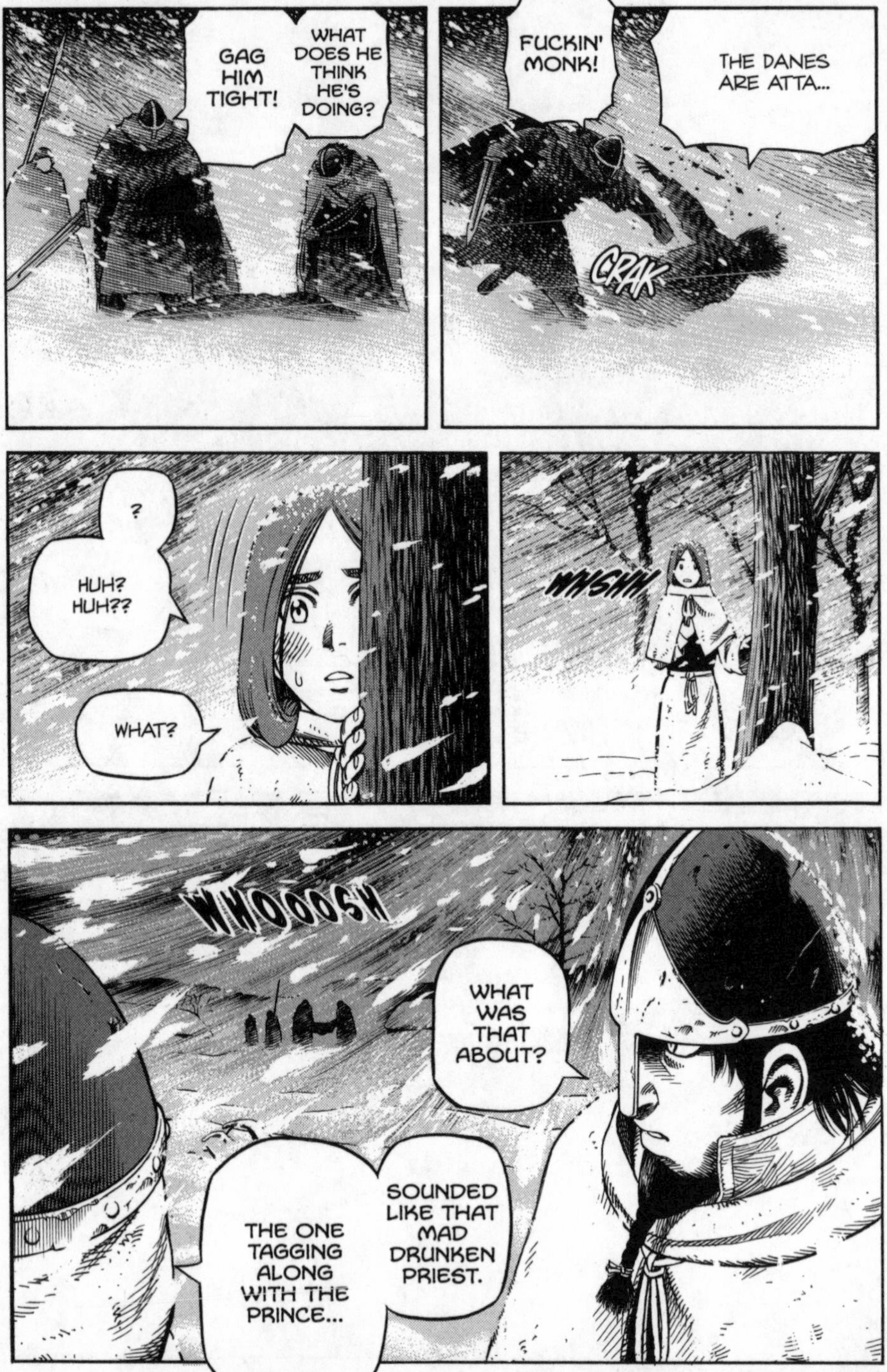
FUCKIN' MONK!
THE DANES ARE ATTA...
CRAK
WHAT DOES HE THINK HE'S DOING?
GAG HIM TIGHT!
WHSHH
?
HUH? HUH??
WHAT?
WHOOOSH
WHAT WAS THAT ABOUT?
SOUNDED LIKE THAT MAD DRUNKEN PRIEST.
THE ONE TAGGING ALONG WITH THE PRINCE...

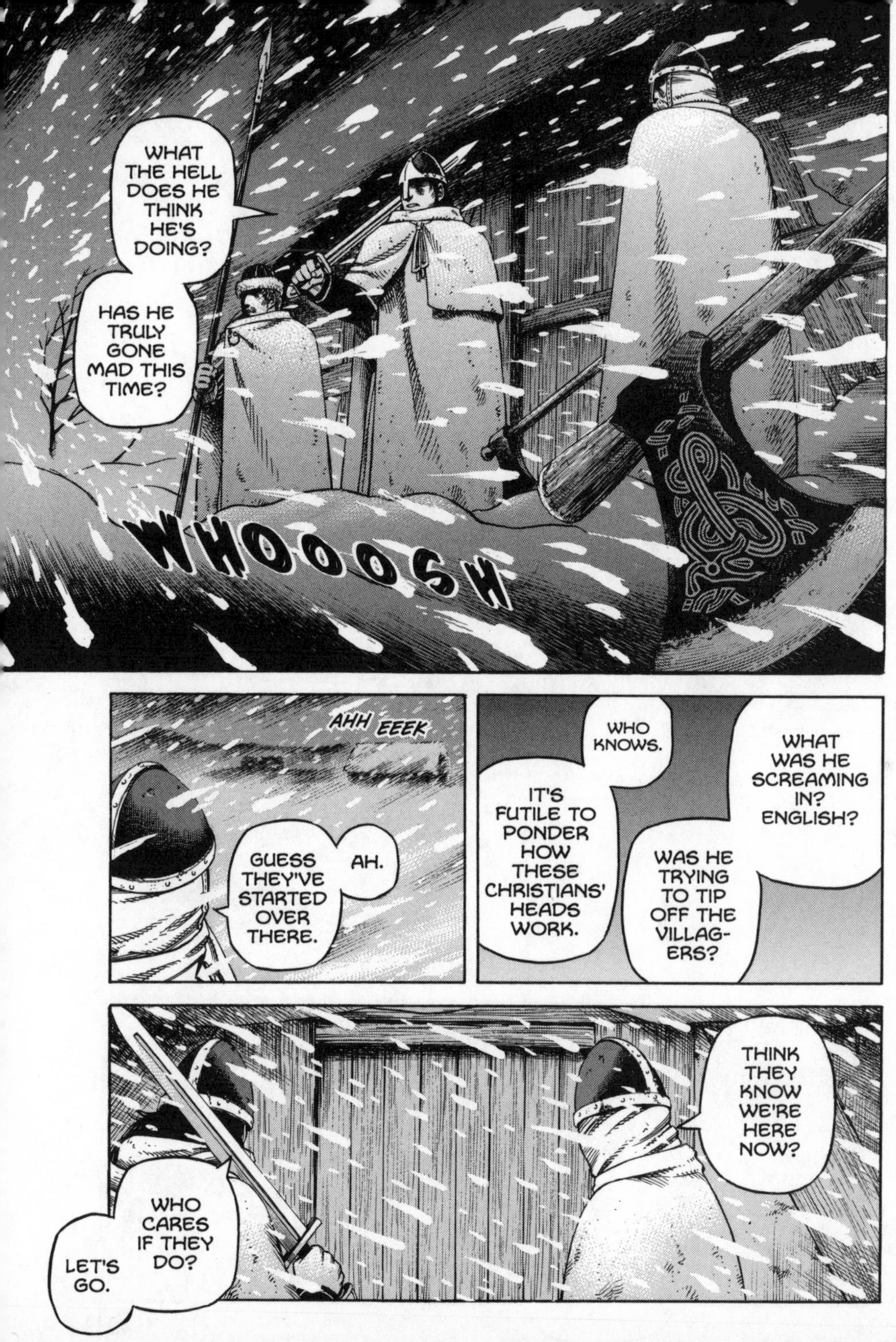
WHAT THE HELL DOES HE THINK HE'S DOING?
HAS HE TRULY GONE MAD THIS TIME?
WHOOOSH
WHAT WAS HE SCREAMING IN? ENGLISH?
WAS HE TRYING TO TIP OFF THE VILLAG-ERS?
WHO KNOWS.
IT'S FUTILE TO PONDER HOW THESE CHRISTIANS' HEADS WORK.
AHH EEEK
AH.
GUESS THEY'VE STARTED OVER THERE.
THINK THEY KNOW WE'RE HERE NOW?
WHO CARES IF THEY DO?
LET'S GO.

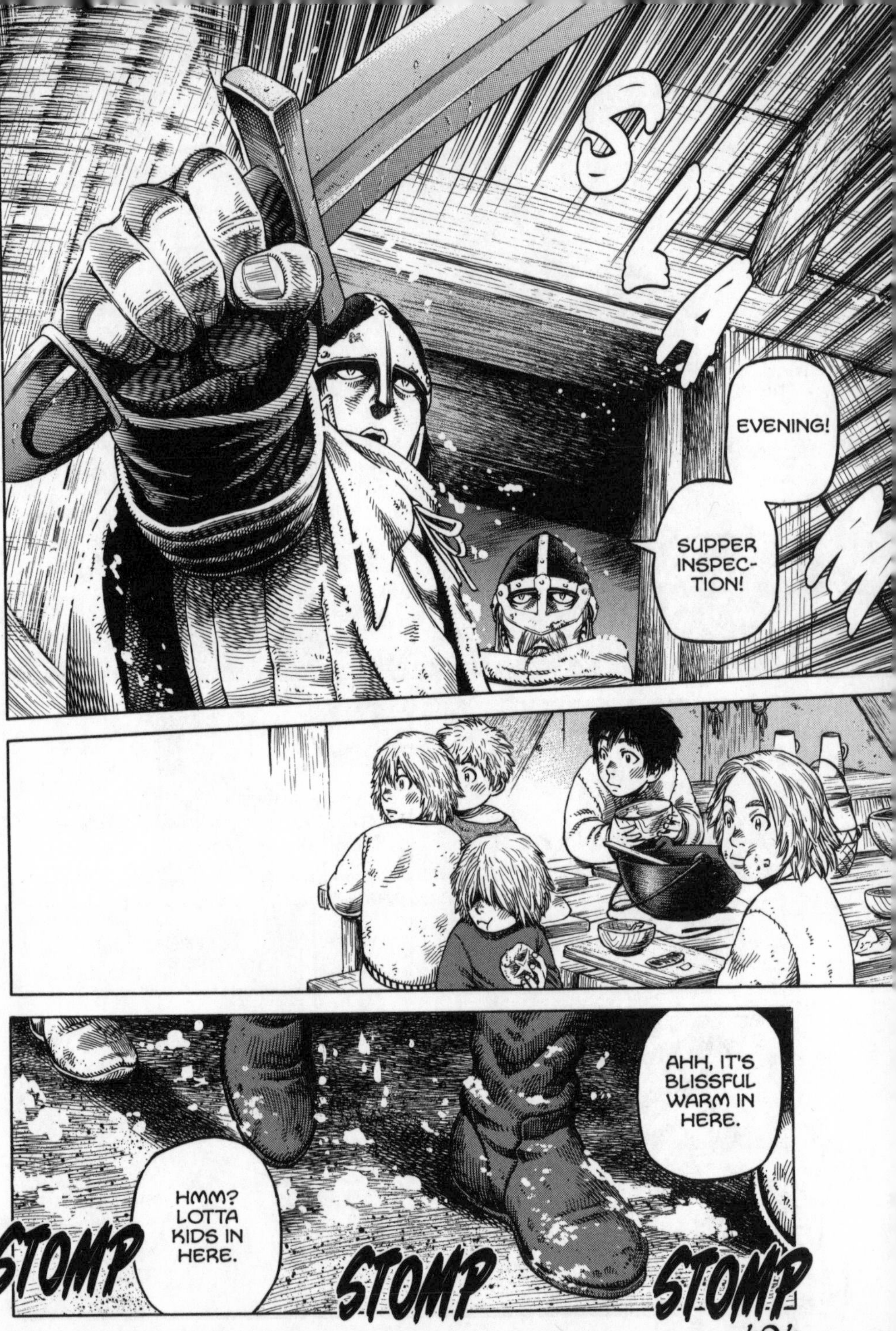
SLAM
EVENING!
SUPPER INSPECTION!
AHH, IT'S BLISSFUL WARM IN HERE.
HMM? LOTTA KIDS IN HERE.
STOMP
STOMP
STOMP

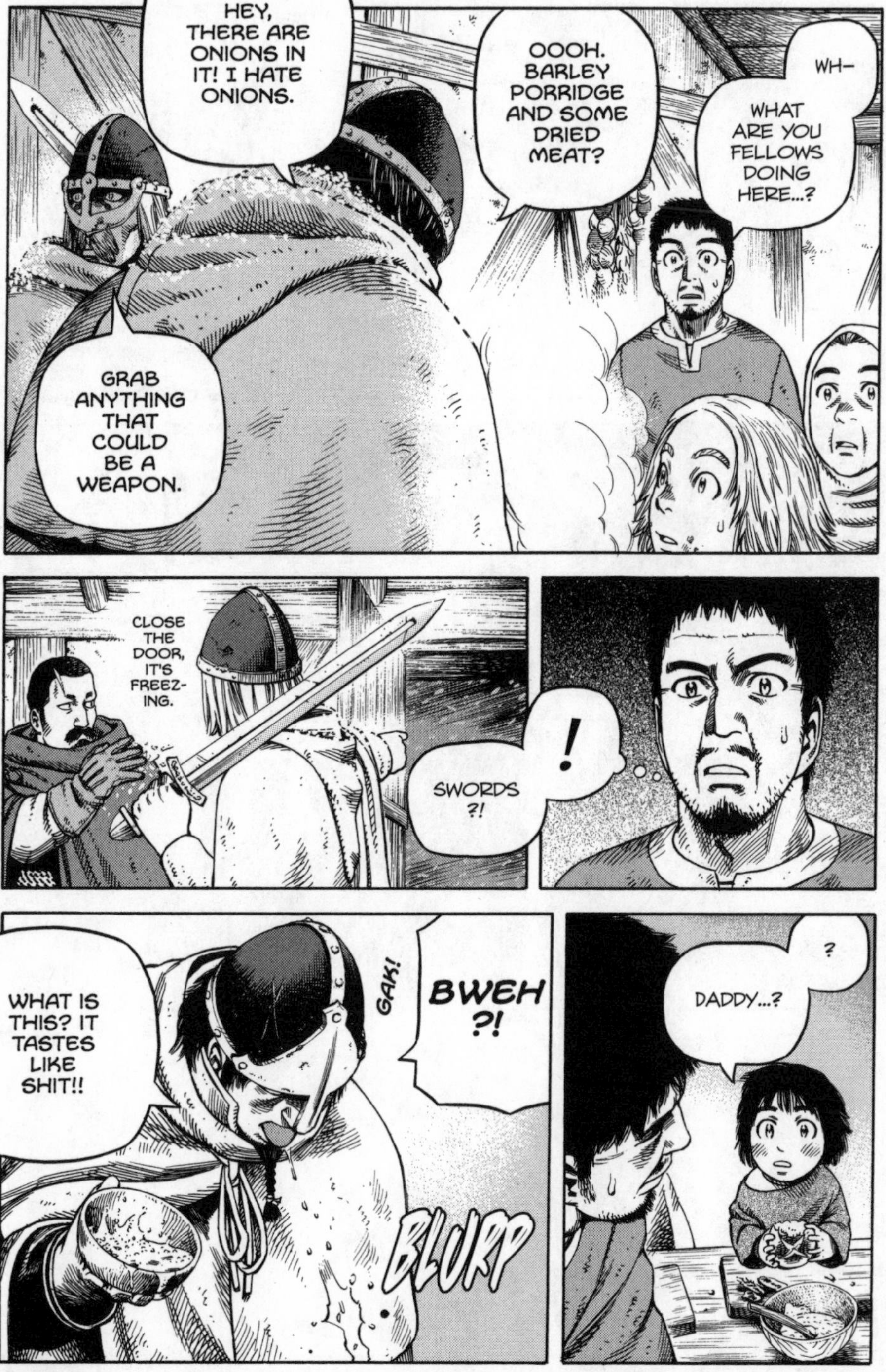
WH—
WHAT ARE YOU FELLOWS DOING HERE...?
OOOH. BARLEY PORRIDGE AND SOME DRIED MEAT?
HEY, THERE ARE ONIONS IN IT! I HATE ONIONS.
GRAB ANYTHING THAT COULD BE A WEAPON.
!
SWORDS ?!
CLOSE THE DOOR, IT'S FREEZ-ING.
?
DADDY...?
BWEH ?!
GAK!
WHAT IS THIS? IT TASTES LIKE SHIT!!
BLURP

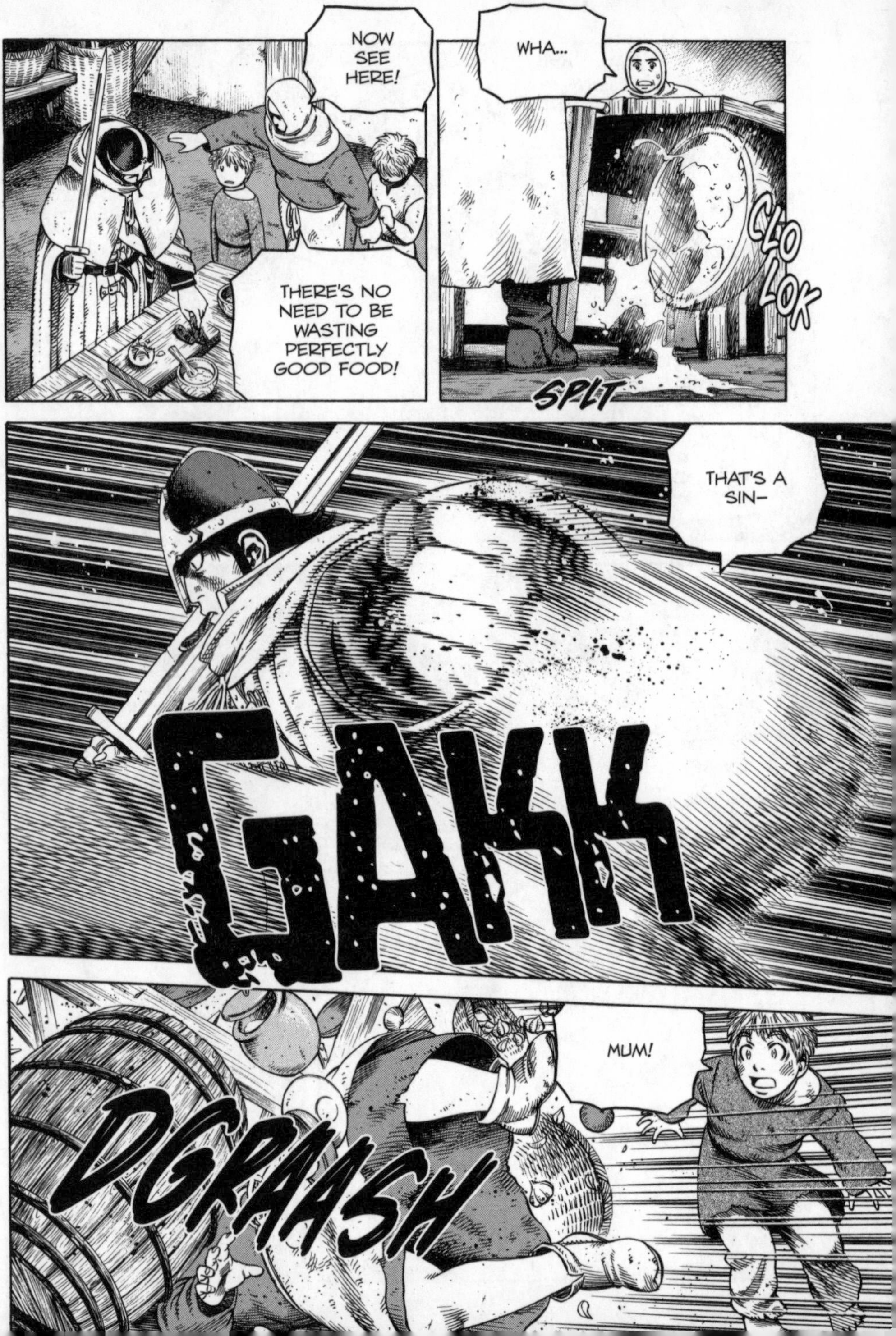
WHA...
CLO LOK
SPLT
NOW SEE HERE!
THERE'S NO NEED TO BE WASTING PERFECTLY GOOD FOOD!
THAT'S A SIN-
GAKK
MUM!
DGRAASH

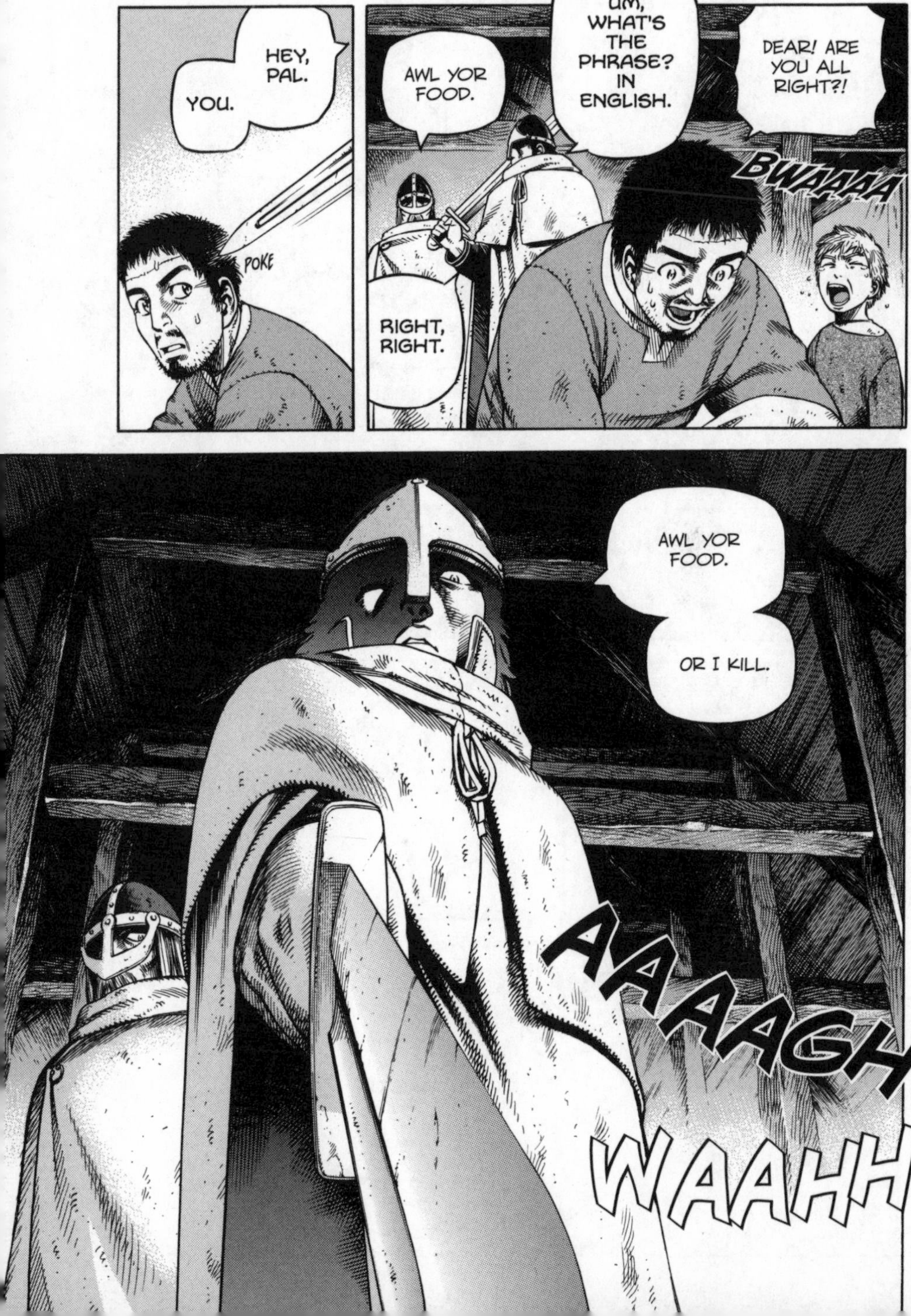
DEAR! ARE YOU ALL RIGHT?!
BWAAAA
UM, WHAT'S THE PHRASE? IN ENGLISH.
AWL YOR FOOD.
RIGHT, RIGHT.
HEY, PAL.
YOU.
POKE
AWL YOR FOOD.
OR I KILL.
AAAAGH
WAAHH

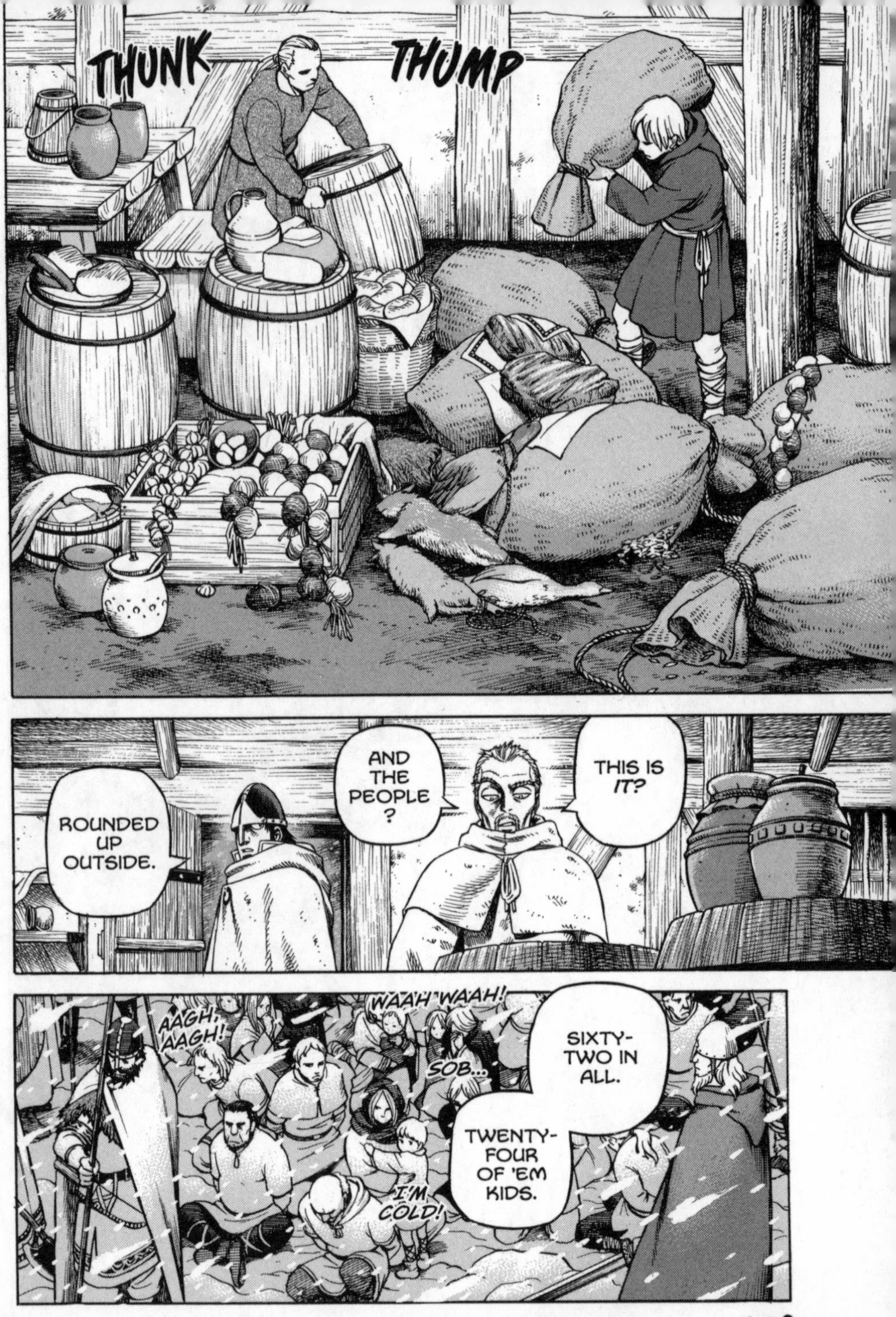
THUMP
THUNK
THIS IS IT?
AND THE PEOPLE?
ROUNDED UP OUTSIDE.
SIXTY-TWO IN ALL.
TWENTY-FOUR OF 'EM KIDS.
WAAH WAAH!
SOB...
AAGH AAGH!
I'M COLD!

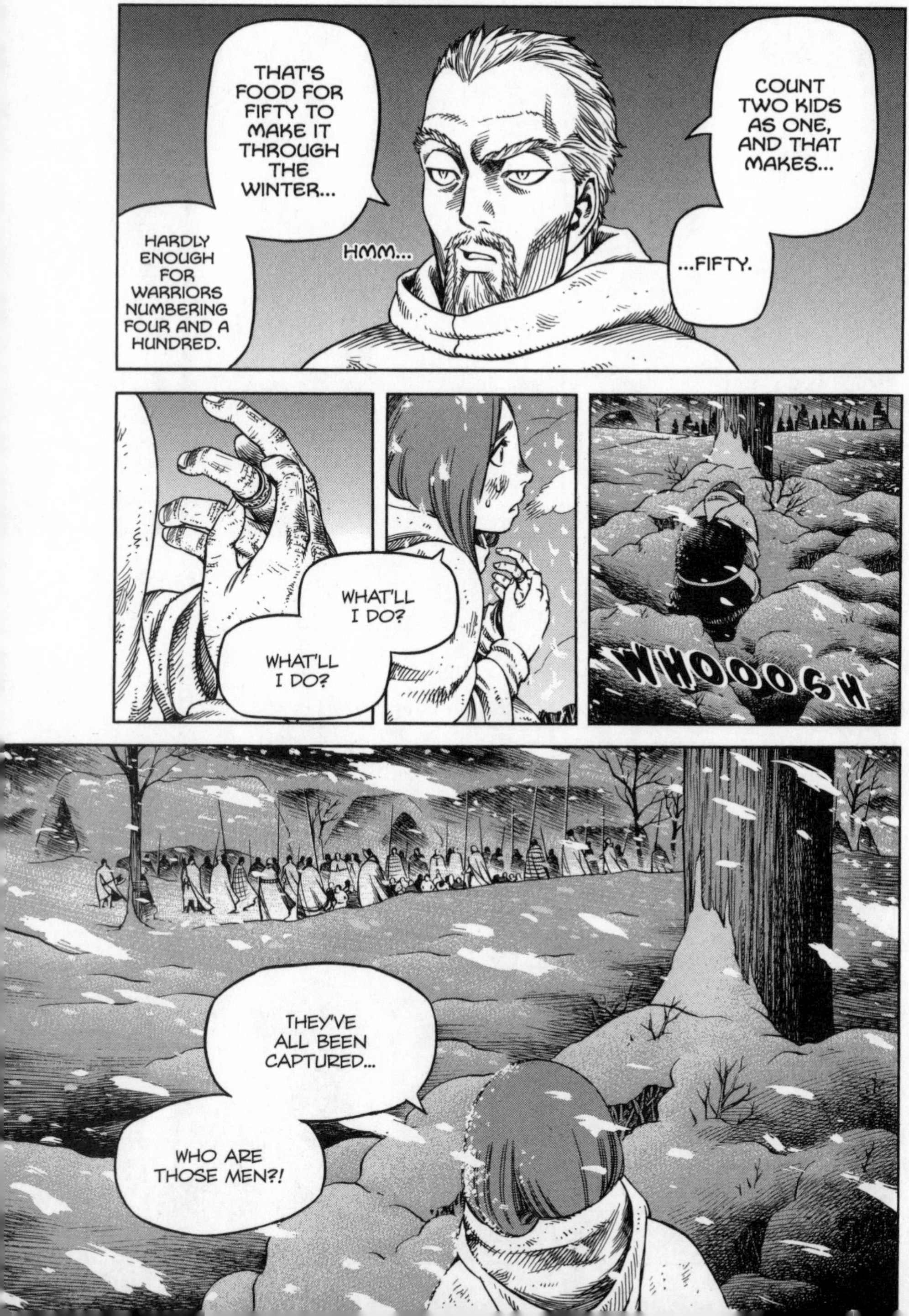
COUNT TWO KIDS AS ONE, AND THAT MAKES...
...FIFTY.
HMM...
THAT'S FOOD FOR FIFTY TO MAKE IT THROUGH THE WINTER...
HARDLY ENOUGH FOR WARRIORS NUMBERING FOUR AND A HUNDRED.
WHOOOSH
WHAT'LL I DO?
WHAT'LL I DO?
THEY'VE ALL BEEN CAPTURED...
WHO ARE THOSE MEN?!

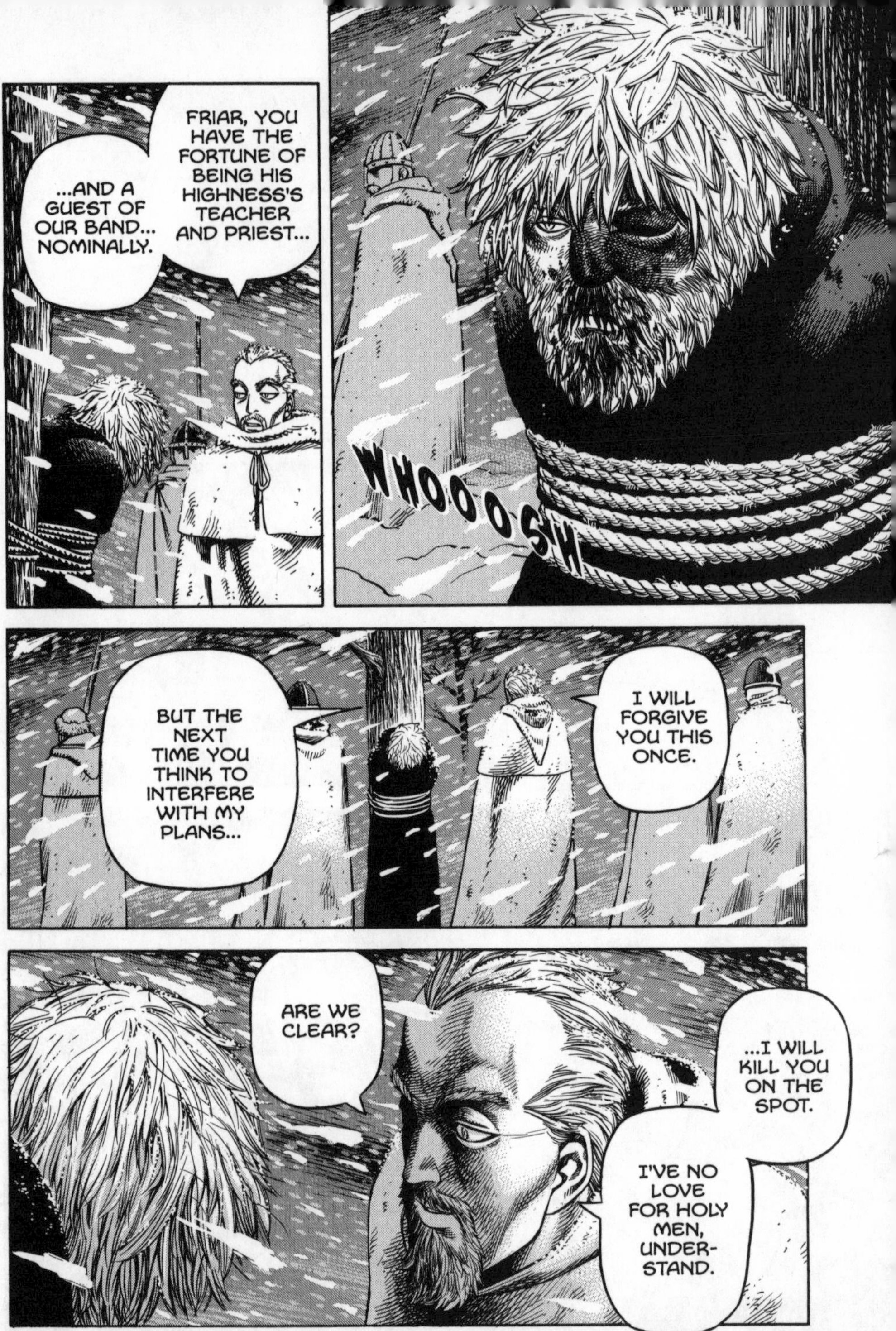
WHOOOSH
FRIAR, YOU HAVE THE FORTUNE OF BEING HIS HIGHNESS'S TEACHER AND PRIEST...
...AND A GUEST OF OUR BAND... NOMINALLY.
I WILL FORGIVE YOU THIS ONCE.
BUT THE NEXT TIME YOU THINK TO INTERFERE WITH MY PLANS...
...I WILL KILL YOU ON THE SPOT.
I'VE NO LOVE FOR HOLY MEN, UNDER-STAND.
ARE WE CLEAR?

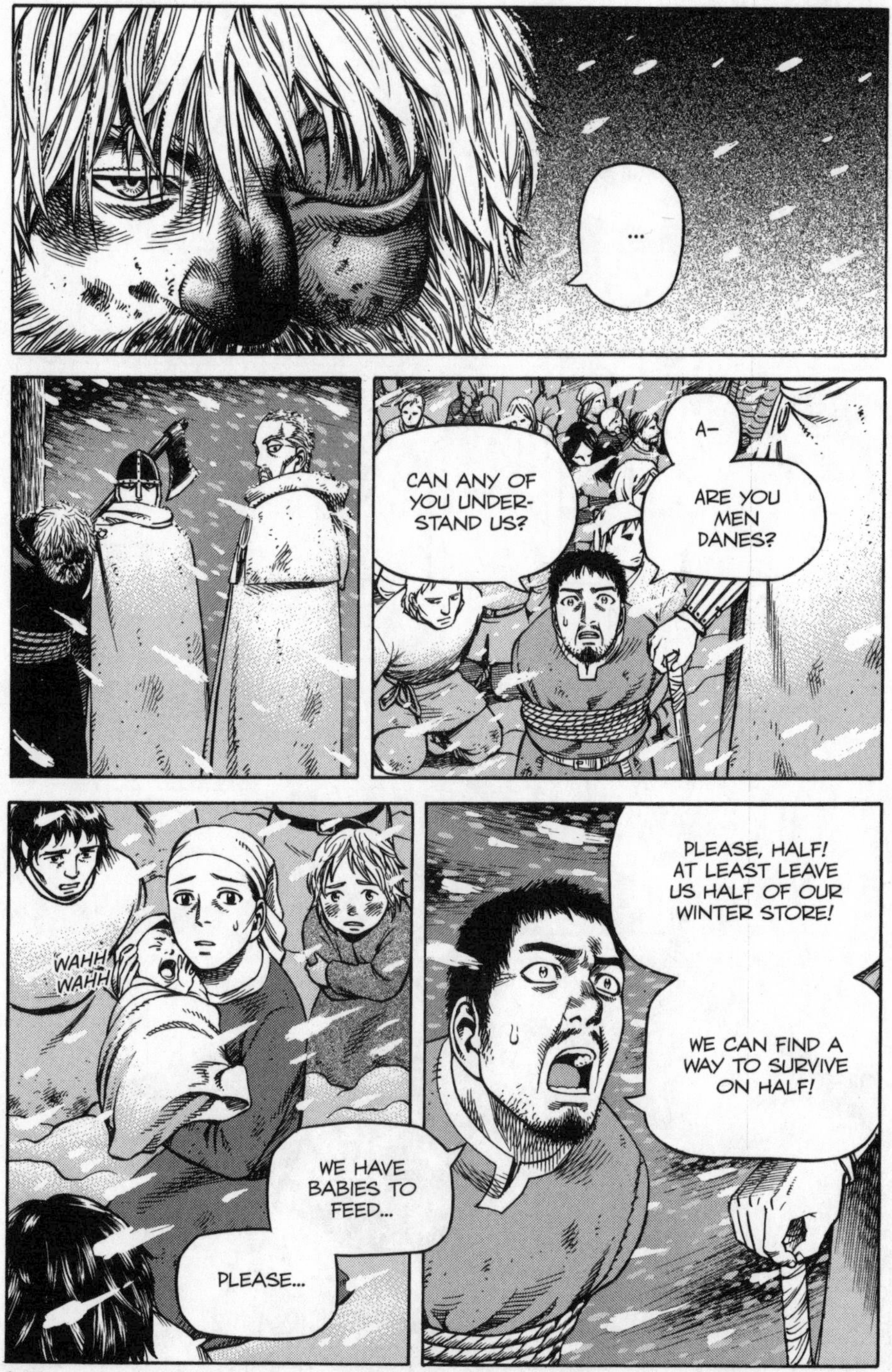
...
A–
ARE YOU MEN DANES?
CAN ANY OF YOU UNDER-STAND US?
PLEASE, HALF! AT LEAST LEAVE US HALF OF OUR WINTER STORE!
WE CAN FIND A WAY TO SURVIVE ON HALF!
WE HAVE BABIES TO FEED...
PLEASE...
WAHH WAHH

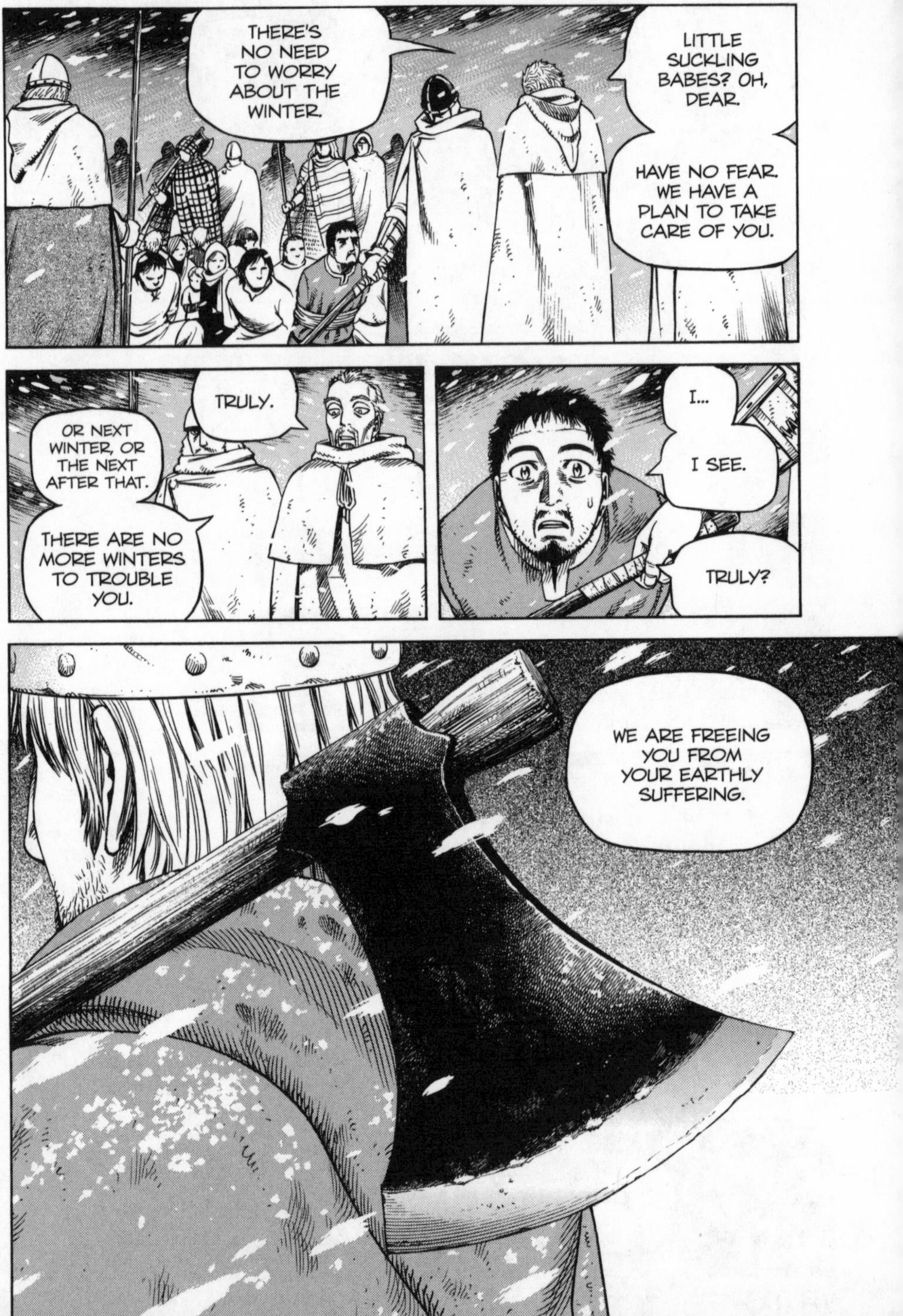
LITTLE SUCKLING BABES? OH, DEAR.
HAVE NO FEAR. WE HAVE A PLAN TO TAKE CARE OF YOU.
THERE'S NO NEED TO WORRY ABOUT THE WINTER.
I...
I SEE.
TRULY?
TRULY.
OR NEXT WINTER, OR THE NEXT AFTER THAT.
THERE ARE NO MORE WINTERS TO TROUBLE YOU.
WE ARE FREEING YOU FROM YOUR EARTHLY SUFFERING.

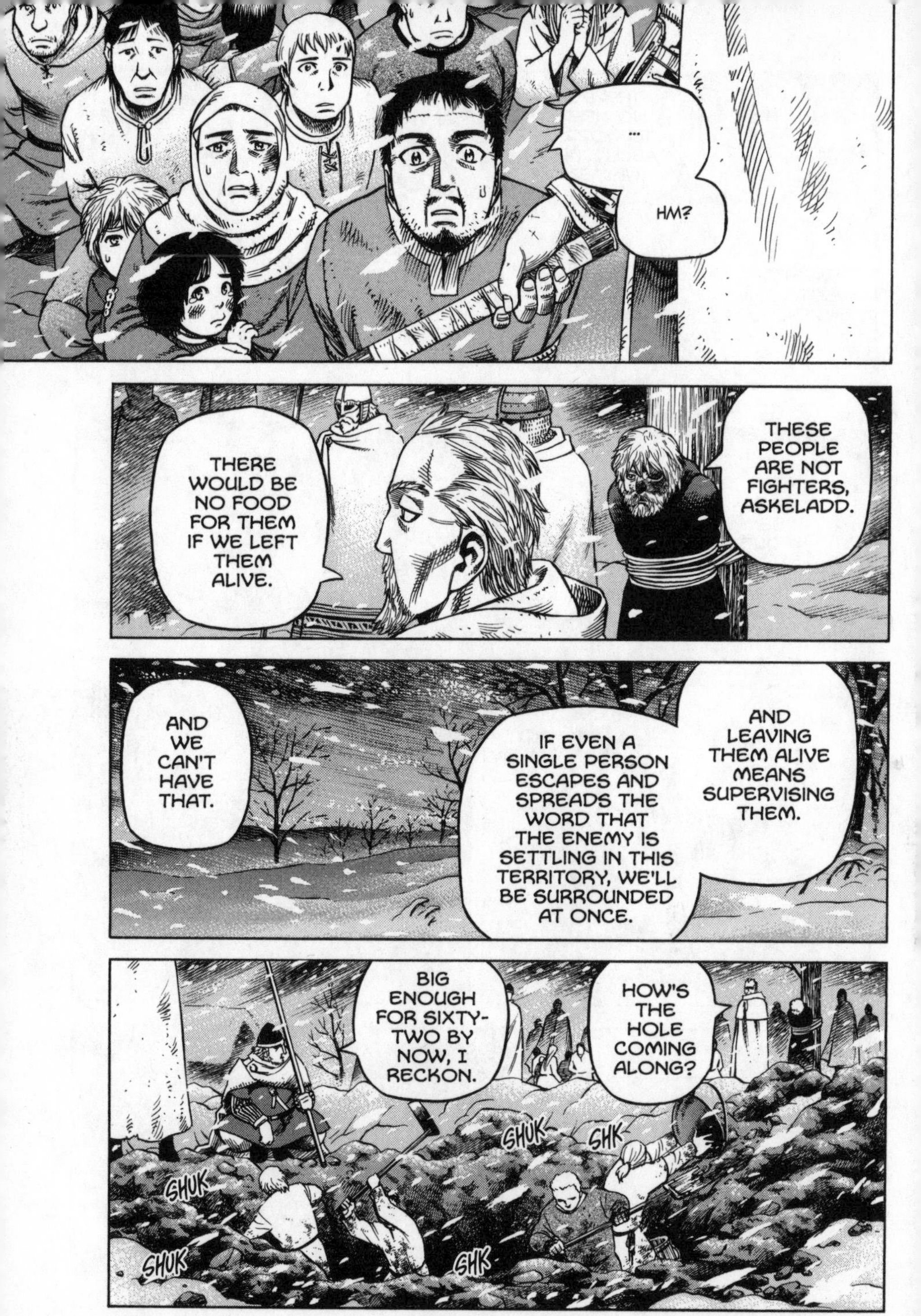
...
HM?
THESE PEOPLE ARE NOT FIGHTERS, ASKELADD.
THERE WOULD BE NO FOOD FOR THEM IF WE LEFT THEM ALIVE.
AND LEAVING THEM ALIVE MEANS SUPERVISING THEM.
IF EVEN A SINGLE PERSON ESCAPES AND SPREADS THE WORD THAT THE ENEMY IS SETTLING IN THIS TERRITORY, WE'LL BE SURROUNDED AT ONCE.
AND WE CAN'T HAVE THAT.
HOW'S THE HOLE COMING ALONG?
BIG ENOUGH FOR SIXTY-TWO BY NOW, I RECKON.
SHK
SHUK
SHUK
SHK
SHUK

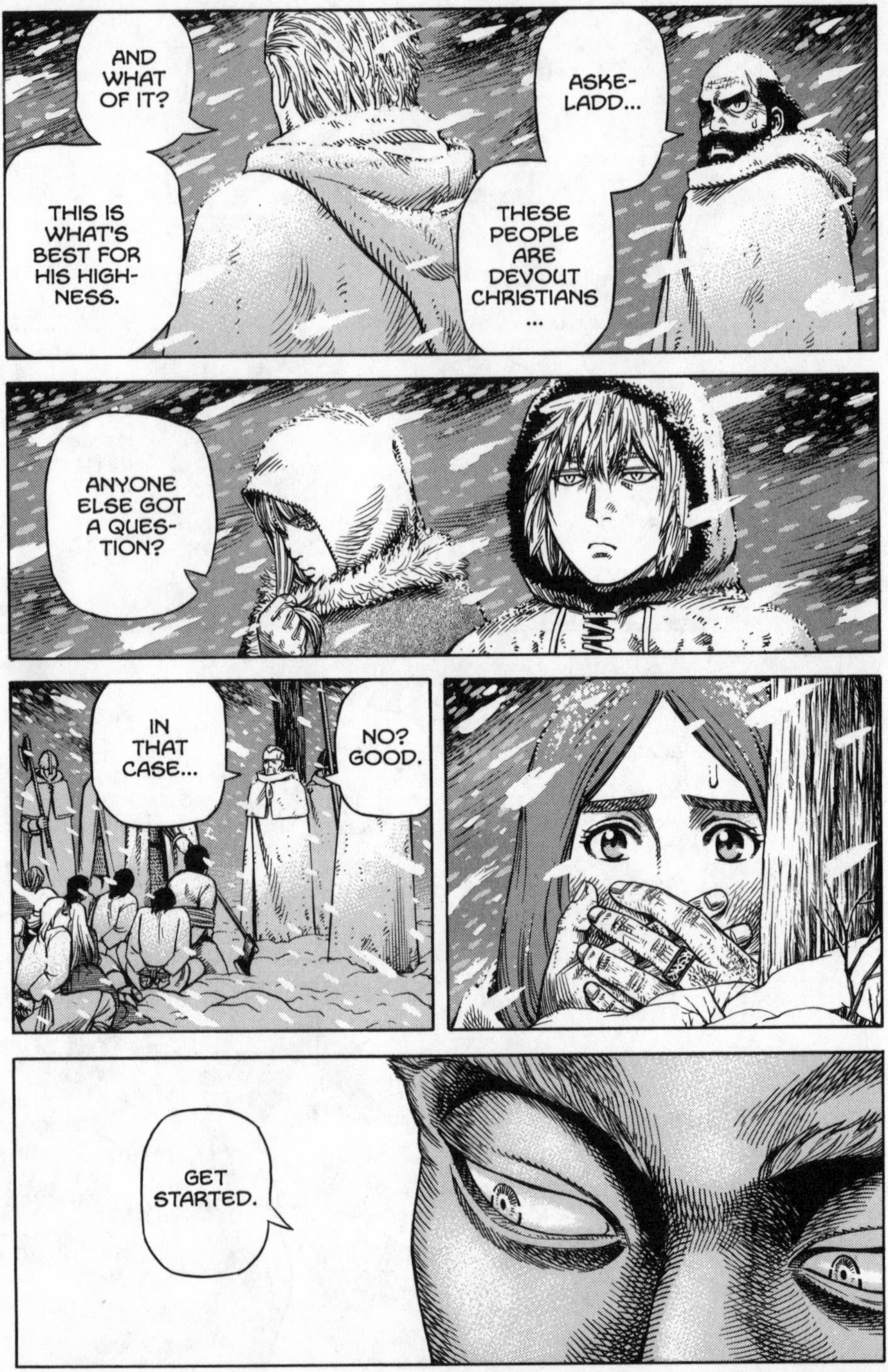
ASKE-LADD...
THESE PEOPLE ARE DEVOUT CHRISTIANS ...
AND WHAT OF IT?
THIS IS WHAT'S BEST FOR HIS HIGH-NESS.
ANYONE ELSE GOT A QUES-TION?
NO? GOOD.
IN THAT CASE...
GET STARTED.

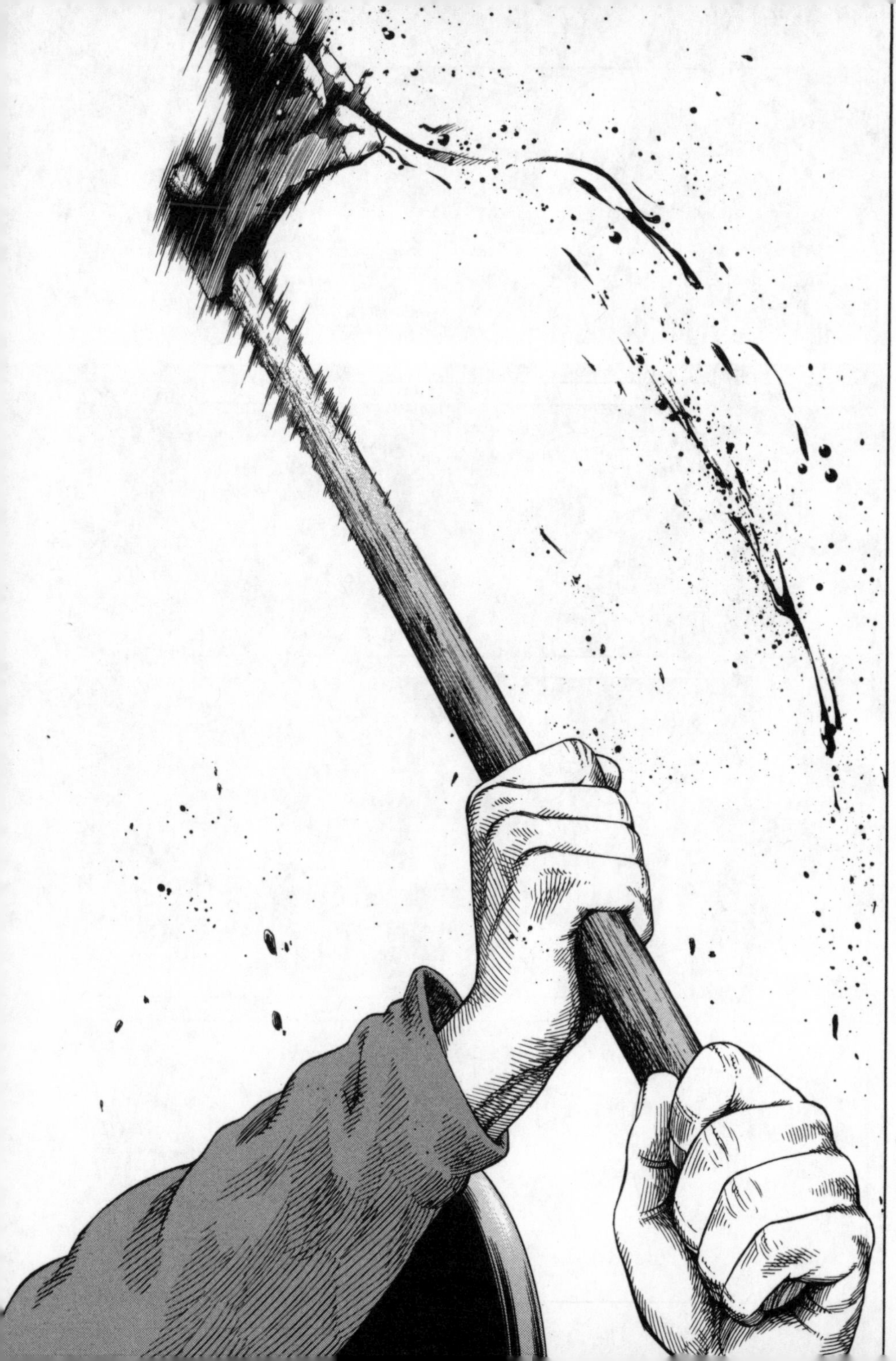

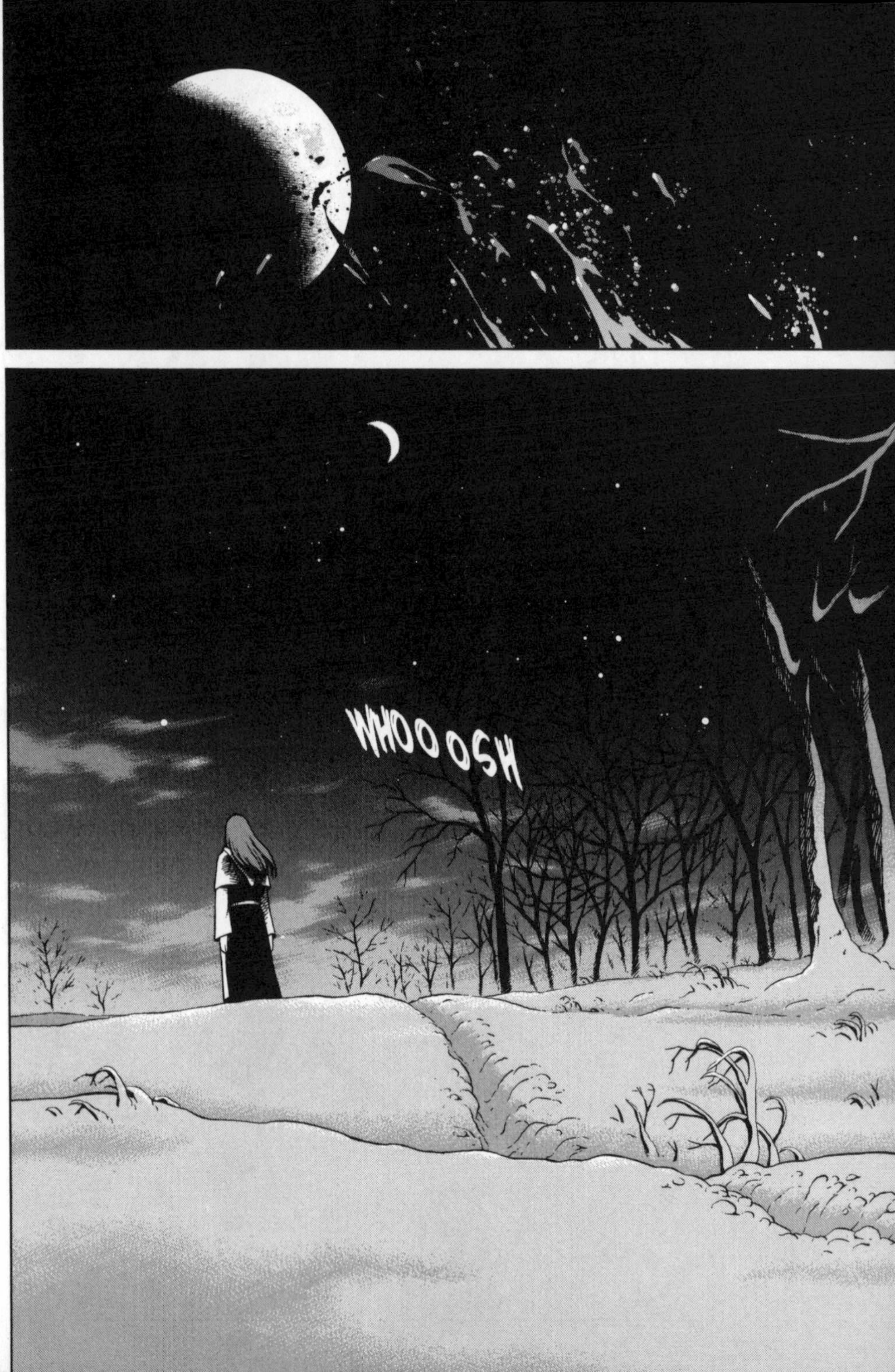
WHOOOSH

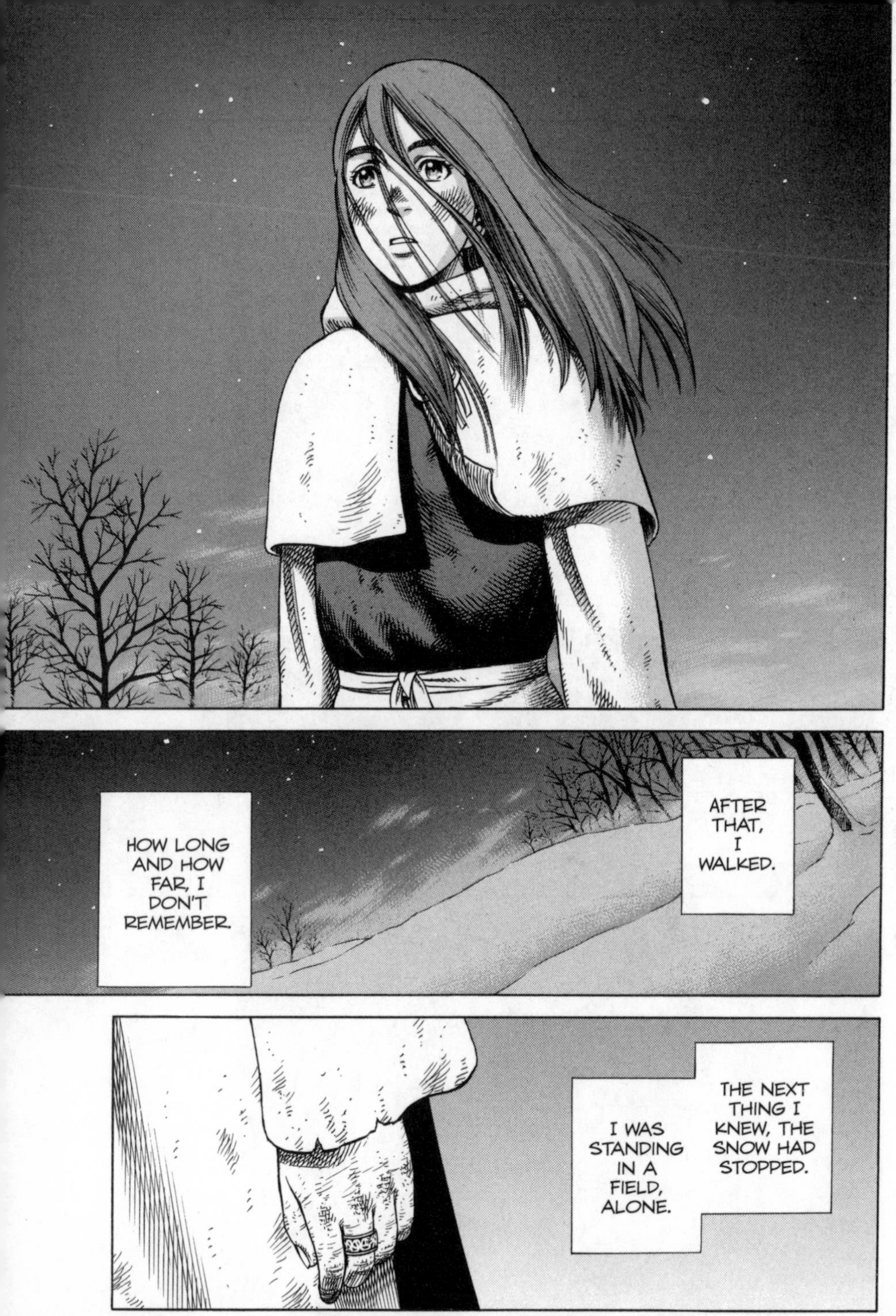
AFTER THAT, I WALKED.
HOW LONG AND HOW FAR, I DON'T REMEMBER.
THE NEXT THING I KNEW, THE SNOW HAD STOPPED.
I WAS STANDING IN A FIELD, ALONE.

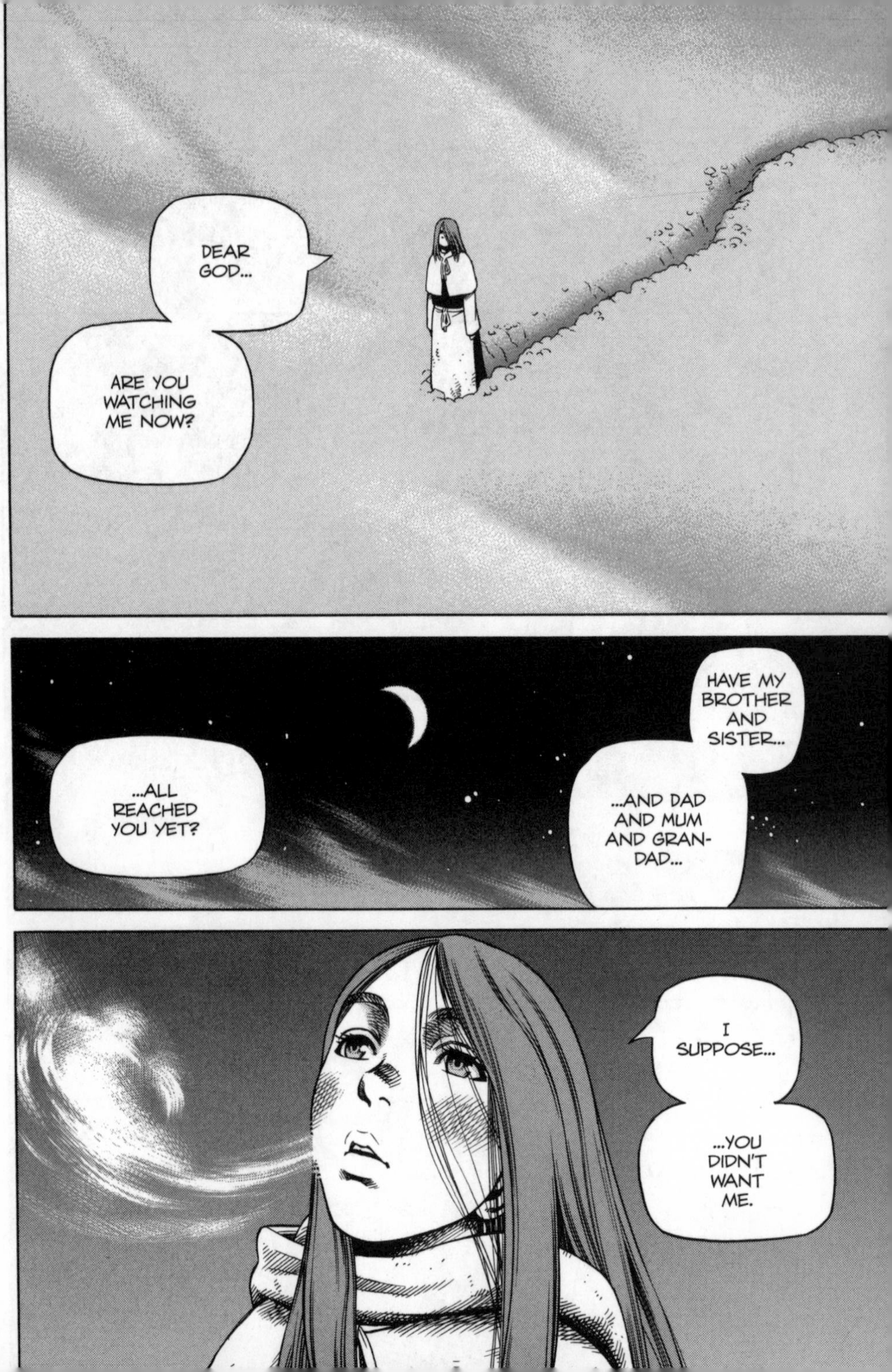
DEAR GOD...
ARE YOU WATCHING ME NOW?
HAVE MY BROTHER AND SISTER...
...AND DAD AND MUM AND GRAN-DAD...
...ALL REACHED YOU YET?
I SUPPOSE...
...YOU DIDN'T WANT ME.

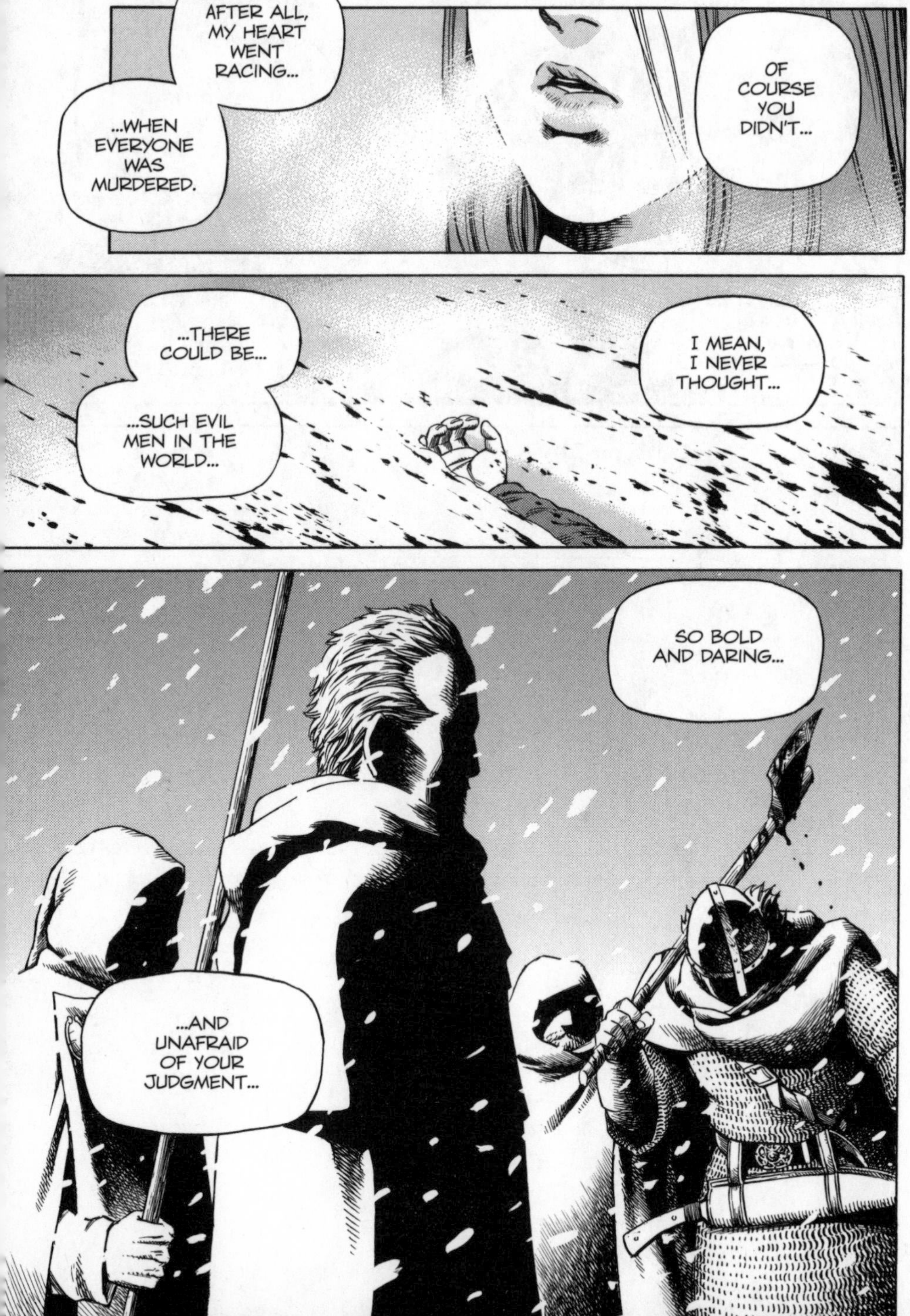
OF COURSE YOU DIDN'T...
AFTER ALL, MY HEART WENT RACING...
...WHEN EVERYONE WAS MURDERED.
I MEAN, I NEVER THOUGHT...
...THERE COULD BE...
...SUCH EVIL MEN IN THE WORLD...
SO BOLD AND DARING...
...AND UNAFRAID OF YOUR JUDGMENT...

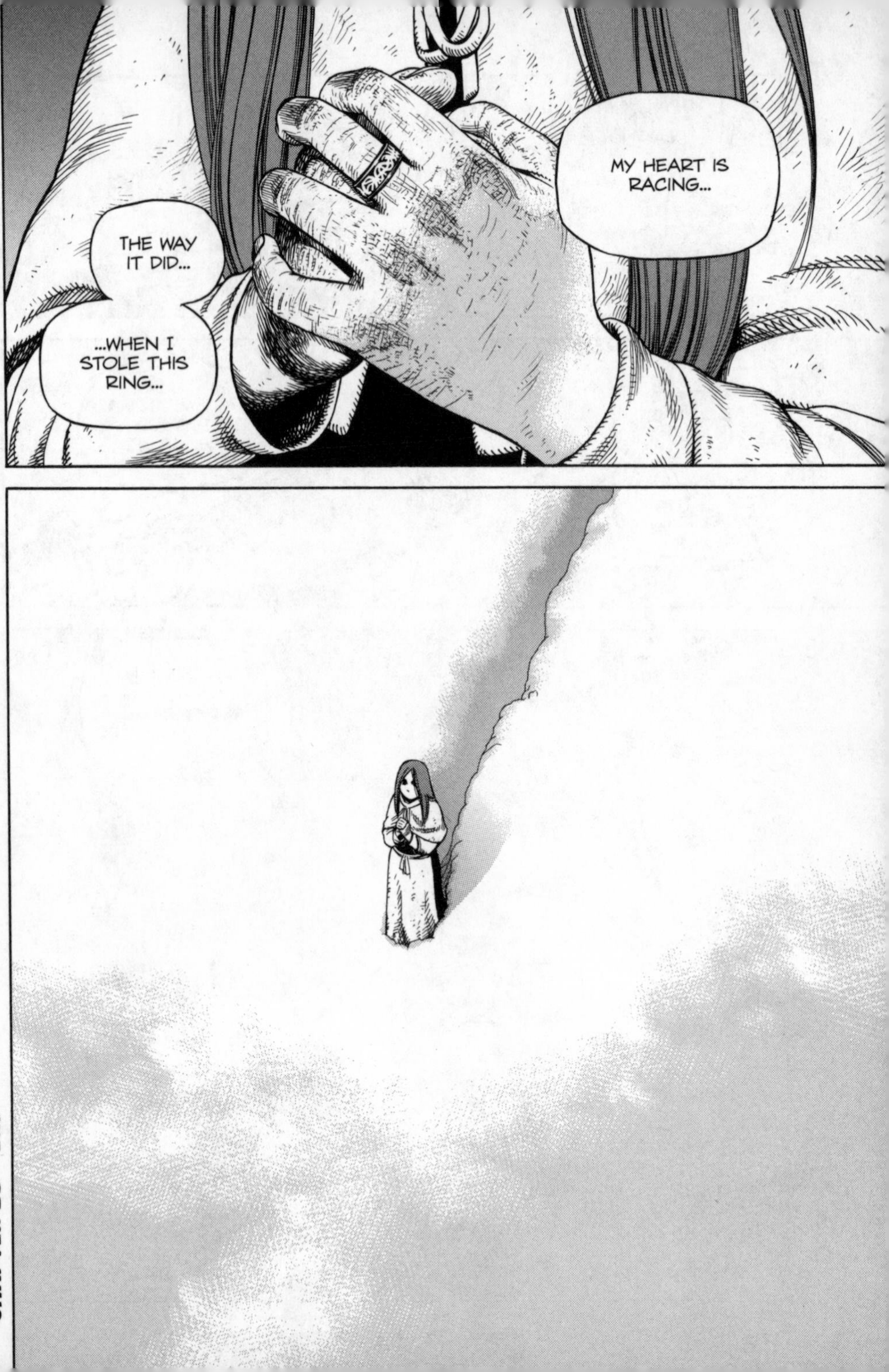
MY HEART IS RACING...
THE WAY IT DID...
...WHEN I STOLE THIS RING...

CHAPTER 28 - END

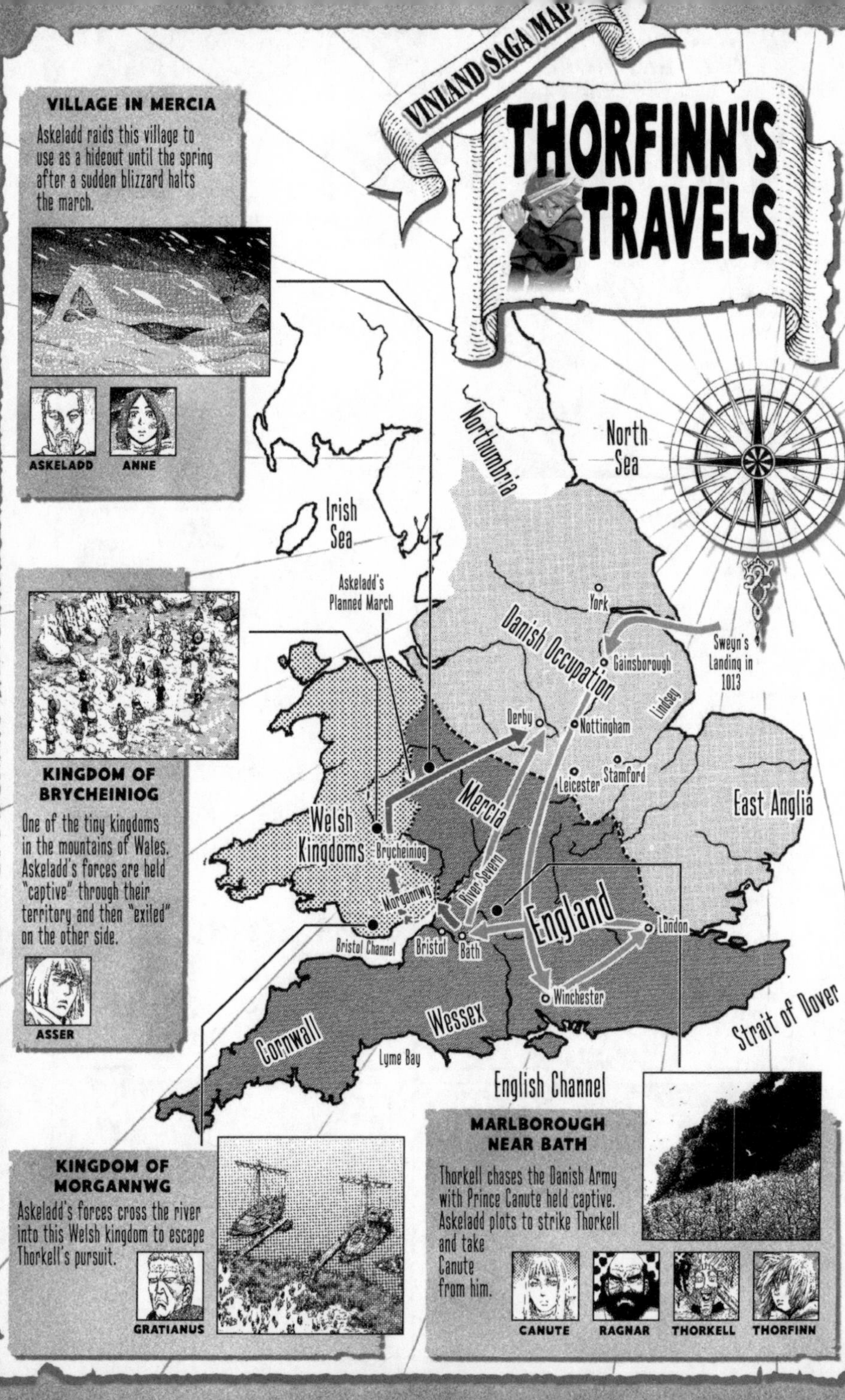

VINLAND SAGA MAP
THORFINN'S TRAVELS
VILLAGE IN MERCIA
Askeladd raids this village to use as a hideout until the spring after a sudden blizzard halts the march.
ASKELADD
ANNE
KINGDOM OF BRYCHEINIOG
One of the tiny kingdoms in the mountains of Wales. Askeladd's forces are held "captive" through their territory and then "exiled" on the other side.
ASSER
KINGDOM OF MORGANNWG
Askeladd's forces cross the river into this Welsh kingdom to escape Thorkell's pursuit.
GRATIANUS
MARLBOROUGH NEAR BATH
Thorkell chases the Danish Army with Prince Canute held captive. Askeladd plots to strike Thorkell and take Canute from him.
CANUTE
RAGNAR
THORKELL
THORFINN
Northumbria
North Sea
Irish Sea
Askeladd's Planned March
York
Danish Occupation
Sweyn's Landing in 1013
Gainsborough
Lindsey
Derby
Nottingham
Leicester
Stamford
East Anglia
Mercia
Welsh Kingdoms
Brycheiniog
Morgannwg
River Severn
England
London
Bristol Channel
Bristol
Bath
Winchester
Strait of Dover
Cornwall
Wessex
Lyme Bay
English Channel

AUTHOR OF "I WON'T DO IT ANYMORE."

HIDEO NISHIMOTO

SPECIAL CONTRIBUTION

VIKING GIRL YLVA

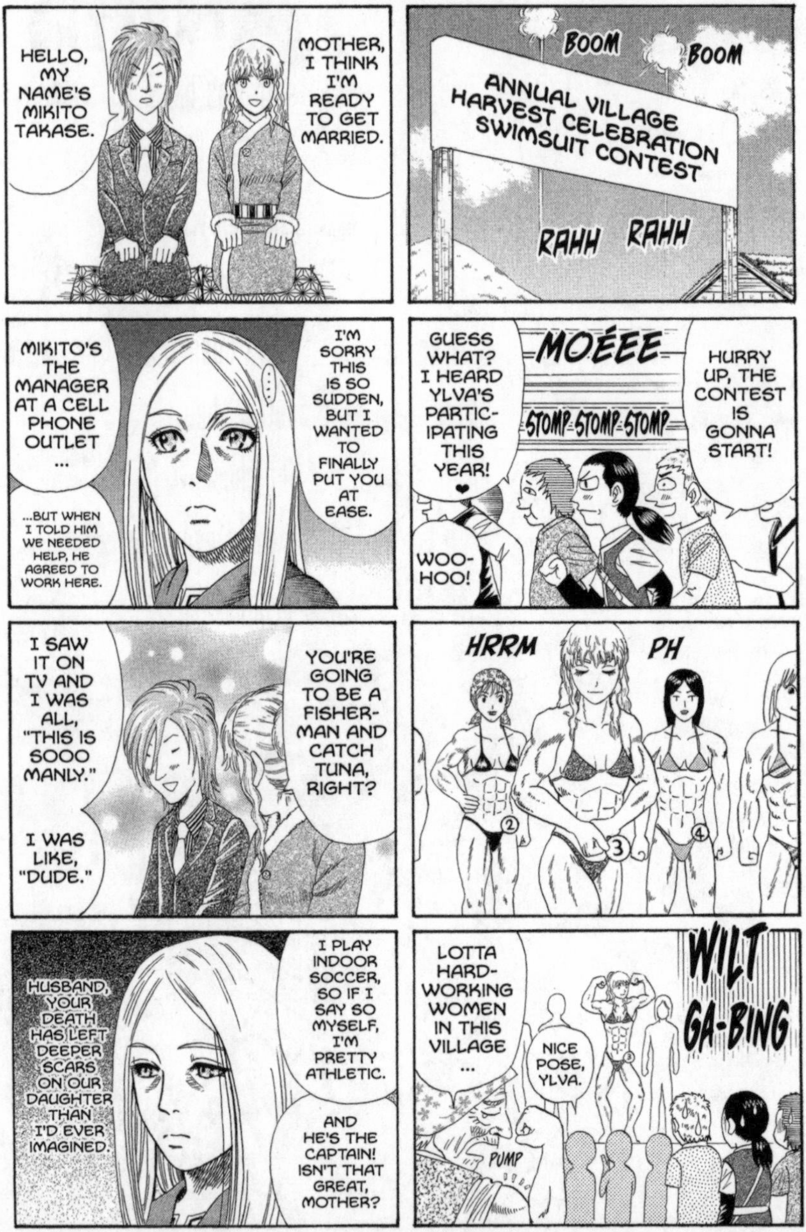
BOOM
BOOM
ANNUAL VILLAGE HARVEST CELEBRATION SWIMSUIT CONTEST
RAHH
RAHH
HURRY UP, THE CONTEST IS GONNA START!
MOÉEE
GUESS WHAT? I HEARD YLVA'S PARTIC-IPATING THIS YEAR! ♥
STOMP STOMP STOMP
WOO-HOO!
PH
HRRM
WILT
GA-BING
LOTTA HARD-WORKING WOMEN IN THIS VILLAGE ...
NICE POSE, YLVA.
PUMP
MOTHER, I THINK I'M READY TO GET MARRIED.
HELLO, MY NAME'S MIKITO TAKASE.
I'M SORRY THIS IS SO SUDDEN, BUT I WANTED TO FINALLY PUT YOU AT EASE.
MIKITO'S THE MANAGER AT A CELL PHONE OUTLET ...
...BUT WHEN I TOLD HIM WE NEEDED HELP, HE AGREED TO WORK HERE.
YOU'RE GOING TO BE A FISHER-MAN AND CATCH TUNA, RIGHT?
I SAW IT ON TV AND I WAS ALL, "THIS IS SOOO MANLY."
I WAS LIKE, "DUDE."
I PLAY INDOOR SOCCER, SO IF I SAY SO MYSELF, I'M PRETTY ATHLETIC.
AND HE'S THE CAPTAIN! ISN'T THAT GREAT, MOTHER?
HUSBAND, YOUR DEATH HAS LEFT DEEPER SCARS ON OUR DAUGHTER THAN I'D EVER IMAGINED.

AFTERWORD

My first son was born in 2006. The labor itself was hard, but raising our child is even harder for my wife. Breastfeeding him, changing his diapers, switching him to solid foods, taking him on walks, comforting him in the middle of the night... All Vikings started as babies, of course, and the same painstaking care must have been taken to raise them into adults. And yet, once they were adults, they rushed to their deaths, killing others and causing misery. I bet those Viking mothers were so exasperated. But even knowing what would eventually happen, they still raised their sons. Mothers are so great. Men are so stupid.

MAKOTO YUKIMURA

VINLAND SAGA

Translation Notes

Fyrd, page 22

IT'S BECAUSE THEY'RE INVADING THAT DAD HAD TO GO AND JOIN THE FYRD, RIGHT?

An Anglo-Saxon militia system in which civilians were called to defend their region for short periods. It was largely developed and practiced as a means of defense against Viking raids. Service was seen as a duty and obligation, with men reporting to fortresses called burhs. By the end of the 11th century, the fyrd system had largely been replaced by standing armies of lifetime soldiers and knights employed by lords and kings.

Thegn, page 27

HE'S ALREADY KILLED TWO OF HIS MAJESTY'S THEGNS.

A personal servant of a lord or king, in this case referring to official soldiers as opposed to militia men. The definition varied depending on the time and place; for example, the Scottish thanes as seen in Shakespeare's Macbeth were royal officials much like counts.

Burh, page 56

A military fort utilized by the Anglo-Saxons to defend against invasion. When a fyrd was called, men reported to the burhs, some of which were built around former Roman settlements. The larger burhs grew into their own towns, forming the basis for the English word "borough."

Yule, page 134

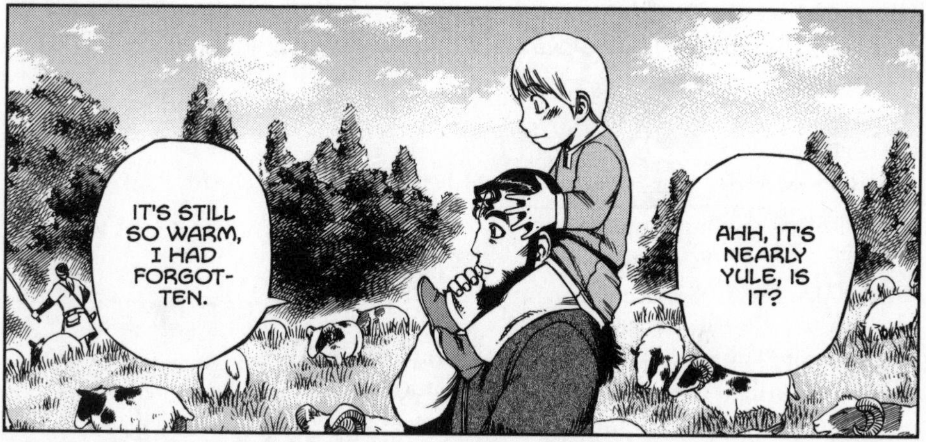
AHH, IT'S NEARLY YULE, IS IT?
IT'S STILL SO WARM, I HAD FORGOTTEN.

A Northern European pagan celebration based around the winter solstice. With the spread of Christianity among Germanic peoples, the traditional Yule holiday was adapted into Christmas, and several remnants of Yule (such as the Yule log) still exist today within the Christmas setting.

Ragnarok, page 158

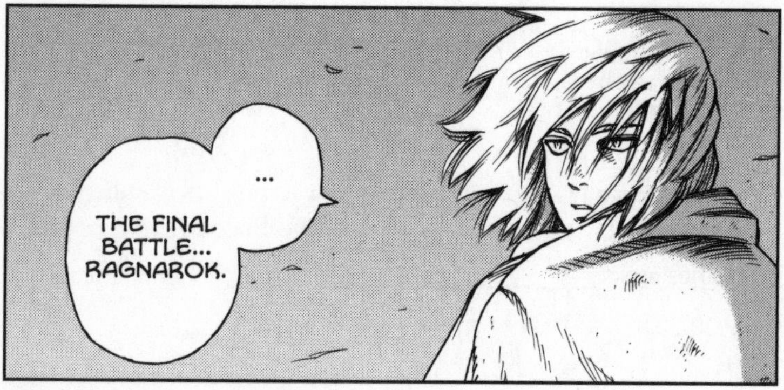
...
THE FINAL BATTLE... RAGNAROK.

The "final battle" in Norse mythology, in which most of the gods will perish and humanity will be wiped out.

Einherjar, page 181

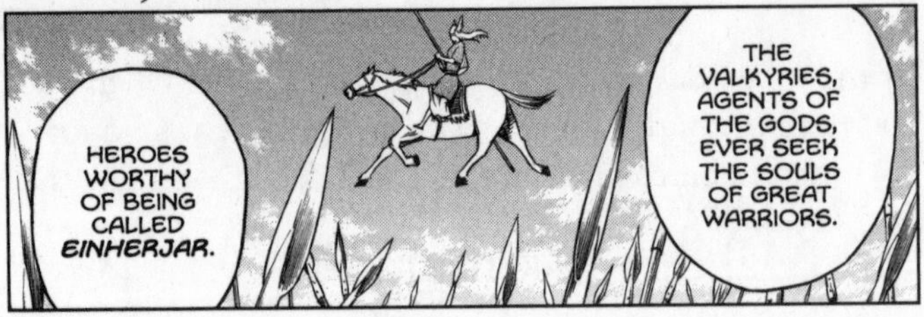
THE VALKYRIES, AGENTS OF THE GODS, EVER SEEK THE SOULS OF GREAT WARRIORS.
HEROES WORTHY OF BEING CALLED *EINHERJAR*.

The worthy warriors who have been summoned to Valhalla by the valkyries after their mortal deaths. The einherjar feast in the great hall day after day, preparing for the coming of Ragnarok.

Bifrost, page 181

The rainbow bridge that connects Midgard (the mortal realm) with Asgard, home of the gods.

Legatus, page 283

The title of a Roman army general, often styled "legate" in English. As the Romans had abandoned Britain (and Wales) by the early 400s, the trappings of Roman culture displayed in the story are merely remnants of the past and not indicative of direct Roman involvement.

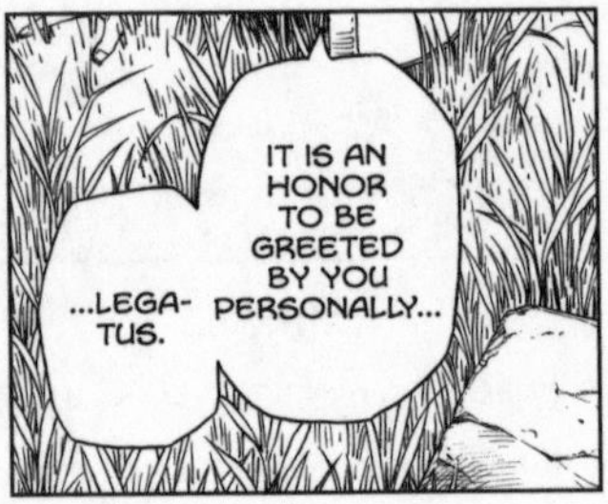
IT IS AN HONOR TO BE GREETED BY YOU PERSONALLY...
...LEGA-TUS.

Córdoba, page 305

The Caliphate of Córdoba was a kingdom extending over most of the Iberian Peninsula and parts of North Africa between 929 and 1031 A.D. As perhaps the height of Moorish power in Spain, Córdoba was at one point the most advanced and enlightened city in Europe before the Muslims were steadily driven south back into Morocco by the Christians by the end of the 15th century.

Gwenhwyfar, page 352

The queen of King Arthur, typically styled "Guinevere" in English. Gwenhwyfar is the Welsh form of the name. The name means "the White Enchantress" or "the White Fairy."

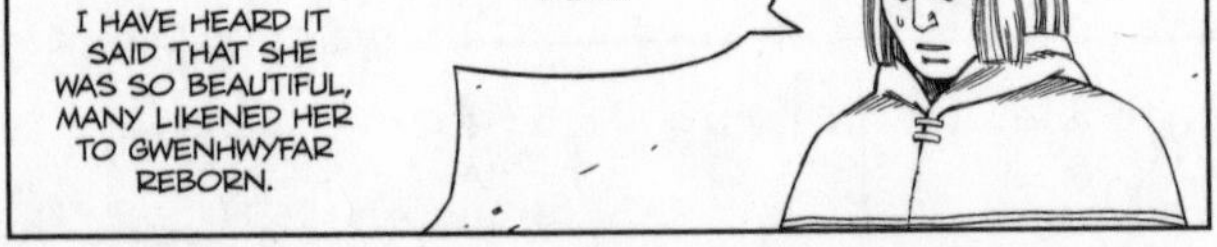
IT IS A TRAGIC TALE...
I HAVE HEARD IT SAID THAT SHE WAS SO BEAUTIFUL, MANY LIKENED HER TO GWENHWYFAR REBORN.

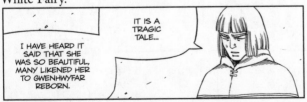

For Our Farewell Is Near Part 2
By Makoto Yukimura

Introduction

At the end of the Edo Period, the arrival of the "black ships" from abroad spelled the end of 260 years of isolation enforced by the shogunate. In response to the shogunate's desire to open the country's borders, disgruntled regional forces loyal to the emperor, such as the Choshu Domain, planned a rebellion. The imperial loyalists massed in Kyoto, where the emperor lived, growing increasingly bold until the city became, in effect, a lawless area. In an effort to restore order, the shogunate recruited ronin (masterless samurai) in Edo (Tokyo) and sent them to Kyoto.

Among these men were Kondo Isami and Okita Soji, students at the Shieikan dojo in Tama. Upon reaching Kyoto, they formed the "Shinsengumi" under the orders of the daimyo of Aizu Domain, who had been charged with keeping the peace in the city. But, unable to reverse the tide of history, the shogunate lost power, and the Shinsengumi were defeated at the Battle of Toba-Fushimi. In 1868, Kondo and Okita had fled to Edo. Okita's body was already wracked with tuberculosis at this time.

To read the first part of For Our Farewell Is Near, pick up a copy of Vinland Saga, Book One.

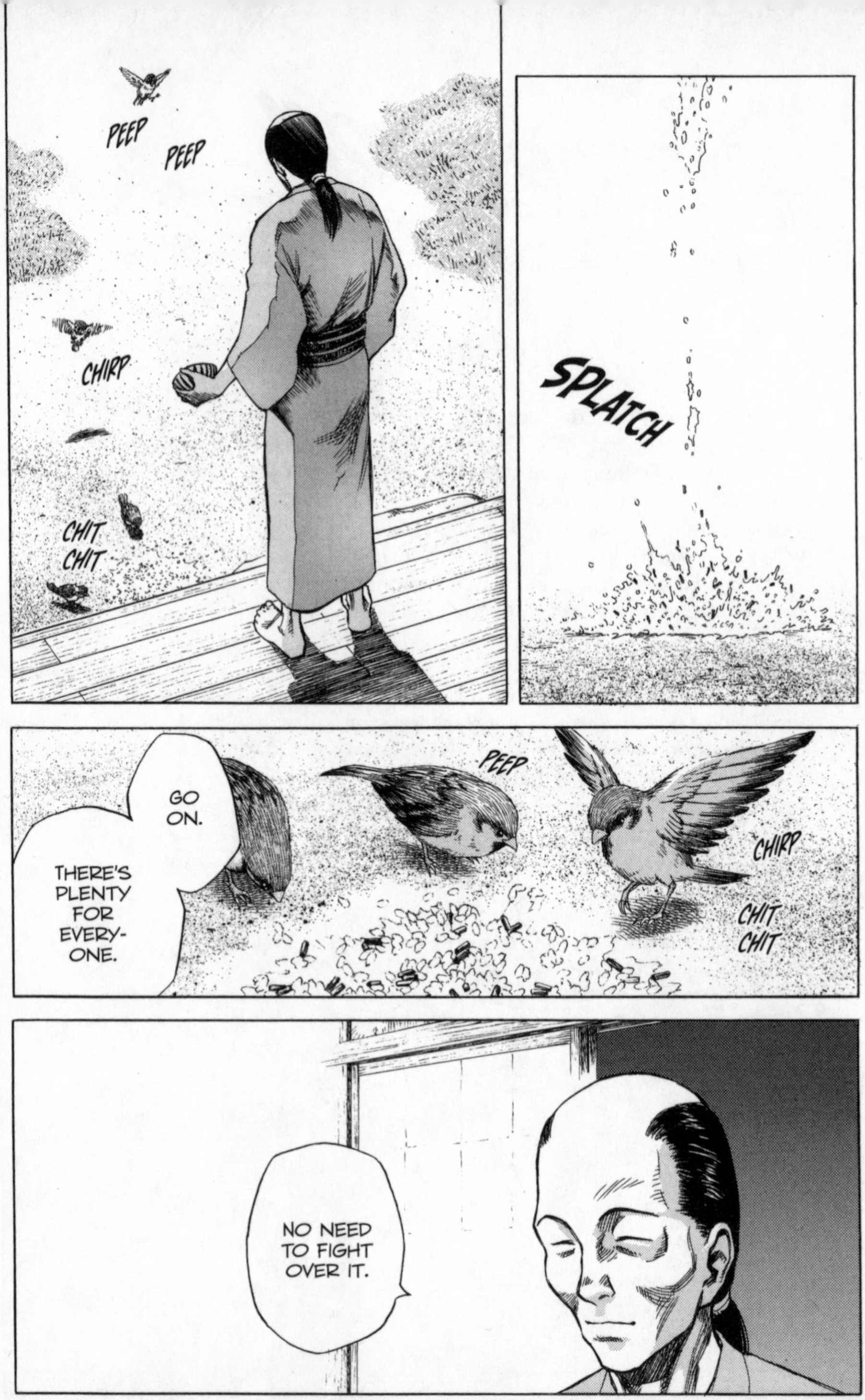
SPLATCH
PEEP
PEEP
CHIRP
CHIT
CHIT
PEEP
CHIRP
CHIT
CHIT
GO ON.
THERE'S PLENTY FOR EVERY-ONE.
NO NEED TO FIGHT OVER IT.

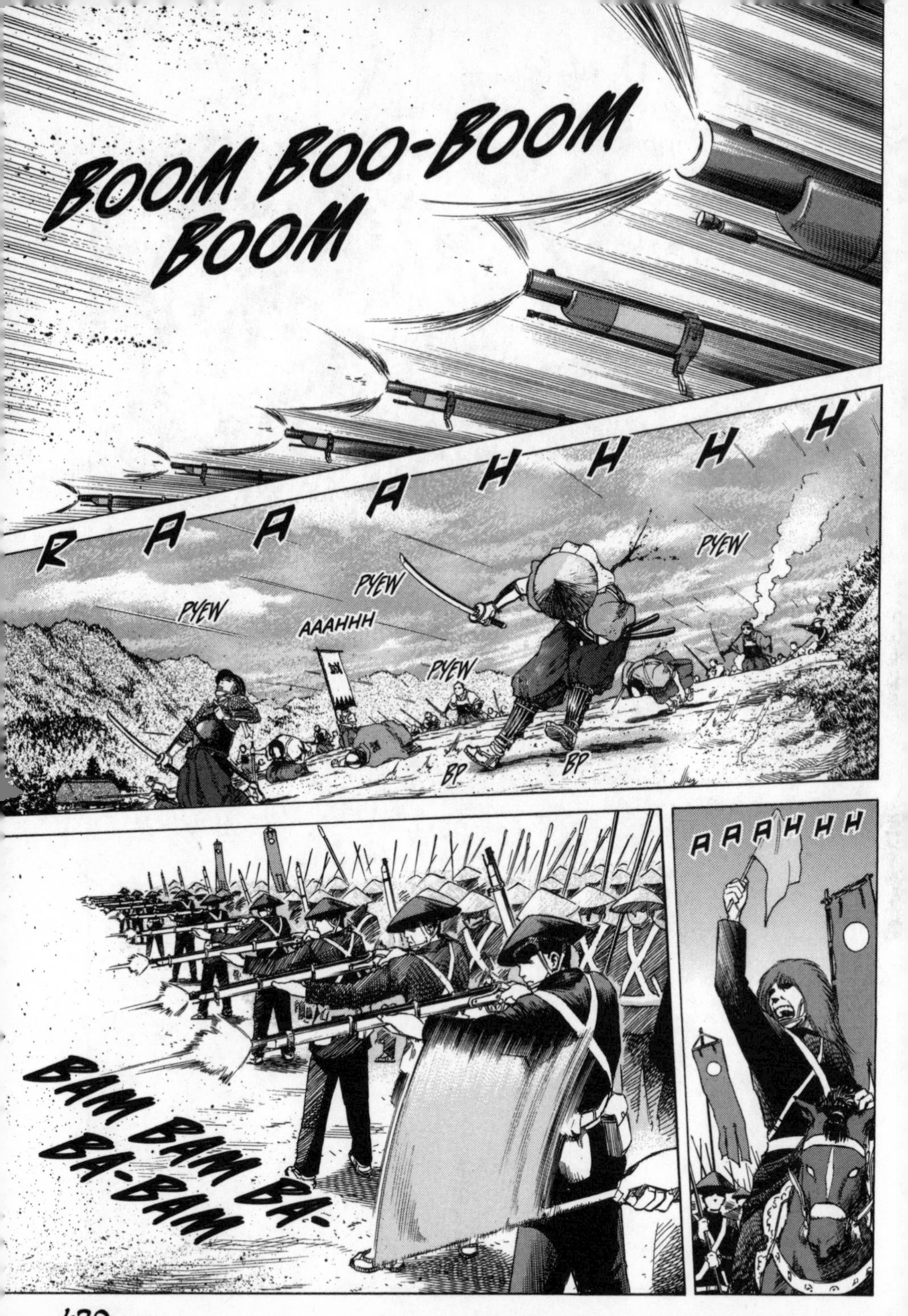
BOOM BOO-BOOM
BOOM
R A A A H H H H
PYEW
PYEW
PYEW
AAAHHH
PYEW
BP
BP
AAAHHH
BAM BAM BA-
BA-BAM

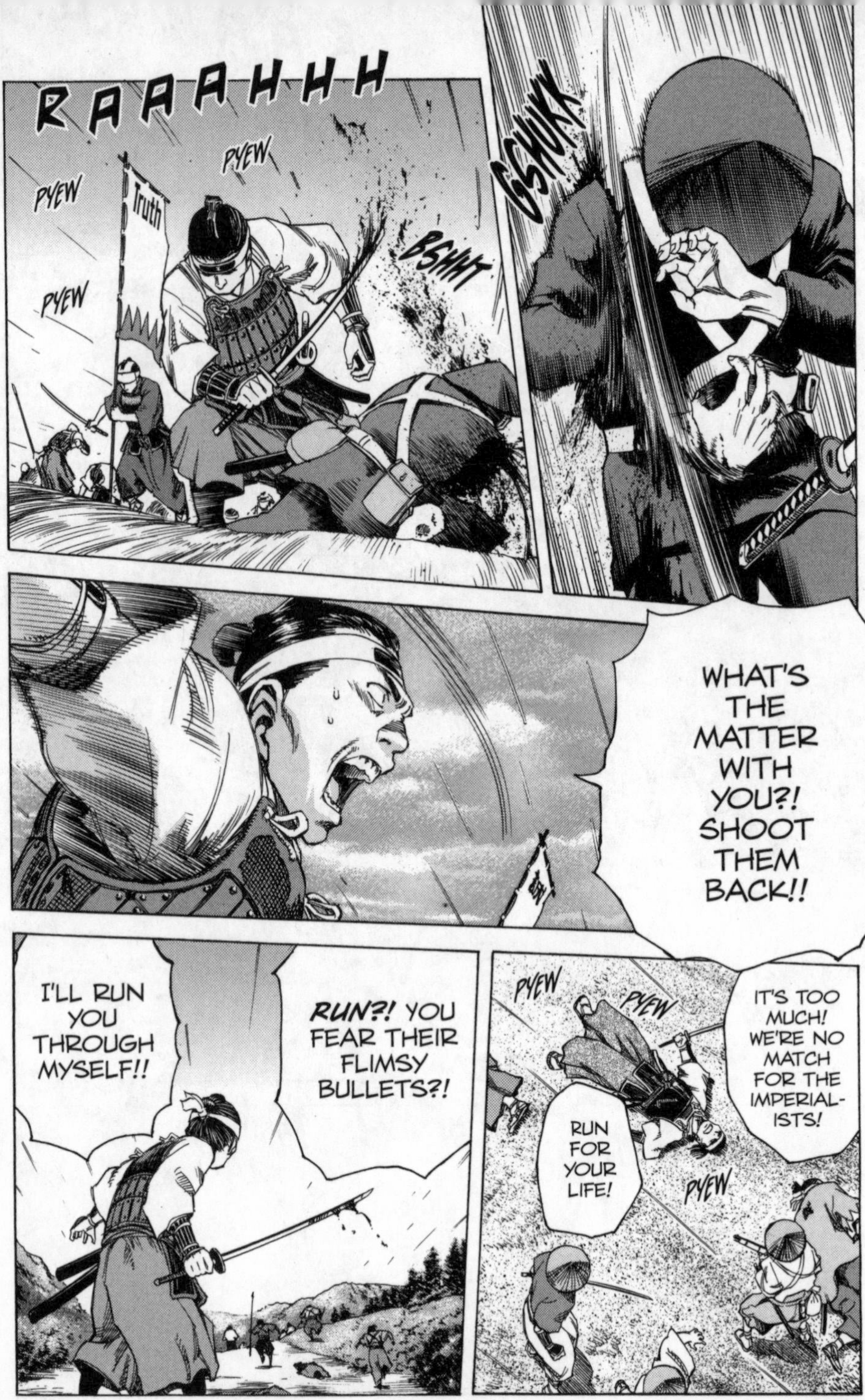
GSHUKK
RAAAHHH
PYEW
PYEW
Truth
PYEW
BSHHT
WHAT'S THE MATTER WITH YOU?! SHOOT THEM BACK!!
PYEW
PYEW
IT'S TOO MUCH! WE'RE NO MATCH FOR THE IMPERIAL-ISTS!
RUN FOR YOUR LIFE!
PYEW
RUN?! YOU FEAR THEIR FLIMSY BULLETS?!
I'LL RUN YOU THROUGH MYSELF!!

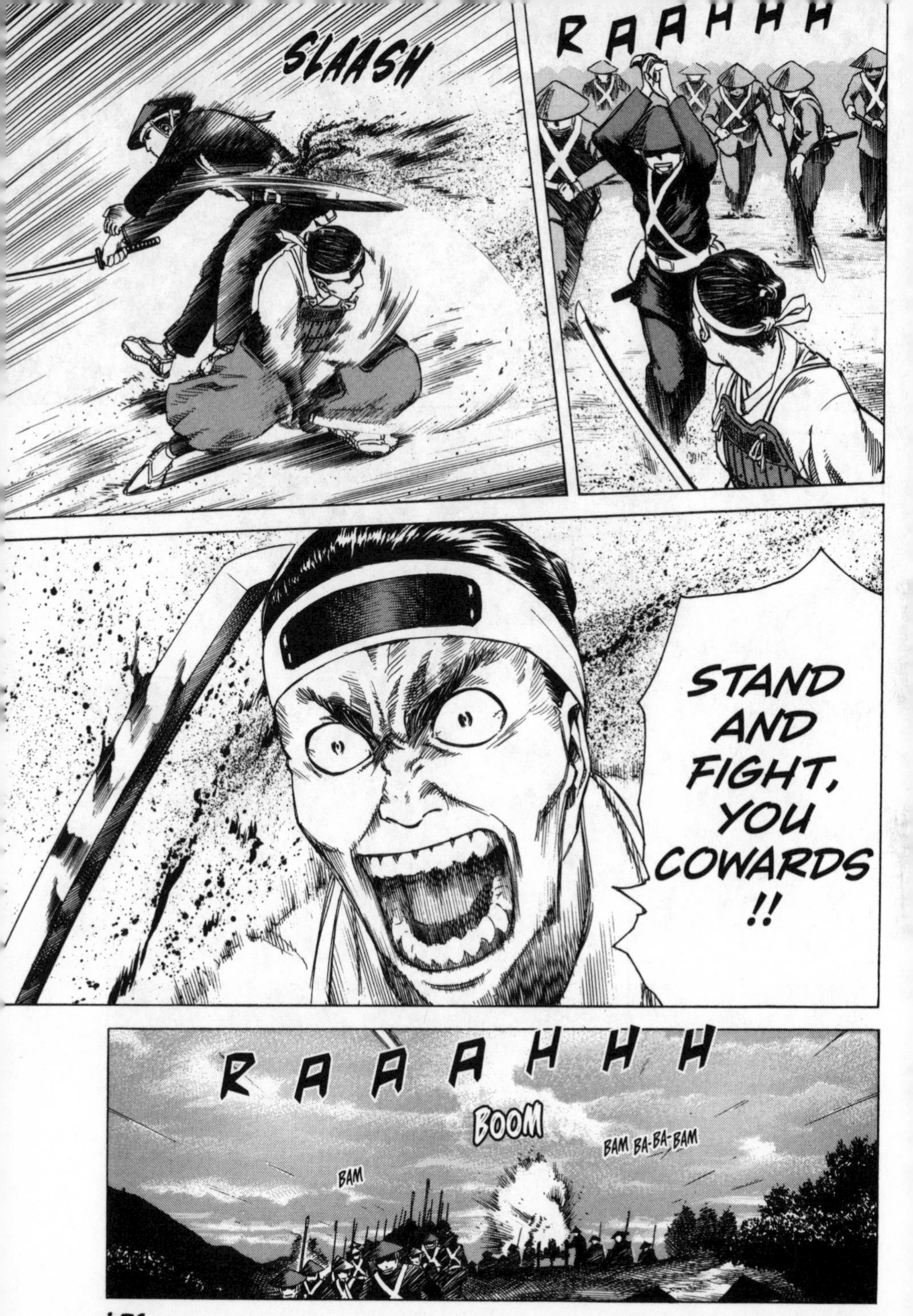
RAAHHH
SLAASH
STAND AND FIGHT, YOU COWARDS !!
RAAAHHH
BOOM
BAM BA-BA-BAM
BAM

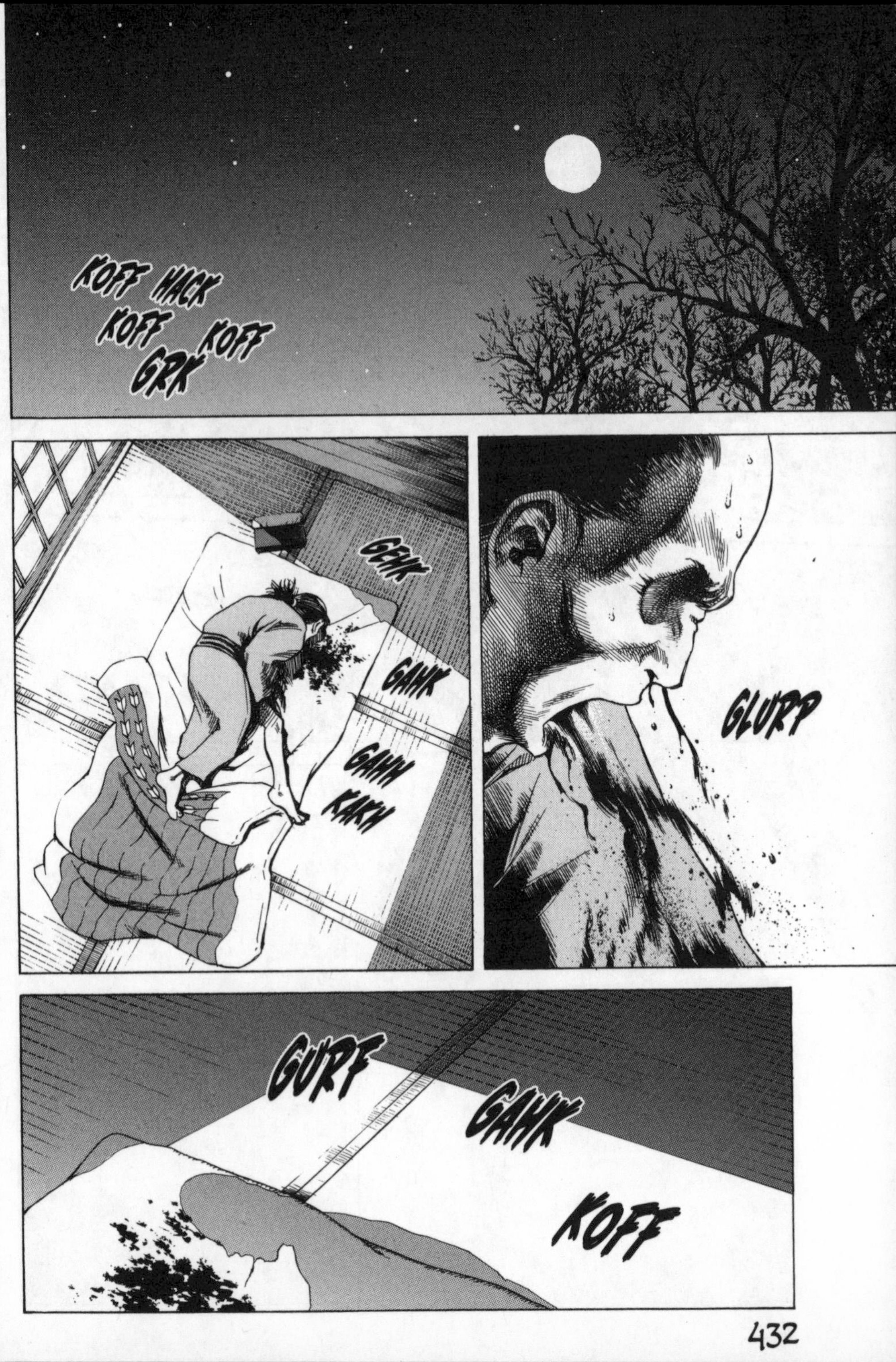
KOFF HACK
KOFF
KOFF
GRK
GLURP
GEHK
GAHK
GAHH
KAKH
GURF
GAHK
KOFF

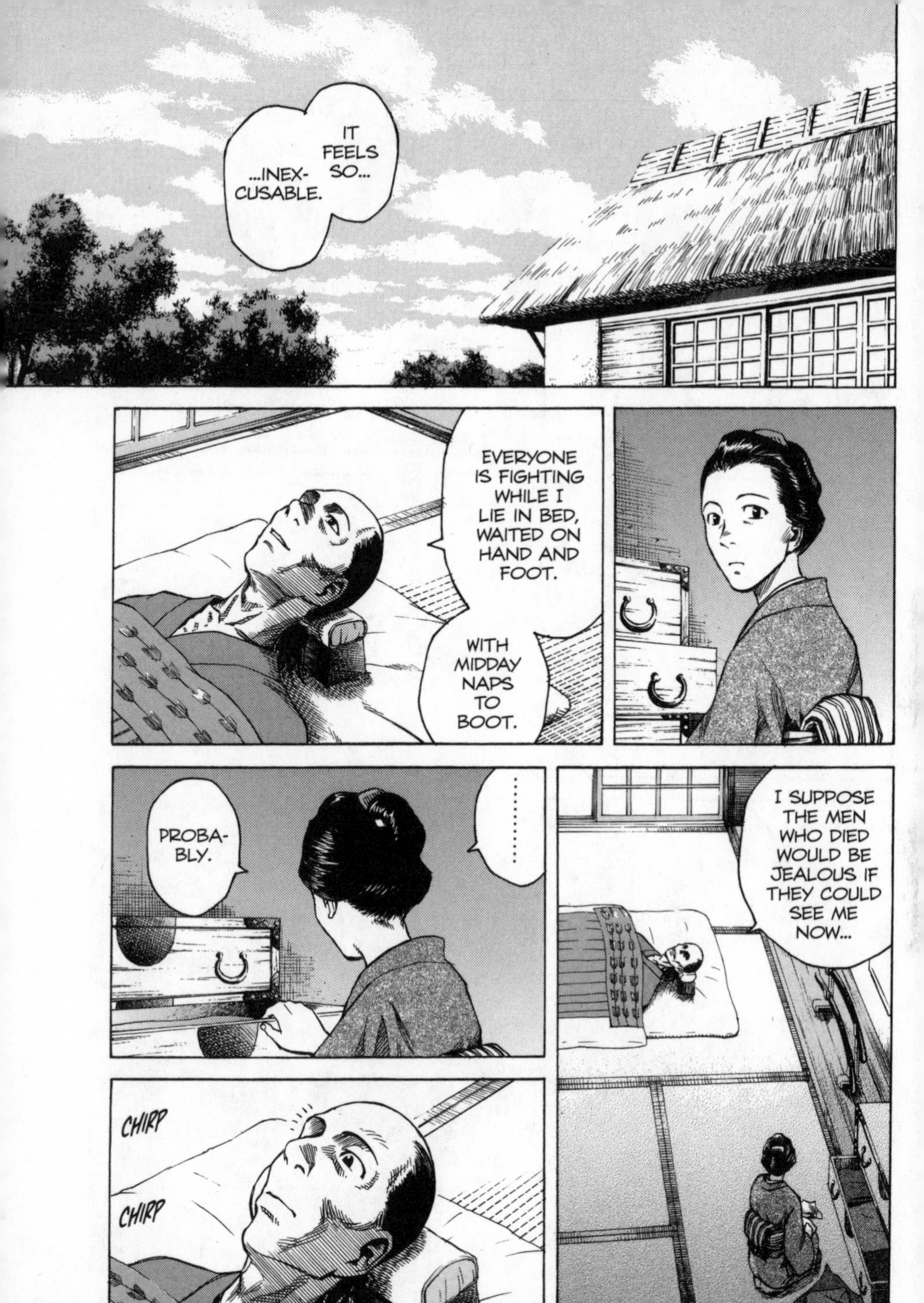
IT FEELS SO... ...INEX-CUSABLE.
EVERYONE IS FIGHTING WHILE I LIE IN BED, WAITED ON HAND AND FOOT.
WITH MIDDAY NAPS TO BOOT.
I SUPPOSE THE MEN WHO DIED WOULD BE JEALOUS IF THEY COULD SEE ME NOW...
......
PROBA-BLY.
CHIRP
CHIRP

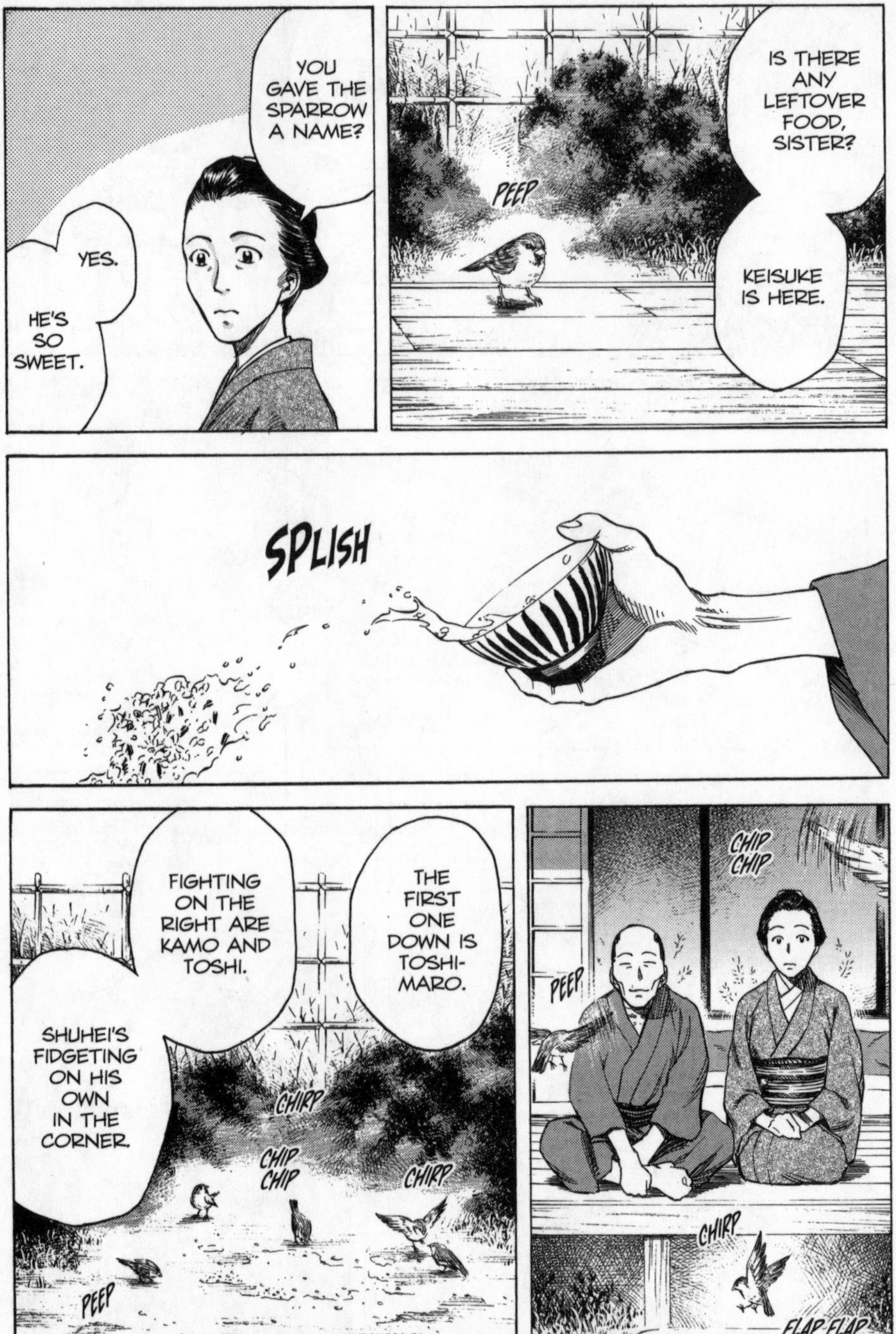
IS THERE ANY LEFTOVER FOOD, SISTER?
KEISUKE IS HERE.
PEEP
YOU GAVE THE SPARROW A NAME?
YES.
HE'S SO SWEET.
SPLISH
CHIP CHIP
PEEP
CHIRP
FLAP FLAP
THE FIRST ONE DOWN IS TOSHI-MARO.
FIGHTING ON THE RIGHT ARE KAMO AND TOSHI.
SHUHEI'S FIDGETING ON HIS OWN IN THE CORNER.
CHIRP
CHIP CHIP
CHIRP
PEEP

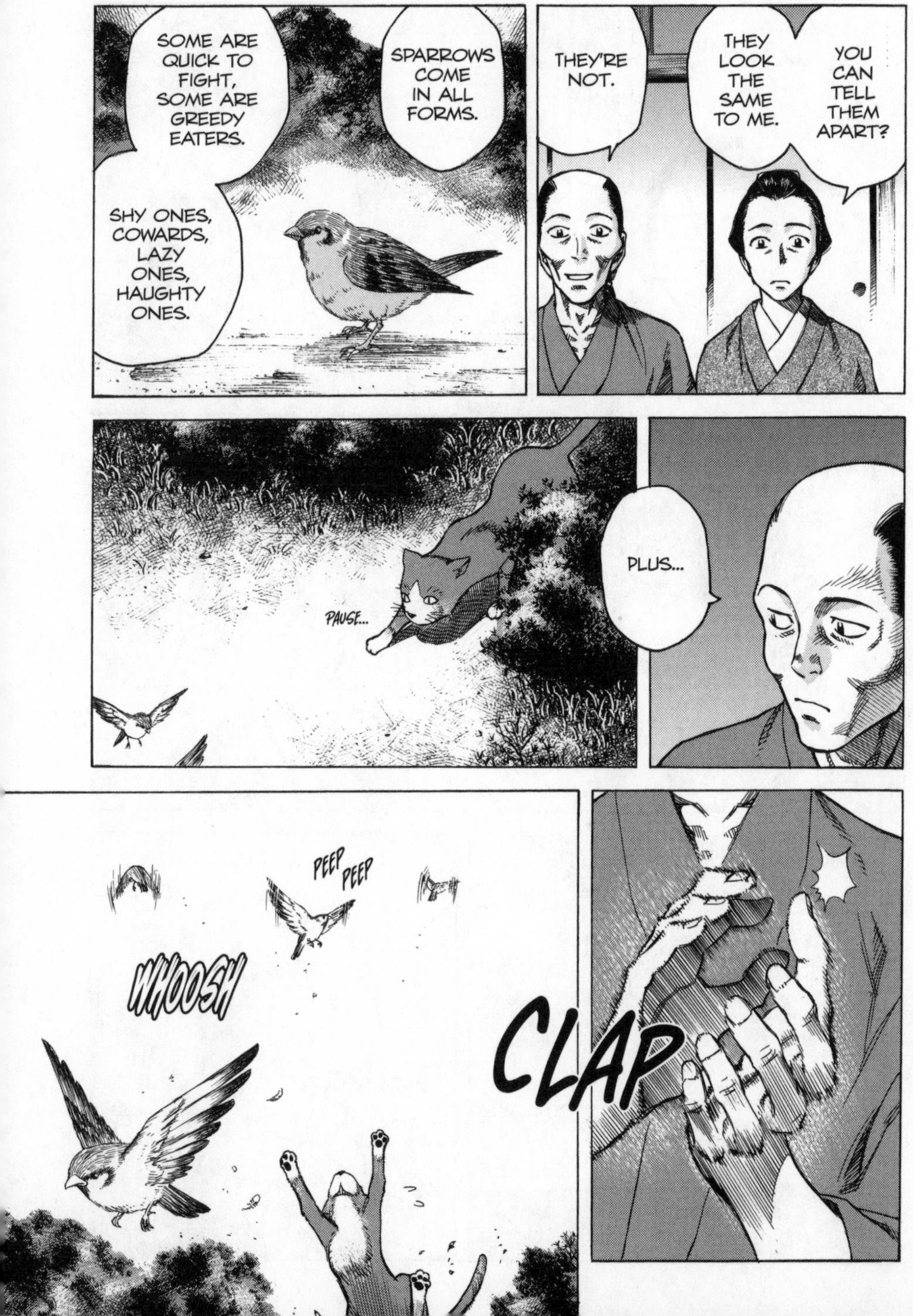
YOU CAN TELL THEM APART?
THEY LOOK THE SAME TO ME.
THEY'RE NOT.
SPARROWS COME IN ALL FORMS.
SOME ARE QUICK TO FIGHT, SOME ARE GREEDY EATERS.
SHY ONES, COWARDS, LAZY ONES, HAUGHTY ONES.
PLUS...
PAUSE...
CLAP
PEEP PEEP
WHOOSH

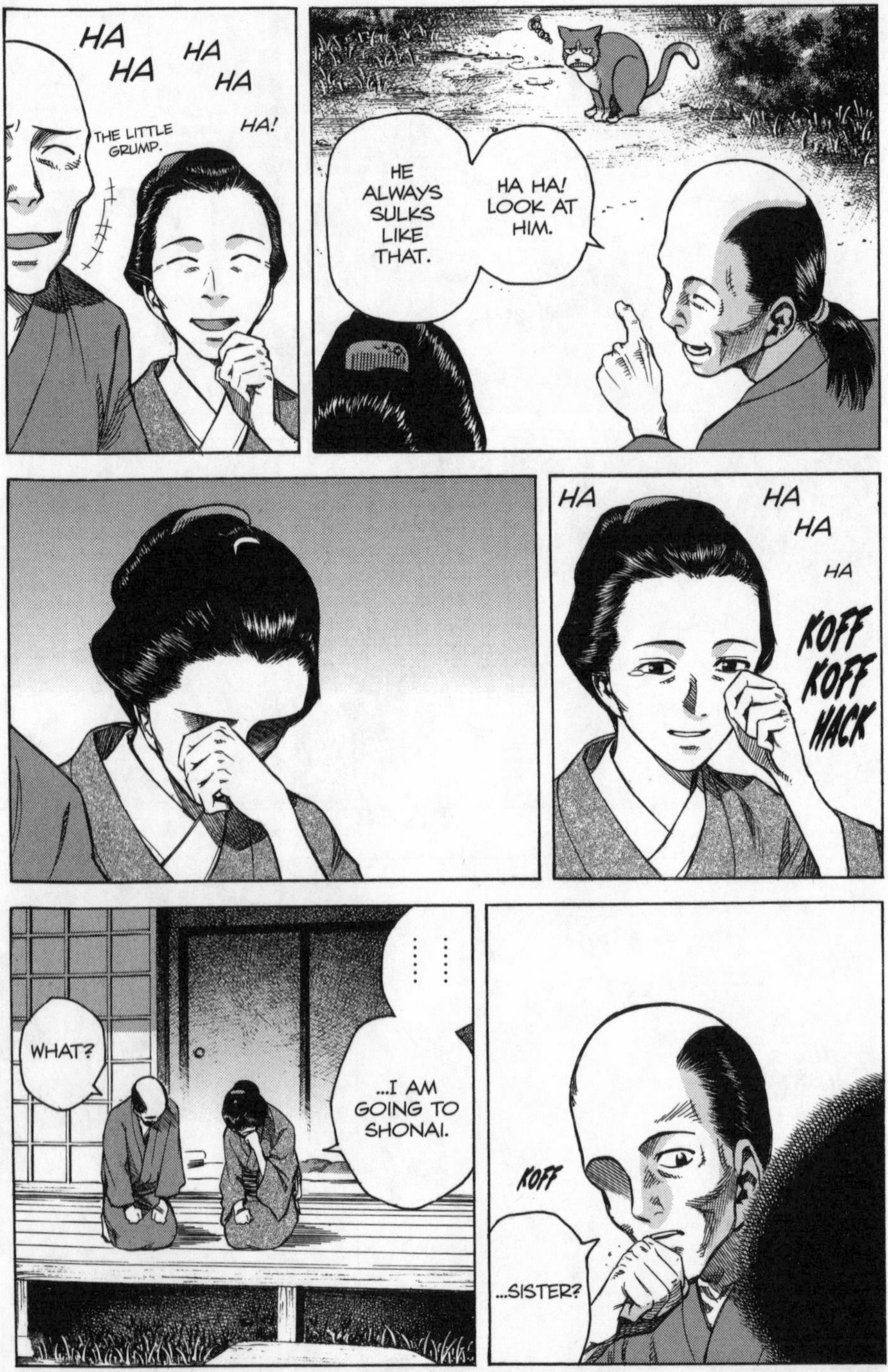
HA HA! LOOK AT HIM.
HE ALWAYS SULKS LIKE THAT.
HA HA HA HA HA!
THE LITTLE GRUMP.
HA HA HA HA
KOFF KOFF HACK
KOFF
...SISTER?
......
...I AM GOING TO SHONAI.
WHAT?

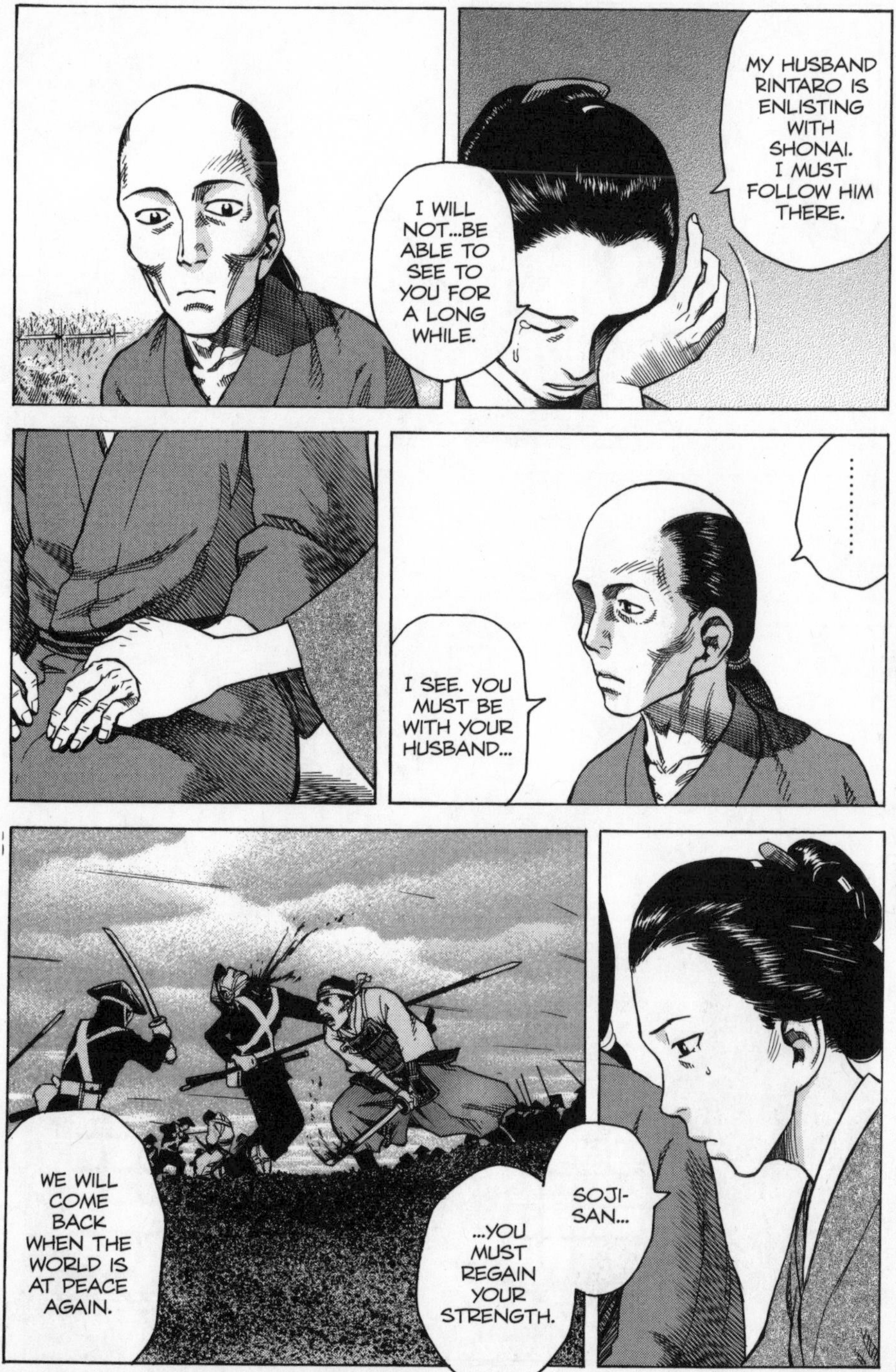
MY HUSBAND RINTARO IS ENLISTING WITH SHONAI. I MUST FOLLOW HIM THERE.
I WILL NOT...BE ABLE TO SEE TO YOU FOR A LONG WHILE.
......
I SEE. YOU MUST BE WITH YOUR HUSBAND...
SOJI-SAN...
...YOU MUST REGAIN YOUR STRENGTH.
WE WILL COME BACK WHEN THE WORLD IS AT PEACE AGAIN.

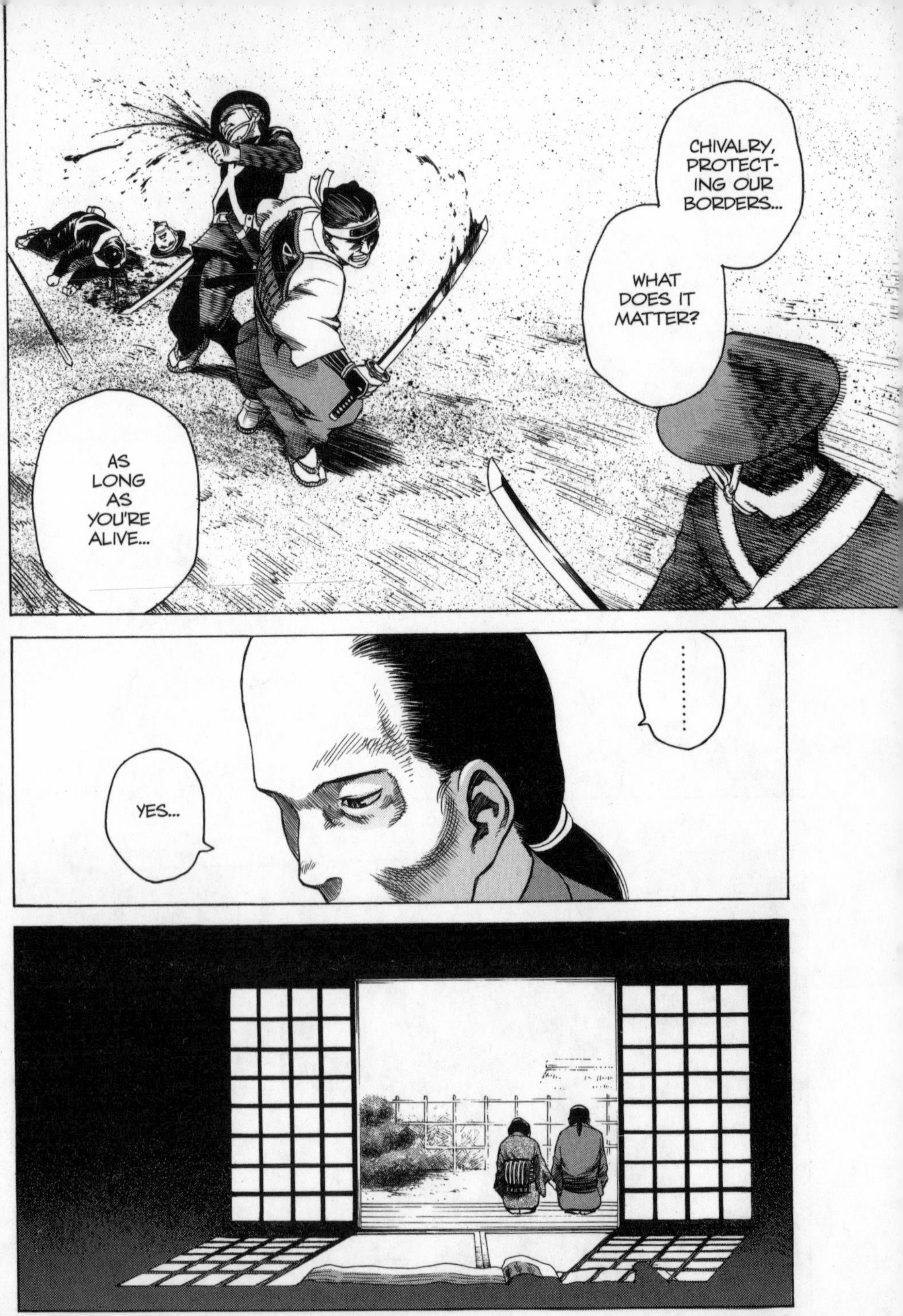
CHIVALRY, PROTECT-ING OUR BORDERS...
WHAT DOES IT MATTER?
AS LONG AS YOU'RE ALIVE...
......
YES...

Continued in Vinland Saga Book Three

A Kodansha Comics Trade Paperback Original.

Vinland Saga volume 2 copyright © 2006, 2007 Makoto Yukimura
English translation copyright © 2014 Makoto Yukimura

Published in the United States by Kodansha Comics, an imprint of Kodansha USA Publishing, LLC, New York.

Publication rights for this English edition arranged through Kodansha Ltd., Tokyo.

First published in Japan in 2006 and 2007 by Kodansha Ltd., Tokyo, as *Vinland Saga*, volumes 3 and 4.

ISBN 978-1-61262-421-1

Printed in the United States of America.

www.kodansha.us

9 8

Translation: Stephen Paul
Lettering: Scott O. Brown
Editing: Ben Applegate

www.kodanshacomics.com/vinland

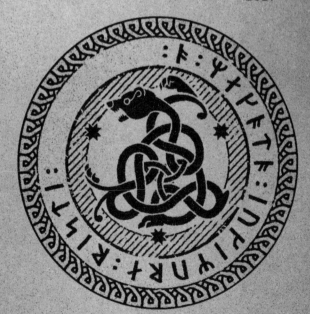